W9-ATF-125

Encyclopedia of
MULTICULTURALISM

Encyclopedia of
MULTICULTURALISM

Volume 5

Names and name changes – Six Nations

Editor

SUSAN AUERBACH

Marshall Cavendish
New York • London • Toronto

Published By
Marshall Cavendish Corporation
2415 Jerusalem Avenue
P.O. Box 587
North Bellmore, New York 11710
United States of America

∞ The paper in these volumes conforms to the American National Standard for Permanence of Paper for Printed Library Materials, Z39.48-1984.

Library of Congress Cataloging-in-Publication Data

Encyclopedia of multiculturalism / editor, Susan Auerbach.
p. cm.
Includes bibliographical references (p. 1767) and index.
Contents: v. 1. A. Philip Randolph Institute–Business and corporate enterprise; v. 2. Mother Cabrini–Estonian Americans; v. 3. Ethnic and minority group names–Inner city; v. 4. Daniel Ken Inouye–Mythology, American Indian; v. 5. Names and name changes–Six Nations; v. 6. Slavery–Zoot-suit riots.
ISBN 1-85435-670-4 (set : alk. paper). — ISBN 1-85435-675-5 (v. 5 : alk. paper)
1. Pluralism (Social sciences)—United States—Encyclopedias. 2. Multiculturalism—United States—Encyclopedias. 3. Ethnology—United States—Encyclopedias. 4. United States—Ethnic relations—Encyclopedias. 5. United States—Race relations—Encyclopedias.
I. Auerbach, Susan, 1956- .
E184.A1E58 1993 93-23405
306.4′46′0973—dc20 CIP
AC

First Printing

PRINTED IN THE UNITED STATES OF AMERICA

Contents

Encyclopedia of

MULTICULTURALISM

N

Names and name changes: Name changes occur in some societies at puberty or initiation into adulthood; at marriage; following special accomplishments or a conversionary experience; or at the option of the individual. Generally a change in name is meant to indicate a change in identity.

Among Americans Indians, given names were traditionally ascribed at birth but last names were not used. A male might change his name several times during his lifetime based on accomplishments or failures. Females did not change their names, even at the time of marriage. Eventually, the U.S. BUREAU OF INDIAN AFFAIRS imposed surnames on native peoples. The late 1900's have seen a renewed interest in traditional Indian names as a badge of ethnic pride.

Many immigrants to the United States underwent name changes. For some this was the natural result of interaction with English speakers who could not pronounce their unfamiliar foreign names; it was common to arrive at ELLIS ISLAND with one name and leave with a new "official" one. Czechs, Slovaks, Serbs, Russians, Ukrainians, and Poles felt the need to

Many immigrants purposely or unwittingly had their names changed in the processing room at Ellis Island in the early 1900's. (Library of Congress)

change or simplify their long family names. Italian names seem to have undergone fewer changes, perhaps because they were easier for English-speaking Americans to pronounce. Jewish immigrants and others also often Anglicized their names to avoid PREJUDICE and DISCRIMINATION.

Since many immigrants were illiterate, they often spelled their names the way they pronounced them. President Herbert Hoover, for example, descended from a family whose name had evolved to include *Hoeber, Hover, Hoofer, and Huber*.

Asian immigrants experienced other types of name transformations. In China, Vietnam, and some other Asian countries, surnames are recorded first, followed by given names. Many Asian immigrants switched this pattern to avoid being called by the wrong name.

Other immigrants changed their given names or surnames to indicate their new membership in U.S. society. They gave their children "American" names; Maria became Mary and Sven became Steven. Some individuals then used two names, one at home with family and another at school or work with outsiders. In an interesting reversal, the ETHNIC HERITAGE REVIVAL of the 1970's and 1980's led some Americans to change their altered names back to their original form in a celebration of ethnicity.

It is widely believed that the family names of African Americans are those of their original slaveowners. Following the Emancipation, however, many blacks simply chose names that were common to their neighborhood or region, and occasionally took names of political heroes. Many contemporary African Americans have selected new names as a way of reestablishing the link with their African heritage or to show religious conversion to Islam. The champion boxer Cassius Clay, for example, became MUHAMMAD ALI; athlete Lew Alcindor became KAREEM ABDUL-JABBAR.

In contemporary American culture, the most common type of formal name change has traditionally been that of a woman taking her husband's surname upon marriage. As an outgrowth of FEMINISM in the latter part of the twentieth century, there is a growing trend among some women to retain their maiden names.

SUGGESTED READINGS. For general information on American names, see Patrick Hanks and Flavia Hodges' *A Dictionary of Surnames* (1988). A detailed treatment of names and name changes among immigrant groups can be found in H. L. Mencken's *The American Language: An Inquiry into the Development of English in the United States* (4th ed., 1936) and *The American Language: Supplement II* (1948). An extensive listing of names and meanings is included in *Names from Africa* (1972) by Ogonna Chuks-orji.

Nation of Islam: Black nationalist religious and social movement founded in 1930 in Detroit, Michigan. Known by the symbol of the star and crescent, the Nation of Islam began with the sudden appearance in Detroit's African American community of Master Fard Muhammad (Wallace D. Fard), who established a cult called the

Under the leadership of Elijah Muhammad, the black separatist Nation of Islam attracted thousands of new adherents. (AP/Wide World Photos)

Temple of Islam. Fard told people that he had been born in Mecca and educated in England. Within three years, he had developed an organization so effective that he was able to withdraw almost completely from active membership. In 1934, Fard vanished without a trace. By then he had begun the process of transforming African Americans' fervor for religious and political nationalism into a mass movement which would become the vanguard of BLACK NATIONALISM in the United States.

Prior to his disappearance, Fard had chosen the Honorable ELIJAH MUHAMMAD (Elijah Poole) to be his Chief Minister and Deputy. Under the successful leadership of Elijah Muhammad, the cult was transformed into a movement. Membership grew from less than eight thousand members under Fard to "a few hundred thousand" by the early 1970's, according to the movement. Black Muslims, as the group's members call themselves, are African Americans who believe in Allah (God) and the Koran; they distinguish themselves from orthodox MUSLIMS in the belief that Elijah Muhammad is the Messenger of Allah (God), directly commissioned by Allah himself, and the "Spiritual Leader of the Lost-Found Nation in the West."

Socioreligious Beliefs. Believing that the "Black Man" is the original man and the primogenitor of all other races, the Black Muslims are committed to the idea that all black men are divine and represent Allah. Allah himself is a Black Man, not a spirit. He is the Supreme Being among a mighty nation of divine black men. Allah's incarnation was Wallace D. Fard, who came to expose the "great enemy of justice and righteousness" before the whole world and to rescue the black man by separating him from his enemy—the white man. To the Black Muslims, the white or Caucasian race is a race of devils whose nature is to be liars, murderers, and enemies of the truth.

The belief that the black race is divine and that the white race is the result of a hybridization experiment by Yakub, a black scientist in rebellion against Allah, is the central myth of the Black Muslim movement. According to this myth, black Americans are descendants of the ancient tribe of Shebazz. The white race, much more recent, began more than six thousand years ago when Yakub, a brilliant but troubled man, was exiled from Mecca because of his preachings in the streets. Embittered toward Allah, Yakub employed recessive-gene experiments to create a bleached-out race of devils who would rule the earth for some six thousand years, until nonwhite people all over the world would rise. The allotted span of white rule ended in 1914, and their "years of grace" will last no longer than is necessary for the chosen of Allah to be resurrected, according to Black Muslim belief.

Historical Background. The roots of this religious nationalism date back to 1913, when the Moorish Science Temple was established in Newark, New Jersey, by Noble Drew Ali, known by his followers as "the Prophet." Believing that the destruction of whites was signified by the appearance in the sky of a star within a crescent moon, the "Asiatics or Moors," as they were called, established temples in Detroit, Harlem, Chicago, Pittsburgh, Philadelphia, and numerous southern cities. At its peak the cult numbered around twenty or thirty thousand. After the mysterious death of the Prophet, the cult split. Many members would become followers of the political nationalism of the Garvey movement, founded by a Jamaican named Marcus GARVEY.

By the summer of 1919, Garvey's UNIVERSAL NEGRO IMPROVEMENT ASSOCIATION (UNIA) claimed more than two million members in its BACK TO AFRICA MOVEMENT. Garvey was deported in 1927 as a result of a felony conviction for using the mails to defraud people in the promotion of stock in his corporation. His movement then faded, leaving a leadership vacuum in the black lower class that Fard seized upon by fusing the religious and political energies into a cult called the Temple of Islam. Fard's disappearance caused a split in his organization, but ELIJAH MUHAMMAD successfully maintained control. Under Muhammad's leadership, the organization became the Nation of Islam. In 1948 Muhammad converted a prison inmate named Malcolm Little into a devoted follower. Little changed his name to MALCOLM X and emerged as the most outspoken minister of the Nation of Islam until he left the organization in 1963 following his unauthorized comment on the assassination of President John F. Kennedy.

In 1975 Elijah Muhammad died, causing the Nation of Islam to undergo drastic fragmentation and transformation. Although Muhammad's son, Warith D. Muhammad, took over the organization, it quickly disintegrated because of his commitment to orthodox ISLAM and his acceptance of whites. In 1976 the charismatic and controversial Louis FARRAKHAN reinstated the policies of Elijah Muhammad when he became the next leader.

Goals of the Movement. The Black Muslims under Elijah Muhammad attained a tremendous vitality. The basis for this vitality and for the Muslim's ability to attract an important segment of the black masses are four of its goals: a united front of black men; racial separation; economic separation; and "some good earth."

The goal of a united front of black men is based on Elijah Muhammad's ideal that black people "will discover themselves, elevate their distinguished men and women . . . give outlets to their talented youth, and assume the contours of a nation." The existence of such a united front would allow blacks to "take the

Malcolm X urged Black Muslims to develop their own separate culture and economy in order to be free of white domination. (Library of Congress)

offensive and carry the fight for justice and freedom to the enemy." Muhammad believed that leaders at every level were needed "to challenge the lies of the white man." To achieve this, the Black Muslims sought scholars to search out the truth independently of what whites have written. They attempted "to reach all black men, those in the colleges and those in the jails."

The goal of racial separation derives from the belief that racial integration with white people is unnatural and unrealistic. The Black Muslims are convinced of their superior racial heritage and believe that a further mixture of white blood will only weaken the Black Nation. They demand absolute separation of the black and the white races, justifying this goal on the basis of historical evils—enslavement, Jim Crow segregation, and *de facto* segregation in the United States—all of which were created by white people.

The goal of economic separation, a fundamental aspect of the movement, is based on the premise that the white race's economic dominance gives whites the power of life and death over blacks. Black Muslims are urged to pool their resources and techniques in merchandising, manufacturing, building, maintenance, and any field in which unity and harmony will contribute to efficiency and effectiveness. They are encouraged to be thrifty, competent, and honest, and above all to "buy black" whenever possible. As an ideal, the Black Muslims advocate a complete economic withdrawal from the white community. This transitional goal hinges on the establishment of black businesses and industries which will reduce interracial contact to a minimum, provide jobs and capital for black workers and entrepreneurs, and offer the sense of community which is essential to an "independent" people. To this end, the Black Muslims maintain numerous small businesses and other enterprises throughout the United States. For example, they operate department stores, groceries, bakeries, restaurants, nursing homes, low-rent housing complexes, large farms, and a hospital.

A fourth goal of the Black Muslims is that of possessing "some good earth." While this goal has never been specifically clarified in terms of where the land would be or how much land would be sufficient, the Black Muslims have always insisted that they must control their own land. Statements made by various ministers regarding this issue have ranged from "two or three states" to "nine or ten states" to a demand for reparations for the injustices done to blacks.

Methods of Reaching the Masses. Elijah Muhammad's strategy for building a mass movement was to put the cult in the public eye wherever there were people. For local action, he placed a small but able corps of ministers in the field. The black press gave him his first major assist. As a columnist in one of the most important black newspapers in the United States, the *Pittsburgh Courier,* he became a controversial topic of conversation for hundreds of thousands of blacks. Thousands of letters were sent to Muhammad and to the *Pittsburgh Courier* which both denounced and defended his positions. People went to the temples to see the man whose columns they read.

The black press helped to supply the initial impetus that brought Muhammad to the attention of potential followers, but the white press made him famous. In the summer of 1959, Mike Wallace presented a television documentary featuring the Black Muslims entitled *The Hate That Hate Produced.* Articles soon followed in *Time, U.S. News and World Report, Readers Digest,* and other publications. Muhammad's total following was then less than thirty thousand. A month after being "discovered" by the mass media, his following doubled, and it continued to climb for most of the 1960's.

In 1959 Muhammad's column was dropped from the *Pittsburgh Courier*. Subsequently, the column began to appear in the *Los Angeles Herald-Dispatch*, which became the official Black Muslim organ until the appearance of *Muhammad Speaks.* Launched in 1960 as "a militant monthly dedicated to Justice for the Black Man," *Muhammad Speaks* was devoted to the general news of Black Muslim interest. *MS*, as it was known, had a national circulation of more than 600,000, making it by far the most widely read paper in the black community. Its news coverage of the Third World was extensive, and its editorial policy was an important instrument of Black Muslim ideology. *MS* photography was generally excellent, and its political cartoons were imaginative and powerful. It was published until Muhammad's death in 1975 and replaced in 1978 by *The Final Call.*

In 1959 and 1960 a number of other publications were launched to bolster the membership of the movement. Among the most important was a treatise called *The Supreme Wisdom: Solution to the So-Called Negroe's Problem.* Other publications were *The Messenger, The Islamic News,* and *Salaam.* In addition, weekly radio lectures, long-playing records, audio and video tapes, and books written by Muhammad and

Black Muslim activist Louis Farrakhan personified the movement in the 1980's and early 1990's. (AP/Wide World Photos)

other ministers have been used to keep the movement vibrant.

The Nation of Islam's mass communication strategies are augmented by their effective recruitment approaches, especially in jails and prisons, where inmates resentment against society increases with each day. The Black Muslims have had impressive success in rehabilitating certain categories of social outcasts, including drug addicts and alcoholics. The real recruitment, however, is done in the temples or mosques. To clinch the conversion of true believers, the lure of personal rebirth is offered. To commemorate the rebirth, the convert drops his last name and becomes known by his first name and the letter X. The X has the double meaning of "ex," which signifies that the Muslim is no longer what he or she was, and "X," which signifies an unknown quality or quantity. Black Muslim parochial schools, with their massive emphasis on education about the Black Man—his resplendent past, his divine nature, and his triumphant future—are also a powerful recruiting device of the movement with long-range effects.

SUGGESTED READINGS. For a firsthand account of the Black Muslim philosophy, see Elijah Muhammad's *Message to the Blackman in America* (1965). *The Autobiography of Malcolm X* (1965) is also important. For a scholarly treatment, see *The Black Muslims in America* (rev. ed., 1982) by C. Eric Lincoln; Clifton E. Marsh's *From Black Muslims to Muslims: The Transition from Separatism to Islam, 1930-1980* (1984) is also informative.—*Michael H. Washington*

National Americanization Committee: Organization founded in 1915 by Frances A. Kellor as a vehicle of the Americanization movement. The group's short history (it was dissolved in 1919) encapsulates the shift in the

AMERICANIZATION movement from progressive, or at least well-meaning, beginnings to coercive patriotism. Initial efforts of the movement to ensure the full participation of immigrants into American society were characterized by concerns for immigrants' welfare and a push for social reform, but the National Americanization Committee soon exploited fears aroused by World War I and the Red Scare to demand that immigrants become "100 percent" Americanized. The group was originally called the National Americanization Day Committee, taking its name from the celebration of the Fourth of July as "Americanization Day." In 1915, more than a hundred U.S. cities marked the holiday with receptions honoring newly naturalized citizens with the slogan "Many Peoples, but One Nation."

National Association for Bilingual Education (NABE): Organization founded in 1975 in Dallas, Texas, and now headquartered in Washington, D.C. The association is composed of educators, interested members of the community, and students. It promotes and publicizes BILINGUAL EDUCATION, compiles statistics, and operates a placement service. In addition, the association holds annual meetings to promote public awareness of outstanding bilingual programs and publishes a quarterly journal.

National Association for Multicultural Education (NAME): Spearheaded by Dr. Rose Duhont-Sells, Dean of Education at Southern University in Baton Rouge, Louisiana, this organization was established in 1990 by scholars, activists, and multicultural educators who strive for social, political, economic, and educational equity in American society. NAME promotes equality for all regardless of race, ethnicity, culture, language, age, gender, or exceptional needs. The association believes that MULTICULTURAL EDUCATION is vital if Americans are to acquire the attitudes, skills, and knowledge to function in various cultures.

National Association for the Advancement of Colored People (NAACP): Pioneering, politically active civil rights organization in the United States. The NAACP works to achieve equal rights under the law for African Americans and other minorities and to eliminate racial prejudice in all aspects of daily life.

It has been said that the history of the NAACP, more so than any other civil, religious, or political

The NAACP was formed, significantly, at the height of the period of lynchings of African Americans. This painting by Jacob Lawrence captures the despair that lynching brought to the black community. (National Archives)

group, best reflects the hopes and desires of twentieth century African Americans. Its single-minded dedication to the elimination of racial discrimination and SEGREGATION placed the association in the vanguard of the struggle for civil rights and integration. Currently criticized by some as being "too conservative" or "out of touch" with the conditions affecting African Americans and other minorities, the NAACP has achieved numerous victories in its long existence that have enhanced the quality of life for people of color. Focused primarily on litigation, legislation, and education, the NAACP has been instrumental in winning landmark legal decisions, obtaining passage of groundbreaking federal laws, and improving the awareness and activity of African Americans in the nation's democratic process.

Beginnings. Founded in 1909, the NAACP was developed in response to the prevailing decline of the status of blacks in the United States. Between 1900 and 1909, 885 blacks were lynched. Nowhere was the senseless victimization of African Americans more apparent than in the 1908 RACE RIOT in Springfield, Illinois. On an August night, a white woman told the police she was dragged from her bed and raped by an African American man who had been working in the neighborhood. The man, named George Richardson, was immediately arrested and jailed. After a special grand jury was convened, the woman confessed that her true assailant was a white man. Unfortunately, the truth came too late. Mobs of whites rampaged through town destroying the homes and businesses of blacks in an attempt to drive them out of Springfield.

During the first night of rioting, the mob killed a black barber after burning his shop to the ground. Following that, they dragged his broken body through the streets and prepared to burn it when militiamen fired into the crowd, breaking it up. On the subsequent night, a mob within sight of the state capitol lynched an eighty-four-year-old black man who had been married to a white woman for thirty years. The sheer ferocity of these events sickened many Americans. In many communities across the country, African Americans perceived they had no legal protection against violence.

The NAACP was brought into being by a group of affluent white liberals and black religious leaders organized by New York social reformer Mary White Ovington in reaction to the Springfield riot. In an open letter—entitled "The Call"—published in the *New York Evening Post,* the group announced the National

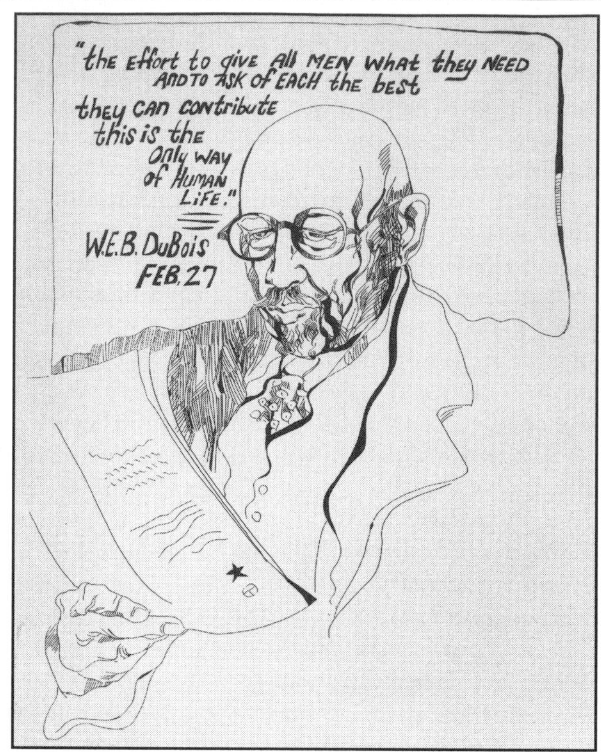

Black intellectual W. E. B. Du Bois, depicted here on a poster, was one of the founders and early officials of the NAACP. (Library of Congress)

Negro Conference to be held February 12, 1909, in New York, the 100th anniversary of Abraham Lincoln's birth. The issue of discussion would be the complete emancipation and full enfranchisement of African Americans. Among the white participants were William English Walling, a free-lance writer, and Oswald Garrison Villard, publisher of the *New York Evening Post* and grandson of the abolitionist William Lloyd Garrison. African Americans who were present included W. E. B. DU BOIS, Ida B. WELLS, and Bishop Alexander Walters of the African Methodist Episcopal Zion (AMEZ) Church. Du Bois, who was a professor at Atlanta University, had been the leader of the NIAGARA MOVEMENT—a group of black intellectuals, opposed to the accommodationist views of Booker T. WASHINGTON, who had met at Niagara Falls, Canada, in 1905, to fight for the abolition of racism in the United States.

Following the National Negro Conference, Villard helped secure funds to establish the initial organization. In May of 1910, the offices of the NAACP were established in New York. Moorfield Storey, a nationally known lawyer, served as the first president, and Walling served as chairman of the executive committee. As director of publicity and research and editor of *The Crisis*, the official publication of the NAACP, Du Bois was the organization's only black officer until the following year, when Bishop Walters was named as one of two vice presidents. *The Crisis* focused on the achievements of blacks in the arts and business, and issues of racial strife inflicted upon African Americans. This included an annual listing of LYNCHINGS in America. By 1919, the circulation of *The Crisis* had surged to 104,000—larger than most black newspapers of the time. As a result of its magazine's growing influence, the association grew in notoriety. By 1921, the NAACP had more than four hundred branches nationwide.

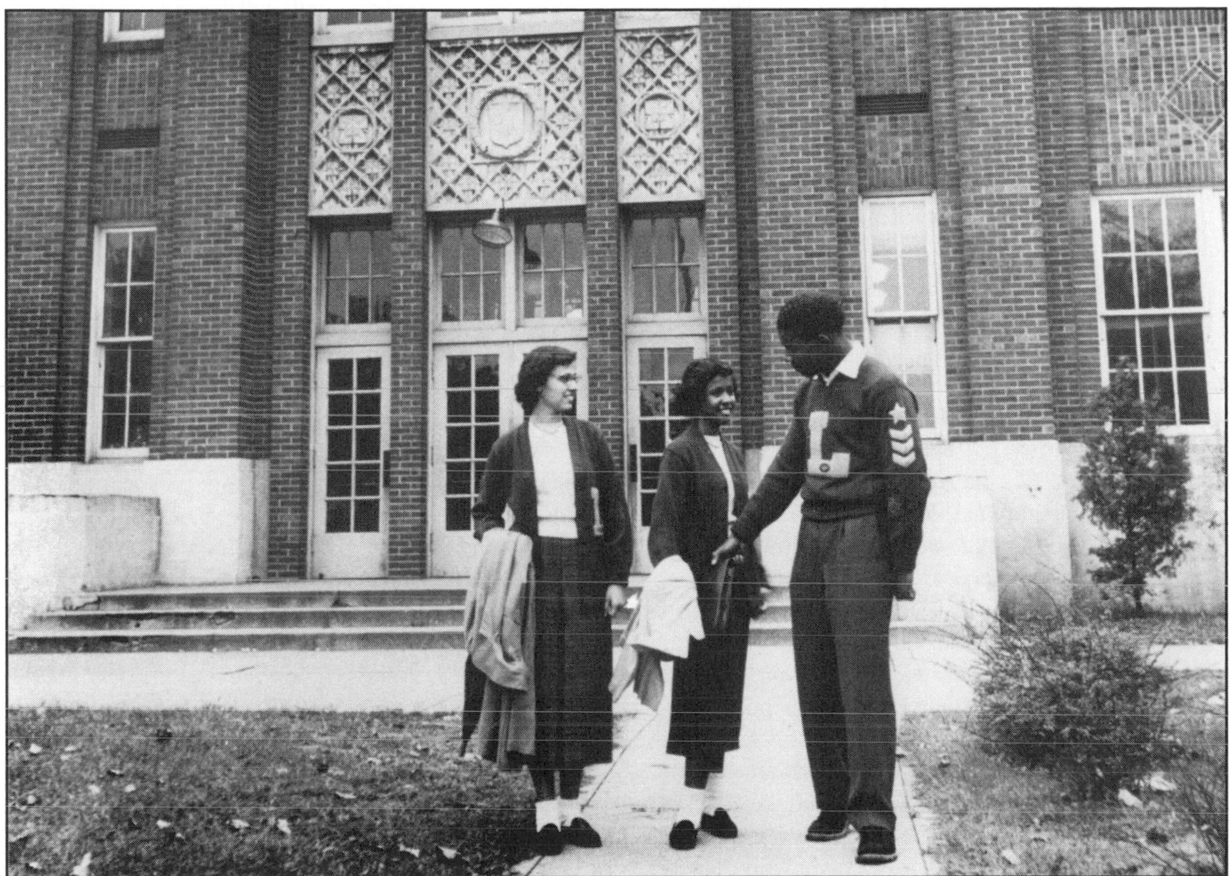

As a result of the NAACP's landmark legal victory in Brown v. Board of Education *in 1954, black students began to attend previously all-white schools.* (Library of Congress)

Legal Battles. The courts have always been the principal arena of the NAACP in the field of empowerment. Early in the group's history, a legal redress committee was developed and was headed by Arthur Spingarn. Distinguished lawyers such as Spingarn, Clarence Darrow, Louis Marshall, and Felix Frankfurter donated free legal services to the committee. Their first important victory came in the celebrated 1915 Supreme Court case *Guinn v. United States*. Examining the Oklahoma and Maryland State constitutions, the Supreme Court declared that so-called grandfather clauses—Reconstruction-era voting provisions that disfranchised blacks—violated the FIFTEENTH AMENDMENT and were therefore unconstitutional.

Following this initial success, many other discriminatory laws were attacked by the committee. In 1917, the NAACP took on a Louisiana city ordinance that upheld segregated residential areas; and in 1923, the committee challenged an Arkansas practice of excluding blacks from juries. Such an act, it was charged, denied a black defendant the right to a fair trial. In both cases, the Supreme Court found the laws unconstitutional. With the creation of the NAACP Legal Defense and Education Fund in 1940, NAACP lawyers won numerous battles on the issue of legal persecution of southern blacks throughout the decade.

The NAACP also achieved many of its goals through legislative action. The group inundated members of the executive and legislative branches—including speakers of the House of Representatives and chairmen of Congressional Judiciary Committees—with demands for restorative legislation. By maintaining such a strong lobby in Washington, D.C., the NAACP enhanced the rights of African Americans. Among the laws it played a major role in passing was the Civil Rights Act of 1957 that protects the right to vote and created the Civil Rights Division of the Department of Justice and the Commission on Civil Rights. The NAACP, through the efforts of Clarence Mitchell and others, also lobbied heavily for the passing of the CIVIL RIGHTS ACT OF 1964 and the VOTING RIGHTS ACT OF 1965. Both legislative acts furthered the protection of African Americans under the law.

The NAACP's most renowned legal victory came from its constant assault on public school SEGREGATION. The fruits of their labors climaxed with the 1954 *BROWN V. BOARD OF EDUCATION* ruling of the U.S. Supreme Court. Thurgood MARSHALL, then an NAACP lawyer, successfully presented the argument that racially segregated schools were inherently unequal, and therefore unconstitutional. This was the most significant triumph the NAACP won in overturning the policy of "separate but equal" facilities which had received legal sanction in 1896 as a result of the Court's *PLESSY V. FERGUSON* decision.

Internal Strife and External Opposition. Criticized continually for the number of whites in positions of authority within the organization, the NAACP has known its share of conflict. William Monroe Trotter, the man with whom DU BOIS had started the NIAGARA MOVEMENT, refused to join in the development of the NAACP because of his distrust of all white people. Du Bois himself had a series of heated disagreements with Villard, the initial chairman of the board of directors. These battles eventually resulted in Villard's withdrawal from active participation in 1914.

Du Bois would prove to be a lightning rod for most of the group's early opposition. His friction with Booker T. WASHINGTON—cultivated prior to 1909—intensified when Du Bois was announced as the only black official of the NAACP. Washington feared Du Bois was now able to challenge his leadership in the African American community. To offset that, he utilized several schemes to undermine the NAACP's efforts, including the use of his influence with the African American press. The conflict ended only after Washington died in 1915 and one of his former protégés, James Weldon JOHNSON, was appointed as field secretary of the NAACP.

During the GREAT DEPRESSION, criticism of the NAACP came from a new group of detractors: young African American intellectuals and activists such as Ralph BUNCHE, Louis Redding, and Abram L. Harris. Disillusioned with Roosevelt's NEW DEAL, these emerging black leaders felt that the solutions to the problems facing African Americans could only be found in the black community. Furthermore, they believed the integration of blacks and whites into a unified labor movement and a philosophy of cultural nationalism in politics and economics should be the new approach in civil rights. Their ideas of black self-determination inflamed an ongoing feud between Du Bois and NAACP executive secretary Walter White. White felt that the tradition of racial integration in the NAACP should not be abandoned; Du Bois believed that BLACK NATIONALISM could ensure the economic survival of African Americans beyond the Depression. Repeatedly in his articles for *The Crisis*, he argued for "voluntary" segregation on the part of African Americans. Finally, seeing that this personal antagonism was undermining the group, Du Bois resigned in 1934 and created the Pan-African Congress. He would return briefly in 1944 to serve in a semi-independent position as consultant, only to leave again in 1948 because of continued conflicts with White.

During the 1960's. Under the leadership of Roy WILKINS, the NAACP found its initiative for change appropriated by new emerging protest groups. The SOUTHERN CHRISTIAN LEADERSHIP CONFERENCE (SCLC), the CONGRESS OF RACIAL EQUALITY (CORE), the STUDENT NONVIOLENT COORDINATING COMMITTEE (SNCC), and the NATION OF ISLAM began to receive national attention that had once seemed reserved exclusively for the NAACP. These groups employed methods of aggressive direct action and street demonstrations that gave them improved media focus and high visibility. In spite of a growing militant call for racial separation, Wilkins strongly reaffirmed the NAACP's pledge to support integration. Nevertheless, at the 1968 NAACP Annual Conference, a group of young revisionists within the association continued to argue that the traditional policies were no longer relevant. The resulting power struggle coincided with the controversial publication of an attack on the U.S. Supreme Court as racist by a white member of the

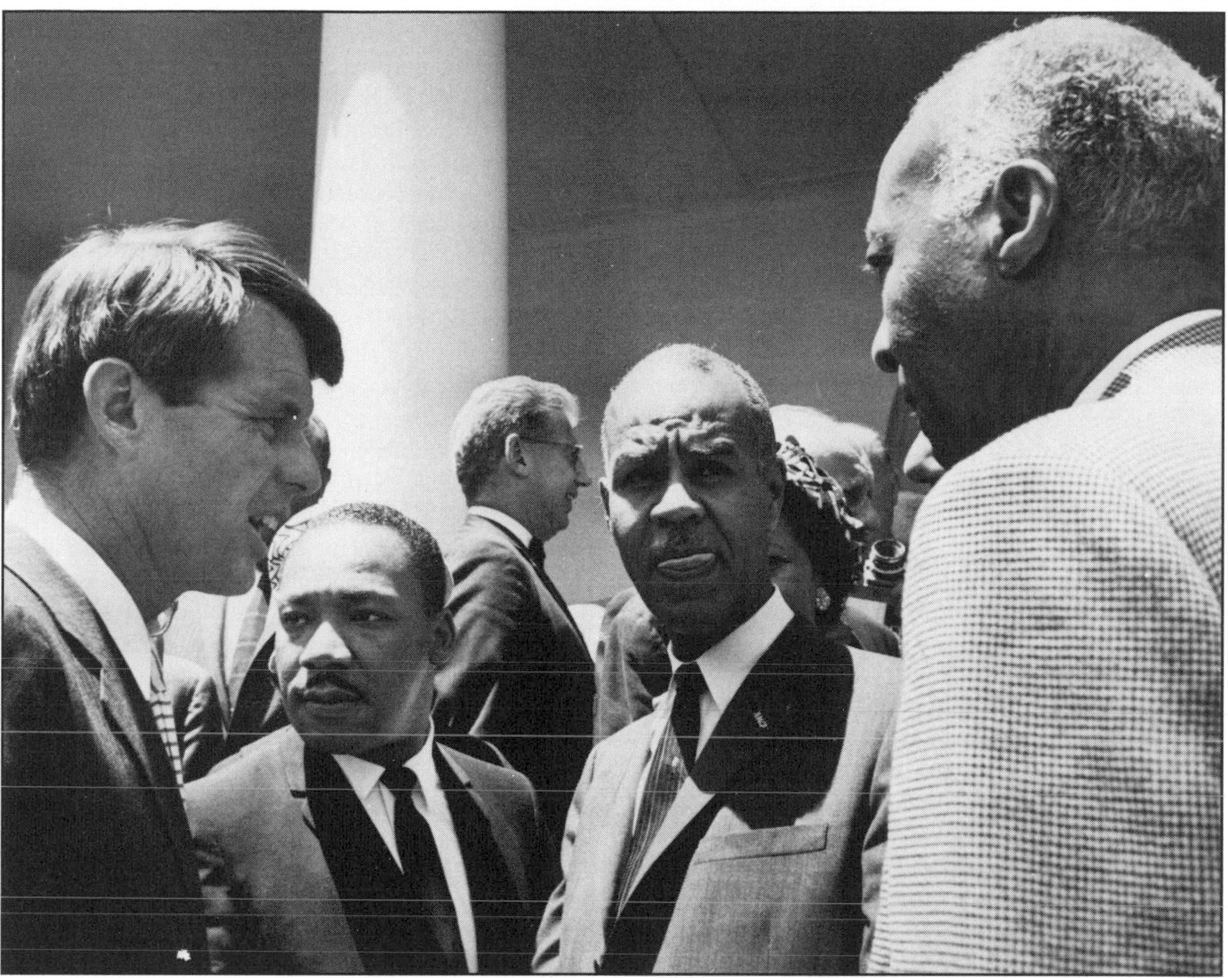

Roy Wilkins (second from right) led the NAACP during the civil rights era of the 1960's. He is pictured here in 1963 with (from left) Attorney General Robert Kennedy, Martin Luther King, Jr., and union leader A. Philip Randolph. (National Archives)

NAACP legal staff. Lewis Steel, an NAACP associate counsel, was dismissed over his article "Nine Men in Black Who Think White," which had appeared in *The New York Times Magazine*. Following his dismissal, the entire legal staff of the NAACP resigned in protest.

Although the revisionists lost their fight to wrest power from the conservative wing of the association, they did succeed in slowly moving the group toward an agenda that emphasized more social programs and less litigation. In 1958, the NAACP worked to diminish poverty and hunger for people of color. With the establishment of the Mississippi Emergency Relief Fund, the organization raised funds to feed poor African Americans in the Mississippi Delta. In 1971, the group's Youth Council created a breakfast program for needy children in Nashville. By 1977, new officers were chosen. Margaret Bush Wilson, an African American lawyer from St. Louis, became president of the board of directors, and Benjamin L. Hooks replaced Wilkins as executive secretary.

In the early 1990's, the NAACP claimed 500,000 members in 2,200 branches across the country, with some seven hundred Youth Councils nationwide. Rupert Richardson served as the group's national president and Benjamin Chavis was named to replace Hooks as executive director in 1993. Among NAACP's many activities are job referrals, day care, seminar sponsorship, maintenance of an extensive law library, and assistance in developing low and moderate income housing provided by NAACP Housing Corporation. Departments include Economic Development and Voter Education and Registration. Among the organization's many subgroups are committees on health and international affairs.

Suggested Readings. There are numerous books and articles on various aspects of the organization. For general histories of the NAACP and discussions of its most significant achievements, see Minnie Finch's *The NAACP: Its Fight for Justice* (1981), Robert L. Zangrando's *The NAACP Crusade Against Lynching, 1909-1950* (1980), and Charles Kellogg's *NAACP: A History of the National Association for the Advancement of Colored People* (1967). In *The NAACP's Legal Strategy Against Segregated Education, 1925-1950* (1987), Mark V. Tushnet chronicles the group's legal triumphs. Mary White Ovington's *The Walls Came Tumbling Down* (1947) and Robert Jack's *History of the National Association for the Advancement of Colored People* (1943) provide early accounts of the group's activities.—*Gary Anderson*

Leaders of NAACP branches such as Ernestine Moss of Dubuque, Iowa, continue to carry the message of the organization into all parts of the United States in the 1990's. (James L. Shaffer)

National Association of Colored Women's Clubs: Political and service organization for African American women. The organization was founded in 1896 as the National Association of Colored Women when the National Colored Women's League combined with the National Federation of Afro-American Women in Washington, D.C. Mary Church Terrell became the organization's first president and led its campaign for voting rights. By 1916, the National Association of Colored Women's Clubs represented fifty thousand women. Under the leadership of Mary McLeod Bethune, who became president in 1924, the group developed educational programs. Other association projects have focused on improving civil rights and community welfare through service and philanthropy. The group also sponsors the National Association of Girls Clubs.

National Association of Latino Elected and Appointed Officials (NALEO): Nonpartisan organization founded in 1975 by Spanish-surnamed politicians to encourage Latino participation in the American political process. Besides encouraging Latinos to exercise their right to vote, NALEO also promoted the development of a national lobby for legislation that benefits Latinos. From its headquarters in Washington, D.C., it publishes a newsletter called *NALEO Washington Report.*

National Association of Manufacturers: Organization founded in 1895 to communicate the manufacturing industry's views on national and international problems at the federal level. In the early 1990's, the association had a membership of about 13,500. Primary goals are to review legislation, judicial decisions, and other administrative rulings and/or interpretations that affect the industry. The association also maintains numerous policy groups and public relations programs.

National Brotherhood. *See* **Assembly of First Nations**

National Consumers League: Organization founded in 1899 that conducts consumer research and encourages citizen participation in governmental and industry decision making. The league maintains educational and advocacy programs on consumer issues such as insurance, credit, health, privacy, the minimum wage, communications, labor standards, telemarketing fraud, air safety, and product safety and standards. In the early 1990's the league had a membership of eight thousand.

National Council of La Raza (NCLR): Private, nonprofit service corporation whose goal is the improved social and economic welfare of Mexican Americans. When founded in 1968 it was called Southwest Council of La Raza, and its purpose was to organize and assist community-based groups to obtain financing for housing and economic development. After the Ford Foundation withdrew funding in 1970, the Council moved to Washington, D.C., and three years later changed the name to reflect its new national focus. The NCLR publishes a bimonthly magazine titled *Agenda*.

National Council of Negro Women (NCNW): Association of African American women's organizations. Founded in 1935 by Mary McLeod BETHUNE, the NCNW is a unifying force for thirty-one national African American women's associations. The group, headquartered in Washington D.C., focuses on racial discrimination and federal laws concerning women and children. Other activities include developing leadership qualities in African American women, helping minority women succeed in nontraditional careers, archiving information about African American women's history, and publishing the periodicals, *Black Woman's Voice* and *Sisters Magazine*. Internationally, the group sponsors projects to help women in Third World countries.

National Federation of Afro-American Women: Association founded by Mrs. Booker T. Washington in 1895. The association was originally formed by members of approximately twenty women's clubs throughout the United States; in 1896 it merged with the National Colored Women's League and was known as the National Association of Colored Women. Mary Church TERRELL served as the newly merged group's first president. In 1977, the group's name was changed to the National Association of Colored Women's Clubs, with a membership of 120,000. In 1990, more than thirty-eight state and one thousand local groups were involved. Their goals are to provide services, educational activities, and raise money for worthy causes, including the National Association of Girls Clubs.

National Indian Youth Council: Group of young, activist American Indians who were among the first to call for self-determination. Formed several months after the American Indian Chicago Conference of 1961, the National Indian Youth Council believed that their elders spent too much wasted time on cautious cooperation with the United States BUREAU OF INDIAN AFFAIRS (BIA) and other government agencies. Ready for a more aggressive policy, the group met and was formed at the Gallup Indian Community Center in Gallup, New Mexico. In their policy statement, they identified the insidious and dangerous weapons used against American Indians: educational, religious, and social reforms that attempted to replace American Indian values with those of the white man. Condemning their conservative elders as "Uncle Tomahawks" who willingly acquiesced to BIA policies, the council backed up their rhetorical call for self-determination with dramatic activism in the form of numerous staged "fish-ins" protesting the loss of tribal fishing rights in the Pacific Northwest.

National Negro Business League: Association of African American business leaders. The National Negro Business League was founded in 1900 by Booker T. WASHINGTON as a black counterpart to white chamber of commerce groups. Its purpose was to help African Americans enter the business world and to encourage African Americans to patronize businesses owned by members of their own race. The league published its own journal, entitled *Negro Business*. In the early 1990's the group's name was changed to the National Business League. The organization has more than 10,000 members in at least 127 local groups and focuses on helping members of all minorities in their business ventures.

National Organization for Women (NOW): Association founded in 1966 to obtain equal rights and opportunities for women in the United States.

Origins. Modern FEMINISM dates back to Europe in the eighteenth century, when the French Revolution included calls for sexual equality, and Mary Wollstonecraft Shelley wrote *Vindication of the Rights of Women* (1792). In the United States, landmarks included the historic 1848 SENECA FALLS CONVENTION and the SUFFRAGE MOVEMENT that led to a constitutional amendment in 1920 giving women the vote. By the 1950's, however, homebound wives and mothers had become well established in what feminist Betty FRIEDAN called the "cult of domesticity."

The CIVIL RIGHTS MOVEMENT for racial equality in the 1960's inspired a parallel campaign on sexual terms. In 1961, President John F. Kennedy convened the first Commission on the Status of Women, and in 1963 Friedan's *The Feminine Mystique* appeared and quickly became a controversial best-seller. The following year, Title VII of the CIVIL RIGHTS ACT OF 1964 officially prohibited sexual discrimination in employment; however, the EQUAL EMPLOYMENT OPPORTUNITY COMMISSION (EEOC) was lax in enforcement. Two issues in particular drew feminists' ire: sex-segregated employment advertisements and age limits for "stewardesses," as female flight attendants were then called. Congresswoman Martha Griffiths of Michigan and prominent feminists such as Wisconsin's Kathryn Clarenbach believed that women needed an organization to pressure the EEOC into action. Even Aileen Hernandez and Richard Graham, two sympathetic EEOC members, concurred. Friedan, a frequent visitor to Washington, seemed to be the perfect person to inspire and galvanize such an organization.

In June of 1966, at the National Conference of State Commissions on the Status of Women, Friedan and others shared their frustrations. Over lunch, they jotted ideas on paper napkins, and before the conference ended, twenty-five women had contributed five dollars each to form a new women's organization. With Friedan at the helm, the National Organization for Women was born.

The fledgling group moved swiftly into action. They immediately sent telegrams to EEOC members demanding enforcement of existing antisexism statutes. On October 29, a two-day conference on women's rights opened in Washington with a press conference announcing NOW's existence. The organization claimed three hundred charter members and had a conventional structure with a hierarchy and procedural rules. The original board of directors included Friedan, Clarenbach, Graham (who had resigned from the EEOC), and Caroline Davis of the UNITED AUTO WORKERS (UAW). From the start, NOW was open to men as well as women.

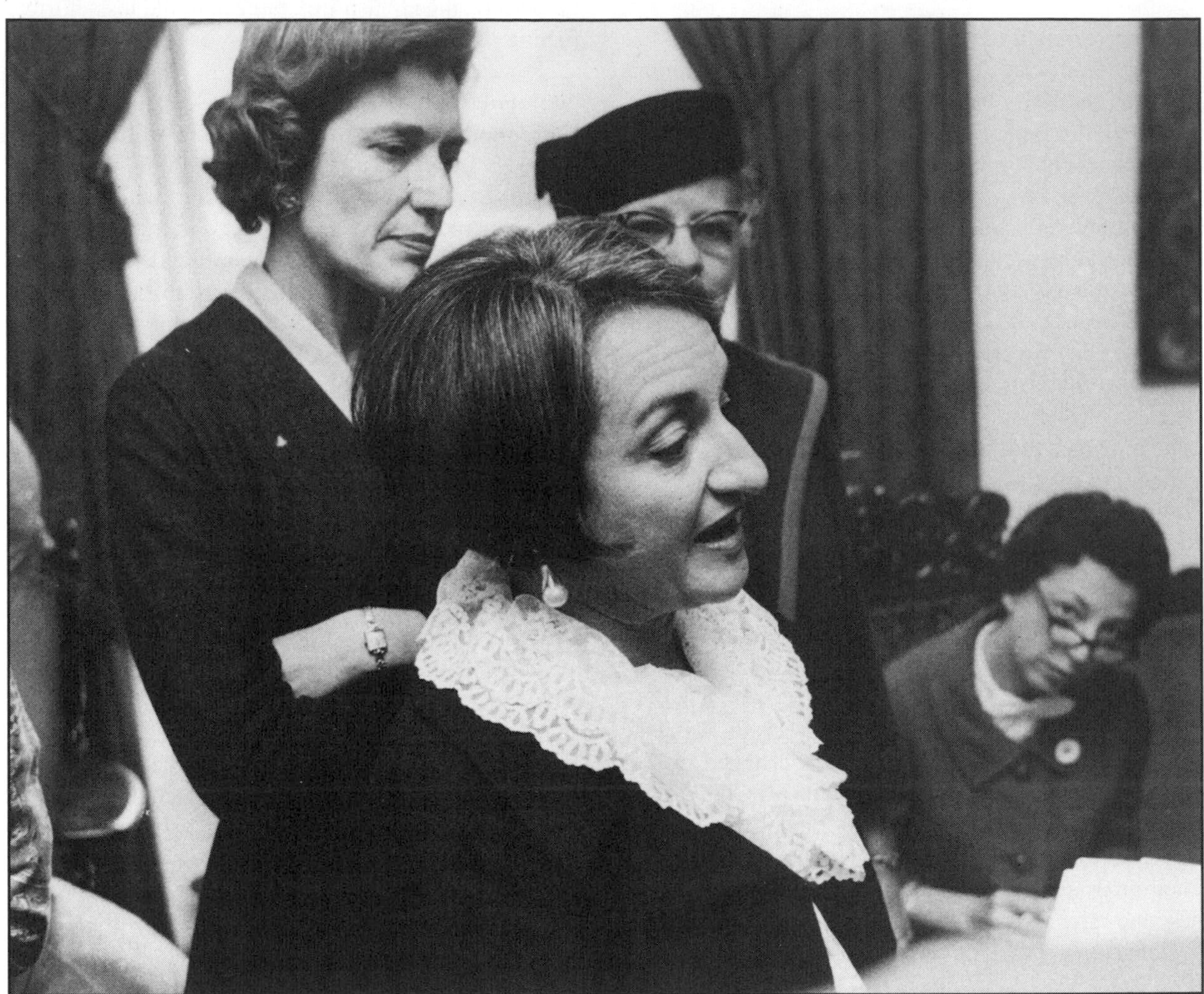

Betty Friedan, who brought attention to women's limited domestic sphere in The Feminine Mystique *(1963), became the first president of NOW in 1966.* (AP/Wide World Photos)

Because of pressure from NOW, the EEOC held hearings on Title VII enforcement the following spring. Still dissatisfied over segregated advertising, on December 14, 1967, NOW members picketed the offices of both *The New York Times* and the EEOC. In early 1968, the organization initiated lawsuits against alleged violators. Under growing pressure, President Lyndon Johnson issued Executive Order 11375 in October of 1968, requiring the Office of Federal Contract Compliance to monitor sexual as well as racial discrimination in employment. Shortly thereafter, the EEOC formulated its Guidelines against Sex Discrimination. Within several years, women's cases accounted for one quarter of the EEOC's complaints.

In November of 1967, at its second conference, NOW articulated its Bill of Rights. The eight planks called for an EQUAL RIGHTS AMENDMENT (ERA) to the U.S. Constitution; an end to employment discrimination; maternity leave and benefits for women workers; tax deductions for child care; child care centers;

NOW's pressure on the government to enforce bans on sex discrimination opened the way for women to enter nontraditional careers. Barbara Barrett became Eastern Airlines' first female pilot in 1973. (AP/Wide World Photos)

equal and unsegregated education; equal job training and allowances for poorer women; and reproductive freedom. The organization's Statement of Purpose emphasized the goal of "true equality for all women in America . . . in truly equal partnership with men."

Growth and Dissent. NOW ranks grew quickly, rising from three hundred at the 1967 conference to three thousand in 1970. From the beginning, however, the organization was steeped in controversy. Because it officially advocated reproductive freedom—contraception and abortion on demand—conservative members withdrew in 1968, led by attorney Elizabeth Boyer, and formed the Women's Equity Action League. Honoring their union's opposition to the ERA, Davis and the UAW contingent ceased active involvement with NOW in 1967. As the UAW members had been providing all of NOW's clerical support, their loss sent the organization into virtual chaos. In the New York chapter in 1968, disapproval of the centralized hierarchy led prominent member Ti-Grace Atkinson to withdraw and begin her own October 17 Movement.

These defections reflected deep ideological conflict. Friedan tried to keep NOW open to all, but reconciling angry women-only radicals with more practical work-with-the-system reformists was no easy task. Though women's liberation in many ways grew out of the Civil Rights movement and had clear ties with both socialist political theory and gay liberation, NOW faced the task of defining its particular breed of activism.

In their 1968 pamphlet "Toward a Female Liberation Movement," Beverly Jones and Judith Brown distinguished the feminist battle from the traditional class struggle. Nevertheless, some feminists viewed NOW as a bastion of bourgeois feminism that did not represent the concerns of poor and working women. Members of the Socialist Workers' Party and the Young Socialist Alliance had become active in NOW toward the end of the 1960's. Concern among the organization's leaders led to a report by Lucy Komisa in 1972 and ultimately a purge of those perceived to be dangerous.

In 1970, another controversy engulfed the New York chapter. Rita Mae Brown, a lesbian, questioned the organization's commitment to LESBIANS, a volatile political issue. When author Kate Millett acknowledged her bisexuality at a Columbia University forum, the press used her admission to propagate the myth of the angry, bra-burning, man-hating feminist. In May of 1970, twenty women disrupted the Congress to Unite Women and presented a position paper on the "Woman-Identified Woman." These self-proclaimed Lavender Menaces—a term denoting the negative impact of lesbians on the feminist image—later went on to become the RadicaLesbians.

Their point was heard, and lesbian inclusion was a

major issue in the New York chapter's 1971 elections. The West Coast regional membership passed a resolution in April to accept lesbians, and that September, at the fifth annual national convention, NOW passed a prolesbian resolution stating that "a woman's right to her own person includes the right to define and express her own sexuality" and acknowledging "the oppression of lesbians as a legitimate concern of feminism."

During the early 1970's, NOW became a pragmatic outlet for women who were also involved in more radical activities elsewhere. In 1972 many of the early NOW members who shared political concerns or aspirations formed the NATIONAL WOMEN'S POLITICAL CAUCUS (NWPC) to encourage female politicians. By 1976, with its advocacy of lesbian rights and the decriminalization of prostitution, NOW had lost its middle-class respectability and was viewed as radically leftist by the political establishment, to the degree that activists Karen de Crow and Artie Scott were asked to leave Kansas City during the Republican Party Convention there. At the National Women's Conference in Houston in 1977, NOW President Eleanor Smeal espoused a populist position that sought to include lower-class women and women of color, and to establish a new direction for the organization. After the conference, NOW grew to an unprecedented 100,000 members.

The Equal Rights Amendment. During the 1970's and 1980's, much of NOW's energy was directed at passage of the ERA. The ERA had first been proposed in 1923, but through the 1960's it failed to pass both houses of Congress. On February 17, 1970, future NOW president Wilma Scott Heide led a group of

Aileen Hernandez, a Jamaican American civil rights official, served as NOW president from 1970 to 1971 in the midst of controversy over NOW's white, middle-class focus. (AP/Wide World Photos)

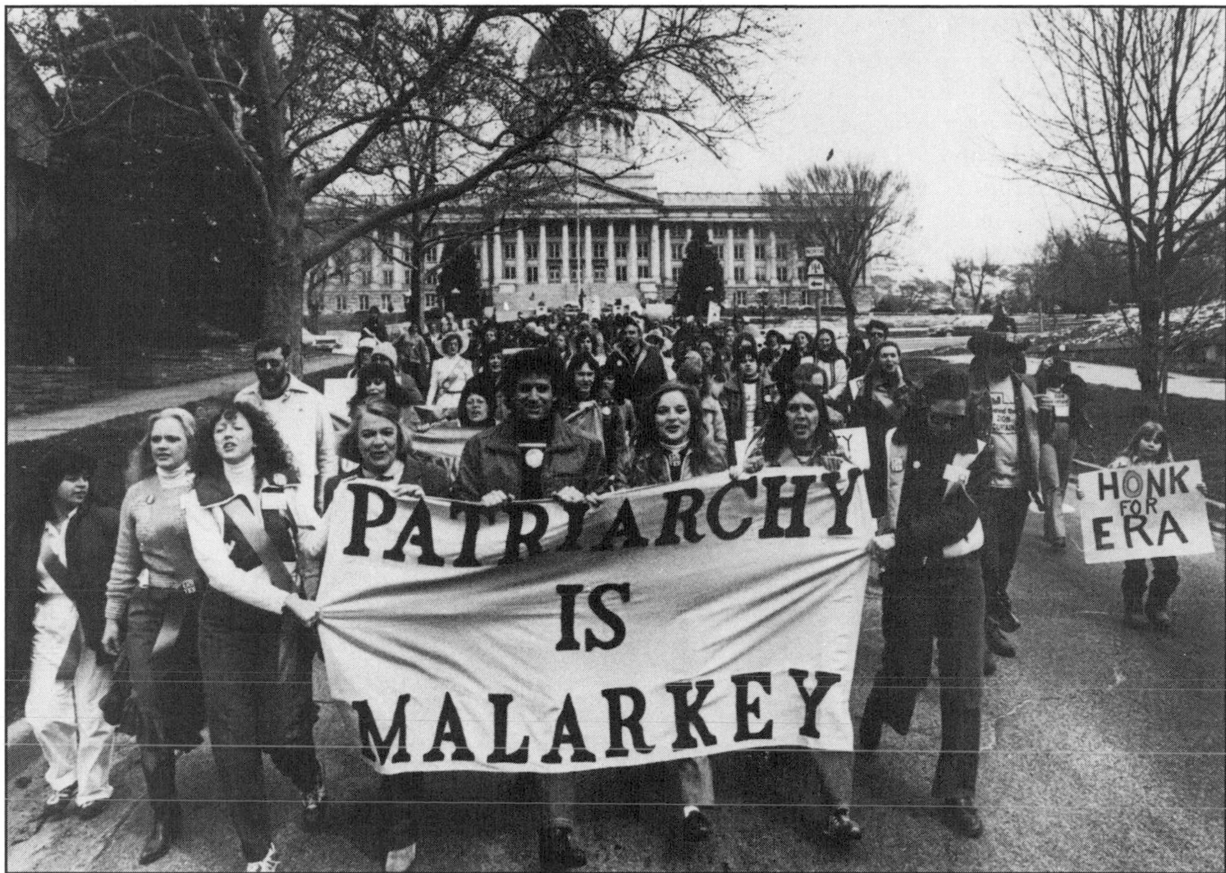

Pro-ERA demonstrators in Utah march to Mormon Tabernacle Square to protest the Mormon church's stand on the ERA. NOW gave support to state efforts to ratify the controversial amendment. (AP/Wide World Photos)

Pittsburgh NOW members into a Senate hearing to lobby directly for the ERA. At last, in 1972, the amendment was passed with a deadline of March 30, 1979, for ratification by the necessary thirty-eight states.

From 1972 on, NOW financed state ERA campaigns and fought at all levels for ratification. Within three years, thirty-three states had ratified, but then the pace slackened. By February of 1978, with the deadline nearing, NOW proclaimed an ERA State of Emergency. Under NOW sponsorship, 100,000 ERA supporters marched on Washington. NOW lawyers, with impressive astuteness and efficiency, obtained a three-year deadline extension. Smeal moved NOW to the ERA vanguard with campus crusades, canvassing, letter-writing campaigns, and media projects to educate the public. NOW called for boycotts of nonratifying states, targeting convention cities such as Atlanta, Chicago, New Orleans, and Las Vegas. Hundreds of organizations joined in the boycott; it is estimated that Miami Beach lost $9 million, Chicago $15 million, and Missouri $18 million because of canceled conventions.

In spite of NOW's prodigious efforts, legislatures in targeted states did not respond. The June 30, 1982, deadline passed, and the decade-long ERA battle became NOW's hardest defeat.

Other Activities. In addition to its larger legal and political struggles, NOW has engaged in a plethora of practical activities. From the beginning, NOW sponsored consciousness-raising groups and speaker service bureaus. In 1966, a committee was established to examine MEDIA PORTRAYALS OF WOMEN, leading to the Barefoot and Pregnant in the Kitchen Award for sexist advertising and to graffiti campaigns against offensive billboards. In 1969, Pittsburgh NOW founded KNOW, Inc., a press for feminist literature, and New York NOW founded New Yorkers for Abortion Law Repeal.

On August 26, 1970, the fiftieth anniversary of the NINETEENTH AMENDMENT, NOW sponsored a national Women's Strike for Equality demanding equal opportunity, CHILD CARE, and ABORTION on demand.

That same year, NOW lobbied for a national child-care program at the White House Conference on Children, and helped to establish the nation's first WOMEN'S STUDIES PROGRAM at San Diego State University. NOW leaders invited George Wiley of the NATIONAL WELFARE RIGHTS ORGANIZATION to speak on the concerns of minority women. In 1972, NOW launched *MS.* MAGAZINE under the editorship of Gloria STEINEM.

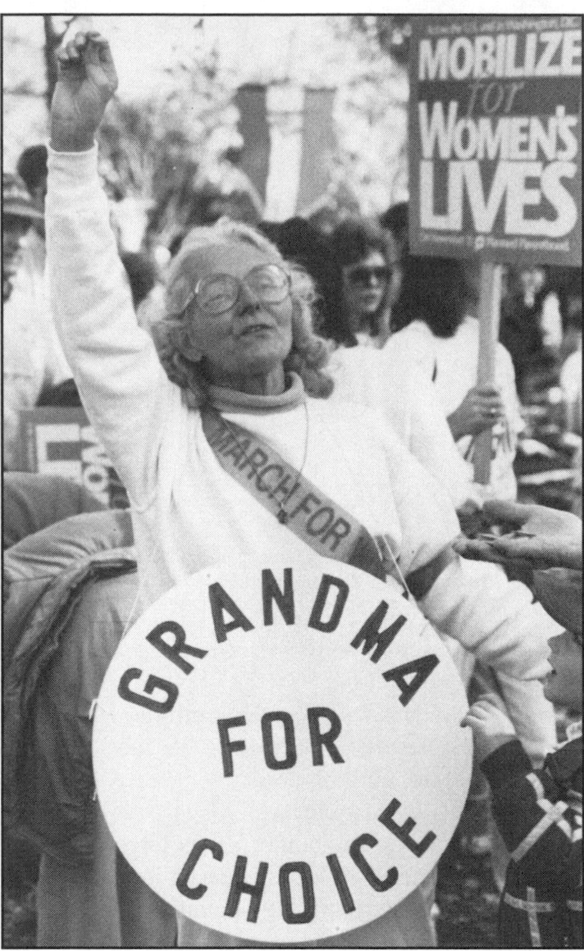

NOW members of all ages and backgrounds have been active in the movement for abortion rights. (Sally Ann Rogers)

Across the United States, NOW established child care, RAPE, and spousal abuse crisis centers; evaluated candidates on women's issues; organized marches, rallies, and fairs; fought gender-based insurance rates; studied SEXISM in schoolbooks; and sponsored public service advertisements. NOW created task forces on consumer credit, on older women, and on women and religion. Mother's Day, 1975, was declared a Day of Outrage against the Catholic church for its sexist dogma. The NOW Legal Defense and Education Fund has worked for child support enforcement, equal scholarship opportunities, and the education of judges.

The 1980's. Throughout the 1970's, NOW membership continued to grow, reaching a high of 210,000 in 1982 before beginning to taper off. Though the emergence of the religious right and the conservatism of the Reagan Administration threatened to halt the momentum of the WOMEN'S MOVEMENT, NOW continued its work on many fronts.

Reproductive freedom had always been a NOW priority; the 1973 Supreme Court decision in *ROE v. WADE* legalizing abortion had been a major victory for the organization and the entire feminist movement. With the issue still raging, NOW sponsored a meeting of antiabortion and pro-choice feminists in 1979 to find common ground. NOW formed its own political action committee in 1980 and coordinated efforts with other abortion rights organizations, such as the National Abortion Rights Action League (NARAL). In April of 1989, NOW played a major role in organizing a march on Washington, D.C., that attracted 300,000 abortion rights supporters. After the U.S. Supreme Court ruling in the *Webster v. Reproductive Health Services* case in July, which again threatened reproductive freedom, NOW gained 50,000 new members. At the national convention, NOW President Molly Yard called for a third party to reflect women's concerns, but NARAL and NWPC opposed the idea. The election of President Bill Clinton in 1992 augured an era of progress for NOW's feminist agenda.

Throughout the 1980's, NOW realigned itself and adapted to changing times. Once careful to avoid partisan politics, NOW became identified with the Democratic Party. In 1981, NOW President Smeal addressed the national convention of the AMERICAN FEDERATION OF LABOR-CONGRESS OF INDUSTRIAL ORGANIZATIONS (AFL-CIO), and the two bodies celebrated a "solidarity day" rally on September 19. Complaints from black members about NOW activities at the 1984 Democratic Convention underscored the organization's traditionally white, middle-class focus. NOW leaders made an effort to include all women, and in 1989 the first multicultural chapter was opened. Dallas Rainbow NOW actively sought minority involvement and addressed issues such as POVERTY, HOMELESSNESS, and discrimination in public clinics. Changing with the times and the political climate, NOW continued to strive for women's rights in a variety of ways.

SUGGESTED READINGS. Thorough examinations of the women's movement can be found in Flora Davis' *Moving the Mountain: The Women's Movement in America Since 1960* (1991) and Barbara Sinclair Deckard's *The Women's Movement: Political, Socioeconomic, and Psychological Issues* (1983). Ginette Castro in *American Feminism: A Contemporary History* (1990) and Vicky Randall in *Women and Politics* (1982) offer more theoretical approaches. In *Sex, Gender, and the Politics of ERA: A State and the Nation* (1990), Donald Mathews and Jane De Hart provide an in-depth account of a state-level battle for ERA ratification.—*Barry Mann*

National Puerto Rican Forum (NPRF): Social action organization that originated in a 1957 meeting of educators in New York City and became incorporated in 1970. Its primary mission is the empowerment of Puerto Ricans/Latinos to achieve socioeconomic and political parity through leadership, education, and economic advancement. The forum established the Puerto Rican Community Development Project, which encouraged and aided the formation of Puerto Rican organizations. It became national with the opening of offices in Chicago, Cleveland, Hartford, Miami, Philadelphia, and Washington, D.C.

National Urban League: Interracial civil rights organization formerly known as the National League on Urban Conditions Among Negroes. Founded in New York City in 1910, the league's original purpose was to help rural African Americans adjust to northern urban life. Until the 1960's, it remained primarily a social services organization with a staff of social workers. During the Civil Rights movement, it also helped with voter registration and promoted health programs and neighborhood improvements for minorities under the leadership of Whitney M. Young, Jr. In the 1970's, it concentrated on obtaining jobs and educational opportunities for minorities. During the 1980's and early 1990's the league addressed issues such as substance abuse and homelessness. The league accepts donations from private sources to finance its operations, many of which are carried out by local volunteers. The league is known for publishing annual "State of Black America" reports since 1975.

National Welfare Rights Organization (NWRO): Organization founded in the early 1960's as a means of empowering welfare recipients—especially poor women and their children—to improve their living conditions. The main impetus for the NWRO came from President Lyndon Johnson's WAR ON POVERTY program and the CIVIL RIGHTS MOVEMENT. Besides agitating for welfare reform and involving the poor in political activities, the organization (no longer in existence) opened the door for the formation of other groups to empower poor people.

National Woman Suffrage Association (NWSA): Organization formed by Susan B. ANTHONY and Elizabeth Cady STANTON in 1869 for woman suffrage. Angered by the Republican Party's deliberate exclusion of women from the FIFTEENTH AMENDMENT, Anthony and Stanton encouraged women to create an independent women's movement. NWSA distinguished itself from the rival American Woman Suffrage Association (AWSA) with a focus on women's leadership and a strategy for a federal amendment, rather than a state-by-state approach. NWSA members believed that women would use the vote to enact laws for other social and labor reforms. In 1890, NWSA merged with AWSA to create the National American Woman Suffrage Association.

Suffragists flank the suffrage association's banner in 1913, seven years before women finally won the franchise. (Library of Congress)

National Woman's Party (NWP): Militant organization that promotes equality for women. Founded in 1913 by Alice PAUL, the NWP built upon the efforts of its predecessor, the Congressional Union, and revived the American women's SUFFRAGE MOVEMENT. It introduced new tactics including picketing the White House and staging hunger strikes while in jail. The arrests and imprisonment of party members brought the public's attention to their cause. After suffrage passed in 1920, the NWP dedicated itself to ending all forms of sex discrimination. It introduced the first Equal Rights Amendment in December, 1923, calling for an end to discrimination on the basis of sex in all laws.

National Women's Political Caucus: Multipartisan organization founded in 1971 to increase women's voice in local, state, and national politics. Among its founders were prominent women politicians such as Bella ABZUG and Shirley CHISHOLM, as well as feminist leaders such as Betty FRIEDAN and Gloria STEINEM. The caucus supports women candidates and promotes women's issues such as the EQUAL RIGHTS AMENDMENT, ABORTION rights, comparable worth, and AFFIRMATIVE ACTION. Its membership grew during the 1980's to a total of seventy-five thousand as a result of political and media attention to the "gender gap" between male and female voters' interests.

National Women's Trade Union League (NWTUL): Organization of working women and social reformers founded in 1903 to unionize women workers. The league's goals were reflected in its motto: "the eight hour day, a living wage, to guard the home." The league developed in Boston, Chicago, and New York City but soon expanded into eleven cities. At first, middle-class members dominated the leadership; however, wage earners took more active roles starting in 1910 and by 1920 had assumed leadership positions. The NWTUL shifted its efforts from organizing to advocating legislation during the 1910's to achieve its goals.

Nationalism—American: Concern for and devotion to the culture and interests of the United States, above concerns for other nations. Historically, the term nationalism can refer to everything from advocacy of American independence to consciousness of a separate national identity within the international community and the ongoing attempt to define the essence and character of that identity. In its more extreme forms, American nationalism has spawned such nativist movements as the Know-Nothings, the KU KLUX KLAN, and the IMMIGRATION RESTRICTION LEAGUE.

Formation of a national identity in the United States has been complicated by a number of historical factors: the tension between political liberalism and religious conservatism in the Colonies; the conflict between the individual states and the emerging federal government; the country's vast geography; and the heritage of immigration. The significant differences between the cultures and values of various American ethnic groups have made the concept of American nationalism especially problematic, as opposed to smaller countries with more homogeneous populations.

The United States has traditionally been viewed as a "MELTING POT" in which immigrants from various parts of the world would be assimilated into a common culture, taking on an "American" identity that would supersede identification with their country of origin. A World War I poster, for example, read, "Americans All!: Du Bois, Smith, O'Brien, Knutson, Cejka, Hauke, Pappandeikopolous, Gonzales, Andrassi. . . ." Yet the issue has never been so simple: Some groups of immigrants were assimilated more readily than others, and immigration laws tended to favor people whose cultures were most similar to the dominant culture in the United States. As the idea of CULTURAL PLURALISM, and later MULTICULTURALISM, took hold, an alternative model was proposed: a view of America as a "salad bowl" in which ethnic groups as diverse as African Americans, Asian Americans, and Latinos would contribute to the national character by retaining their ethnic identity instead of giving up or suppressing it.

Nationalistic impulses have spawned resistance to multiculturalism in areas such as education and social policy. Some argue that BLACK HISTORY MONTH, college courses in women's literature, and elementary school classes taught in Spanish foster separatism instead of unity. Similarly, an "ENGLISH ONLY" MOVEMENT has sought to bolster national identity by legislating English as the official language of the United States. Yet advocates of multiculturalism point to another keystone of American nationalism—individualism—to support their view that in the contemporary United States complete cultural ASSIMILATION may be neither desirable nor possible.

SUGGESTED READINGS. Hans Kohn's *The Idea of Nationalism* (1944) documents the history of nationalism. Barbara Ward's *Nationalism and Ideology* (1966) addresses questions of nationalism and world order. The United States' "melting pot nationalism" is scrutinized in Louis Snyder's *The New Nationalism* (1968). In *Holding Fast the Inner Lines: Democracy, Nationalism, and the Committee on Public Information* (1980), Stephen Vaughn discusses the perils of American nationalism during the World War I era. Lawrence Fuchs presents a very thorough account of the effects of nationalism in *The American Kaleidoscope: Race, Ethnicity, and the Civic Culture* (1990).

Nationalism—black. *See* **Black nationalism**

Nationality parishes: Catholic churches that are dominated by a particular ethnic group and still practice the language and customs of the country from which they or their ancestors originated. The parish is the smallest unit in the Catholic organizational structure that extends from the local level to the Vatican in Rome. Church members within a geographically designated parish are assigned to attend a particular church. Parishes have been extremely important in the North American Roman Catholic church because they are the religious counterpart of neighborhoods. Nationality parishes were created over the years of immigration to the United States, as communities attempted to re-create the makeup and spirit of their original communities. Initially, the nationality parishes were European, primarily German, Polish, Italian, and Irish, among others. Later some of the most prominent of the nationality parishes have been Latino.

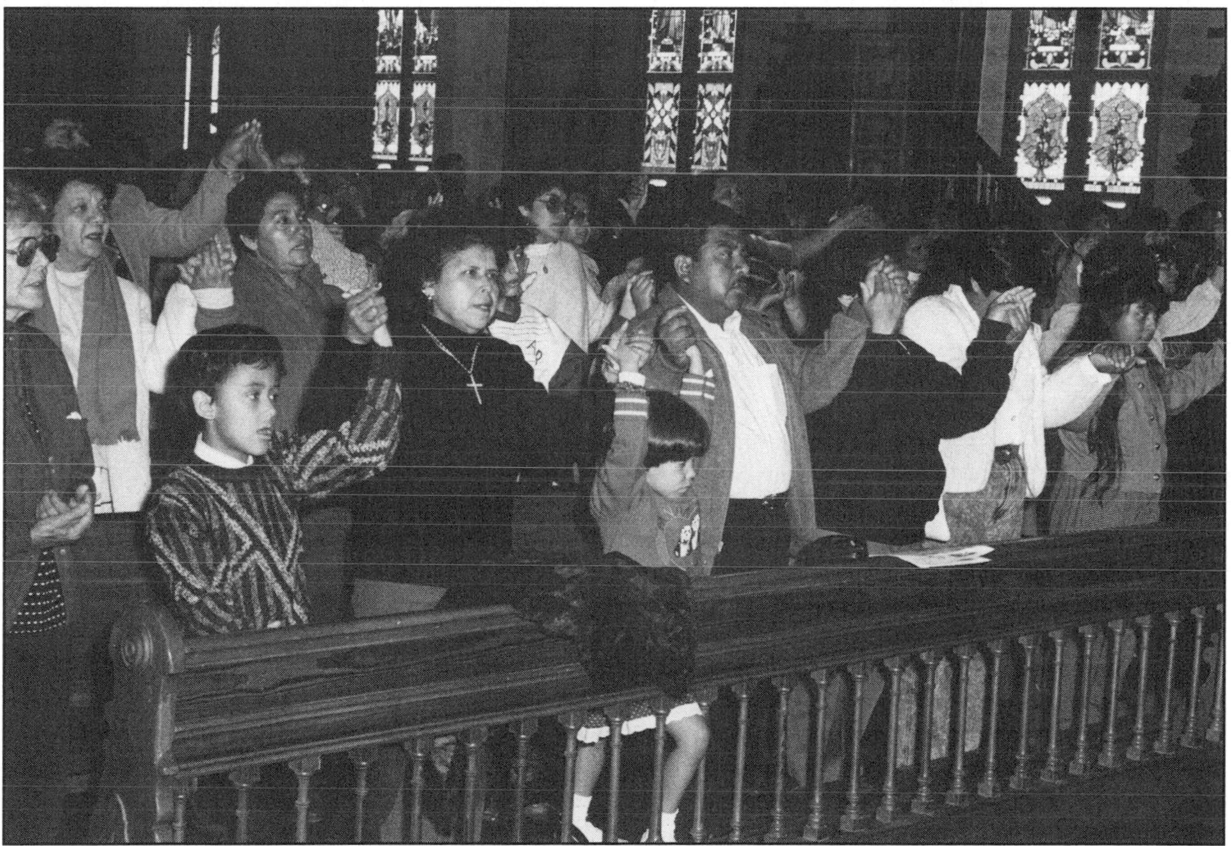

Some of the largest ethnic parishes, like this one in San Antonio, Tex., are Mexican American. (James L. Shaffer)

Nationality parishes have traditionally served four basic purposes. They are an important social center in which the members find identity in the midst of an alien world that often discriminates against them because of their ethnic background. They also offer members recreational opportunities in basketball and baseball, keeping youth off the streets. They allow parishioners to engage in the political and cultural life of the community and the world beyond, building up political power and uniting to fight discriminatory practices. Finally, nationality parishes serve as the locus for the celebration of the major sacramental events of the immigrant's life.

Education and employment opportunities are organized for members of nationality parishes. Parish parochial schools take into consideration language needs of recent immigrants and help them prepare themselves for employment, both within and without the parish. Thus, nationality parishes integrate religion and the life of the local community and serve to protect immigrant groups in urban areas.

Large, influential nationality parishes, such as the Irish parishes in Boston and Chicago, have had a major impact on both local and national politics. Since the 1980's Latino nationality parishes in major cities such as Los Angeles, New York, and Washington, D.C., have represented the needs of their members to the larger community, although many Latinos have left the church because they claim that it has not adequately addressed the needs of the immigrants.

Suggested Readings. Five famous nationality parishes that have received great publicity regarding their adaptation of Catholicism to their ethnic traditions include: Old St. Patrick's Church, Church of Our Lady of the Angels, Our Lady of Mount Carmel, St. Ladislaus Church, and St. Charles Boromeo. Their story can be read in Tim Unsworth's "How Five Ethnic Parishes Celebrate a Tailor-Made Faith," in *U.S. Catholic* 53 (December, 1988), pp. 23-30. A historical perspective on nationality parishes can be found in *How to Save the Catholic Church,* by Andrew M. Greely and Mary Greeley Durkin (1984). Nationality parishes in relation to recent trends in Catholicism are described in Penny Lernoux's *People of God* (1989) and more broadly in Jap D. Dolan's *The American Catholic Experience (1985). The problems of the Latino nationality parish, which is the dominant contemporary ethnic parish, are explained in Alan Figueroa Deck's "The Crisis of Hispanic Ministry: Multiculturalism as an Ideology," in America* 163 (July 14, 1990), pp. 33-37.

Native American. *Use* **American Indian**

Native American Church: Pan-Indian religious movement emphasizing brotherhood and solidarity among American Indians of all backgrounds. Thought to have originated among the Kiowa and Comanches in Oklahoma around 1885, the Native American Church is widespread among American Indians, especially in the Southwest. While there are many local variants of the church, all groups adhere to an ethical code composed of four main themes: brotherly love and mutual aid among members; a strong, monogamous family; personal self-reliance; and the avoidance of alcohol. Members are expected to earn their own living, take care of their families, and help one another out in time of need.

The Native American Church is described by social scientists as being both nativistic and syncretistic. A nativistic movement is one that attempts to revive a destroyed way of life. The Native American Church is one of several movements that arose in the late nineteenth century as a response to the destruction of the lifestyles of American Indians by whites. The church offered a supernatural means of restoring some of the social patterns of precontact life, while at the same time helping individual members adjust to the new social environment.

The Native American Church is a syncretic movement in that it blends elements of Christianity with American Indian spiritual beliefs. Among the concepts taken from Christianity are the idea of a Trinity of God as father, son, and holy spirit; of Jesus as a mediating figure between God and humanity; of the Bible as a collection of important beliefs (though church members select which parts of the Bible they wish to use, emphasizing what they see as passages of particular importance to American Indians); and of Christian rituals, especially communion. These concepts are merged with American Indian custom, for example, when communion is held as part of an all-night ceremony in a tipi with peyote substituted for the Christian sacramental elements of bread and wine. Members emphasize that the Native American Church is only for American Indians; casual onlookers, tourists, and non-Indians seeking religious experience are turned away from church ceremonies. Members also assert the superiority of their version of Christianity.

As noted, the Native American Church uses peyote as part of its rituals; in fact, the church is sometimes called the Peyote Church or the Peyote Way. During rituals, members consume peyote buttons which are the rounded tops of a cactus (Lophophora williamsii) found in northern Mexico and Texas. The buttons, which may be consumed green or dried, contain a powerful alkaloid called mescaline. Consuming the buttons produces an altered state of consciousness—after an initial period of extreme discomfort—characterized by euphoria, distorted senses, and visions. Church members use peyote to heal and to teach. Peyote is thought to give power to ill members, thus healing them. Through visions and heightened sensibility, peyote is thought to guide church members in their lives and to encourage self-examination. Although classified as a narcotic and a hallucinogen by state and federal law, the use of peyote in Native American Church rituals is permitted by the American Indian Freedom Act of 1978. The church vigorously opposes the sale or use of peyote for purposes outside church ritual.

Suggested Readings. Recommended books include *Peyote Religion: A History* by Omar C. Stewart (1987); *Peyote, The Divine Cactus* by Edward F. Anderson (1980); *The Peyote Religion* by J. S. Slotkin (1956); and *The Peyote Cult* by Weston LaBarre (1938).

Native American Grave and Burial Protection Act (1990): Legislation that established guidelines for the return of Indian skeletal remains and ceremonial grave goods. The remains were to be returned to the decedents' lineal descendants or to the decedents' respective Indian tribes for reburial on ancestral lands. Funeral goods, sacred objects, and other artifacts were also ordered to be returned. In addition, the bill provided for the protection of various Indian and Native Hawaiian burial sites throughout the United States from excavation without tribal consent. Museums and universities receiving federal funds were ordered to comply with these provisions or face fines or civil lawsuits. A special amendment excluded the Smithsonian Institution, which holds numerous Indian skeletons and ceremonial grave goods, from compliance with act's provisions.

Native American Rights Fund (NARF): Nonprofit organization, founded in 1970 and headquartered in Colorado, that is devoted to representing Indian individuals and tribes in legal cases of national significance. The organization takes interest in legal cases involving efforts of American Indian tribes to achieve rights to sovereignty guaranteed by treaties with the United States. Various tribes' efforts toward that end have been stalled by lengthy legal battles carried out in U.S. courts at the federal, state, and local level. Because reservations are exempt from sales and property taxes and from restrictions on gambling, many state governments are seeking to tax the income generated by the commercial activities that take place on Indian reservations.

Of greater importance to individual Indians is the NARF's assistance in achieving formal recognition of many Indian groups not previously acknowledged as legitimate tribes. By the early 1990's, more than three hundred tribes and bands of American Indians were recognized by the federal government and were qualified to receive federal and state aid. NARF's work in convincing the Bureau of Indian Affairs (BIA) to accept the legitimacy of tribal claims brought before the agency as the administrator of the congressionally authorized Acknowledgment Project has led to the formal recognition of several tribal groups.

Native Sons of the Golden West: Anti-Japanese organization. The group, founded in 1875, had its peak influence between 1900 and 1930, although it was influential through the World War II years, producing an inflammatory publication called *The Grizzly Bear*. The Native Sons wanted to revoke the citizenship of all Japanese Americans and were among the founders of the Japanese Exclusion League of California in 1920. The Native Sons and other groups successfully pressured the U.S. government just after the start of World War II to move all people of Japanese ancestry—both citizens and noncitizens—from the West Coast. They feared that Japanese Americans would not be loyal to the United States once the United States was at war with Japan.

Nativism: Policy of favoring people born in a country over those who have immigrated. There have been significant nativism movements in the United States at times of economic hardship when native-born Americans felt threatened by immigrant groups and tried to restrict immigration. Nativism gives rise to prejudice and discrimination against immigrant groups that are easily identifiable by race, language, or customs. The strong anti-Chinese sentiments among Anglo Americans in the late nineteenth and early twentieth centuries, which included anti-Chinese violence, is one example; another is the discrimination against Irish immigrants that was common in the Northeast around the same time.

Naturalization: Process of conferring citizenship. Naturalization may be based on either the principle of ascription, in which one's political membership is determined by an objective circumstance such as place of birth or parents' citizenship, or the principle of consent, in which one chooses and applies for political membership. Both principles have been applied in different ways to American naturalization law over time.

Since 1907, some 12.5 million people have become U.S. citizens through naturalization, including 270,000 in 1990. Normally aliens can apply five years after becoming permanent residents (that is, after acquiring their "green card"). If married to a U.S. citizen, they can apply after three years. Applicants must also have lived for at least six months in the state where they apply. Like some other procedures of the IMMIGRATION AND NATURALIZATION SERVICE (INS), the paperwork involved may bring long delays.

Applicants must also pass an oral exam. In the 1990's, candidates for naturalization were required to know "simple words and phrases" in English and to understand questions given to them in "ordinary English" by a naturalization examiner. Aliens who are illiterate because of physical incapacity and aliens over fifty years of age who have lived in the United States for twenty years are excused from the literacy requirement. Applicants are asked questions on American government and history, including major provisions of the Constitution and leading historical figures. There is usually a group ceremony before a federal or state court for those who pass, which includes an oath of allegiance to the United States.

Immigrants take the oath of citizenship at a group ceremony in Miami in 1984. (AP/Wide World Photos)

Historical Background. The first Congress in 1790 passed the first American naturalization law, which set the pattern of excluding some groups from the process. Citizenship was possible only for "free white persons"; blacks were excluded until passage of the FIFTEENTH AMENDMENT in 1870. Though some Asians had been admitted to U.S. citizenship over the years, in the 1920's the Supreme Court found this illegal in cases such as *OZAWA V. UNITED STATES*. Because of the American role in the Philippines, Filipinos could become naturalized if they served in the U.S. military for at least three years.

The ALIEN AND SEDITION ACTS of 1798 included a Naturalization Act which extended the residency requirement for aliens applying for citizenship from five years residence in the United States to fourteen years. The act also barred from citizenship anyone from a country with which the United States was at war. The Federalists were afraid that the new foreign citizens would give the Jeffersonians an advantage in the 1800 elections. President John Adams did not invoke the 1798 laws, but they likely had some effect in discouraging immigration and causing some foreigners to leave the United States. After Jefferson's victory, the residence period was returned to five years.

The FOURTEENTH AMENDMENT declared that those born or naturalized in the United States, and subject to the jurisdiction thereof, are citizens of the United States and of the state where they reside. The 1898 Supreme Court decision of *U.S. v. Wong Kim Ark* confirmed that this amendment extended citizenship to the American-born sons of permanent residents of California who were Chinese subjects. This applied despite the provisions of a treaty between China and the United States as well as the 1790 naturalization statute that had expressly disqualified nonwhites from becoming naturalized citizens. The 1898 decision overturned the 1873 *Slaughter House Cases* opinion that a child born to parents who were subjects of a foreign state would not acquire citizenship by birth. At the same time, however, the CHINESE EXCLUSION ACT was in effect, and a similar effort was being made to bar Japanese immigrants. In 1922 the Supreme Court held that Japanese were ineligible for American citizenship. The 1924 Quota Act declared that those ineligible for citizenship should be excluded from American shores. During World War II, after the attack on Pearl Harbor, the NATIVE SONS OF THE GOLDEN WEST in California unsuccessfully sought a reversal of the *Wong Kim Ark* case as it applied to Japanese children.

The NINETEENTH AMENDMENT guaranteeing women's suffrage led to a change in the policy regarding female citizenship. Until 1922, a woman had gained citizenship by marriage to an American but lost citizenship by marriage to an alien. If an alien husband became naturalized, his wife and children would acquire U.S. citizenship. With the Cable Act of 1922, marriage would neither confer nor forfeit citizenship, although marriage to an American could expedite

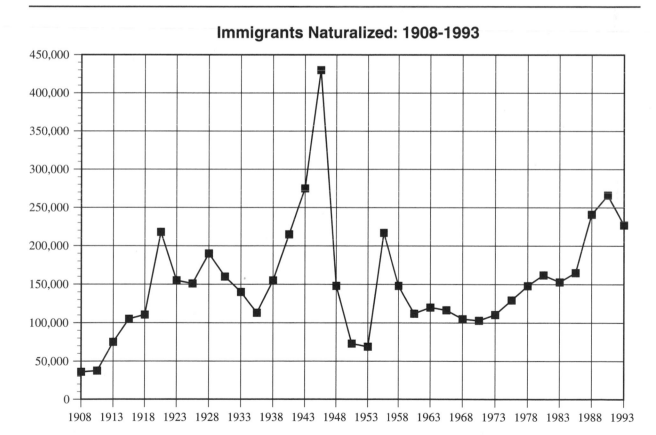

Immigrants Naturalized: 1908-1993

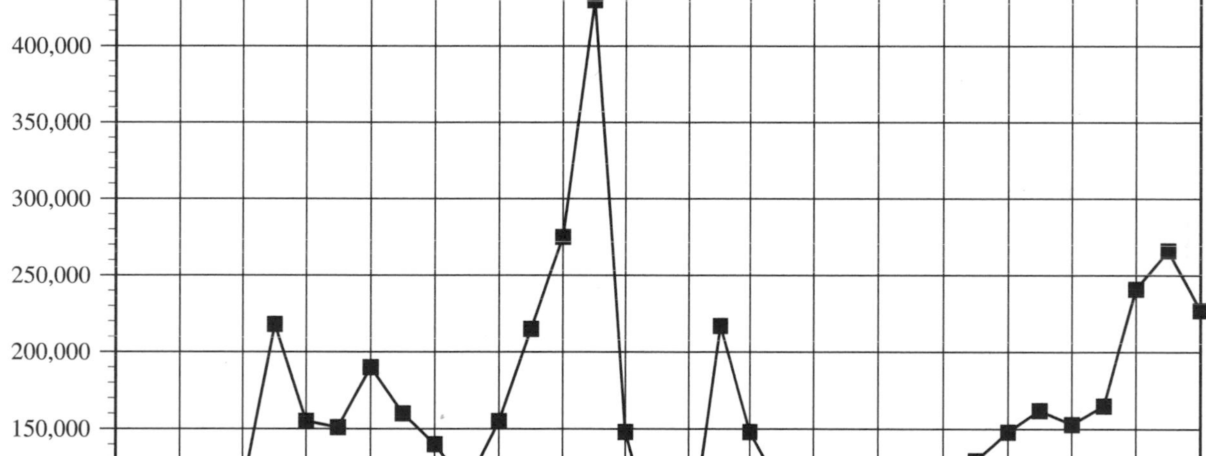

Source: Adapted from Immigration and Naturalization Service, *An Immigrant Nation: United States Regulation of Immigration, 1798-1991*, p. 19. Washington, D.C.: Department of Justice, 1991.

one's acquiring citizenship through naturalization.

The Naturalization Act of 1940 permitted the naturalization of descendants of peoples indigenous to the Western Hemisphere. Chinese became eligible for naturalization in 1943; natives of India and the Philippines in 1946; and Japanese, Koreans, Polynesians, Thais, and other persons of Asian ancestry in 1952.

State Citizenship and Restrictions. At one point in the 1800's, more than twenty states allowed aliens to vote before their U.S. naturalization process was complete. This practice presumably offered the states certain political advantages in close elections.

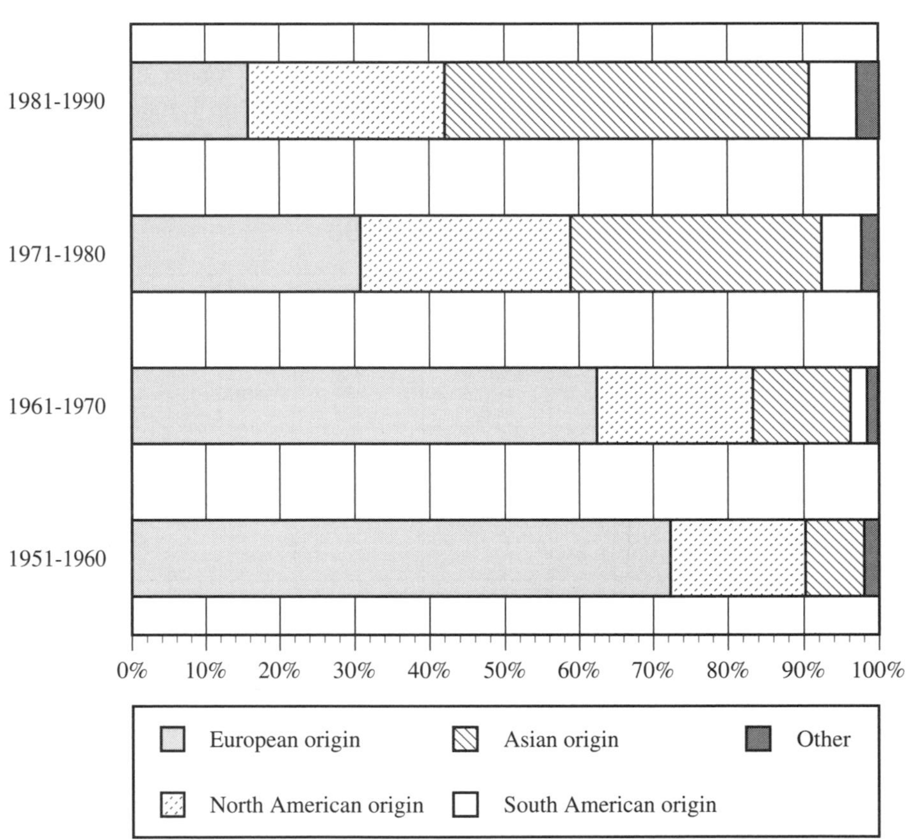

Source: Adapted from Allison Landes, ed. *Immigration and Illegal Aliens*. Figure 2.5. Wylie, Tex.: Information Plus, 1991.

Expeditious state naturalization sometimes came about through partisan fraud and corruption. For example, after the Civil War the Tammany Hall Democratic machine in New York City had its hack judges, Barnard and Cardozo, look the other way when confronted by irregularities in procedure. The New York Printing Co., which Boss Tweed owned, printed 105,000 blank applications and 69,000 certificates for naturalization. The Hall also paid the naturalization fees and gave foreigners red tickets that enabled them to obtain their papers free of charge. More than forty thousand such tickets were issued in 1868, a presidential election year. (The Republicans, also in the business of naturalization, gave out a different colored ticket.)

Limiting and Revoking Citizenship. Theoretically, naturalization confers upon aliens all of the rights of native American citizens except eligibility for the presidency. Over the years, however, there have been efforts to undermine the equal footing with native-born citizens that the U.S. Constitution seems to suggest. For example, the Hartford Convention of 1814 called for a constitutional amendment to prohibit naturalized citizens from holding federal office. In the 1850's, the Know Nothing Party tried to extend the residence requirement for naturalization to twenty-one years. Massachusetts amended its constitution to prohibit immigrants from voting until two years after their naturalization.

Aliens were also subject to various forms of discrimination, as in alien land laws that limited their rights to own property. Special interest groups convinced state governments to bar aliens from certain professions ranging from lawyers, dentists, and bankers to plumbers, pawnbrokers, and boxing promoters. In 1918, Congress doubled the income tax on nonresident aliens. Other bills were introduced to deport aliens who failed to apply for U.S. citizenship or who failed to learn

English within a specified period.

In some cases, aliens have been denied citizenship because of their political or religious beliefs. In 1929, the Supreme Court in *U.S. v. Schwimmer* allowed the rejection for citizenship of a fifty-year-old pacifist woman who would not take an oath to bear arms in defense of the country. The ruling was overturned by the 1946 case *Girouard v. U.S.*, involving a Seventh-day Adventist on the grounds that Congress did not expressly require bearing arms as a prerequisite to citizenship. Justice William O. Douglas wrote, speaking for the Court, "We cannot believe that the oath was designed to exact something more from one person than from another." (Girouard was willing to serve in the army as a noncombatant.)

In 1969, a federal judge declined to grant citizenship to two Jehovah's Witnesses. He ruled that citizenship requires responsibilities and that the applicants relied upon a religious code that they claimed forbade participation in voting, serving on juries, or pledging allegiance.

Citizenship can be taken away from naturalized citizens if they have concealed a material fact (such as complicity in World War II atrocities) or willfully misrepresented their case. A 1961 Supreme Court case involving racketeer Frank Costello concluded that he had lost his citizenship for swearing in his 1925 application that his occupation was real estate when it was actually bootlegging. In a later decision, the Court held that Costello's two crimes involving moral turpitude, which justified deporting an alien, had taken place during the years when he was still a citizen (1925-1959), and so could not be made the basis of his deportation.

During the COLD WAR, Congress provided that persons who refused to testify before a congressional committee regarding their "subversive activities" could be denaturalized for obtaining citizenship fraudulently. Membership in an organization within five years following naturalization that would have been a basis for the denial of citizenship was another ground for denaturalization.

Leaving the United States after naturalization and becoming a permanent resident of a foreign country was said to create a presumption of fraudulent intent. The Citizenship Act of 1907 provided that "when any naturalized citizen shall have resided for two years in the foreign state from which he came, or for five years in any other foreign state, it shall be presumed that he had ceased to be an American citizen." In *Schneider v. Rusk* (1964), however, the Supreme Court held that the rights of citizenship of native-born and naturalized persons are the same and that denaturalization of naturalized citizens for living abroad constitutes an unreasonable and arbitrary discrimination in violation of the Fifth Amendment. The Court rejected the "impermissible assumption" that "naturalized citizens as a class are less reliable and bear less allegiance to this country than do the native born."

At one time, holding an office in another country that could only be held by a national of that country or voting in a foreign election were grounds for termination of American citizenship. The 1967 *Afroyim v. Rusk* decision overturned a deprivation of citizenship for voting in a foreign election. Afroyim had become a U.S. citizen in 1926, and then voted in an Israeli election in 1951. His passport renewal request was rejected by the State Department in 1960, but in another five-to-four decision, the Supreme Court rejected such a drastic penalty.

SUGGESTED READINGS. Those wishing further knowledge of legal precedents of naturalization should consult Milton R. Konvitz's *The Alien and the Asiatic in American Law* (1946). A more up-to-date treatment of immigrants' legal rights may be found in *The Rights of Aliens and Refugees* (1990), written by David Carliner and others, which was published by the American Civil Liberties Union. For information on contemporary rules, see the *Basic Guide to Naturalization and Citizenship* (1990) prepared by the outreach program of the Immigration and Naturalization Service (INS).—*Martin Gruberg*

Navajo Code Talkers: Nickname given to some of the Navajo Indians recruited into the Marines during World War II. More than four hundred Navajo communications specialists were given the name "code talkers" because they regularly outwitted Japanese eavesdroppers in the South Pacific by using transmissions with phrases from the Navajo language. This secret language associated military terms with certain Navajo words, broken into code. For example, their word for "owl" meant an observation plane, and "iron fish" meant torpedo. The use of these coded messages enabled U.S. Marines to seize the island of Iwo Jima. In 1982 a presidential proclamation declared August 14 to be National Navajo Code Talkers Day.

Navajo–Hopi Land Dispute: Disagreement that resulted from the federal government's Executive Order of 1882, establishing a new reservation for the Hopi Indians on lands situated on and around three mesas (flat-topped mountains) stipulating that this Hopi land could be utilized by "other Indians as the Secretary of the Interior may see fit to settle thereon." This arrangement has displeased both the Hopis and the Navajos for more than a hundred years.

In part the dispute is the result of different lifestyles of the HOPIS and NAVAJOS on adjoining or overlapping lands. Historically, the Navajos lived as herders of livestock, surrounding the less numerous Hopis. The Hopis lived as farmers congregated in villages, using outlying land for grazing and religious rites.

In 1910, four-fifths of the Hopi reservation's 3,863 square miles was utilized by Navajos. Although the Hopi population had doubled since the reservation's founding, the federal government compressed the Hopis into a fourth of their reservation lands in 1943. Hopis were permitted to graze their livestock only in District 6, the Hopi Grazing Unit. The remainder was left to Navajos. This land reduction resulted in livestock reduction. The dispute over land jurisdiction then centered on a 1.5 million-acre area of desert, termed "the Gap," south of Tuba City, Arizona. The modern legal battle over land ownership centers on the Hopi claim to 128,000 acres west of the 1882 Hopi reservation boundary line in the Gap, with the Navajos prepared to accept Hopi rights to 40,000 acres of that land. A key question is whether land ownership should be determined by the residence of Navajos on fifteen sites inside the proposed Hopi partition line—an issue that dates back to the 1934 Boundary Act.

The 1934 Boundary Act, designed to establish Navajo reservation boundaries, provided for recognition of the rights of other Indians already located there. A unique twist to the Navajo-Hopi land dispute occurred in the 1960 *Healing v. Jones* federal court decision giving the Hopis exclusive right to land within District 6, and the Hopis and Navajos "joint, undivided and equal rights" to land in an area south of Keam's Canyon, Arizona. More recently the Navajos proposed to buy out Hopi land to avoid relocation; the Hopi refused to sell. The dispute continued in the early 1990's, with the Hopi land official refusing Navajo-initiated improvements on the disputed land that might contribute to Navajos' legal claims to the land.

SUGGESTED READINGS.The dispute is sympathetically discussed from the Hopi perspective in Frank Waters' *Book of the Hopi* (1963). The Navajo perspective on this issue is detailed in Bertha P. Dutton's *American Indians of the Southwest* (1983).

Navajos: Largest American Indian group in the United States, numbering 200,000 in the early 1990's. Dwelling on a 32,000-square-mile reservation in northeastern Arizona and northeastern New Mexico, the Navajos call this region Dinétah (the Land of the People) and themselves Diné (the People). The Diné origin legend claims that Navajos (in Spanish *Nabajó,* derived from the Tewa

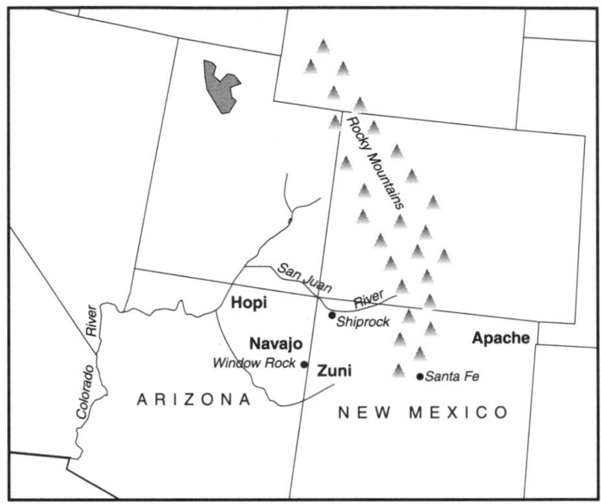

NAVAJO TERRITORY

Návahu'u, "the arroyo with the cultivated fields") came to earth through a progression of underworlds, grouped together into layers identified as the Black World, the Red World, and the Blue World. Contemporary chronological evidence defines Navajos as an Athabascan language-speaking group that lived in northwestern Canada two thousand years ago, then migrated to the American Southwest through the intermountain region west of the Rocky Mountains over a period of four hundred years. By the mid-fourteenth century they occupied an area on tributaries of the San Juan River, northwest of Santa Fe, New Mexico.

The Navajos' rich and often tragic history includes early wars with the Spanish and their Pueblo Indian allies, the PUEBLO REVOLT OF 1680, the LONG WALK (1864), and the return to Dinétah (1868). The community was maintained over the years through elaborate ceremonies and a matrilineal clan system. Navajo communities were organized into chapters during the 1920's and were hurt by the compulsory livestock-reduction programs of the 1930's and 1940's targeted at the traditional source of Navajo wealth.

Navajos are governed today by a chairman and an eighty-eight member tribal council located at Window Rock, Arizona. Formed in 1938, the tribal council oversees 109 chapters on a reservation the size of West Virginia. Navajo tribal government at Window Rock developed under leaders such as Henry Chee Dodge, the first chairman of the Navajo Tribal Council. Navajo business interests have diversified since the mid-1900's.

Ansel Adams photograph of Navajo woman and child in Canyon de Chelly, Ariz. (National Archives)

Traditionally, the Navajo lifestyle centered on herding livestock. Contemporary Navajos (called the Navajo Nation after a 1969 Tribal Council resolution) have attempted to attract industrial firms to the reservation, and to develop an annual $75 million budget from coal, oil, and uranium mineral rights, as well as taxation and timber. Educational opportunities for Navajo youth have increased as well, exemplified in two reservation-based institutions: the Navajo Community College in Tsaile, Arizona, and Shiprock, New Mexico; and the Rough Rock Demonstration School and its Navajo Curriculum Center in Rough Rock, Arizona.

Known for their traditional hexagonal dwellings called hogans, their rugs woven on an upright loom, and their silver and turquoise jewelry, Navajos attend Pueblo ceremonies in Zuñi, New Mexico, and at Hopi villages in Arizona. Each September they hold the Navajo Nation Fair, the largest American Indian fair in the United States. They are a people who endeavor to remain *hozho*, the Navajo term for beauty, goodness, happiness, and harmony.

Suggested Readings. The rich traditions of this proud people are aptly presented in Peter Iverson's *The Navajos* (1990). Other helpful sources include Clyde Kluckholm and Dorothea Leighton's *The Navaho* (1974) and Ruth Underhill's *The Navajos*

(1967). The Navajo origin legend is perceptively told in Paul G. Zolbrod's *Dine bahane: The Navajo Creation Story* (1984).

Negritude movement: Literary and social movement among intellectuals of the African diaspora. Centered in Francophone Africa and the French West Indies, the Negritude movement was led by Aimé Césaire, Léopold Senghor, and Leon Damas in the 1930's. The movement emphasized the unique world view expressed by African peoples in their music, literature, dance, art, and other cultural expressions. Similar themes were expressed in the Black Awakening in Haiti, which urged blacks to learn African history and culture, and in the HARLEM RENAISSANCE in the United States. The Negritude movement reached the height of its popularity in the 1960's; during the 1970's and 1980's, its views merged into AFROCENTRISM.

The first World Series of the Negro Leagues in 1924 featured the Kansas City Monarchs. (National Baseball Library, Cooperstown, NY)

Negro American Labor Council (NALC): Labor organization formed in May, 1960, by A. Philip RANDOLPH, who was president of the BROTHERHOOD OF SLEEPING CAR PORTERS. Although Randolph had become a member of the executive council of the AMERICAN FEDERATION OF LABOR-CONGRESS OF INDUSTRIAL ORGANIZATIONS (AFL-CIO) in 1955, he believed in the necessity of establishing the NALC as a pressure group to eliminate racial discrimination within unions. Although the major unions supported passage of important civil rights legislation in the 1960's, they were slow to integrate their own leadership and often did not understand the plight of their minority members. The NALC worked to help all minorities in any union achieve fair pay and equal opportunity for promotion. Randolph resigned his presidency of the NALC in 1966 and was succeeded by Jamaican-born Cleveland Robinson.

Negro League baseball: Term loosely used to refer to a number of organizations that sponsored and coordinated games and leagues for African American players. Early black baseball clubs were formed in the 1860's and participated in regional tournaments by the 1880's. The Negro National League was begun February 13, 1920, through the efforts of popular black pitcher Andrew "Rube" Foster. The league included member teams from cities such as Cincinnati, Kansas City, Chicago, Detroit, and St. Louis, all of which had large African American populations. The Eastern Colored League was formed in 1923. Although the Negro National League folded within a few years, the Negro Leagues continued to field teams through World War II. In the 1930's, the financial support of racketeers enabled some black teams and leagues to survive the Depression. After Jackie ROBINSON broke the color barrier in 1947 and African Americans were allowed to play in the white major leagues, many talented players left and interest in Negro League baseball diminished. The last all-black team, the Indianapolis Clowns, became inactive in the early 1960's.

Neo-Nazis: Term used for various American white supremacist groups and organizations, including actual American Nazi Parties, skinheads (urban youth gangs modeled after British gangs), the KU KLUX KLAN, and the Posse Comitatus, among others. The groups share the belief that "aliens"—particularly Jews, African Americans, and homosexuals—are inferior and evil, and that violence against such people is justified, even necessary. No neo-Nazi group has a national organization; rather, small groups have sprung up locally throughout the country. By the 1990's, approximately twenty to fifty thousand Americans were official members of these groups, with many thousands more passive supporters. The HATE CRIMES and other activities of neo-Nazis are closely monitored by their opponents such as the ANTI-DEFAMATION LEAGUE.

New Deal: Large-scale, wide-ranging series of programs and activities initiated by President Franklin Delano Roosevelt to combat massive unemployment during the GREAT DEPRESSION. The New Deal brought millions of Americans into the mainstream of public life for the first time.

New Deal programs helped put the nation back to work after the Great Depression. (AP/Wide World Photos)

In 1932, when Roosevelt was elected president, the United States was mired in the worst depression in its history. One-quarter of the work force was unemployed, the economy had practically collapsed, and the nation seemed to have lost hope. Once in office, Roosevelt embarked on a whirlwind of activity that created projects, programs, and agencies designed to put Americans back to work. Together, these groundbreaking programs became known as the New Deal and changed the shape of American society.

SOCIAL SECURITY, one of the New Deal's most enduring programs, provided a previously lacking social safety net for older Americans and disabled people, who could now depend upon at least minimal assistance from the federal government. In many ways, Social Security was the first step in bringing these two groups into fuller participation in modern American life.

Programs such as the Works Progress Administration (WPA), the Civilian Conservation Corps (CCC), and the Tennessee Valley Authority (TVA) hired and trained millions of unemployed Americans to repair roads and bridges, recover land lost to erosion, and construct massive public power projects. These activities of the Roosevelt Administration deliberately included minority groups as program recipients and participants. This aspect of the New Deal was encouraged by Eleanor ROOSEVELT, the First Lady, who was a tireless champion of the rights of women, minorities, workers, and children.

The influence of the New Deal extended into the arts, for the WPA created innovative programs for writers, artists, and theaters that likewise included minorities. In New York City, for example, African American theater entered a vibrant new phase, funded in large part by the federal government.

The New Deal's impact on MULTICULTURALISM in the United States was profound and lasting. Many elements of American society that had been ignored or neglected received the chance to participate in economic, political, and cultural life. Urban blacks in the North, rural poor whites in Appalachia, displaced MIGRANT WORKERS in California: all these and many more found that FDR's New Deal offered them hope and opportunity as part of a more generous, multicultural society.

SUGGESTED READINGS. Frank Burt Freidel's *Franklin D. Roosevelt: A Rendezvous with Destiny* (1990) provides the personal context for the New Deal, while Anthony Badger's *The New Deal: The Depression Years, 1933-40* (1989) is a comprehensive view of its programs and activities. For an intimate, common person's approach to the New Deal and what it meant, the reader can turn to Page Smith's *Redeeming the Time: A People's History of the 1920's and the New Deal* (1987).

New Harmony, Ind.: Utopian community in southwestern Indiana founded by British social and economic reformer Robert Owen in 1825. Owen envisioned communities in which people could live and work together in a cooperative society; they would share the results of their work equally. Unfortunately, many of the thousand or so people who responded to Owen's call were misfits and troublemakers. The community was in constant disarray, even anarchy. After three years, Owen gave up and returned to England. His sons stayed on, however, and the town remained a cultural center of the pre-Civil War United States.

New World exploration. *See* **Exploration and explorers of the New World; Spanish Empire and the New World**

New York, N.Y.: Since its colonial years (1626-1776), New York has been a diverse, multicultural community. Originally the Dutch Calvinist colony of New Amsterdam, the city welcomed Europeans of various religions, such as French Huguenots and Portuguese Jews. After the English took over the city and renamed it New York in 1664, there were periodic waves of Scots-Irish and German immigration. About eight hundred African American slaves lived in New York in the 1720's; they were gradually replaced by Irish indentured servants.

New York saw a great infusion of New England Yankees in the late 1700's. After 1820, however, the City began to feel the effects of the great unprecedented waves of nineteenth century immigrants. Between 1820 and 1880, approximately 80 percent of immigrants who settled in New York were "old immigrant" groups from Ireland, the United Kingdom, Scandinavia, or Germany (including German Jews). Between 1880 and 1920, the total number of immigrants per decade increased greatly and their origins also shifted dramatically. New York City absorbed an enormous influx of Italians, Russian and Polish Jews, and various peoples from Austria-Hungary.

In the early years of the twentieth century, especially during World War I, the city experienced the effects of the GREAT MIGRATION of African Americans from the South in search of jobs in the northern industrial states. This influx greatly stimulated the growth of Harlem as an African American ghetto in Manhattan and as a renowned cultural center during the HARLEM RENAISSANCE of the 1920's.

After World War II, the African American migration to New York City resumed, coinciding with a very large migration of Puerto Ricans to East Harlem (later known as Spanish Harlem). By the 1950's and 1960's, African Americans and Puerto Ricans had become the dominant ethnic groups in other large districts such as the South Bronx, Bedford-Stuyvesant, and East New York in Brooklyn.

The IMMIGRATION AND NATIONALITY ACT OF 1965 removed longstanding restrictions against immigrants from non-European countries. This resulted in a wave of new immigrants, who often moved into neighborhoods vacated by "older" groups such as the Italians, Irish, Jews, and Germans, who had moved to the suburbs. Thus, a massive immigration of Koreans (supplemented by large numbers of Chinese and some Japanese) rescued Flushing, Queens, from its decline in population and economic activity. Thousands of Dominicans and other Latin American immigrants have settled in Washington Heights and Inwood in Manhattan, north of Harlem. Arabs have developed an enclave around Atlantic Avenue in Brooklyn. Asian Indians and Pakistanis have concentrated in Jackson Heights, Queens, in large numbers. The largest West Indian community in the United States is located in Jamaica, Springfield Gardens, and St. Albans in Queens, as well as in various African American neighborhoods of Brooklyn.

A massive influx of Greeks since the 1950's has turned Astoria, Queens, into the second largest Greek community in the world after Athens. Even the National Mortgage Bank of Greece has established a branch there. Similarly, the North Central Bronx has attracted a steady flow of Albanians since the 1960's. Perhaps the most surprising example of the great diversity of the new immigration is that of Brighton Beach, Brooklyn. As the Soviet Union gradually relaxed its barriers to emigration by Soviet Jews in the 1970's and 1980's, approximately fifty thousand Rus-

Through its Ellis Island reception center (shown here in 1902), New York City became the chief point of entry for immigrants to the United States in the late nineteenth and early twentieth centuries. (Library of Congress)

sian and Ukrainian Jews settled in this neighborhood, which has been given the affectionate nickname "Odessa by the Sea."

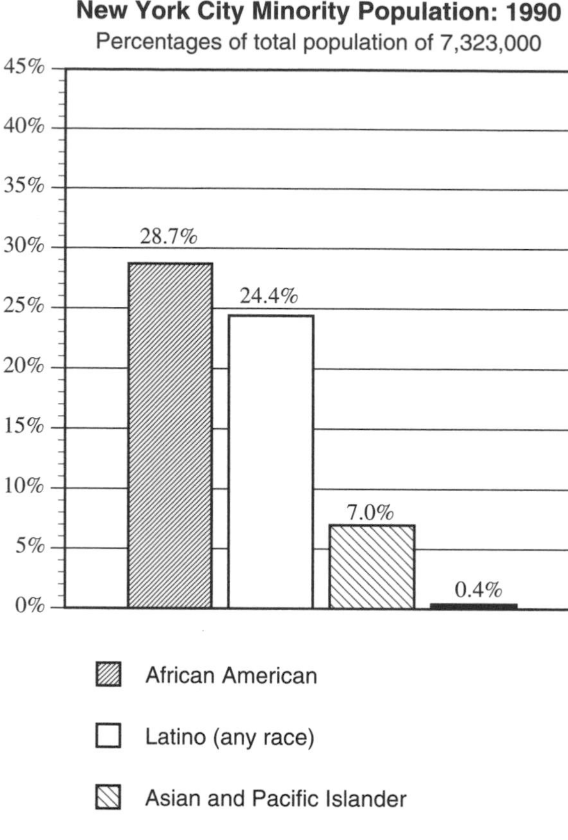

Source: Data are from *Statistical Abstract of the United States, 1992.* Table 38. Washington, D.C.: U.S. Government Printing Office, 1992.

New York City politics have been dominated at various times by the Irish, the Italians, the Jews, and the African Americans. The city has been at the center of numerous crises in intergroup relations, such as conflicts between blacks and Koreans, or blacks and Jews. It has also been the site of numerous reform efforts such as SETTLEMENT HOUSES and programs for CULTURAL PLURALISM. Despite its many urban problems, New York City continues to serve as a beacon and a gateway to the United States for large numbers of immigrants from a truly amazing range of nations.

SUGGESTED READINGS. Further insight into the Jewish experience in New York City may be found in *World of Our Fathers* (1976) by Irving Howe. *Beyond the Melting Pot: The Negroes, Puerto Ricans, Jews, Italians, and Irish of New York City* (1963) by Nathan Glazer and Daniel Patrick Moynihan is a classic work. *This Was Harlem: A Cultural Portrait, 1900-1950* by Jervis Anderson (1982) presents a sensitive, in-depth look at the nation's most famous African American community. *Chinatown: A Portrait of a Closed Society* (1992) by Gwen Kinkead and *New Urban Immigrants: The Korean Community in New York* (1981) by Illsoo Kim both are profound studies which present invaluable information on the Asian American experience in New York City.

New Zealander Americans: New Zealanders have a very similar culture to Australians. New Zealand, like Australia, is known for the people who migrate to it, rather than for emigrants who leave to seek a better life elsewhere.

New Zealand was originally settled by an aboriginal people who called themselves Maori, which means "normal," to contrast themselves with the European settlers who first arrived in 1642. Europeans arrived in greater numbers after the exploratory voyages of Captain James Cook in the 1770's. By the middle of the nineteenth century there were more Europeans than Maori in New Zealand.

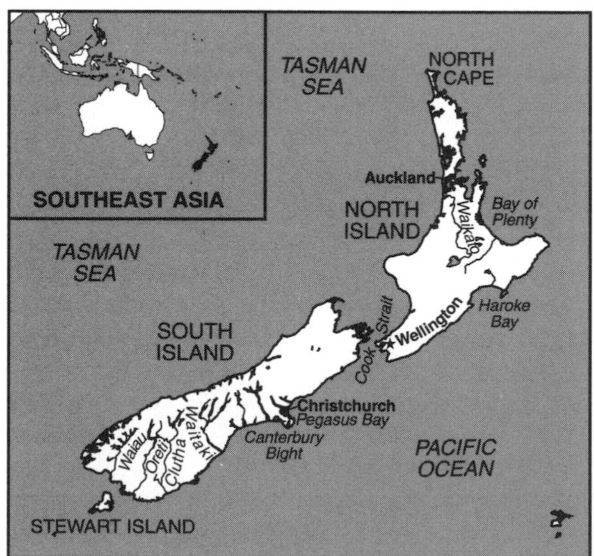

NEW ZEALAND

The Europeans exposed the Maori to diseases to which they had no resistance and fought with them for control of the land. These two factors wiped out four-fifths of the Maori population by the beginning of the twentieth century.

Almost all of the few New Zealanders who come to the United States are of European descent, especially of English, Irish, or Scottish background. Their immigration peaked in the early 1900's, with significant numbers also arriving during the California GOLD RUSH or as war brides after World War II. Their westernized, industrial culture allows New Zealanders to assimilate rapidly into American society. New Zealanders and Australians often settle in California because it is similar in lifestyle and climate to their homelands.

Nez Perce: Indian tribe that inhabited present-day eastern Oregon. The Nez Perce had a sophisticated culture in the mid-nineteenth century, with a population of approximately 3,000.

The Nez Perce believed in a spiritually animate universe, with deities populating every dimension of experience. Holy men acted as mediators between people and deities, but the emphasis was on the individual's relationship with the divine. Each person had a *wyakin*, or totem (such as an eagle, a rock, or a cloud), from which spiritual power could be drawn. Beginning in 1834, both Protestant and Catholic missionaries attempted to convert the Nez Perce, and elements of Christianity were grafted onto the native religion. The missionaries had highly negative effects on the culture by, for example, introducing flogging and capital punishment to the Nez Perce, who had previously settled their disputes through fines.

The Nez Perce was a nomadic tribe that moved in search of food. They depended on fishing, especially for salmon, in the Northwest, and on hunting big game (elk, deer, mountain sheep, bear, and buffalo) at home and on the eastern plains of Montana. Their material culture reflected their diverse food-gathering activities: they lived in skin or brush lodges, like the small fishing groups of the Northwest, and dressed in decorated skins, like the buffalo-hunting SIOUX of the Great Plains.

Social organization of the Nez Perce was highly individualistic, with no clearly recognized source of centralized power or authority. The chiefs "ruled" more by example than by executive fiat, and the family had priority over the dicta of the chiefs. Although the Nez Perce was not a warlike tribe, their approach to warfare—primarily though not exclusively with Indian tribes from the south—emphasized individual confrontations with the enemy.

Chief Joseph led the Nez Perce in peaceful relations with European Americans until they were forced onto reservations in the 1870's. (National Archives)

Relations with the whites were tempered by Nez Perce tolerance and restraint, although the tribe's peacefulness was continually tested by broken treaties and racial incidents. Chief JOSEPH, called "Thunder Coming up over the Land" by his people, could justly claim that since first meeting the whites in the early 1800's, the Nez Perce had never killed a white man.

Throughout the 1860's and 1870's, the Nez Perce were pressured onto reservations; in June, 1877, after receiving a thirty-day ultimatum to move to a reservation in Idaho, three warriors killed four settlers, precipitating war.

The war, in turn, led to the most heroic trek of the INDIAN WARS: a fifteen-week, 1,700-mile journey over the Rockies to the safety of Canada. With General Oliver Otis Howard in hot pursuit, Chief Joseph led more than 800 people to Snake Creek, forty miles from Canada, where he was attacked and defeated by Colonel Nelson A. Miles. Joseph's surrender was immortalized by his poetic declaration: "Hear me, my chiefs! I am tired. My heart is sick and sad. From where the sun now stands, I will fight no more forever."

The surrender was conditional on Miles's promise that the Nez Perce would go back to the Idaho reservation. Miles broke his promise, however, and the Nez Perce were sent to INDIAN TERRITORY in Oklahoma, not to return to the Northwest until 1884.

After suffering great hardship and loss of life in Oklahoma, the Nez Perce were relocated to the Colville Reservation in Washington State. Others were eventually located on the Nez Perce Reservation in Idaho. In the early decades of the twentieth century, the Nez Perce were forced to cede title to communal grazing lands they controlled in Idaho; INTERMARRIAGE with whites led many tribal members to leave the reservations. During the 1950's and 1960's, mixed-blood members struggled for greater control of tribal income and sought a lowering of the blood requirement for tribal membership to give mixed-blood members majority control in tribal matters. Some 2,200 individuals were entered as Nez Perce in the 1980 U.S. Census, and the tribe continues to sponsor religious and secular events on the reservations. The tribe has been successful in pursuing legal claims before the U.S. Indian Claims Commission.

SUGGESTED READINGS. Consult Robert M. Utley's *The Indian Frontier of the American West, 1846-1890* (1984). For specialized studies, see Merrill D. Beal's *"I Will Fight No More Forever"* (1963), Mark H. Brown's *The Flight of the Nez Perce* (1967), and R. Ross Arnold's *The Indian Wars of Idaho* (1932).

Ng Poon Chew (Mar. 14, 1866, Sun Ning, China—Mar. 13, 1931, Oakland, Calif.): Chinese American journalist. Ng came to the United States in 1881 after having been orphaned as a young child and groomed by his grandmother to become a Taoist priest. Once in California he began working as a houseboy on a ranch near San Jose and learned English at the local Chinese Presbyterian Mission. He converted to Christianity and attended the San Francisco Theological Seminary. In 1892 he was ordained as a Presbyterian minister. By 1899 he resigned the ministry and moved to Los Angeles, where he established *Hua Mei Sun Yat Po*, America's first Chinese language daily newspaper. In 1900 he returned to San Francisco, where he continued to publish the newspaper under the name *Chung Sai Yat Po.* Ng became an expert on Chinese American issues and served as adviser to the Chinese Consulate General in San Francisco from 1906 to 1913, becoming vice consul in 1913. His writings include *A Statement for Non-Exclusion* (1905), coauthored with Patrick J. Healy, and *The Treatment of the Exempt Classes of Chinese in the United States* (1908).

Ngor, Haing (b. 1947, Samrong Yong, Cambodia): Cambodian American doctor and actor. Ngor was a surgeon and obstetrician in Cambodia's capital, Phnom Penh. When Cambodia was taken over by the Khmer Rouge in 1975, he was sent to a forced labor camp and

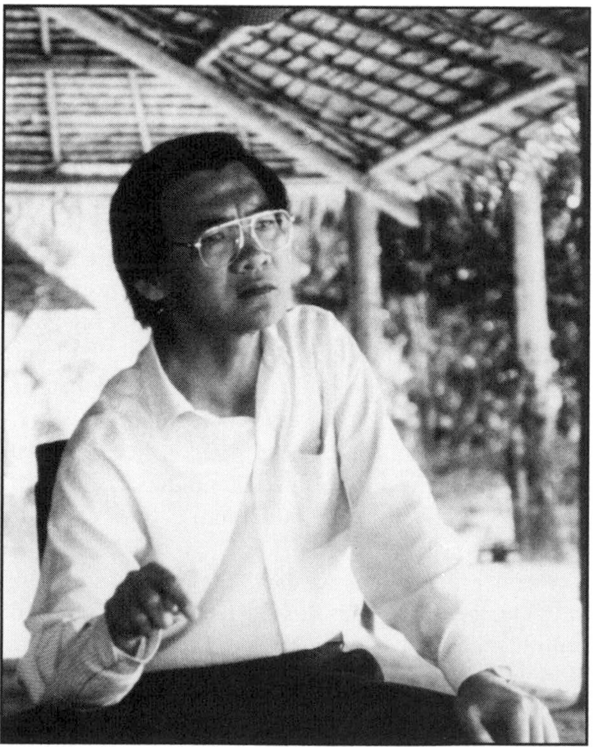

After starring in the The Killing Fields *(1982), Haing Ngor became a spokesman for and inspiration to the Cambodian American community.* (AP/Wide World Photos)

had to hide his education and skills in order to avoid being killed. During the next four years, Ngor was tortured, his wife died in childbirth, and several members of his family were executed. In 1979, he escaped to Thailand, and he later came to the United States. In 1982, he began a new career as a film actor and won an Academy Award for his first role, portraying a photojournalist in *The Killing Fields*. He played Dith Pran, an educated Cambodian who had escaped from the Khmer Rouge.

Niagara movement: Group begun in 1905 under the leadership of W. E. B. Du Bois during a period when physical and legal attacks on African Americans were on the rise throughout the country. Members held meetings at historic sites such as Faneuil Hall and Harpers Ferry to emphasize their continuation of an activist tradition dating back to the American Revolution. Their purpose was to seek equal voting and civil rights plus equal economic and educational opportunities. In 1909 they called for a conference to discuss the status of the Negro in the United States, on the centennial of Abraham Lincoln's birth. This national conference led to the founding of the National Association for the Advancement of Colored People (NAACP).

Nicaraguan Americans: This relatively small Central American community is made up of immigrants who fled their country during political upheavals and civil war in the 1970's and 1980's. Most Nicaraguans are mestizo, a mixture of Spanish and Indian, but some are of Caucasian, African, or Indian ancestry.

History. Nicaraguans originated from various indigenous tribes and more sophisticated Indians who migrated from Mexico and Guatemala. The colonial period began in 1522 when a Spanish expedition from Panama explored the Pacific region and founded a few settlements. There was frequent fighting between the Spanish on the Pacific and the Indians and the British on the Caribbean. The large Indian population was greatly reduced because of this fighting and diseases brought by the Spanish, who sold many of them into slavery.

Nicaragua became an independent republic in 1838. Civil strife between the liberals of Leon and the conservatives of Grenada led the Leonese to seek aid from William Walker, an American adventurer, who came into the country with a small band of followers and took over as president the next year. He was driven out in 1857 by conservatives, who ruled for some forty years. When uprisings occurred in 1912, the government requested help from the U.S. Marines. The marines remained there until 1925 and returned again from 1926 until 1933. This foreign intervention led to resentment by many Nicaraguans. One of those who opposed the presence of the marines and led a guerrilla war against them was Augusto César Sandino. His courage and daring feats made him the inspiration for the later revolutionary group known as the Sandinistas. Eventually he was captured and executed by the National Guard, a U.S. trained Nicaraguan army that took control when the marines left.

NICARAGUA

The English-speaking commander of the National Guard, Anastasio Somoza García, a member of a powerful Nicaraguan family, seized the government in 1936. This began the corrupt forty-two-year reign of the Somoza family, who maintained control over the people by supporting the hated National Guard, currying the favor of the United States, and favoring the wealthy. The family's blatant disregard for the suffering of its people paved the way for later rebellion.

With the murder of Pedro Joaquín Chamorro, the respected editor of one of Nicaragua's leading newspapers, violent clashes erupted between the people and the National Guard. The fighting continued until July, 1979, when the Sandinista National Liberation Front

(FSLN) brought down the Somoza dictatorship and took over the country.

The Sandinista Years. The new government, headed by a junta representing various ideologies, was faced with a country ravaged by war and an economy almost totally looted by the Somoza family. One of the first acts of the new government was to restore basic personal freedoms and a new judicial system. In the beginning the government made great strides in bringing about reform, particularly in the areas of literacy, health care, and land management. At the same time, it nationalized large segments of the economy.

Because the government leaned heavily on aid from Cuba and other Soviet-supported countries, some Nicaraguans became disenchanted with the Sandinistas and began to form opposition groups. The largest of these was the counter-revolutionary group known as the Contras. By the time Daniel Ortega Saavedra was elected president in 1984, the U.S. government was openly supporting the Contras with arms, equipment, and aid; the aid became covert later when Congress voted to suspend support. During this civil war, thousands of Nicaraguans were tortured and killed; many families were divided. In 1989 a regional peace plan committed the government to democratic changes, including elections in 1990.

Democratic Government. Violetta Barrios de Chamorro, the wife of the murdered newspaper editor, won the election in a surprise upset. Amnesty was granted to both sides, the embargo was lifted, and the Contras were to be disbanded. The transition to a democratic government has not been easy because of continuing animosity between the former Contras and the Sandinista soldiers, as well as a failing economy.

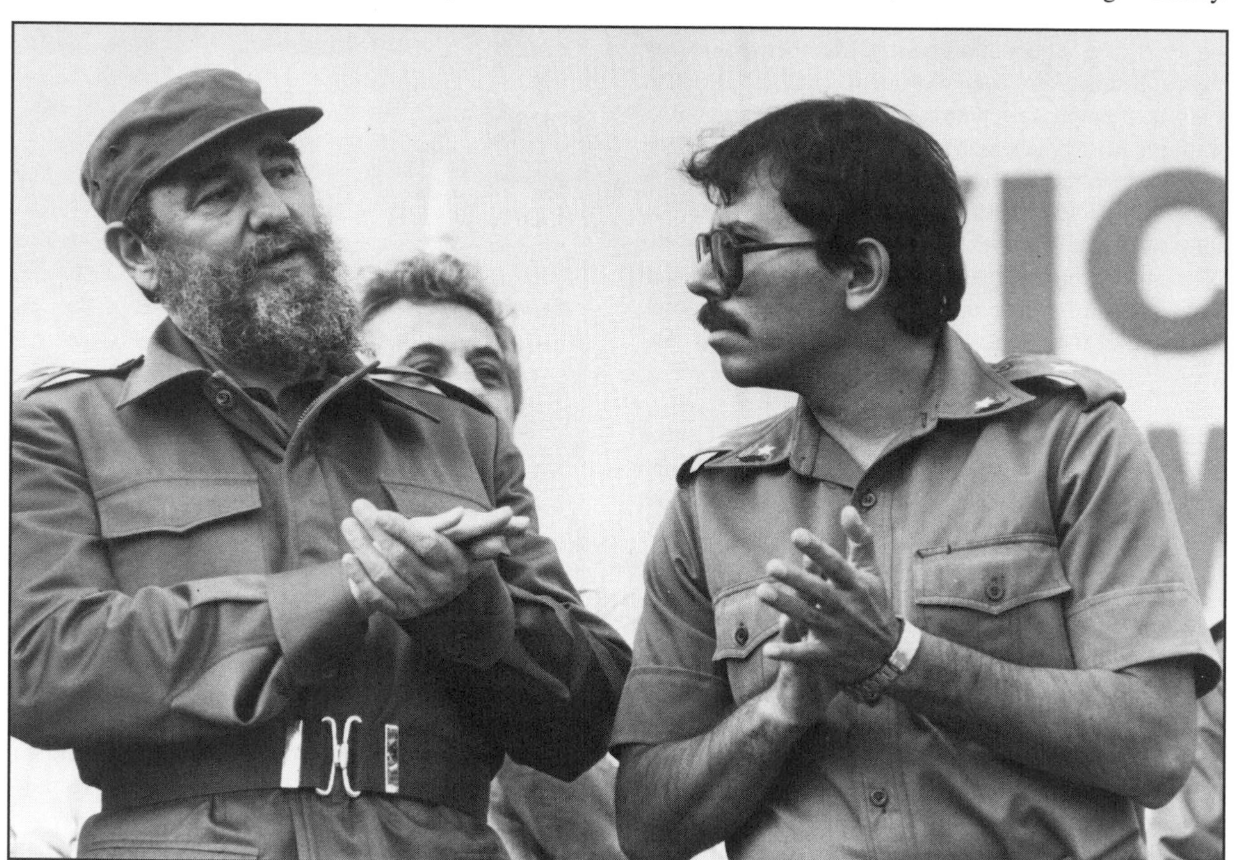

The victory of the Sandinistas in 1979 and the election of Daniel Ortega (right, with Fidel Castro, left) in 1984 prompted many wealthier, more conservative Nicaraguans to leave the country. (AP/Wide World Photos)

Immigration. Some of the wealthy supporters of Somoza fled the country after his overthrow in 1979, but they were relatively few. Most of those who left at that time were members of the National Guard, who fled to Honduras, Costa Rica, or Miami, Florida.

Later, however, many other Nicaraguans left because of increasing dissatisfaction with the government and the Contra war. Exact figures for people migrating to the United States are not readily available, since the movement was often clandestine and since until the mid-1980's immigration records did not classify Nicaragua as a separate country (they listed it under "other Caribbean countries"). It has been estimated that by 1987, approximately 188,000 Nicaraguans came into the U.S. The number of arrivals increased each year during the Contra war from approximately 19,000 in 1984, the first year for which separate figures are available, to approximately 44,000 in 1989. From statements of intended residence, it appears that the largest number of immigrants came into the states of California, Florida, and Texas, most arriving in the cities of Miami and Los Angeles.

In 1988, U.S. immigration officials ruled that the entering Nicaraguans must remain in the ports of entry until their refugee status could be determined. This resulted in many of the immigrants camping in the open because the IMMIGRATION AND NATURALIZATION SERVICE (INS) provided no housing and the shelters sponsored by local churches were filled. Frequently, the immigrants had to wait a long time because the process of applying for refugee status was complex and time-consuming. For example, at the beginning of 1989 the INS had received 35,431 applications. By the end of the year, only 3,252 applicants had been admitted; 10,486 were denied approval; and 21,693 applications were still pending. Interestingly, the Nicaraguans were not readily granted refugee status even though the U.S. government considered Nicaragua a Marxist state. Seventeen percent of applicants were approved from 1981 to 1984, for example, only slightly higher than the figure for legally admitted Salvadorans and Guatemalans, who were fleeing rightist governments, but much smaller than the number of approved Cubans, who were also fleeing a Marxist government. This pattern is also reflected in the small number of Nicaraguan Americans who have been naturalized. During the years 1980 to 1989, the number varied only from 616 (1983) to 1,363 (1988).

For the most part, the Nicaraguan immigrants have blended into the Spanish-speaking communities where they have settled. After the election of Chamorro, it was thought that many might return to Nicaragua, but this was not proven true. A relatively small number, mostly the wealthy or former National Guardsmen, returned to reclaim their land, but economic and political conditions in Nicaragua made this difficult. The majority of Nicaraguans who have immigrated since the revolution have adjusted to American life. Though they may not have learned fluent English, their children have done so, and they hope to make a better life for themselves and their families while still maintaining some aspects of their Nicaraguan culture.

Culture. There is a common heritage that almost all Central Americans share. It is rooted in the SPANISH LANGUAGE, the ROMAN CATHOLIC religion, and a deep love for the family. The Nicaraguans also have their own unique characteristics, including a distinctly Nicaraguan Spanish language.

The Somoza family had promoted foreign culture, most notably that of North America, but the Sandinistas took pains to recapture and rejuvenate that which was intrinsically Nicaraguan. Nicaragua has a rich literary tradition, particularly in poetry, finding its inspiration in the country's most acclaimed poet, Rubén Darío (1867-1916), who has been widely translated and has instilled a poetic sensibility that the ordinary people have brought with them to the United States.

Most Nicaraguan organizations in the United States were founded and flourished in the 1980's, but few remained active after the 1990 elections. They came into existence in response to U.S. intervention in Nicaragua—the majority in support of the Sandinista revolution and against U.S. aid to the Contras, although there were a few, such as the Nicaraguan Information Center, dedicated to the support of the U.S. position on Nicaragua. The purpose of most of the groups, composed largely of Americans, was to provide medical, technical, or humanitarian aid to the people of Nicaragua. Other groups concentrated on human rights problems and attempted to educate American citizens and the U.S. government regarding abuses according to their political perspective. Their programs included education, dissemination of information, and speakers' bureaus. In cities with large Nicaraguan populations, such as Los Angeles, Nicaraguans also have social organizations to maintain community and cultural ties.

SUGGESTED READINGS. For historical background on the Nicaraguan people, see Thomas Walker's *Nicaragua: The Land of Sandino* (1986) or Eduardo Crawley's *Nicaragua in Perspective* (1984). For various viewpoints on the revolution, see *Nicaragua: Unfinished Revolution, the New Nicaragua Reader* (1986), edited by Peter Rosset and John Vandermeer, or Stephen Kinzer's *Blood of Brothers* (1991). Steven White's *Culture and Politics in Nicaragua* (1986) presents the views of some of the Nicaraguan poets and writers.—*Lucille Whalen*

9 to 5 National Association of Working Women: An organization founded in 1973 to promote better pay and working conditions for women office workers. The early years of the organization coincided with the heyday of contemporary FEMINISM, and represented a spread of feminist concerns to the "pink collar ghetto" of female secretaries. Over the years, the group's agenda has expanded to include concerns with sexual and racial discrimination, the health hazards of video display terminals (VDTs), and issues such as family leave for working women.

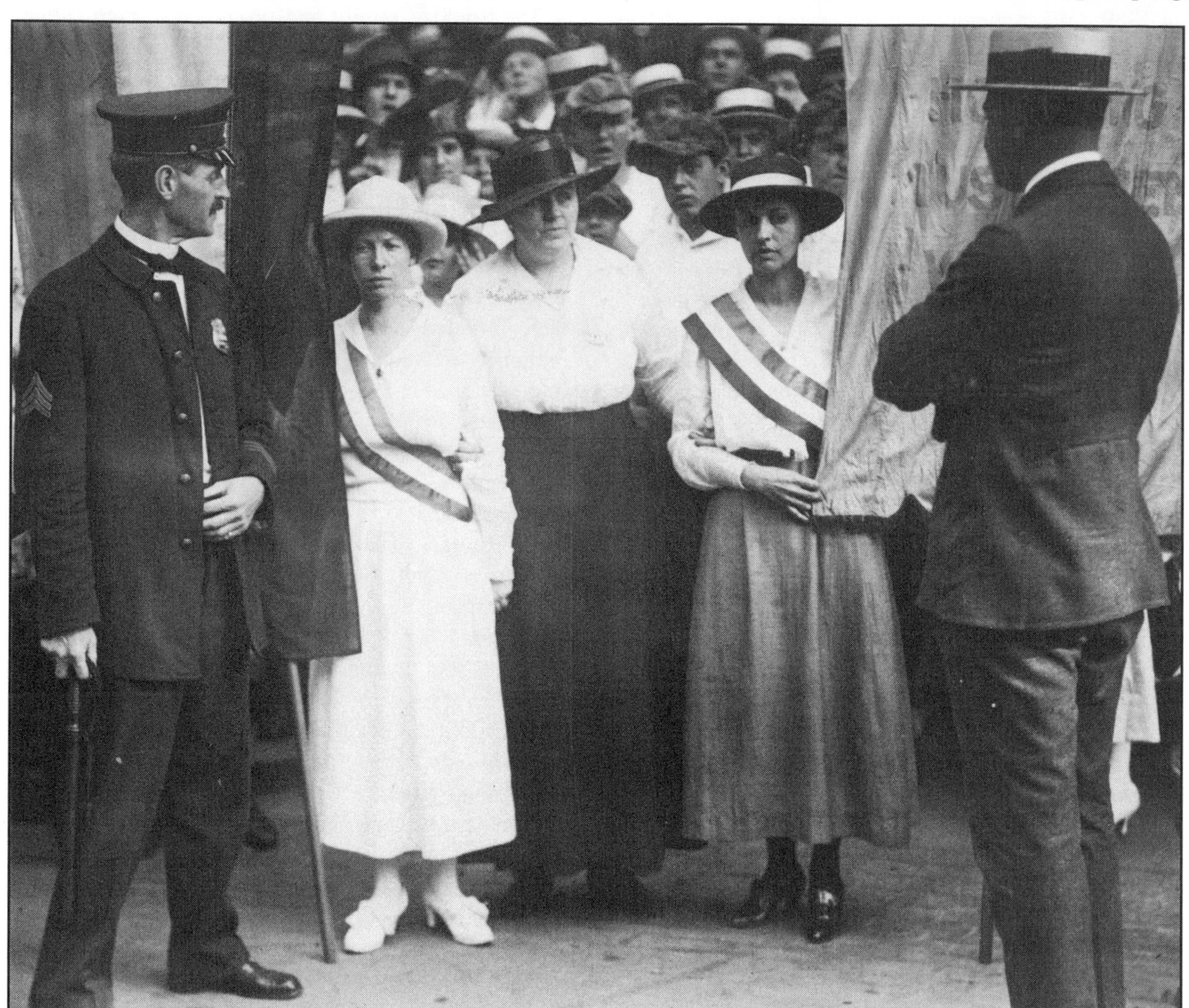

Women are arrested for picketing at the White House for the right to vote in 1917. (Library of Congress)

Nineteenth Amendment (1920): On August 26, 1920, the Nineteenth Amendment, giving women throughout the United States the right to vote, became part of the U.S. Constitution. While certainly a fundamental right, woman suffrage did not guarantee anything like full legal equality. Indeed, some have argued that winning the vote broke the momentum for equal rights and slowed women's social, economic, and even political progress.

Early feminist leaders had come from the ABOLITIONIST MOVEMENT and sought to end African American slavery. The Civil War accomplished that goal but failed to win new legal rights for women. In fact, the FOURTEENTH AMENDMENT explicitly added the word "male" to the Constitution for the first time, prompting some feminists to oppose its ratification: The FIFTEENTH AMENDMENT granted the vote to African American men while withholding it from women who had worked to free them. Feminists such as Elizabeth Cady STANTON and Susan B. ANTHONY concluded that other rights depended on the vote and organized the NATIONAL WOMAN SUFFRAGE ASSOCIATION (NWSA) in 1869. The American Woman Suffrage Association (AWSA) also organized that year. Both groups agreed on the goal of suffrage, but NWSA saw it as part of a broad range of rights requiring a constitutional amendment, while AWSA focused more narrowly and worked state by state (the two groups merged in 1890).

The SUFFRAGE MOVEMENT and suffragists used various tactics. Some, risking imprisonment, attempted to vote in federal elections in the 1870's. As women became active in more public roles such as organizers of unions and SETTLEMENT HOUSES, suffragists sought alliances with them, stressing the need for suffrage to accomplish their other goals.

Nonetheless, men would ultimately decide if women could vote. To persuade men that the vote would not bring social and domestic revolution, the suffrage movement increasingly portrayed itself in conservative terms, implying that women sought the vote not for themselves but to protect home and family. In truth, many suffragists were socially conservative, resenting African American and immigrant men's superior political rights and seeking to maintain the prerogatives of their own privileged group.

Suffrage came in stages, as suffragists adapted their tactics to changing forms of opposition. Women first won the vote in the territories of Wyoming and Utah in 1870. The so-called "Anthony amendment" was proposed in 1878 but languished in Congress until the Progressive era. Action moved to the states, a handful of which had granted women the vote by 1910. In 1912, the Progressive Party endorsed a woman suffrage amendment, reflecting the suffragists' new activism and political skills. Grassroots efforts won the vote in several states during the Wilson Administration, and new prosuffrage representatives finally helped force Congress to submit an amendment to the states in 1919. Within a year, the requisite thirty-six states had ratified the Nineteenth Amendment.

SUGGESTED READINGS. Both Eleanor Flexner's *Century of Struggle* (1975 ed.) and William L. O'Neill's *Everyone Was Brave* (1969) provide stirring accounts, while Steven Buechler's sociohistorical *Women's Movements in the United States* (1990) and William Chafe's *The Paradox of Change* (1991) view suffrage's legacy more ambivalently. There are also many fine biographies of individual suffragists.

Nisei: Second-generation Japanese Americans. Nisei were born in the United States of Japanese immigrant parents (ISSEI). Nisei were considered Americans by the Japanese, unlike their immigrant parents, who were generally considered Japanese. Many Nisei reached adulthood in the 1930's and had to contend with the Great Depression, Japanese American INTERNMENT by their own government during World War II, and continuing discrimination after the war. After World War II, Nisei held most of the power and influence in Japanese American communities. Awareness of generation is very important to Japanese. Issei and Nisei tend to form separate organizations and to worship separately.

Dancers at annual Nisei Week celebration in Los Angeles. (Alon Reininger, Unicorn Stock Photos)

Northwest Ordinance: One of the most important acts passed by Congress under the Articles of Confederation. The ordinance, which was approved in July of 1787, mapped out steps by which an area could achieve statehood and set limits on the expansion of slavery by prohibiting its existence in territory north of the Ohio River and east of the Mississippi. It included a clause stating that good faith would always be observed toward American Indians and guaranteeing that their lands and property would never be taken away without their consent. Although this stated policy toward American Indians was later little heeded, the ordinance was approved into law by the first Congress to convene in 1789 after ratification of the U.S. CONSTITUTION.

Norton, Eleanor Holmes (b. Apr. 8, 1938, Washington, D.C.): African American attorney and political leader. Norton was called "one of the most powerful women" in Washington, D.C., in 1989 by *Washington Magazine.* After attending segregated schools in Washington, D.C., she studied law at Yale University (M.A., 1963; LL.B., 1964). She held jobs with the American Civil Liberties Union (1965-1970), New York Commission on Human Rights (1970-1977), and the Equal Employment Opportunity Commission (1977-1981). She also taught at Georgetown University Law Center (1982-1990), served on the board of Yale (1982-1988), and won a (nonvoting) seat in the U.S. House of Representatives from the District of Columbia (1990).

Norwegian Americans: Of all Scandinavian immigrants to the United States, Norwegians probably have kept the closest ties to their homeland. Norwegians have always been a traveling and seafaring people; their country has the longest seacoast in all of Europe. In the eleventh century, Norwegian and Icelandic adventurers, led by Leif Ericsson, established colonies in Greenland and in North America at least as far south as Newfoundland. These settlements did not survive, but individual Norwegians began coming to the Dutch New Netherlands colony in the early 1600's.

Immigration. Apart from Ireland, Norway has contributed the largest percentage of its population to American immigration. Between 1820 and 1975, some 855,000 Norwegian immigrants arrived. Significant Norwegian settlement of the United States began in 1825, when a ship left Stavanger, Norway, for New York with fifty-two religious dissenters aboard. Like many European countries, Norway experienced a major increase in population in the nineteenth century, especially among the poor. Many had no opportunity for improving their lives, apart from emigrating. Also in the nineteenth century, the Lutheran state church of Norway was in tumult, challenged by dissenting sects and called upon to defend an unjust social system. During the 1840's and 1850's, Norwegian religious and political dissenters settled in New York, Iowa, Illinois, and Texas, often guided by a charismatic leader who was also a land speculator and promoter. Best known of these was violinist Ole Bull, whose failed colony in Pennsylvania, called Oleana, is still satirized in Norwegian songs and jokes.

After the Homestead Act opened the Great Plains in 1862, Norwegian immigration began in earnest. Much of the upper Midwest was first settled by Norwegians, including parts of Iowa, Minnesota, Nebraska, Wisconsin, and the Dakotas. As O. E. Rölvaag's novel *Giants in the Earth* (1927) reveals, many failed and even died in the harsh conditions. Others succeeded, and some of the Midwest's most prosperous farmers are of Norwegian ancestry. Many Norwegians were attracted to life in the United States by letters from friends or family who had gone before.

Later in the nineteenth century, numerous Norwegian tradespeople came to the cities, especially Chicago, Minneapolis, and other major midwestern centers. Others settled in Brooklyn, New York (especially Bay Ridge) and in San Francisco. Young Norwegian men often went to sea and thus were familiar with

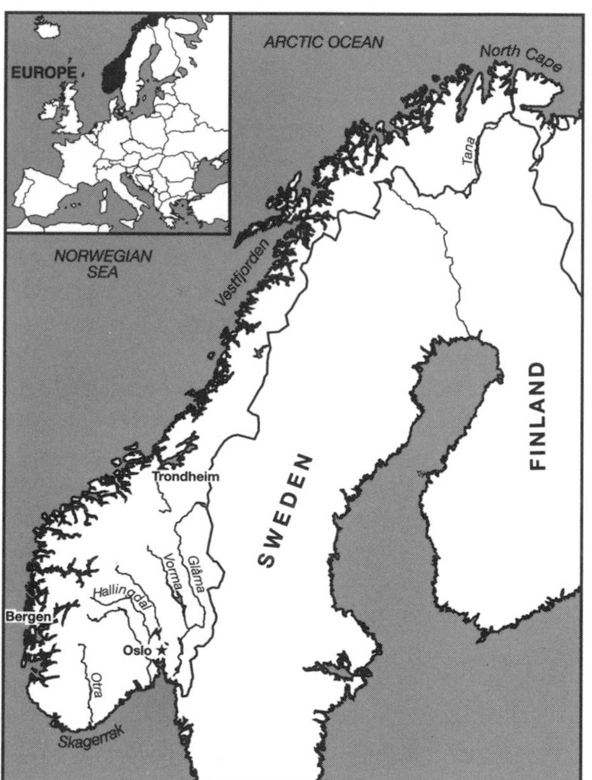

NORWAY

New York and other seaports. The Pacific Northwest, southeast Alaska, and the shores of Lake Superior attracted Norwegian fishermen and loggers. For a long time, most of the sailors on the merchant fleet of the Great Lakes were Norwegians. Seattle once had the largest urban concentration of Norwegian Americans in North America, and Norwegians still dominate the maritime trades around Puget Sound.

Community Life. Of all Scandinavian immigrants,

the Norwegian Americans were most active in organizing clubs, churches, and associations. The national fraternal order, Sons of Norway, had more than three hundred lodges and 85,000 members in 1974. Many early Norwegian Americans joined *bygdelag*, clubs organized around the district or *bygd* in Norway from which they had come. The immigrants also organized male choruses and public songfests to perform the choral music of Norwegian composers. *Torskeklubber* ("cod clubs") were dining associations that served Norwegian ethnic food, including the celebrated *lutefisk*, a hard-dried cod softened with lye before eating.

Young Norwegian Americans don national costume for a Norwegian Independence Day parade. (Frances M. Roberts)

Norwegian Americans, far more than other Scandinavian immigrants, have kept their language alive in the United States through language classes at Norwegian clubs and, until recently, in churches. Many cities with large Norwegian American populations, including Chicago, Minneapolis, and Seattle, hold parades on *Syttende mai* (May 17), Norway's constitution day. Some communities also celebrate October 9 as Leif Ericsson Day, an alternative to Columbus Day for those loath to credit the Italian navigator with being the first European in North America.

Cultural Contributions. Norwegian Americans have established educational institutions in the United States, including St. Olaf's College in Northfield, Minnesota; Augsburg College in Minneapolis; Concordia College in Moorhead, Minnesota; and Pacific Lutheran University in Parkland, Washington. Since 1847, when *Skandinavia* was founded in New York City, there have been dozens of Norwegian-language newspapers in the United States. By the 1990's, there were still three, *Western Viking*, in Seattle; *Nordisk Tidene*, in Brooklyn; and *Minnesota Posten*, in Minneapolis. All now print articles in both English and Norwegian.

Among leading Norwegian Americans of the twentieth century are the following. Thorstein Veblen, author of *Theory of the Leisure Class* (1899), was one of the founders of modern sociology. Norwegian-born

Knute Rockne was an outstanding football player and coach, under whose leadership University of Notre Dame's squad became the most famous American college football team. "Babe" Didrikson ZAHARIAS was called the greatest woman athlete of all time. Both Henry M. Jackson of Washington state and Walter Mondale of Minnesota carved out distinguished careers in the U.S. Senate, and Mondale also served as vice president, presidential candidate, and ambassador to Japan. Naval architect H. C. Hanson designed minesweepers and other naval craft and fishing boats and tugs used all over the northern Pacific. Kathryn Forbes's *Mama's Bank Account* (1943) became the long-running Broadway play *I Remember Mama* (1945). Most Norwegian American men and women, however, made modest but lasting contributions to American life in the building trades, agriculture, education, and the professions.

SUGGESTED READINGS. Dorothy Burton Skårdal's *The Divided Heart* (1964) surveys Scandinavian American immigrant culture. O. E. Rölvaag's *Giants in the Earth* (1927) is the classic novel of the Norwegian sodbuster. Among the many histories of Norwegian immigration and immigrant life are Arlow W. Andersen's *The Norwegian-Americans* (1975), Theodore C. Blegen's *Norwegian Migration to America* (1969), and Ingrid Semmingsen's *Norway to America* (1978). Kenneth O. Bjork's *West of the Great Divide* (1958) is about Norwegians on the West Coast. Arlow W. Andersen's *The Immigrant Takes His Stand* (1953) discusses Norwegian Americans in politics. A fine anthology of immigrant letters home is *Land of Their Choice* (1955), edited by Theodore C. Blegen.—*Jens Lund*

Novello, Antonia Coello (b. Aug. 23, 1944, Fajardo, Puerto Rico): Latina physician and U.S. Surgeon General. Having overcome a debilitating chronic childhood condition, Novello became a doctor at the University of Puerto Rico in 1970. She came to the mainland United States to study pediatrics and nephrology at several leading universities, and then practiced and conducted research at the National Institutes of Health from 1978 to 1990. In 1990, she was appointed Surgeon General, the first woman and the first Latino to hold the top medical position in the nation. Novello has been a leader in children's health, smoking, and ACQUIRED IMMUNE DEFICIENCY SYNDROME (AIDS) issues. Her honors include a Lifetime Achievement Award form the Puerto Rican Coalition in 1990 and a Simón Bolivar Award in 1991.

O

Oberlin College (Oberlin, Ohio): Independent, coeducational private college. Oberlin College was founded by Rev. John J. Shipherd and Philo Penfield Stewart in 1833 to train students for ministerial positions in the West. It was the first college in the United States to adopt coeducation. In 1835, Oberlin also adopted the policy of admitting students without regard to color. Oberlin has been a center for many American reform movements as a source of antislavery sentiment during the pre-Civil War years and the birthplace of the Anti-Saloon League in 1893. The college is composed of two divisions containing a College of Liberal Arts and a Conservatory of Music, founded in 1865.

Ochoa, Severo (b. Sept. 24, 1905, Luarca, Spain): Spanish American biochemist and Nobel laureate. Ochoa attended Malaga College and the University of Madrid and was head physician at the Institute for Medical Research in Heidelberg, Germany, before coming to the United States in 1940. He worked his way up the hierarchy at New York University Medical School, from research associate in 1942 to full professor and chair of the Department of Biochemistry in 1976. Ochoa shared the 1959 Nobel Prize in Medicine and Physiology with Arthur Kornberg for their synthesis of RNA and DNA. He received the National Medal of Science and Japan's Order of the Rising Sun.

Spanish American biochemist and Nobel laureate Severo Ochoa shared in synthesizing RNA and DNA. (The Nobel Foundation)

O'Connor, Sandra Day (b. March 26, 1930, El Paso, Tex.): U.S. Supreme Court justice. After passing the bar exam, O'Conner served as deputy county attorney for San Mateo County, California. Unable to find a private law firm in Los Angeles that would accept her as a woman attorney, she set up a practice in Phoenix, Arizona. In 1965 she was elected attorney general for the state of Arizona. She served in the state senate beginning in 1970, and in 1972 became the first woman elected majority leader. In 1979 she was appointed to the Arizona Court of Appeals. In 1981 she was appointed to the Supreme Court by President Ronald Reagan, becoming the Court's first female justice.

Office of Minority Business Enterprise (OMBE): Established in 1968 by an executive order issued by President Richard M. Nixon to help stimulate minority business ventures by African Americans, Puerto Ricans, American Indians, Aleuts, Inuits (Eskimos), Asian Americans, and Latinos. As part of the Department of Commerce, the OMBE provided grants, advice, and contracts to nonprofit organizations who were willing to use the money to help minority-operated small businesses which were already in existence or in the planning stage. The program was criticized because it did not provide continuing support for many of these businesses, some of which failed. Other OMBE programs provided credit and capital to minority businesses. The agency was superseded by the Minority Business Development Agency, which was established in 1979 to provide management and technical assistance to minority business enterprises through a national network of assistance centers.

O'Keeffe, Georgia (Nov. 15, 1887, Sun Prairie, Wis.—Mar. 6, 1986, Santa Fe, N.Mex.): Artist. O'Keeffe's work first appeared in photographer Alfred Stieglitz's Gallery 291 in New York, in 1916. In 1924 she married Stieglitz, who encouraged her unique style and promoted her career. Beginning in 1929, O'Keeffe spent long periods alone at Ghost Ranch in New Mexico, where she painted cow skulls, adobe buildings, and the stark hills infused with the vivid colors of the Southwest. When Stieglitz died in 1949, the independent O'Keeffe moved permanently to Ghost Ranch and continued to paint into her nineties. O'Keeffe's paintings are like dreams with bold objects floating in space. A number of her abstracts of flowers are thought to evoke female sexuality. Among her famous paintings are *Pelvis with Moon* (1943), *Cow's Skull—Red, White, and Blue* (1931), and *Black Iris* (1926). O'Keeffe inspired a generation of women artists and poularized images which became part of the Southwest style.

Oklahoma land runs (1889-1903): Rush by white settlers to occupy land in Indian Territory that the government made available.

Encouraged by the HOMESTEAD ACT of 1862, white settlers began moving in great numbers to settle the West after the Civil War. White cavalry were employed to destroy and remove Plains Indians, some into Indian Territory where the CHEROKEES and other tribes had been relocated in 1838. Against this ominous background, the Cherokees, CHOCTAWS, Chickasaws, Creeks, and Seminoles were rebuilding their societies according to principles which had earned them the title "FIVE CIVILIZED TRIBES."

In 1870 the railroads were poised to move across Indian Territory, and within two years they had done so. Now it would be impossible for the tribes to stop the "final solution" to their existence: Ownership of the Indian lands would be challenged by railroaders and others, until the U.S. Congress finally agreed to open great sections of the territory for white settlement in 1889. These were the "unassigned lands," mainly in the western half of the territory. On April 22, 1889, thousands of white settlers lined up to charge into these lands at the sound of cavalry guns (some, the "Sooners," had arrived earlier). The Cherokees were forced to sell a strip of land just below the Kansas border, called the "Cherokee Outlet," in 1893 at $1.25 per acre. This was opened for a "run" by white settlers on September 16, 1893.

First train and wagons crossing the line for the "run" on land formerly belonging to the Cherokees on September 16, 1893. (National Archives)

Indian nations had traditionally occupied land in common, but in 1887 the DAWES ACT directed that

Indian lands be divided into 160-acre allotments and shared out to individual tribe members; all land not allotted would be available for white occupation. Not only was this a move toward elimination of tribal identities, it was also an assault upon cultural ties between people and nature. Indians of the Five Civilized Tribes were opposed to such divisions of the land as a violation of their "Mother" Earth, and many (especially full-bloods, known as the "irreconcilables") hid in the tree-covered hills, refusing to select their land allotments. Yet this federal policy continued unabated until 1934. In 1893 Senator Henry Dawes of Massachusetts was sent by President Grover Cleveland to negotiate with the tribes, and in 1898 Congress passed the Curtis Act, which ended tribal laws in Indian Territory.

Land of the Five Tribes was surveyed, and all tribal members were recorded by name, tribe, and percentage of blood. This record, or "roll," was to become the basis for land assignment and compensation; full-bloods were to be treated differently than mixed-bloods, for whom white law was more lenient. Indians of all the tribes were thus brought under federal law, and their schools were administered by the Department of the Interior. There was some resistance, led by the Cherokee Redbird Smith, but it did not have serious effects. Mixed-blood leaders agreed to the treaty of 1905, which established a final roll of the Indian Nations in order to compensate for lands which would be ceded to create the new state of Oklahoma in 1907.

Suggested Readings. Morris L. Wardell's *Political History of the Cherokee Nation, 1838-1907* (1938) provides a detailed study that includes events of the land runs as experienced by the Cherokees. Grant Foreman's *History of Oklahoma* (1942) is a more comprehensive view. Succinct accounts sympathetic to the plight of the Indians can be found in Angie Debo's *A History of the Indians of the United States* (1970), and in Peter Collier's *When Shall They Rest? The Cherokees' Long Struggle with America* (1973).

Older Americans: Because gerontologists tend to designate the ages of sixty-five to seventy-four years and older as advanced old age, the age of sixty-five years is generally used as an arbitrary dividing line between middle age and old age. Nevertheless, this particular age has very little relevance in describing aspects of functioning such as general health, mental capacity or capabilities, psychological or physiological endurance, or creativity. Age in years is not an accurate indicator of an individual's physical and mental status, but it is used as a convenience in discussing human developmental stages. The wide variability among individuals is at least as great at age sixty-five as it is at any other time. It must be remembered that there are sixty-five-year-old people whose activities, interests, and vitality are quite comparable to those of an average fifty-year-old person.

At an age when many people would be considered "old-old," this eighty-two-year-old Chinese American woman is graduating from college. (Frances M. Roberts)

Because there is a significant spread of years between those at age sixty-five and those at age eighty-five or ninety, several researchers in the field of gerontology have decided to divide this range of the human life span into two categories—the "young-old" and the "old-old." The "young-old" are those people who are still highly active physically, mentally, and socially even though they might already be retired. These people are generally found between the ages of 55 and 75. Beyond this age range are the "old-old"—those for whom physical activity is more limited or among whom the effects of decline have become more obvious and rapid. These loose and somewhat rather arbitrary labels are indicative of modern society's lack of precise vocabulary for discussing older Americans. It is also an indication of how, until very recently, American society has shown very little interest in the aging process.

The Senior Population. The numbers of older Americans have increased dramatically both in absolute years as well as a proportion of the overall U.S. population. For example, while the overall population increased almost two and a half times during the first six decades of the twentieth century, the number of people older than sixty-five increased by a factor of five. This increase can be attributed in part to a high birthrate early in the century, as well as to early immigration policies that enabled large numbers of young people to come to the United States. Other factors that have contributed to the high increase in the number of older people are advances in medical research and changes in nutrition that have enabled people to live longer. These factors have succeeded in increasing people's life expectancies. The net result of this phenomenon was that by 1989, more than 12 percent of the U.S. population was sixty-five or older—a total of approximately 31 million individuals. This percentage continues to increase steadily, according to researchers. Demographic projections for the end of the twentieth century estimate that nearly 14 percent of the population will be above the age of sixty-five; that percentage is expected to increase by the year 2030, according to a 1988 report by the U.S. BUREAU OF THE CENSUS.

One of the reasons for this increase is the postwar baby boom that occurred between 1946 and 1964. As these baby boomers move into old age, the ratio of older people to younger people will increase dramatically. The net effect of this situation will increase even more by declining birthrates.

Seniors, while numerous, constitute a minority group in the American society. As with any other minority, they experience overt and covert discrimination. Unlike discrimination against other minority groups, discrimination against older Americans is perpetrated by individuals who themselves will become seniors and may eventually face discrimination based upon their own age.

Characteristics of Older Americans: 1970-1990

	1970	**1980**	**1990**
Total population	19,900,900	24,200,000	29,600,000
Marital status			
Percent single	7.6	5.5	4.6
Percent married	51.3	55.4	56.1
Percent widowed	38.8	35.7	34.2
Percent divorced	2.3	3.5	5.0
Living arrangements			
Percent alone	25.5	30.3	31.0
Percent with spouse	49.0	53.6	54.1
Percent with other	20.7	15.9	14.6
Education			
Percent completed high school	15.7	24.0	32.9
Percent completed college	6.3	8.6	11.6
Economic status			
Percent below poverty level	25.3	15.2	11.4
Percent employed	16.4	12.2	11.5

Source: Data are from *Statistical Abstract of the United States, 1992.* Table 40. Washington, D.C.: U.S. Government Printing Office, 1992.

Stereotypes and Misconceptions. Older Americans are often stereotyped as rigid in thought and manner, and old-fashioned in morality and skills. Beyond these stereotypes, there are also three basic misconceptions that society tends to hold regarding older Americans. Seniors are assumed to be sick or infirm, senile, and nonproductive. Concerning the third misconception, researchers in the area of gerontology have found that older Americans are as productive as young workers, are less prone to job turnover, and have lower accident and absentee rates.

Retirement can be a period of significant adjustments. Here two older men visit in a San Francisco park. (Robert Fried)

Seniors are discriminated against in many areas that affect their well-being. Many employers discriminate against them in hiring and retention. Most senior citizens live on limited incomes and consequently are at greater risk of becoming impoverished. In addition, many medical personnel admit that they prefer not to treat seniors. These realities of life, coupled with philosophical beliefs and moral values different from those held by younger generations, create an environment conducive to ageism—prejudice against people because they are old.

As a group, seniors are understandably concerned about political issues dealing with the maintenance and enhancement of Social Security and health care benefits. They are among the nation's most regular voters, whom politicians routinely try to woo. Seniors are more likely than other groups to support taxpayer "revolts" and to resist efforts toward revenue enhancement that might diminish their incomes. They are also more likely than other minority groups to resist attempts to increase school revenue through taxes, since typically they are no longer involved in rearing or financially supporting school-age children.

Adjustment to Old Age. Adjustment to old age is, for the most part, a function of a number of variables such as gender, socioeconomic status, ethnic background, adequacy of social support systems, and whether an individual faces old age alone or with a spouse. Women tend to adjust to old age much more smoothly than men. For men, retirement marks a dramatic change in life and is therefore likely to cause a lot of psychological or even physical problems. Widowers tend to face even greater adjustment problems than widows. This difference is not surprising, since fewer men than women anticipate losing a spouse. As a group, older men are often unprepared to assume household responsibilities and are hard pressed to find men in similar situations able to provide support or companionship. Older widows, however, have a large potential support group of other widows.

As a microculture, only some older Americans seem to have a sense of group identity. Many of them use chronological criteria to determine the advent of old age, while the remainder generally use criteria such as retirement or health conditions to determine old age. Some are ashamed of their age and, in some cases, resist the idea of being identified as "senior citizens."

One of the major factors involved in adjustment to old age is socioeconomic status. Seniors' income can influence, among other things, their longevity, social status, housing situation, and physical health. Seniors with high incomes have a number of advantages associated with their greater financial resources, including their ability to afford such leisure activities as traveling that help make the retirement years much more pleasurable. In light of these advantages, it is understandable that people from high socioeconomic backgrounds tend to view old age more favorably than those from low socioeconomic backgrounds.

Sensory Changes Associated with Aging. As one gets older, beginning in early adulthood especially, there are some changes that take place in the sensory systems. One of these is the sense of sight. Virtually all individuals require at least one pair of prescription eyeglasses by the end of middle age, with men generally requiring them at a younger age than women. The most common problem is far-sightedness, which is usually linked to decreasing elasticity and thickening of the eye lens. With age, the lens also becomes less transparent. When this happens, peripheral vision, depth perception, color vision, and adaption to the dark become poorer.

Another major sensory change associated with aging is the loss of hearing. Symptoms often begin during middle age and become more serious after the age of sixty. These symptoms are more common in men than in women and are most evident in decreasing sensitivity to higher tones and a difficulty in discriminating between different sounds. The desire that many older Americans have for quiet environments may well be related not to an aversion to noise but rather

An intergenerational art project provides a means of expression for older and younger participants. (Hazel Hankin)

Active in business, community work, or hobbies, many older Americans do not wish to be called "senior citizens." (Skjold)

to a desire to follow normal conversation without strain. The loss of hearing may have some serious psychological consequences. Older people whose hearing impairments severely limit their ability to understand speech are often prevented from enjoying such pastimes as playing cards, watching television, attending films and concerts, and other activities.

A number of seniors gradually lose their sense of taste. Many of them frequently find that food does not taste as good as it once did. Some use far more salt, pepper, and other spices than they did when they were younger.

Longevity—Men Versus Women. The twentieth century has created conditions causing a marked difference between the life expectancies of men and women. In the United States, women live approximately eight years longer from birth and five years longer after age sixty-five. Women outlive men every place in the world where hard physical labor and reduced maternal mortality are present.

Women outlive men because of men's higher mortality risk from arteriosclerotic heart diseases, as well as from lung cancer and emphysema, which are associated with smoking. Other sources of men's problems are industrial accidents and toxicity, motor vehicle and other accidents, suicide, and cirrhosis of the liver (associated with alcoholism). Lifestyle, stress, hormonal differences, genetic differences in immune resistance, and other differences between the sexes are still being studied.

Abuse of Seniors. Older Americans face the increasing risk of abuse from their children, relatives, or acquaintances. This abuse may be physical or mental in nature. In some cases, adult children of older people deprive them of their social security benefits, while other seniors are deprived of food or proper living conditions. Older Americans are also prime targets of robberies and muggings as well as money-swindling schemes in which they are persuaded to invest their life savings or real estate holdings with the false promise of making more money.

The victimization of older Americans must be placed within the context in which aging itself has been made into a progressive victimization. There is no doubt that in American society, becoming old means becoming less of something on the way to losing everything. That seniors have become more popular targets of victimization than others may be explained by the perception that their diminishing usefulness and productivity somehow justifies their victimization. While studies, debates, reforms, and innovations are still under way in areas such as sexual assault, domestic violence, child abuse and neglect, the sheer number of Americans moving toward old age dictates that society also confront the issue of victimization of seniors.

Suggested Readings. For a discussion of issues dealing with older people and mental health, see Robert N. Butler's *Aging and Mental Health* (1991). Donna Gollnick and Philip Chinn's *Multicultural Education in a Pluralistic Society* (1990) has a good section on older Americans and people's prejudices toward them. For more on societal attitudes toward senior citizens, see Guy Lefrancois' *The Lifespan* (1987). A source of information on abuse of senior citizens is Jordan Kosberg's *Abuse and Maltreatment of the Elderly* (1983).—*K. Paul Kasambira*

Olmos, Edward James (b. Feb. 24, 1947, East Los Angeles, Calif.): Latino actor, director, and producer. Olmos studied sociology at California State University and began performing with his own rock band. His first major Broadway role was in *Zoot Suit*, for which he received a 1978 Tony Award nomination. He produced and acted in the films *The Ballad of Gregorio Cortez* (1982) and *American Me* (1992), and he was nominated for an Academy Award for his portrayal of schoolteacher Jaime Escalante in *Stand and Deliver* (1988). From 1984 to 1988, he was a regular on television's *Miami Vice*. Deeply concerned with conditions in Los Angeles' Latino communities, Olmos was a major public figure urging peace and rebuilding after the 1992 Los Angeles riots and is an important role model for Chicano youth.

Controversial educator Jaime Escalante (right) compares notes with actor Edward James Olmos, who plays Escalante in the film Stand and Deliver. (AP/Wide World Photos)

Olympians and the Olympic Games: The modern Olympic Games, begun in 1896 in a spirit of multinational cooperation, have served as a stage on which notable American athletes of diverse backgrounds have displayed their abilities. In the first half of the twentieth century, when rigid segregation ruled many aspects of American culture, Olympic competition offered a somewhat unusual chance for Americans of different races and cultures to compete for athletic glory on a more or less equal basis.

In 1904, for example, at a time when African American boxing great Jack Johnson was not allowed to fight for the world heavyweight title, and nearly a half century before Jackie ROBINSON broke the color line in major league BASEBALL, George Poage became the first African American Olympian, winning bronze medals in the 200- and 400-meter hurdles at the St. Louis Olympics. (Robinson himself would win a gold medal as a member of the 1948 U.S. BASKETBALL team.) African American athletes such as Jesse Owens (four gold medals at the 1936 Berlin Olympics), Wyomia Tyus (three golds and a silver in 1968 at Mexico City), and Carl Lewis (a total of eight golds in the 1984, 1988, and 1992 games) have provided many of Olympic history's most memorable performances.

An American Indian, Jim THORPE, became perhaps the first Olympic superstar in 1912, when he won gold medals in the pentathlon and the decathlon. Although he was later forced to return his medals when his amateur status was questioned, he was generally acknowledged as the greatest athlete of his time. In 1964, another American Indian, Billy Mills, provided one of the highlights of the Tokyo Olympic Games with a surprising victory in the 10,000-meter race.

Meyer Prinstein, a Jewish American, became one of the first repeat gold medalists by winning gold medals in the hop, step, and jump (the forerunner of the triple jump) in the 1900 and 1904 games; he also won the 1904 broad jump competition. Another Jewish American, Mark Spitz, turned in perhaps the greatest performance in Olympic history when he won gold medals—and set world records—in all seven of the swimming events he entered at the 1972 Munich Olympics.

Latino athletes who won Olympic gold medals include boxer Paul Gonzales in 1984, boxer Oscar de la Hoya in 1992, and swimmer Pablo Morales in 1992. Asian Americans who achieved Olympic success include diver Sammy Lee (gold medals in 1948 and 1952) and figure skater Kristi YAMAGUCHI (a 1992 gold medalist). Hawaiian swimmer Duke Kahanamoku won gold medals in 1912 and 1920, as did Warren Kealoha in 1920 and 1924.

Women have competed in the Olympics since the 1900 Paris Games, although their early participation was limited to such SPORTS as tennis and archery.

Japanese American figure skater Kristi Yamaguchi from Fremont, Calif., won a gold medal in the 1992 Winter Olympics. (AP/Wide World Photos)

Women's events in swimming, gymnastics, track and field, and other sports were added gradually over the years to the Summer Olympics, and women's figure skating became a highlight of the Winter Olympics soon after their establishment in 1924. Norwegian American Mildred "Babe" Didrikson ZAHARIAS won recognition as the world's greatest female athlete by capturing two golds and one silver in track and field at the 1932 Los Angeles Games. Since then, American women, including Wilma RUDOLPH, Peggy Fleming,

Mary Lou Retton, and Florence Griffith-Joyner, have been among the biggest stars in Olympic history.

SUGGESTED READINGS. For a general history see Bill Henry's *An Approved History of the Olympic Games* (1984). John M. Hoberman's *The Olympic Crisis: Sport, Politics, and the Moral Order* (1986) discusses controversies that have plagued the games. For an account of African Americans who have come to dominate several of the Olympic Games' events and won seats on the U.S. and International Olympic Committees, see *The Black Olympians, 1904-1984* (1984) by Lonnie G. Bunch and Louie Robinson.

Oneida Community: Utopian society founded in 1848 in Putney, Vermont, and later relocated in Oneida, New York. The society's founder, John Humphrey Noyes (1811-1886), taught that Perfectionism, freedom from sin, was attainable.

Activities of the Oneida Community were run by committees, including a central committee of Noyes's closest disciples. Until dissension struck the community, however, Noyes, as the representative of God, was the unchallenged leader. Since the Perfectionists led a comfortable and somewhat affluent lifestyle, many people sought admission. Noyes removed dissidents and invited wealthy individuals and skilled craftsmen and farmers to join. This enabled the community to be nearly self-sufficient. Noyes, his wife, and several relatives invested in the community when losses were totaling about four thousand dollars annually.

This changed when Sewell Newhouse joined: Marketing a trap that he had invented proved highly profitable. By 1860 the Oneida factory, using an assembly line and hiring nonmembers, was producing 300,000 traps yearly. In 1877 it began manufacturing the plated silverware that is still produced.

Community members spent three hours daily in Bible reading and prayer. At evening meetings, Noyes often preached. Individuals subjected themselves to self-criticism and to mutual criticism from the group. Noyes was never subjected to group criticism but occasionally subjected himself to self-criticism.

The main community lived at Oneida in the Mansion House, which had sleeping areas and a dining room, meeting hall, photographic studio, chemical laboratory, library, and Turkish bath. More than two hundred "family" members lived together peacefully, adopting a "we" rather than "I" orientation. They enjoyed academic learning and had concerts and theatrical productions. Children were considered to belong to the entire community.

Prior to founding the community, Noyes had married Harriet A. Holton and had five children. He later had at least ten more. The central committee, including Noyes and his wife, practiced complex marriage, a form of communal marriage controlled by the committee. Other pairings were not allowed to stay together for prolonged periods.

Noyes was often away, and the central committee lacked leadership qualities. The community became increasingly secular. Some younger men objected to being paired with older women. James W. Towner claimed that Noyes was too autocratic. Along with outsiders, he had been gathering data to charge Noyes with statutory rape. After appointing a committee headed by his son, Theodore, to succeed him, Noyes fled to Canada. With Noyes's agreement, the community abolished complex marriage.

On January 1, 1881, the Oneida Community disbanded, forming a joint stock company, Oneida Ltd., which distributed $600,000 in assets among the members. Oneida Ltd. continues, a worldwide organization with net sales of over $300,000 annually.

SUGGESTED READINGS. Primary sources include Noyes's writings. See also *Oneida: Utopian Community to Modern Corporation* (1969) by Maren Lockwood Carden.

Onizuka, Ellison (June 24, 1946, Kealakekua, Hawaii—Jan. 28, 1986, Cape Canaveral, Fla.): Asian

Ellison Onizuka, the first Japanese American astronaut, died in the Challenger space shuttle explosion. (NASA)

American astronaut. Onizuka studied aerospace engineering at the University of Colorado at Boulder and spent eight years as an Air Force test pilot. With a strong interest in education, Onizuka taught test pilots at Edwards Air Force Base and also devoted much time to sharing his enthusiasm for space with children. He became a National Aeronautics and Space Administration (NASA) astronaut candidate in 1978 and as mission specialist on the 1985 flight of the Discovery was the first Hawaiian or Japanese American to fly in space. Onizuka died on his way into space in the tragic explosion of the Challenger space shuttle in 1986.

Operation PUSH: National social, political, and economic organization started in 1971 by the Reverend Jesse JACKSON. Operation PUSH (PUSH is an acronym for People United to Save Humanity) grew out of Jackson's earlier involvement with Operation Breadbasket, an economic assistance campaign spearheaded by the SOUTHERN CHRISTIAN LEADERSHIP CONFERENCE (SCLC).

Jackson's organization focuses on economic issues, believing that it does little good to have the rights to an education, to eat at a restaurant, or to live in any neighborhood if a person does not have the economic means to take advantage of these rights. In addition to other civil and human rights programs, the organization sponsors PUSH-EXCEL programs in several U.S. cities to motivate and assist high school students in building up their skills so that they can succeed in academics and in the job market.

Operation Wetback: IMMIGRATION AND NATURALIZATION SERVICE (INS) program created in 1954 in response

During Operation Wetback in 1954, a border guard reenacts discovering an illegal immigrant hiding under an automobile hood. (AP/Wide World Photos)

to the swelling number of Mexican immigrant laborers who had entered the United States illegally, or who had remained in the country past the legally specified time contained in their entry contract with the Department of Labor.

In April, 1954, Joseph Swing, a retired army general and personal friend of President Dwight Eisenhower, was appointed commissioner of the INS. Drawing upon his military experience, Swing quickly mobilized a campaign that involved hundreds of BORDER PATROL officers and police forces in Mexican communities in a mass deportation operation. Full-scale military resources, including boat and plane forces, were used in order to deliver the deportees deep into the Mexican interior. The campaign, dubbed "Operation Wetback" ("wetback" is an ETHNIC SLUR referring to illegal immigrants' swimming across the Rio Grande border from Mexico to the United States), began in Southern California and was subsequently extended along the entire U.S. border with Mexico.

Much of the considerable popular support for Operation Wetback was based on an unfortunate confluence of conservative, racist rhetoric that blamed Mexican people for subversion, disease, labor strife, and a variety of other alleged activities. Agricultural employers were among the few who spoke out against the campaign, since their businesses were threatened by the evaporation of the migrant labor supply.

The success of Operation Wetback in terms of fulfilling the goals set forth by immigration authorities was instrumental in solidifying the reputation of the INS. By acting on the threat of deportation, the INS was able to convince employers that it was not good business to employ illegal migrants. In turn, the INS moved to improve employer access to the existing channels of legally available contract laborers (*braceros*) and took significant measures to simplify the process of contracting laborers. In the process, however, the INS virtually eliminated the responsibilities of employers to their contracted laborers, leaving the *BRACERO* PROGRAM with few mechanisms of protection for the migrants.

By 1955, the INS commissioner declared that the problem had been solved, with Mexican immigration becoming renormalized under the terms of the *bracero* program still in effect with Mexico. The traumatic impact of the program upon established MEXICAN AMERICAN communities was severe, however, with many naturalized U.S. citizens experiencing harassment simply because of their Mexican heritage.

SUGGESTED READINGS. Juan Ramón García's *Operation Wetback: The Mass Deportation of Mexican Undocumented Workers in 1954* (1980) provides a detailed account of the deportation campaign. Julian Samora's *Los Mojados: The Wetback Story* (1971) and Peter N. Kirstein's *Anglo over Bracero: A History of the Mexican Worker in the United States from Roosevelt to Nixon* (1977) provide background information on the treatment of legal and illegal migrant workers, and Mario T. Garcia's *Mexican Americans: Leadership, Ideology and Identity, 1930-1960* (1989) explores the implications of U.S. immigration policy on the established Mexican American community. Silvia Pedraza-Bailey's *Political and Economic Migrants in America: Cubans and Mexicans* (1985) analyzes the vast differences in U.S. policy in the treatment of Cuban and Mexican immigrants.

Oral history: Historical information gleaned from interviews with both ordinary and famous people to gain insight into a time, place, or population group. Oral history is especially useful for documenting those outside the mainstream, such as women and minorities, whose lives are often left undescribed in conventional history texts. Between 1938 and 1942, the Federal Writers' Project sent writers across the country to interview people ranging from former slaves to urban immigrants about their daily lives and the important events that had influenced them. The ETHNIC HERITAGE REVIVAL of the 1970's sparked widespread interest in tape recording oral history interviews as a way of learning more about one's family or group history. Many American universities, MUSEUMS, AND RESEARCH CENTERS have conducted special oral history projects, housed in tape archives, to document twentieth century social movements and ethnic communities.

Organization of Afro-American Unity (OAAU): Black nationalist organization. The OAAU was begun in 1964 by MALCOLM X. In addition to its militant black nationalist ideology, the OAAU embraced many reform-oriented goals that appealed to a broad base of African Americans. It advocated programs to help African Americans become registered voters, to help form black tenant organizations to lobby for better living conditions, and to help initiate black community educational institutions to promote awareness of African American history and culture. Unlike some other civil rights organizations at the time, OAAU was run by African Americans. Malcolm proposed that the OAAU present a petition to the United Nations Human Rights Commission detailing the crimes against the African Americans committed by the United States government. The organization became the center of Malcolm's secular political activities until his assassination in 1965. After his death Malcolm's sister Ella Mae Collins assumed leadership of the OAAU but was unable to keep it going.

Treasury Secretary Katherine Ortega delivered the keynote address to the Republican National Convention, in Dallas, Tex., 1984. (AP/Wide World Photos)

Ortega, Katherine Davalos (b. July 16, 1934, near Tularosa, N.Mex.): Latina banker and U.S. treasurer. After graduating from New Mexico University in 1957, Ortega worked for Peat, Marwick, Mitchell and Pan American National Bank. In 1975, she became the first female president of a California commercial bank. In 1983, she became the first woman or Latino to serve as treasurer of the United States. In 1989 she returned to private life, going into business and consulting and serving on the boards of numerous financial organizations and professional groups.

Orthodox Jews. *See* **Jews—Orthdox**

Osceola (c. 1804—Jan. 30, 1838, Charleston, S.C.): Leader of the Seminole Indians of Florida, who protested the 1832 and 1833 treaties that forced Indians to move west. After the killing of an Indian agent by his warriors, Osceola and his band were driven southward to the Everglades. He accepted peace overtures by General T. S. Jesup and went to see the American under a flag of truce in 1837. Jesup had Osceola seized and imprisoned at Fort Moultrie at Charleston, South Carolina, where he died.

Our Bodies, Ourselves (1973): Self-help book on women's health which became the bible of the women's HEALTH movement in the 1970's. The book, written by the Boston Women's Health Book Collective, developed from a 1969 study group on women's medical concerns. Frustrated by the lack of available information, eleven women began to research and teach others about women's health issues. In 1973, the collective published their findings commercially. The book covers a wide array of topics, from body image, sexuality, and birth control to the aging process. The emphasis throughout is on self-education, preventive health care, and reform of the health care delivery system to better serve women. The collective issued an updated edition of the book in 1984 and has also sponsored national conferences on women's health to further these goals.

In 1973, Seiji Ozawa was named the permanent musical director of the Boston Symphony Orchestra. (AP/Wide World Photos)

Ozawa, Seiji (b. Sept. 1, 1935, Hoten, Japan): Japanese American orchestral conductor. Beginning his professional studies at the Toho School of Music in Tokyo during the 1950's, Ozawa studied with such musical figures as Leonard Bernstein, Herbert von Karajan, Hideo Saito, and Eugene Bigot. During the 1960's, he conducted for the New York Philharmonic, the Ravinia Festival near Chicago, and the Toronto Symphony Orchestra, and he conducted the San Francisco Symphony Orchestra from 1970 to 1976. In 1973 Ozawa became permanent musical director of the Boston Symphony Orchestra. While based in Boston, he has continued to make frequent guest appearances with major European and American symphonies and operas, and in 1984 he cofounded Japan's Saito Kinen Orchestra.

Ozawa v. United States (1922): U.S. Supreme Court decision on whether persons of Japanese ancestry were eligible to become U.S. citizens. Japan-born Takao Ozawa had applied for citizenship in Hawaii on October 16, 1914, after living for twenty years in the United States. He had attended high school as well as college in Berkeley, California, and had educated his children in American schools. His family attended American churches and used the English language at home. Ozawa therefore believed he had the character, motivation, and education for citizenship.

Section 2169 of the Revised Statutes of the United States, however, limited citizenship to aliens who were white or of African descent. The original wording in 1790 only mentioned whites; the African section was added in 1870. On June 29, 1906, however, the Naturalization Act took effect with a uniform rule for NATURALIZATION that did not mention race or color. Ozawa argued that this negated Section 2169.

In a unanimous opinion authored by Justice George Sutherland, the Court construed the 1906 act to bar those of Japanese ancestry from American citizenship. Sutherland noted that the act had thirty-one sections, all having to do with procedure, with no intent to modify policy. If Congress had desired to alter a rule so long and well established, it would have done so; there can be no repeal by implication. The Court found it inconceivable that a rule which had been in force from the early years of the government could be deprived of its force in such a dubious and casual fashion.

Sutherland went on to say that those who wrote the original 1790 act did not foresee precisely who would be excluded from citizenship in the future. A zone of acceptability had been established, and individual cases within the zone would still have to be decided, but Ozawa was clearly outside the zone as construed by federal and state courts and sustained by numerous scientific authorities. Despite the culture and enlightenment of the Japanese, the Court must support the will of Congress. The Court concluded, however, that there is no implication in the legislation or its interpretation of any individual unworthiness or racial inferiority on the part of Japanese people.

Two years later the Court was vindicated when Congress passed a law specifically forbidding Japanese aliens from becoming U.S. citizens, further stigmatizing the Japanese immigrant community. Not until the 1950's did immigration law allow people of all races to become U.S. citizens.

SUGGESTED READINGS. The Ozawa decision can be read in its entirety in the *United States Supreme Court Reports*, vol. 260. See also Robert A. Wilson and Bill Hosokawa's *East to America: A History of the Japanese in the United States* (1980) and Ronald Takaki's *Strangers from a Different Shore: A History of Asian Americans* (1989) for good historical overviews.

Pachuco: A term of uncertain origins applied in the 1940's and 1950's to Mexican American youths in urban areas of the Southwest, especially Los Angeles. Young males who adopted a certain lifestyle that usually included a "zoot suit" as a kind of uniform, hand tattoos, special slang, and membership in a gang were commonly known as pachucos. They saw themselves as defenders of their barrios, their women, and their culture. The term received national publicity in 1943 because of the infamous ZOOT-SUIT RIOTS. In parts of New Mexico, a shortened version, chuco, was sometimes used.

Pacific Islander Americans: As of 1990, 365,024 Pacific Islanders from the various islands of Oceania (the central and South Pacific) lived in the United States. The largest number are of Hawaiian descent. In descending order of population, Pacific Islander Americans include Samoans, Guamanians, Tongans, Fijians, and Palauans. Technically, not all these people are immigrants; for example, because Guam is a territory of the United States, Guamanians are U.S. citizens, while people from American Samoa are considered U.S. nationals. Because no census information was collected on them until 1980 and because they represent only 5 percent of the Asian/Pacific population in the United States, Pacific Islanders are a little-known, relatively invisible community.

Origins. Pacific Islanders are the peoples of Oceania. They do not constitute one homogeneous ethnic group; rather, they speak linguistically related but distinct languages, practice different religions, and come from various islands. Their cultures share in common histories of vast ocean voyages, dependance upon the sea and sometimes agriculture for food, and extensive use of natural resources for artistic and functional items. They also share a recent history of colonization and occupation by various world powers. Many of these islands are now becoming or have become self-governing while facing major economic and educational changes.

Geographers and anthropologists divide Oceania into three major regions: Micronesia, Melanesia, and Polynesia. Each of these major divisions may be broken down into yet smaller, more distinct island groups.

Micronesia ("tiny islands"), located north of the equator and about 2,500 miles west of Hawaii, covers an area about the size of the continental United States. The major island groups include the Marianas, the Carolines (Yap, Palau, Truk, Ponape, and Kosrae), the Marshalls, and the Gilberts. Guam, southernmost in the Marianas, has been a territory of the United States since 1898, except for the years of World War II. All but the Gilberts were administered by the United States following the war, but since then each has negotiated differing political statuses.

Pacific Islander Americans are natives of Oceania. Here a Hawaiian man wears a magnificent lei. (AP/Wide World Photos)

Melanesia ("black islands") includes the islands of the southwestern Pacific: New Guinea, the Solomon islands, and Fiji. The peoples of this area are linguistically diverse; more than seven hundred different languages are spoken on Papua New Guinea alone. Of the Pacific Islanders migrating to the United States from this region, Fijians seem to be most represented.

Polynesians, who account for the vast majority of Pacific Islander Americans, include the indigenous peoples of Hawaii, New Zealand, Tahiti, Tonga, and both Western and American Samoa. Polynesia ("many islands") is bounded on the north by Midway, on the east by Easter Island, and to the west by New Zealand and Tuvalu. The biggest percentage of Polynesians in the United States are Hawaiians, although sizable numbers of Samoans and Tongans have also migrated. According to one study of Pacific Islander immigrants, of all the different island groups, Tongans increased most (by 183 percent) in the decade between 1980 and 1990.

Migration and Immigration. People are motivated to leave the Pacific Islands for a number of reasons, most of which involve hope for better economic conditions and educational opportunities. Generally, the living standard on the islands is low compared to that of the United States.

The U.S. Navy administered to American Samoa from 1900 to 1951, during which time it provided jobs to many Samoans at an American military base. When the base was closed in 1951, Samoans connected to the military were allowed free entry into the United States, resulting in the first major wave of Samoan migration. Later, economic problems, drought, and higher expectations prompted more Samoans to leave for the mainland. A number of Western Samoans also came to the U.S., often by way of American Samoa.

In Tonga, Mormon missionaries offered free education and access to Mormon universities in Hawaii and Utah. This opportunity was welcome for many residents of the economically depressed island kingdom. As a result, one-fourth of all Tongan Americans lived in Utah in the early 1990's.

Hawaiian dancers perform at the Polynesian Cultural Center on Oahu, Hawaii. The Hawaiian cultural renaissance that began in the 1970's has also affected communities on the mainland. (Marshall Prescott, Unicorn Stock Photos)

Guamanians took advantage of U.S. citizenship received in 1950 to come to the United States. Micronesian high schools became what some observers have called education mills to prepare students for American colleges. Once in the United States, it is difficult for many Micronesian college students to return home—partly because of the weak economy in the islands and the lack of skilled jobs, partly because they have become attached to American lifestyles. Besides winning educational grants, another common pattern of entry for Micronesian immigrants has been to join the U.S. military.

Many Pacific Islanders speak of an eventual return to their homeland and of their longing for familiar language, foods, and customs. Samoans and Guamanians typically come and go freely between the United States and the islands, especially for important family occasions.

Community and Family Life. Most Hawaiians are clustered in Hawaii, while most Samoans, Guamanians, and Fijians in the mainland United States are concentrated in California. One in four Tongan Americans lives in Utah. Cities with important Samoan communities include Los Angeles, San Francisco, San Diego, and Oceanside in California and Seattle, Washington. In Carson, outside Los Angeles, the city government has an Office of Samoan Affairs to advocate for the needs of the community and help it become better integrated in urban life. Significant numbers in some communities speak their native language at home; such was the case with 70 percent of Samoans and 35 percent of Chamorros (the indigenous people of Guam) in the 1980's.

Pacific Islanders are a mostly young population. They tend to maintain their traditional extended family structures in the United States, with large households and a relatively high number of children per family. In Salt Lake City, Utah, for example, it is not unusual for five families to pool their resources and share a home. Large households and extensive social obligations can be a drain on the islanders' finances. Migrants are typically expected to send remittances home to the islands, to share cash or goods with needy family members, and to be generous at important occasions such as weddings and funerals.

Unemployment is a major problem in most Pacific Islander communities, despite 11 percent of the males being college graduates. Many people arrive in the United States with few job skills and inadequate English, thus ending up in low-paid, entry-level positions. Some rely on public assistance programs. In 1979, 29 percent of Samoans and 38 percent of Micronesians lived below the U.S. poverty line. In some inner-city areas, Samoan and Tongan youth have been involved in GANGS AND CRIME, leading to STEREOTYPES that victimize the entire community. Various social service agencies have been created to help Pacific Islander Americans deal with their socioeconomic problems.

As their communities have grown, islanders have tended to cluster themselves in affiliated groups. Among Samoans and Tongans, churches provide an important cultural and religious focus, with ministers serving the former function of chiefs and congregations acting as a village. Samoan church dedication ceremonies are large, lively affairs, with guest appearances by choirs from other churches, participatory dancing, and originally composed songs about the history of the church, all in the effort to inspire donations to a new church. Through the church, young people often learn traditional songs, dances, and other cultural traditions. A different sort of group is the Association of Pacific Island Educators, which raises and disperses funds for college scholarships.

The case of Tongans in Utah reveals key trends in Pacific Islander community life. Tongans, numbering about twelve thousand, are the state's second largest minority group after Latinos. They are well represented in the Church of Latter-day Saints (Mormons), where there are five Tongan-language wards, or parishes. Many attend Brigham Young University, including Filia (Phil) Uipi, who immigrated in 1973 and served in the Utah legislature. Young people may get involved in Tongan rugby teams or the gang Tongan Crips or both, yet gang members are rarely involved in drugs. Some Tongan men have continued the custom of all-night all-male gatherings over a homemade, slightly intoxicating brew called *kava*.

In some urban areas, Pacific Islanders have begun to find ways to increase communication among different groups, thereby raising their profile in the general population as well as providing their children with avenues for learning about cultural practices their parents left behind. For example, in 1989 representatives from a number of Pacific Islander communities in the Los Angeles area that had never worked together before helped the city plan a Pacific Islander festival. Presentations included music and dance performances as well as demonstrations of cooking, traditional medicine, and storytelling. Some young people took the opportunity to learn arts, such as weaving pandanus mats, that they had not been able to practice since migrating from their home islands. With more such efforts, Pacific Islanders and their culture will become better known to other Americans.

SUGGESTED READINGS. Although extensive published materials exist regarding the lives of Pacific Islanders in the Pacific, relatively little has been published detailing the lives of those who have migrated to the

United States. For an analytical treatment 1980 census findings on the lives of Pacific Islander Americans, see Herbert Harringer, Robert Gardner, and Michael Levin's *Asians and Pacific Islanders in the United States* (1993). General accounts of immigration can be found in the *Harvard Encyclopedia of American Ethnic Groups* (1980), edited by Stephan Thernstrom.—*Judith E. Haut*

Padrone system: Means by which many immigrants, particularly Italians, secured employment once they reached the United States. *Padrone* is Italian for "patron," sometimes translated as "boss." Although an artifact of the mass Italian immigration to the United States, characteristics of the *padrone* system can be found among many other contemporary immigrant groups, including Latinos and Asians.

The *padrone* system flourishes among immigrants who cannot speak English and who therefore require mediation in order to obtain employment in even the most menial work. Many scholars have emphasized the exploitive nature of the Italian *padroni*, who as middlemen took advantage of the newly arrived immigrants, and preyed upon their meager earnings. Many Italian immigrants worked exclusively on the construction of the railroads. They were organized into work gangs formed and directly supervised by their *padroni*. The *padrone* in turn contracted with employers to supply them with the labor they required, freeing the employer of the laborious task of interviewing and screening prospective laborers.

In some cases, *padroni* actually traveled to Italy and recruited laborers to come to the United States. The *padrone* would advance some portion of the fare for overseas passage to the immigrant and then, upon arrival, would find the immigrant work for a "bossatura" or fee. In many cases, the immigrant was compelled to purchase goods from a store run by the *padrone*. At every step, the *padrone* profited from the complex set of transactions, extracting interest on all advanced monies and profiting from marked-up prices on all goods and services provided. Although estimates vary, it is clear that a very large percentage of Italian immigrants — well over half in large communities such as New York — were working under the "sponsorship" of the *padrone* system during the latter years of the nineteenth and early twentieth century.

The dominant perception of *padroni* was negative: They were viewed as unscrupulous ethnic businessmen who were abusing their countrymen for profit, often providing labor at below the established wage level or for firms experiencing labor strikes. In 1886, a bill was introduced in Congress specifically aimed at criminalizing the *padroni* for engaging in the recruitment of "slave labor," although some viewed this bill as more an expression of anti-Italian sentiment than a concern with the well-being of immigrants.

Suggested Readings. Joseph Lopreato's *Italian Americans* (1970) provides an overview of the conditions of Italian Americans as they arrived and assimilated into the United States, including a description of the *padrone* system that emphasizes its exploitive character. Sharing Lopreato's view of the *padrone* system, Erik Amfitheatrof's *The Children of Columbus* (1973) also provides an overall history of the arrival of Italians in the New World. Luciano J. Iorizzo and Salvatore Mondello's *The Italian Americans* (1980) provides an alternative view that stresses the positive contributions made by *padroni* in assisting the arriving Italian immigrants. Salvatore J. LaGumina's collection of documents entitled *Wop: A Documentary History of Anti-Italian Discrimination in the United States* (1973) provides primary sources on the perceptions of *padroni* during the peak of Italian immigration.

Pakistani Americans: The country of Pakistan was created in 1947 as a Muslim nation. The land area—more than 307,000 square miles situated in southern Asia and bordered by Afghanistan to the north, China to the northeast, India to the southeast, the Arabian Sea to the south, and Iran to the west—was carved out of India for the purpose of giving religious independence to Muslims who were in constant conflict with India's Hindu population.

Most Pakistani immigrants arrived in the United States after the reforms of the Immigration and Nationality Act of 1965. According to U.S. Census reports, by 1980 approximately thirty thousand Pakistanis lived in the United States. Although some were in the country as students or diplomats, a majority were either already U.S. citizens or waiting to become naturalized. In the next decade, an additional sixty thousand Pakistanis arrived.

Pakistani immigrants tend to be the best educated members of the society they have left. Typically they have settled in urban areas, creating large communities in New York City, Chicago, Los Angeles, San Francisco, Newark, Houston, and Washington, D.C. Their arrival in these cities has spawned at least two hundred Pakistani American cultural and social organizations (such as the Pakistan League of America and Pakistan Students' Association of America), several Pakistani publications and media broadcasts, educational facilities to teach children their history and the Punjabi or Urdu language, and mosques.

The family remains the center of the relocated community. Pakistani American men, who usually immigrate as young adults or adults, have found success and stability in professional careers as physicians, scientists, businessmen, engineers, and academics. Very few work as unskilled laborers. In accord with their Muslim traditions, the immigrant families are hierarchical and male-dominated; women manage the home and care for the children. Traditional roles, however, continue to be challenged by the first and second generations of Pakistanis born in the United States. With regularity, more and more women are attending universities and establishing careers outside of the home.

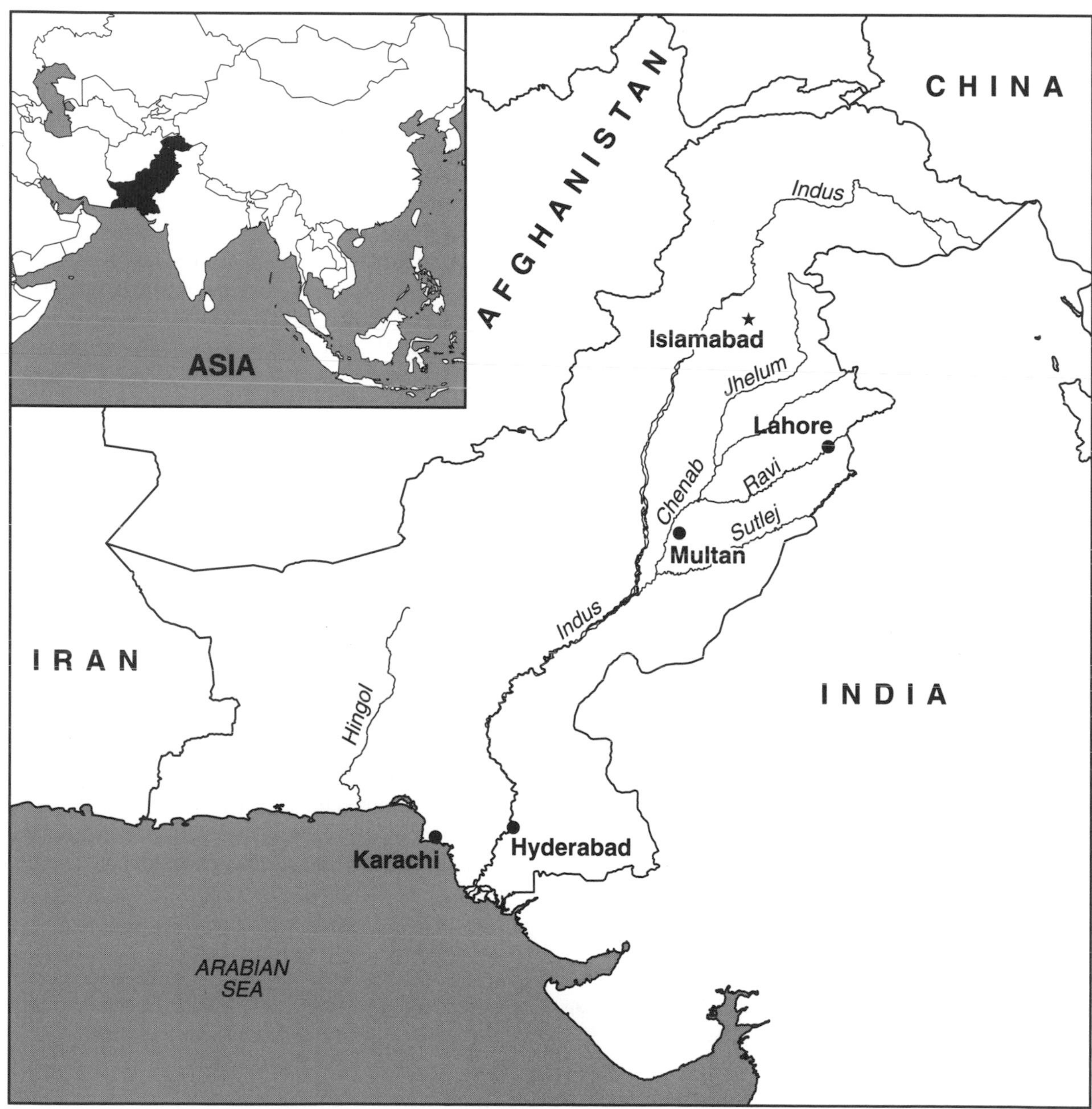

PAKISTAN

Pakistani Americans have formed a tight-knit community. They have maintained their religious and cultural traditions, observing the Ramadan fast and celebrating various Pakistani holidays and festivals, including Pakistan Independence Day on August 14.

Palestinian Americans: The Palestinians constitute a tiny but rapidly growing ethnic community in the United States. As in the case of other Arab immigrants from Greater Syria, as much of the Middle East was once called, Palestinian immigration began during the final decades of the nineteenth century. The largest influx—similar to that of the Yemeni Arabs—began during the late 1960's. It is estimated that the Palestinian American population exceeded 87,000 in 1984; by the late 1980's it reached between 130,000 and 165,000.

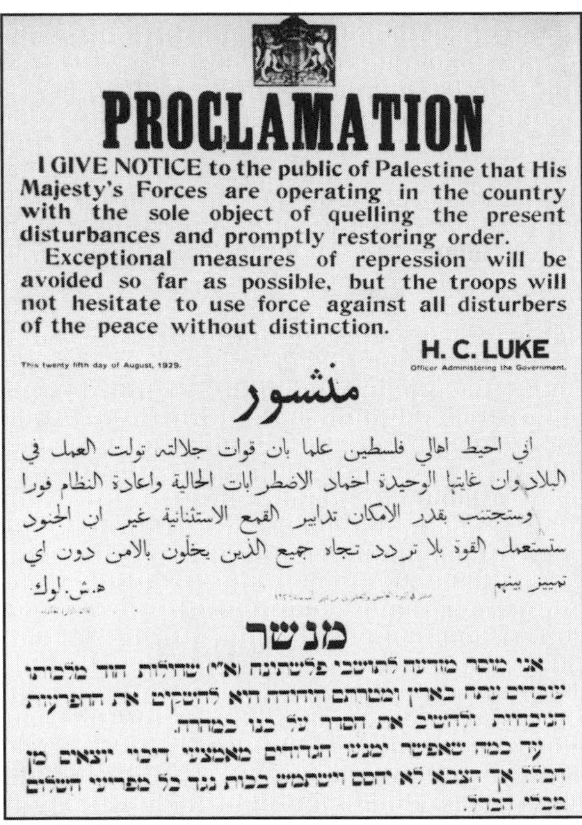

Poster from 1929 proclaims British intention to use force to put down disturbances in Palestine. Most Palestinian Americans came to the United States as a consequence of displacement from their land after Israeli independence. (National Archives)

From the 1890's to the 1960's. The great majority of Palestinian Americans are recent immigrants from Eastern Palestine which, in the wake of Israel's creation in 1948, remained under Arab sovereignty until the June, 1967, Arab-Israeli War. This area was called the West Bank by the Hashemite Kingdom of Jordan after it was formally annexed to Jordan in 1950, following the Arab-Israeli War of 1948. The Hashemite Kingdom offered Jordanian citizenship to Palestinian refugees of the 1948 war and to the Palestinians residing on the West Bank. Consequently, many Palestinians arriving in the United States have been designated as Jordanian citizens by the U.S. Immigration and Naturalization Service (INS).

Between 1820 and 1899, the INS classified Palestinian immigrants in the general category of persons from Turkey and Asia. This classification referred to all persons—not necessarily Arabs—who lived in the Ottoman province called the administrative unit, or *sanjak*, of Syria. In 1899, the INS instituted the racial category Syrian. This was applied until after the Great Depression of the 1930's to categorize Arabs from Greater Syria. Of the approximately 100,000 "Syrian" immigrants admitted to the United States between 1899 and 1921, less than 6 percent are estimated to have been Palestinians.

The overwhelming majority of Palestinian immigrants until the late 1940's and early 1950's were Christians from the town of Ramallah near Jerusalem, which became part of the Israeli-occupied West Bank in 1967. Like the Syrian Christians, the Palestinians in their ancient homeland were essentially shopkeepers, merchants, artisans, and owners of small family farms. After being exposed to the Western world and its ideals through Christian missionaries, Ramallah's Christians were motivated to leave. Another "push factor" prompting them to leave their homeland was the hardship imposed by the stringent Ottoman requirements of military service and heavy taxation. Though the Palestinian Christian Arabs, like the Jews, were tolerated and protected as *dhimmis* under the Ottoman Empire, they nevertheless viewed it as oppressive.

The Palestinian Muslim immigrants who came during the years preceding World War II were inhabitants of the villages in Eastern Palestine, geographically contiguous to both Ramallah and Jerusalem. They were essentially small farmers or farm laborers with a lower socioeconomic background. They came to the United States to escape their mounting difficulties of surviving through farming. They intended to alleviate their miseries by settling in a rich country and doing business with their Christian compatriots who had already immigrated and begun to prosper. Thus, whereas the Christian Palestinians immigrated for both economic and political reasons, inspired by their exposure to some form of Westernization, their Muslim counterparts left the Middle East for purely economic reasons. They hoped to return to their homeland after accumulating some capital. Both Christian and Muslim Palestinians were considered unskilled in the United States; many became peddlers and shopkeepers. The Christian immigrants fared better economically, eventually entering larger businesses.

continued to increase markedly in 1977, reaching even higher levels during the 1980's. The post-1967 Palestinian influx is largely explained by Israel's establishment of military rule in the West Bank and the Gaza Strip where Palestinian Arabs lived. As was the case during the 1948 war, Israel's military victory led to the exodus of many Palestinians from the West Bank into Jordan and Lebanon. A smaller proportion immigrated to the United States. Frustration among Palestinians in both the West Bank and Jordan also increased following the Camp David Accords (1978) and Egypt's peace treaty with Israel, which bypassed Palestinian participation and nationalist aspirations.

Palestinian Americans wear traditional headdresses as they rally in Chicago. (James L. Shaffer)

Since the 1960's. The Palestinians who immigrated to the United States beginning in the 1950's and 1960's were generally far more skilled and better educated than those who arrived earlier. According to one study, young men from the Jerusalem-Ramallah area were sent to the West for a university education during the mid-1950's. Indeed, Palestinians are generally considered the best-educated Arabs in the Middle East, many holding professional positions such as doctors and engineers. Accordingly they have also been active in the leadership of Arab American organizations.

In the immediate aftermath of the 1967 war and Israel's capture of East Jerusalem and the West Bank from Jordan, Palestinian immigration accelerated and

Moreover, in the 1980's, when the political climate and economic conditions for Palestinians in the Arab Gulf states and other Arab countries worsened, Palestinians could no longer turn automatically to the oil-rich Gulf states for employment. Simultaneously, there were not enough universities and colleges in the West Bank and Arab countries to admit all educated Palestinians seeking higher education in order to guarantee support for their families remaining in the Occupied Territories. In 1990, the effects of Iraq's annexation of Kuwait and the Persian Gulf War deprived Palestinian Arabs residing in the Gulf states of employment, status, and security.

While before 1967 the more politicized Palestinian immigrants tended to be the MUSLIMS, this situation changed with political developments in the Middle East since that time. The Palestinian American Christian communities began to exhibit adaptive patterns similar to those of the Muslims and expressed their opposition to the continued Israeli presence in the West Bank and Gaza. After 1987, mutual support for the *intifada* (the Palestinian uprising against Israel in the Occupied Territories) brought about greater solidarity between Christian and Muslim Palestinians. The community, its organizations, and publications avidly follow current events in the Middle East, such as the peace talks in the early 1990's. Although an agreement between the Israelis and Palestinians was signed in 1993, questions remain as to whether further confrontations might occur, spurring increased Palestinian immigraiton to the United States.

A Case Study: Muslim Palestinians in Chicago. The Muslim Palestinian community in Chicago is at least eighty-five years old. In 1988, it was one of the four largest Palestinian American communities, numbering between twenty and thirty thousand people in the city and as many as sixty thousand in the greater Chicago area. The majority of its members came from the West Bank, especially the Jerusalem-Ramallah region. According to Louise Cainkar, who studied the community, Palestinian Muslims have gone from being sojourners to semi-adapters to alienated exiles who tend to be ideologically resistant to nearly everything considered American.

Prior to 1945, the community was almost exclusively male. Its members earned their livelihood by peddling dry goods door-to-door. They had little interaction with other Chicagoans except their African American clientele. They made no attempts to become American or to emulate American customs. Consequently, they differed sharply from the Syrian and Palestinian Christian immigrants who, by the 1920's, were determined to stay in the United States and gradually assimilated.

Following World War II and the 1948 war, including events surrounding the creation of the state of Israel, Muslim Palestinian immigrants brought their wives and children to Chicago compelling the Muslim Palestinians to find suitable homes for them.

By the late 1940's, those who had accumulated sufficient capital began opening dry goods stores and small businesses. Palestinian Muslims continued to maintain their traditional clientele among African Americans. Relations were generally cordial between these two ethnic groups. For example, the Arab Club, founded mostly by Palestinian Muslims from the village of Betunya (near Ramallah), met in the African American Muslim Temple. African Americans and Palestinian Muslims coordinated lectures on topics of mutual understanding and increased social contact.

These Palestinian MUSLIMS remained isolated from mainstream American society for a few decades. They tended to be suspicious of AMERICANIZATION as a form of Christianization. Gradually, however, they diversified their occupational patterns by opening food and liquor stores; providing services such as real estate, insurance, and travel agencies; and managing gas stations or fast food restaurants. With a new influx of better educated immigrants, and some who have obtained a higher education in the United States, a growing force of Palestinian Muslims held professional jobs in the 1990's. By 1992, this urban community had a number of organizations characterized by class, educational, and ideological differences, and a growing segment of first-generation American children.

SUGGESTED READINGS. Information on Palestinian Americans is limited. *The Muslims of America* (1991), edited by Yvonne Yazbeck Haddad, is an overview of the larger Arab Muslim community of which some Palestinians are a part.—*Michael M. Laskier*

Pan-Africanism: Both an ideology and a political movement aimed at unifying and liberating the peoples of Africa and all those of African descent. Its ideological basis is linked to the African diaspora and the colonization of Africa. The ideology implies a common cultural and political conception and a unity of purpose among those of African descent. Pan-African ideas have been expressed in the Caribbean, North America, Europe, and Africa. Although the term was not used until the First Pan-African Congress in 1900, related concepts were evident in eighteenth century resistance to SLAVERY. Ottobah Cugoano and Olaudah Equiano were among the first Africans to articulate objections to slavery.

African repatriation in the nineteenth century gave rise to Pan-African ideology, supported by black missionaries from the Caribbean, such as Thomas Keith of Jamaica and John Duport of St. Kitts, as well as by black Bostonian Paul CUFFEE. British endeavors to relocate former slaves in Sierra Leone in 1808 were paralleled by the establishment of Liberia in 1847 by the AMERICAN COLONIZATION SOCIETY.

Edward Wilmot Blyden, originally of St. Thomas, was perhaps the most prolific nineteenth century advocate of early Pan-African ideas. He resettled in Liberia in 1850 and published *Christianity, Islam and the Negro Race* (1887). Other spokesmen included Martin DELANY, Reverend Henry McNeal TURNER, Reverend Alexander CRUMMELL, and John B. Russwurm, who founded the *Liberia Herald* in 1830. James JOHNSON and James Africanus Horton, both of Sierra Leone, advocated repatriation. Horton published *West African Countries and Peoples, British and Native* (1868). Other turn-of-the-century proponents included Haitian Benito Sylvain, Egyptian Yahub Pasha, Trinidadian Henry Sylvester Williams, and Nigerian Orishatuke Faduma.

W. E. B. Du Bois launched the Pan-African Congress in London in 1900 and in Paris in 1919. (The Associated Publishers, Inc.)

In the twentieth century, Pan-Africanism developed through a series of international congresses. W. E. B. DU BOIS was one of the leading African American exponents, launching Pan-African congresses in London in 1900 and in Paris in 1919. During the 1920's the Jamaican Marcus GARVEY also started a Pan-African organization, the UNIVERSAL NEGRO IMPROVEMENT ASSOCIATION (UNIA), which promoted a BACK TO AFRICA MOVEMENT. Other leading figures of the twentieth century included Trinidadians George Padmore and C. L. R. James.

"The First Pan-African Conference on African Soil" was held in Ghana in 1958 through the efforts of Kwame Nkrumah, the most prominent African advocate, along with Nnamdi Azikiwe of Nigeria, Ahmed Sékou Touré of Guinea, and Julius Nyerere of Tanzania (the site of the 1974 Congress). During the 1960's, the BLACK POWER MOVEMENT under Stokely CARMICHAEL reflected Pan-Africanist ideas, as did the ORGANIZATION OF AFRO-AMERICAN UNITY founded by MALCOLM X.

SUGGESTED READINGS. Pan-Africanism has been a subject of much scholarly investigation. Imanuel Geiss's *The Pan-African Movement: A History of Pan-Africanism in America, Europe and Africa* (1974) defines Pan-Africanism with a reliance on European sources. *Pan-Africanism* (1974), edited by Robert Chrisman and Nathan Hare, contains essays on a variety of topics. P. Olisanwuche Esedebe's *Pan-Africanism: The Idea and Movement, 1776-1963* (1982) employs Pan-African documents as primary source material; Tony Martin's *The Pan-African Connection: From Slavery to Garvey and Beyond* (1983) focuses on Garvey's contribution. An analysis of the movement in Africa is contained in Opoku Agyeman's *Nkrumah's Ghana and East Africa: Pan Africanism and African Interstate Relations* (1992).

Panamanian Americans: The Republic of Panama lies on the S-shaped isthmus that connects North and South America. This land was under Spanish colonial rule from the sixteenth to the beginning of the nineteenth century. Panama broke from Spain and joined Colombia in 1821. Aided by the United States, it finally became an independent republic on November 3, 1903.

Fifteen days later, Panama granted the United States the right to construct and control the Panama Canal, the only water route between the Atlantic and Pacific oceans. Since that time, the United States has been intimately involved in Panamanian affairs and has influenced the Panamanian economy and culture.

Possibly because of this close relationship, Panamanians make up the largest group of Central American immigrants in the United States. These immigrants are mostly people of color: indigenous people from the Guaymí, Cuna, or Chocoe tribes; mestizos, of mixed Spanish and Indian heritage; and Panamanians of African ancestry, who are descendants of slaves brought in during the colonial era.

Panamanians tend to settle in the urban areas of the northeastern United States, particularly in New York City. Female immigrants outnumber males two to one. Many of these women find work as domestic servants. Few Panamanian Americans are agricultural laborers. More than one-third of the new arrivals are white-collar workers or professionals.

Like their Central American counterparts, Panamanians speak Spanish and most consider themselves Roman Catholic. Panamanians and other Central Americans tend to hold middle-class values. Their relatively high levels of education and income often hasten their ASSIMILATION into American society.

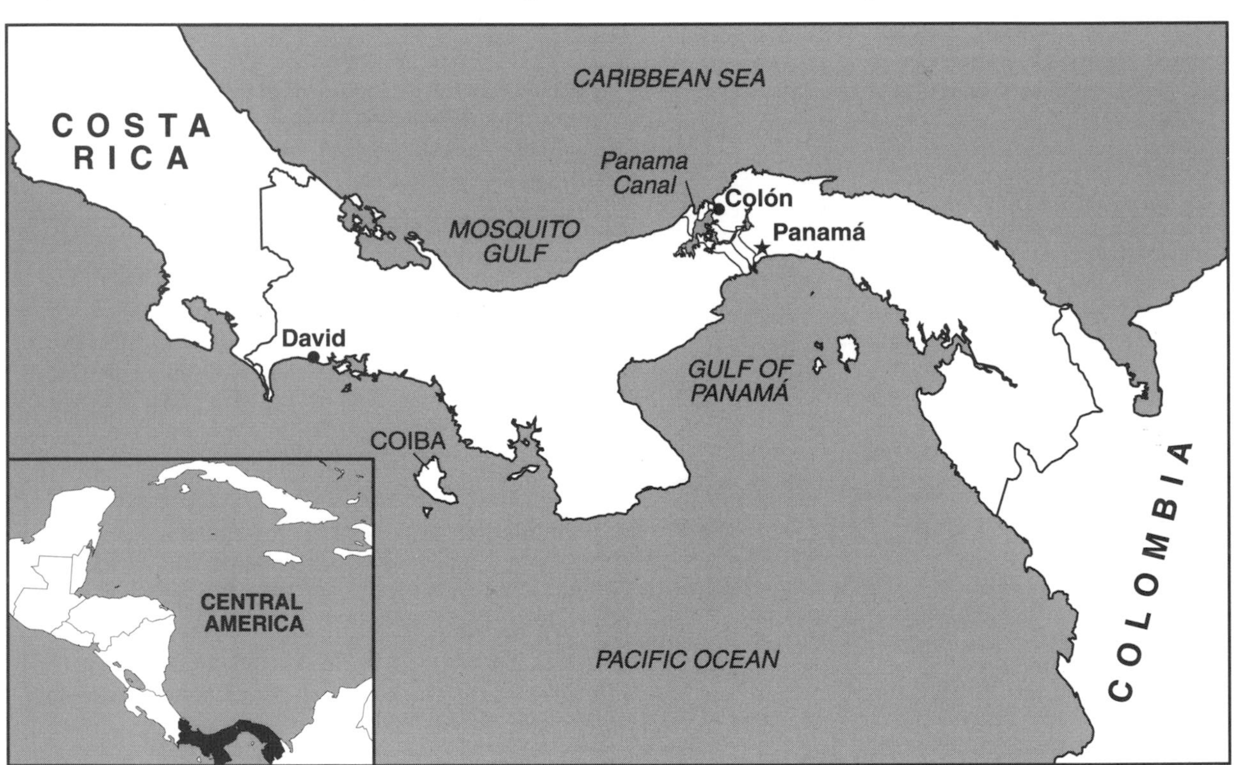

PANAMA

Pan-Indianism: American Indian cultural identity as "Indian" that supersedes individual tribal identities. While in the nineteenth century Pan-Indianism took spiritual and military forms, in the twentieth century it led to new religious, cultural, and political movements.

Prior to European contact, Indian identity was dispersed among allegiances to hundreds of distinct groupings. Any homogeneity existed only in the perception of whites. Distinct tribal cultures created bonds in order to resist the incursion of alien European society. The earliest pan-Indian movements were warlike religious and military responses. The PUEBLO REVOLT OF 1680 and PONTIAC'S REBELLION (1763-1765), led by the Ottawa leader, based intertribal confederacies on the messages of American Indian prophets. Other pre-twentieth century pan-Indian movements, such as Handsome Lake's New Religion and the GHOST DANCE of 1890, took more spiritual, less militaristic orientations.

Several historical patterns established a climate for contemporary Pan-Indianism. These included the breakdown of traditional Indian subsistence bases, the mass removal of indigenous peoples to reservations, and the educational practices at Indian schools, such as the CARLISLE INDIAN SCHOOL in Pennsylvania, which combined students from different cultures and sought the eradication of tribal identities. Indians developed new religions that both drew on traditional practice and accommodated new social situations. One such religion was the peyote cult, which was synthesized from Christianity and traditional Indian (particularly Plains) religions. In the first half of the twentieth century, various branches of the faith coalesced into the pantribal NATIVE AMERICAN CHURCH. The religion provides an identity that cuts across tribal affiliations, and congregations provide a setting for pan-Indian interactions that bond persons of diverse cultural backgrounds.

Pan-Indian political coalitions also emerged later in the twentieth century, particularly after World War II. The first major coalition was the politically moderate National Congress of American Indians (NCAI), established in 1944. This was followed in the early

Powwows are intertribal gatherings where Pan-Indianism influences can be seen. (Arni Katz, Unicorn Stock Photos)

1960's by the NATIONAL INDIAN YOUTH COUNCIL, which took a more radical stand than the NCAI. This incipient "Red Power" movement culminated in the formation of the activist and characteristically confrontational AMERICAN INDIAN MOVEMENT (AIM) in 1968. Failing to achieve its ends by direct confrontation, pan-Indian political activism returned to mainstream tactics after the late 1970's.

The POWWOW phenomenon, which has been characterized by some commentators as pop cultural, serves as a vehicle for pan-Indian sentiments on yet another level. These gatherings, featuring costumed dances and singing (and often sales of crafts and food, rodeos, or other events), provide opportunities for intertribal communication and participation in performances based to a greater or lesser degree on generalized Plains models. These gatherings have drawn criticism for blurring cultural distinctions and inviting the participation of non-Indian enthusiasts of the INDIAN HOBBYIST MOVEMENT.

SUGGESTED READINGS. Hazel W. Hertzberg's *The Search for American Indian Identity* (1971) carefully examines the sources of Pan-Indianism. Both *Indian Americans: Unity and Diversity* (1971) by Murray Wax and *The Ghost Dance: Ethnohistory and Revitalization* (1989) by Alice Kehoe provide substantial sections on nineteenth and twentieth century pan-Indian movements. James H. Howard presents an early analysis of the phenomenon in "Pan-Indian Culture of Oklahoma," in *Scientific Monthly* (November, 1955), pp. 215-220.

Paper sons: Illegal Chinese immigrants who falsely claimed to be sons of Chinese people who had attained U.S. citizenship. The term, which originated within CHINATOWNS, eventually became an integral part of the vocabulary of Chinese immigration history.

The passage of the CHINESE EXCLUSION ACT in 1882 barred nearly all Chinese immigration to the United States, and a small amount of illegal immigration began almost immediately. Then, in 1906, the San Francisco earthquake and fire destroyed the city's immigration and birth records. This event provided the opportunity for many Chinese men to fraudulently claim, and be granted, United States birth and citizenship. Under the citizenship law of 1855 (amended in 1938), such American citizens could freely go abroad and return without any restrictions. Men also had the privilege of bringing any children they fathered abroad back into the United States and claiming derivative American citizenship for them.

A number of enterprising Chinese individuals initiated a business of selling fraudulent documents in China and bringing to the United States young Chinese men who could afford the passage as their own sons. The surnames of these fabricated sons were changed to match those of their fathers on paper, so these illegal entrants were known in U.S. Chinatowns as paper sons. Chinese communities in the United States had populations that were mostly men, primarily because the original immigrants had come as laborers. The paper son phenomenon further contributed

After the 1906 fire in San Francisco's Chinatown district destroyed public records, many Chinese men were able to obtain false documents to immigrate as "paper sons." (Library of Congress)

to the unbalanced sex ratio of these populations, which continued well into the twentieth century.

It is difficult to ascertain the actual number of paper sons who entered the United States. The IMMIGRATION AND NATURALIZATION SERVICE (INS) estimated the number of legal Chinese entries between 1883 and 1943 to be about ninety-five thousand. This number, however, is not very accurate because it includes multiple entries by the same individuals. Moreover, there were illegal entrants who arrived by other means such as jumping off boats, entering via Mexico, or continuing to stay on (in hiding) after their visa terms had expired.

After an initial period of success, the paper son business came under heavy scrutiny by the INS and the federal court system. Chinese people claiming citizen status or seeking entry into the United States were subjected to interrogation and gruelling examination. Some Chinatown residents were hired by the INS as informers. Counterschemes were soon devised in the Chinatown community, however, in the form of "crib sheets" running to hundreds of pages. These were to be memorized by the paper sons, and they provided detailed information about their supposed lives—their village, family history, relatives, and particular incidents—in order to outsmart the INS.

This influx of paper sons decreased greatly when the U.S. government introduced blood tests to determine paternity. Several paper sons were deported, and several Chinese men in the United States were stripped of their citizenship.

Following the repeal of the Chinese Exclusion Act in 1943 and the passage of the McCarran-Walter Act, or the IMMIGRATION AND NATIONALITY ACT OF 1952, which restored naturalization privileges to Asians in the United States and established a national origin quota, steps were taken by the American government to provide for the legalization of paper sons and other illegal Chinese immigrants. Under a congressional act of September 11, 1957, a confessional system was provided for illegal residents to regularize their status if such individuals had a spouse, parent, or child who was a citizen or a permanent resident of the United States. During this Cold War period, however, when anticommunist and xenophobic hysteria was at its peak in the United States, few cared to "confess" before the much-distrusted INS.

SUGGESTED READINGS. A scholarly account of paper sons is to be found in Roger Daniels' *Asian America* (1988). Other informative sources on this subject are Victor G. Nee and Brett de Bary Nee's *Longtime Californ': A Documentary Study of an American Chinatown* (1973), and Diane Mei Lin Mark and Ginger Chih's *A Place Called Chinese America* (1982).

Paredes, Américo (b. Sept. 3, 1915, Brownsville, Tex.): Mexican American folklorist, educator, and journalist. He received a doctorate from the University of Texas at Austin in 1956, taught at the University of Texas, El Paso, and in 1967 became director of the Center for Intercultural Studies in Folklore and Oral History at the University of Texas at Austin. He was significant not only in bringing scholarly attention to BORDER CULTURE but also in inspiring a whole generation of Chicano students and activists in the CHICANO MOVEMENT. His many publications include the well-known *With a Pistol in His Hand* (1958), *Folk Music in Mexico* (1966), *Folktales of Mexico* (1970), *A Texas-Mexican Cancionero* (1976), *George Washington Gomez* (1990), and *Between Two Worlds* (1991). Paredes has been the recipient of numerous prestigious awards.

Paris, Treaty of (1763): Treaty between England, France, Spain, and Portugal that restored most colonies to their prewar owners. France gave Canadian territory to England on the condition that French inhabitants would be allowed to practice Catholicism. Free access to the Mississippi River was given to both England and France, and all land on the "left side of the River Mississippi" except New Orleans and its island was ceded to England. England returned Cuba to Spain; in return, Spain relinquished claim to Florida and other parts of North America.

Parker, Charlie "Bird" (Aug. 29, 1920, Kansas City, Kans.—Mar. 12, 1955, New York, N.Y.): Groundbreaking African American jazz composer and musician. A great improviser on alto saxophone, a creator of the bebop style, and a lasting influence on jazz, Parker was prominent during the 1940's and 1950's. He cut his first records in 1941 in Kansas City and played with the original Billy Eckstine band. Parker's bebop duos with Dizzy Gillespie defined the freewheeling, sharply accented style and generated controversy in the music world. After 1946, Parker worked mostly with a quintet. The club Birdland was named in his honor. Among his compositions are "Now's the Time" and "Yardbird Suite" ("Yardbird" was another of Parker's nicknames). The film *Bird* (1988) popularized Parker's music and tragic life story.

Parker, Ely Samuel [Donehogawa] (1828, Indian Falls, N.Y.—Aug. 31, 1895, Fairfield, Conn.): Seneca Iroquois U.S. government official. The son of a Seneca chief, Parker trained as an engineer after being denied admission to the bar because he was an American Indian. As General Ulysses Grant's military secretary from 1864 to 1866, he was famous for transcribing the documents at Appomattox that ended the Civil War. He served as Commissioner of Indian Affairs from 1869 to 1871.

Parker, Quanah (c. 1845, Tex.—Feb. 23, 1911, Fort Sill, Okla.): Comanche Indian chief and businessman. Son of the Comanche chief Peta Nocone and a white captive, Cynthia Ann Parker, he became chief of a band of Kuahadi Comanches. Quanah Parker led raids on frontier settlements and against white buffalo hunters in the 1860's and 1870's. He instigated a short war against white settlers in Texas in 1874; his group was defeated in 1875. He promoted housing, agriculture, and education for Indians. Quanah Parker became a successful Oklahoma businessman and was reported at one time to be the wealthiest Indian in the United States. When he died, he was buried with military honors and was the most esteemed and influential member of his tribe.

Parks, Rosa (b. Feb. 4, 1913, Tuskegee, Ala.): African American integration pioneer. A tailor's assistant who had attended Alabama State College, Rosa Parks secured her place in the history of the American Civil Rights movement by a courageous act on a city bus in Montgomery, Alabama, on December 1, 1955: She took a seat toward the front of the bus in the section "reserved for whites" under southern segregation laws. She refused to relinquish her seat to a white man. For this she was jailed, provoking the black community to organize the MONTGOMERY BUS BOYCOTT—an event which mobilized support for the early Civil Rights movement. Dr. Martin Luther KING, Jr., came to Montgomery to help the cause and promote the principle of nonviolent "passive resistance" to discriminatory laws.

Parochial schools: Alternatives to public school education sponsored by religious organizations. Public schools serve the general public, which is composed of adherents to diverse creeds, and cannot, by law, offer any religious instruction. Parochial schools are centrally based around a religion and aim to instill religious values. They have been established by many denominations since the colonial era and especially since the nineteenth century. Parochial schools are autonomous in nature; they are not supported by public funds, and they are responsible only to the parents of their students and any other supporters.

The first Catholic parochial school was established in St. Augustine, Florida, in 1606. With the dramatic growth of the Catholic population through immigration in the 1800's, Vatican bishops encouraged each parish to build schools in order to offer a Catholic belief-based education. This was the Catholic church's response to what it viewed as a Protestant orientation and anti-Catholic bias in the public school system, as evidenced by a daily reading from the King James version of the Bible and certain textbooks. By 1985, there were 9,397 Catholic schools in the United States with an enrollment of 2,933,657 students.

Many religious groups—such as the AMISH, QUAKERS, PRESBYTERIANS, LUTHERANS, and JEWS, to name a few—formed their own schools to combine religious instruction and general education in order to protect children from outside influences that might challenge their belief in a particular religion and to safeguard their culture. Some parochial schools were established as a reaction against the CULTURAL PLURALISM of the

Integration pioneer Rosa Parks is honored on her seventy-fifth birthday, 1988. (AP/Wide World Photos)

Girls enjoy a recreation period at a parochial school in the Midwest. (James L. Shaffer)

public schools. While the public schools concentrated on serving the needs of a diverse society, parochial schools concentrated on the need some ethnic groups felt to preserve their own culture, language, and ethnic heritage, as in the Jewish day schools or Protestant fundamentalist Christian day schools.

Parochial schools have been accused of being formed to maintain SEGREGATION in that many people flocked to them after courts ordered public school integration and a majority of their students tended to be Caucasian. In answer to that charge, most schools maintain that their goal is to ensure quality religious education and that they, too, are subject to federal antidiscrimination laws. In fact, some parochial schools have thrived on the admittance of minority students. For example, some Catholic schools remained in inner-city areas in the 1960's and 1970's after their traditional white clientele had left for the suburbs; these schools admitted many Latino and African American students, often as an incentive to receive more money from the diocese. The proportions of minority students in Catholic schools grew from 10.6 percent of enrollment in 1983 to 23 percent in 1989. By 1990, approximately 10 percent of all African American schoolchildren attended private schools, mostly Catholic.

Although religion and preservation of culture were once the basis for enrollment in parochial schools, dissatisfaction with public schools has prompted more parents of all backgrounds to turn to parochial education in the late 1900's. Parochial schools usually offer more individualized instruction and more advanced curriculum than public schools, and many parents equate a parochial education with a greater opportunity for higher education and upward mobility.

SUGGESTED READINGS. To read more about particular

Private School Enrollment and Tuition: 1988

Type of School	Students Enrolled	Number of Schools	Average Tuition
Catholic schools	2,902,000	9,527	$1,327
Other parochial schools	1,715,000	12,132	$1,941
Nonsectarian private schools	863,000	5,148	$3,839

Source: Data are from *Statistical Abstract of the United States, 1992.* Table 247. Washington, D.C.: U.S. Government Printing Office, 1992.

cases involving parochial schools, and the controversial question of religion in public schools, read *Religion and Morality in American Schooling* (1981), edited by Thomas Hunt and Marilyn Maxon, and *Religion and the Schools* (1963) by Paul Blanshard. On federal regulations concerning religion and education, see *Government and Campus* (1982) by Edward Gaffney and Philip Moots. The *Encyclopedia of Education Research* (1992) includes statistics on parochial schools.

Partido de la Raza Unida (PRU): Latino political party founded in 1970. One of its primary leaders in the 1970's was José Angel Gutiérrez. The party (often abbreviated to La Raza Unida) intended to work as a third party in a number of ways. In areas where there were large Latino concentrations, La Raza Unida sought to elect Latino candidates; where the Latino population was smaller but still significant, it sought to swing the balance of power toward candidates who would best serve the Latino community. The party achieved some notable success in 1972 elections in Texas, but it generally failed to gain the political influence it sought on a national level. In local elections, the party succeeded in placing candidates on school boards and city councils. La Raza Unida was viewed as too radical by many voters, however, and its influence declined as the DEMOCRATIC and REPUBLICAN parties ran more Latino candidates on their own tickets.

Passover: Jewish holiday in either March or April (depending on the Jewish lunar calendar) which commemorates the deliverance of the Israelites from Egypt. Exodus 13:3 instructs, "Remember the day on which you went forth from Egypt, from the house of bondage, and how the Lord freed you with a mighty hand." This Feast of Unleavened Bread celebrates the miraculous exodus from slavery more than three thousand years ago, the seminal event in Jewish history.

In the home or at a communal gathering of synagogue members, Jews celebrate Passover with a special service and meal called the Seder. REFORM JEWS usually have one Seder the first night, whereas ORTHODOX and CONSERVATIVE JEWS have a Seder on both the first and second nights. Jews read from a book called the Haggadah, recounting with family and friends the story of Passover. The Haggadah explains the symbolic objects on the Seder table, and contains passages from Exodus as well as prayers, psalms, hymns, and songs rejoicing in the miracle of God's delivering the enslaved Jewish people. The observance of this festival each spring, the season of renewal, reminds Jews of their people's ancient heritage and renews the human spirit.

The Seder begins with the rituals of blessing the festival candles and the wine, sanctifying the event. Symbolic foods assembled on a special Seder plate are explained and then eaten. Greens (such as celery or parsley) represent renewed life. A Pascal lamb bone recalls the ancient sacrificial lamb and the marking of Jews' homes with blood of the lamb to signify those whom God would spare (pass over) during the plague of the first-born. A roasted egg symbolizes fertility. Perhaps the most representative Passover food, *matzoh* (unleavened bread), recalls that the Jews left Egypt in such haste they did not wait for their bread to rise. Salt water and bitter herbs (horseradish) remind Jews of their forebears' bitter tears and suffering; *haroset* (a mixture of apples, nuts, cinnamon, and red wine) symbolizes the mortar the slaves used to make bricks for the Egyptian pyramids. Drinking four cups (or sips) of wine represents the four expressions of redemption. The cup of Elijah, a special chalice of wine, is for the prophet, who is invited in as a child opens the door.

Passover offers many rich traditions. The youngest child asks the "Four Questions" about the symbolic nature of the Seder, and the leader responds. After a sumptuous meal and singing, children search for the Afikomon—a matzoh hidden at the beginning of the service, with the child who finds it receiving a present. The Seder ends with sharing pieces of the *matzoh*, the bread of affliction which symbolizes the bond of humanity with the oppressed everywhere. Jews are supposed to refrain from eating leavened foods for the eight days of the holiday.

SUGGESTED READINGS. Books on Passover's history and traditions include Theodor Herzl Gaster's *Passover: Its History and Traditions* (1962); *A Passover Haggadah: Home Service for the Passover* (1978), illustrated by Leonard Baskin; and Philip Goodman's *Passover Anthology* (1961). An excellent Passover children's book is Uri Shulevitz's *The Magician* (1973).

Jewish American family observes Passover with the Seder meal. (James L. Shaffer)

Paul, Alice (Jan. 11, 1885, Moorestown, N.J.—July 9, 1977, Moorestown, N.J.): Suffragist. Paul was arrested six times in England between 1907 and 1912 for various women's suffrage activities. On her return to New York, she became involved in organizing suffrage parades. In 1913 she was elected head of the National American Woman Suffrage Alliance but split off from the group a year later to form the Women's Party, her own congressional committee. The outspoken Paul was a master propagandist and brought many new recruits into the suffrage movement. In 1928 she founded the World Party for Equal Rights for Women.

Well-known suffragist Alice Paul, c. 1920. (Library of Congress)

Peace activism: Although peace activism is commonly associated with the antiwar movement of the 1960's and 1970's, the organized protest of war has a long history in the United States. QUAKERS, among the earliest settlers in colonial America, have always been pacifist in their orientation and sought alternatives to war. Their important role in the ABOLITIONIST MOVEMENT of the early and mid-1800's brought the cause of peace together with that of eradicating slavery. Many leaders of the women's SUFFRAGE MOVEMENT also pressed for world peace in the latter half of the 1800's. Jeanette RANKIN, the first woman to be elected to Congress, was an avowed pacifist during World War I at a time when such a stance was extremely unpopular.

The Quakers formed the American Friends Service Committee (AFSC) in 1917 to provide humanitarian relief for victims of the war and to develop opportunities for alternatives to military service for conscientious objectors. The pacifist AFSC remains one of the oldest peace organizations in the United States, often supporting and working in coalitions with newer groups that arise in response to particular conflicts. From its beginnings it also set the precedent of combining peace activism and education with efforts for social justice and reform.

Peace activism in the United States has generally been dominated by European Americans. Relatively few African Americans were incorporated into the AFSC ranks. One black Quaker, Bayard Rustin, became a maverick peace activist who advocated Mahatma Gandhi's philosophy of nonviolence, arguing for the inseparability of peace and civil rights. Rustin was active during the early 1940's, working alongside A. Philip RANDOLPH and his trade union in the struggle to build black support for peace.

During the early 1940's, roughly one out of six federal prisoners was a conscientious objector. In mid-1943, a strike at Danbury Federal Correctional facility led by imprisoned pacifists protested racial SEGREGATION in prison dining halls. This strike led to a concerted alliance of pacifist organizations, the NATIONAL ASSOCIATION FOR THE ADVANCEMENT OF COLORED PEOPLE (NAACP), and legal advocacy organizations. By December, the prison gave in, becoming the first federal prison to desegregate dining facilities. Similar actions soon occurred at other prisons, registering remarkable successes in prison reform and initiating a legacy of cooperation between peace and civil rights activism.

Following World War II, Peace and civil rights activists focused their attention on racial segregation in the military. By 1947, Bayard Rustin and A. Philip Randolph began to agitate for an end to this practice, declaring that they would organize black youths to resist the draft unless segregation was unconditionally abolished. As a result, President Truman issued an executive order in mid-1948 which ordered an end to racial segregation.

During the Cold War era, anti-Communist hysteria made peace activism unpopular and extremely difficult. Even civil rights organizations witnessed "red-baiting" within their ranks as hawkish new leaders, seeking to win support from the mainstream, denounced "unpatriotic reds and pacifists." Ironically, many African Americans now sought personal advancement through service in the newly desegregated military.

The political leadership of Martin Luther KING, Jr., initiated a revival of peace activism in minority communities. Throughout 1965, the CIVIL RIGHTS MOVEMENT reluctantly grappled with the Vietnam War issue as King, a committed pacifist, lobbied hard for a strong antiwar stand. In January of 1966, King decisively spoke out in a scathing attack on the war, denouncing it as disastrous for the African American community. The STUDENT NONVIOLENT COORDINATING COMMITTEE (SNCC) supported King's antiwar position, followed later by the more conservative SOUTHERN CHRISTIAN LEADERSHIP CONFERENCE (SCLC). King's principled stand against the military destruction being unleashed against the poor of Vietnam had profound and persistent echoes in the African American community.

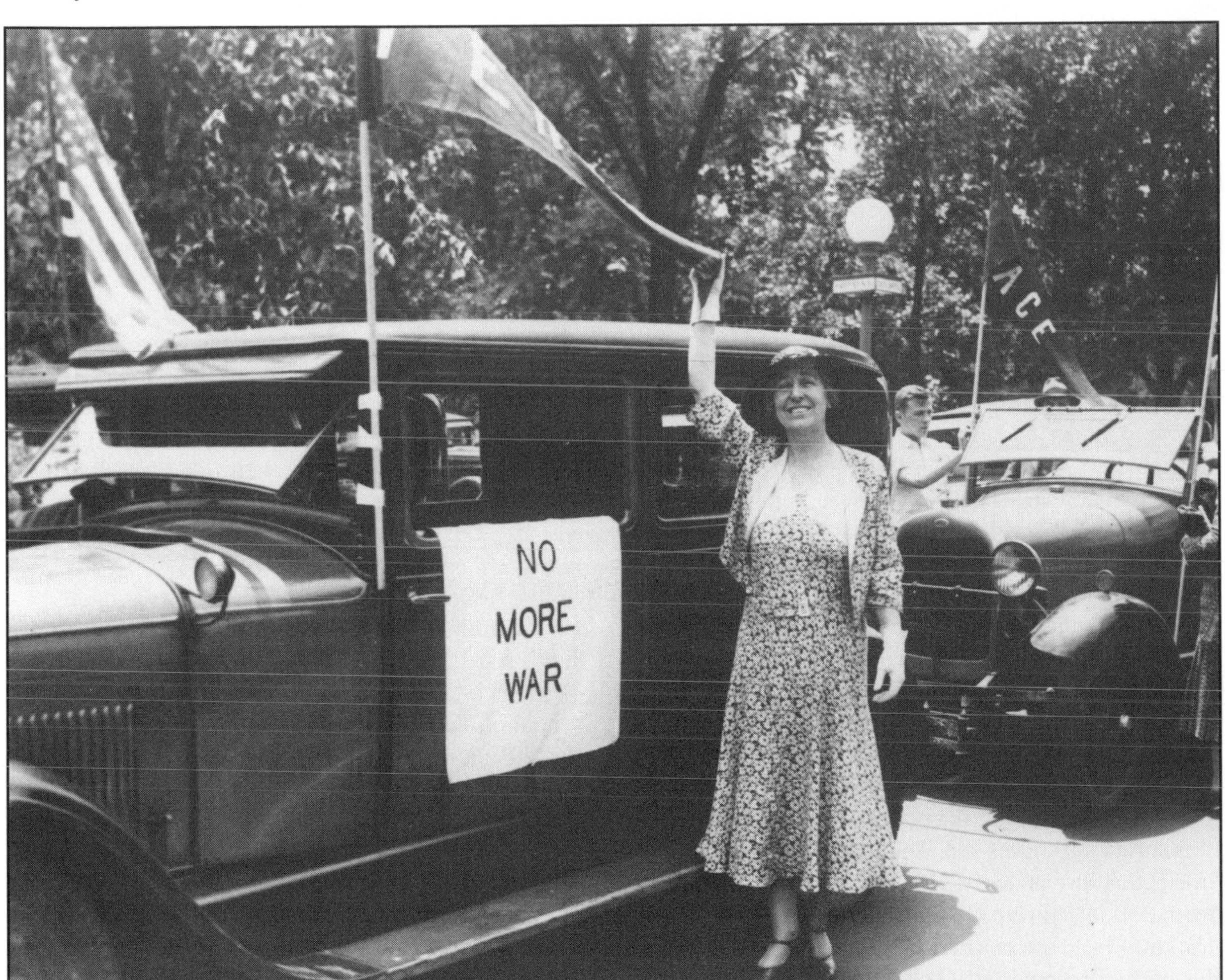

Jeanette Rankin, pacifist and first woman member of Congress, pictured here in 1932. (AP/Wide World Photos)

Peace activism was at the center of student protests on numerous college campuses during the 1960's and 1970's. Like civil rights protestors, antiwar protestors were often arrested or mistreated—and occasionally killed—by the police and National Guard. The peace movement exerted pressure on the U.S. government during the final years of the VIETNAM WAR and its aftermath, greatly influencing public opinion. During the 1970's and 1980's, the movement shifted its attention to limiting nuclear weapons and protesting U.S. involvement in Central America. In the early 1990's, peace activism continued quietly on a variety of fronts, generally attracting support and attention only in times of crisis such as the Gulf War in 1991.

Suggested Readings. Lawrence S. Wittner's *Rebels Against War: The American Peace Movement, 1941-1960* (1969) describes the overlapping concerns of peace and civil rights. *Peace Movements in America* (1973), edited by Charles Chatfield, highlights historical aspects of peace activism, while Merle Eugene Curti's *The American Peace Crusade, 1815-1860* (1965) focuses on peace and abolitionism. James A. Colaiaco's *Martin Luther King, Jr.: Apostle of Militant Nonviolence* (1988) and John G. Ansbro's *Martin Luther King, Jr.: The Making of a Mind* (1982) discuss King's contributions to peace activism.

Pearl Harbor: Site of attack by Japan on December 7, 1941, that thrust the United States into World War II. It is located on the Hawaiian island of Oahu. The Hawaiian islands are strategically located approximately halfway between Japan and the United States, making them desirable as a way station or fueling center for both the United States and Japan. In a seemingly impossible strategic maneuver, Japan successfully bombed the unsuspecting Pearl Harbor Naval Shipyard.

Although there were rumors that an attack might be forthcoming, the isolation and topography of the harbor made such a feat seem improbable and gave the men and women stationed there a false sense of security. Approximately nine square miles of water are contained in the circular harbor, which has Ford Island at its center. The narrow, shallow entrance was impenetrable by conventional torpedoes and protected by submarine nets. Even top military personnel were confident that any attack would be from individual saboteurs seeking to destroy the air fleet housed at nearby Hickum Field rather than Pearl Harbor. Indeed, the Japanese also attacked Hickum Field during their air raid. To make guarding the planes against sabotage easier, the American military was housing them close together on the airfield, which ironically made their annihilation relatively easy for the Japanese air patrol.

The early morning surprise attack sent a wave of shock and xenophobia throughout the United States, which officially entered World War II the next day. Particularly on the West Coast, anti-Japanese sentiment had never been far below the surface. Unfounded fears of spying and sabotage by Japanese Americans were undoubtedly inflamed by the attack. Japanese Americans on the West Coast, viewed as security risks, were soon incarcerated in remote internment camps—a flagrant violation of their civil rights.

Suggested Readings. Three objective historical accounts of Pearl Harbor are Walter Lord's *Day of Infamy* (1957), Gordon W. Prange's *At Dawn We Slept: The Untold Story of Pearl Harbor* (1981), and John Toland's *Infamy: Pearl Harbor and Its Aftermath (1982).*

Pecan shellers' strike (1938): On February 1, 1938, pecan shellers in San Antonio, Texas, most of whom were Mexican American, went on strike because management declared a one-cent reduction in pay rates from five or six cents a pound. Local law authorities supported management and arrested more than a thousand strikers, including Congress of Industrial Organizations (CIO) organizer J. Austin Beasley when he arrived to assist union members. The Mexican Chamber of Commerce, League of United Latin American Citizens (LULAC), and church leaders all refused to support the strikers because their leadership was considered communist. The strike ended when an arbitration board required management to comply with the Fair Labor Standards Act (1938) requiring a minimum wage of twenty-five cents an hour.

Peck, Annie Smith (Oct. 19, 1850, Providence, R.I.—July 18, 1935, New York, N.Y.): Mountain climber. In 1885 Peck was the first woman to be admitted to the school of classics in Athens, Greece. She climbed her first mountain, Mt. Shasta in California, in 1888. In 1904 she climbed Huascaran, a peak in the Peruvian Andes, then the highest point climbed in the Western Hemisphere. In 1911, at sixty-one years old, she climbed Mount Coropun in Peru and planted a sign at the summit that read "Votes for Women." Her last climb, at age eighty-two, was Mount Madison in New Hampshire. Peck is the author of *A Search for the Apex of South America* (1911) and *Flying over South America* (1932).

Pei, I. M. [Ieoh Ming] (b. Apr. 26, 1917, Guangzhou, China): Chinese American architect. Pei came to the United States to study architecture in 1935. He earned his master's degree from Harvard University in 1939, and then alternated between private practice in New York, Boston, and Los Angeles and teaching at Harvard.

He became an American citizen in 1954 and the following year established his own firm, I. M. Pei & Associates in New York, with a distinctly modern architectural style. Among Pei's notable buildings are the Mile High Center in Denver (1955), Kips Bay Plaza in New York (1962), the John F. Kennedy Library in Boston (1979), and the 1988 expansion of the Louvre Museum in Paris. Pei has won numerous honors, including the Pritzker Prize in 1983, the National Medal of Art in 1988, and Japan's Praemium Imperiale in 1989.

Noted Chinese American architect I. M. Pei has a distinctly modern style. (Serge Hambourg, courtesy of Pei, Cobb, Freid and Partners)

Penitentes: Loosely organized lay religious society of the Roman Catholic church established in northern New Mexico and southern Colorado around 1800. The official name is the Brothers of Our Father Jesus Nazarite, and its two primary functions are the commemoration of the passion of Jesus and the practice of Christian charity. Members and their auxiliaries are best known for their penitential processions during Holy Week that involve self-flagellation, carrying the cross, and other types of self-mortification. The society has been condemned for its excessive practices. In 1947, however, an official reorganization and reinstatement was proclaimed by Archbishop Edwin Byrne.

Pentecostal congregations. *See* **Evangelical and Pentecostal congregations—African American**

Pentecostals: Adherents of a Protestant movement originating in the United States in the nineteenth century and subsequently spreading throughout the world, which teaches that all Christians should seek "baptism with the Holy Spirit" after conversion. They believe that this experience parallels the first descent of the Holy Spirit upon the twelve disciples of Christ, who had assembled in Jerusalem on the day of the Pentecost (seventh Sunday after Easter, or the Resurrection of Christ). They further maintain that this experience is accompanied by the same sign that appeared to the disciples: the ability to speak in a language entirely unknown and foreign to the speaker and rarely comprehended by the listener—that is, to "speak in tongues" (glossolalia).

Pentecostals believe that speaking in tongues often strengthens individual Christians and that, when accompanied by interpretation, this activity edifies the church, becoming a vehicle of the loftiest kind of spiritual praise. Speaking in tongues is intended to be a commencement of a new life in the Spirit that is distinguished by certain charismatic (spiritually inspired) gifts, such as the ability to speak wisely or prophetically, the power to heal or work miracles, and the ability to discern error or control demons.

In matters of doctrine, Pentecostals can be described as Evangelicals whose theology is akin to Fundamentalism. Almost universally, they believe in the infallibility of the Bible, the Trinity, the virgin birth, the absolute deity of Christ, the atoning sacrifice of Christ's death for the sins of the world, the resurrection, and the return of Christ in bodily form to earth.

Despite a common belief in certain doctrines such as baptism of the spirit, speaking in tongues, and healing, Pentecostals are not united in a singular denomination. With roots that are numerous and varied, this charismatic movement consists of numerous groups that differ in size, church government, modes of worship, and ordinances. The major denominations of Pentecostalism in the United States are the Churches of God; the Church of God in Christ; the Pentecostal Holiness Church; the Pentecostal Church of God of America; the United Pentecostal Church; and the International Church of the Foursquare Gospel.

There has been a tendency among Pentecostals to divide into smaller groups that follow a particular gifted leader, who may be very charismatic and spontaneous or, conversely, ritualistic and controlling. The movement as a whole has grown phenomenally since its inception to become one of the fastest growing religious movements in the Western hemisphere. In the late 1980's authorities within the movement estimated the total membership to be between 8 and 12 million worldwide.

SUGGESTED READINGS. John Thomas Nichol's *Pentecostalism* (1966) describes the worldwide scope of Pentecostalism and attempts to classify the varieties of Pentecostalism in the United States. *Suddenly from Heaven* (1961) by Carl Brumback is an authoritative history of the Assemblies of God. Klaude Kendrick's *The Promise Fulfilled* (1961) is an extensive history of the eight most prominent American Pentecostal bodies. In *They Speak with Other Tongues* (1964), John L. Sherrill presents one of the best treatments of the revival of the charismatic phenomena in non-Pentecostal circles.

Perkins, Frances (Apr. 10, 1882, Boston, Mass.—May 14, 1965, New York, N.Y.): Federal official. Perkins was the first female cabinet member of the United States, serving as Secretary of Labor from 1933 to 1945. One of her early jobs was at HULL HOUSE, JANE ADDAMS' settlement house in Chicago. From 1907 to 1909, as secretary of the Philadelphia Research and Protective Association, she investigated sweatshop conditions. After the TRIANGLE SHIRTWAIST COMPANY FIRE of 1911 in New York killed 146 workers, mostly women and children, Perkins did investigative work for the State

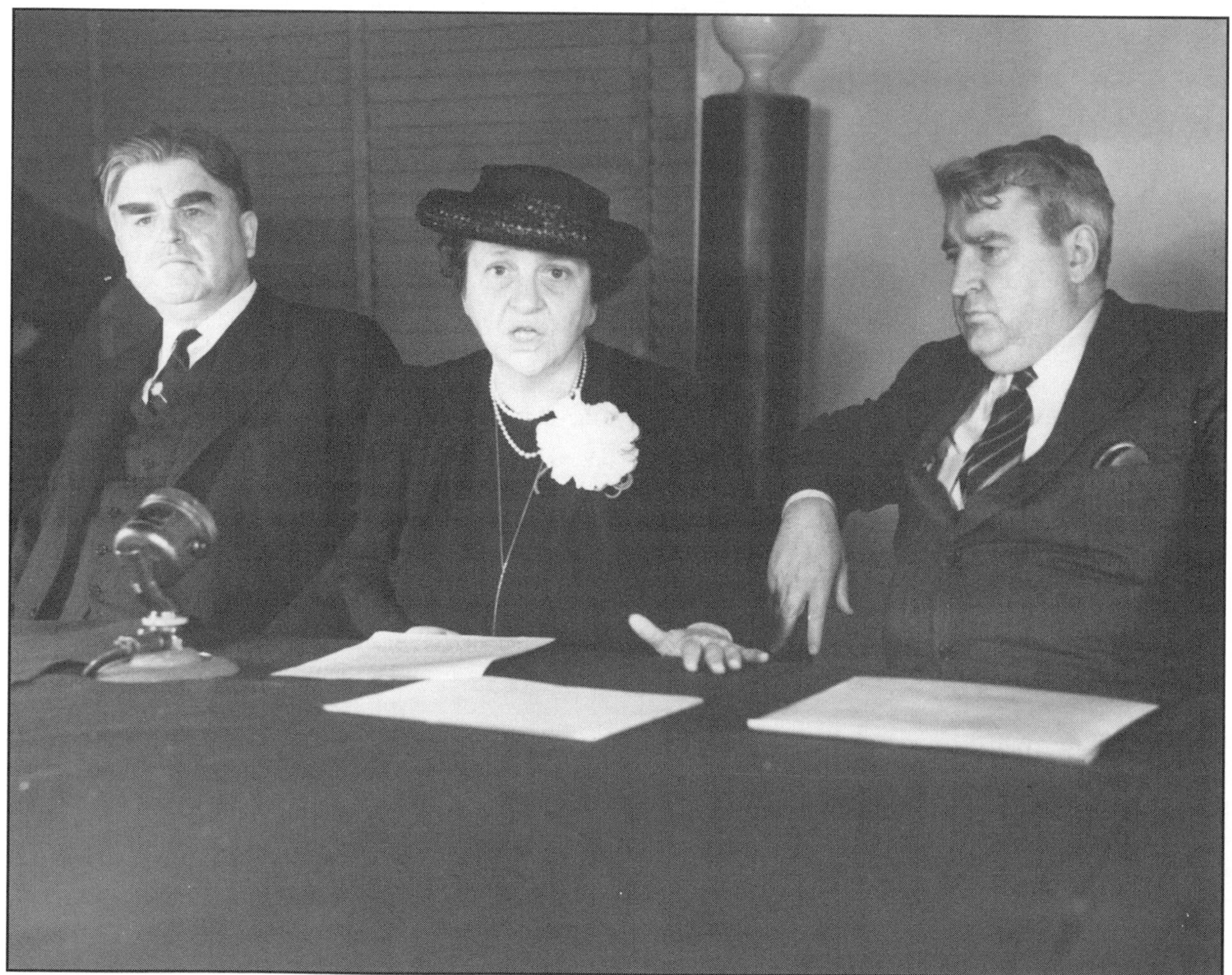

Secretary of Labor Perkins (center) confers with United Mineworkers' John L. Lewis and Charles O'Neill of Appalachian Soft Coal Operators regarding a strike in 1939. (AP/Wide World Photos)

Factory Committee. As Secretary of Labor she was responsible for prompting passage of the SOCIAL SECURITY ACT (1935), the National Labor Relations Act (1935), and the Wage and Hour Act (1938).

Perry, Matthew Calbraith (Apr. 10, 1794, South Kingstown, R.I.—Mar. 4, 1858, New York, N.Y.): Naval leader. As commodore of the African Squadron of the U.S. Navy from 1843 to 1845, Perry opposed the slave trade and helped to establish the state of Liberia as a haven for free blacks. He took command of the India Squadron in 1852 and set his sights on Japan, which had traditionally been closed to American interests. On July 8, 1853, Perry brought four ships into Tokyo Bay to a lukewarm welcome. The following winter, he returned with seven ships and an impressive display of American technological achievements. On March 31, 1854, the Treaty of Kanagawa was signed, establishing Japanese-American trade, port rights, and consular privileges.

Persecution: Acts of oppression, violence, or harassment often directed at groups or individuals who are different from oneself. Acts of persecution are caused by BIGOTRY and hatred, which are most often fueled by insecurity, fear, and misinformation. Persecution consists of actions such as HATE CRIMES that are deliberately intended to harm others because of their race, ethnicity, beliefs, or sexual orientation. (Some forms of discrimination, on the other hand, may be thoughtless or unintentional.) At its most extreme, persecution can involve individual acts of murder such as LYNCHING (as once perpetrated by the KU KLUX KLAN) or mass destruction such as the annihilation of six million Jews by the Nazis during the HOLOCAUST. Persecution also includes actions that, although not life-threatening, systematically undermine confidence and self-esteem.

Peruvian Americans: Peru lies on the Pacific coast of South America, south of Ecuador and north of Chile. Before the Spanish conquistador Francisco Pizarro arrived in 1532, the territory that is now Peru was the center of the Inca empire. The Incas had developed sophisticated agricultural and architectural skills. Before the Spanish arrived, the Inca population reached approximately twelve million. In the first fifty years of Spanish domination, nearly ten million Incas died.

Peru has a history of ethnic diversity. During the colonial period, the Spaniards imported slaves from Africa. In 1824, Peru achieved independence from Spain and welcomed a substantial number of Chinese immigrants into the country to work on Peruvian farms. Other post-revolution Peruvian immigrants included more Spanish, some northern Europeans, and numerous Japanese.

PERU

The indigenous people of Peru—the Cuzco, Arequipa, Tarma, Cajamarca, and the Huancavelica, among others—intermarried with the immigrants and created new racial types. These included mestizo (white and Indian), injerto (white and Asian), mulatto (white and black), zambo (black and Indian), and chinocholo (black and Asian). As the generations passed, racial intermingling became so complex that today there are no Peruvians of unmixed white heritage.

Among the relatively few Peruvian immigrants who come to the United States, there are slightly more men than women. Peruvians, like other South Americans, tend to settle in the metropolitan areas of the northeastern United States, particularly in New York City. Some also settle in Los Angeles, San Francisco, and Chicago. A high percentage of these newcomers are professionals who therefore assimilate into American society in a relatively short time.

Peyote: Cactus well known for its mescal buttons, which produce hallucinogenic effects when eaten or chewed. Peyote has figured prominently in the religious practices of certain American Indian tribes; it is an important element in the ceremonies of the NATIVE AMERICAN CHURCH. Peyote is found in the limestone soil of the Chihuahuan desert of southern Texas and northern Mexico. The principal element of peyote is mescaline, an alkaloid drug, and the sale, use, or possession of live plants or dried mescal buttons is prohibited by law in some areas.

Philadelphia, Pa.: In the early 1600's, the site of Philadelphia was occupied by the Delaware (or Lenni Lenape) Indians. The Delawares were gradually pushed inland by the Swedish and Finnish settlers of New Sweden, who were in turn conquered by the Dutch (1655) and the English (1664). Ownership of the land ultimately passed to William Penn, a wealthy Englishman who, in 1682, named his new city Philadelphia (Greek for "City of Brotherly Love") in keeping with his Quaker faith and his utopian vision for the city as a "holy experiment." From the beginning Penn guaranteed that settlers and investors of all religious persuasions would be welcome.

The 1700's were a period of rapid growth for Philadelphia. It continued to be the chief port of entry for immigrants to the English colonies until the nineteenth century, when it was displaced by New York. Numerous waves of Mennonites, Lutherans, Moravians, and other Protestants from the various German states and Switzerland passed through Philadelphia on their way to what would become known as the "Pennsylvania Dutch" country in southeastern Pennsylvania. Similarly, thousands of Scots-Irish Presbyterians immigrated from Northern Ireland to the area.

For most of the nineteenth century, the largest immigrant group in the city of Philadelphia was the Irish Catholics. Among much of the settled white Protestant population, nativist fear of the growth of Roman Catholicism and economic competition from the Irish resulted in periodic anti-Irish, anti-Catholic riots. The year 1844 was especially representative of this violence.

The African American population in Philadelphia dates back to 1684, when those present were slaves. Quakers' moral doubts about slavery, however, and a 1780 Pennsylvania law providing for its gradual phasing out, led to a large population of free African Americans. During the 1700's, the African American community grew rapidly both in numbers and in social status.

By 1830 Philadelphia had a population of 14,447 free blacks and only thirteen slaves. This was by far the largest population of free African Americans anywhere in the nation at the time. The energy and zeal of these people is indicated by their leadership of religious denominations. Philadelphia was home to the first African Protestant Episcopal church, the first African Presbyterian church, the first African Methodist church, and the first totally independent African American denomination—the AFRICAN METHODIST EPISCOPAL (AME) CHURCH. Unfortunately, many white Philadelphians felt threatened by the growing population of free African Americans. There were serious outbreaks of antiblack rioting each year from

Philadelphia Minority Population: 1990

Percentages of total population of 1,586,000

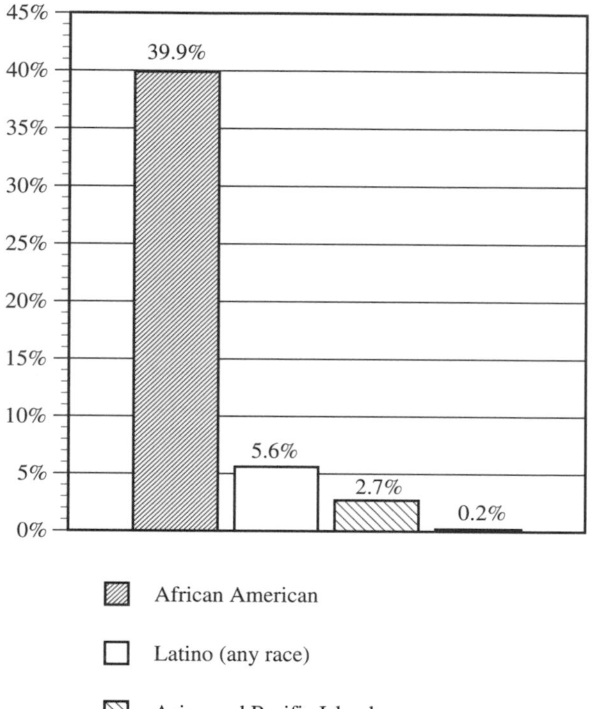

Source: Data are from *Statistical Abstract of the United States, 1992.* Table 38. Washington, D.C.: U.S. Government Printing Office, 1992.

1834 to 1838 and again in 1849. Nevertheless, the free African American population continued to grow in both numbers and influence.

During World War I, thousands of African Americans came to Philadelphia from the South as part of the GREAT MIGRATION. This process resumed after World War II. As a result, by the 1980's African Americans had become a majority of the city's population and its citizens elected W. Wilson Goode as its first mayor of African American descent. This period also saw the development of a confrontation between the municipal government and police force with MOVE, a small, militant African American group. In May, 1985, a standoff between MOVE and the police resulted in the bombing of MOVE headquarters, which left several people dead and destroyed virtually an entire block of housing. The city continues to support numerous African American social, cultural, educational, and political organizations.

The largest white ethnic group in modern Philadelphia is the Italian Americans, who arrived mainly between 1890 and 1920 and settled in South Philadelphia. The city is also home to large populations of Slavs and Jews.

SUGGESTED READINGS. For an excellent comprehensive history of Philadelphia see *Philadelphia: A 300 Year History* (1982), edited by Russell F. Weigley. For excellent ethnic studies see *The Irish in Philadelphia* by Dennis Clark (1973), *Jewish Life in Philadelphia* (1983), edited by Murray Friedman, and *Forging Freedom: The Formation of Philadelphia's Black Community, 1720-1840* (1988) by Gary B. Nash (1988). Finally, unrest in the African American community in the 1980's is thoroughly presented in *Burning Down the House: MOVE and the Tragedy of Philadelphia* (1987) by John Anderson and Hilary Hevenor.

Philadelphia riots of 1844: Disturbances that began with minor confrontations between Irish Catholics and local political organizations in May and escalated into fighting in the streets from July 5 through July 8, as Protestant workers, agitated by antipapal propaganda, launched attacks on all foreigners. Although far more destructive, the events recalled earlier riots in Philadelphia in which skilled workers vented their rage against new immigrants to the city in 1828, 1834, 1835, 1840, and 1842. Attempts by Catholics to end Bible-reading in the public schools had alarmed Protestants and further agitated the Protestant members of the working class. As a result of the violence, Catholic churches were burned and hundreds of immigrant homes were destroyed.

Picture brides: Japanese women who came to the United States to marry Japanese immigrants in a marriage system based on the exchange of pictures. These women constitute an important part of the history of the first-generation Japanese Americans, or ISSEI. While picture brides are mainly associated with immigration from Japan to the United States, about a thousand picture brides were permitted to enter Hawaii from Korea as Japanese subjects between 1910 and 1924, when Korea was under Japanese occupation.

The early Japanese immigrants who arrived in the United States between the late nineteenth century and the mid-1920's were mainly unmarried single men. Since economic hardships and the presence of anti-Asian prejudice and laws made it difficult for these bachelors to return to Japan to get married, a majority of them secured their spouses as picture brides in the United States.

Picture-bride marriages were an offshoot of the arranged marriage system in Japan, which was primarily a relationship between two families rather than two individuals. In other words, a marriage could be legally performed in the physical absence of the bride and the bridegroom by entering the woman's name in her prospective husband's family register, at the local government office. A large number of Issei bachelors made use of this custom to obtain Japanese brides from their villages. These men would send their pictures home with impressive details about their lifestyle and accomplishments in the United States. Their families in Japan would find a suitable match, send the picture of the prospective bride to the groom, and conduct the formal marriage. The picture brides were then shipped to the United States, often in groups, with pictures of their grooms, whom they were to meet at the ports.

The picture brides made a significant difference in the demographic pattern of the Japanese American immigrant history. Unlike other Asian immigrant groups, particularly the Chinese Americans, the Japanese immigrants were not subject to legal exclusion until 1924 because of the GENTLEMEN'S AGREEMENT of 1908 between the governments of Japan and the United States. Therefore, the immigration of women, mainly as wives and picture brides, continued, creating a balanced sex ratio in this population. The picture brides

Japanese picture brides enter the United States at Angel Island, Calif., in the 1920's. (National Archives)

helped provide stability to the Japanese American family as well as the benefit of a second American-born generation or NISEI.

The arrival of the picture brides, however, caused a mixed reaction in the United States. On the one hand, they stimulated cross-cultural interest and sympathy. Yet at a time when anti-Asian and anti-Japanese hysteria was gaining ground in the United States, the unfamiliar Japanese marriage system and the institution of picture brides were viewed as immoral. Public pressure mounted during the first couple of decades of the twentieth century on the government to halt the immigration from Japan, like it had for other Asian countries. Some Americans saw the picture brides as threatening because they were viewed as "breeders" who would produce more "unassimilable" persons, while others suspected that the women were actually laborers who violated the provisions of the Gentlemen's Agreement.

SUGGESTED READINGS. A detailed account of the immigrant experience and struggle of the picture brides can be found in Emma Gee's "Issei Women," in *Counterpoint: Perspectives on Asian America* (1976), edited by Gee. For details of the legal controversy surrounding the arrival of picture brides, see Milton R. Konvitz's *The Alien and the Asiatic in American Law* (1946) and Roger Daniels' *The Politics of Prejudice* (1967). Roger Daniels' *Asian American* (1988) is a useful source for a comprehensive overview of the Japanese American history.

Pierce, Sarah (June 26, 1767, Litchfield, Conn.—Jan. 19, 1852, Litchfield, Conn.): Educator. Pierce started a school in Litchfield in her dining room with only a few students. In 1827 it became the Litchfield Female Academy, offering reading, writing, grammar, geography, history, arithmetic, needlepoint, watercolor, dance, and drama. The school received religious instruction from Reverend Lyman Beecher, and consequently, Harriet Beecher STOWE, Henry Ward, and Catherine Beecher attended. In 1814 John Pierce Brace, Sarah's nephew, added philosophy, logic, botany, and mineralogy to the course list. At its height the school enrolled close to 130 females ranging from age seven to about twenty-five.

Pietists: Members of sects that began to flourish at the end of the seventeenth century in Europe in an attempt to revitalize religious feeling. Although the theology of pietism is diffuse, the sects have had a lasting effect on Western culture.

After the Treaty of Westphalia, which ended the Thirty Years War (1618-48), there was a pervasive sense in Germany that religion had lost its meaning, and had become dry and empty. Philipp Jackob Spener (1635-1705), raised as a Lutheran, became the evangelical force of Pietism as he protested against theological intellectualism, ecclesiastical formalities, and ethical quietism. Opposed to precise doctrinal distinctions, Spener and his supporters attempted to revive Christian piety and intensify a sense of moral purity. This revivalism was a reaction against the rationalism of the Enlightenment; the Pietists instead stressed the experiential nature of faith—the experience of being reborn—and the seriousness of the Christian calling in the social world.

In general, the Pietists stressed the feelings of the heart. These intense feelings of conversion and regeneration should inevitably lead the Christian to an emotional relationship with Christ as the redeemer of the world. This personally felt connection, in turn, should lead to works of charity and love in the community; thus, there is a pietistic emphasis on charitable works.

Spener and another influential Pietist, Count Nickolaus Zinzendorf (1700-1760), inspired many pietistic sects throughout Europe, which were eventually transported to the American colonies. One of the most important developments of pietism in England was John Wesley's society, organized at Oxford. Wesley (1703-1791) had his group meet regularly to study the Bible, partake of communion, observe fasts, and perform acts of charity, such as visiting jail prisoners. The group's moral strictness, however, alienated other students at Oxford, and they were derisively called "Methodists"—an appellation that remains today.

The Wesley brothers and the remarkable preacher George Whitefield (1714-1770) made missionary journeys to the American colonies, and established Methodism there. The work of Whitefield, particularly, contributed to a revival of American religious fervor in the mid-1700's called the GREAT AWAKENING.

Other important pietistic sects also emigrated to America. These include the Dunkers, organized by Christopher Sauer (1693-1758); the Moravian Brethren, led by Augustus Gottlieb Spangenberg (1704-1792); and the Schwenckfelders, named after their leader, Kaspar Schwenckfeld von Ossig (1489-1561). As Sydney E. Ahlstrom writes, "Taken as a whole, pietism performed an immense revivifying role in all Protestant churches during the eighteenth century."

SUGGESTED READINGS. For literature on the pietistic sects, see Sydney Ahlstrom's magisterial *A Religious History of the American People* (1972). Other important studies include Garnest Stoeffler's *The Rise of Evangelical Pietism* (1965); Edwin Scott Gausted's *The Great Awakening in New England* (1957); Richard Cameron's *The Rise of Methodism* (1954); and Robert Monk's *A Study of the Christian Life: John Wesley, His Puritan Heritage* (1966).

Planned Parenthood Federation of America (PPFA): Founded in 1916 by Margaret SANGER, the mission of Planned Parenthood is to ensure people's fundamental right to plan when they want children and to prevent unwanted pregnancies. PPFA clinics throughout the nation offer contraceptive services, low-cost ABORTIONS, prenatal care, and sterilization, as well as educational programs on human sexuality and the prevention of adolescent pregnancy. Throughout its history PPFA has been an unyielding advocate of widespread access to family planning services.

Plessy v. Ferguson (1896): Landmark U.S. Supreme Court decision upholding the constitutionality of racial SEGREGATION under the "separate but equal" doctrine. It may be viewed as a part of a deliberate pattern to deprive the African American population of many of the rights it had gained through the abolition of slavery. By constitutionally sanctioning JIM CROW LAWS, the decision remained the principal legal obstacle to civil rights for African Americans for half a century.

The case grew from a challenge to an 1890 Louisiana statute requiring "equal but separate accommodations for the white and colored races" on its railroads. In 1892, Homer Adolph Plessy, seven-eighths white and one-eighth black, boarded the railroad to make the 60-mile trip between New Orleans and Covington, Louisiana. According to a prearranged plan, he refused to ride in the Jim Crow car and was arrested as soon as he sat down. He was brought to trial before Judge John H. Ferguson of the Criminal Court of New Orleans, who found him guilty of violating the state law. Several of Louisiana's African American leaders retained New York lawyer Albion W. Tourgee, a former North Carolina carpetbagger judge, as counsel to challenge the decision in the U.S. Supreme Court. The argument for instituting an action to restrain enforcement of the statute was based on the dual claims that it violated both the prohibition of involuntary servitude stated in the THIRTEENTH AMENDMENT and the rights and privileges of national citizenship guaranteed by the FOURTEENTH AMENDMENT.

The Supreme Court, by a seven-to-one vote, ruled Louisiana's statute constitutional. For the majority, Justice Henry B. Brown wrote that "the underlying fallacy" of Plessy's argument was its "assumption that the enforced separation of the two races stamps the colored race with a badge of inferiority." A law that "implies merely a legal distinction" between blacks and whites did not violate the Thirteenth Amendment. The Court decided that the Fourteenth Amendment "in the nature of things . . . could not have been intended to abolish distinctions based on color, or to enforce social, as distinguished from political equality, or a commingling of the two races upon terms unsatisfactory to either." While there was, in fact, no real legal authority upon which the Court could base such a conclusion, there were many so-called scientific, sociological, and psychological theories of race at the time that appeared to support the Court's view.

Justice John Harlan, a former slaveowner from Kentucky, wrote the lone dissent. Echoing the language of Tourgee's brief, he wrote: "Our Constitution is color-blind. . . . In respect of civil rights all citizens are equal before the law." While the Supreme Court heard several challenges over the next half century that severely weakened a state's power to mandate the separate-but-equal doctrine, restrictive legislation based on race increased steadily. Not until the 1954 decision of *BROWN V. BOARD OF EDUCATION* did the court overturn *Plessy v. Ferguson*, ruling, in the original brief's words, "Compulsory racial segregation is itself an unconstitutional discrimination."

SUGGESTED READINGS. For further information, consult Otto Olsen's *The Thin Disguise: Plessy v. Ferguson, a Documentary Presentation* (1967) and Robert Harris' *The Quest for Equality* (1960).

Plyler v. Doe (1982): U.S. Supreme Court decision involving the rights of undocumented aliens. This decision established that children of illegal immigrants could not be excluded from access to free public school education without violating the principle of equal protection of the law guaranteed by the FOURTEENTH AMENDMENT of the U.S. Constitution.

This case arose after the state of Texas enacted a statute denying local school districts funds for the education of undocumented alien children and allowing school districts to exclude such children from their public schools unless the students paid a tuition fee. A class action suit was brought in the name of certain school-age Mexican children illegally residing in Texas against James Plyler, a school superintendent, and other state officials. On appeal, the U.S. Supreme Court struck down the statute as a violation of the Fourteenth Amendment. The relevant clause in this amendment says that no state shall "deny to any person within its jurisdiction the equal protection of the laws." The state of Texas argued, in part, that undocumented aliens were not persons "within its jurisdiction" and were therefore not entitled to equal treatment by the laws of Texas. By a vote of five to four, the Court rejected this argument, noting that the equal protection clause was intended to bring about "the abolition of all caste-based and invidious class-based legislation."

The majority opinion by Justice William Brennan stressed the importance of education to the individual, to democracy, and to society in general, but it stopped short of declaring education a fundamental constitutional right. The state of Texas argued that the objectives of the statute were to protect itself from an influx of illegal immigrants, to improve the overall quality of education in the state, and to avoid spending public monies on children unlikely to remain productively employed in the state. The Court regarded all of these as insubstantial state interests that did not outweigh the costs to the individual and to society of denying children access to an education.

In *Plyler v. Doe*, the Court majority seemed to hold that the mere physical presence, and not the legal status, of persons within a state's borders entitled them to equality under the law. Yet Brennan also implied that states might be allowed to deny full equality under law to undocumented adults because, unlike their children, they are responsible for their illegal status. The Texas statute was judged to deny equal protection in this case because it imposed "a lifetime hardship on a discrete class of children not accountable for their disabling status." The ruling in *Plyler v. Doe* has since been narrowly construed by the Court to apply strictly to undocumented alien children in the area of public education. It is doubtful that this decision will become the basis for expanded rights of undocumented alien adults.

SUGGESTED READINGS. For a good analysis of the legal status of aliens, see Kenneth Karst's *Belonging to America: Equal Citizenship and the Constitution* (1989). Patrick Henry Kellough and Jean L. Kellough's *Public Education and the Children of Illegal Aliens* (1985) is a useful bibliography of that subject. Other relevant sources include Elizabeth Hull's *Without Justice for All: The constitutional Rights of Aliens* (1985); Linda J. Wong, John Huerta, and Morris J. Baller's *The Rights of the Immigrant Poor: A Legal Analysis* (1983); and Peter H. Schuck and Rogers M. Smith's *Citizenship Without Consent: Illegal Aliens in the American Polity* (1985).—*Philip Zampini*

Pocahontas [Matoaka] (c. 1596, Werowocomoco, Va.—Mar., 1617, Gravesend, Kent, England): Powhatan Indian who probably saved the life of Captain John Smith, prominent member of the Jamestown council, as

Pocahontas saved Captain John Smith of the Jamestown settlement from execution by her father, Chief Powhatan. (Library of Congress)

her father, Chief POWHATAN, was about to execute Smith. She became a Christian and in 1614 married the English colonist John Rolfe, who introduced tobacco cultivation to the colonies. This union brought peace for eight years. Rolfe took her to England in 1616, where she was received as a princess. Pocohontas died while preparing to return to America and was buried at Gravesend, England.

Poets and poetry: Poetry, like recorded history, has always been published primarily by those groups of people who have achieved the greatest degree of influence and control in a particular society. Whereas the writing of history requires a course of training and some academic experience, the practice of poetry is much less limited, dependent more on individual experience and the personal involvement with language that is available to any member of a cultural community. It is not necessary to be connected to any formal educational system or even to be literate in a written fashion. From the earliest moments of recorded time, the speaking or singing voice of the poet has expressed the widest and most varied thoughts and impulsesof the culture from which it springs.

Poets Stanley Kunitz and Lucille Clifton chat at a conference in New York City. (Hazel Hankin)

The English Tradition. Until the late twentieth century, the academic establishment presented an essentially monocultural description of American poetry. Poetry was fundamentally defined by the rules of form and structure delineated in poems written in Great Britain more than four centuries before the declaration of American independence. The "British" strain of American culture was so strongly dominant that in the eighteenth century, African American Phillis WHEATLEY, brought to the United States as a slave child at about the age of seven, achieved fame by mastering the modes of English verse and publishing her work in London in 1773. The British model, as well as the power exerted by an English mind-set in the early days of the American colonies, led American poets such as William Cullen Bryant, John Greenleaf Whittier, and Henry Wadsworth Longfellow to write poetry that ostensibly had an American setting but that spoke in a familiar English voice and maintained the restricted conception of a poem common to the British tradition.

This conception effectively excluded the oral poetics that had thrived on the North American continent since pre-Columbian times. The oral tradition in poetry has been described by Jerome Rothenberg as "deeply rooted in the powers of speech and song, breath and body, as brought forward across time by the living presence of poet-performers, with or without the existence of a visible/literal text." Such poetry may include sermons, blues, gospels, narratives, chants, spells, and other forms of poetry often dismissed by narrowly conventional academic commentators. In addition, the British persuasion implied that poetry was primarily the work of men intellectually trained in the New England Renaissance, making it difficult for women poets to be taken seriously and nearly impossible for poets of other ethnic communities to be noticed at all.

The American Indian Tradition. The original form of oral presentation and even the original language of much American Indian poetry have been either lost or transmuted in fragmentary transcriptions. Yet it is evident that a vital poetics combining history, myth, religion, and lyric expression was a part of the culture of many tribal groupings prior to the arrival of Europeans on the North American continent. William Brandon's adaptation of the Iroquois "The Tree of the Great Peace" stems from a poem created in the mid-fifteenth century. The "Walam Olum," a chronicle of the Lenni Lenape Delaware Indians, was developed as a "painted record" (the title means "red score") on a bundle of sticks. It relates tribal history from a moment of emergence (as in a creation myth) through the migration from Asia and Alaska until the arrival of Europeans in the region. Although the original sticks have been lost, the range of the narrative suggests the duration of its existence in tribal memory. Similarly, a combination of pictures and sound/symbols cut into rocks in Hopi settlements in the Southwest—including those in Oraibi, site of the oldest continuous habitation in the United States—demonstrate the methods of commemoration used by a poem such as the Hopi "Song of the Humpbacked Flute Player" to register the continuing history of a people.

Most of the older American Indian poetry that remains was translated in the nineteenth century or later. Yet some of the poets' concerns with biological richness and splendor of the natural world were still strikingly relevant to poets of various backgrounds at the close of the twentieth century. Santo Blanco, a Seri Indian living off the coast of Baja California, wrote a series of whale songs which find parallels in the work of the contemporary poet Gary Snyder, while the traditional song/stories about the trickster-figure Coyote (such as the Nez Perce "Three Songs of Mad Coyote") and the Winnebago prankster/god legends have been sources of inspiration for Simon Ortiz and Peter Blue Cloud. The celebratory poetry of Smohalla (Nez Perce), which honors the Earth as a benevolent entity; Ojibwa songs by Wabezic, Gawitayac, and Meckawigabau (as their names have been phonetically transcribed); Teton Sioux songs by Brave Buffalo and Teal Duck; and the Inuit "improvised greeting" on the theme "The lands around my dwelling/ Are more beautiful" convey an appreciation of the landscape akin to the writing of Anglo Americans such as John Muir, Edward Abbey, and other more familiar figures in the American tradition of terrain exploration.

More recently, the poems of Louise ERDRICH (Chippewa) combine a contemporary sensibility with the sacramental qualities of visionary or sacred poetry such as Ghost Dance songs and the peyote songs of the Comanche from circa 1870. Modern poets such as William Oandasan, a member of the Ukomnóm tribe of northern California, and Linda Hogan, a Chickasaw from Oklahoma, use elements from the history of their communities as well as a full command of the poetic techniques available to any American writer in the midst of the postmodern epoch. These two poets, along with Roberta Hill Whiteman (Oneida), Joy Harjo (Creek), and others, offer a unique perspective. Their fusion of realism and the "philosophy of American Indian spirituality . . . recalls the wounds of the past, the agony of the present and dream visions of a better future," according to C. B. Clark.

African American Poets. Unlike American Indian poets, whose disruptive contacts with European civilizations still left them immersed in their own cultural contexts, the violent wrenching of Africans away from their homeland into slavery in the United States produced a severe fracture in cultural continuity. Although the AFRICAN CULTURAL SURVIVALS the slaves brought with them were not sufficient to sustain a complete literary tradition, these elements helped shape the direction of African American poetry. Since enslaved African Americans were denied an education, a very strong oral tradition developed, ranging from song and story to "drum languages." Nineteenth century field chants, hollers, work songs, and spirituals led to BLUES MUSIC in the twentieth century, with its bitingly ironic rhymed texts. The verbal dexterity of "the dozens," "signifying," and eventually RAP MUSIC,

Gwendolyn Brooks was named Poet Laureate of Illinois. (AP/Wide World Photos)

indicate a love for language and rhythm that is at the heart of poetic expression.

At the same time, in defiance of the constraints placed upon formal education among African Americans, writers such as Phillis WHEATLEY and Jupiter Hammon (a slave born in New York) mastered the "British" formal verse expected of competent poets or versifiers of the time. Hammon's religious poems have the familiar ring of other quatrains composed by devout colonials, while Wheatley's poems are so "English" that only titles such as "To His Excellency General Washington" even suggest their American origins. The educated British style of Wheatley, Hammon, or Frances Harper and the singularly "American" textures of the oral tradition produced twin tracks in African American poetry that ran in the same direction with almost no interlinkage—a muted version of the mainstream and a powerful undercurrent.

When the essentially artificial division between conventional poetry and more distinctly American forms began to dissolve, the first real flowering of African American poetry took place in what has come to be called the HARLEM RENAISSANCE. This literary movement propelled into prominence writers such as Countée Cullen, who wrote romantic lyrics expressing a black personality; Claude McKay, who used the sonnet form; Sterling Brown, who combined vernacular speech with narrative song; and Langston HUGHES, who mastered every modern poetic mode available. Since the 1930's, more contemporary African American poets have drawn on the oral traditions and historical experience of the community, as well as a range of universal contemporary or postmodern poetics. Writers such as Sonia Sanchez, Amiri BARAKA, Gwendolyn BROOKS, Alice WALKER, and Michael Harper, among numerous others, have solidified the position of African American poets in the central current of American literature.

The Submerged Ethnic Tradition. In spite of the availability of small presses, duplicating machines, and even hand-written, self-circulated broadsheets, poetry written in communities where English was not a first language has frequently vanished into a limbo of "lost languages" in the United States. Occasional instances of generally forgotten writing, such as the poems carved on barracks walls by Chinese immigrants awaiting acceptance or deportation in San Francisco Bay's Angel Island between 1910 and 1940, stand as evidence of what is probably a much larger body of work. In the poetry of contemporary Asian Americans such as Janice Mirikitani, Ai, and Wing Tek Lum, and in the poetry of Latinos such as Miguel Algarin, Tato Laviera, and Lorna Dee Cervantes, there is, in William Oandasan's words "the voice of an ancient age/ dreaming of breath"—the hidden history of a people emerging in an ethnopoetics that is responsive to the world in which it is written and may reflect cultural traditions maintained by oral transmission. In the 1990's, for example, a collection of poems by Asian Americans was described as very diverse but united by the writers' awareness of race in American life.

As Ishmael Reed has stated, "American literature is an ocean" more than a mainstream, and the rich cultural diversity of life on the North American continent has rarely been realized in artistic expression more completely than in the work of the poets who inhabit it.

SUGGESTED READINGS. A number of excellent collections offer samplings of multicultural poetry. A comprehensive view of American literature from a multicultural perspective is provided by *The Heath Anthology of American Literature* (1990), edited by Paul Lauter and a team of scholars. An excellent discussion of the issues involved in multicultural literary expression is found in Jerome Rothenberg and Diane Rothenberg's *Symposium of the Whole* (1983), a collection of essays by poets, anthropologists, philosophers, and others. For a more specific sample of minority poets, see Jerome Rothenberg's anthologies *Technicians of the Sacred* (1968), with selections from Africa, America, Asia, and Oceania, and his *Shaking the Pumpkin* (1972), a collection of traditional American Indian poetry. Rothenberg and George Quasha's innovative *America, a Prophecy* (1973), which they describe as "a new reading of American poetry from pre-Columbian times to the Present," is an especially interesting and eclectic gathering of poems, suggesting by juxtaposition how much merging there has actually been between supposedly separate types of poetic expression. *The Before Columbus Foundation Poetry Anthology* (1992), edited by Ishmael Reed, J. J. Phillips, Gundars Strads, and Shawn Wong, contains a perceptive selection of poetry, brief essays, and a sound introduction.—*Leon Lewis*

Poitier, Sidney (b. Feb. 20, 1924, Miami, Fla.): African American actor. A star of screen and stage, Poitier was the first black actor to be nominated for an Academy Award (for *The Defiant Ones* in 1958) and the first black to win one (for *Lilies of the Field* in 1963). Poitier got his start after World War II with the American Negro Theatre in New York. During the 1950's he made nine Hollywood motion pictures, including *Blackboard Jungle* (1955) and *Porgy and Bess* (1959), and then starred in the stage and film versions of *Raisin in the Sun* (1959, 1961). Later he appeared in films such as *In the Heat of the Night* and *To Sir with Love* (both 1967); he also directed films. His memoirs are titled *This Life* (1981).

Polish Americans: In the early 1990's, Polish Americans were by far the most numerous among the many Slavic nationalities in the United States. Although estimates vary considerably, more than nine million Americans claimed Polish ancestry in the 1990 census. It should be noted, however, that this figure encompassed many individuals of mixed ethnicity. Approximately two million Polish Americans continued, in the early 1990's, to belong to strongly Polish ethnic religious organizations, in particular the hundreds of Roman Catholic parishes organized to meet their spiritual and social needs, as well as hundreds of fraternal insurance associations, social clubs, and cultural groups active throughout the country. This well-defined community with enclaves in many major industrial cities of the Northeast and Midwest (Chicago, Detroit, Buffalo, New York, Milwaukee, and Philadelphia) has long been

POLAND

Polish American young people attend dedication at Memorial Square in Brooklyn for Father Jerry Popieluszko, a Polish priest killed under the Communist regime in Poland. (Odette Lupis)

known as "Polonia." In 1990, there were approximately 400,000 first-generation (Polish-born) Polish Americans.

History. The Polish presence in the New World dates to the founding of the first permanent English settlement at Jamestown, Virginia (1607). Polish craftsmen joined the colonists and helped establish two key early American industries: glassmaking and woodworking. A few Polish immigrants were also settlers in William Penn's colony of Pennsylvania. In the 1730's, Anthony Sadowski explored the frontier and the Mississippi River and set up a trading post that later became the industrial city of Sandusky, Ohio.

For centuries, a recurrent theme in the history of the Polish people has involved the struggle for liberty, both at home and abroad. Along with Lafayette, two of the most famous foreigners to have fought in the American Revolution were the Polish noblemen Tadeusz Kosciuszko and Casimir Pulaski, who was mortally wounded in the battle of Savannah (1779).

To honor their exploits, Polish Americans have erected monuments and established foundations in their names, and each year on October 11 (Pulaski Day) they march in festive parades.

Between 1795 and 1918, Poland, at one time one of Europe's largest states, was partitioned and subsumed within the empires of its powerful and hostile neighbors Prussia, Russia, and Austria. Throughout the nineteenth century many Polish émigrés to the United States were revolutionary nationalists, dedicated to restoring Poland's independence by marshaling support among the growing number of Poles in the United States. No one worked with greater zeal for this cause than Henry Kalussowski (1806-1894), who founded or facilitated the founding of the first immigrant patriotic organizations committed to Poland's independence, in particular the Polish National Alliance (1880). The group is the largest of Polish American FRATERNAL ORGANIZATIONS.

Polish Americans celebrate Pulaski Day with a parade in New York City. (Frances M. Roberts)

Following World War I, in which thousands of Polish Americans fought, President Woodrow Wilson provided for an independent Poland in his 1918 peace plan, the Fourteen Points. Independence, however, proved to be short-lived. Nazi Germany's invasion of Poland in 1939 precipitated World War II, and the Tehran and Yalta agreements among the victors led to decades of Soviet domination of Poland.

Two historic events in the late twentieth century changed the face of Europe and the image of Poles everywhere, including in the United States, where some Polish Americans had altered their surnames to avoid discrimination and negative ethnic STEREOTYPES. The astonishing election of Karol Wojtyla, the archbishop of Krakow, as pope of the Roman Catholic church in 1978 and the courageous struggle for freedom mounted by Solidarity, the revolutionary Polish labor union led by Lech Walesa with strong support of the Polish American community, claimed the attention and admiration of the Western world. The long COLD WAR came to an end, and a Polish pope and Polish workers were instrumental in this momentous, largely bloodless revolution.

Immigration. In 1854, some eight hundred Polish Catholics made their way to the United States from Prussian Poland and established a farming community named Panna Maria in east Texas. There they built the first Polish parish church and school in the country. Other Polish towns named Polonia, Czestochowa, and Kosciuszko soon were founded in Texas. Soon after, the mass migration of Poles from Prussian, Russian, and Austrian Poland began in earnest, peaking in the decades between 1870 and World War I. Perhaps two million of these mostly peasant farmers, known in Poland as the *za chlebem*, or bread-seeking emigrants, fled poverty, famine, and in some cases military conscription and religious persecution.

Though they had been villagers in the homeland, these newcomers soon discovered they could earn more by staying and finding work in or near burgeoning American cities. Poles became miners in Pennsylvania, meatpackers in Chicago, steelworkers in Pittsburgh, and autoworkers in Detroit. As with other ethnic enclaves, Polish American communities and American smokestack industries grew up together. In time Poles played a key role in the U.S. labor movement and assumed leadership positions in some major American trade unions, as in the case of Joseph Yablonski of the United Mine Workers union.

The restoration of an independent Poland in 1918, the imposition of U.S. IMMIGRATION QUOTAS in the 1920's, and the Great Depression in the United States in the 1930's all served to curtail Polish immigration between the wars. Following WORLD WAR II and the havoc that it wreaked on Europe, thousands of Poles were among the many refugees admitted to the United States under a series of displaced persons acts. The rise of Solidarity and the collapse of the Communist Party in the 1980's brought a new wave of Polish émigrés, swelling the numbers and challenging the character of the old community.

Cultural Contributions. The stereotypical image of Polish Americans as blue-collar, working-class members of an insulated community, while rooted in historical fact, has tended to obscure this group's rich contributions to American culture. Many early immigrants originally intended to stay only briefly in the United States and took whatever work they could find so they might save money to return home with funds to buy land for themselves and their families in Poland. Coming to the United States without a knowledge of English was also a decisive factor in determining the kinds of work they could perform.

For second-generation Polish Americans, many of them coming to adulthood during the GREAT DEPRESSION, opportunities for advancement were also scarce. Things changed markedly for third-generation Polish Americans, however, especially after World War II. Prosperity and opportunities to pursue higher education and advanced degrees combined to make Polish Americans among the most economically and professionally successful of Americans of European ethnic heritage. Thus, while traditional terms such as "polka" and "kielbasa" continue to be used to describe aspects of Polish American culture, the "blue collar" image of Polish Americans has clearly become outmoded.

Two of the twentieth century's greatest musicians were the conductor Leopold Stokowski (1882-1977), maestro of the Philadelphia Orchestra, and acclaimed concert pianist Artur Rubinstein (1887-1982). Gene Krupa set the standard for jazz drummers. Many Polish-born entrepreneurs and performers helped develop vaudeville and the American cinema as producers (Harry and Jack Warner of Warner Bros.); as entertainers and actors (Sophie Tucker, Pola Negri, Mike Mazurki); and as directors (Richard Boleslawski, Roman Polanski, and Andrzej Wajda). Expatriate poet Czeslaw Milosz, who became an American citizen in 1970, won the Nobel Prize in Literature in 1980.

In anthropology and linguistics, Boleslaw Malinowski and Alfred Korzybski made distinguished contributions to their fields at American universities and research centers. In nutrition, Casimir Funk discovered and coined the term "vitamin," and the bacteriologist Albert Sabin developed the oral polio vaccine.

Classic names in cosmetics and fashion include Helena Rubinstein and Oleg Cassini (Polish Italian). Polish American members of the Baseball Hall of Fame include St. Louis Cardinal superstar Stan Musial, Boston Red Sox star Carl Yastremski, and Philadelphia Athletics star Al Simmons. Many Poles have made their mark on the gridiron. Mike Ditka, for example, was a Hall of Fame football player and coach of the Chicago Bears.

Politics and Government. In the post-World War II era, Polish Americans have taken an increasingly visible interest in national politics. Named as special prosecutor in November of 1973, Leon Jaworski handled a tense assignment in the Watergate scandal and the Richard Nixon impeachment deliberations. As national security adviser and secretary of state, respectively, Zbigniew Brzezinski and Edmund Muskie were among the most influential members of the Carter Administration (1977-1980). Three prominent Polish American members of Congress were Representatives Dan Rostenkowski and Roman Pucinski (D.-Ill.) and Senator Barbara Mikulski (D.-Md.).

SUGGESTED READINGS. An excellent overview essay is Victor Greene's "Poles," in *The Harvard Encyclopedia of American Ethnic Groups*, edited by Stephan Thernstrom. For more comprehensive treatments, see *The Poles in America, 1608-1972: A Chronology and Fact Book* (1973), edited by Frank Renkiewicz, and John J. Bukowczyk's *And My Children Did Not Know Me: A History of the Polish-Americans* (1987). For the interaction of the Polish American community and Poland, consult Donald Pienkos' *For Your Freedom Through Ours: Polish-Americans' Efforts on Poland's Behalf, 1863-1991* (1991).—*David McClave*

Political Association of Spanish-Speaking Organizations (PASSO): Organization based in Texas, influential in the 1960's, whose stated goal was to use political means to help solve the economic and social problems of Latinos. PASSO grew out of Mexican Americans for Political Action, a permanent Texas organization that had been an outgrowth of the "Viva Kennedy" clubs formed in 1960 to work for the election of John F. Kennedy. Mexican Americans for Political Action changed its name to PASSO to broaden its appeal. Cofounder Dr. Hector Garcia, organizer of the American G.I. Political Forum, became the first president. After success in 1963 in Crystal City, Texas, PASSO worked with African American organizations in San Antonio and Houston to elect minority candidates. Membership declined with the rise of other Latino organizations such as PARTIDO DE LA RAZA UNIDA, and it remained basically a Texas organization.

Political asylum: Permission to stay in a country of refuge when political turmoil forces one to leave one's home country. The United States grants asylum only for political REFUGEES—that is, for those who are fleeing persecution or a "well-founded fear of persecution" at home. The U.S. government does not grant asylum to refugees who flee because of extreme poverty, even if the poverty is caused by political unrest. Traditionally, those fleeing Communist countries have had an easier time gaining asylum, while the United States has been hesitant to accuse allies of political persecution. Thus, for example, during the early 1980's, Polish refugees were more readily granted asylum than those fleeing the civil war in El Salvador, in which the United States supported the Salvadoran government. A 1990 federal court ruling ordered the IMMIGRATION AND NATURALIZATION SERVICE (INS) to reconsider 150,000 applications from Central Americans who had been denied fair treatment.

Numbers of asylum applications jumped dramatically after passage of the REFUGEE ACT OF 1980 from a few thousand per year in the 1970's to an average of 39,000 per year in the 1980's. By 1993, the INS had a backlog of 300,000 cases and 120,000 people were expected to apply for asylum that year.

Political correctness: Term of derision, used primarily by conservatives to dismiss the concerns of liberals for greater inclusion of women and minorities. The issue arose in the academic debate on MULTICULTURALISM in colleges and universities in the late 1980's. Many on the left believed that literature and history courses should include more material by and about women, African Americans, Latinos, homosexuals, and other minority groups. They further wished to set up official policy to punish faculty and students who attacked members of minorities in their speech or actions. Conservatives thought that these efforts were misguided and placed unconstitutional limits on the right to free speech. They labeled as "politically correct" (or "PC") anything that they thought took the cause of multiculturalism too far.

Political organizations: In the multicultural United States, political organizations permit groups to preserve

Mainstream and special interest political organizations give a voice to all Americans. (A. Gurmankin, Unicorn Stock Photos)

their specific identities while influencing the direction of national policy.

Mainstream Political Parties. Although the U.S. Constitution does not mention political parties and the Founders warned against the dangers of "factions," parties formed quickly in colonial America. Before the end of the eighteenth century Thomas Jefferson had founded the DEMOCRATIC PARTY, the oldest continuous political organization in the world.

From the beginning, the major parties wrestled with questions of inclusion and exclusion. As early as 1800, the conservative Federalists favored exclusionary policies, pushing through the notorious ALIEN AND SEDITION ACTS to counterbalance the "foreign ideas" of the French Revolution.

After the demise of the Federalists in the early 1800's their exclusionary bent was adopted by the Whigs, who exhibited a bias against immigrants, especially Irish Catholics and southern Europeans. With the decline of the Whig Party, the REPUBLICAN PARTY, while founded in the 1850's on an antislavery platform, continued this philosophical tradition.

The Democratic Party has generally been more receptive to immigrants and minority groups. During the first great wave of European immigration in the 1820's, the Democrats brought the newcomers into their ranks, establishing the Irish political organizations that still exert considerable influence in cities such as Boston, New York, and Chicago. During the presidency of Franklin Delano Roosevelt, the Democratic Party further broadened its ranks and policies, incorporating African Americans, Asian Americans, Latinos and other groups.

This tendency has intensified since the 1950's, bringing the Democratic Party a greater diversity and proportion of almost all religious, racial, and national groups than the Republican Party. Throughout most of the twentieth century the Democratic Party has become more African American, Latino, and Asian in both its candidates and its voters. While fewer minorities tend to vote for or run for office within the Republican Party, it, too, has attempted to woo voters of color with campaign stops in ethnic neighborhoods and an improved record on balancing its ticket and political appointments in the 1970's and 1980's. A large sector of the Latino population, including wealthier Cuban and Mexican Americans, are loyal Republicans.

Nativist Organizations. In the years preceding the Civil War, the backlash against immigrants produced the phenomenon of NATIVISM, which found expression in political organizations of its own, most notably in

Russell Means (left) and Dennis Banks, American Indian Movement leaders, spearheaded the revolt at Wounded Knee. (AP/Wide World Photos)

Democrats and Republicans in Congress and the White House: 1961-1993

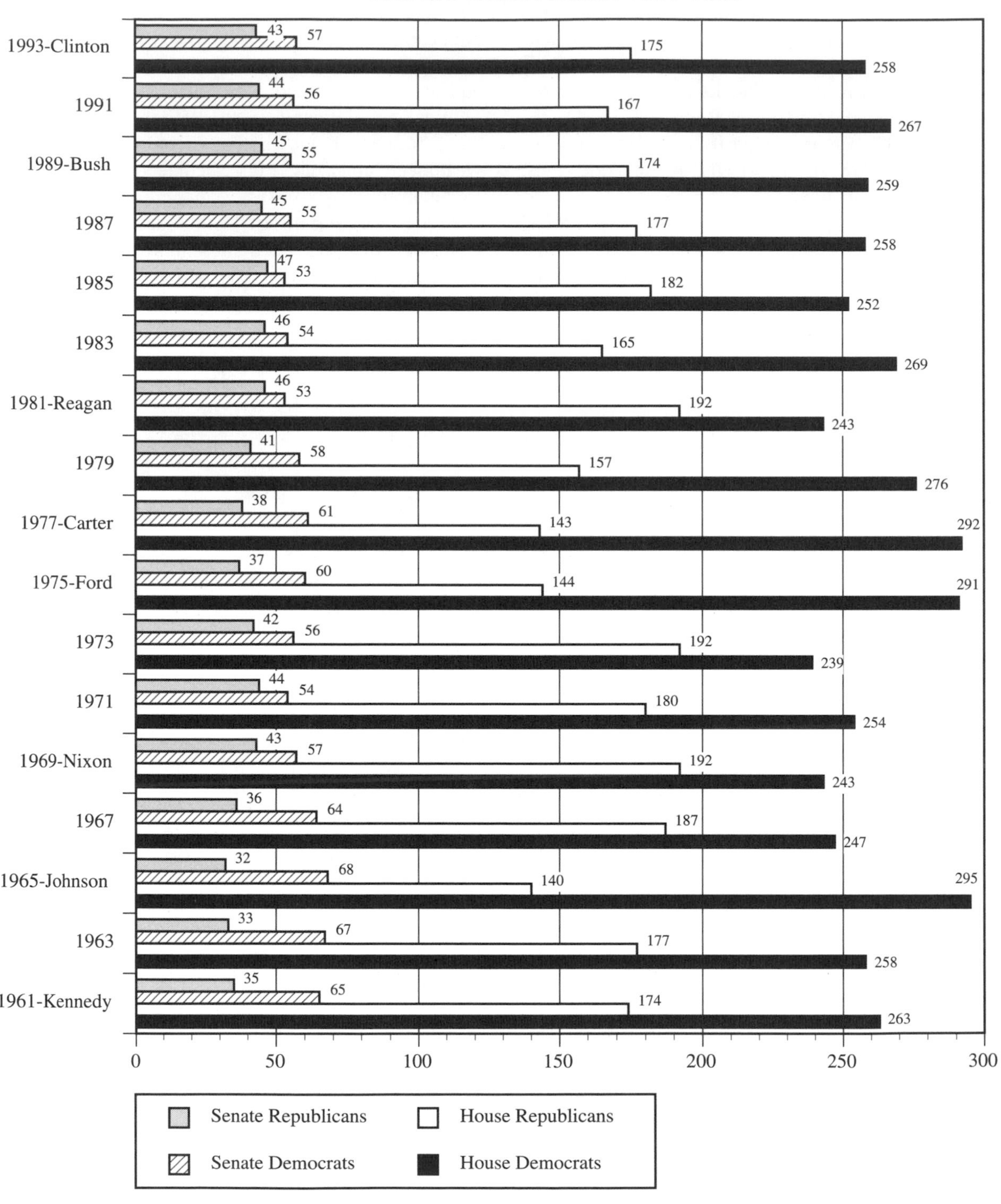

Source: Data are from *Statistical Abstract of the United States, 1992.* Table 421. Washington, D.C.: U.S. Government Printing Office, 1992.

the Know Nothing Party of the 1850's. In part the nativists were motivated by irrational prejudices and senseless fears, such as the belief that the Catholic church planned to overthrow the American government. On the other hand, nativists were also responding to the growing political power which the newcomers actually possessed; by the late 1820's, for example, the dominant political organization in New York City, Tammany Hall, was already an Irish stronghold.

The most successful nativist organization was the Order of the Star Spangled Banner, established in 1850, with membership restricted to native-born, white Protestants. It was popularly known as the Know Nothing Party because its members were sworn to secrecy and instructed to reply "I know nothing" when asked about the group and its activities. By the mid-1850's, the Know Nothings had achieved considerable success in state and congressional elections, and even made a bid for the presidency. By 1856, however, the party had self-destructed, prey to internal divisions and rejection by a majority of Americans.

Since the end of the Know Nothings, nativism has remained a constant but muted undercurrent in American political life. During the 1920's the KU KLUX KLAN achieved some degree of success with its message of fear and hate against foreigners, Catholics, African Americans and Jews. The Klan's extremism, however, and the virulence of its perverted vision were rejected by most Americans.

American Indian and Asian American Organizations. While the national parties have grappled with the politics of inclusion and exclusion, political organizations of various racial, ethnic, and national groups have flourished. They follow a consistent pattern, drawing together first for economic survival and social support, then expanding to claim a share of the political process. The history of each group's political movements reflects their unique historic experience.

American Indians have the longest history of political organization since they were already well established before the arrival of the Europeans. The conflicts between existing inhabitants and the newer arrivals, however, resulted in an almost unbroken string of defeats for the native tribes and their gradual dismemberment and resettlement on reservations.

During the second half of the 1900's there was a considerable resurgence in American Indian identity and pride, this found its political voice in a number of organizations ranging from the radical AMERICAN INDIAN MOVEMENT to groups closer to the political center. These mainstream organizations have demonstrated substantial ability in electing American Indian candidates to local, state, and even national offices.

Although Asians have been present in large numbers in the United States since the 1840's, it was only in the second half of the twentieth century that they made dramatic strides with their political organizations. Not surprisingly, the greatest gains have been on the West Coast and in Hawaii, where Asian Americans are found in the largest concentrations. During the 1930's, Chinese and Japanese Americans transformed their traditional self-help, mutual aid societies into the nucleus of political organizations. These were crucial in electing such officials as Hiram FONG, a Hawaiian of Chinese ancestry, who entered the Hawaiian House of Representatives in 1938 and became its Speaker in 1949. Following World War II, Japanese American veterans—the most highly decorated ethnic group of U.S. fighting forces—formed a remarkably effective political organization that refashioned Hawaii's Democratic Party into a truly multicultural alliance. The "Democratic Revolution" of 1954 brought to office leaders such as Daniel K. INOUYE, who have made their state one of the most progressive in the nation. Asians have also gained important seats in state and local government in California.

Latino political organizations. For a century after the 1830's, Mexican Americans formed a largely agrarian underclass with little political power or influence. World War II changed that. The war industries needed workers, and Mexican American leaders made it clear to the Roosevelt Administration that they expected fair, nondiscriminatory labor practices. Pressure from groups such as the LEAGUE OF UNITED LATIN AMERICAN CITIZENS (LULAC) and the Mexican American Movement (MAM), both established during the 1930's, led FDR to issue an executive order to this effect in 1941.

LULAC and MAM were only two of the many Latino political organizations that grew out of community self-help efforts. Often politically sophisticated and diverse in their culture and backgrounds, Latinos have created a wide variety of groups whose keynote is a concentration on practical efforts and social betterment. Thus, the Community Service Organization, founded in 1947, not only sought to increase Latino voter registration but also worked on fund-raising, civil rights, and economic self-determination projects.

Overtly political Latino organizations have had undeniable impact on national politics. The MEXICAN

United Farm Workers head César Chávez built support for broader Chicano and Latino causes with his championing of workers' rights. (AP/Wide World Photos)

American Political Association, founded in 1959 in Fresno, California, stressed ethnic identity and electoral involvement; it was a major voice of the Latino community from 1960 to 1965 and continues to be important in some areas. The Viva Kennedy organizations of 1960 may well have provided the impetus needed to swing the Mexican American community behind the Democratic ticket, thus bringing Texas into Kennedy's column and winning him the presidency. A further indication of this group's influence is the fact that nationally Kennedy received an impressive eighty-five percent of the Latino vote.

As Latinos have moved into the mainstream of national life and become financially secure, many have embraced the generally more conservative policies of the Republican Party. Cuban Americans have been especially responsive to the Republicans' anti-Castro, anti-Communist message. At the same time, more activist organizations such as Partido de la Raza Unida and César Chávez's United Farm Workers have continued to struggle for social justice and a fuller integration of all Latinos into the national tapestry.

The African American Experience. African Americans have had by far the most dramatic and lasting influence on American political life of any traditional minority group. Because of slavery, it was not until the Reconstruction period after the Civil War that American blacks could form open, effective political organizations. From 1867 to 1877, African Americans held many elective offices in the South and accomplished many long-needed social reforms, including the creation of a comprehensive public school system, supported by fair taxes and available to every child.

The end of Reconstruction, however, brought a system of strict segregation to the South, and similar discrimination in the North, pushing African Americans out of the political mainstream. Yet especially in the cities, African Americans dealt with the white power structure in a realistic and often effective fashion. During the 1920's, for example, black political leaders such as Robert R. Church in Memphis, Ferdinand Morton in New York City, and Oscar DePriest in Chicago delivered a consistent and reliable number of black votes to white politicians, who in return supported black issues. These black leaders also won elective office, with DePriest becoming the first black alderman in Chicago and, in 1929, its first black member of Congress.

Black political organizations functioned well in cities because of the concentration of the African American population and relative ease of transportation and communication. The task of such groups was much more difficult in the rural South, where political power was possible only after educational and health needs had been met. Successful black political organizations in the South addressed these and other needs in their communities—problems then ignored by the conventional political system.

Many African American political organizations grew out of, or were actual parts of, the black churches. One of the most potent forces in American democracy, the black church has repeatedly demonstrated its effectiveness in articulating and realizing the social and political desires of its congregation. This role dates back to the first AFRICAN METHODIST EPISCOPAL CHURCH, founded in 1787. In the years before the Civil War, when southern black organizations were almost always illegal, church leaders combined the roles of spiritual guides, teachers, and political organizers.

African American educational bodies, such as the TUSKEGEE INSTITUTE in Alabama, have likewise been key to black political success. The so-called Tuskegee Machine conducted voter registration and education drives that were essential to the Civil Rights movement and the election of blacks to public office.

Since 1909, the NATIONAL ASSOCIATION FOR THE ADVANCEMENT OF COLORED PEOPLE (NAACP) has been tremendously politically influential though active in areas that transcend the purely political. From the landmark *BROWN V. BOARD OF EDUCATION* case in 1954, which led to the outlawing of "separate but equal" segregated schools, to massive get-out-the-vote drives, the NAACP has had a profound and lasting impact on the American political process. Other national organizations, such as the CONGRESS OF RACIAL EQUALITY (CORE) and the NATIONAL URBAN LEAGUE have also played and continue to play major roles in African American and national political life. These groups have acted as a conscience to politicians, reminding them on the one hand of the contributions of African American voters while pressuring officials to remedy inequalities and injustices. More militant groups, such as the NATION OF ISLAM, and the BLACK PANTHERS, have made the headlines over the years but have not achieved the enduring political influence of mainstream African American organizations.

SUGGESTED READINGS. A general overview of American politics, which covers the role of the major parties, is John Bibby's *Governing by Consent* (1992). The nativist movement is well documented in David Bennett's *The Party of Fear* (1988), while Asian American political organizations are briefly discussed by Sucheng Chan in *Asian Americans: An Interpretive History* (1991). Juan Gómez-Quiñones examines Latino organizations in *Chicano Politics: Reality and Promise, 1940-1990* (1990); the collection of essays edited by Chris Garcia, *La Causa Política* (1974), explains many of these groups in more detail.

There are numerous books and essays on the African American political experience. Among the most useful are *Black Political Life in the United States* (1972), edited by Lenneal J. Henderson, Jr.; *From Exclusion to Inclusion* (1992), edited by Ralph Gómes and Linda Faye Williams; and Manning Marable's leftist study *Black American Politics* (1985).—*Michael Witkoski*

Politics: American mass media coverage generally presents multicultural politics as women and people of color challenging the power of white males by competing for political office. This perspective ignores both the many types of political involvement of people in various ethnic, religious, racial, and sexual groups and the political diversity within these groups. Ethnicity has been woven into the very fabric of American political life; indeed, there has never been politics devoid of ethnicity.

In a republican system, legitimate power lies in the ability to win electoral office. Yet the scope of political power goes far beyond elections. It lies in the ability to influence decisions—specifically the making, implementing, and adjudicating of laws. Perhaps most important, power is the ability to influence the basic values of a society.

The likelihood that any ethnic or other minority group might achieve political power in the United States depends on several factors. These include the group's level of political experience, political resources such as wealth and education, integration into the larger community, cultural congruence with the dominant culture, period of arrival, and location. Other important factors are group attitudes toward their new country or the dominant culture, and the dominant culture's attitudes toward the minority group. No groups are completely homogeneous; important internal dif-

The inauguration of President-elect Bill Clinton (second from right) in 1993 focused on symbols of inclusion and diversity in American political life. (AP/Wide World Photos)

ferences exist, especially in the volatile political arena.

American Indians. Long before the Europeans heard about the Americas, millions of American Indians roamed the land as members of various tribes. Although certain traits clearly differentiated them from the Europeans, enormous political differences also existed among the tribes. Some tribes were aggressive and violent (Apache, Mohawk) while others were pacifist (Hopi and some California tribes); some allowed a measure of individual usage of land (Southeastern) while others believed in tribal usage rather than any form of ownership (Plains). In many, women were the possessions of their husbands, while in others women had their own councils that had a say in tribal decisions (Iroquois).

For the conquering Europeans, the most politically important groups were the five Iroquois nations, who formed a loose political confederation that allowed them to maintain individual tribal integrity while they traded with one another and formed a defensive alliance. The founding fathers used the IROQUOIS LEAGUE as a model for constructing the first American government in the Articles of Confederation.

In the nineteenth century, many tribes were dispossessed of their lands and forced to move to reservations in the West. They lost much of their autonomy as federal government agencies took control over their lives. Most were not granted citizenship until 1924.

Because of poor education and lack of identification with issues outside the reservation and the Indian community, contemporary Indians have a low rate of involvement in American politics. When they do vote, it is primarily for the Democratic Party, a reflection of that party's response to their widespread poverty. Many American Indians have put their faith in tribal government, business and corporate enterprise, or the INDIAN RIGHTS MOVEMENT to address their needs rather than standard electoral politics.

Changes began to percolate among American Indians in the late 1900's. Their numbers were increasing dramatically, and they were starting to form more pan-Indian associations that overcome tribal differences. Positive attention was drawn to the 1992 election of Ben Nighthorse CAMPBELL (Northern Cheyenne), a Democratic senator from Colorado and, in 1993, the only American Indian in Congress.

Early European Settlers. From the establishment of the American colonies in the 1600's, the English became the dominant group. By 1790, they constituted 60 percent of the American population. Afterward, that proportion decreased but because they arrived first, they generally left their imprint on the political system.

Many basic American customs, such as language, dress, and religion, follow those of the English, and so do the nation's fundamental political principles. These are summed up by the tenets of classical liberalism: the right of the people to create a representative government that they control through elections, and the right of the individual to limit the potential abuse of power by the government. The Madisonian fear of tyranny by the majority led to a seeking for consensus that would satisfy not only the majority but also the minority. With the addition of the fundamental French principle of universal equality, the basic dynamics of American political thought were in place.

Many European colonists had a strong distrust of government, having been persecuted in Europe for their religious beliefs. The official separation of church and state encouraged the settlement of various minority religious sects, both before and after independence. The Quakers, for example, imposed their views about religious tolerance on the founding principles for the state of Pennsylvania in the 1680's. In the 1830's, German and Swiss Mennonites and Amish brought their Anabaptist spirit of separation from the secular world of government to settlements in Pennsylvania, Iowa, and Indiana. These groups remain among the most culturally isolated and politically unintegrated of all American ethnic groups.

Other non-English, non-Protestant Europeans established their own patterns of settlement and interaction with the emerging English-dominated politics of COLONIAL AMERICA. For example, the early French Catholic presence in North America was dispersed around the periphery of the United States—in the bayous of Louisiana, in northern New England, and in Canada's eastern province of Quebec. French political impact is still felt in Louisiana's legal system, the only one in the country derived from the Napoleonic code, which allocates little power to the judge. Likewise, vestiges of Spanish legal and political tradition can be noted in parts of the Southwest.

Ethnic differences also appeared in the South. The first Africans in the South were indentured servants, most of whom—like whites—were freed after their term of service was fulfilled. Slavery developed relatively slowly because it was antipathetic to the English idea of liberalism. Under the pressure of economic need, however, even the Puritans found a rationalization allowing them to own and staff slave ships.

The South has long been divided into two fairly distinct regions: the large-plantation, slave-holding, once strongly Democratic tidewater (eastern) areas, and the small, nonslave, independent, and noticeably Republican Appalachian (western) region. Some historians suggest that the two regions reflect ethnic differences between the obedient, law-upholding English and Scottish Highlanders along the coast and the more individualistic, anti-government Scots-Irish in the mountains. The Scots-Irish Americans' scorn for organized government was displayed in their illegal liquor stills, refusal to pay taxes, and outlawed religious practices such as the handling of poisonous snakes. All were evident in the hollows and forests of the southern Appalachians. Fearing that these and other foreigners might grow in numbers and support the egalitarian Jeffersonian Republicans, the more entrenched English Federalists passed the ALIEN AND SEDITION ACTS in 1798, extending the citizenship residence requirement from five to fourteen years and allowing the president to deport dangerous foreigners. This was the first in a series of anti-immigration legislation based on XENOPHOBIA and ethnic prejudice.

Three groups—the Scandinavians, Germans, and Irish Catholics—came in large numbers in the mid-1800's, leaving their distinct political stamp. Scandinavian farmers who settled in the upper Midwest and the Northwest developed a strong cooperative tradition. Concerned with a spirit of fair play, they organized to oppose the monopolistic railroads and big banks that dominated the small farmer. At the turn of the twentieth century many Scandinavians supported the Progressive movement, a home-grown version of SOCIALISM. They helped create a very liberal Farm Workers Party in Minnesota that, allied with the DEMOCRATIC PARTY, maintained power in what its opponents called the "independent socialist Swedish state of Minnesota." That tradition still lives on in a generally liberal set of senators such as former vice president Walter Mondale, the grandson of Norwegian immigrants.

Early twentieth century political conventions were just beginning to include women and a greater variety of European Americans. (Library of Congress)

Many of the second wave of German immigrants came to the United States in response to the failure of the 1848 revolution in Germany. The largely liberal lower middle-class carried with them a strong anti-slavery sentiment, gave strong support to Lincoln and the Republicans, and in several cases went on to found major civic-cultural organizations in cities such as San Francisco, Cincinnati, and Milwaukee—the only major city in American history with a mayor who served for twenty-eight years—Henry Maier (Democrat-Socialist), of German heritage, mayor from 1960-1988.

In history, temperament, socioeconomic status, and religion, the Irish Catholics were the most radically different European group to arrive in the pre-Civil War period. These were poor tenant farmers escaping the potato famine, accustomed to but not accepting British oppression in their native land, steeled to fatalism by underproduction and starvation.

In spite of their British Isles background, the Irish Catholics encountered enormous prejudice related to their religion and large numbers. The anti-immigrant Order of the Star Spangled Banner flourished, later to coalesce with other nativist elements to form the Know Nothings. This eventually became a major third party that elected seventy-five people to Congress and contended seriously for the presidency in 1856. Violence against the Irish was periodic and intense, sufficiently so that in 1870 Irish American miners organized their own infamous vigilante group, the MOLLY MAGUIRES.

Irish Americans started moving to the city in large numbers just as the city started to expand. Partly because of their clannishness and their ability to draw on friends and neighbors, the Irish were able to organize politically. Control over the big-city party was aided by a corrupt system of control over government jobs and assorted business contracts. With Irish American help, the Democrats were able to nominate and run a strong campaign in 1928 for "one of their own," Al Smith of New York, the first major-party Catholic presidential candidate. Eventually, powerful Irish Americans were able to steer the Democratic nomination in 1960 to John Fitzgerald Kennedy. The last of the great urban political machines was presided over until the 1970's by the last of the great Irish bosses, Democrat Richard Daley of Chicago.

African Americans. By the time of independence, the issue of African American slavery had divided the country, and compromises had to be reached to secure the adoption of the U.S. Constitution. Alternative solutions to slavery appeared early. In 1817 the AMERICAN COLONIZATION SOCIETY starting repatriating free Africans in the South to the new African nation of Liberia. The BACK TO AFRICA MOVEMENT has resurfaced periodically among African Americans, although it has never successfully sent many people back.

Despite a strong abolitionist movement in the North in the 1800's, the courts upheld the rights of the slave owners and deprived slaves of any legal standing. Eventually, the conflict was resolved on the battlefield, where the defeated South fell under northern rule. During RECONSTRUCTION, new constitutional amendments outlawed slavery and granted blacks citizenship and black males the right to vote. Many African Americans won political office in this period. Under the BLACK CODES, however, which appeared shortly after Reconstruction, they were treated as second-class citizens whose voting rights could be denied.

Politically, where they could vote, African Americans supported the party of the Great Emancipator, Republican Abraham Lincoln. That pattern changed abruptly in 1932 when Franklin Roosevelt's NEW DEAL Democrats offered more programs to meet the economic concerns of the poor. That switch was so complete that since 1968 African Americans have been, by far, the staunchest Democratic voters; about 90 percent of black Americans vote Democratic. African Americans in general are not likely to change their overwhelmingly Democratic affiliations in the near future, although the substantial growth of the African American middle class and the rise of conservative black politicians suggests that there are pockets of support for the Republicans.

Until the VOTING RIGHTS ACT OF 1965 and the Twenty-fourth Amendment, African Americans, especially in the South, found local government obstacles to voting. They still have relatively low rates of political participation, which have been linked to low education and income. Compared with white and minority citizens of similar socioeconomic status, African Americans have similar if not higher levels of participation, although that may be changing as larger numbers of Caribbean blacks—many without a strong political tradition—migrate to the United States. Whatever their rates of voting, however, African Americans have made substantial strides in attaining public office since the 1970's. In 1990, there were 7,335 black elected officials, mostly in city, county, and educational posts, compared with 1,479 in 1970 and 4,963 in 1980. These included 440 African Americans in federal and state legislatures.

David Dinkins (center) campaigns for mayor of New York City in 1987. Also pictured are former New York mayor John Lindsay, publisher Earl Graves, and former city council president Carol Bellamy. (AP/Wide World Photos)

Southern and Eastern European Immigrants. After the Civil War, political life in the United States changed dramatically. New immigrants, primarily from southern and eastern Europe, began flocking to the newly industrializing cities of the Northeast and Midwest. These new arrivals were noticeably physically, linguistically, culturally, and religiously different from earlier immigrants. They served as a convenient scapegoat during hard times. As urban outsiders, they were likely to be courted by the party of the outsiders, the Democrats.

Polish immigrants split among those who went to urban and rural areas. Because they did not emphasize education, this largely blue-collar work force tended to stay together as family and as neighbors, often in the Northeast and northern Midwest. They stayed Democratic longer than most of the predominantly New Deal Catholics. As a group, early Polish Americans did not develop a strong commitment to American political activism. Slavic Americans tended to follow a parallel path. One of their characteristics, especially for the later immigrants, has been a concern with politics in the homeland, particularly among Serbian Americans and Croatian Americans.

The largest group of "new" immigrants was the Italians, most of whom were from southern Italy, where they barely eked out a subsistence living from the soil or the sea. Their different ways, Catholicism, and dark complexions drew much prejudice, especially during the recession of the 1890's and in an antiforeign campaign following World War I. The politically biased murder trial in Massachusetts of two Italian anarchists, Nichola Sacco and Bartolomeo Vanzetti, added fuel to the fire for the resurgent nativist movement and xenophobic activities of the KU KLUX KLAN.

The Italians also battled with their earlier-arriving Catholic brethren, the Irish, who held on to their control of both the Democratic Party and the Roman Catholic church hierarchy in spite of being outnumbered. The tenacious hold of the Irish on party power drove some Italian Americans into the Republican fold, especially in New England. Eventually, however, they made some headway in the Democratic Party. By the 1990's one Italian American, Geraldine FERRARO, had run for vice president (in 1984), and another, Mario Cuomo, was considered regularly for the presidential nomination.

Politically, one of the most important immigrant groups was the Jews. Unlike many other European immigrants, they were neither farmers nor fishermen but literate, semiskilled craftsmen accustomed to living in moderate or large towns.

A number of Russian Jews had been touched by the nascent socialist and communist ideologies that would soon revolutionize eastern Europe. Thus, the Jews brought an awareness of political ideas that helped explain the misery that they and other working-class immigrants faced in sweatshops and overcrowded, unsanitary, dilapidated ghettos. Memories from eastern Europe of a hostile church, an oppressive government, and an exploitative landed gentry also tended to push Jews into the liberal and socialist camps.

Because they were largely city dwellers and took advantage of educational opportunities, Jews became interested and active in American politics. Because few Jewish immigrants seriously considered returning to their crumbling homelands, Jews also had very high rates of citizenship. Yet it was not until the second or third generation, after World War II, that important Jewish political leaders arose.

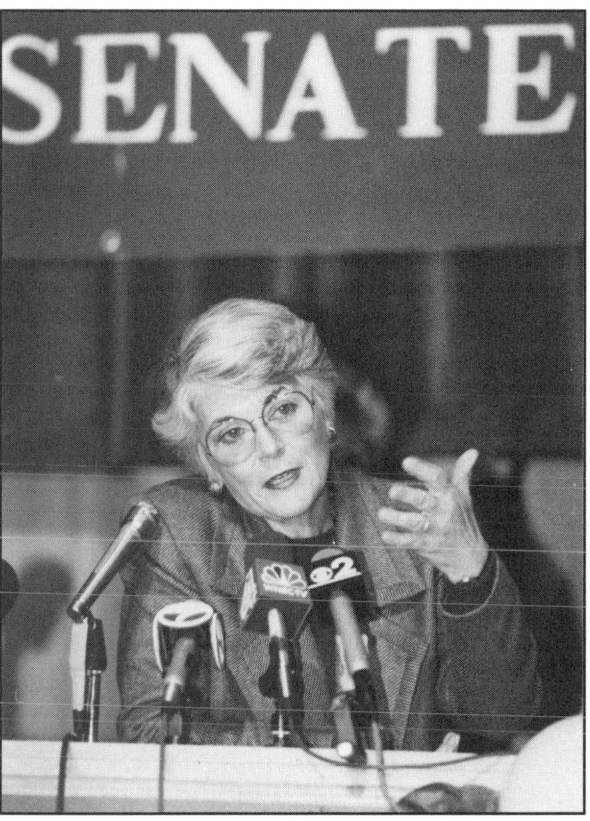

Italian American Geraldine Ferraro, Democrat and former vice-presidential candidate, announces her run for the U.S. Senate in 1991. (AP/Wide World Photos)

The other large European group that maintained a passionate cultural interest in politics was the Greeks. In the big cities where they settled, the Greek American community was unusually well-organized and self-regulating, giving its members practical experience in the political world. A number of Greeks attained major political positions, including Republican vice president Spiro Agnew as well as Democratic presidential candidate Michael Dukakis and Senator Paul Tsongas.

Asian Americans. The Asian American presence did not become significant until the latter half of the nineteenth century. Their early impact on the political system generally was small, in part because many originally came as SOJOURNERS. Because the cultural gap between them and other Americans was enormous, they suffered deep-seated and pervasive prejudice in addition to legal discrimination.

The Chinese came first, hoping to make enough money to buy land in China. Their numbers increased as they were recruited as cheap ("coolie") labor for the railroads. Partly because of perceived racial and cultural differences, made worse during periods of economic downturn, the Chinese were attacked, often violently, by the Irish, themselves the victims of ethnic violence a generation earlier. Limited economic, educational, and residential opportunities as well as racist laws affecting their citizenship and immigration (the CHINESE EXCLUSION ACT of 1882) effectively kept Chinese Americans out of mainstream political life.

Years later, especially during the 1960's, when local community organizing of poverty programs was encouraged, Chinese Americans, especially in San Francisco, began playing an active political role. As Chinese communities became more wealthy, individuals moved into more mainstream political life at the local level. Los Angeles City Council member Mike Woo, for example, made an unsuccessful bid for mayor in 1993.

Early Japanese immigrants were fewer in number and somewhat more educated, and they made better economic progress than many of their other Asian neighbors. The Japanese suffered much of the same prejudice as the Chinese, including ALIEN LAND LAWS that banned them from owning land—a serious liability for people who farm. The first two generations of Japanese Americans were largely segregated. Just as the second generation (Nisei) was beginning to ascend economically, the Japanese American internment in the West during World War II dealt the community a severe blow. Their experience in the camps, however, led some to political and civil rights activism in the late 1900's.

The Japanese Americans survived what might have been a catastrophic war experience and by virtue of hard work and educational success achieved considerable assimilation and economic success. The generally low interest and low rates of participation in politics among the Japanese is noteworthy, especially given their relatively high economic status.

One important exception is the Japanese Americans who live in Hawaii. There the Japanese have long had an active role in state politics in large part because they arrived—for field work in the sugar and pineapple plantations—before there was an established modern political system. They quickly became the state's power brokers and have filled most of the state's Democratic major elected offices as well as some national seats, such as that held for many years in Congress by Daniel INOUYE.

Among the Asian groups arriving in the U.S. since the relaxed immigration laws of 1965, the Koreans and Filipinos deserve special note. The majority of Korean Americans came for economic opportunity and were largely apolitical. Some had a strong anti-Communist orientation, but others were opponents of the right-wing dictatorships in South Korea and remained concerned with Korean politics. Many were preoccupied with making a living as owners of small businesses in poor, often African American neighborhoods where the rent was cheap. Tense African American-Korean American relations sometimes plunged the new immigrants into political conflict, violence, and civil unrest. In the Los Angeles riots of 1992 scores of Korean stores were burned and looted. This experience, and their difficulties getting government aid to rebuild, alerted many Koreans to the importance of political empowerment. At least one Korean has run in the congressional primaries, and in 1992, Jay KIM, a Republican from Diamond Bar, California, became the first Korean elected to the House of Representatives.

Filipino Americans are the second largest Asian group in the United States after the Chinese. Many arrived in the 1970's and 1980's with professional skills as nurses and accountants; gradually, they are applying for citizenship in large numbers. They tend to be hard-working, socially conservative middle-class people with strong family values. Yet by the 1990's they had not yet developed an organized political interest group.

Latinos. The single largest group of Latinos, Mexicans, has a presence in North America that antedates the coming of the Spanish conquerors. New Mexico, in particular, has a very old and established Mexican community that plays an important political and cultural role in the modern state. The majority of Mexican Americans have always lived in California and Texas. Two of the earliest mayors of Los Angeles (1865-1872) were José Mascarel and Cristobar Aguilar. After the influx of large numbers of Anglos in the late 1800's, however, the political power of Mexicans declined in the city. At times Mexican immigrants were legally forced out of California, only to reemerge when employers, such as the large farmers of the Central Valley, wanted cheap labor. In the

Japanese American senator Daniel Inouye has represented Hawaii in the U.S. Congress since the 1950's. (AP/Wide World Photos)

1940's, growing prejudice led to the infamous ZOOT SUIT RIOTS in which public officials allowed Anglo street attacks on innocent citizens of Mexican and Filipino background.

Meanwhile, economic problems in Mexico continued to prompt immigration, both legal and illegal, to the north. Despite the fact that some long-settled immigrants have moved up the socioeconomic ladder, the constant influx of poor, uneducated newcomers keeps a majority of Mexican Americans at the bottom. Immigration has long been a major issue in California politics, especially during periods of economic recession.

One of the dilemmas facing Mexican Americans in the 1980's and 1990's was their low rates of citizenship and even lower rates of political participation. This reflects several factors: the Catholic church has not served as a political instrument for Mexican participation as it did for the Irish; many Mexicans come as sojourners; the ease of travel to northern Mexico allows immigrants to maintain strong ties with the homeland; and the insularity of life in Mexican American barrios may act as a disincentive to pursuing U.S. citizenship. Efforts such as the SOUTHWEST VOTER REGISTRATION EDUCATION PROJECT (SVREP) have brought more Mexican Americans into the polling booth, however, and both citizenship and participation rates are bound to increase with increasing general education.

Among Mexican Americans, CLASS is politically important, as is a fundamental conservatism on social and family issues. Thus, wealthy and middle-class Mexican Americans are likely to be conservative and Republican whereas the poor, by far the largest proportion, lean to the Democrats. Mexican Americans in political office range from the liberal Gloria MOLINA, the first Latina Los Angeles County Supervisor, to the conservative Linda CHÁVEZ, who served in the Reagan Administration.

The other two major Latino groups stand politically to the right and left of the Mexicans. The Cubans who arrived in the United States in the 1960's were primarily lower middle-class bourgeoisie who came with strong anticommunist views, an attachment to capitalism, and a conservative culture. They made significant economic gains while their children achieved considerable educational success. Cuban Americans became a solidly conservative Republican force, especially in Florida politics. As they relinquished their dreams of returning to Cuba, they invested more energy in local issues, becoming the dominant force in Miami politics since 1980. The sole Cuban American member of Congress, Ilena Ros-Lehtinen, is a solid conservative

Liberal politician Gloria Molina, shown here at a campaign victory rally, was the first Latina to become a Los Angeles County Supervisor. (AP/Wide World Photos)

Republican representing a formerly liberal district that has become increasingly Cuban. Some Cubans in the United States are passionately involved in efforts to "liberate" or—more rarely—to support Communist Cuba.

On the other side of the political spectrum, the Puerto Ricans in the mainland United States came from poor agricultural backgrounds. They found low-paying jobs in the country's two largest Democratic cities, New York and Chicago, so their political orientations naturally were pro-Democratic. The early Puerto Ricans who moved to the mainland, however, were not active participants in the political process. This may be traced to the discrimination and housing segregation they faced, as well as to their generally low education, frequent returns to Puerto Rico, and greater political interest in the debate on the status of their homeland (commonwealth, state, or independent nation). By the 1980's, local Puerto Rican institutions had started to grow. The annual Puerto Rican Day Parade in New York draws hundreds of thousands of viewers and all political candidates. The inclusion of Puerto Rican former Congressman Herman BADILLO in the second spot in Rudolph Giuliani's 1993 New York mayoral campaign attests the growing political strength of Puerto Ricans.

The last and fastest-growing group of Latinos are those from South and Central America, a very heterogeneous group of economic and political refugees, some running from left-wing or right-wing oppression, but most from violence and abject poverty. Because they have been in the United States for a short period of time, most have not yet voted. As long as they remain poor and of low education, they are likely to be politically uninvolved but to prefer the Democrats and domestic programs to aid the poor.

Women. Like racial and religious minorities, American women suffered legal discrimination, although this varied by region and marital status. Generally, women in the West—where they were few in number—had more equality than those in the more traditional East, especially the South. Married women—in some areas treated as the property of their husbands—had fewer rights than those unmarried. In most places, women did not have the right to vote until 1920. In addition to their legal inequality, women were less educated, less wealthy, less likely to work outside the home, and less powerful than men.

FEMINISM historically grew out of women's involvement in other movements; first, the ABOLITIONIST MOVEMENT, which led to the first major women's political conference, the SENECA FALLS CONVENTION, in 1848; later the SUFFRAGE MOVEMENT which borrowed leaders from the anti-alcohol temperance movement. The modern WOMEN'S LIBERATION MOVEMENT was closely tied to the CIVIL RIGHTS MOVEMENT, student protest, and PEACE ACTIVISM in the 1970's. Women learned to lead and participate in politics by honing their skills in movements on behalf of others. Then they used that experience to defend their own rights.

Although the campaign for the EQUAL RIGHTS AMENDMENT failed, important liberal groups such as the NATIONAL ORGANIZATION FOR WOMEN (NOW) have pressed their views on equal wages in the workplace, abortion rights, and payment of child support by absentee fathers. They have also strongly supported women candidates for office. In 1993-1994, a record forty-seven women served in the Congress and seven in the Senate; California, for example, had two women U.S. senators for the first time. In 1992, Carol Moseley BRAUN of Illinois was the first African American woman elected to the United States Senate—an en-

Carol Moseley Braun was the first black woman elected to the U.S. Senate. (AP/Wide World Photos)

couraging sign for the many women of color in the United States who have felt doubly oppressed by race and gender.

In the 1992 election, there were some signs that the gender gap in party voting was decreasing from what it had been during the 1980's, when women first became significantly more Democratic. One impetus for women to vote for Democrats had been that women are more likely than men to oppose heavy defense spending, preferring to see funds go to domestic needs such as education and social services—priorities for northern Democrats. With the end of the Cold War and greater parity in the educational level of the sexes, their political ideas and partisanship may grow more similar, erasing any noticeable gender gap.

Homosexuals. Unlike women and ethnic minorities, gay men and lesbians have the advantage of being able to hide their identity in a world that often punishes them socially, economically, and legally. Being closeted, however, hurts any potential political movement by minimizing public support. As increasing numbers of homosexuals began to "come out" in the 1970's and 1980's, liberal politicians began to court gay groups and individuals for their support and openly gay politicians began to emerge. The GAY AND LESBIAN RIGHTS MOVEMENT took on both specifically gay and broader political issues, becoming very well organized in some cities.

As American society has become more educated about and somewhat more tolerant of diversity, the opportunities for gay people improve. Openly gay San Francisco supervisor Harvey Milk was respected for his support of women's rights and civil rights, but he was assassinated in his office in 1978. The U.S. Supreme Court has let stand state laws that prohibit homosexual behavior in the home and that sanction the firing of teachers because they are homosexual.

If gays chose a party simply according to its level of tolerance and political support, it would be the Democrats. The only two openly gay Congress members in the early 1990's (Barney Frank and Gerald E. Studds) were both Democrats. Democratic presidential candidate Jesse Jackson and President Bill Clinton are the only important national leaders to have sought the homosexual vote openly. On the other hand, rich gays who vote with their pocketbook tend to vote Republican. As is the case for so many other groups, political life is defined by a combination of factors and influences.

SUGGESTED READINGS. The most comprehensive overview and source is *Harvard Encyclopedia of American Ethnic Groups* (1980), edited by Stephan Thernstrom. On the interaction between immigrants and older American groups, see John Higham's *Strangers in the Land: Patterns of American Nativism, 1860-1925* (1955). A textbook that covers many groups is Vincent N. Parillo's *Strangers to These Shores* (1990). For insight on the intersection of several groups, see Abraham D. Lavender's *Ethnic Women and Feminist Values* (1986). Other useful sources are *The Struggle for Influence: The Impact of Minority Groups on Politics and Public Policy in the United States* (1985) by Michael C. Le May and *Blacks in Southern Politics* (1987), edited by Laurence W. Moreland, Robert P. Steed, and Tod A. Baker.—*Alan M. Fisher*

Pontiac (c. 1720, Ohio—Apr. 20, 1769, Cahokia, Ill.): Chief of the Ottawa Indians based near present-day Detroit, Michigan. Under Pontiac the Ottawa Indians, along with other tribes, fought against British rule at the end of the French and Indian War in PONTIAC'S REBEL-

Pontiac, an Ottawa chief, opposed British rule. (Library of Congress)

LION (1763-1766). After some of his strongest allies petitioned for peace, Pontiac signed a peace treaty and was pardoned. He was later slain in Illinois by an Indian presumably bribed by an English trader.

Pontiac's Rebellion (1763): Indian uprising sparked by the transfer of French territories in North America to British control in the wake of the Seven Years' War (1756-1763). Pontiac, chief of that Ottawas, had supported the French and realized that his people would no longer enjoy the same benefits or be welcomed in the British forts. The Ottawas might ultimately be deprived of their hunting grounds once the British were in charge. On May 23, 1763, Pontiac enlisted the support of tribes from Lake Superior to the lower Mississippi River and instructed them to attack a string of British forts. These attacks destroyed nearly every British fort west of the Niagara River. After several months without receiving aid from the French, however, many of the tribes decided to make peace. While still trying to reinforce his shaky alliance by gathering support from other tribes, Pontiac eventually realized that the British would be victorious. Pontiac signed a treaty of peace and amity pledging loyalty to the British on July 25, 1766.

Popé (1655-1690): Pueblo medicine man from Tewa Pueblo. He led the PUEBLO REVOLT OF 1680, which temporarily liberated New Mexico from the Spanish. Of the total Spanish population of twenty-five hundred, nearly one-fifth was killed; the rest made their way to El Paso del Norte (El Paso, Texas). With Taos as headquarters, Popé sought to obliterate all Spanish influence on Pueblo life. He did not live to see his efforts destroyed by the Spanish reconquest of the province in 1692.

Popular music: Mass marketed music of mass audience appeal. It differs from both art music and FOLK MUSIC by its shift from pure style to a more moderate and predictable sound.

Popular music is generally associated with cities and commercialism. In ancient Greece and Rome, minstrels played wherever crowds gathered for special occasions, usually at circuses, theaters, markets, and religious ceremonies. In the Middle Ages, professional roving minstrels of all classes entertained throughout Europe and Asia, mingling exotic styles that over the years were formalized into a stock repertoire. When the European bourgeoisie emerged as the economic power of the post-Renaissance years, the demand for popular entertainment grew along with the increased amount of leisure time created by the merchant classes. This demand for popular entertainment intensified during the periods of urbanization that followed the Industrial Revolution.

In the United States, popular music has borrowed heavily from diverse cultures. Popular styles evolved from a blend of European folk musics and African American SPIRITUALS, then were standardized by itinerant minstrels and traveling vaudeville theater troupes. Later, the songs from burlesque and vaudeville would be further developed into "musicals," elaborate dramatic productions of unrealistic situations.

The most powerful influence on popular music in the second half of the twentieth century came from a fusion of BLUES MUSIC and JAZZ—hybrids derived from slave ballads and traditional African American spirituals. These mixed with bluegrass and various folk styles to produce, on the one hand, mainstream country and western music, and on the other hand, RHYTHM AND BLUES, ROCK AND ROLL, and SOUL MUSIC. With the advent of electronic musical instruments and the proliferation of commercial radio stations, rhythm and blues, country, and soul music dominated the popular music scene of the 1950's and 1960's.

The contribution of African American musicians in the development of American popular music cannot be overstated. From the mid-1800's through the dominance of the "MOTOWN sound" in the 1960's, popular music was shaped by African American styles. Motown produced dynamic talent such as Smokey Robinson, the Supremes, and Marvin Gaye, as well as songwriters Eddie and Brian Holland and Lamont Dozier. Earlier artists such as minstrel music pioneer James A. Bland, ragtime composer Scott Joplin, Broadway entertainer Bert Williams, and singers Josephine BAKER, Billie HOLIDAY, and Ethel Waters—all were indispensable in the development of modern popular music, theater, and film.

Many American ethnic groups also enjoy their own forms of popular music ranging from Latino SALSA to Armenian American love songs. These forms of music, like mainstream popular music, are featured on recordings and ethnic radio programs as well as at concerts, dances, and other events in ethnic communities.

SUGGESTED READINGS. For a general history of popular music, read *Popular Music in America* (1991) by Michael Leckrone. For a more comprehensive study, try Timothy E. Scheurer's *Born in the U.S.A.: The*

Myth of America in Popular Music from Colonial Times to the Present (1991). Two books that discuss in detail the evolution of popular musical styles are *American Popular Song: The Great Innovators, 1900-1950* (1972) by Alec Wilder and *Popular Music Perspectives: Ideas, Themes, and Patterns in Contemporary Lyrics* (1991) by B. Lee Cooper. For a review of the African American experience in shaping American popular music, see Arnold Shaw's insightful *Black Popular Music in America* (1986).

Porter, Katherine Anne (Maria Veronica Callista Russell; May 15, 1890, Indian Creek, Tex.—Sept. 18, 1980, Silver Spring, Md.): Writer. Porter is best known as a southern short story writer. In 1966 she won the Pulitzer Prize and the National Book Award for *The Collected Stories of Katherine Anne Porter* (1965) which describes, through the eyes of children, the secrets that run counter to the appearances of aristocratic southern families. Among her other books are *Flowering Judas and Other Stories* (1930), *Pale Horse, Pale Rider: Three Short Novels* (1939), *The Leaning Tower and Other Stories* (1944), and the novel *Ship of Fools* (1962). Her last book, *The Never-Ending Wrong* (1977), covers the trial and execution of SACCO AND VENZETTI.

Pulitzer prize-winning author Katherine Anne Porter. (Washington Star)

Portuguese Americans: The influence of the Portuguese in the Americas began in the age of exploration, when Portugal was a major world power. The Portuguese were well known for their nautical and map-making skills. It was partly because of the nautical leadership of the Portuguese that Christopher Columbus became involved in the exploration of the New World. He learned navigational and map-making skills from the Portuguese while living in Lisbon, and he later married a Portuguese woman from Madeira. The presence of the Portuguese in the United States can be traced back to the early 1500's when Miguel Côrte-Real, a Portuguese explorer from the Azores islands, was shipwrecked off the New England coast in Berkley, Massachusetts. Another Portuguese explorer, João Rodrigues Cabrillo, discovered San Diego Bay in 1542. This age of exploration spread Portuguese culture throughout the world.

Immigration History. The Portuguese emigrated to the United States, Canada, and Brazil in the seventeenth and eighteenth centuries for economic and religious reasons. For example, Mathias de Sousa, a Portuguese Jew escaping persecution, arrived in Maryland in 1634, and the American Jewish community was founded by Portuguese Jews from Brazil who were refugees of religious persecution in Portugal. Other Portuguese adventurers settled in New Amsterdam in the 1700's, and in New Orleans and the Carolinas in the early 1800's. Some of the latter group intermarried with American Indians and African Americans.

Greater numbers of Portuguese began arriving in the United States around 1830. Most of these immigrants were from the Azores, nine islands located in the Atlantic Ocean 800 miles from Lisbon. By the mid-1800's many Azoreans settled as fishermen in New Bedford, Massachusetts, or went to work in the mines and lumber mills of California. Other Portuguese Americans settled in Rhode Island and Hawaii.

The second wave of Portuguese immigration took place between 1880 and 1920. It consisted of 200,000 Azoreans, Madeirans, and Cape Verdeans. The island of Madeira is located in the North Atlantic approximately 350 miles west of Morocco. Cape Verde, an independent nation formerly under Portuguese rule, lies in the Atlantic approximately 400 miles west of Senegal. These second-wave immigrants (mostly from coastal areas) arrived in whaling ships and became fishermen, farmers, or workers in textile mills. Many were involved in California's dairy farming and wine making industries. They settled in Boston, New Bedford, and Fall River, Massachusetts; Providence,

Rhode Island; Oakland, California; New York; New Jersey; and several other areas. In the 1900's, the Portuguese became a major source of unskilled labor in the United States.

After World War II, around 4,000 Portuguese immigrants from Macao (an island southwest of Hong Kong) settled in California near San Francisco and Los Angeles. They were counted as Chinese immigrants. Many Portuguese also emigrated to Canada at this time to work as farmers in Quebec. The third major wave of Portuguese immigration occurred in the mid-1950's, when 10,000 Azoreans from the island of Faial left as a result of the devastation from a major earthquake. Senator John F. Kennedy of Massachusetts, along with Senator John Pastore of Rhode Island, sponsored the Azorean Refugee Act of 1958, allowing an additional 1,500 visas beyond the regular quota. Another earthquake in the Azorean island of São Jorge prompted action from Senator Edward Kennedy allowing more Portuguese to enter the United States in 1964. After the 1965 IMMIGRATION AND NATIONALITY ACT, a greater number of Azoreans emigrated to the United States.

Except for a small number of middle- and upper-class émigrés, most Portuguese immigrants were from a working-class background. Many had not completed education beyond elementary school and lacked the skills needed for factory work. They were hardworking people, however, with expertise in whaling, fishing, and farming. Used to braving the harsh Atlantic weather, they were ready for the challenges facing them in the new country. Many Portuguese Americans were happy to come to a democratic country where individuals could move up the socioeconomic ladder by their own efforts—a marked contrast to the rigid hierarchical divisions of Portuguese society. New opportunities were available to the Portuguese immigrant in education and employment. In the late twentieth century, some Portuguese Americans still look forward to visits to the Old Country; others, after accumulating a certain amount of economic independence, decide to reestablish residence in the Azores or continental Portugal.

Acculturation. Most Portuguese Americans live in ethnic communities, surrounded by those who share their language and culture, yet are well-adjusted to the American way of life. A trip to Cambridge, Massachusetts, for example, reveals a typical Portuguese community where grocery shopping revolves around various specialty stores: The bakery offers fresh Portuguese bread, while the butcher shop, the fishmarket, and other small family-run grocery stores fulfill the needs of the immigrant. In many of these stores people speak both Portuguese and English. Words in Portuguese (a romance language based in Latin) have become Anglicized—a common sign of ACCULTURATION. For example, *loja* becomes *estoa*, taken from the English "store."

Portuguese American attorney (c. 1940's) has decorated his office with a portrait of Abraham Lincoln and a map of his native Azores islands. (Library of Congress)

Portuguese American Catholic religious celebrations, such as the saints' days of Santo António, São João, and São Pedro, are well known in Massachusetts and California. The most famous celebrations revolve around *As Festas do Espirito Santo*, or Holy Ghost Festivities, which take place yearly in May. Church services and street processions (*croações*) carrying images of Jesus are followed by eating, drinking, music, and dancing. Homemade sweet breads (*massa sovada*); beef soup (*sopa de carne*); boiled beef with sausage, potatoes, and cabbage (*cozido a portuguesa*); oven-baked stewed beef (*alcatra*); and rice pudding (*arroz doce*) are among the delicacies served. Fine Portuguese wines accompany the meal.

Some areas with a high concentration of Portuguese

immigrants have *fado* (literally, fate) restaurants featuring the traditional melancholic folksong accompanied by guitar. Traditional Portuguese foods served at such restaurants include kale soup, codfish, Portuguese sausage, and flan pudding.

Portuguese Americans keep abreast of events in their homeland through Portuguese-language newspapers published within the immigrant communities such as *Portuguese Times*, *Azorean Times*, and *Portuguese Heritage Journal*. Some local bookstores specialize in Portuguese literature with works by continental Portuguese authors such as Camões' Lusiados and Azorean writers such as Antero de Quental. Radio and television programs in Portuguese are also available in some communities.

Many Portuguese Amer-icans rely on community groups that assist fellow immigrants in the acculturation process and in maintaining socioeconomic ties with their close-knit communities. Such groups include, for example, União Portuguesa Continental dos Estados Unidos da America (Portuguese Continental Union of the United States of America) in Boston, União Portuguesa do Estado da California (UPEC), and the Luso American Educational Federation. The American Portuguese Society in New York City was founded to bring a cultural appreciation of Portugal to the United States. Roman Catholic parishes such as Cinco Chagas (Five Wounds) in San Jose, California; Nossa Senhora de Fátima (Our Lady of Fatima) in Ludlow, Massachusetts; and Saint John the Baptist in Boston are also important community centers. Many of these parishes also have established parochial schools that offer bilingual education to immigrant children.

Later arrivals are better educated and more attached to their homeland than earlier immigrants. They feel equal pride in being Portuguese and in being American. Several second- and third-generation Portuguese Americans are graduates of Boston, Harvard, and Princeton universities, as well as other prestigious institutions of higher education.

The biggest leap in the acculturation process of Portuguese Americans seems to occur when the children of second-generation immigrants wish to become "Americanized." Conflicting values between the old and the new cultures often result in misunderstandings between parents and children. Traditional Portuguese Amer-ican families view the father as the head of the household, while the mother has a supporting role. Peer pressure and other American cultural influences on young people lead to less parental control. Similarly, Portuguese American women's roles are changing as more women enter the work force. Third generation immigrants are usually more secure as Americans, and therefore more interested in tracing and preserving their Portuguese heritage.

Portuguese immigrants, like other minorities of non-Anglo Saxon background, have not been immune to prejudice and discrimination. Cape Verdean Portuguese from the island of Brava were victimized because they were of mixed African descent. Many fearful Portuguese immigrants, especially those of Mediterranean appearance, tried to hide their ethnic background. Like other immigrants, many were forced to Anglicize their names; for example, the name Rosa would be changed to Rogers. Nowadays, Portuguese immigrants no longer hide their ethnicity and are proud of their background. Typical Portuguese American surnames such as Andrade, Carvalho, Dias, dos Passos, and Sousa are recognized in American culture.

Portuguese immigrants' parade in New York City. Portuguese Americans also proceed through the streets in some towns for annual saint's day celebrations. (Richard B. Levine)

Contributions. Portuguese Americans have made outstanding contributions in a variety of fields in the United States and abroad. John Philip Sousa, the renowned composer of marching band music, was a third-generation Portuguese American. Joe Raposo was another famous composer of Portuguese descent. Born of Portuguese immigrants in Connecticut, Elmar de Oliveira is a well-known concert violinist. The celebrated writer John dos Passos, who had Portuguese roots in Madeira Island, became quite interested in his heritage in later years.

Tony Coelho of Merced, California, became the first Portuguese American elected to the House of Representatives in 1979. Ben Nighthorse CAMPBELL, elected a Democratic senator from Colorado in 1992, is of both American Indian and Portuguese descent. Born on the island of São Miguel, Cardinal Humberto Medeiros became Boston's Catholic spiritual leader. Meredith Vieira is a well-known CBS television journalist. Dr. Artur da Cunha Oliveira, born in the United States, returned to Portugal to become a deputy from the Azores in the European Community. Many other Portuguese Americans have attained high positions in education, science, and the humanities. Although a minority, the Portuguese have become major contributors to the American pluralistic democracy.

SUGGESTED READINGS. Additional information on Portuguese immigrants can be found in *The Portuguese Americans* by Leo Pap (1981; a 1992 paperback is available from the Portuguese Continental Union of the USA in Boston), *The Portuguese in America* by Manoel da Silveira Cardozo (1976), and *And Yet They Come: Portuguese Immigration from the Azores to the United States* by Jerry R. Williams (1982).—*Maria A. Pacino*

Posadas, Las (Dec. 16-24): Traditional religious procession in preparation for CHRISTMAS that reenacts the search of Mary and Joseph for an inn on their journey to Bethlehem. Formerly, Las Posadas took place outside churches and convents during the Mexican colonial period as part of a miracle play originally used to teach

San Antonio, Tex., girls portray Virgin Mary (left) and angel in a Las Posadas procession. (Robert Fried)

Christianity to Indians. Contemporary Mexican American celebrations begin on December 16 and last for nine days. Participants carrying statues of Mary and Joseph form a procession through a neighborhood, knock on doors, and request admittance in a sung dialogue but are refused. When finally a door is opened to them, all enter singing and enjoy refreshments, games, dancing, and the breaking of a piñata. Las Posadas are often organized by groups of neighbors as well as churches, community organizations, and even museums.

Post-traumatic stress disorder—Indochinese refugees: Psychological and other health problems which have surfaced as a delayed reaction to extreme stress during and after the VIETNAM WAR. The problem became a subject of great concern for health professionals serving the tens of thousands of REFUGEES who began to arrive in the United States from Southeast Asia after 1975. A disturbingly high number of Indochinese immigrants seemed prone to serious depression, psychological dysfunction, and varying degrees of difficulty in dealing with everyday life. Many complained of physical ailments and a general feeling of poor health.

Research on migration and mental health suggests that refugees experience greater psychological stress than other immigrants. After all, a refugee's decision to abandon the homeland is based on a combination of necessity and fear. Most Vietnamese and Cambodian immigrants arrived in the United States with the burden of having been exposed to years of war, displacement, severe daily hardship, and unspeakable horrors. Most had suffered family losses during escapes over land or by sea, and endured months of privation in the refugee camps. In addition, they left their homelands with no sure destination and little preparation for their new lives.

Once resettled, the refugees faced the tremendous tasks of getting accustomed to new values and life in a complex—and alien—Western industrial society. Learning a new language was in itself an enormous task. For some refugees, learning to cope with harsh winters was just as challenging as suffering a loss of social or economic status. Family members mourned for loved ones who were lost or left behind. Some refugees were predisposed to mental disorders because their sense of security, identity, and self-esteem had been shattered.

In most places Indochinese refugees settled, there was no existing ethnic community to give them cultural orientation and emotional support. This lack of solace compounded the emotional and social isolation felt especially by refugees in rural areas.

Post-traumatic stress syndrome in Indochinese refugees is characterized by symptoms of emotional withdrawal, lack of expression, severe depression, anxiety, incoherent speech or incommunicative behavior, and sometimes violent or antisocial behavior—all of which might take years to surface. Adolescents and the elderly are especially susceptible. Although the condition may be treatable with psychiatric counseling, many refugees are suspicious of Western medical practices and tend to avoid doctors. Commonly, even to admit mental illness within the family is a social stigma for Indochinese families. In a typical clash of cultures, the health worker and refugee are often at odds. While the professional may be insensitive to cultural taboos, the refugees lack an understanding of Western medical practices that could ease their anxiety over seeking treatment. Language problems, social habits, and general uncertainty about the future can complicate treatment.

Increasing numbers of Southeast Asian MUTUAL AID SOCIETIES have set up programs staffed by fellow refugees to help those suffering from the syndrome in a culturally sensitive manner. Recent studies have emphasized the need to understand cultural differences in mental health treatment programs. For example, Indochinese child-rearing practices, family dynamics, and sources of self-esteem can differ greatly from those in mainstream American society.

SUGGESTED READINGS. "Psychiatric Symptoms in Refugee Families from South East Asia: Therapeutic Challenges" by Soma Ganesan et al. appeared in vol. 43, no. 2 (April, 1989) of the *American Journal of Psychotherapy* and includes two case studies. *Mental Health Issues: Indochinese Refugees: An Annotated Bibliography* (1985) by Barbara J. Silver and Josephine Chui lists books and social services addressing the problem. For more informal life stories detailing refugee traumas, see *Voices from Southeast Asia* (1991) by John Tenhula.

Potlatches and giveaways: Ceremonies among American Indians of the Pacific Northwest at which there is a distribution of gifts or valuable possessions to affirm or reaffirm social status. Those in attendance were required by tradition to reciprocate by demonstrating their generosity in their own subsequent potlatches. The term potlatch was derived from a Chinook Indian word meaning "to give." Potlatches were characterized by the generosity of gift giving as well as the large number of people invited from differing tribes to share in the festive atmosphere, and were given for a variety of reasons: marriages, births, deaths, and everything in between. The primary importance of the potlatch was the assertion and validation of social rank, not the occasion itself. Among American Indian tribes of the Pacific Northwest, traditional potlatches had virtually stopped by the 1960's because families lacked sufficient economic resources to indulge in lavish ceremonies.

Poverty: Poverty is a global social problem which has generally been worse in the less industrialized Southern Hemisphere than in the Northern Hemisphere. Poverty has been an enduring social problem in the United States even though it is one of the world's richest countries. The American poor were rediscovered in the 1960's with the publication of Michael Harrington's book *The Other America* (1962). This sparked the "WAR ON POVERTY" of the Johnson Administration of the mid-1960's and continued concern over poverty in the United States.

In 1964, when the problem of poverty was being analyzed, the Council of Economic Advisors established the poverty line at a maximum income level of $3,000 per year. The official poverty level for a nonfarm family of four in the 1990's rounds off to approximately $10,000. In 1984, Michael Harrington estimated that there were approximately 40 to 50 million Americans living in poverty. Some official statistics undercount the American poor by more than 25 million. Contrary to popular belief, most poor Americans are white.

Many of those living in poverty have done so for more than one generation. This persistent poverty has developed into a culture of its own, dubbed the "culture of poverty" by anthropologist Oscar Lewis. The CULTURE OF POVERTY has been said to exist in various forms among about one in five poor people in both rural and urban areas. Its economic characteristics include a constant struggle for survival; unemployment or underemployment; low wages; and child labor. In addition, there is an absence of savings, a chronic shortage of cash, the pawning of personal goods, and borrowing from local money lenders at usurious rates of interest. Rather than keeping large food reserves in the home, poor people tend to buy small quantities of food frequently as the need arises. Many only buy second-hand clothing and furniture.

Lewis represents one theoretical explanation of the causes of poverty. A second general perspective of poverty focuses on external factors such as problems with the society or the economy. From this perspective the poor are poor because they do not have fair access to education, health care, adequate housing, or good jobs. DISCRIMINATION and the "dual labor market" may both be contributing factors to poverty. For example, in the dual labor market (one black and one white), black workers typically receive lower wages than white workers for comparable work. Blacks are also usually consigned to the lower occupational levels and suffer disproportionately from underemployment (employment below education level, usually in dead-end jobs) and unemployment. Through improved education and training for blacks, an end to discriminatory hiring practices, and maintenance of high overall demand for labor, income inequality in the United States could be reduced. Yet research has shown that even if employment discrimination were sufficiently reduced, there would still be a difference between white and black income because of the low quality of schooling received by many nonwhites.

Rural Poverty. Poverty and inequality have always been features of many rural people's lives. Poor rural communities tend to have two social classes, those who have control and those who are powerless: the haves and the have-nots. The rural poor in the United States are a diverse group. They include rural blacks in the South; Appalachian whites in the coal mines; American Indians on scattered reservations; Latino and other MIGRANT WORKERS; and low-wage farm and manufacturing workers.

The rural problems of low-wage and part-time or seasonal employment are regarded as the inevitable cost of a changing economy and as major contributors to poverty. Remote rural areas, like inner cities, appear to have continuous high unemployment and high poverty rates, which have their greatest impact on young people. Nevertheless, it is generally believed that rural poverty has always reflected a limited opportunity structure rather than limited ambitions.

About half of the estimated 9 million rural poor live in the South. Persistent long-term poverty is greater in rural areas than in urban. For example, one-third of all rural blacks are persistently poor. Although conditions have improved since the 1960's, 4 million Americans in rural areas are still persistently poor.

Older Americans in rural areas have higher poverty rates than older people in urban areas. An increasing number of female-headed households are also experiencing long-term poverty in rural areas.

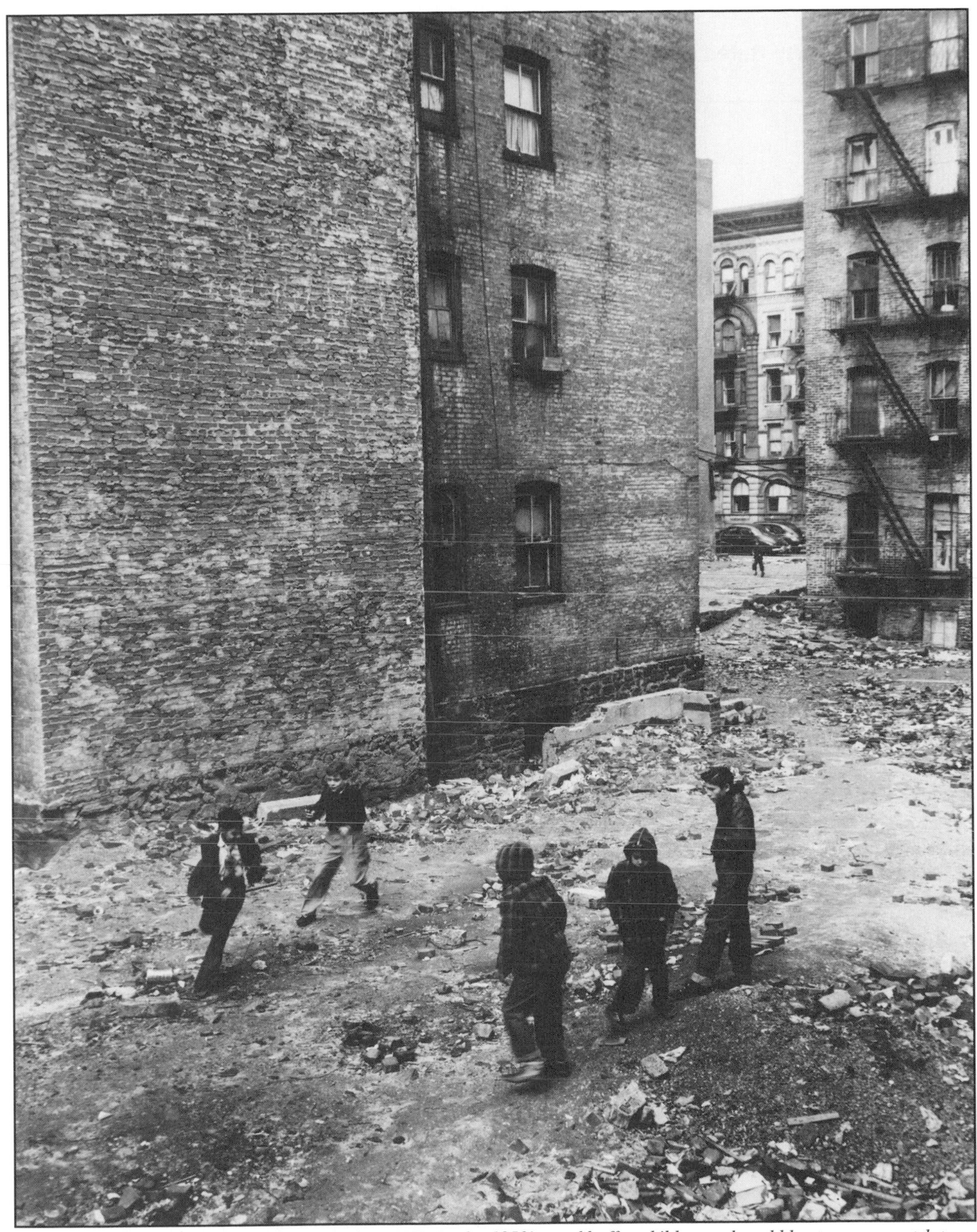

Poor inner-city areas such as Spanish Harlem, N.Y., in the 1950's, could offer children only rubble-strewn vacant lots as playgrounds. (AP/Wide World Photos)

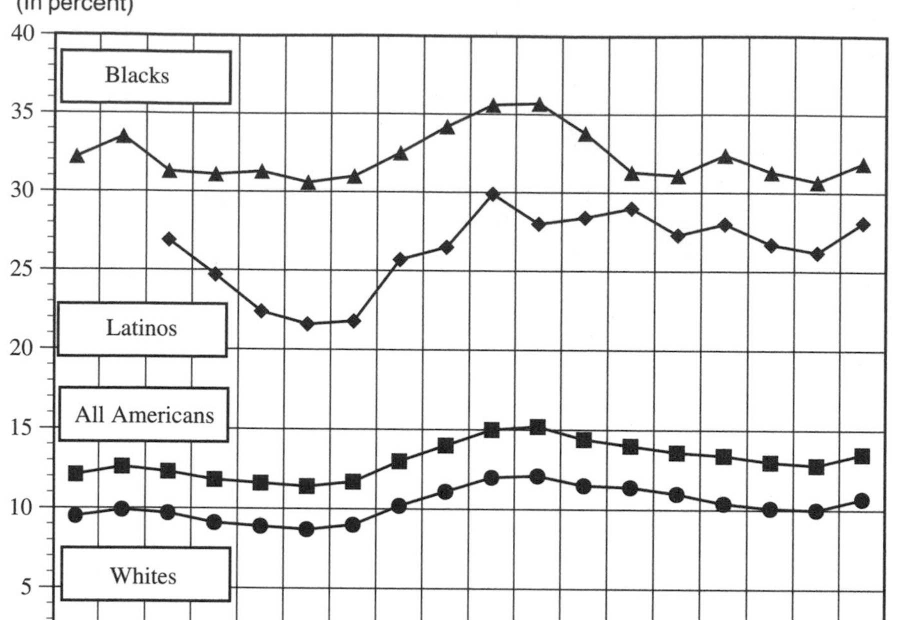

Sources: Adapted from Anna Wilson, *African Americans Struggle for Equality.* Discrimination series, p. 36. Vero Beach, Fla.: Rourke Corp., 1992. Additional data are from *Statistical Abstract of the United States, 1992.* Table 717. Washington, D.C.: U.S. Government Printing Office, 1992.

Urban Poverty. The number of poor people living in the inner city in the United States has increased drastically since the late 1960's. In 1969 there were 8 million people (12.7 percent) in the central city population who were poor; by 1985 there were 14.2 million people (19 percent) in the central city population living in poverty. Sociologists attribute this increase to economic and industrial changes that have taken place in metropolitan areas. In the past, jobs were located in the inner city for people with few or no skills, and little education. Now industries have moved to industrial parks located outside the central city. What is left in the cities are low-paying clerical, domestic, or service jobs for inner city residents.

People with skills and education are fleeing the BARRIOS and GHETTOS, so the central city population remains disproportionately young, uneducated, unskilled, and poor. Middle-class flight to better jobs, schools, and neighborhoods leads to social isolation for those left behind. With insufficient ties to the labor market and inferior schools, inner city residents may become locked in a cycle of poverty. Temptations to engage in the drug trade and other crime that is rife in the inner city also generate behavior that is not favorable to good work histories.

Feminization of Poverty. The feminization of poverty was recognized in the 1970's. This term refers to the fact that in the United States, women head half of all poor families. Recent studies estimate that two out of three poor adults are women and that one out of five children lives in poverty. Fifty percent of white children and 68 percent of black and Latino children living in female-headed households are also faced with oppressive poverty.

In the late 1900's, women were participating in the labor force more than at any other time in history. More than half of all women are employed outside the home. Work, however, is not the answer to female poverty. The jobs available to women are actually part of the problem; they are centered in service, retail sales, clerical, and domestic work in which the pay is very low. These jobs often do not have benefits such as health insurance and retirement programs. These traditional female jobs have given rise to the "pink collar" ghetto in which single working mothers are living in, or on the edge of, poverty.

Many FEMALE HEADS OF HOUSEHOLDS would like to work full-time but are unable to do so because of health problems or lack of child care. Those who can work part-time may become a part of the working poor.

The Working Poor. One of the contradictions of American society is that simply having a job does not mean an end to poverty. Some people may work six or seven days a week and still remain poor. Either their wages are too low to support their families, or their families are so large that they must work more than one job barely to break even.

According to Sar A. Levitian and Isaac Shapiro, the working poor are not an isolated few. Some 2 million people work full-time year round but live in poverty; another 7 million work full-time for part of the year or in part-time jobs. Most disturbing is that the number of working poor is growing substantially. In the 1980's the number of working poor was 50 percent higher than in the 1970's.

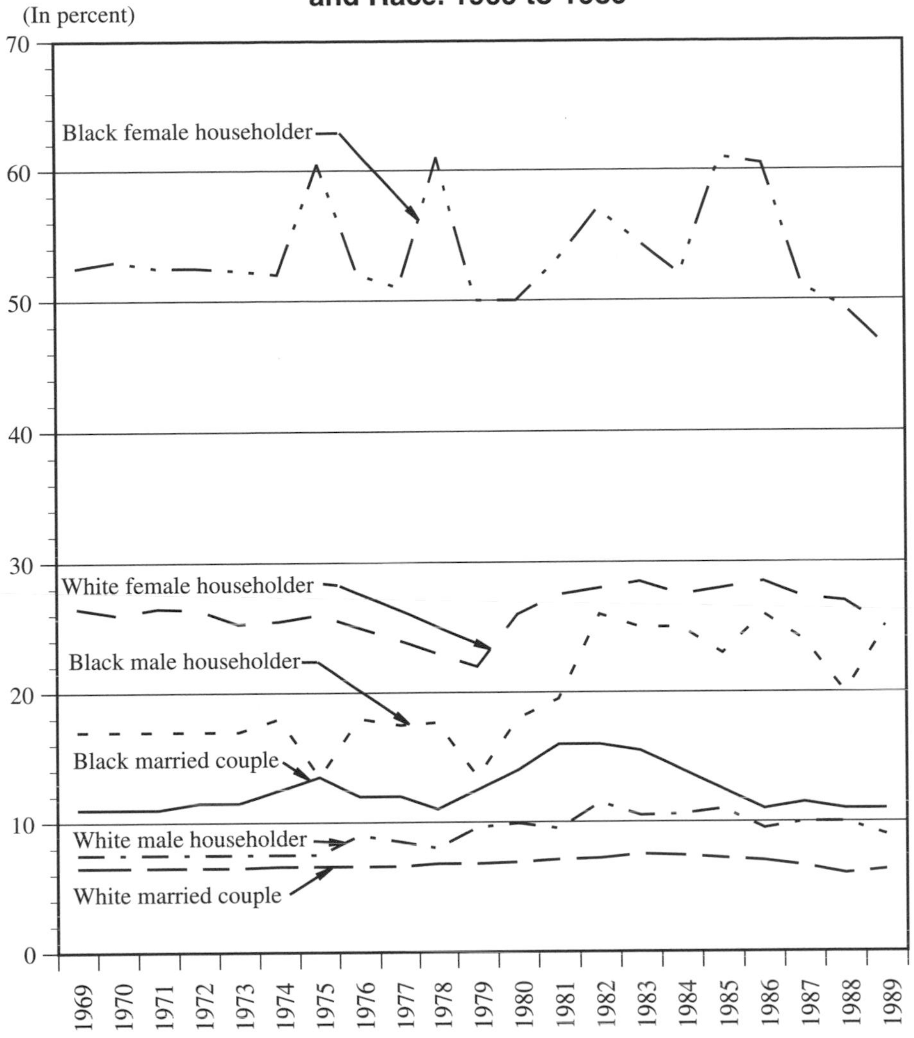

Source: Adapted from Anna Wilson, *African Americans Struggle for Equality*. Discrimination series, p. 15. Vero Beach, Fla.: Rourke Corp., 1992.

The majority of the working poor, like the poor in general, are white. Males usually work full-time throughout the year; females constitute the majority of the poor who work full-time for part of the year or who work part-time.

The working poor are highly concentrated in nonmetropolitan areas in the United States. Their educational levels are lower than the working nonpoor. The working poor are also disproportionately represented among the estimated 13 percent of Americans who are illiterate. Of the full-time year round working poor, 4 percent suffer from physical disabilities. Such factors contribute greatly to the perpetuation of the working poor. Another factor is the exemptions from and weak enforcement of the FAIR LABOR STANDARDS ACT, which allow employers to pay many workers less than the federal minimum wage.

Present economic trends do not suggest a good prognosis for the working poor. In addition to the high unemployment rate, the income distribution is becoming more skewed in favor of the affluent. Current federal policies are likely to lead to continued high levels of poverty among individuals and families who are committed to work.

SUGGESTED READINGS. Michael Harrington, a pioneer

in the study of poverty, has written two excellent works: *The Other America* (1962) and *The New American Poverty* (1984). Anthropologist Oscar Lewis, who coined the term "culture of poverty," has enlightened the world on the enduring nature of poverty over generations. His fine study of poverty in a family in Mexico is *The Children of Sanchez* (1963).

On recent problems among the rural poor, see *Rural Poverty in America* (1992), edited by Cynthia M. Duncan. Other specialized studies of poverty include *Poverty in the American Dream: Women and Children First* (1983) by Karin Stallard, Barbara Ehrenreich, and Holly Sklar; *Quiet Riot: Race and Poverty in the United States* (1988), edited by Fred R. Harris and Roger W. Wilins; and *The Working but Poor: America's Contradiction* (rev. ed., 1993) by Sar A. Levitian.

For further study, the student may want to see Richard D. Bingham, Ray E. Green, and Sammis B. White's edited work *The Homeless in Contemporary Society* (1987), Ken Auletta's *The Underclass* (1982), and *The Black Underclass* (1980) by Douglas G. Glasgow.—*Paul T. Lockman, Jr.*

Joint Chiefs of Staff Chairman General Colin Powell discusses the future of the military during a news conference in 1993. (AP/Wide World Photos)

Poverty, War on. *See* **War on Poverty**

Powell, Colin Luther (b. Apr. 5, 1937, New York, N.Y.): African American chairman of the Joint Chiefs of Staff. Born in Harlem to Jamaican immigrants, Powell was commissioned as a second lieutenant following his graduation from City College of New York in 1958. Powell served two tours of duty in Vietnam (1962-1963 and 1968-1969) and received numerous awards throughout his military career, including the Legion of Merit (1972). In 1987, he was asked to serve as national security adviser by President Ronald Reagan. Powell was promoted to four-star general in 1989 shortly before he was named by President George Bush to be chairman of the Joint Chiefs of Staff. Powell became the first black officer and the youngest man to achieve that position. Having served with distinction as a chief coordinator of military strategy during the Persian Gulf War, Powell was reappointed to a second two-year term in 1991. He announced his intention to retire at the end of his term in September of 1993.

Powhatan [Wahunsonacock] (c. 1550, Powhata, near Richmond, Va.—Apr., 1618, Powhata, Va.): Chief of the Powhatans of present-day Virginia. Powhatan was head of a confederacy of thirty American Indian tribes of the Eastern Woodlands when Jamestown was settled by white colonists in 1607. The English seized some of the Indians' best land, but peace was secured through the marriage in 1614 of John Rolfe and Powhatan's daughter POCAHONTAS. Following Powhatan's death, Indian attacks on the English increased; after 1665, the chiefs were appointed by the governor of Virginia, and the POWHATAN CONFEDERACY was dissolved.

Powhatan Confederacy: Group of Algonquin tribes united by their allegiance to the Indian chief Wahunsonacock, known to the British colonists of Virginia as Powhatan. Early British settlers of Jamestown eventually discovered that tobacco was a highly profitable export crop and were encroaching on the confederacy's territory for new, rich land to cultivate. During his lifetime, Powhatan managed to preserve peace. His half brother and successor as chief, Opechancanough, was angered by the settlers' encroachment and the murder of one of his subjects. In 1622, Powhatan Indians attacked British colonists in settlements along the James River, massacring one-fourth of their total population. Periodic warfare occurred for years between the confederacy and the settlers. In 1644, Opechancanough launched a final

By the time of English colonialism in the New World, Powhatan was chief of a confederacy of thirty tribes of the Eastern Woodlands. (Library of Congress)

uprising in which 500 whites were slain. Although the attack was costly, the total British population of 8,000 colonists was far too numerous to eradicate. The confederacy quickly backed down and accepted a peace settlement in 1646.

Powwows: Communal celebrations characterized by dancing, arts and crafts, and traditional American Indian tribal costumes. Powwows had their origin in religious ceremony. In the Algonquian language, powwow means "he dreams," suggesting communication with the spirit world. The dancing, singing, and praying performed at powwows celebrated manhood, renewed friendships, commemorated the dead, and sought to expel sickness. Speeches, gift giving, and pipe smoking were also common characteristics of the powwow. These celebrations were held to unite the minds and spirits of the tribe for the common good. In the late twentieth century, powwows still were held to reinforce tribal identity and solidarity.

Singers gather around the drum in the center of a circle of dancers at a Springfield, Mo., powwow. (Terry Barner, Unicorn Stock Photos)

Prejudice: Literally, "prejudgment"; any like or dislike that is formed before facts are examined to determine whether the opinion is valid. In common parlance, the term usually refers to negative prejudice—unfavorable opinions about others, specifically about other racial, ethnic, or religious groups. RACISM, SEXISM, and ageism are all forms of prejudice, as are antipathies directed toward people of a certain religion, gay people, or people with disabilities. Sociologist Gordon Allport defined it as "an antipathy based upon a faulty and inflexible generalization" that could either be "felt or expressed." When expressed or acted upon, prejudice may lead to DISCRIMINATION or even to persecution.

Prejudice results from a lack of knowledge of and contact with groups different from one's own. It is exacerbated by rumor and misinformation as well as by insecurity and fear of competition from members of other groups. One odd aspect of prejudice is its perseverance even when new information contradicts the incorrect prejudicial belief that a person holds. Once a person's prejudices are formed, he or she often tends to discount or reinterpret any new experience that would modify those prejudices.

Presbyterians: Adherents of a church of essentially Calvinistic Protestant principles, which is governed by presbyters, or elders. Presbyterianism developed in England during the Civil War (1642-1645). The Westminster Assembly produced the Westminster Confession, approved by the Puritan Parliament in 1648. This Calvinistic document became the basis of English and American Presbyterianism.

Like CALVINISTS, the Presbyterians believed strongly in Original Sin and predestination. The Confession proposed a theology based on a contract with God, a "covenant of grace," holding that salvation should be granted to believers in Christ through faith alone rather than good works. Regarding Calvinistic predestination, the Westminister Confession proposed "infralapsarianism." This doctrine holds that God decided who should be saved and who should be damned after (not before) Adam's disobedience in the Garden of Eden.

The church itself was organized by a hierarchy of courts: Above the local "session" were the "presbytery," the "synod," and the general assembly. Presbyterian ministers met in 1706 to create the first American presbytery under Frances Makemie (1658-1708). With an influx of Scots-Irish immigrants, the number of Presbyterian churches grew quickly, and a synod was formed in 1716. In succeeding decades, there was considerable controversy regarding doctrine and the source of authority—whether ecclesiastical authority is based in presbyteries or synods.

Large waves of Scots-Irish immigration at the end of the eighteenth century increased Presbyterian membership and changed the character of the church in the United States, in effect severing the ties to specific churches in the home country. Furthermore, the GREAT AWAKENING, an emotional revival of religious fervor in the mid-1700's, also led to a vast increase in adherents of the American Presbyterian church.

The first African American Presbyterian churches were formed early in the nineteenth century, beginning in Philadelphia in 1807. White churches were active in missionary work among slaves in the South, but they had less success than did some other Protestant denominations. One reason was that the church did not come out in opposition to slavery. After the Civil War, however, a number of northern Presbyterian churches were active in RECONSTRUCTION, establishing schools for African Americans in the South.

The church was active in the CIVIL RIGHTS MOVEMENT of the 1960's; in 1963, it created a Commission on Religion and Race. Two white Presbyterian ministers were killed in the course of their civil rights activities. In the 1980's, some Presbyterian churches were heavily involved in the SANCTUARY MOVEMENT, which evolved to provide safety to refugees from civil war in Central American countries, most notably El Salvador. Activist Presbyterian minister Jim Fife was one of the first members of the clergy to become involved in the movement.

SUGGESTED READINGS. For a complete discussion of Presbyterianism's development in the United States, see Sydney E. Ahlstrom's magisterial *A Religious History of the American People* (1972). Carl Bridenbaugh, in *Mitre and Sceptre: Transatlantic Faiths, Ideas, Personalities, and Politics, 1689-1775* (1962) discusses the intersection of American/English religion and politics. Leonard J. Trinterud discusses Presbyterianism specifically in *The Forming of an American Tradition: A Re-examination of Colonial Presbyterianism* (1949).

Price, Leontyne (b. Feb. 10, 1927, Laurel, Miss.): African American opera singer. A lyric soprano and operatic prima donna, Price is a world-class singer who has helped break racial barriers. After college she studied voice at the Juilliard School in New York City, singing in George Gershwin's *Porgy and Bess* (1952) on Broadway, while performing opera elsewhere. In 1961, as Leonora in *Il Trovatore*, Price became the first black woman to sing a major role at the Metropolitan Opera in New York City. She had turned down the role of Aida (1959) because it seemed stereotypical. A specialist in Giuseppe Verdi's operas, Price continues to hold her high place among the world's great performers.

Leontyne Price stars in Aida *at New York's Metropolitan Opera in 1979.* (AP/Wide World Photos)

Priests and social activism: Particularly since the 1970's, an increasing number of Catholic priests have become involved in supporting the social causes of parishioners who believe they are the victims of discrimination. These priests are going beyond their traditional spiritual role by acting within a political arena to effect legal change and support those whose human rights have been abrogated. The movement started after the reforms of the second Vatican Council (Vatican II) in the early 1960's, which radically changed the Catholic church, making it more supportive of its members seeking worldwide democracy, justice, and peace.

The involvement of priests in social issues is a worldwide phenomenon in Catholicism, catalyzed in large part by the liberation theology movement in Latin America in which priests took on the causes of the exploited poor and began to fight against the repressive governments of the region. The movement grew in the 1970's in the United States and became quite militant in its pressure on the U.S. government in the 1980's to respond to the murders in El Salvador of Archbishop Oscar Romero and four female American missionaries.

Whereas Catholicism had previously encouraged fatalism, the post-Vatican II church taught the poor that they should seek political and economic change to improve their conditions. The U.S. Catholic Conference and the American Bishops Conference have both played a significant role in arguing for the rights of the poor rather than merely accepting the political line of the Vatican. A bishop's pastoral letter written in 1986 argued that economic rights belonged in the list of fundamental human rights and called on the middle class to substitute their desire for wealth with the desire to live a Christ-like life, fighting for justice for all.

Priests who advocate social causes have received considerable opposition from the Restoration movement in the church that is attempting to push the church back to its traditional narrow, authoritarian doctrine. One noteworthy case is the punishment of Seattle's Archbishop Raymond Hunthausen, who was stripped of his powers in 1986 by the Vatican because of his stand on social issues. He had recommended, among other things, that Catholics take action against the U.S. arms buildup by withholding part of their federal income tax and that they support a county ordinance protecting the job rights of minorities, including homosexuals. Hunthausen's reprimand caused a public outcry which included a statement signed by 140 priests, as well as religious and lay leaders and a demand by a group called Concerned Catholics supported by 13,500 signatures to restore his power. Whereas the Restoration argues for a European-centered Catholicism, other currents in American Catholicism see the necessity for a world Catholicism that respects and promotes MULTICULTURALISM.

SUGGESTED READINGS. The shift in the Catholic church toward more social action is explained in detail in Penny Lernoux's *People of God* (1989) and *Cry of the People* (1982). Leonardo Boff's *Church, Charisma, Power: Liberation Theology and the Institutional Church* (1985) argues that the fundamental issue facing Catholicism is human rights. *The Non-Violent Cross* (1968) by Jim Douglass presents his view of how politicized Catholics should act. Jay P. Dolnan's *The American Catholic Experience* (1985) shows how American Catholicism emerged and looks at its relationship to the Vatican.

Property rights—married women's: In the United States, the laws governing married women's property rights are derived from several sources. These laws varied depending on whether English, Spanish, or French legal traditions predominated in the region where a particular woman lived. In addition, a married woman's rights depended on whether she herself was considered to be property—that is, a slave.

English Common Law and the Doctrine of Coverture. English common law formed the basis of family law in the former English colonies, the Old Northwest territories, and most of the Louisiana Purchase. According to this tradition, which drew its justification from the Old Testament, husband and wife were one person and that one was the husband. Upon her marriage, a woman experienced "civil death"—she ceased to exist in the eyes of the law and had no separate legal identity. According to the eighteenth century English jurist Sir William Blackstone, a wife's legal identity was absorbed in her husband's, as if she were "under his wing"; hence the use of the terms "coverture" and *feme covert* (from the French word for "hidden") to describe the legal status of married women.

Since a wife had no separate legal identity, she could not hold property, whether goods, money, or real estate, in her own name, nor could she transfer property by contract, gift, deed, or bequest. Everything a woman possessed at the time of her marriage, both assets and debts, became her husband's, as did any property she received after marriage, whether inheritance, gifts, or wages. A wife could not sue or be sued in court and could not make a binding will.

Marriage and Slavery. Some early women's rights advocates compared the legal status of wives with that of chattel slaves, and not only in terms of property rights. Like a slave, a wife had no legal say in determining the guardianship of her children; a husband could designate someone else in his will to rear the children after he died. He could also apprentice their children away without her consent. A wife might legally be "chastised" with a stick, so long as it was no bigger around than her husband's thumb. Ironically, a wife could sometimes escape liability for crimes she might commit or debts she might incur, since acts committed in a husband's presence were considered to be under his orders and hence his responsibility.

Married women who went to work in factories in the early 1800's were not allowed to keep their wages. (Culver Pictures, Inc.)

In truth, there were significant differences between the status of wives and slaves. For one, a wife recovered her separate legal identity when the marriage ended, whether by the death of her husband or, much more rarely, by divorce. A husband could bequeath his whole estate to his wife for use during her lifetime; whatever other provisions he might make, a widow was always entitled to at least one-third of her husband's estate (a widower inherited the entirety of his wife's property). A widow sometimes enjoyed a legal and social status superior to that of both wives and unmarried women.

In addition, American wives actually had more legal rights than the common law implied. From colonial times into the nineteenth century, the practice of dowry was not uncommon. The money, property, and goods that a woman brought to her marriage protected her from an improvident or abusive husband. Although he could use her dowry during the marriage, that portion was always considered to be exclusively hers when the marriage ended, and she could recover it from her husband's creditors or other heirs. Moreover, wives could seek and win legal remedies in courts of equity (or chancery), many of which were established as early as 1776. Wives could also protect their property through various equitable devices, such as antenuptial contracts (agreements between the prospective spouses before the marriage itself) and trusts (which placed a woman's property under the control of a third party, thereby avoiding having her possessions merged with her husband's). Courts of equity specifically addressed situations in which neither common law nor statute provided any fair recourse.

Most important, wives, unlike slaves, had the option of removing themselves from intolerable relationships. Divorce that allowed both parties to remarry was rare until the twentieth century, but arrangements comparable to legal separation offered a way out and restored some of a married woman's rights. Slaves had no such option, unless their masters let them buy their freedom or voluntarily emancipated them. Slave marriages themselves existed under a different set of rules altogether from those governing marriages between free individuals. Slave marriages had no legal validity and could be abrogated when either party was sold or traded to a new master. In the eyes of the law, slaves were considered to be property, so neither husband nor wife had any superior property right. Paradoxically, this lack of property rights may have promoted more equality between the sexes in slave marriages.

Community Property. A third tradition, derived originally from Roman civil law, existed in parts of the United States as well. Unlike English common law, Roman law explicitly recognized that families consisted of separate individuals, all of whom had distinct rights and responsibilities within the family. In this tradition, property was owned jointly by both husband and wife, a pattern that forms the historical basis for modern community property statutes.

Early settlers in North America from the mainland of Europe brought with them laws derived from this tradition. Acadians from French Canada were relocated to Louisiana following France's defeat by Britain in the mid-eighteenth century. There they developed a distinctive Cajun culture while continuing French legal traditions. By the time the United States purchased the Louisiana territory from France in 1803, these laws had been further modified by the French Revolution but remained fundamentally different from English common law.

Likewise, Spain transplanted its legal traditions to a vast empire in North and South America. Mexico won independence from Spain in 1821 but soon lost much of its territory, first in the struggle for Texas independence (1836) and then later in the Mexican-American War (1846-1848). Although settled predominantly by Anglo Americans, Texas decided in 1840 to maintain the earlier Mexican tradition of community property. Similarly, the Treaty of GUADALUPE HIDALGO, which concluded the Mexican-American War, asserted that the property of Mexican residents and nonresidents was to be "inviolably respected." To accomplish this and avoid confusion, the community property system that had prevailed before the war was soon adopted in most of the states formed from the Mexican Cession.

Although other states have experimented with community property, this system has been most firmly entrenched in states where French and Spanish traditions set the pattern—Arizona, California, Louisiana, Nevada, New Mexico, and Texas, plus the western States of Idaho and Washington. In theory, wives enjoyed more rights under this system, since it recognized the separate property that each party brought to the marriage and the joint, common ownership of property acquired during the marriage. In reality, however, community property has ensured far less equality of property rights than one might expect. Although both husband and wife might own property jointly in both their names, the husband had the sole right to manage or dispose of the property. The justification for this policy was that only one person in a family should have decision-making power, since disagreements over the management of property might disrupt marital harmony. This approach, which designated the husband as "head of the family," was not so different in effect from declaring the husband to be the one person in a marriage; by this logic, only a husband, not a wife, could sue in cases involving the community property, for example. Moreover, a wife had no right to bequeath her portion of the community property, although a husband could do so. Should a wife die before her husband, all community property reverted to him; in other words, a wife was distinctly limited in her ability to make a valid will, just as under common law.

Early Married Women's Property Statutes. Married women gained greater control over their property for various reasons, many having little or nothing to do with a commitment to women's rights. The first married women's property law was passed in Mississippi in 1839. The law referred to only one sort of property—slaves—and was designed to protect slaveholding families from economic ruin. By classifying the slaves that a wife either brought to her marriage or inherited afterward as her separate property, the law limited creditors' ability to seize all of a family's slaves. Similar acts in Maryland (1843) and Arkansas (1846) also focused on protecting family property in slaves; new laws in the Midwest left management and

Susan B. Anthony's activist efforts led to passage of a New York law that gave women control over their own earnings. (AP/Wide World Photos)

control of a wife's property (especially real estate) in a husband's hands while safeguarding it from creditors. In the volatile economy of the early nineteenth century, these new laws maximized a husband's assets for taking risks while protecting him and his family from the full consequences of those risks.

In the Northeast, however, other influences were at work. In New York and New England, for example, a key factor was the codification movement, which held that laws should be simple and clear enough for ordinary people to understand and which rejected the niceties of equity rulings as inherently undemocratic. Codification's very emphasis on democracy complemented the nascent women's rights movement. New York passed its first married women's property act in 1848. Although it reflected the common concern with protecting family property, it was seen as revolutionary by some contemporaries and soon was rejected by the courts (largely on the grounds of violating the implicit property rights of the marriage contract). Its passage three months before the first women's rights convention, the SENECA FALLS CONVENTION, signaled a shift in perspective from a concern with family property to a focus on women's rights. By the mid-1850's, activists such as Susan B. ANTHONY and Ernestine Rose were lobbying for married women's control over their own wages, and in 1860 New York passed a married women's earning act, which also increased wives' rights in matters of guardianship. A Massachusetts act in 1854 and an Ohio act in 1861 addressed the legal disabilities of wives as well as the protection of family assets.

By the end of the 1870's, most of the common law states had enacted married women's property legislation that usually protected wives' wages and sometimes other forms of property. The agitation for these rights indirectly stimulated a women's rights movement that increasingly focused on suffrage rather than on further economic gains. In the community property states, change occurred in less clearly marked stages. In California, for example, the legislature began modifying family law in favor of wives around 1891, initially by requiring a wife's consent before a husband could give away parts of their community property; in 1901, her written consent was required before he could sell household furnishings or her clothes.

Imbalances continue to exist under both systems in the late 1900's. Several former common law states still limit the ability of wives to engage in a business in their own right; some community property states consider a wife's inheritance of community property taxable, whereas a husband's is not. In short, the struggle to win equal economic rights for wives is far from over.

SUGGESTED READINGS. Mary R. Beard's path-breaking *Woman as Force in History: A Study in Traditions and Realities* (1946), a long-neglected classic, is an excellent introduction to this topic. Marylynn Salmon's *Women and the Law of Property in Early America* (1986) and Norma Basch's *In the Eyes of the Law: Women, Marriage, and Property in Nineteenth Century New York* (1982) provide detailed and clear studies of the early laws in action. Articles in *Women and the Law: A Social Historical Perspective*, edited by D. Kelly Weisberg (1982), synthesize much research. Finally, Leo Kanowitz' *Women and the Law: The Unfinished Revolution* (1969) discusses women's property rights throughout the country, past and recent, in the context of all their legal rights.—*Susan Wladaver-Morgan*

Prosser, Gabriel (1775, Henrico County, Va.—Oct. 7, 1800, Richmond, Va.): African American slave insurrectionist. Prosser—the slave of Thomas Prosser—was a literate coachman and blacksmith. He planned and then helped to lead a large, unsuccessful slave revolt in Richmond, Virginia, on August 30, 1800. Inspired by the DECLARATION OF INDEPENDENCE, he aimed to free his fellow slaves in Virginia by overpowering whites around Richmond. After bad weather and security leaks doomed the slaves' attack, Prosser and other rebel leaders were hanged. The insurrection did much to heighten southern whites' fears of blacks.

Prostitution: Practice of engaging in sexual relations for payment. Prostitution has existed in the United States since the colonial period; among the first prostitutes were English, Scots, and Irish female INDENTURED SERVANTS and African female slaves. Prostitution was outlawed in colonial America as early as 1672, but the rate of prostitution increased in direct proportion to population growth. It increased significantly in the late nineteenth century with the spread of industrialization and dramatic changes in economic and family life. The rapid growth of cities, westward expansion, and the flood of immigration are all conditions which created populations that patronized prostitutes.

Because prostitution was illegal in the United States and because it was widely condemned as immoral, few women in the nineteenth century willingly revealed their participation in prostitution. Many public officials believed that prostitution was a necessary evil that helped to preserve the virtue of pure women by providing a sexual outlet for their husbands. In most cities, prostitution flourished in more or less officially designated "red-light districts." Directories to houses of prostitution were widely available and circulated among businessmen and male travelers. New Orleans' French Quarter and Storyville district and San Francisco's Barbary Coast, for example, were among the best-known districts.

Many American prostitutes worked in brothels, where the madams in charge proved themselves adept as businesswomen, frequently amassing considerable money and property and existing in cooperation with local law enforcement, to whom they often paid bribes. Some women turned to prostitution in order to supplement income because they could find no other work; others had been ostracized by their communities because of a perceived lapse in virtue; still others seem to have viewed prostitution as simply work. In the early twentieth century, several well-publicized cases revealed that women had been forced into a "life of vice" with the aid of drugs. The outcry against "white slavery" ultimately resulted in the Mann Act (1910), which outlawed transporting women across a state line for immoral purposes. This law, however, did not have much impact in San Francisco's Chinatown, to which women purchased in China were routinely imported for prostitution.

Despite the efforts of social reformers of the 1800's and 1900's to put an end to prostitution or create new economic opportunities for prostitutes, the practice continues. It thrives not only in desperate inner-city neighborhoods but also in wealthy suburbs and business districts. Not only women but also some men work as prostitutes. Some feminists in the late 1900's expressed concern over prostitutes' health, well-being, and civil rights, believing that the practice should be humanized if it could not be eliminated. Yet attempts to unionize prostitutes have been largely unsuccessful. Prostitution remains illegal in the United States, except in Nevada.

SUGGESTED READINGS. Barbara Meil Hobson's *Uneasy Virtue: The Politics of Prostitution and the American Reform Tradition* (1987) provides what is probably the best comprehensive history of the politics of prostitution in the United States. Eleanor F. Miller's *Street Woman* (1986), Ruth Rosen's *The Lost Sisterhood: Prostitution in America, 1900-1918* (1982), and Charles Winick's and Paul Kinsie's *The Lively Commerce: Prostitution in the United States* (1971) are all excellent sources on this subject. Anne Butler's *Daughters of Joy, Sisters of Misery: Prostitution in the American West* (1985) offers an excellent account of prostitution from a regional perspective, while Mark Thomas Connolly's *The Response to Prostitution in the Progressive Era* (1980) examines prostitution between 1890 and 1917.

Protective legislation for women: Laws passed during the "sweatshop era" of the early twentieth century as part of an overall social reform effort to improve working conditions for women. These laws varied from state to state, but they typically limited the hours that women could work, prohibited work at night, or even prohibited women from working in certain occupations. This type of law is now considered a form of sex discrimination and is illegal under Title VII (1972) of the CIVIL RIGHTS ACT OF 1964.

These laws were viewed as a means of relieving some of the worst aspects of industrialization, namely overwork and exploitation among women workers, during a time when all forms of labor legislation were likely to be struck down by the courts as unconstitutional. Employers opposed these laws, calling them a violation of the right of "freedom of contract" of the worker as well as the employer. According to the then-current economic doctrine of laissez-faire, the state had no business interfering with the "wage bargain."

After the 1890's, state legislatures also passed laws affecting men workers in dangerous jobs (such as mining) or in particular occupations (baking or cigarmaking). Sometimes they were upheld by the courts; sometimes they were struck down. The same was true of laws directed at women workers specifically. For example, in 1907 a New York court invalidated a law which would have prohibited women from working at night, saying the law was "certainly, discriminative against female citizens, in denying to them equal rights with men in the same pursuits." In 1910, however, Illinois upheld a law restricting women's working hours to ten per day. No clear pattern had yet emerged.

Legislation designed to protect women workers also served to keep women out of higher-paying jobs. (Culver Pictures, Inc.)

It could be argued that laws affecting women specifically protected women who were weaker than men economically and were not in an "equal" situation with their employer to bargain over wages and working conditions. A law which, for example, regulated hours for women but not men might be justified on the grounds that women were physically frailer than men, especially because of health concerns regarding pregnancy and childbirth. This reasoning was used in *MULLER V. OREGON*, the landmark 1908 Supreme Court decision which successfully argued that a law limiting women's work to "only" ten hours per day and sixty per week was constitutional.

These laws were intended to protect women workers by defining their main function as maternal and domestic and restricting their paid work. The effect of the laws was to reinforce women's subordinate position in the workforce. They also limited women to lower-paid jobs and tended to eliminate women from traditionally male skilled trades. It was not until the 1920's that effective feminist opposition to "protection" in favor of "equality" for women emerged among social reformers.

SUGGESTED READINGS. For an account of legal arguments and a broad analysis of the social movements favoring and opposing these laws, see Susan Lehrer's *Origins of Protective Labor Legislation for Women, 1905-1925* (1980). For a historical discussion of women's work and protective laws, see Alice Kessler-Harris' *Out to Work* (1982).

Protest organizations. *See* **Activist and protest organizations**

Protestant–Catholic relations. *See* **Catholic–Protestant relations**

Protestants: Protestantism was the second major form of Christianity to arise in western Europe and is the majority religion of the contemporary United States. Originating in the sixteenth century as a radical reform movement within the ROMAN CATHOLIC church in Germany and Switzerland, Protestantism quickly formed itself into four distinct church traditions.

LUTHERANS set down roots in Germany and spread to Scandinavia and North America. The Reformed and PRESBYTERIAN churches flourished in France, Holland, Hungary, Scotland, England, North America, and Switzerland. Arising at this same time on Swiss soil were the historic peace churches known as Anabaptists and including today's MENNONITES, AMISH, HUTTERITES, and Brethren. Finally, the Church of England, or Anglicanism, began as a national church under Henry VIII, whose daughter Elizabeth I gave to Anglicanism a comprehensive character as a Protestant church within the Catholic tradition. The comprehensive approach of the official church of England was not congenial to all English Protestants, and the seventeenth century saw the beginnings of an important new family of Protestant churches, the English free churches. The free church tradition reflected Anabaptist influence and featured congregational church order, the separation of church and state, a "puritanism" in worship and life, and a noncreedal biblicism in theology. These churches were important in shaping American Protestantism and include the CONGREGATIONALISTS, the Society of Friends (QUAKERS), and the BAPTISTS.

Methodist pastor meets with his youth choir to offer guidance and encouragement. (Jeff Greenberg, Unicorn Stock Photos)

The METHODISTS were another church family to separate from Anglicanism, but their spiritual life was significantly informed by seventeenth century continental Pietism (a renewal movement among German Lutherans). Methodism emphasizes heartfelt religious experience, personal sanctity leading to Christian perfection, and warm Christian fellowship expressed in hymn singing. Included in this family are the Holiness and the PENTECOSTAL churches which arose directly or indirectly from Methodism and which give prominence to Christian sanctification or holiness. The Holiness group includes such denominations as the Church of God, the Church of the Nazarene, and the Salvation Army. African Americans were prominent in the formation and growth of the Holiness church movement. They were also instrumental in the emergence of the Pentecostal church movement in the interracial Azusa Street revival in Los Angeles (1906). Pentecostalism subsequently divided along racial lines to form a number of different denominations, the largest black Pentecostal group being the Church of Christ in God, founded by Charles H. Mason. Perhaps because it encourages lay leadership, Pentecostalism assumed a variety of forms such as the "sign preaching" of Appalachian Pentecostals, which involves the handling of poisonous snakes and the drinking of poison. What generally distinguishes these churches is the belief that a Spirit baptism and the gift of tongues are essential signs of Christian experience.

The Christian belief that Christ is to come a second time is an important feature of the millennialist family of churches. In the United States, belief in the anticipated return of Christ and the thousand year reign of peace that is to accompany the millennium was especially intense in the nineteenth century. Early in that century among revivalists such as Charles Finney there was a widely held belief that Christ's coming would be hastened by a general spiritual awakening and moral reform. Thomas and Alexander Campbell were even convinced that the millennial age would commence with the restoration of the church to its primitive condition. With Barton Stone, the Campbells established a new Protestant denomination, the Disciples of Christ. Utopian experiments also flourished in this millennialist climate and added to the rich diversity of American Protestantism. For the SHAKERS and the ONEIDA COMMUNITY, the future age was thought to be a present reality. The Shakers hailed their founder, Mother Ann Lee, as the female Messiah and Christ's second appearing on earth. The Oneida communitarians created a society governed by the ideal of millennial freedom, equality, and morality within the context of a system of "complex marriage." The modern SEVENTH-DAY ADVENTISTS represent the largest and most influential millennialist church denomination. The JEHOVAH'S WITNESSES represent the most radical member of this family with their conviction that the present age is under Satan's dominion and is soon to be superseded by the age of the saints, the "elect of Jehovah," who will be the sole members of the Messianic Kingdom.

A final diverse group of churches includes MORMONS, CHRISTIAN SCIENTISTS, and UNITARIAN-Universalists. These churches are characterized not by what they have in common but rather by their divergence from normative Protestant beliefs and practices. Mormonism, or the Church of Jesus Christ of the Latter-day Saints, has a strong Adventist element. Mormons believe that centuries ago America was visited by Christ and that Zion will be built in that country, and they believe they have a special revelation in the *Book of Mormon*. Christian Science was founded by Mary Baker EDDY, who taught that Divine Mind is the only reality and that sickness and death are the effects of false thinking. Unitarianism is a type of rational Christianity that rejects trinitarian teachings and the divinity of Christ and subscribes to congregational principles of church order.

Protestantism and Immigrant Communities. Of these families of Protestant churches, some came into existence in America. Important among these are the Mormons, the Christian Scientists, the Seventh-day Adventists, and the Shakers. Most Protestants, however, immigrated to North America from Europe. During the American colonial period, the English free churches established themselves along the eastern seaboard. Pennsylvania was particularly notable for attracting immigrant groups from Europe in the seventeenth century. The colony's policy of religious toleration encouraged the settlement of Mennonites, Baptists, Baptist Brethren (Dunkers), Seven-day Baptists, and Calvinists from Germany as well as Dutch Quakers and Swiss Amish.

Lutherans were to be an especially prominent ethnic Protestant enclave in the United States. The waves of German and Scandinavian immigrants after the 1840's led to the multiplication of independent Lutheran organizations, as many as sixty-six at one time. Often these immigrant communities sought to preserve not only their confessional integrity but also their linguistic and national identities. Others advocated bringing Lutheranism into closer contact with the main currents of American religious thought. While tensions still exist within this family, the end of the nineteenth century saw a movement toward an intrafamily ecumenism which culminated in a major merger of Lutheran synods in the 1960's with the formation of the Lutheran Council.

Immigration from the south has contributed to the modest growth of Protestant churches among the traditionally Catholic peoples of Central and South America. Though Seventh-day Adventists, Methodists, and Baptists have all sought to establish a Protestant presence among these Spanish-speaking peoples, the Pentecostal movement has registered the greatest successes. As early as 1917, the Mexican-born Francisco Olazabal experienced a Pentecostal baptism of the Holy Spirit and resolved to leave the Methodists to become a pastor of the Assemblies of God. In 1936 he organized the Concilio Olazabal de Iglesias Latino Americano. Other Spanish-speaking churches include the Defenders of the Faith, the Iglesia Bando Evangélico Gedeón, and the Latin-American Council of the Pentecostal Church of God of New York.

Protestantism and American Indians. As early as 1644, Thomas Mayhew, a New England Puritan minister, began missionary work among the Algonquian-speaking Indians on the islands of Martha's Vineyard and Nantucket. Puritan John Eliot, known as apostle to the Indians, learned the Massachuset language so that he would be able to preach among them. Even more typical of the Protestant approach to missionary activity was Eliot's preparation of the first translation of the Bible into the language of an American Indian people. Roger Williams, cofounder of Rhode Island and defender of religious conscience, also found time to write a dictionary of Indian words and phrases. Interest in converting the native populations of North America preoccupied Protestants in the middle and southern colonies as well. Pennsylvania Quakers evangelized among the Delawares, and Baptists preached among the Cherokees of the Carolinas. In the eighteenth century, a colony-wide spiritual revival known as the GREAT AWAKENING sought to extend the Protestant presence among American Indians by establishing mission or charitable schools, the most famous of which became Dartmouth College.

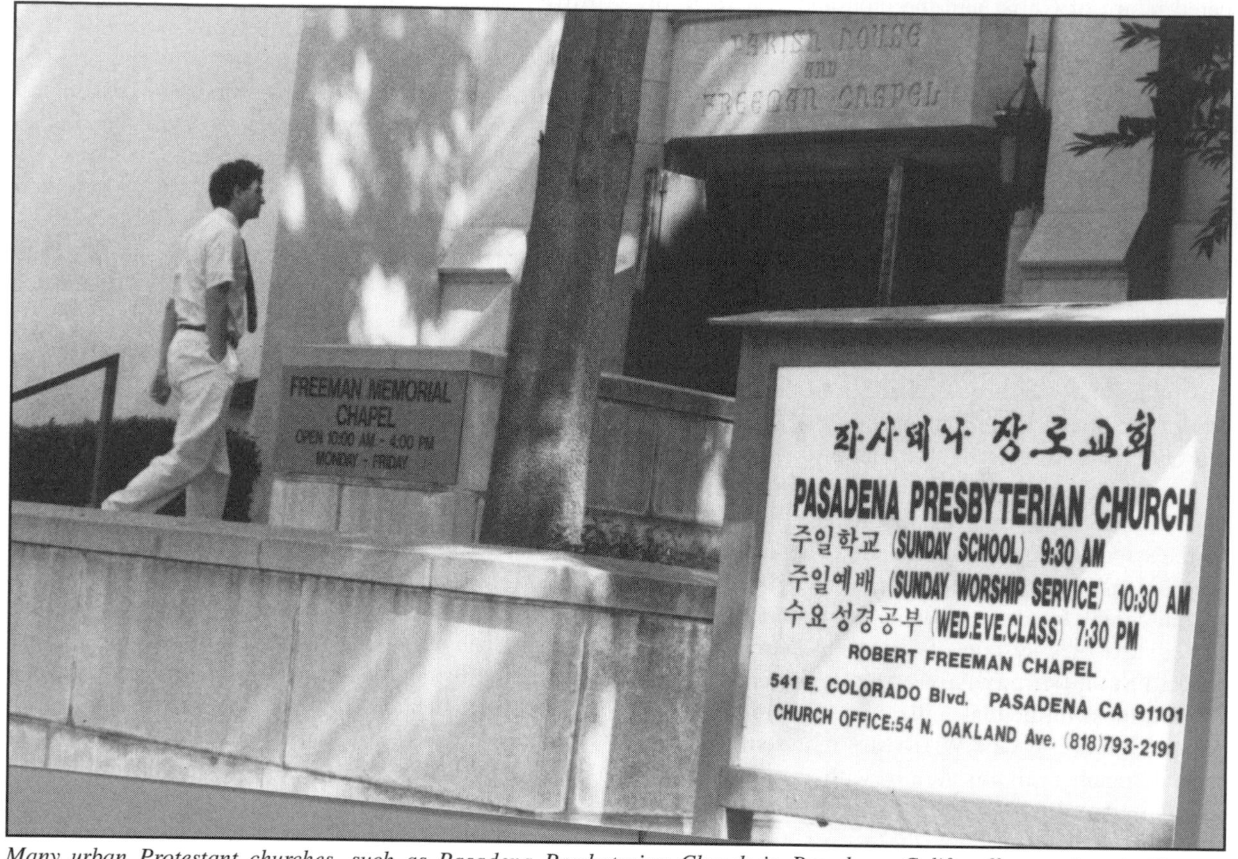

Many urban Protestant churches, such as Pasadena Presbyterian Church in Pasadena, Calif., offer services in Korean, Spanish, or other languages for large immigrant populations. (Valerie Marie)

This process of conversion continued throughout the nineteenth century in connection with the reservation system; consequently, today it is impossible to find a reservation without one or more Christian churches. Yet in spite of the Euro-American presence that Christianity represents, American Indian peoples continue to preserve the integrity of the traditional ways. Some have sought to revive their religious heritage; others have appropriated Christian elements to reexpress their own religious vision. Even where denominational Christianity is found on reservations today, American Indian religious experience and heritage makes itself felt in worship and belief. On the Qualla Boundary Reservation in North Carolina, for example, the Christianity of the Eastern Cherokees is Baptist. Yet the ordinance of baptism, so central to the Baptist family of churches, recalls the traditional Cherokee purification act known as "going to the water." A similar tendency to integrate Christian beliefs and practices with indigenous traditions is evident among African American churches.

African and African American Traditions. Protestantism has always proven adaptable to new experiences and circumstances, as is evident in its adoption by African Americans before the Civil War. By the 1760's the conversion of blacks to Protestantism had already begun. Baptist and Methodist churches, with an emphasis on conversion, personal experience, and congregational governance, were especially popular among black slaves and former slaves. In the North, black churches formed independent denominations at an early date. The AFRICAN METHODIST EPISCOPAL (AME) CHURCH was organized in 1816; the African Methodist Episcopal Zion church was founded in 1820. After the Civil War, most blacks in the South also formed their own separate churches.

Protestant experience in the antebellum South among African Americans found perhaps its most impressive expression in what has been called the "invisible institution" among African slaves. A church or churches without official membership rolls, ordained pastors, official meeting places, or approved ceremonies, these clandestine slave churches adapted Protestant forms of religion to African American experience. This process of religious enculturation resulted in "spiritual preaching," communal hymn singing, rhythmic movement, and dance becoming basic features of African American churches. Many of these features gained renewed and transformed expression among the twentieth century Holiness-Pentecostal churches. The spiritual, for example, became GOSPEL MUSIC when blues and jazz were added to the formula. In the twentieth century, some black Protestant churches promoted black consciousness, the image of Jesus as a black Messiah, and the development of a black theology and a theology of liberation.

Protestant Belief. The cardinal principles of Protestantism can be summarized in three phrases: Salvation is by Scripture alone, by grace alone, and by faith alone. The first of these beliefs arises from the conviction that sinners are personally and powerfully addressed by God's redemptive Word, which is the instrument of God's grace or saving power. It is thus through the encounter with the biblical word in private devotion or public worship that sinners are forgiven and enter into a living fellowship with Christ, a fellowship defined by an unreserved trust called faith. Scripture, grace, and faith are no less important for the Protestant conception of the church than they are for the Protestant understanding of the Christian life. Having given priority to the Bible in the drama of Christian redemption, Protestants from the beginning thought of the church as a Bible-centered reality, as a community of believers gathered for the purpose of hearing the Gospel preached. Protestants also looked to the Bible as the final authority in matters of faith, discipline, practice, ethics, and church order.

Protestant experience and belief required a redefinition of Christian ministry and vocation. Protestants believe that, by virtue of God's saving power and a common baptism, there is only one priesthood of all believers and only one Christian vocation. Instead of the special Christian monastic vocation of Catholicism, every Christian is called to witness to the faith in word and moral action in the world. Protestants also believe that there is no special sacramental priesthood. Every Christian has a priestly authority to appear before God, to pray for others, to teach and bear witness to the Gospel, and to confess, repent, and be forgiven. There is thus no "higher" calling for Christians, and the only difference between lay Protestants and their clergy is one of function.

SUGGESTED READINGS. For a thorough presentation of the central religious beliefs, practices, and cultural expressions of Protestantism, see Martin E. Marty's *Protestantism: Its Churches and Cultures, Rituals and Doctrines, Yesterday and Today* (1974). A standard treatment of the history and theological development of Protestantism is found in John Dillenberger's and Claude Welch's *Protestant Christianity: Interpreted Through Its Development* (1988). A concise presentation of Protestant beliefs, worship, church order, and families is found in Thomas E. Helm's *The Christian Religion: An Introduction* (1991). A valuable one-volume reference book of American religion is J. Gordon Melton's The Encyclopedia of American Religions (1987). This volume contains essays on the major religious groupings in part 1 and short entries on individual religious groups in part 2.—*Thomas E. Helm*

Public housing developments: Housing built with government support and intended for occupation by low-income families or individuals. Low-cost housing built in the 1930's by the Public Works Administration to eliminate slum conditions might be considered the first set of housing projects. Plans called for African American management staffs and for rents below market rates. By 1936, the federal government had spent \$130 million on public housing in more than thirty cities. Black architects, contractors, and builders were hired to plan and construct many of these housing projects.

Over the next several decades, most public housing

projects were segregated, constructed for all-black or all-white occupancy. Until 1962, the decision of whether to segregate was at the discretion of local housing authorities. Even when what was called urban renewal began around 1949, discrimination by private developers continued without much government interference. In December, 1972, the U.S. Supreme Court ruled that residents of racially segregated housing projects could sue to integrate the projects.

High rise public housing developments dot the horizon in New York City. (Photo Agora)

On August 1, 1968, President Lyndon B. Johnson signed the Housing and Urban Development Act. The act authorized more than $5 billion for a three-year program to provide 1.7 million units of new or rehabilitated housing for low-income families. A home ownership assistance program was to provide eligible low-income purchasers with interest-rate subsidies that would lower their mortgage payments. Other subsidies assisted with construction or rehabilitation of rental or cooperative housing. The Department of Housing and Urban Development gave grants and direct loans to local housing authorities or authorized public agencies. It also aided in home purchases by allowing for transfer of ownership to tenants who could obtain financing or who had developed equity through performing maintenance on housing structures.

President Gerald Ford signed the Housing and Community Redevelopment Act on August 22, 1974. It consolidated many of the housing programs that had proliferated since 1949. The act provided for block grants to local governments based on the population, degree of overcrowding, and degree of poverty within their jurisdiction. The grants could be used at community discretion to meet such needs as urban renewal, aid to displaced families, housing code enforcement, and provision of water and sewer facilities. The act also authorized a rent subsidy program of $1.23 billion. The act was designed to shift control of housing projects from the federal to the local level.

About one million black households lived in public or subsidized housing in 1980. That number included about one-fourth of all the black households that were renting in that year. During the fiscal year ending on September 30, 1990, the Department of Housing and Urban Development allocated $7.37 billion for low-income housing assistance. Those funds went for public housing as well as housing payments to public agencies and college housing. Older Americans occupied an increasing percentage of low-income public housing units. They filled less than 1 percent of the occupied units in 1960, with that proportion rising to about 16 percent in 1970 and about 27 percent in 1980 and 1988.

Suggested Readings. John Pynoos' *Breaking the Rules: Bureaucracy and Reform in Public Housing* (1986) looks at some of the problems of public housing and its management; *Critical Perspectives on Housing* (1986), edited by Rachel G. Bratt, Chester Hartman, and Ann Meyerson, is a collection of papers from a conference on public housing. Mary A. Vance has compiled two bibliographies on the subject, *Public Housing* (1982) and *Low Cost Housing* (1983). A number of government studies and reports are also available.

Pueblo Revolt of 1680: Uprising by the Pueblo Indians against Spanish colonial rule in New Mexico. It was the most successful American Indian revolt against European occupation in American history.

When the Spanish came to New Mexico in 1598, they established themselves principally along the Rio Grande Valley. They founded the capital of Santa Fe in 1609. Spanish settlers and missionaries soon established ranches and missions that depended on Indian labor. Pueblo Indian villages in the region became subject to Spain. Spanish policy toward the natives was based on exploitation rather than expulsion. Indian groups kept their lands but had to pay heavy Spanish taxes in the form of crops, woven goods, and labor.

The Spanish system was especially oppressive of native religion. The PUEBLOS' religion was outlawed and driven underground. Religious paraphernalia, such as masks and KACHINAS, was seized and publicly burnt. Shamans were punished, even executed, for holding to the old faith. The Pueblos' suffering became more intense in the 1660's, when drought parched the land and Apache raids terrorized the people.

POPÉ, a Tewa shaman from the Pueblo of San Juan, gave the Indians leadership in the crisis. He was faithful to the old religion; not even beatings by the Spanish could make him change his ways. Popé realized that the only hope of rebellion against the Spanish rulers was to strike everywhere simultaneously. After years of planning and preparation, he set the date of August 10, 1680, for the uprising. As a ruse to trick the Spanish, Popé sent Christian Pueblo chiefs the wrong date. The chiefs informed the Spanish authorities, as Popé expected, that the attack would fall on August 13.

The surprise was total. All over New Mexico, Spanish missionary priests, ranchers, and soldiers were killed in Indian raids. One by one, Pueblo communities joined the rebellion. Soon, only Santa Fe remained in Spanish hands. Governor Antonio de Otermin and the town's surviving citizens and soldiers were besieged by a Pueblo army of five hundred warriors. After heavy fighting, the Indians were repulsed, but it was a costly victory for the Spanish: They abandoned the province and fled south.

The Pueblo Revolt thus ended in victory for the Pueblo people. Out of some twenty-eight hundred Spanish, around four hundred were killed, including twenty-one out of thirty-three missionary friars. Never before, and never since, had Indians gained so total a triumph over a European colonial power.

Pueblo independence lasted a dozen years. If later accounts are to be believed, Popé became a tyrant, demanding a complete renunciation of all aspects of European civilization, even beneficial imports such as fruit trees. Popé died before the Spanish returned to the region in 1692.

SUGGESTED READINGS. An absorbing account of the Pueblo Revolt can be found in Alvin M. Josephy's *The Patriot Chiefs* (1962). Less colorful, but no less informative, are sections of Arrell Morgan Gibson's *The American Indian* (1980) and Alice B. Kehoe's *North American Indians* (1992). Another fine narrative retelling is John Upton Terrell's *Pueblos, Gods, and Spaniards* (1973).

Pueblos: Group of Southwest Indian tribes who lived in permanent villages made of stone or adobe. Pueblo is derived from the Spanish word for village. Village dwellings were often multistory "apartment house" arrangements, giving a distinctive stamp to the culture. Pueblo peoples were not united politically or linguistically, but shared similar lifestyles.

Culturally, Pueblo peoples are divided into two groups: the western Pueblos, and the eastern Pueblos. The western Pueblos are represented by the HOPIS, Zunis, Acomas, and Lagunas. The eastern, or Rio Grande, Pueblos include the Tewas, Tiwas, Towas, and Keresans.

The Pueblo peoples are of great antiquity. They are considered descendants of the ANASAZI (Navajo for "ancient ones"), whose culture reached its peak from about 1100 to 1300. Also known as "cliff dwellers," the Anasazi often built their villages atop ledges on the sides of cliffs. An example of an Anasazi settlement can be seen at Mesa Verde, Arizona.

Before the Spanish colonial period, Pueblos were theocratic societies, ruled by the heads of religious societies. Religion was supremely important, and it was largely the domain of men. Much religious ceremony was devoted to placating the gods so they would send rain to a dry country and ensure a good harvest. Social and religious activity centered around the kiva, a round underground structure used for ceremonies.

Kachina (or katchina) societies were essential to Pueblo life. KACHINAS were spirit beings—not necessarily gods—who could help bring rain and ensure good crops. Male society members impersonated kachinas with elaborate masks and costumes at religious rituals.

The Pueblos were farmers who grew corn, beans, and squash. The eastern Pueblos in the Rio Grande valley had more access to irrigation. The western

Pueblos such as the Hopis and Zunis practiced so-called "dry" farming with great success.

First white contact came as early as 1539, when Father Marcos de Niza visited the region. Serious Spanish colonization did not begin until 1598, however, when a major expedition under Juan de Oñate pushed north from Mexico. At the time of Oñate's arrival, it is estimated there were sixty-six separate Pueblo settlements with an estimated total population of forty thousand. Spanish control largely centered in New Mexico's Rio Grande valley.

Historic Taos Pueblo in Taos, N. Mex., photographed in 1941 by Ansel Adams. (National Archives)

Spanish colonization was based on the exploitation, not the expulsion, of American Indian populations. The Spanish imposed high taxes and persecuted native religions. In 1680, the Pueblos rose in revolt, and New Mexico was free from Spain until 1692.

During the 1700's and early 1800's, disease and raids from Shoshonean (COMANCHE and UTE) and Athabascan (APACHE and NAVAJO) tribes depleted Pueblo populations. Just prior to the United States' takeover of the Southwest, the Tewas of the Taos pueblo rose up against the occupying American forces on January 19, 1847. The revolt was suppressed at the cost of some 150 Tewa lives. Later, Pueblo-American relations improved as the Pueblos cooperated with the U.S. government against the Apaches and others.

In 1975, the Pueblo peoples joined with the Navajo, Jicarilla Apache, and other tribes to form CERT, the COUNCIL OF ENERGY RESOURCE TRIBES. CERT monitors oil, gas, and coal production on the reservations, giving the tribes a voice in the regulation of those industries. In the 1990's, the Pueblos numbered more than thirty thousand people and continued to practice many of their ancient ceremonies and rituals.

SUGGESTED READINGS. Alvin M. Joseph, Jr.'s, *The Indian Heritage of America* (1968) contains material on Pueblo life. A good historical overview of the Pueblos is provided by John Upton Terrell's *Pueblos, Gods, and Spaniards* (1973), and in a chapter of Alice B. Kehoe's *North American Indians* (2d. ed., 1992).

Puerto Rican Family Institute: Organization in New York City founded in 1971 to provide a range of services to Spanish-speaking families. These include support to those with acute domestic problems to enable them to keep their children at home, preventive programs to keep youth out of trouble with the law, and assistance for new arrivals from Puerto Rico. The institute maintains a mental health clinic and gives technical assistance to other agencies in New York City.

Puerto Rican Legal Defense and Education Fund (PRLDEF): Nonprofit organization founded in 1972 to assist and protect the rights of Puerto Ricans and other Latinos. It undertakes class-action suits protesting civil rights violations in housing, education, employment, health, and political participation. PRLDEF also maintains a placement service for Latino lawyers and offers advice as well as financial assistance to Latinos who are considering a career in the legal profession. It puts out a publication entitled *Civil Rights*.

Puerto Rican Traveling Theater: Theatrical group founded in New York City in 1967 by Miriam Colon Valle, known as the first lady of Puerto Rican popular theater. Its main purpose is to make the dramatic arts available to those who would otherwise not have access to them, such as low-income Puerto Ricans. This goal is accomplished by taking productions to the streets and barrios of the cities. The group primarily performs plays by Latino playwrights, and it presents works written in both English and Spanish. It also conducts bilingual training programs and a playwrights' program.

Puerto Ricans: By 1990, about 40 percent of the more than six million Puerto Ricans resided on the United States mainland, composing about 13 percent of U.S. Latinos. Centuries of Spanish and U.S. colonialism in Puerto Rico have made Puerto Ricans unique in their dual identity as Latin Americans and legal citizens of the United States. Puerto Ricans have proudly conserved their rich cultural heritage and continue to display an extraordinary level of nationalism.

Early History. The Caribbean island of Puerto Rico was first inhabited around the first century by an indigenous fishing and gathering people whose origins are unclear. By the second century, a more advanced culture known as the Igneris arrived in Puerto Rico from Venezuela via the Caribbean Antilles. Part of a larger group of Arawak Indians, the Igneris made great achievements in ceramic pottery until their gradual disappearance in the sixth century. Subsequent groups of migrating Arawaks (Ostinoids) had more complex social organization and are remembered for their strong emphasis on ceremonial rites.

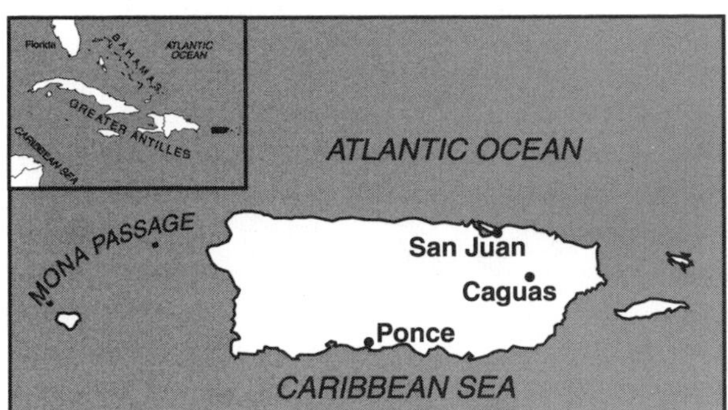

PUERTO RICO

Beginning around the eleventh century, successive Arawak migrations brought increasingly more technologically advanced peoples known as TAINOS to Puerto Rico. Their highly developed agricultural and nautical abilities were matched by their complex tribal organization, which established local village chiefs or *caciques* who served on regional councils governed by a supreme island *cacique*. The Tainos flourished for centuries throughout the Caribbean, moving easily from island to island, and were among those encountered by Christopher Columbus on his second voyage in 1493. Their rich cultural heritage left a significant mark on Puerto Rican culture, in food, language, architecture, and place names. By the time Juan Ponce de León established a permanent Spanish colony on Puerto Rico in 1508, the island's Tainos were under repeated attack by the Caribs, another native people from the Antilles known as fierce warriors.

Spanish Colonialism in Puerto Rico. Ponce de León first named the naturally protected harbor of San Juan "Puerto Rico," destined later to become the Spanish name for the island. Under military pressure from the Caribs, Taino island chief Agueybana formed a pact with Ponce de León, seeking to maintain his rule by paying tribute to the Spanish in the form of food and Indian labor for the gold mines. By 1511, however, the Spanish intentions to colonize and enslave the Tainos became clear.

The defiant Agueybana led an unsuccessful rebellion in which thousands of TAINOS were slaughtered. Survivors were either enslaved or forced to join the retreating Caribs, who later harassed colonialists throughout the Caribbean. By the mid-1500's the Tainos were virtually wiped out as a result of war, disease, and slavery engendered by the conquest.

The island became fortified as a strategic Spanish outpost and remained sparsely populated until the latter 1700's, when African slaves were utilized to increase agricultural activity. The island's agricultural base gradually expanded through the 1700's and 1800's, particularly during periods when Spain relaxed its trade restrictions on the island. Coffee, sugar, and tobacco production became increasingly lucrative for Puerto Rican producers.

A day for celebration at the Puerto Rican Day Parade, New York City. (Hazel Hankin)

In Puerto Rico, African slaves always remained a relatively small percentage of the total population and thus never posed a serious threat to Spanish domination. Instead, political challenge eventually came from the descendants of the Spanish settlers themselves. Those Puerto Ricans born and reared on the island, who had defended it for decades against Spain's European enemies, became known as Criollos. Increasingly resentful of the tight hold that the Spanish throne kept over the island, Criollos began in the mid-1800's to form various secret societies. Led by Puerto Rican patriots such as Ramón Emeterio Betances and Segundo Ruíz Belvis, their goal was to foment an insurrection with the ultimate aim of acquiring the island's independence from Spain.

In 1868, an uprising in the town of Lares briefly set up a provisional government, but the rebellion was decisively repressed, its leaders either killed or forced into exile. Just decades later, however, Spain became beleaguered by internal strife with the fear of renewed revolts among its colonies, leading it to grant considerable autonomy to Puerto Rico in 1897. The effort proved futile since one year later, Spain was drawn into the brief but disastrous Spanish-American War. The defeated Spanish were compelled to cede Puerto Rico as well as Cuba and the Philippines to the United States.

U.S. Colonialism in Puerto Rico. Following the withdrawal of Spanish troops, U.S. military forces quickly overwhelmed sporadic armed resistance from Puerto Rican patriots and installed a military government that ruled for two years. Civilian authority began with the Foraker Act of 1900, which established that Puerto Rico now "belonged to but did not form part of the United States of America." The United States would henceforth appoint a governor to wield executive power over the "unincorporated territory." With U.S. congressional control over Puerto Rico's trade and tariff structures along with federal jurisdiction over the island's judiciary system, Puerto Rico had become a colony of the United States.

In 1917, the Jones Act further defined the contours of U.S. colonialism by creating a popularly elected, Puerto Rican consultative legislature and imposing U.S. citizenship on all Puerto Ricans. Unfortunately for Puerto Ricans, the "gift" of citizenship stipulated mandatory military service in the U.S. armed forces only months prior to the bloody trench battles of World War I. Puerto Ricans would later fight and die in disproportionately large numbers in every subsequent American war.

The Jones Act created political tensions that remained unaddressed for thirty years. In 1948 the Truman Administration asserted the need for Puerto Rican self-determination. The first step, Truman argued, was for Puerto Ricans to elect their own governor. The Elective Governor Act was passed in 1947 at Truman's behest, transferring a significant amount of local power to the colonial establishment of Puerto Rico, and Puerto Ricans installed their first freely elected governor in 1949. Governor Luis Muñoz Marin proposed a political formula whereby Puerto Rico would "freely enter" for an indefinite period into a "compact" of political association with the United States. Public Law 600 of 1950 permitted Puerto Rico to submit a draft of a constitution for approval by the U.S. Congress. With the implementation of limited constitutional rule under federal supervision, the island became known as the Freely Associated State of Puerto Rico and the United States informed the United Nations that Puerto Rico could no longer be considered a colony.

Puerto Rican Migration to the Mainland United States. Under U.S. domination, Puerto Rico's economy was transformed by a heavy penetration of largely unregulated, American corporate investment. A once-fertile agricultural base was replaced with an industrialized, capital-intensive manufacturing sector. With special federal tax exemptions, corporations profited greatly while large numbers of Puerto Rican laborers were displaced from the island's traditional economy. Lax environmental standards resulted in ecological damage and roughly 13 percent of the island remained occupied by U.S. military bases.

The result was increasing unemployment throughout the island, leaving migration to the mainland United States as the only viable option for many Puerto Ricans. The Puerto Rican exodus that ensued eventually led to the creation of "two Puerto Ricos" in which more than two out of every five Puerto Ricans—already U.S. citizens—became residents of the U.S. mainland. While mass migration provided a political "relief valve" to island unemployment, Puerto Ricans who settled first in New York City, and later in Chicago and other major cities, soon emerged as one of the poorest ethnic groups in the United States.

Puerto Rican girls, proud of their heritage, seen here in New York City. (Hazel Hankin)

Puerto Rican Political Movements. Worsening conditions on the island inevitably led to popular discontent. By the 1930's, the Nationalist Party of Puerto Rico, led by Pedro Albizu Campos, openly rejected adherence to electoral strategies of change and became the voice of a militant Puerto Rican independence movement. When Albizu was arrested and convicted of seditious conspiracy in 1936, the effects reverberated throughout the island and the mainland. Before long, the Puerto Rican community in New York formed pro-independence organizations and organized collections for the cause on the island.

By the 1960's, Puerto Ricans living in the United States drew inspiration from growing civil rights struggles and began to openly protest racist discrimination. Piri Thomas, a radical Puerto Rican poet, wrote *Down These Mean Streets* (1967), which chronicled the poverty and degradation of *El Barrio* (the New York Puerto Rican community). By decade's end, a Puerto Rican youth gang known as the Young Lords became transformed into a political activist organization in New York and Chicago, declaring their militant support for the Puerto Rican independence movement. On the island, the independence struggle likewise grew in strength, fueled by opposition to the Vietnam War which was taking a particularly high toll on Puerto Rican youth.

By the mid-1970's, a revolutionary nationalist organization known as the Fuerzas Armadas de Liberación Nacional Puertorriqueño (FALN) became active in the Puerto Rican communities of New York and Chicago, carrying out hundreds of clandestine bombings against American corporate and military targets associated with U.S. colonialism in Puerto Rico. Although Federal Bureau of Investigation (FBI) and police crackdowns imprisoned most of the underground movement or drove it into exile by the early 1980's, the FALN's legacy inspired the formation of new, militant independence organizations such as the Movimiento de Liberación Nacional Puertorriqueño (MLN), which mobilized support of imprisoned Puerto Rican *independentistas* both on the mainland and in Puerto Rico.

Cultural Contributions. The radical nationalism of this period led to the creation of highly politicized Puerto Rican cultural centers in virtually all large Puerto Rican mainland communities, including New York, Chicago, Philadelphia and Hartford, Connecticut. These centers display an impressive level of community organization, sponsoring alternative high schools, day care centers, cultural events, legal support networks, AIDS prevention and treatment programs, and other activities, all of which stress pride in Puerto Rican culture and the need for self-determination of the Puerto Rican nation. Yearly "Puerto Rican Day" parades organized by the community centers display the extraordinary attachment of Puerto Ricans to their national culture.

With a strong cultural attachment to the island, Puerto Ricans on the mainland have made a substantial impact upon North American culture. The immense Roberto Clemente Public High School of Chicago bears the name of one of the many Puerto Rican greats who have played major league baseball. Tragically, Clemente was killed in a 1972 plane crash while volunteering in a relief effort to help victims of an earthquake in Managua, Nicaragua.

Beloved Puerto Rican baseball star Roberto Clemente died in a plane crash in 1972 on a relief mission to aid Nicaraguan refugee victims. (National Baseball Library, Cooperstown, NY)

Countless *bodegas* (corner grocery stores) and eating establishments in the streets of the New York Bronx and elsewhere have introduced other Americans to the island's cuisine. This is typified by creole-style pork dishes, *plátanos* or *tostones* (cooked or deep fried plantains), the popular *queso con pasta de guayaba* (cheese and guava paste delicacy), and a variety of pastry and desserts such as *brazos gitanos* ("gypsy arm" jelly rolls) and *flan de coco* (milk custards). The deep aroma of *café bustelo* or other Puerto Rican-style espresso coffees are never far behind.

Generations of Puerto Rican musicians and dancers have produced influential styles that testify to the subtle differences between the arts of Puerto Rico and those of Cuba and the Dominican Republic. Bandleader Charlie Palmieri helped to popularize the *pachanga* rhythm in the early 1960's, helping to pave the way for subsequent generations of Puerto Rican SALSA musicians to play to wider audiences. Andrés Jimenez and Roy Brown became two popular figures in the 1970's and 1980's for their expression of both Puerto Rican folk traditions as well as protest and pro-independence FOLK MUSIC.

Geographically split between their homeland and the impoverished conditions of the largest slums in the United States, Puerto Ricans have retained an extraordinarily strong sense of cultural awareness and nationalism. Puerto Rico's political future remains uncertain in view of persistent demands from a vocal and long-standing independence movement.

SUGGESTED READINGS. For a comprehensive overview of Puerto Rico's history, see Arturo Morales Carrión's *Puerto Rico: A Political and Cultural History* (1983). For emphasis on the political history of U.S. colonialism in Puerto Rico, see Raymond Carr's *Puerto Rico: A Colonial Experiment* (1984). Manuel Maldonado-Denis' *The Emigration Dialectic: Puerto Rico and the U.S.A.* (1980) provides an excellent analysis of Puerto Rican migration. An anthology treating many aspects of the Puerto Rican experience can be found in *The Puerto Ricans: Their History, Culture and Society* (1980), edited by Adalberto López. For statistical data concerning mainland Puerto Rican communities, see Clara E. Rodríguez's *The Puerto Ricans: Born in the U.S.A.* (1989).—*Richard A. Dello Buono*

Puritans: Separatist Protestant group that left England to found early American colonies. Puritanism arose as a

Massachusetts woman portrays a Puritan settler in Plymouth, Mass. (Cleo Freelance Photo)

renewal movement within the Church of England in the 1500's. Early Puritans were largely Calvinist in theology, and thus stressed human sin, divine grace, biblical authority, preaching as the heart of Christian worship, and personal piety.

While the movement was fundamentally religious, it took on political overtones with Oliver Cromwell's revolt, which briefly took control of England in 1649. Resistance to the Puritan desire for religious reform caused some Puritans to separate from the Church of England. Some of these separatists left England to seek greater religious and political tolerance for a time in Holland, where they were influenced by Dutch Mennonites. Returning to England briefly, these separatist Puritans (later known as the Pilgrims) set sail for the New World, founding Plymouth Colony in 1620 and Massachusetts Bay Colony in 1629. They became the prototypical WHITE ANGLO-SAXON PROTESTANTS (WASP) and the mythological founders of American society, even though other groups had preceded them.

New England Puritans were noted for their extreme piety, which emphasized both personal and public religious devotion to God, and disapproved of "sinful" behavior such as gambling, dancing, drunkenness, adultery, and any unnecessary work or frivolity on Sunday. The Puritan fear of eternal damnation was captured in Jonathan Edwards' classic sermon, "Sinners in the Hands of an Angry God" (1741). The guilt associated with sexual sin was immortalized in Nathaniel Hawthorne's novel *The Scarlet Letter* (1850).

New England Puritans, like their coreligionists in England, viewed the Bible not only as the authoritative guide to personal life and matters of religion but also as a foundation text for Christian government. They attempted to structure a holy commonwealth around their interpretation of the Bible. Ironically, although the Puritans in New England had themselves suffered considerable persecution in England, they began to exhibit extreme intolerance for persons and groups holding alien beliefs or behaviors. The Salem witch trials of the 1690's are well-known. Less well known is the Puritans' persecution and banishment of QUAKERS and of BAPTISTS, such as Roger Williams.

Directly or indirectly, Puritanism gave birth to or influenced major denominations such as the CONGREGATIONALISTS, UNITARIANS, BAPTISTS, METHODISTS, and PRESBYTERIANS. Puritans founded Harvard and Yale universities as schools for preparing ministers.

In a broad sense, Puritanism set its stamp on North American Protestantism as a whole. Thus "puritan" has come to be associated not with membership in a specific religious denomination, but rather with extreme asceticism in personal life and with an associated intolerance for unchaste sexual behavior, drunkenness, gambling and card-playing, movie-going, and dancing, especially among conservative or evangelical Protestants. Puritan vision and influence clearly survived in the modern efforts of Jerry Falwell's Moral Majority, Pat Robertson's Christian Coalition, and other groups associated with the Christian Right political movement of the 1980's and 1990's. Their general goal of restructuring the United States as a Christian nation, free of abortion, homosexuality, and other perceived evils, can be seen as an attempt to build a Christian commonwealth across the United States.

SUGGESTED READINGS. See Alden T. Vaughan's *The Puritan Tradition in America, 1620-1730* (1972), Kai Erikson's *Wayward Puritans* (1966), and Jerry Falwell's *Listen, America!* (1980).

Pushmataha (1764, near Noxubee County, Miss.—1824, Washington, D.C.): Choctaw chief who opposed TECUMSEH's efforts to form an Indian Confederacy and led Choctaw warriors against Creeks in the campaign under Andrew Jackson. Jackson described Pushmataha (also written Apushmataha) as the greatest and bravest Indian he had ever known. In 1824 Pushmataha led a delegation to Washington, D.C., where he met with the president, the secretary of war, and members of the Cabinet. He was buried with full military honors.

Quakers: Christian sect that believes in simplicity, pacifism, and the "inner light" in every human being. Officially called the Religious Society of Friends, the movement began in England around 1652 under the inspiration of George Fox (1624-1691). As members of one of the more radical PURITAN sects, Quakers endured considerable persecution, both in England and colonial America. For example, a law provided a stiff fine for any ship's captain bringing a Quaker into the Massachusetts Bay Colony, and four Quakers were hanged between 1659 and 1661.

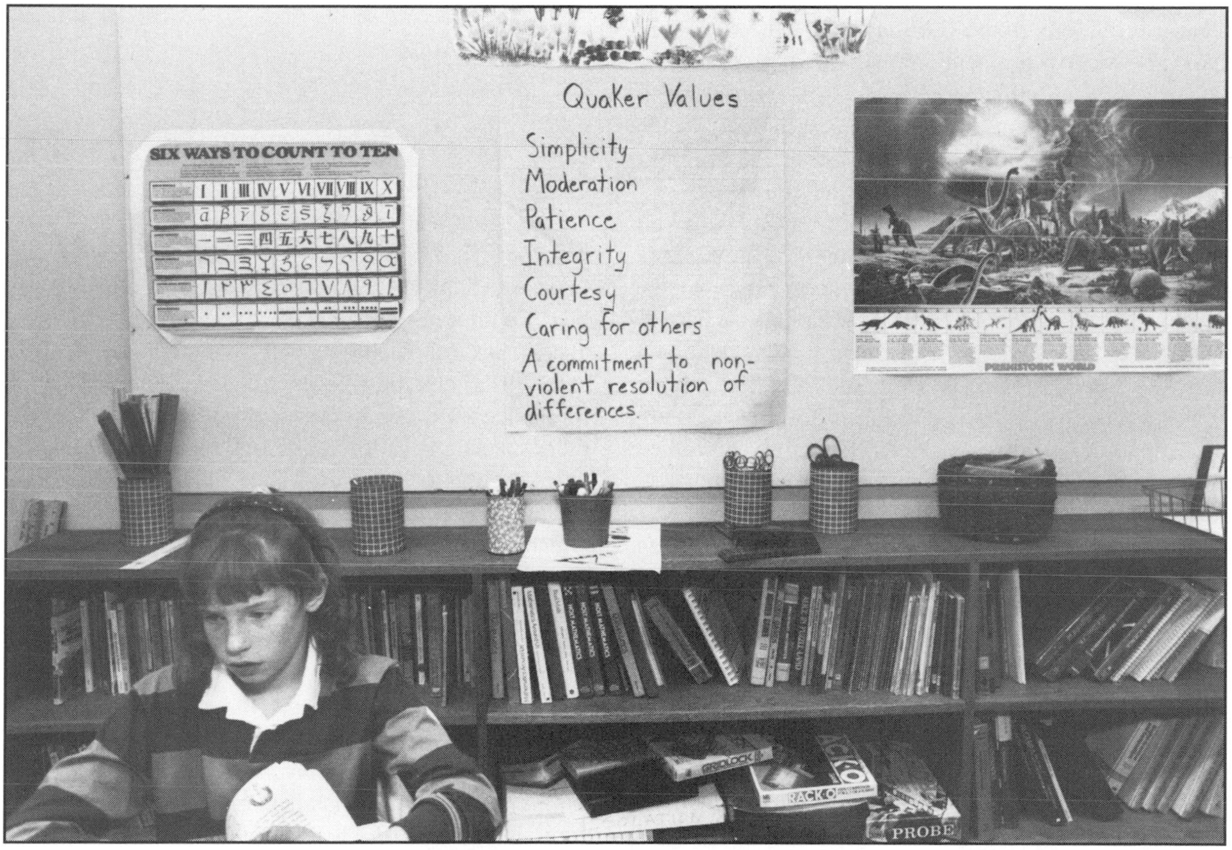

Toleration improved after 1672, when George Fox visited Rhode Island, at that time a refuge from religious persecution. In other areas at this time, notably Virginia and North Carolina, Quakers met less resistance, and by 1680 more than fifteen hundred had settled in New Jersey and begun organizing their religious community.

The greatest stimulus to Quaker expansion in colonial America was the founding of Pennsylvania by William Penn in 1681, and the rapid growth of Philadelphia in the 1680's. By the end of the century, Pennsylvania was thriving and the Quakers had become a powerful religious movement second only to the Massachusetts Puritans. The decline of the Quakers in Pennsylvania was hastened by the influx of other groups, the sect's intensifying commercialism, and a schism brought on by the attacks of George Keith (1639-1716), a convert from Presbyterianism. By 1750 Quaker zeal for reform had subsided and the Quaker faithful had become more insular.

The Quaker tradition of social activism, from abolitionism to the sanctuary movement, has been motivated by such "Quaker values" as a "commitment to nonviolent resolution of differences." (Hazel Hankin)

Modern Quakers consider themselves somewhat

apart from Roman CATHOLICS and PROTESTANTS, rejecting all formal dogma, clergy, and sacraments. Quaker services, called Meetings for Worship, traditionally take place in simple Meeting Houses without the adornment of steeples, altars, stained glass, or other decoration; the gatherings are silent except for spontaneous prayers, readings, or personal reflections.

American Quakers have a long tradition of commitment to social justice. They have opposed war, capital punishment, SLAVERY, and discrimination. John Woolman (1720-1772) speaks eloquently against slavery in his famous journal, and the Massachusetts Quaker poet John Greenleaf Whittier (1807-1892) was one of the leaders of the ABOLITIONIST MOVEMENT. Known for their important role in helping slaves escape through the UNDERGROUND RAILROAD, the Quakers also established a home for freed slaves after the Civil War at Frogmore, South Carolina. In the 1980's, some Quakers were prominent in the SANCTUARY MOVEMENT to aid Central American refugees. The American Friends Service Committee, formed in 1917, puts Quaker values to work in social justice and community development projects around the country.

In Quaker theology God's love is available to all through each individual's "inner light." The Bible is of central importance to Quakers, who generally praise Jesus' example without agreeing on his precise nature. Quakers emphasize spiritual growth in atonement, and they substitute for Heaven, Hell, and Purgatory a hope for achieving the good life in this world. Quakers are unsympathetic to divorce, have always given women full equality, do not have a unified stand on abortion, and tend to support full rights for homosexuals.

SUGGESTED READINGS. *The Journal of John Woolman* (1871, repr. 1972) is one of the masterpieces of spiritual autobiography. Margaret Hope Bacon's *The Quiet Rebels: The Story of the Quakers in America* (1969) is a good survey. For a quick sketch, see "The Society of Friends" by Melvin B. Endy, Jr., in *Encyclopedia of the American Religious Experience: Studies of Traditions and Movements* (1988). The essay "What Is a Quaker?" in *Religions of America* (1975), edited by Leo Rosten, is an excellent analysis of the beliefs of modern Quakers.

Quinceañera: Semipublic celebration to mark the fifteenth birthday of Mexican, Mexican American, and some Central American girls. It functions in much the same way as an Anglo debutante ball, allowing girls to be introduced to potential marriage candidates in a formal, socially acceptable way. The fiesta traditionally began with a religious ceremony at church for family and friends, followed by a party with food and dancing at the girl's house or a rented hall. The young girl, called the quinceañera, begins the dance with her father or some other special male. Some Catholic church authorities in cities such as Los Angeles have objected to the trend toward lavish, expensive quinceañera celebrations, which impoverish poor families and stress social rather than religious aspects. Yet the tradition persists in most sectors of the Mexican American community.

The quinceañera celebration, marking a girl's fifteenth birthday, is sometimes quite lavish. (Robert Fried)

Quinn, Anthony (b. Apr. 21, 1915, Chihuahua, Mexico): Latino actor. Quinn began his acting career in 1936 in the play *Clean Beds*. Among his notable stage performances were *A Streetcar Named Desire* in 1961 and *Zorba* in 1983. Quinn has performed in more than 175 films, including *Irish Eyes Are Smiling* (1944), *The Guns of Navarone* (1961), *Lawrence of Arabia* (1962), *Zorba* (1964), and *The Greek Tycoon* (1978). He received Academy Awards for his performances in *Viva Zapata!* (1952) and *Lust for Life* (1956). In addition to acting, Quinn is a published author and produced screenwriter, and his paintings, sculptures and serigraphs have been exhibited in the United States, Paris, and Mexico City.

Anthony Quinn in a scene from the stage musical Zorba, *in which he reprised a film role from nearly twenty years earlier.* (AP/Wide World Photos)

Quotas—admissions: Allocation of a specific number or percentage of college enrollments based on such criteria as race, gender, religion, or national origin of applicants. Though originally used to limit the number of minorities admitted, quotas have more recently been instituted to benefit minorities and limit white enrollment, according to critics.

Unofficial quota systems have been used to shape the student bodies and faculties of some colleges and universities in the United States. At times, quotas have served to maintain a group's enrollment below a certain ceiling. Between the world wars, for example, qualified Jewish applicants in excess of a 10 to 15 percent quota were subjected to discriminatory admissions practices at various Ivy League universities and medical schools. In the 1980's, Asian Americans charged they were the victims of similar quotas at Stanford University, Harvard University, and the University of California at Berkeley, among other institutions. Berkeley officials asserted that Asian Americans were "overrepresented" in the student body, revealing an admissions policy based on proportional shares of the state and national population.

Should college admissions be based solely on merit, on preferential treatment, or on some combination of both? The question of quotas is part of the intense debate on this subject. As AFFIRMATIVE ACTION and outreach programs became institutionalized in the 1970's and 1980's, colleges and universities aimed to create a student body more reflective of an increasingly multicultural society. Many institutions reserved a set number of places for those whom affirmative action was designed to help: originally women and African Americans, later other minority groups. Diversity was written into the mission statements of many higher educational institutions, and it even became a factor in accreditation decisions.

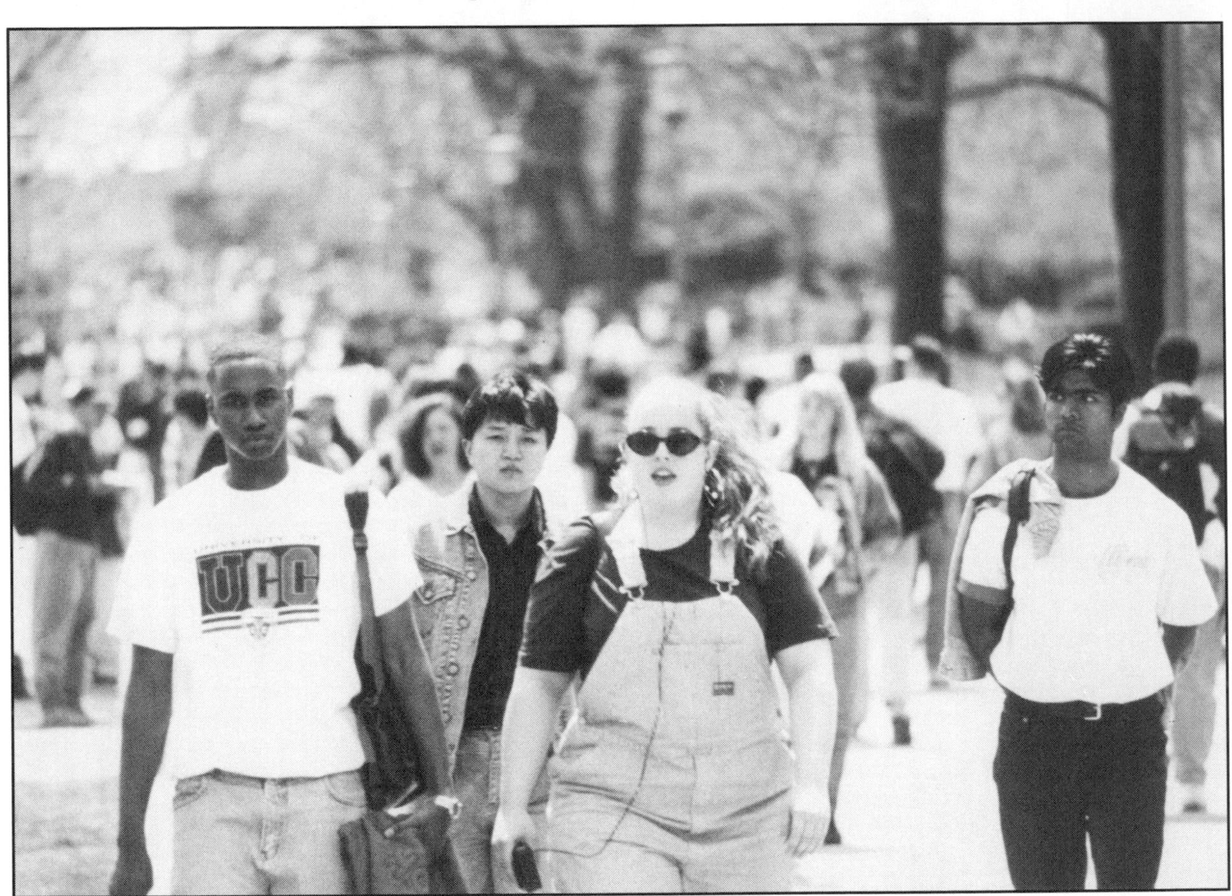

College admission quotas have been controversial, but they have helped many minority students achieve their educational goals. (Joel Dexter, Unicorn Stock Photos)

It was only a matter of time, however, before qualified white applicants charged institutions with REVERSE DISCRIMINATION. In a landmark decision (*RE-*

GENTS OF THE UNIVERSITY OF CALIFORNIA V. BAKKE, 1978), the U.S. Supreme Court ruled against a university plan that set aside a specific number of places (racial quotas) for minority applicants. Allan Bakke (who was white) got into medical school, but the Court, in Solomon-like fashion, said that race could be taken into consideration by an institution in pursuit of the goal of greater ethnic diversity. Thus, affirmative action goals were upheld.

As a means of promoting greater diversity and making HIGHER EDUCATION in the United States a multicultural experience, affirmative action has clearly had a salutary effect. In 1992, women, minorities, and foreign students were studying at American universities, and at their law and medical schools, in record numbers. From 1970 to 1990, women displaced men as the majority among American students. Though not as dramatic, the gains of African Americans and Latinos have been substantial as well. The makeup of the 1992-1993 freshman class at Berkeley provides a good indication of changes in admissions trends: 35.1 percent Asian American, 30.3 percent white, 19.3 percent Latino, 7.5 percent African American, and 1.4 percent American Indian.

SUGGESTED READINGS. For an overview of admissions quotas and affirmative action, see Stephanie Witt's *The Pursuit of Race and Gender Equity in American Academe* (1990). For the Bakke perspective, see Frederick R. Lynch's *Invisible Victims: White Males and the Crisis of Affirmative Action* (1989). Articles in the weekly *Chronicle of Higher Education* offer a constantly updated perspective on these issues.

Quotas—immigration: Allocation of a specific number of entry visas to immigrants based on such factors as hemisphere or country of origin, family relationship to U.S. citizens, or occupation. Quotas have been the cornerstone of the selection system limiting immigration into the United States since 1921. In 1990, the official term for quotas was "worldwide limitation."

No force has been more influential in making the United States a multicultural society than IMMIGRATION. By 1992 more than 55 million documented immigrants and unknown numbers of illegal immigrants had come to colonial America and the United States from all over the world.

Although it is sometimes called a "nation of immigrants," the United States has not always welcomed newcomers. Politicians responded to nativist and xenophobic Americans who feared that they would lose their jobs, religion, way of life, and even health to suspect foreigners. At various times in the 1800's, U.S. immigration law excluded certain nationalities such as the Chinese and certain classes of people such as the poor, sick, or politically radical. Restrictionist groups pressed the government to use LITERACY TESTS to keep out "undesirables," a step it took in 1917.

As the United States population grew and the frontier "closed," the number of applicants for admission seemed to some too great for the country to absorb. Outspoken opponents of immigration were especially alarmed by the record number of immigrants admitted between 1900 and 1920 (14.5 million), and sought new ways to restrict immigration.

After World War I, their efforts culminated in the temporary quota acts of 1921 and 1922. This legislation limited annual immigration to 3 percent of the number of a particular nationality residing in the country as counted in the 1910 census. These measures were aimed at reducing mass migration from southern and eastern Europe and increasing arrivals from northern and western Europe, the sources of earlier immigration. Canada and Mexico were among a few countries exempted from the quotas.

In subsequent major U.S. IMMIGRATION LEGISLATION (1924, 1952, 1965, 1986, and 1990), numerical limitations or quotas have regulated the flow of legal immigration into the United States. For example, after forty years, the quota system based on national origins was replaced in 1965 by unified quotas of 120,000 for immigrants from the Western Hemisphere and 170,000 for those from the Eastern Hemisphere. In 1978 the hemisphere-based system was replaced by a single worldwide total of 290,000. Two years later the figure was lowered to 270,000, with greater allowances made for REFUGEES.

The IMMIGRATION ACT OF 1990 introduced some key changes. It increased the available number of worldwide immigrant visas to an annual level of 700,000 until 1994 and 675,000 thereafter, and it made some visas available through a lottery system. A quota system still gave preference to family members and those with certain occupational specialties, and it created a new category of immigrants for wealthy foreigners willing to invest at least one million dollars in a new American business.

In the early 1990's there were still far greater numbers of applicants than available entry visas. This ensured that some form of preferential system—whether called quotas or something else—would remain an es-

European immigrants crossing the Atlantic in 1902. The huge influx of newcomers between 1900 and 1920 led to quota acts in 1921 and 1922. (Library of Congress)

sential part of U.S. immigration policy.

SUGGESTED READINGS. An excellent standard reference is *American Immigration Policies: A History* (1963), by Marion Bennett. For details of the 1986 act, see Nancy Humel Montwieler's *The Immigration Reform Law of 1986* (1987). For more recent information in this rapidly changing field, consult *The Guide to American Law Supplement 1990* (1990).

Quotas—racial: Allocation of a specific number or percentage of jobs or school enrollments, based on the race of applicants. Since the 1960's, restrictive racial quotas, when proved, have been declared illegal.

From 1875, when the Chinese and Japanese began to be denied entry into the United States, until 1952, there was a racially based discriminatory immigration policy that clearly favored white European immigration. The Immigration Act of 1917 and the Immigration Act of 1924 established an Asiatic barred zone and a rigid system of immigration quotas to put an end to what Senator Hiram Johnson called "the day of indiscriminate acceptance of all races." Only in 1952 did new legislation remove racial barriers to immigration and naturalization.

Racial quotas have also affected minority access to education. Between the two world wars, racial and religious quotas were used to restrict the number of black and Jewish students at American institutions of higher learning.

In the 1960's, the Civil Rights movement and accompanying legislation focused the country's attention on gross inequities in American society. To redress these, affirmative action and equal employment opportunity programs were widely established. Both types of program sought to create opportunities for the victims of past discrimination, especially African Americans and women, in arenas formerly closed to them, such as corporate boardrooms, trade unions, and even the Supreme Court. In promoting these objectives, temporary preferential treatment for racial groups was permitted. Schools and companies set up goals for recruiting and hiring more minorities based on proportional group representation in the population. Other measures to compensate for inequality and lack of opportunity, such as busing, involved balancing numbers of white and nonwhite students in an effort to integrate public schools.

Busing students to distant schools in an attempt to balance the racial makeup of the schools was a controversial effort. Opponents called busing programs a form of quota system. (Cleo Freelance Photo)

Over time, these remedies became viewed as racial quotas by critics of affirmative action, and lawsuits charging reverse discrimination were filed against employers and educational institutions. In 1978 in the famous Bakke case (*Regents of the University of California v. Bakke*), the Supreme Court determined that the University of California's admissions policy giving preference to minorities amounted to a system based on racial quotas and was therefore in violation of civil rights laws. The Burger court, however, did not prohibit using race as a consideration in admissions policy.

Backers and opponents of affirmative action have debated the issue of gender and racial preferences and their relation to unlawful quotas. In the 1980's, the Supreme Court—itself more diverse as a result of heightened race and gender consciousness—showed a willingness to restrict the application of preferential treatment.

Judicial and legislative differences over civil rights and affirmative action culminated in new civil rights legislation in the 1990's. President George Bush vetoed the first version of the Civil Rights Act in 1990, objecting that the bill would "introduce the destructive forces of quotas into our nation's employment system." With a clause disavowing quotas, the revised 1991 act was signed into law by the president.

With few exceptions (import/export restrictions and immigration quotas), quotas have been very unpopular with Americans. Yet most Americans support the broad aims of including greater numbers of minorities and women in traditionally exclusive institutions such as the U.S. Congress and local country clubs. Many difficult questions remain unanswered: When does racial representation become a quota? How much affirmative action is enough? When will the United States be able to rely on a color-blind merit-based system to fill vacancies on the Supreme Court, in prestigious law and medical schools, or in local police and fire departments?

Suggested Readings. For a critical view of affirmative action, see Frederick R. Lynch's *Invisible Victims: White Males and the Crisis of Affirmative Action* (1989). For justifications of affirmative action and discussion of its problems, consult *Affirmative Action in Perspective* (1989), edited by Fletcher Blanchard and Faye Crosby. The U.S. Equal Employment Opportunity Commission's *Indicators of Equal Employment Opportunity: Status and Trends* (1990) covers fair employment issues.

R

Race—scientific theories: Race commonly refers to a group of people who are socially defined as distinct on the basis of shared physical traits. Physical differences such as skin color were readily noticed by ancient peoples and became, throughout history, the subject of much philosophical and scientific speculation. With the growth of the field of biology, and then psychology and anthropology, early European scientists began to attempt to classify racial groups, explain their origins, and measure the differences between them. Their theories both reflected and justified the prevailing belief that some racial groups (specifically Caucasians) were inherently superior to others.

The term "race" arrived relatively late in human discourse. It was coined by French naturalist George Louis Leclerc Buffon in 1749. Yet race, according to Ashley Montagu and other social scientists, is actually a social category used to determine status rather than a legitimate biological concept. Early scientists (notably in the eighteenth and nineteenth centuries) assumed that race was biologically based, inherited, and immutable. Modern scientists, on the other hand, have not been able to agree on the number of races that exist in the world, and geneticists have had trouble identifying the gene or sets of genes responsible for race. Because of such issues and because race is such an emotional and frequently misused term, many scientists have come to believe that the term has outlived whatever scientific usefulness it may once have had. If members of society refused to believe that skin color and certain other physical traits were important, the concept of race would not exist.

Race is at once both social ideology and social reality. Racial designations, interacting with historical, social, economic, political, and cultural factors, promote the development of racial identity; racially ascribed cultural products (such as music, art, and linguistic patterns); and, invariably, RACISM and discrimination. Racial and cultural diversity is characteristic of contemporary American society, yet race itself defies precise definition. Race and the intense emotions that it provokes have plagued American scholars, politicians, and citizens for more than two centuries.

Scientific theories about race must be understood in their social context. Scientists, in spite of their claim to objectivity, are affected by prevailing cultural and religious beliefs. For example, the idea of a common origin for humankind (monogenesis) went against the teachings of the Bible and was therefore rejected by many early scientists. The eighteenth century Enlightenment assumption that all people were potentially good and intelligent prompted scientists to explain what they saw as the "primitive" state of nonwhite peoples and the "civilizing" influence of white blood. For centuries, scientists persisted in theorizing about innate racial differences in spite of conflicting and inadequate evidence. It was not until cultural anthropologists such as Edward Burnett Tylor and Franz Boas started seriously studying nonwhite societies in the late 1880's that these biologically based theories were challenged. As the social sciences became more sophisticated in explaining the effect of social environment (rather than nature and heredity)

As members of a racially diverse society, Americans can either celebrate their differences or use them as a wedge to keep people apart. (Cleo Freelance Photo)

on human development, the scientific justification of racism began to crumble. Thus, scientific theories of race are products of their time, coinciding with early stages in the growth of the natural and social sciences until the latter half of the 1900's.

Racial Categories. The first attempt to classify human races was made in 1684 by François Bernier, a French doctor. Besides the Europeans, Far Easterners, and "blacks," he singled out the Lapps as a separate race. In the next century, the Swedish botanist Carolus Linnaeus made a great step forward in declaring that all humans were members of one species on the grounds that they could produce fertile offspring. He divided humans into four "varieties": Homo Europaeus, Homo Asiaticus, Homo Afer, and Homo Americanus—divisions that roughly correspond to the perceived skin colors of white, yellow, black, and red/brown. In the late 1700's, Johann Friedrich Blumenbach coined the term "Caucasians" for European whites and noted the presence of Mongolians, Ethiopians, Americans, and Malays.

Three large racial groups are often recognized today: Caucasians, Mongoloids, and Negroids. These correspond in the United States to European Americans; Asian Americans and American Indians; and African Americans and others of African ancestry, respectively. Technically, Latinos may belong to any race; many Mexican Americans, for example, are of mixed race. In practice, however, Latinos are often viewed by European Americans as a separate "race" because of their relatively brown skin color.

Attempts to describe racial characteristics are overgeneralized but nevertheless provide some boundaries. Caucasians, originating in Europe, northern Africa, and western Asia, are distinguished by a lighter (whitish, pinkish, or reddish) skin complexion; blond or brunette, wavy or straight hair, with a marked tendency toward balding; blue or green eyes; straight, hooked, or pug noses; conspicuous jaws; and relatively long torsos. Mongoloids, tracing their origins to northern and eastern Asia, are distinguished by a yellow to brown skin complexion; straight black hair; wide cheekbones; low or unpronounced nose bridges; and almond-shaped or slanted eyes caused by epican-

The racial variety among Latinos is evident in members of this Brazilian band in New York. (Hazel Hankin)

thic folds of the eyelids. Negroids, originating in Africa, are distinguished by light tan to dark brown skin complexion; brown to black hair that is typically described as kinky, curly, or woolly; thick lips and noses; and high foreheads. These broad racial groupings are taught in some school textbooks and have been incorporated into U.S. Census forms as white, American Indian/Alaska Native or Asian/Pacific, and black.

Yet modern scientists cannot agree on the exact number of races in the world or even on an acceptable definition of race. For example, Polynesians and Australian aborigines defy simple categorization. While some people of presumed Caucasoid stock, such as Asian Indians with dark skins, were physically more like Negroid peoples, others classified as Negroid, such as the Kalahari Bushmen, were light-skinned. This confusion has led many to attempt to develop more precise classification systems, which resulted in the identification of as few as four and as many as two thousand racial groups. Even if there were agreement on exactly how many racial groups exist, there would remain the question of how persons of mixed ancestry would be classified. Moreover, the complexity of genetic structure that scientists began discovering in the late 1900's suggests the untenable notion of millions of potential "races" in the world. Most modern biologists have discarded the use of racial categories altogether in favor of a study of "populations."

These teenagers represent the three racial groups traditionally accepted by scientists: Mongoloid, Caucasian, and Negroid. (Skjold)

Early Scientific Theories. Bias against nonwhite peoples was evident in the natural history of Buffon, who first used the term "race" in the mid-1700's. He believed that the white race represented "the real and natural color of man." Like many before him, dating back to the ancient Greeks, he believed that race depended on the geographical climate in which people lived and was variable. Blumenbach in the late 1700's did not rank the races in terms of superiority but did begin the practice of extensive study of skulls (craniology) in search of racial differences. It was Charles White, an English surgeon, who in 1799 advanced the idea of separate origins for each race (polygenesis) in a "great chain of being." Each race was thought to have its own place in the system, with blacks at a "station" between whites and apes.

Race was gradually used to categorize specific groups along this evolutionary continuum, in which increasing gradations of whiteness were viewed as signs of superior development. By 1818, for example, Sir William Lawrence, a physician in the Royal College of Surgeons in London, argued that Europeans embodied a specific human type that was inherently superior to Asians and blacks. Although Lawrence insisted that this was not a reason to enslave people of color, his theory of purported inferiority was used to buttress arguments for the continuance of American SLAVERY. Similar racial theories were expanded and given universal expression by the Scottish anatomist Robert Knox in *The Races of Men* (1850), by the French Count Arthur de Gobineau in *Essay on the Inequality of Human Races* (1853-1854), and by the Americans J. C. Nott and G. R. Gliddon in *Types of Mankind* (1854). It was not until the theories of biologist Charles Darwin gained eminence, however, that these statements began to assume the status of science.

Darwin's *On the Origin of Species by Means of Natural Selection: Or, the Preservation of Favored Races in the Struggle for Life* (1859) verified that all people were of one species on the basis of observable structural similarities. Darwin himself did not discuss a hierarchy of the races and did not believe that racial differences could be measured. His theories, however, prompted great interest in such measurements in the late 1800's. More important, Darwin's work was used to explain how racial groups developed as a process of evolutionary selection. While Darwin described the process of selection, he did not identify the instrument of this selection. The identification of the gene as the instrument of natural selection came later, and it owed much to the work of Austrian botanist Gregor Mendel. His work became the basis for the development of population genetics in the 1930's. Such studies led to W. C. Boyd's *Genetics and the Races of Man* (1950), which defined races as specific human populations possessing one or more combinations of genes. Studies in the 1980's and 1990's have suggested that there are as many as a million possible combinations of genes, leading to the conclusion that potentially a million different races could be identified.

Darwin's theories also led to new efforts in craniometry. Samuel George Morton, the leading American advocate of polygenesis in the 1800's, attempted to study the cranial capacity of some eight hundred skulls from around the world on the assumption that larger skulls meant higher intelligence. He and other scientists tried many methods of measurement with frustrating results; even the differences between individual skulls within one racial group were hard to measure and explain. Similar problems were found in research on brains, hair, and skin color. The eugenics movement began in the late nineteenth century in the effort to "improve" racial stock and ensure more geniuses and fewer criminals, paupers, and mentally deficient persons. This led to the development of early intelligence tests and twentieth century debates between the hereditarians, who believed that intelligence was inherited, and the environmentalists, who believed it was affected by the social and cultural environment.

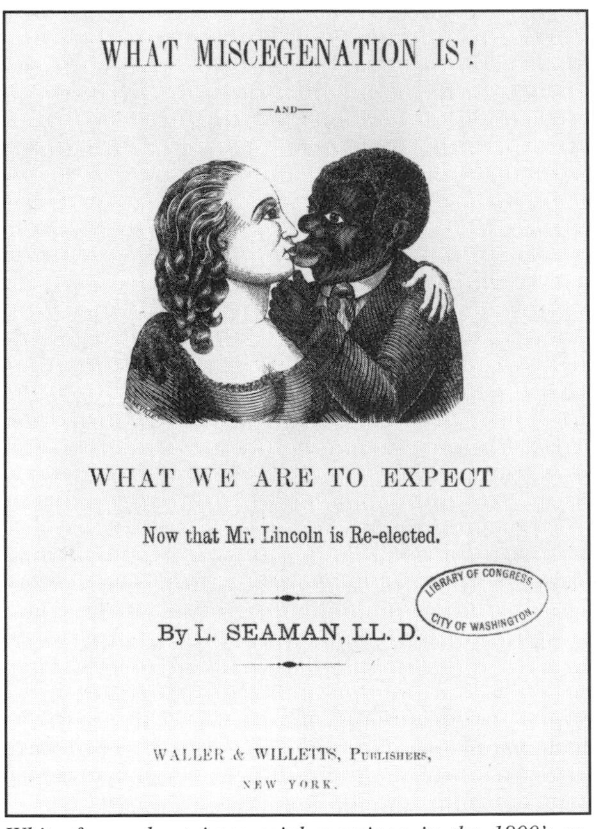

White fears about interracial marriage in the 1800's reflected prevailing beliefs about the inherent inferiority of blacks. (Library of Congress)

Race and Intelligence. Intelligence testing began in the early 1890's. The first intelligence quotient (IQ) tests, promoted as accurate and objective measures of intelligence, were developed by Alfred Binet and Theophile Simon of France in 1905. By World War I, such tests, particularly Stanford-Binet scales and

Yerkes Alpha and Beta tests, were being used to assess intelligence among American soldiers. Scientists used these and later tests to compare the intellectual development of various racial groups. Leading the charge into this abyss were both geneticists and psychologists. They utilized IQ tests to determine the most important influence on behavior: those factors considered innate (such as race) or those determined by environment and socialization (such as class, education, religion, and other cultural values).

Psychologists such as Carl C. Brigham, who assumed that blacks were intellectually inferior to American-born whites, drew on data from the army tests to prove their claims. Early test results demonstrated a wide variation among and within all racial groups. The lowest results have consistently been obtained by minorities, in general, and African Americans and the poor, in particular. Research conducted by Henry Goddard, a pioneer of IQ testing in the United States, concluded that such results were grossly inaccurate. In 1912, he gave intelligence tests at ELLIS ISLAND, finding that at least 80 percent of newly arriving southern European immigrants would be classified as "feeble-minded." Based upon these and other findings, the government created IMMIGRATION LEGISLATION that severely restricted all but northern European arrivals, such as the IMMIGRATION ACT OF 1924.

Later research has suggested that IQ tests are not objective measures of innate capacity or intelligence, but rather are culturally biased measures of access to certain social and intellectual resources. American racial minorities have a long history of being both socially isolated and racially segregated. Therefore, they have had less access to educational or social environments that would promote higher performance on IQ or other standardized tests. Moreover, these tests have traditionally been designed by middle- to upper-class European Americans.

Other social scientists, attempting to minimize the influence of environment, began testing infants to judge the relationship between race and intelligence. Ironically, when black infants scored lower than whites, their lower performance confirmed theories of lesser evolutionary development, and their lower levels of adult achievement were said to result from inferior racial development. Those tests or cases that deviated from this norm were explained as the extremes that prove the rule. The notion of African Americans being inherently less intelligent, as advanced by eugenicist/physicist William Bradford Shockley and Harvard psychologist Arthur Jensen in the 1960's, became highly controversial. By the 1990's, there was still no proof that intelligence is linked to race. The debate regarding the link between race and IQ still rages in academic circles, as does the controversy on racial or cultural bias in standardized tests.

Post-World War II Developments. As intelligence tests came under critical scrutiny and as scientists learned more about the origins of *Homo sapiens* and the nature of cultural and psychological differences, early scientific theories based on racist assumptions were discredited. Franz Boas, a pioneering cultural anthropologist breaking new ground in the understanding of "primitive" cultures, had challenged scientists who believed in innate racial differences to show modern scientific proof in the 1920's. The trend in the second half of the twentieth century was increasingly to look for social and environmental explanations of race and racial differences, rather than biological or hereditary causes.

Race took on urgent meaning for the world with Adolf Hitler's HOLOCAUST, in which some fifteen million people were systematically exterminated solely on the basis of their "racial" designation. The Nazis believed in the physical, moral, and intellectual superiority of the Aryan race, and they attributed genetically determined inferiority to non-Aryan populations such as Jews, Slavs, and Gypsies. Because of the Nazis' fanatical political and racial policies, disastrous world war was waged, more than six million Jews were murdered, and much of Europe was destroyed.

After the Holocaust, the UNITED NATIONS EDUCATIONAL, SCIENTIFIC, AND CULTURAL ORGANIZATION (UNESCO) asked world experts to develop a formal statement regarding the connection between race and behavior. Biologists and physical anthropologists attending the UNESCO meeting in 1952 declared that race as a concept had limited usefulness in describing and classifying human beings. A more useful term, they stated, was the general concept of populations. Human population groups are continuums in which genetic differences are probably as great within groups as those between groups. The scientists further stated that observable differences between human groups are a result of both biology and social environment. The only characteristic related to biological heredity among human groups was blood types, and these do not coincide with typical racial groupings. Those characteristics generally understood to be racial and trans-

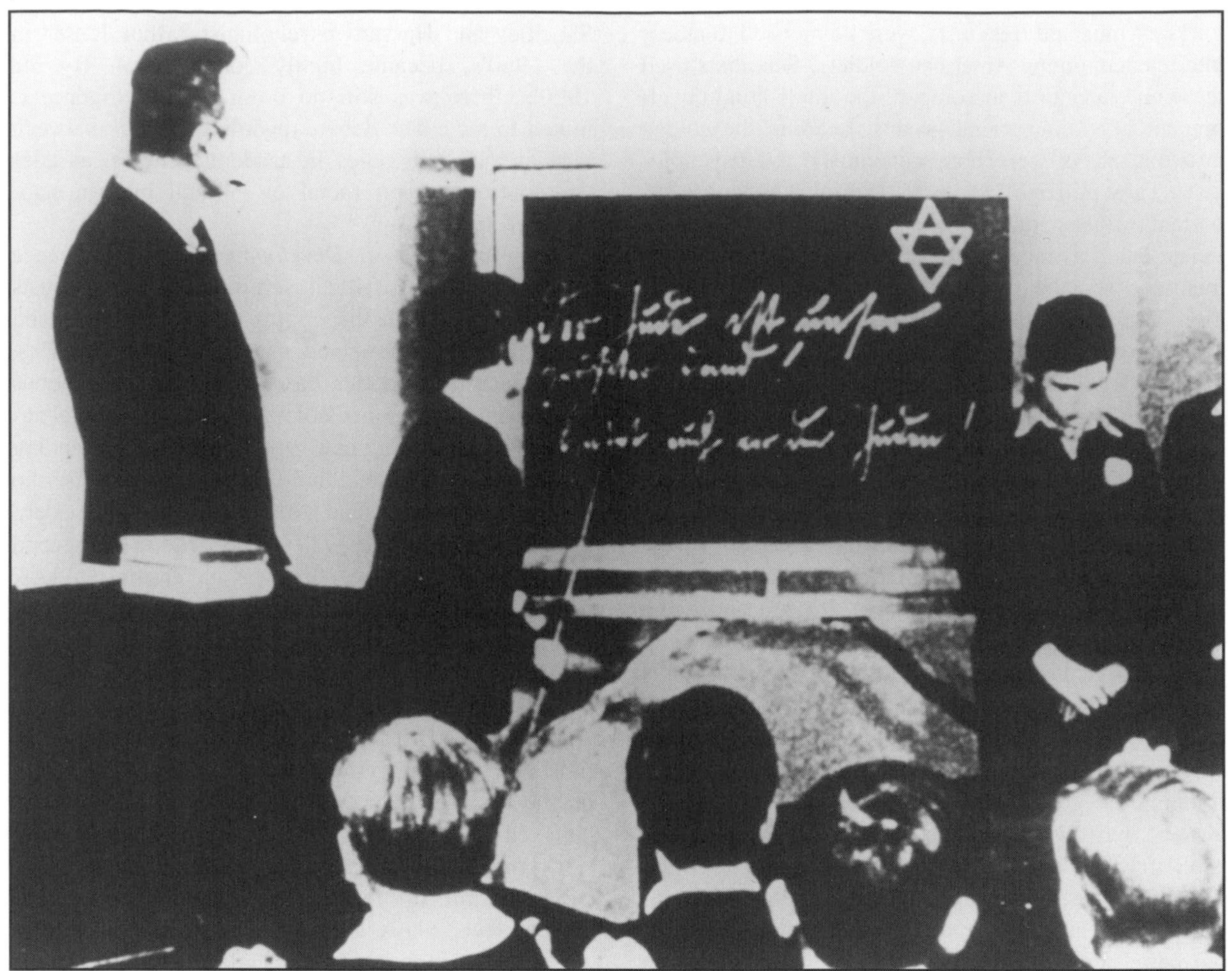

Nazi school forces Jewish student to read blackboard saying "The Jews are our greatest enemies." Hitler's attempt to exterminate entire peoples on the basis of race provoked Americans' reconsideration of the question of race. (Simon Wiesenthal Center)

mitted to the group as a whole are, in fact, transmitted "either independently or in varying degrees of association."

Thus, the UNESCO group concluded, all humanity is derived from a common stock, a single human race. There is no justification for linking cultural, behavioral, or achievement outcomes to genetic inheritance. All humanity shares the ability to advance culturally—a capacity far greater in significance than anything that may result from the accident of birth that society calls race.

SUGGESTED READINGS. A wide assortment of books is available for those who would like to pursue the complex subject of race. One of the finest intellectual histories of the concept of race is Thomas F. Gossett's *Race: The History of an Idea in America* (1963). See also Ashley Montagu's *Man's Most Dangerous Myth: The Fallacy of Race* (1942). Another view of the interaction between Europeans and Africans is provided in Winthrop D. Jordan's *White over Black* (1968). Selected essays by John Hope Franklin in *Race and History* (1989) also provide a historical analysis of how race has helped mold contemporary American society. For a broader view, Stephen Molnar's *Human Variation: Races, Types, and Ethnic Groups* (1992) is an excellent anthropological analysis of the concept of race that covers both historical and contemporary issues.—*Rodney D. Coates*

Race—sociological debate: For sociologists, race has always been a relative social concept rather than an objective physical reality. In other words, society divides people into social groups and assigns meaning to those groups based on physical characteristics. This meaning differs in various parts of the world and in different regions of the United States. What interests sociologists are not racial characteristics per se, but how society defines race, how individuals come to identify with their assigned racial group, and how racial groups interact in the broader society.

This point of view implies that race is not something fixed and absolute but is to a large extent in the eye of the beholder, subject to changes in definition over time. Perhaps this partly is why race has been such a poorly understood and controversial idea in American society. The term "race" has, in the past, been loosely applied to linguistic, religious, and national groups to denote lineage, as in "the Italian race" or "the Jewish race." Some Americans, including many scientists, reject any categorization of people into races, insisting that there is only one human race. By the 1990's, the term "race" had become taboo in certain circles, replaced by the more generic term "culture" or by observations about "color." Yet contemporary racial groups in the United States exhibit such ethnic, economic, political, religious, and other diversity that it is sometimes difficult to define what culture they share. The complexities of public perceptions of race continue to fuel the sociological debate.

The field of sociology developed in the late nineteenth and early twentieth centuries at a time when issues of race were becoming explosive matters of public concern and debate in the United States. The numerical dominance and social privilege of WHITE ANGLO-SAXON PROTESTANTS (WASPs) were challenged by demographic shifts and new opportunities for minorities. African Americans, who had only been freed from SLAVERY since the 1860's, were increasingly mingling with European Americans as a result of the GREAT MIGRATION to cities and to the North, but they were victims of JIM CROW LAWS and other forms of discrimination. They began to fight this situation through CIVIL RIGHTS organizations. Urban areas were grappling with a large influx of southern and eastern European immigrants who, like the Chinese and Japanese already present in the United States, were seen as members of alien races. Restrictive IMMIGRATION LEGISLATION shut the door, and AMERICANIZATION programs were put in place for those who had already arrived.

Sociological theories about race often reflected the prejudices of the day. Indeed, Herbert Spencer's nineteenth century popularization of the idea of SOCIAL DARWINISM, which posited that human society is ruled—like nature—by the "survival of the fittest," influenced many people to enter the new field of sociology in the 1870's and 1880's. Eventually the focus shifted from a view that accepted the alleged inferiority of nonwhite races to theories that attempted to explain or eradicate the scourge of RACISM.

The Biological Perspective. Historically, biological theories dominated the debate on race. The biological model claimed that races are collectivities whose members display common, innate, and unchangeable characteristics. These range from the obvious physical differences among groups designated as races to—more controversially—intellect and culture. Such ideas escaped serious challenge for decades because, ironically, their supporters and opponents shared the same underlying assumptions: They generally believed that races are hierarchically ordered in terms of capabilities and achievements with whites at the top and nonwhites, in varying degrees, at the bottom.

A fundamental shift in ideas about race occurred in the late 1800's and early 1900's, when anthropologists

Anthropologist Franz Boas (1858-1942) laid the groundwork for the sociological debate on race by rejecting biological theories. (Library of Congress)

such as Edward Burnett Tylor and, especially, Franz Boas challenged the biological assumptions undergirding racist thinking. Boas argued that groups designated as races exhibit wide variation and that, therefore, the idea of a "typical" representative of such a group is really only an approximation. Within any race, one can expect to find many deviations from the ideal type, since inheritance occurs in families and not in the larger aggregate group known as a "race." This approach helped to weaken the intellectual foundations of traditional hierarchical pseudoscientific theories of race. Ironically, Nazi Germany's genocidal attempt to implement racist ideas by eliminating entire "races" struck an even stronger blow against the concept of race, since people the world over were shocked by the consequences of its policies.

The Sociological Perspective. As a result of these factors, the sociological perspective on race became more influential in the postwar period. The essence of this perspective is the idea that race is a socially constructed concept rather than an objective phenomenon. The biological perspective treats race as objective, because, from this point of view, "racial" characteristics are fundamentally physiological, permanent, and observable using scientific techniques. The sociological perspective, however, rests on the idea that an individual's biologically based racial characteristics are often not intrinsically important. Instead, they derive their significance from the society in which they occur. It is how other people interpret these characteristics, rather than the characteristics themselves, that is important. Societies may choose to ignore some characteristics as inconsequential while simultaneously stressing others as significant. Since historical and cultural factors guide this process, and since societies vary with respect to their history and culture, the possibility arises that similar biological characteristics can be interpreted differently in different societies. Thus, unlike the biological perspective, the sociological perspective views race as relative rather than absolute.

The Fluidity of Race. Sociologist Max Weber pointed out that groups will use anything to try to set themselves apart from other groups. Physical differences certainly qualify as potential boundary markers, but not all physical differences are equally effective. Skin color is, perhaps, the most widely used boundary marker between human groups. It has the advantage of being obvious and tends to encapsulate all of the supposed differences between the various "races." Skin color, however, also serves to illustrate the idea that race is relative.

The classic racial distinction in American society has been between "whites" and "blacks." Yet even these categories are so fluid that they leave room for much ambiguity. For instance, European Americans have tended to view individuals with even minimal African ancestry as "black." These same individuals, however, might be viewed as "colored" or "white" in societies with different conceptions of "whiteness" and "blackness," such as South Africa, Brazil, and the Caribbean. Traditionally, the general wisdom in Brazil and the Caribbean has been that "money whitens": thus, dark-skinned individuals are seen as becoming "whiter" with upward mobility while poor whites—such as the "Redlegs" of Barbados—seem less "white." Another example of the plasticity of race involves Asian Indians. Anthropologists regard them—along with people of European descent—as Caucasian. Yet when they migrate to England, the British consider them to be "colored."

In the United States the seemingly obvious black-white distinction is muddled by regionalism, interbreeding, and politics, among other factors. Among themselves, African Americans have long made distinctions about degrees of darkness in skin color, traditionally giving greater prestige and privilege to those with lighter skin. CREOLES, French-speaking people of mixed racial heritage in Louisiana, are variously seen as black or white, depending on the context; some Creoles identify themselves as one or the other race while others proudly refuse to identify as anything but Creole. Since the 1980's, the MULTIRACIAL MOVEMENT has brought attention to the fact that large numbers of Americans are actually not wholly black, white, brown, or yellow but the products of mixed ancestry. Many such people cannot accept the racial labels commonly used by government and the general public and seek, instead, the development of new multiracial categories and identities.

Clearly, race is a relative concept that may change over time, across space, and among groups. Furthermore, group identity is a complicated matter: Self-identification is important, but how society views the individual is even more crucial, especially in matters of race.

The Sociological Study of Race. Early sociologists did not question the inferior status that American society assigned to nonwhite races. For example, they accepted claims of blacks' lower intelligence at face value rather than examining the Eurocentric bias of the IQ tests that were the basis of the claims. They looked to European history to show how less powerful groups were typically dominated by and absorbed in more powerful groups. They theorized a cycle of intergroup contact, assimilation, and amalgamation, which became known as the "MELTING POT THEORY." Only gradually did psychologists and sociologists

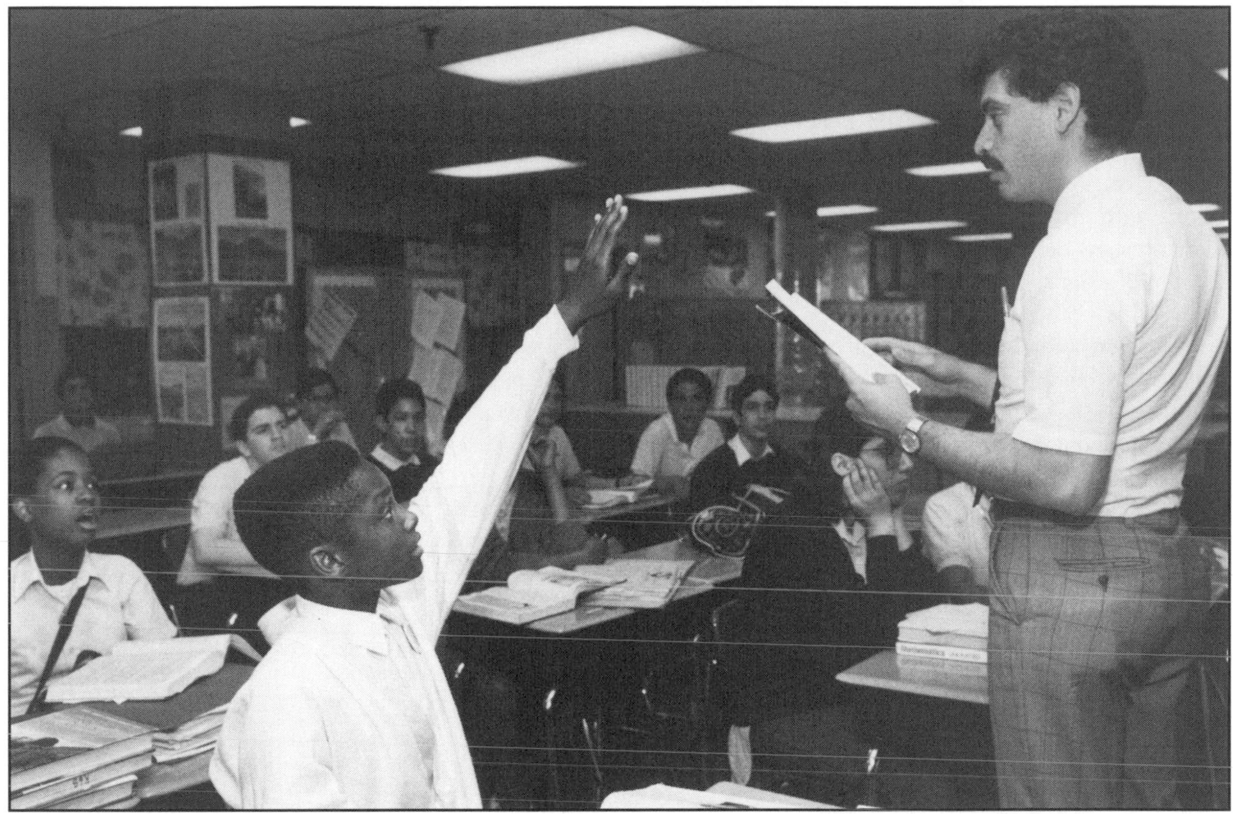

Integrated classrooms became commonplace only after the 1960's. Sociologists noted the effects of prejudice and discrimination in seeking to explain socioeconomic differences between racial groups. (Hazel Hankin)

come to study the effect of the social environment, including PREJUDICE and discrimination, on intelligence or achievement. Rather than blaming the victim, they began to seek reasons for the lack of ASSIMILATION among African Americans in social, political, and economic structures.

With the growth of this approach came a new interest in racial prejudice and race relations. Whereas social scientists in the 1920's had attempted to measure levels of prejudice, after World War II they began to look for ways to explain it. During the height of the CIVIL RIGHTS MOVEMENT in the 1950's and 1960's, some sociologists devised theories and methods devoted to combating RACISM and improving intergroup relations. This direction took on greater prominence and sophistication as nonwhite researchers entered the field and as sociologists began to compare race relations among various groups.

Most modern sociologists subscribe to the idea of race as socially constructed. A number of issues have yet to be resolved in this model, notably the problem of the relationship between race and ethnicity.

Race Versus Ethnicity. Racial identity is only one of a number of identities that individuals and groups can possess. Others include ethnic, gender, and religious identity. Both racial and ethnic identity are socially constructed. While social race arises out of biological features that a society believes are relevant boundary markers, ETHNICITY arises from the cultural commonalities that are shared by a number of individuals. These commonalities serve as focal points around which groups can coalesce, but their mere existence does not automatically bring ethnic groups into existence. That happens only when a consciousness develops among a body of individuals that they form a distinct group because of shared nationality, religion, language, or cultural heritage. Thus, ethnic groups are self-conscious, culturally based social units.

In studying race and ethnicity, social scientists must

confront the question of whether and how racial and ethnic groups overlap. In the United States, the answers to these questions are politically charged because they affect the allocation of resources among competing groups. Generally speaking, defining a group as "ethnic" rather than "racial" implies that it will follow the pattern of European immigrants to the United States, who all eventually assimilated to the dominant culture to greater or lesser degrees. The "ethnicity" model of intergroup relations views ASSIMILATION as desirable and achievable through self-effort, with government playing a minimal role. This view presents racial groups as being essentially similar to ethnic groups, thus using the term "ethnic group" to describe both types of groups.

This viewpoint is controversial because not all racial groups share the historical experience of European ethnic groups. In fact, U.S. history shows that the American Indians, African Americans, and early Asian Americans had far more limited options for participation in the mainstream because of exploitation, enslavement, and exclusion. The fact that people such as Afro-Cubans can belong to both an ethnic and a racial group complicates the issue. In cases such as this, however, society tends to assign a primary identity based on skin color. Opponents of the ethnicity model emphasize the distinction between racial groups and ethnic groups, arguing that each group's formation reflects different responses to the problem of group conflict. Moreover, being defined racially carries more severe consequences than being defined ethnically. Thus, the cycle of assimilation does not work as well for racial groups as it does for white ethnics. Consequently, racial minorities may need special help such as AFFIRMATIVE ACTION to achieve success and overcome a legacy of racial discrimination.

Practically, the evidence suggests that more adverse consequences result from being defined by one's race

Affirmative action officer (left) reviews policies with a city government employee. Some sociologists believe that special opportunities must be created for racial minorities to encourage their assimilation and success. (Mary M. Langenfeld)

rather than ethnicity. Groups defined by race become easier targets for discrimination in such areas as employment, housing, education, and financial services. For instance, one sociological study showed that dark-skinned Caribbean Latinos experience high levels of segregation not only from whites, but also from lighter-skinned members of their own Latino ethnic group. The study concluded that dark skin color, per se, significantly affects the life chances of some people in the United States. This study is important for the race versus ethnicity debate because it implies that race is more important than ethnicity in determining opportunities; if that were not the case, one would not expect to find high levels of segregation between members of the same ethnic group.

In her book *Ethnic Options* (1990), sociologist Mary C. Waters suggests that racial identity leads to more severe consequences than ethnic identity because it is more permanent. White Americans are usually defined in ethnic terms and often have ancestors from different nationalities. This gives them a wide range of ethnic identities from which to choose, and they often change identities over the course of their lives or as they move from region to region. For instance, an individual with parents of French and Dutch background could choose to be either French American, Dutch American, or simply "American." In contrast to this, individuals who are defined racially have less latitude to change their identity because it is based on physical, rather than cultural, criteria. For example, in the United States, an individual with one parent from Nigeria and another from Barbados would usually be viewed as "black" rather than Nigerian American or Barbadian American. Whereas white individuals can initiate an identity change by anglicizing their ethnic-sounding names, dark-skinned individuals cannot because their identity derives from their physical appearance. Thus, racial identity is more fixed than ethnic identity.

Suggested Readings. For an insightful discussion of the historical development of the idea of race from a largely biological concept to a social one, see Thomas F. Gossett's *Race: The History of an Idea in America* (1963) and the first chapter of Robert Miles's *Racism* (1989). E. Ellis Cashmore's *Dictionary of Race and Ethnic Relations* (2d ed., 1988) provides a useful overview of the distinctions between biological race, social race, and ethnicity. Mary C. Waters' *Ethnic Options* (1990) also discusses some of the differences between race and ethnicity. For a review of modern sociological research on racial identity, see *Black and White Racial Identity* (1990), edited by Janet E. Helms.—*Milton Vickerman*

Race riots: Violent civil disturbances caused by racial tensions. Such incidents have a long history in the United States, reflecting problems in intergroup relations and affecting members of diverse minority groups as well as the dominant culture. In the late twentieth century, race riots have come to be associated with African Americans expressing anger and frustration at conditions such as police brutality and discrimination in the inner city. Until the 1960's, however, white citizens were the main instigators of race riots, directing violence against African Americans, Asian Americans, or Latinos. Historically, race riots occurred when ethnic minorities were seen as competing with the white majority for jobs and housing; when the Anglo community needed scapegoats for real or imagined societal ills; or when members of minority groups were accused of certain crimes.

Antiblack Riots Before Emancipation. One of the more famous early antiblack riots occurred in Cincinnati, Ohio, in 1829. Because of an increased influx of African Americans into the city, officials announced that they would strictly enforce laws that required blacks to post a $500 bond as a guarantee of good conduct and as an assurance that they would not become a public charge. Leaders of the African American community realized that they would have to move and received a time extension while they sent a delegation to Canada searching for a safe haven. Local whites, however, became impatient. Mobs formed and roamed through the black section of the city, beating African Americans and burning their homes. On hearing of the riot, the governor of Canada immediately announced that he would allow colonization. Subsequently, an estimated fifteen hundred to two thousand African Americans left town.

Ohio was not the only northern state to experience race riots. By the late 1820's a series of riots had occurred in Philadelphia, Pennsylvania, the "city of brotherly love," whenever black residents paraded to Independence Square for Fourth of July celebrations. On August 12, 1834, white residents who resented the strong African American presence in the city stormed through the black section of town, finding and beating several African Americans. The next day, the mob returned to burn homes, wreck the African Presbyterian Church, and beat yet more blacks. Only as the rioting extended into a third day did the heretofore passive police restore order. In 1842, during a severe economic depression, a white mob broke up a parade of African Americans celebrating the abolition of slavery in the West Indies. The whites beat scores of blacks and burned the Presbyterian Church again and the New African Hall. This time, state troops had to help the police restore order.

Other riots erupted in the North and the West in the 1830's and 1840's—in Utica, Palmyra, and New York, New York, in 1834 and 1839; in Columbia, Pennsylvania, in 1834, and Pittsburgh in 1839; in Cincinnati in 1841; in several towns in Connecticut in the 1840's; in California in 1849; and in many other places.

Anti-immigrant Riots. While Anglo American hostility was usually directed against the African American community, that community was not the only one to feel the wrath of white rioters. For example, the

The contempt for the Chinese among many European Americans, as seen in this magazine cover from 1880, erupted in a series of anti-Chinese race riots. (Library of Congress)

1870's and 1880's saw much ANTI-CHINESE VIOLENCE and hostilities directed at other Asian immigrants on or near the West Coast. Chinese immigrants first came to the United States in significant numbers to toil on the western portions of several of the transcontinental railroads, the first of which was begun in 1862 and completed in 1869. By 1877 many of the Chinese followed the mining frontier and settled in western states such as California, Oregon, Washington, Wyoming, and Colorado.

Major organized violence was first committed against Asians in San Francisco, California, in 1877. The regional economy was suffering a recession, and many people were unemployed. Some white workers blamed the Chinese for glutting the labor market. When white workers met to protest long working hours and to demand an eight-hour day, rabble-rousers led the group in condemning their Chinese competitors. The white activists marched into Chinatown and commenced rioting and looting; several Asians were killed or wounded before authorities could restore order.

In subsequent years, white riots against Chinese occurred in such diverse places as Tacoma and Seattle, Washington; Denver, Colorado; and Rock Springs, Wyoming. Clearly getting the message of the rioters, the federal government expressed its own official hostility and bigotry when it passed the CHINESE EXCLUSION ACT in 1882 to stop Chinese immigration.

The last decades of the nineteenth century were a time of vastly increased immigration from southern and eastern Europe. Many of the riots of this period were directed against the new immigrants. For example, in the LABOR MOVEMENT, especially during union strikes, intergroup violence flared often. A typical pattern was that newer, poorer immigrants were used as "scabs" to replace striking workers who had been fired; this situation heightened the resentment of newcomers by longtime residents and union members.

From the Civil War to World War II. As long as slavery defined southern race relations, there were few riots. Once the slaves were freed, however, rioting occurred often. For example, in 1875 in Mississippi, the African Americans and white citizenry seemed to be virtually at war, with the black militia and Democrats both heavily armed. Riots occurred in Columbia, Charleston, and other towns until after the state elections, when the Democrats returned to power and suppressed the disorder. In 1874 competition between the Union League and the Democratic "White League" led to a riot in New Orleans, Louisiana, that saw forty people dead and one hundred more wounded.

Hamburg, South Carolina, became the scene of one of the worst race riots of the day. As the Republican

African American militia paraded, celebrating July 4, 1876, the Democratic police arrested several soldiers for blocking traffic. After the trial was delayed, a mob of white activists assembled, determined that the black detainees must be punished. In the riot that followed, several black militiamen were killed and five others were captured (and later murdered while in custody).

Mob violence against black citizens seemed to become more frequent around the turn of the twentieth century. In 1898 eight black residents were killed in a riot in Wilmington, North Carolina. In 1904, authorities in Statesboro, Georgia, accused two African Americans of the murder of a white family. They received the death sentence by hanging, but local racist white residents wanted the prisoners killed sooner. A mob formed, surged into the courtroom, took the black prisoners out, and burned them alive. Then the white mob began a wholesale reign of terror in the black community, beating, killing, and wrecking many black homes. The incident left African Americans in such a terrified state that many left the county.

In August of 1906, the BROWNSVILLE INCIDENT in Brownsville, Texas, was notable because black citizens fought back. Race relations in the town had been strained for some time because white locals objected to the presence of nearby African American troopers and heaped insults upon them. On one occasion, a white mob accosted several black soldiers. Three companies of the Twenty-fifth Regiment assembled, went back to town, and indiscriminately started shooting, killing one white man and wounding several others.

The next month, Atlanta, Georgia, became the scene of a larger riot with even more disastrous consequences. The ongoing drive to disfranchise black residents had led to demagoguery on the part of white politicians. Newspaper editors spurred hatred in the white community and created a frenzy by printing loose talk and rumors. A white mob beat blacks in the streets after a fight began in a segregated saloon. When African Americans in a nearby suburb began to take arms to protect themselves, local white authorities sent police to arrest black residents who were carrying weapons. When one policeman was killed in a skirmish, some Atlanta whites began wholesale destruction. As police joined in, the mob killed four blacks, wounded countless others, looted, and burned homes. Many black victims later sold their property at a greatly reduced value and left town. Despite the protests of African Americans, authorities refused to punish the white rioters.

A riot that caught national attention occurred in Springfield, Illinois, in August of 1908. A white woman accused African American George Richardson of rape, and authorities duly arrested him. The woman later told a grand jury that she had been beaten not by Richardson but by her white lover. Nevertheless, a white mob began agitating, becoming furious upon learning that the prisoner had been taken away as a precaution. The mob surged through town shouting, "Lincoln freed you, but we'll show you where you belong." Looting stores and drinking, they secured guns, axes, and other weapons and began to rampage through the black section, destroying businesses and homes. They set fire to one barbershop and lynched the barber, later dragging his body through the streets. The governor called in the militia, which finally dispersed the mob. The next night whites lynched an eighty-four-year-old African American whose crime was having been married to a white woman for more than thirty years. One beneficial result of this riot was that it mobilized black leaders and white "race liberals" to begin the NIAGARA MOVEMENT. This, in turn, led to the founding of the NATIONAL ASSOCIATION FOR THE ADVANCEMENT OF COLORED PEOPLE (NAACP), an organization that would play a large role in the twentieth century CIVIL RIGHTS MOVEMENT.

Race riots continued to break out sporadically. For example, in 1919, there were antiblack disturbances in Longview, Texas; Washington, D.C.; Chicago; Knoxville, Tennessee; Omaha, Nebraska; Somerville, Texas; Elaine, Arkansas; and a particularly violent incident in Tulsa, Oklahoma, in 1921. In the World War II era, riots occurred in places such as Detroit and New York City, often led by Polish Americans who resented African Americans competing with them for housing and jobs.

Anti-Latino Riots. In the Southwest, authorities usually lumped black and Latino residents together. Thus Chicanos were excluded from or segregated in most public accommodations; for example, they were barred from certain restaurants, hotels, and other accommodations, including public swimming pools. They also typically lived in segregated housing and were discriminated against in the job market.

During World War II, violence against Latinos flared on the West Coast, with the most brutal events occurring in Los Angeles. In the early 1940's, some Mexican American youths, calling themselves *pachucos*, joined local gangs, which sometimes fought one another over territory. Especially noticeable were the

White servicemen search streetcar looking for Latinos wearing "zoot suits" during the 1943 riots in Los Angeles. (AP/Wide World Photos)

pachucos who adopted zoot suits—a fashion that had originated in the black sections of northern cities—as their "uniform." Long, loose coats with padded shoulders, balloon pants pegged at the ankles, wide-brimmed hats, ducktail haircuts, and long watch chains created the look. Some of the Los Angeles *pachucos* eventually angered Anglo servicemen who were stationed near the city. Large groups of servicemen on weekend passes from their bases typically roamed Los Angeles looking for excitement. Some found it by attacking the *pachucos*. These Mexican American teenagers seemed too independent and proud to the white soldiers; racism was undoubtedly the cause of the clashes. Consequently, young military men made a habit of assaulting the zoot suiters whenever they could. The ZOOT-SUIT RIOTS began in the spring of 1943, reaching a peak on June 7, when gangs of soldiers and sailors banded together in taxicabs and cars and roamed the city looking for zoot suiters and anyone else who looked Latino. Joined by other white locals, the servicemen beat all the young Mexican Americans they could find, stripped them of their nonconformist clothes, and gave them short haircuts. White police and senior military officers had generally looked the other way during the riots (occasionally arresting young Latinos but ignoring the soldiers' provocations). The day after the June 7 violence, however, the Army and Navy finally announced that servicemen were not to go into Los Angeles, and on June 11 the Navy sternly warned its personnel not to become involved in any altercations with the zoot suiters.

Contemporary Race Riots. In the 1960's, partially because of the "revolution of rising expectations" that accompanied President Lyndon B. Johnson's WAR ON POVERTY, there were 150 major riots between 1965 and 1968, with the first and most notorious the WATTS RIOTS in a section of Los Angeles. These riots were different from the previous "white" riots; it was the African Americans who took to the streets to violently protest continuing discrimination. The federally appointed KERNER COMMISSION issued a report that suggested root causes of the riots in patterns of injustice. A benefit of these events may have been furthering the cause of CIVIL RIGHTS LEGISLATION.

Even at the end of the twentieth century, race riots continued to occur. For example, in the 1970's violence approaching rioting occurred in states such as California, Texas, and Colorado where Vietnamese refugees successfully competed for jobs and housing. Those who resented the Vietnamese presence included not only whites but minorities such as Latinos who were vying for places in low-income housing projects.

The most destructive riot in U.S. history occurred in Los Angeles in 1992. Black motorist Rodney King had been seriously beaten by police in 1991 in an episode captured on videotape by a witness. When a jury in a suburb of Los Angeles found the police officers not guilty, African Americans spilled into the streets in anger. Together with large numbers of Latinos and whites, they began several days of looting and destruction that was not contained until soldiers arrived to help the local police. The King verdict and

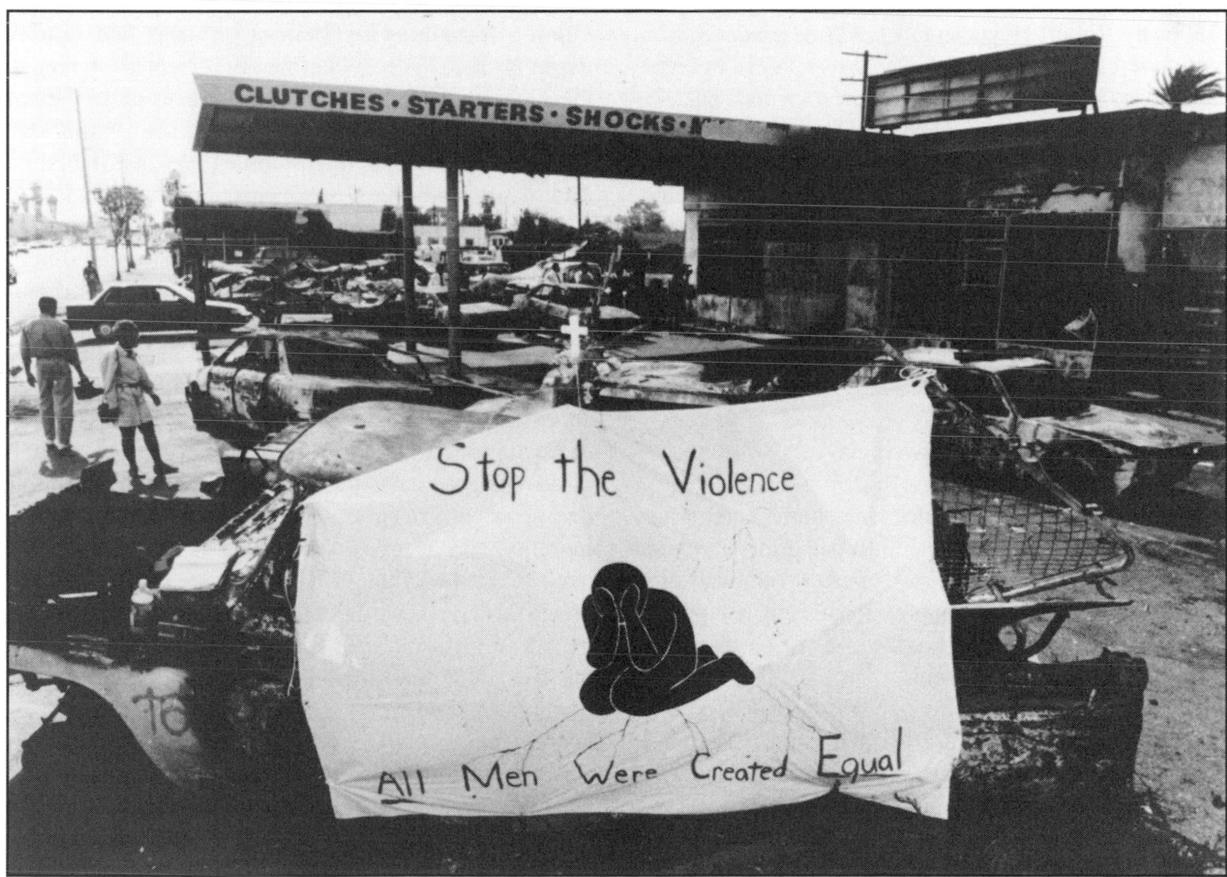

Banner in South Central Los Angeles calls for peace after the 1992 riots. (AP/Wide World Photos)

the Los Angeles riots set off smaller disturbances in other cities across the nation, reminding Americans of what many black citizens saw as an inherently unjust legal system and continued gaps between privileged Americans and a growing underclass. Among more radical African Americans and others, both the unrest in Watts in 1965 and the events in Los Angeles in May, 1992, have come to be known as "rebellions" rather than "riots." This terminology suggests a planned intention of protest, rather than opportunism and anarchy, in response to what activists see as social injustice.

Suggested Readings. For more information on race riots, which seem endemic in the multicultural United States, the interested reader might consult the general studies *From Slavery to Freedom* (1988) by John Hope Franklin and Alfred Moss, Jr., or Peter and Mort Bergman's *The Chronological History of the Negro in America* (1969). Studies that examine certain riots in depth include *Carnival of Fury: Robert Charles and the New Orleans Race Riot of 1900* (1976) by William Hair; *A Night of Violence: The Houston Riot of 1917* (1976) by Robert Haynes; and *The Brownsville Affair: National Crisis and Black Reaction* (1971) by Ann Lane. Also see *Becoming American: An Ethnic History* (1983); *The Huddled Masses: The Immigrant in American Society* (1982); and *The History of Violence in America* (1969), edited by Hugh Davis Graham and Ted Robert Gurr. Other studies include Robert Brisbane's *Black Activism: Racial Revolution in the United States. 1954-1970* (1974); James Button's *Black Violence: Political Impact of the 1960's Riots* (1978); and James Forman's *The Making of Black Revolutionaries* (1972).—*James Smallwood*

Racial quotas. *See* **Quotas—racial**

Racism: Belief that race determines human capacities and that some races are inherently superior to others. White racism, linked to forms of prejudice and discrimination, has led to the oppression of racial minorities in the United States and has been a major source of contemporary social problems.

Although the United States was founded on the principle that "all men are created equal," all races have not been treated equally. Ideological explanations were invented to justify racist practices such as the enslavement of African Americans and the exclusion of Chinese immigrants. The inferiority of nonwhites was "proved," for a time, by scientific theories such as polygenesis (the idea that the races all developed from different sources). Such theories were shown to be based on false assumptions, but not until after racism had been tightly woven into the fabric of American life.

Over the course of the twentieth century, the rise of various civil rights movements, the increased participation of racial minorities in the mainstream, and government intervention all posed challenges to racism. Overt racism gradually disappeared as an official policy of the U.S. government and other institutions. By the late 1900's, racism had become a complex and explosive issue of public debate, subject to numerous interpretations. Some whites began to accuse militant nonwhites of reverse discrimination and antiwhite racism. Meanwhile, white racism persisted in subtle forms in many sectors of American society. It was expressed through speech, acts of avoidance of people of color, discrimination, and occasionally, violence.

Definitions and Functions. Meyer Weinberg in *A Chance to Learn: The History of Race and Education in the United States* (1977) provides a poignant definition of racism as a system of privilege and penalty based on race. The system has two facets: a belief in the inherent superiority of some people and inherent inferiority of others, and the acceptance of the way goods, services, and opportunities are distributed in accordance with these judgments. James M. Jones, in *Racism and Prejudice* (1972), divides racism into three categories: individual, institutional, and cultural. Individual racism is closest to the idea of racial prejudice in which an individual believes in the superiority of his or her own race over another and exhibits behavior that reflects this belief. Institutional racism is an extension of such prejudice to the manipulations of institutions so as to benefit some racial groups and disadvantage others; this form of racism supports institutional practices that restrict the choices, rights, mobility, and access of groups or individuals on the basis of race. Although not sanctioned by law, these practices are nevertheless real (this is sometimes called de facto racism). Cultural racism is defined as the individual and institutional expression of the superiority of one race's cultural heritage over that of another race. People and institutions such as schools and governments can exhibit what some perceive to be racism in their words or actions, even if those people and institutions are not aware of holding racist attitudes or policies.

Like other forms of prejudice, racism arises from

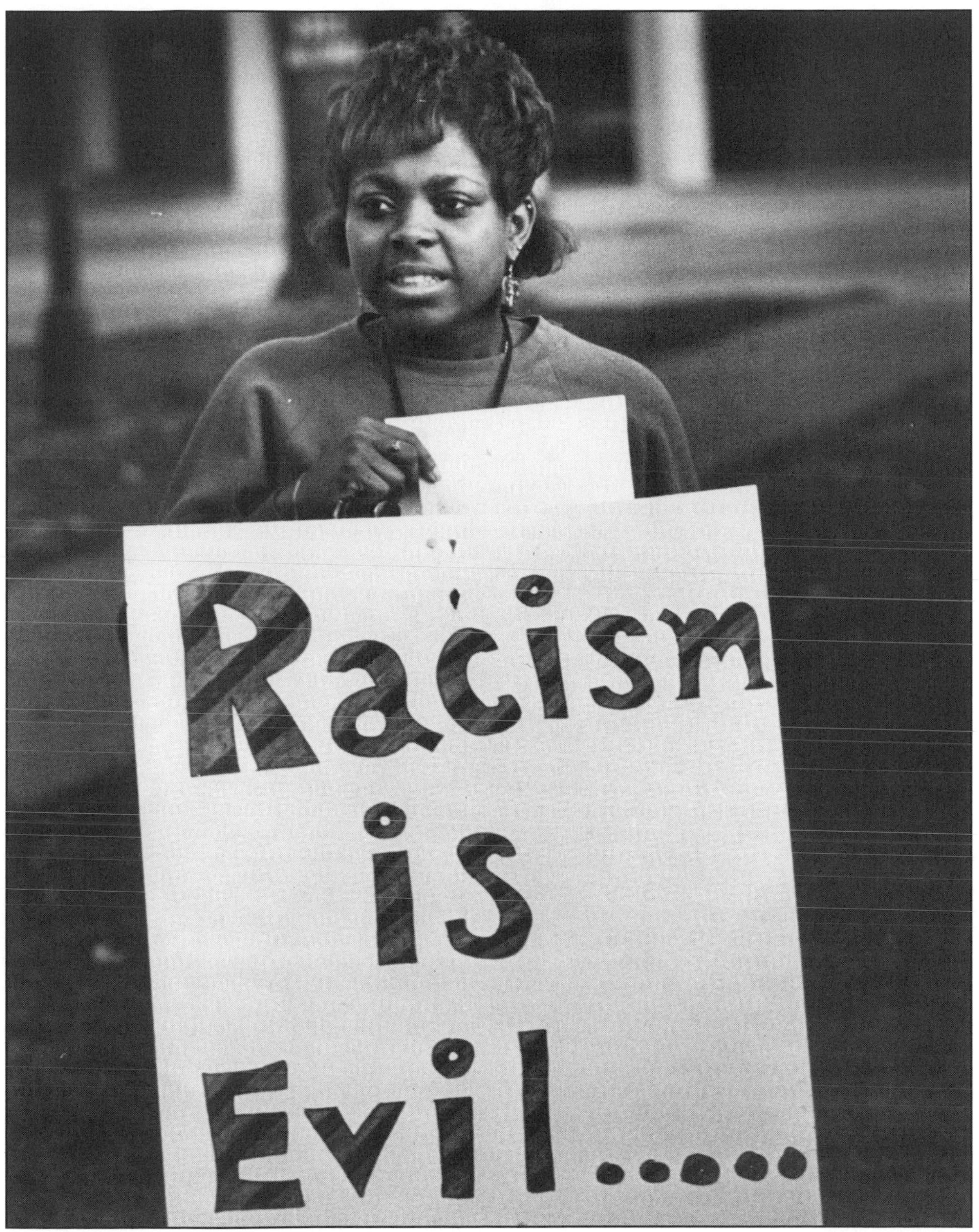

By the late 1990's, most Americans agreed with this demonstrator's sign, but they differed on their view of what constituted racism. (James L. Shaffer)

and gives rise to STEREOTYPES. Racists may generalize about an entire race of people on the basis of one encounter—or on the basis of no encounters or knowledge whatsoever. These generalizations are then used to victimize the group as a whole, ensuring that they remain in an inferior social position. In her book *Racial Prejudice* (1985), Ellen Pascoe traces the origin and perpetuation of certain stereotypes in American culture, such as that of the "shiftless" black male. She notes how the conditions of SLAVERY, SEGREGATION, and employment discrimination helped to create certain behaviors on the part of African Americans and certain perceptions on the part of European Americans. Thus, racism fosters a vicious circle: born of prejudice and stereotypes, it breeds discrimination, which in turn perpetuates the conditions that lead to continued prejudice.

Sociologists theorize that if white racism had no function in American society, it would cease to exist. Over time it has put Caucasians at an advantage compared with other races, providing convenient scapegoats and minimizing competition between groups for scarce resources. It has also been tremendously economically useful, as in treaties that showed little regard for American Indian land rights in order to make land available to European settlers and in the cotton economy of the South that was dependent on slave labor. Religious and cultural beliefs as well as scientific theories have been used to justify American racism.

Scientific Justifications of Racism. The nineteenth century saw the development of a number of scientific and pseudoscientific theories that were used to justify racist practices. Blacks were seen as a link between whites and lower animal forms in an evolutionary continuum known as the "great chain of being." Darwin's *On the Origin of Species* (1859) made a case for all people being part of one human species rather than members of different species, as previously supposed. Some of his ideas, however, provided a rationale for what became known as SOCIAL DARWINISM under Herbert Spencer. Spencer claimed that different races represented different stages in the evolutionary "struggle for existence" and "survival of the fittest," with the superior white race destined to prevail. Related to social Darwinism is the theory of biological determinism. According to Stephen J. Gould, this theory holds that "shared behavioral norms, and the social and economic differences between human groups—primarily races, classes, and sexes—arise from inherited, inborn distinctions, and that society is an accurate reflection of biology." This doctrine became manifest in both individual and institutional racism in the United States.

Another theory used to uphold racism was that of recapitulation. This idea, developed by a French anatomist around 1860, held that higher creatures repeated the adult stages of lower animals during their own growth. It was argued that warmer climates tended to arrest human physical and mental development at a "primitive" stage, imposing an earlier but incomplete maturation on people such as Italians. Thus, the "primitive" or "lower" races could be compared with Caucasian children. This view offered scientists such as paleontologist E. D. Cope a criterion for ranking the races. In the 1880's, he identified four groups of lower human forms: nonwhites, women, southern Europeans, and the lower classes among northern Europeans. The pseudoscience of craniometry (measurement of the skull to determine intelligence) and biased intelligence tests were also used in the twentieth century to prove the hereditary bio-

Portrait of Christopher Columbus attributed to Rodolfo Ghirlandaia. Early European explorers considered native peoples in the Americas to be "savages" in need of "civilizing" European control. (AP/Wide World Photos)

logical inequality of the races. The eugenics movement to "improve" racial stock, originally developed in the late 1800's, exploited people of color for experimentation in the 1930's. It was not until genetic advances later in the century that scientists discovered there was no genetic basis for racial categories.

Origins of European and European American Racism. Racial differences were noted in the literature, art, and historical chronicles of ancient peoples such as the Chinese, Egyptians, Greeks, and Hebrews. Black skin, for example, was sometimes associated with enemies or suspect character. Many ideas were promoted to explain racial differences. In early instances of ETHNOCENTRISM, each people tended to extol its own customs and values while perceiving other peoples as strange and awkward. Thus, the ancient Greeks saw the Asians as cowards, and the Romans considered themselves politically sophisticated and humane compared to the fierce Celts and Germans. These national prejudices were often based on ignorance and perpetuated STEREOTYPES, much like modern racism.

The modern concept of race and the origins of white racism can be traced to the European "age of discovery." Beginning in the fifteenth century, European EXPLORATION and colonization in the New World brought unprecedented contact with nonwhite peoples. The Europeans viewed these unfamiliar people as savages and saw themselves as Christians who were destined by God to rule over other races. Some colonizers believed that the heathens could be civilized and attempted religious conversion, while others saw the only option as subjugation through war or enslavement. Concepts of color also influenced the European view of race; in Elizabethan England, for example, black was associated with something "wicked" or "foul," and physical defects were considered reflections of defects in the soul.

In Europe the most loathsome heritage of racism was the quintessential quality attributed to the slave: that of nonhumanness. According to Aristotle, a slave was only a partial man who lacked the "governing element of the soul and therefore needed to be ruled by those possessing this element." By the time the Portuguese initiated the African slave trade in the 1400's, slaves were considered human beings but were treated as caste inferiors because they had been captured. Ironically, according to Ashley Montagu, it was only when the trafficking in slaves was declared immoral and inhumane by influential people in both Europe and the United States that the supporters of SLAVERY were forced to claim the biological inferiority of slaves on the basis of race. Their racialist ideas asserted that slaves were less human because of innate differences in character, ability, and intelligence.

Racial prejudices were well entrenched in European thought by the time Europeans colonized North America. As they dealt with various nonwhite populations, such as American Indians, Africans, and Chinese, or with unfamiliar European immigrant groups, such as Irish Catholics or Polish Jews, the issue was often whether or not such peoples were capable of ASSIMILATION into northern European-dominated American culture. Throughout U.S. history, influential members of the dominant culture claimed that other "races"—such as the Japanese, Mexicans, or Italians—were "unassimilable." This was tantamount to saying, "they are not like us; they cannot become like us." Once designated as "unassimilable," nonwhite peoples were persecuted and marginalized, often with the full consent of the law.

Racism Against American Indians. With the coming of Spanish, French, and English explorers and settlers to the New World came colonization, Christianity, disease, and destruction for the indigenous American Indian population. In the Spanish-ruled Caribbean Islands, for example, the native populations were nearly, if not entirely, devastated by disease and their exploitation as slave labor. Although the Catholic church and the Spanish crown did not advance the belief that native peoples were less than human, they endorsed the subjugation of a people by their own perceived ethnocentric superiority. This made for a growing disparity between those with power and privilege—the Spanish—and those without—the African and native populations. Consequently the practice of privilege of one racial group over others was formalized.

In the American colonies, the early English contact with and view of American Indians ensured that Indians would not be perceived as a lower caste but rather as lesser human beings—as savages or, at best, "noble savages." Initially, the English, like the Spanish, tried to convert the Indians. After an Indian massacre in 1622, however, the Virginia colonists reported that conquering the Indians was much easier than civilizing them. After KING PHILIP'S WAR inflicted heavy casualties on both sides, the colonists believed they were confirmed in their hostility and their view of Indians as "bloodthirsty savages."

This strong Anglo prejudice against native peoples

The Trail of Tears was only one instance of forced removal of American Indians resulting in death and hardship. This 1942 depiction by Robert Lindneux discounts the fact that most of the Indians made the difficult journey on foot. (Woolaroc Museum, Bartlesville, Okla.)

was expressed not only in efforts to control their sovereignty and way of life but also in extermination and systematic displacement of Indians from their homelands, as in the notorious TRAIL OF TEARS. Removal to western reservations marked U.S. policy toward Indians in the 1800's. The Commissioner of Indian Affairs, General Francis C. Walker, commented in 1871: "When dealing with savage men [Indians], as with savage beasts, no question of national honor can arise. Whether to fight, to run away, or to employ a ruse, is solely a question of expediency." Such attitudes fueled institutional racism in the U.S. government against Indians well into the twentieth century.

Racism Against African Americans. The first Africans were brought to colonial America in 1619 as INDENTURED SERVANTS. As it became more difficult to obtain bond servants from Europe and as the actual time served in bondage was shortened, other labor pools were needed to support the growing colonial economy, and more Africans were brought in. Originally, the white colonists based their subjugation of blacks, like that of Indians, on the alleged "heathenism" of these peoples. By the 1660's, however, the Africans were singled out for special treatment on the grounds of their race by Maryland and other colonies. Whereas white indentured servants served a specified number of years, those from Africa were compelled to serve in bondage until death. Thus began a two-hundred-year period of the most harsh form of institutional racism against African Americans.

The system of SLAVERY, besides meeting economic needs, fit prevailing European American views about the racial inferiority of blacks. Accordingly, African Americans were treated as less than human. The U.S. CONSTITUTION stated that each slave was to count as only three-fifths of a person in calculating the apportionment of state seats in federal government. Enslaved blacks were bought, sold, traded, and accounted for as property. They were forbidden to marry and prevented from keeping their families together. They were caricatured in the popular press as subhuman beasts of labor or as meek children who shared no humanity with their white masters. Even the minority of free blacks found their lives severely restricted. Because slavery was an integral part of the economy of many states, the generation of racist theories was actively supported by scientific, religious, and political leaders to maintain the prosperity of the system.

One of the key tactics of the ABOLITIONIST MOVE-

MENT was to showcase the speaking and literary abilities of educated African Americans such as Frederick DOUGLASS and Phillis WHEATLEY to disprove theories of blacks' inferiority. Harriet Beecher STOWE's novel *Uncle Tom's Cabin* (1851-1852), while relying on certain STEREOTYPES, nevertheless won compassion for the enslaved population among many European Americans because of its sympathetic portrayals.

Institutionalized racism against African Americans did not end with the official end of slavery in the 1860's but continued under other guises in spite of early CIVIL RIGHTS LEGISLATION. During RECONSTRUCTION, southern states instituted BLACK CODES to maintain the status quo. South Carolina's code of 1866 stated that the races were "separate and distinct, the one the highest and noblest type of humanity, the other the lowest and most degraded." Official SEGREGATION policies and JIM CROW LAWS relegated blacks to separate but inferior public facilities, and *PLESSY V. FERGUSON* (1896) established a precedent for "separate but equal" institutions that would remain in place for more than half a century. Meanwhile the KU KLUX KLAN and other groups terrorized blacks with frequent LYNCHINGS.

Beginning with *BROWN V. BOARD OF EDUCATION* in 1954, the U.S. government began to combat racism systematically and to open opportunities for African Americans through legal channels. Earlier in the century, the achievements of black athletes in the Olympic Games, black writers and artists in the HARLEM RENAISSANCE, and black activists in the NATIONAL ASSOCIATION FOR THE ADVANCEMENT OF COLORED

Perhaps the most overt case of anti-Japanese racism was the internment of Japanese Americans in the West during World War II. Here a family is transported under armed guard to a train that will take them to the Manzanar camp. (National Japanese American Historical Society)

People (NAACP) had already begun to affect white attitudes toward blacks. This change took on greater momentum with the Civil Rights movement of the 1950's and 1960's. With the introduction of affirmative action programs in the 1970's and 1980's, however, African Americans experienced a backlash of hostility from some European Americans who resented what they called preferential treatment for minorities in education and employment. Debates on race in the 1990's were still primarily focused on black-white relations, as this remained the most obvious division between the races in American society.

Racism Toward Other Groups. Various waves of immigration prompted racist responses from the white Anglo-Saxon Protestant (WASP) majority. Even Catholics and Germans were suspect and subject to discriminatory treatment in some areas in the eighteenth and nineteenth century because their culture was viewed as alien and threatening. New immigrants from southern and eastern Europe, whose appearance and customs were even less familiar, were denounced as inferior "races." Thus, during the peak immigration years from about 1880 to 1925, Jews, Poles, Serbians, Hungarians, Greeks, and other non-Teutonic peoples from Europe endured prejudice on "racial" grounds from established white Americans. Yet the most severe forms of racism were reserved for people of color such as Asian and Latino immigrants and migrants.

Since they began arriving in the United States in the mid-1800's as railroad workers, the Chinese endured overtly racist treatment. White supporters of nativism who resented the economic competition posed by the newcomers spread myths about Chinese people, predicted a disastrous invasion of the Chinese "race," and fomented anti-Chinese violence in a number of race riots. Anti-Chinese sentiment in the West pressured Congress into passing the Chinese Exclusion Act of 1882, effectively keeping out Chinese immigrants for sixty years and disqualifying those already in the country from U.S. citizenship.

Similar resentment and discrimination greeted the Japanese in California. For example, the city of San Francisco instituted segregated schools for them, and alien land laws prevented them from owning land. The worst form of institutional racism directed at this population was the Japanese American internment during World War II. Solely on the basis of their ancestry, they were expelled from the West Coast, forced to dispose of their property and businesses, and held for up to four years in internment camps in desolate areas. This injustice was not redressed until the U.S. government formally apologized and offered reparations to internees and their descendants more than forty years later.

Mexicans who had settled the Southwest before the Mexican-American War (1846-1848) felt the impact of various forms of racism that were linked to white Americans' contemptuous views of the Mexican nation. According to Arnoldo De León, many whites believed that Mexicans were "descended from ancestors who exhibited depraved and barbarous conduct"; moreover, some American leaders expressed the view that "backward" Mexico was "easy prey of the more adventurous enemy." Exploitation in the form of land grabbing from well-established Mexican families became routine in the Southwest after the war. Nor were Anglos in nineteenth century Texas troubled by the frequent killings of Mexicans. They were bolstered by what historian Rodolfo Acuña calls an "attitude of righteousness" that came to a climax during the war and the subsequent settlement of the Southwest. The war reinforced Anglos' sense of technological superiority and furthered the doctrine of Manifest Destiny.

A pattern for the exploitation of Mexican labor was established long before the large-scale border crossings that occurred in the twentieth century. In the 1880's, Mexican miners were paid less than half the wages of Anglo miners doing the same work. According to one mine owner, "They [the Mexicans] have been peons for generations. They will always remain so, as it is their natural condition." Such attitudes bolstered negative stereotypes and justified the unequal treatment of Mexican laborers well into the late 1900's. During the 1960's, farm labor leader César Chávez and the Chicano movement brought attention to the injustices suffered by Mexican Americans. Inspired by the Civil Rights movement, they made a case for Chicanos being treated as subhumans who, it was assumed, did not need a living wage or decent working conditions.

Technically, Latinos may belong to any race; the terms "Hispanic" and "Latino" are considered ethnic or cultural designations. Yet Latinos have often been treated as a subordinate racial group. Puerto Ricans in New York City were long consigned to the ghetto of Spanish Harlem rather than permitted to live in white neighborhoods. Those of African descent among both Puerto Ricans and Cuban Americans have been particularly affected by racism. Latino activists believe that brown skin per se puts Latinos at risk for racist treatment. For example, some Latino citizens have reported being mistreated by border officials or potential employers because they are suspected of being undocumented immigrants. Mexican appearance was enough to provoke the rage of European American soldiers during the ZOOT-SUIT RIOTS in Los Angeles in the 1940's.

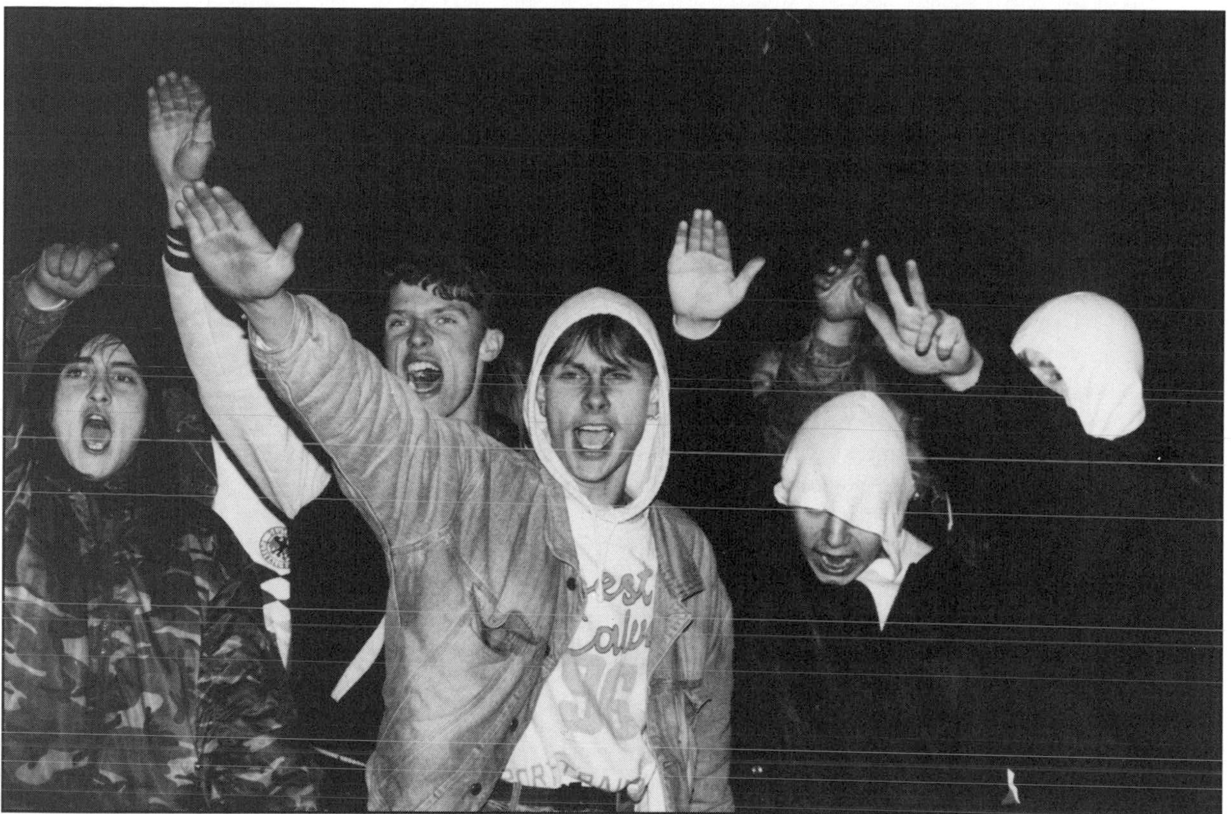

Neo-Nazis making Third Reich salute in 1991. White supremacist groups continue to flourish throughout North America and Europe. (AP/Wide World Photos)

Racism in a Multicultural Society. Great strides have been made toward abolishing white racism in the United States in the late twentieth century. Many court battles have been fought to ensure equal opportunity for people of all races. CIVIL RIGHTS LEGISLATION and the issues surrounding it have continued to be part of the national dialogue. Policies have been altered to promote equal rights in virtually all social institutions, although such policies are not always enforced. Public officials from corporate executives to baseball commissioners who make racist remarks are immediately criticized and are often forced to resign.

Changes have been made in the field of EDUCATION in the effort to socialize children to appreciate racial diversity. MULTICULTURAL EDUCATION documenting racism and celebrating the contributions of all racial groups has been absorbed into many school curricula. Most accredited teacher training institutions require some training in intergroup relations and multicultural education. ETHNIC STUDIES programs have become an established feature of most large colleges and universities, and research on racism has been enriched by the work of increasing numbers of sociologists of color. Educational efforts have extended to interracial dialogue and exchange in the workplace, in RELIGIOUS ORGANIZATIONS, and in youth programs that bring groups together for shared work projects. Human relations councils have been set up in cities and counties to encourage racial tolerance and help resolve intergroup conflicts. MUSEUMS have mounted exhibits devoted to racism-related themes, and the Museum of Tolerance in Los Angeles, which opened in 1993, is exclusively focused on the topic. (Visitors are given the choice of entering by doors for racists and nonracists, but only the one marked "racists" can be opened, illustrating the pervasiveness of racism.)

In spite of this progress, the subtle racism of the present day remains greatly influenced by the overt racism of the past. Racist echoes from the past can be heard whenever a white family removes its children from a predominantly black school, a politician claims that undocumented Latino immigrants are stealing "American" jobs, or a business leader engages in Japan-bashing. Numerous racial and ETHNIC SLURS remain part of many Americans' speech patterns, reflecting attitudes that are, at best, insensitive, or at worst, racist. Latino and African American leaders continue to blame racism and its consequences for various problems in their communities, including rates of education, EMPLOYMENT, and income that are lower than those of European Americans.

Nor has overt racism disappeared. It remains the policy of a number of white supremacist American organizations. HATE CRIMES have been well documented and scrutinized by a noted Filipino intellectual, E. San Juan, Jr., in his highly critical volume, *Racial Formations/Critical Transformations: Articulations of Power in Ethnic and Racial Studies in the United States* (1992). He identifies several manifestations of racism in the 1980's as violent as those documented in the past. These include the killing of African Americans in the Howard Beach and Bensonhurst incidents; various antibusing attacks; the 1982 killing of Chinese American Vincent CHIN by unemployed auto workers who thought he was Japanese; the racist harassment of students of color at several university campuses; the slaying of a man of Ethiopian descent by NEO-NAZI skinheads in Portland, Oregon; and the wanton murder of five Southeast Asian children and the wounding of thirty others at a Stockton, California, schoolyard by a white gunman with a hate psychosis. Organizations that monitor hate crimes contended in the early 1990's that such acts were on the rise, although this may be an indication of improved reporting and monitoring.

The U.S. CENSUS OF 1990 demonstrates the status of the diverse American population: One out of every four Americans is a person of color, and one out of three will be a person of color in the year 2000. It becomes incumbent upon everyone living in a multicultural society to understand racism and its devastating effects on groups and individuals, and to take all necessary steps to eliminate racism in themselves and others.

SUGGESTED READINGS. For a comprehensive historical perspective on race and racism, see Thomas F. Gossett's *Race: The History of an Idea in America* (1963). Both Stephen J. Gould and Ashley Montagu provide penetrating analyses of the fallacies of biological determinism in their respective books, *The Mismeasure of Man* (1981) and *Man's Most Dangerous Myth: The Fallacy of Race* (1942). In his primer, *Racism and Prejudice* (1972), James M. Jones writes with keen insights into those topics. Institutional racism and its role in public education is well documented in Meyer Weinberg's *A Chance to Learn: The History of Race and Education in the United States* (1977). Rodolfo Acuña in *Occupied America: The Chicano's Struggle Toward Liberation* (1972), Arnoldo De León in *They Called Them Greasers: Anglo Attitudes toward Mexicans in Texas, 1821-1900* (1983), and Ronald Takaki in *Iron Cages: Race and Culture in Nineteenth Century America* (1990) offer superb historical analyses of racism toward various American groups. See also Thomas Powell's *The Persistence of Racism in America* (1992) and Robert Miles's *Racism* (1990). For ordinary people's views, consult Studs Terkel's *Race: How Blacks and Whites Think and Feel About the American Obsession* (1992).—*Rudolfo Chávez Chávez*

Radical feminism. *See* **Feminism—radical**

Rain Dance: Ceremonial dance summoning rain from the gods to guarantee an abundant harvest. Performed chiefly by the PUEBLO Indians of New Mexico and Arizona, the Rain Dance differs from other American Indian dances. The Rain Dance is simply structured and its performers remain stationary throughout, unlike the corn dances, in which performers move in elaborate designs within a pattern of slow and fast dances. The songs that accompany the Rain Dances combine traditional music forms with complicated tonalities and rhythm. Male dancers sing and provide their own instrumental accompaniment using rattles while performing their dance.

Rainbow Coalition: Progressive, multicultural, black-led mass movement in American electoral politics that developed in 1983 around the leadership of Jesse JACKSON and remained an important political force throughout the 1980's.

Racial and ethnic groups in the United States experienced different levels of participation in formal political institutions depending on a number of factors including their geographic location, population size, and history. The result of these experiences was substantial inequality in political power among various groups in the multicultural society. African Americans, for example, were historically excluded from participation in institutional political processes through legal and extralegal agencies such as poll taxes, intimidation, and GERRYMANDERING.

African Americans usually acquired symbolic political power through appointments of intermediary black leaders in high profile positions. This tradition led to the development of a black elite that was committed to being junior partners in the process of achieving racial integration throughout the society. Historically, most of this leadership came from nonelected positions and usually from extrapolitical movements such as strikes, boycotts, and civil disobedience.

Jesse Jackson had become a clergyman after working with Dr. Martin Luther KING, Jr., during the CIVIL RIGHTS MOVEMENT. He went on to lead OPERATION PUSH in Chicago and took an increasingly vocal stand on national and international issues.

In the 1980's, the Democratic presidential primaries became an arena to present African American grievances inside the framework of the organized DEMOCRATIC PARTY. Jackson organized a united front of liberal integrationists, socialists, trade unionists, feminists, gays and lesbians, and racial minority constituencies around the presidential campaign of 1984. By banding together, these diverse groups hoped to find greater power and government responsiveness to their needs. The Rainbow Coalition platform was based on four claims: that Jackson had a base among the "black masses," that he was a central figure in southern black politics, that the campaign would stimulate black voter registration, and that Jackson's candidacy would generate significant "coattail" effects that would propel other outsiders into the electoral process at state and local levels. None of these claims was proven true by events that followed.

Jesse Jackson addresses members of the Rainbow Coalition at a rally in Washington, D.C. (Hazel Hankin)

To maintain national political positioning, Jackson had to pull the left-leaning Rainbow more toward the political center by the time of the 1988 presidential campaign. This process required that Jackson purge its activist tendencies by blocking democratic elections of local Rainbow leadership and by placing gag orders on socialist and radical black nationalist dissenters. In 1989 Jackson called for the right to appoint all Rainbow Coalition leaders at the congressional district rank. Thousands of local and community-based activists left the coalition in protest, and several splinter groups organized.

Although the coalition earned support from traditional African American political elites, in the 1990's Bill Clinton was able to undermine Jackson's leadership role in the African American community, severely diminishing the power of the Rainbow Coalition. Clinton's presidential victory in the 1992 general election resulted in the rise of Ron Brown, one of Jackson's protégés, who had become the chair of the Democratic National Committee and was appointed Secretary of Commerce. This resulted in many workers, activists, and young people leaving the Rainbow Coalition and in its leadership closely adhering to Clinton's policies.

SUGGESTED READINGS. Manning Marable's *Black American Politics* (1985) and Adolph L. Reed, Jr.'s *The Jesse Jackson Phenomenon* (1986) provide detailed accounts of the development of the Rainbow Coalition. Additional information can be found in Frank R. Parker's *Black Votes Count* (1990) and Sheila D. Collins' *The Rainbow Challenge* (1986).

Randolph, A[sa] Philip (Apr. 15, 1889, Crescent City, Fla.—May 16, 1979, New York, N.Y.): African American labor unionist and activist. From his teens until his death at the age of ninety, Randolph actively protested injustice. In 1917 he helped found *The Messenger*, which opposed black support of World War I. In 1925 he organized porters and maids against the Pullman Company. His protests during the 1940's helped establish the Fair Employment Practice Committee and end segregation in the army. From 1955 to 1968, Randolph was a vice president of the AMERICAN FEDERATION OF LABOR and CONGRESS OF INDUSTRIAL ORGANIZATIONS (AFL-CIO) and was prominent in the 1963 MARCH ON WASHINGTON.

Rankin, Jeanette (June 11, 1880, Grant Creek Ranch, near Missoula, Mont.—May 18, 1973, Carmel, Calif.): Congresswoman and pacifist. Rankin was the first woman elected to the House of Representatives (1917 and 1941), and she was the only member of Congress to oppose United States entry into World Wars I and II. In 1913 Rankin was Secretary for the National American Woman Suffrage Association (NAWSA). In 1919 she and Jane ADDAMS were delegates to the Second International Congress of Women. She was a strong follower of Mahatma Gandhi; on visits to India, she noted the heavy U.S. involvement in Third World nations. She opposed the Cold War and the Korean War, and during the Vietnam War set up the "Jeannette Rankin Brigade" to protest the war.

Jeannette Rankin, pictured here in 1968, was elected to Congress three years before women won the right to vote. (AP/Wide World Photos)

Rap music: Type of African American popular music marked by the rapid delivery of rhymed text over a prerecorded rhythmic track.

Perhaps the most innovative form of African American music since bebop, rap combines two distinctive African cultural features: verbal jousting (known in African American culture as "playin' the dozens") and music in which rhythm—not melody—is the key element. Like its Jamaican ancestors, "talk over" and "toasted" reggae, in which disc jockeys (DJ's) insult one another and boast of their sexual prowess over instrumental breaks in records, rap music is characterized by its reliance on prerecorded sounds rather than live performances on musical instruments.

For the rap artist, the cassette recorder, drum machine, and record turntable have replaced the traditional drums-bass-guitar-piano format of popular music and ROCK MUSIC. Sampling—digitally recording music and sounds from audio tape, records, or radio—is at the center of the rap "attitude," which insists on the public domain of all music. Aside from undermining and reshaping conventional concepts of music, the rap artist's reliance on cheap, everyday consumer products radically democratizes the concept of music "performer": Not everyone can learn to play the piano, but almost anyone can learn to rap or tape and spin records.

Rap had its roots in the late 1960's with Kool DJ Herc, a Jamaican immigrant who specialized in "talk over" reggae at house parties in the West Bronx in New York City. Herc quickly discovered that African Americans would not dance to reggae, so he began talking over the instrumental breaks on records, urging on dancers with verbal pyrotechnics. Other house party DJ's adapted and refined Herc's popular methods. DJ Theodor invented scratching: spinning a record backward and forward at rapid speeds with the needles in the grooves, thus transforming the record into a percussion instrument. Grandmaster Flash became an expert at punch phrasing: hitting a particular break on one turntable while the same record plays on another turntable, thus allowing the DJ to punctuate rhythmic phrases.

The first rap records came out in the mid-1970's, issued by bands such as Fatback and the Sugar Hill Gang. It was not until the early 1980's with "The Breaks" by Kurtis Blow, "The Message" by Grandmaster Flash and the Furious Five, and "Walk This Way," an Aerosmith song turned inside out by Run-D.M.C., that rap began to have an impact on popular music.

The late 1980's witnessed the popularity of rap with mainstream audiences, most of whom were introduced to the form through music videos. The subsequent growth of rap into a dominant force in popular music was related to its proliferation into a number of subgenres, almost one for every kind of taste: boast raps, insult raps, news raps, message raps, nonsense raps, party raps, and advice raps. Influential rap artists can be found in virtually every one of these categories: respectively, L. L. Cool J., Ice Cube, Public Enemy, Arrested Development, Kriss Kross, Hammer, and Queen Latifah. Rap music also gained notoriety in the early 1990's when Ice-T's "Cop Killer" was confiscated from some record stores and widely condemned for inciting violence. Rap remains the rebellious voice of youth culture and an almost exclusively African American music form, despite the occasional successes of white rappers such as the Beastie Boys and Vanilla Ice, or Latino rappers such as Rico, Mellow Man Ace, and Kid Frost. Despite the prevalence of misogynistic lyrics and imagery in rap music, many female artists have attained popularity as rappers, including such stars as Queen Latifah, MC Lyte, Salt-N-Pepa, and TLC.

SUGGESTED READINGS. The best historical and analytical studies of rap music can be found in David Toop's *The Rap Attack: African Jive to New York Hip Hop* (1984) and *Rap Attack 2: African Rap to Global Hip Hop* (1992), Dick Hebdige's *Cut 'N' Mix* (1987), and Charles Gillet's *The Sound Of The City* (1983). African American cultural critic Nelson George provides his own perspective on rap in *Fresh, Hip Hop Don't Stop* (1985), and Michael Small analyzes the newest generation of rappers in *Break It Down: The Inside Story from the New Leaders of Rap* (1992).

Rape: Rape, or sexual assault, is any behavior used to force (or attempt to force) sexual contact with another person against that person's will. Sexual abuse, a more general term, refers to attempted rape, fondling, inappropriate touching, or even verbal harassment. Although rape is not inherent in the nature of males or females, there are few societies free of rape, sexual assault, or abuse.

Rape in the United States is a legal term, its meaning defined somewhat differently from one state to another. Before the 1980's, rape was defined almost entirely as a crime against females. As part of an effort to rid society of sexist laws, most states have replaced rape statutes with more generic and neutral sexual assault statutes. Whatever the label, forced sex is overwhelmingly a crime against females, and whatever the legal definition, there are always "informal" or "working definitions." These definitions vary from one culture to another but are used on a daily basis with such regularity and consistency that they are largely responsible for the public's understanding of rape and its reactions to rape victims. These definitions even influence the treatment of rape cases in the criminal justice system.

The incidence of reported sexual assault is higher in the United States than in other, comparable industrialized societies, but this could be a result of greater

Rise in Forcible Rape: 1970-1990

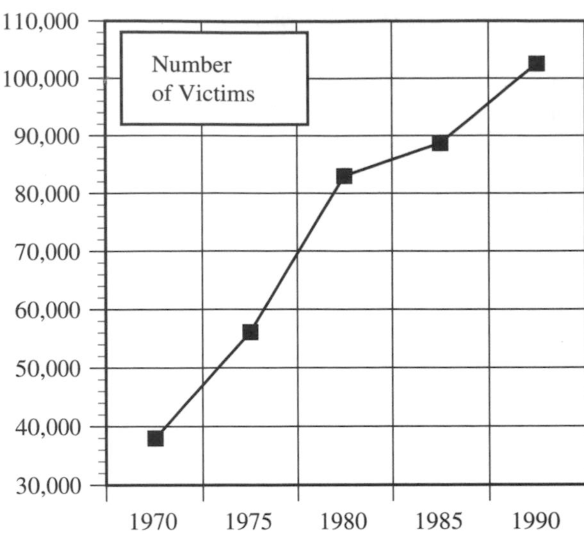

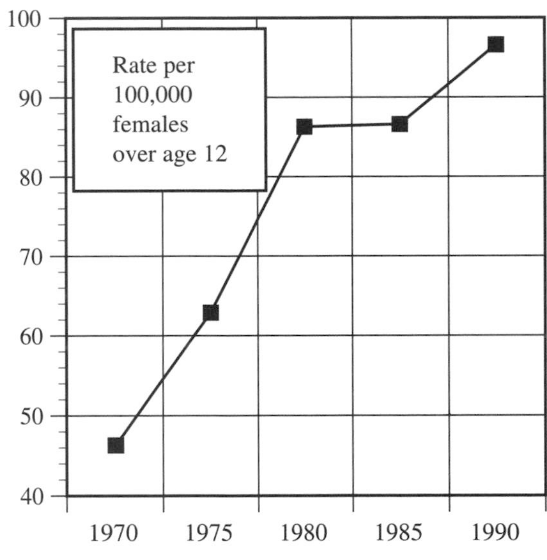

Source: Data are from *Statistical Abstract of the United States, 1992.* Table 293. Washington, D.C.: U.S. Government Printing Office, 1992.
Note: Includes reports of forcible rapes and rape attempts.

awareness of sexual assault as a crime and of the higher prevalence of reporting. Proponents of FEMINISM and the WOMEN'S LIBERATION MOVEMENT brought greater public attention to the problem of rape beginning in the 1970's with workshops and rape crisis centers. By the 1990's, even popular women's MAGAZINES were discussing "date rape." Sexual assault certainly is not unique to the United States; it has occurred in some form throughout history and is found to be present in most societies. In general, societies with a high frequency of rape are those in which sexual assault and sexual abuse are culturally allowed, dismissed as "natural," or simply ignored. Upon closer examination, the few societies reported to be rape-free have simply not defined or labeled a certain abusive behavior as rape or sexual assault according to Western standards.

Almost any behavior can be perceived as the norm if it has been learned as such. Even within the United States, definitions of rape vary greatly in terms of use of force, consent, and relationship between victim and assailant. There is, however, a commonly accepted STEREOTYPE of what constitutes actual rape: a stranger-to-stranger assault, taking place in a setting where the victim is engaging in socially acceptable behavior (for example, going home from work), and involving physical violence or use of a weapon.

Rape-Prone Societies. There are many explanations of rape and of why some environments are relatively rape-free while others pose high rape risks. Research into the causes and incidence of sexual assault has produced no simplistic cause-and-effect relationships, but it has yielded some understanding of the kinds of social and cultural settings associated with a high frequency of rapes. Several characteristics of rape-prone societies are singled out for discussion here because research findings are consistent if not always conclusive.

Where women live in an unequal relationship with men, they tend to live at risk of violence (including rape or sexual assault) being perpetrated against them. Inequality of females in relation to males means that women have not attained the same status (position or power) in society as males. Inequality may manifest itself in differences in decision-making authority (inside the home versus outside the home), in political and economic power, and in patriarchal social institutions supported by patriarchal social values.

One apparent repercussion of gender inequality in diverse settings is in the incidence of violence against women (including rape). For example, in *Family Violence in Cross-Cultural Perspective* (1989), David Levinson reported a high incidence of wife beating in preliterate societies characterized by male-female inequality. In *Four Theories of Rape in American Society* (1989), Larry Baron and Murray Straus report rape rates in the United States to be highest in states where women hold the lowest position in relation to men.

Male dominance is often an integral part of male-female inequality and such dominance may, in its most negative manifestation, sanction violence against women or, at the very least, treat women as the property of males. War is a good example. Not only is war a legitimizer of violence, but it also sets up a situation where the usual moral and normative constraints and inhibitions are temporarily suspended. Where male dominance is prevalent, the lifting or temporary suspension of social controls may be all that is needed to usher in an open season for raping women. In *Against Our Will: Men, Women, and Rape* (1975), Susan Brownmiller documents that rape historically has been an inevitable by-product of war. From ancient times through the reports of "sex camps" in Bosnia in the former Yugoslavia in 1993, where there is war, there is rape of women. Rape is the ultimate act of victory in war, since rape "by a conquering soldier destroys all remaining illusions of power and property for men of the defeated side."

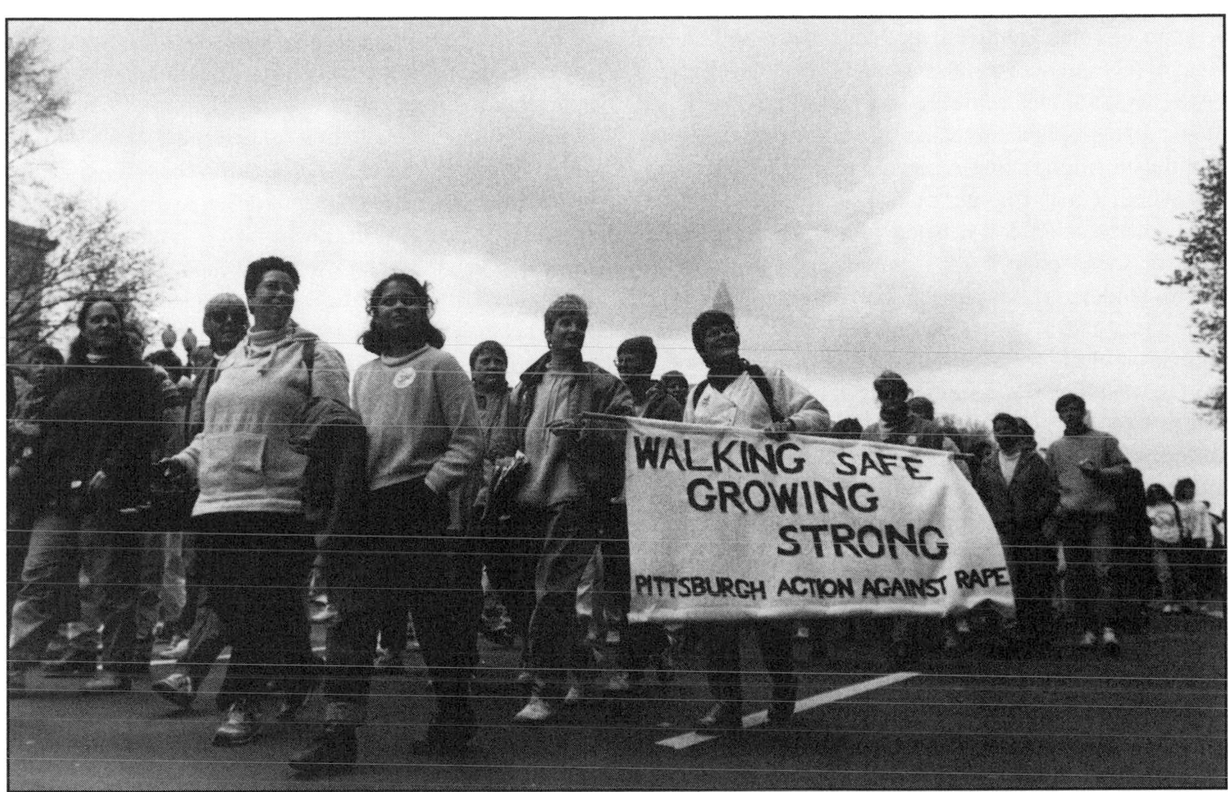

Beginning in the 1970's, women staged marches and "take back the right" rallies to bring public attention to the problem of rape. (Sally Ann Rogers)

Cultural Variations on Rape in the United States. If rape is a product of culture, there are obviously variations, not only in frequency and pattern but also in how women react and survive as victims and in how communities treat offenders and survivors. Among the various racial and ethnic groups in the United States, there is evidence of cultural diversity with regard to how rape is defined and how these groups deal with rape victims, survivors, and perpetrators. Groups such as African Americans, Mexican Americans, and European Americans present the most obvious examples of diversity.

A two-part research project reported in *The Second Assault: Rape and Public Attitudes* by Joyce Williams and Karen Holmes (1981) compares community attitudes about rape, rapists, and survivors in sample populations of European Americans, African Americans, and Mexican Americans in San Antonio, Texas. The work also examines the responses of adult rape survivors in these populations. The findings clearly demonstrate that across all groups, rape is a devastating experience, leaving its survivors feeling stronger for having survived yet extremely angry and vulnerable. As one woman put it, "The absolutely worst thing about rape is knowing that you will never again feel safe." Although all survivors shared a devastating experience, there were, nevertheless, some obvious cultural variations among victims that were linked to community attitudes about rape. These are rooted in each group's unique history in relation to sex roles, male-female relationships, and the meanings assigned to forced sex.

For example, there is a certain tension about rape in the African American community. The reason for such tension is historically based: The accusation of raping a white woman has been routinely used as a weapon of social control over black males. Often the charge of rape was a false one, but in the criminal justice system, any white person had more credibility than a black person. Because of this history, there is skepticism among some African Americans about rape and whether it is in fact "real" as opposed to a fictitious charge used for reasons of racism, vindictiveness, or social control.

The tendency to approach the charge of rape with skepticism and to assess its authenticity based on the reputation of the female often results in judgments that are less than fair for victims of rape. The San Antonio research suggests, however, that once blacks make their initial assessment of a victim's reputation and integrity, they tend to be more accepting of the reality of the crime of rape and less judgmental in their attitudes toward victims than the other two populations. They recognize the harsh reality of rape—both for falsely accused males and for women as victims. Two things apparently contribute to a supportive environment for rape survivors in the African American community: the common awareness that rape risks are real and the fact that traditional male-female sex-role stereotypes and expectations are less rigid among African Americans than among some groups. Consequently, the fact that a woman may fall victim while engaged in behavior that is socially unacceptable (hitchhiking, for example) makes her no less a victim.

Of the three community samples, Mexican Americans in San Antonio were found to have the greatest difficulty in coping with rape. The Mexican American community generally holds more rigid traditional expectations for women than do African Americans or European Americans and therefore tend to place blame for rape on the woman if she is not following her prescribed roles. Even when a woman was not blamed, she was often urged by those around her to forget what happened rather than talk about it. Where men were given responsibility for rape, they were perceived as being "sick" or mentally ill, thus escaping many of the negative consequences women experience. Not unexpectedly, Mexican American females tend to be more supportive of victims and more accepting of the reality of rape than males. In this context, Mexican American women may become victims rather than survivors, suffering more adverse effects from the assault than either African American or European American women.

In San Antonio, the European American community was found to hold more negative attitudes toward women than the other two groups. Females, more than males in this group, were found to hold women responsible for rape and to display skepticism about the reality of any alleged rape except an assault carried out by a stranger against a victim who was engaged in traditional, socially acceptable behavior or activities (such as working). There was also a tendency to view violent rapes involving use of a weapon as more "real" than others. Perhaps the higher level of female over male skepticism about rape was a type of self protection, a false sense of security that it "can't happen to me."

In summary, groups tend to define rape in different ways based on experience and socialization. The extent to which a society is rape-prone is influenced by the degree of equality between males and females and the tendency of a community or society to allow rape simply by failing to acknowledge and ensure the right of every person to choose his or her sexual partner and to engage in sex only by mutual consent.

SUGGESTED READINGS. *Against Our Will: Men, Women, and Rape* (1975) by Susan Brownmiller is feminist in perspective and strident in tone. It is, however, a carefully documented historical record of rape across time and cultures that has influenced scholars, researchers, and service-providers alike. In *Forcible Rape: The Crime, the Victim, and the Offender* (1977), editors Duncan Chappell, Robley Geis, and Gilbert Geis pull together a collection of scholarly works dealing with rape from the perspectives of social scientists, therapists, and criminal justice professionals. Joyce E. Williams and Karen A. Holmes's *The Second Assault: Rape and Public Attitudes* (1987), a study of public attitudes about rape in San Antonio, Texas, is the first empirical work to compare attitudes across ethnic groups. In *Rape* (1986), editors Sylvana Tomaselli and Ray Porter present a collection of works that explore rape from a variety of perspectives. Lee Ellis, in *Theo-*

ries of Rape (1989), and Larry Baron and Murray A. Straus, in *Four Theories of Rape in American Society* (1989), test various theoretical propositions in order to formulate models for rape prediction and prevention.—*Joyce E. Williams*

Reconstruction (1867-1877): Reorganization of politics and society in the southern states following the Civil War. At the beginning of the period, the South was physically devastated; it had lost its system of railroads, for example, and many of its farm lands were overgrown with weeds and saplings. The former slaves, or freedmen, were celebrating their independence, but they had no land, tools, draft animals, homes, income, or legal rights. It was left to the military, the president, Congress, and state and local governments to rebuild the South and to settle questions about the future place of blacks in society.

Presidential Reconstruction. Serving in Congress was considered a part-time job in the nineteenth century, and accordingly Congress went home on a long recess after the surrender of Confederate troops in 1865. This left President Andrew Johnson in Washington, D.C., to grapple alone with the questions of just how the southern states should be readmitted to the Union, what early steps should be taken to rebuild the war-ravaged South, and what the new role of African Americans would be in the South. Although President Abraham Lincoln had made some conciliatory statements about Reconstruction in the months before his death, these statements were designed in part to induce the southern states to lay down their arms. It seems likely that Lincoln would have pursued a more aggressive Reconstruction policy after seeing the failure of his conciliation efforts.

Through a strange quirk of fate, Lincoln—a Repub-

Gatherings were held in both the North and South to celebrate the official end of slavery, ushering in the tumultuous Reconstruction period. (Library of Congress)

The Freedmen's Bureau's efforts to aid former slaves in their arduous shift to freedom provoked the anger and resentment of some European Americans, as seen in this extreme cartoon. (Library of Congress)

lican, a Northerner, and an opponent of slavery—was succeeded in April, 1865, by Johnson, a lifelong Democrat, a Tennessee resident, and a man uninterested in rights for black people. Lincoln's decision to "balance his ticket" in the 1864 election by including a vice-presidential candidate very different from himself played a major role in the early shaping of Reconstruction policy.

Johnson encouraged the southern states to call conventions to write new state constitutions; then new state governments would be formed and new congressmen elected. Johnson made few demands of the southern states except that they admit secession had been illegal and that they ratify the THIRTEENTH AMENDMENT to the U.S. CONSTITUTION, permanently ending all SLAVERY in the United States. The southern states did the things Johnson asked of them and sent congressmen to Washington to claim their seats. Johnson took the attitude that by December, 1865, Reconstruction was largely at an end.

As they watched southern events from their home districts, however, northern congressmen were infuriated. The new southern state governments had begun passing BLACK CODES, which were modeled on the old Slave Codes and were designed to control the freedmen in certain ways. These new state laws typically made it illegal for black people to own guns, be out late at night, serve on juries, and—perhaps most ominously—testify against white people in a court of law. Northerners in Congress began to feel that the great sacrifices of the Civil War years had been for naught, and that the South was emerging from the war completely unchanged. This impression was reinforced when congressmen looked at the names of the newly elected southern members. The list included former Confederate generals, colonels, members of

Congress, and even the vice president of the Confederacy.

Congressional Reconstruction. When Congress returned to Washington in December, 1865, it vowed to ensure that the Civil War sacrifices would bring genuine change to the South. The first step was to refuse admittance to the newly elected Southerners. Then, in passing the Civil Rights Act of 1866, Congress nullified the Black Codes by requiring equality before the law for all citizens. Congress also enacted a law extending the life of the FREEDMEN'S BUREAU, a government agency designed to help the most destitute Southerners by providing written labor contracts and setting up schools for the former slaves.

Johnson vetoed both the Civil Rights Act of 1866 and the renewal of the Freedmen's Bureau. He argued that these laws gave too many powers to the national government and urged the states to protect black citizens. Johnson's arguments rang hollow after major RACE RIOTS in Memphis, Tennessee, and New Orleans, Louisiana, in 1866, which state and local authorities were unable to suppress. Congress passed versions of the two contested laws over Johnson's veto. To ensure that a future Congress would not repeal the Civil Rights Act, members of Congress framed the FOURTEENTH AMENDMENT to the CONSTITUTION. This amendment declared that every person born in the United States was a citizen of the United States and was subject to equal protection before the law.

In the Military Reconstruction Act, Congress refused to recognize the southern state governments fostered by the president, instead remanding the South to military control. Under this act states would be readmitted to the Union when they had written new constitutions satisfactory to Congress and when they had ratified the Fourteenth Amendment. Once again Johnson vetoed the law and Congress overrode his veto.

Finally, Congress considered forbidding state disfranchisement of persons because of race. The lawmakers' motivations for such a move were clearly mixed. On the one hand, they wanted to give African Americans a tool with which they might protect themselves. Using the army to protect black rights was expensive and could not continue forever. If black people could vote, congressmen reasoned, they could help choose legislators sympathetic to black rights and sheriffs who would be just enforcers of the law. The Republican majority in Congress undoubtedly had a partisan motive as well. Their party had never existed in the South and would continue to be a regional (northern) party unless they could find a way to attract southern voters. Most southern whites were unlikely to embrace the party of Lincoln, but southern blacks undoubtedly would. In 1869 Congress framed the FIFTEENTH AMENDMENT, which declared that states could not limit the right to vote on account of race. This amendment brought change to many northern states as well, since only six northern states had previously introduced black voting.

Reconstruction in the South. Under Congress' plan, the southern states quickly reorganized their governments and ratified the Fourteenth and Fifteenth amendments. With one exception, all the new state governments were controlled by the REPUBLICAN PARTY. Black citizens provided the great bulk of southern Republican votes; important leadership also came from two groups of whites in the South. One was a group of men of northern birth, most of them Union veterans who had fought in the South and then decided to stay there. The other was a small group of native white Southerners, mostly former Whigs, who decided to battle the Democrats by joining the Republican Party.

Robert De Large was one of a number of U.S. representatives from South Carolina during Reconstruction. (Library of Congress)

Reconstruction was a peak of African American political power in the United States, featuring black voting and office-holding at a level that would not be equalled until late in the twentieth century. Thousands of blacks were elected to local office, hundreds to state legislatures, twenty to the U.S. House of Representatives, and two to the U.S. Senate. Together, the black and white southern Republicans founded the first system of public schools in the region, funded the railroads, and built up state institutions including universities, hospitals, and asylums. Citizens' tax bills increased, although the amount Southerners paid in taxes never equalled that paid by Northerners.

Southern white Democrats (also called "Conservatives") reacted with horror as they saw themselves losing control of their states. They were angry at seeing African Americans holding public office and perhaps angrier at the election of white Union veterans. In an attempt to regain control of their states, Democrats turned to the KU KLUX KLAN, which became almost an arm of the DEMOCRATIC PARTY at the time. By using threats, beatings, and assassinations, the Klan saw to it that Republicans began to lose elections in the South. Congress reacted by passing a series of Enforcement Acts (1870-1871), making it a crime to hinder a citizen's constitutional rights, including the right to assemble, speak freely, and vote. The Enforcement Acts had the desired effect of breaking up the Ku Klux Klan, but interference with black voting continued. As Democrats regained control of many counties, they found they could control elections by more peaceful means, including ballot-box stuffing.

By 1876 only three southern states remained in Republican hands. After a presidential election that year, the victor, Rutherford B. Hayes, made it clear that U.S. troops would no longer play a major enforcement role in the South. Yet it is simplistic to say that Reconstruction ended with this declaration in 1877. In some counties of the South, black voting and Republican victories had ended much earlier. In other areas, ranging from Norfolk, Virginia, to Jackson, Mississippi, the Republicans controlled county or city governments well into the 1880's.

The Reconstruction Amendments. Among the most important achievements of Reconstruction were the addition to the CONSTITUTION of three amendments designed to ensure equality of citizens regardless of race. The THIRTEENTH AMENDMENT abolished SLAVERY, the FOURTEENTH promised equality before the law for all citizens, and the FIFTEENTH prohibited states from denying the right to vote on account of race. All three amendments became virtual dead letters between 1875 and 1900, at least as they pertained to the rights of members of minority groups. Although these amendments were designed to protect the rights of African Americans in particular, other groups, including women and Asian Americans, would later attempt to use the amendments to secure rights before the courts.

Although the old system of bond slavery never reappeared in the United States after passage of the Thirteenth Amendment, many blacks were returned to a system in which they worked for white plantation owners without cash payments and with their rights to leave the plantation severely limited. Under this system of peonage (debt servitude), former slaves and their descendants were advanced credit at the plantation store but then found that their year's income did not erase their debt. State law forbid them moving on to other employment until the debt was cleared. The system of peonage also appeared in lumbering and mining camps. Although federal statutes prohibited it, the practice continued despite occasional prosecutions.

The Supreme Court backed away from any real commitment to equal rights before the law in several cases of the late nineteenth century. In the *Civil Rights Cases* (1883), the SUPREME COURT ruled that the Fourteenth Amendment forbade states to discriminate because of race but did not bar private individuals or companies from discriminating. Thus, SEGREGATION by individual hotels, restaurants, and theaters was permissible under the Fourteenth Amendment. In *PLESSY V. FERGUSON* (1896), the Court ruled that even if a state law called for racial segregation (in this case on railroads), the requirement of separate facilities was not an abridgement of anyone's rights, so long as the facilities provided for the two races were equal in quality.

In the area of voting, southern states introduced a variety of devices for preventing blacks (and many poor whites) from voting. Preventive strategies included requiring payment of a poll tax before a citizen could register to vote and certain intelligence and LITERACY TESTS that were often administered in a racially biased way. The U.S. Supreme Court ruled that Mississippi's 1890 constitution, with its provisions for a poll tax, literacy test, and understanding test, was not in violation of the Fifteenth Amendment because the document did not mention race (*Williams v. Mississippi*, 1898). Black voting in Mississippi, and elsewhere in the South, was almost nonexistent by 1900.

Although the failures of Reconstruction left the South a region of one-party politics with a large group of second-class citizens, the Reconstruction amendments to the U.S. Constitution did lay the legal foundation for progress toward CIVIL RIGHTS for blacks and other minority groups, especially after the 1950's.

SUGGESTED READINGS. A good comprehensive treatment of Reconstruction is Eric Foner's *Reconstruction: America's Unfinished Revolution, 1863-1877* (1988). The period of congressional Reconstruction and its aftermath is covered well in William Gillette's *Retreat from Reconstruction, 1869-1979* (1979). —*Stephen Cresswell*

Reconstructionist Jews. *See* **Jews—Reconstructionist**

Red Cloud [Makhpía-Lúta] (1822, near North Platte, Nebr.—Dec. 10, 1909, Pine Ridge Reservation, S.Dak.): Chief of the Oglala Sioux Indians who led opposition to the Bozeman Trail through Indian lands in Colorado and Montana. The FETTERMAN MASSACRE (1866) and Red Cloud's raids finally led to the abandonment of the trail (1868). Red Cloud later made peace with the white settlers but was removed as chief (1881) and retired to Pine Ridge Reservation, South Dakota.

Red scare: Fear in the early twentieth century that Soviet Communism would spread in the United States. In 1917, a Communist government took control of Russia. Because Communists ("reds") vowed to lead an international revolution, U.S. leaders became worried that they were secretly working to undermine American society and overthrow the U.S. government. Even

Alleged German Communists await deportation during the 1919-1920 red scare. (Library of Congress)

though there was very little evidence to support such fears, in 1919 and 1920 the U.S. attorney general tried to jail or expel all "Bolsheviks." These actions involved direct violations of CIVIL RIGHTS. The red scare led to censorship and a sometimes hysterical fear and distrust of immigrants from eastern Europe. It reinforced feelings of American NATIONALISM and NATIVISM. A second red scare occurred in the 1950's, when Senator Joseph McCarthy led congressional hearings attempting to ferret out Communists in the government and the entertainment industry.

Mortgage Disclosure Act requiring lenders to make public the locations of their loans; and the growth of community development banks such as South Shore Bank in Chicago.

Redlining has continued to be an issue in local politics across the United States, as when Los Angeles mayoral candidate Richard Riordan was accused in 1993 of having interests in banks that rarely made loans to minorities.

Reform Jews. *See* **Jews—Reform**

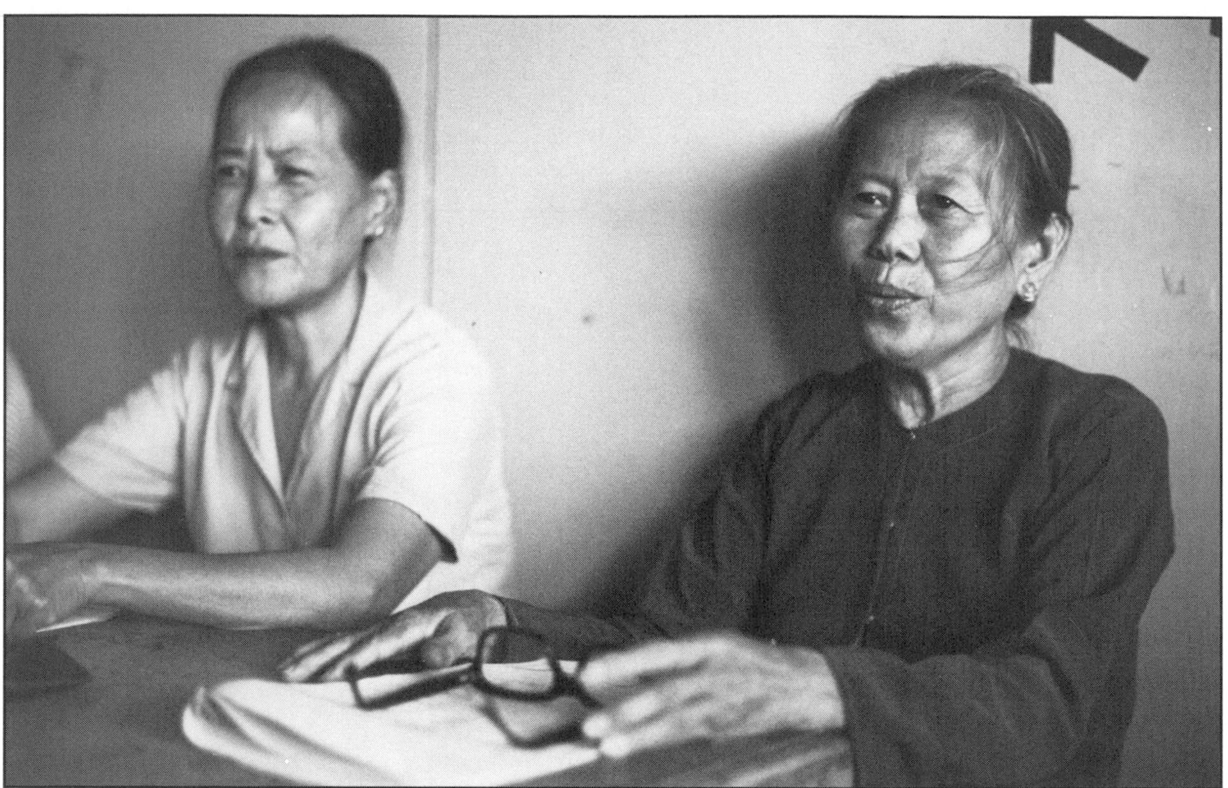

The Refugee Act of 1980 eased the way for the admission of large numbers of Vietnamese boat people such as these two women in a Malaysian refugee camp. (A. Hollmann/UNHCR)

Redlining: Practice employed by some financial institutions of refusing to grant loans in INNER-CITY and other so-called high risk neighborhoods. Attacked as discriminatory by CIVIL RIGHTS and neighborhood organizations since the 1960's, redlining has contributed to problems of unemployment, substandard housing, and economic underdevelopment in many urban areas.

Efforts to combat the practice include the 1977 Community Reinvestment Act urging banks to make home loans in low-income areas and to publicize their lending policies to the community; the 1985 Home

Refugee Act of 1980: Act of Congress that changed the definition of the term "refugee" and opened the door for easier admission of REFUGEES to the United States. Previously, only people fleeing countries in the Middle East or those ruled by Communists could be classified as refugees. This legislation made it possible for one who had left her or his home country and who could not return because of persecution or a "well-founded fear of persecution" to be considered for refugee status. The act was pushed through by President Jimmy Carter in response to the vast numbers of displaced Southeast Asian refugees and particularly to the plight of Vietnamese BOAT PEOPLE.

The increased limit on numbers did not apply to Cubans, most Haitians, or illegal entrants arriving from Mexico (including Salvadorans and Guatemalans). In the first decade, most refugees came from Southeast Asia, Eastern Europe, and the Soviet Union, but the passage of the act made it possible for people from Africa, the Near East, and Central America to come as well. The act entitled all refugees to certain federal benefits and reimbursed states for the cost of assisting refugees during their first three years of resettlement. It also authorized the attorney general to grant work permits to those seeking asylum pending the outcome of their request.

Refugee Relief Act (1953): Authorized 205,000 nonquota immigrant visas to refugees (people in non-Communist countries who could not return to their home countries), escapees (people who fled from Communist-dominated areas of Europe who could not return because of their political beliefs), and German expellees (people of German ethnic origin living in the German Federal Republic who fled from Albania, Bulgaria, Czechoslovakia, Estonia, Hungary, Latvia, Lithuania, Poland, Romania, the Soviet Union, Yugoslavia, and areas within these countries' control). The secretary of the Treasury could make loans to defray immigrants' transportation costs. The law was in effect until December 31, 1956.

Refugees: People fleeing war, persecution, famine, or other danger. Although the United States has traditionally been portrayed as a land of refuge, it had no official refugee policy until the mid-1900's. Then, refugees from Communist regimes were favored. Increasingly since the post-World War II period, American immigration laws have defined "refugees" as people who have been forced to leave their homelands because of persecution or well-founded fears of persecution on account of political beliefs, race, religion, or nationality. More than two million people thus classified as refugees have entered the United States.

Historical Background. As early as 1783, George Washington declared the new United States to be a place of refuge, "open to receive the persecuted and

One of the largest waves of refugees ever admitted to the United States consisted of Southeast Asians fleeing the chaos that followed the Vietnam War. Here, Laotian workers in Merced, Calif., sample corn on the cob as they adjust to American life. (L. Gubb/UNHCR)

oppressed of all nations." Until the early twentieth century, this view of the country as a safe haven was fairly realistic. Although the U.S. government had no programs to help oppressed people migrate, those who could manage to enter the United States on their own were able to settle and make new lives.

As the United States began to restrict immigration, however, it became less open to those escaping hardships of all kinds, political as well as economic. At first, the restrictions were directed primarily at Asians. The CHINESE EXCLUSION ACT of 1882 denied virtually all Chinese the right to enter the United States. The unwritten GENTLEMEN'S AGREEMENT between the American and Japanese governments ended most Japanese immigration beginning in 1907.

After WORLD WAR I, the United States entered a period that historians often refer to as "the era of isolation." The IMMIGRATION ACT OF 1924 limited total immigration from Europe to 164,667 people per year and set quotas for migrants from each country that were intended to severely restrict migration from southern and eastern Europe.

Restrictive immigration policies, NATIVISM, and XENOPHOBIA (fear of foreigners) worked together to keep the door closed to refugees during the years between the world wars. In 1939, Congress failed to pass a bill that would have helped twenty thousand German refugee children, most of whom were Jewish victims of the Nazi regime. That same year, the S.S. *St. Louis*, carrying more than nine hundred German Jewish refugees, approached the coast of Florida, where it was met by a Coast Guard patrol boat sent to prevent refugees from jumping off the boat and swimming ashore.

Beginnings of a Refugee Policy. By 1945, millions of people in Europe and elsewhere had been driven from their homes by the devastation of WORLD WAR II. The situation of German Jews was especially desperate. President Harry S. Truman urged Congress to pass special legislation to allow those languishing in refugee camps to resettle in the United States. Congress passed the DISPLACED PERSONS ACT of 1948, which Truman criticized for excluding more than 90 percent of displaced Jews and for the practice of "mortgaging" national quotas (subtracting the number of displaced persons admitted from the future yearly immigration quotas allotted to a specific country). In 1950, Congress revised the act and removed much of its discrimination against Jewish refugees. By the time the act expired in December, 1951, a total of 409,696 Poles, Germans, Lithuanians, Latvians, Estonians, Russians, and other refugees, including many Jews, had been admitted under its provisions.

Refugee Policy and the Cold War. Although American refugee policy was born largely as a response to the effects of Nazism, it soon became closely associated with anti-Communism. President Truman's appeal to Congress to help escapees from the Communist countries of Eastern Europe led to the passage of the REFUGEE RELIEF ACT of 1953, which authorized more than 200,000 new visas that were not counted as part of the national quotas. The anti-Communist focus of American refugee policy became even clearer in 1956 when Soviet tanks rolled into Hungary to overthrow the new Hungarian government that had been placed in power by a popular uprising.

American-Soviet COLD WAR rivalry created a powerful stimulus for the administration of President Dwight D. Eisenhower to assist the approximately 200,000 Hungarians who escaped into Austria and Yugoslavia. Yet the yearly quota of immigrants set for Hungary was only 865, and about half of these opportunities for migration had already been given away by the practice of "mortgaging" national quotas in the Displaced Persons Act. The Eisenhower administration therefore defined the Hungarian refugees as "parolees," individuals who could be temporarily admitted to the United States for emergency reasons but who would have no legal claims to remain in the country as immigrants. In 1958, the Hungarian Refugee Adjustment Act changed the status of the more than thirty thousand Hungarian parolees in the United States to that of permanent resident aliens.

On January 1, 1959, Fidel Castro established a revolutionary government in Cuba. Cubans fleeing from the new regime were seen, like the Hungarians, as "freedom fighters." Since the Refugee-Escapee Act of 1957 had ended the "mortgaging" of national quotas for the admission of refugees, the American government now had greater freedom of action. President Eisenhower and his successor, President John F. Kennedy, established the Cuban Refugee Program to provide welfare benefits and to assist in resettlement for the Cubans streaming into Florida.

The connection between refugee policy and anti-Communist foreign policy became even closer in late 1962 when the U.S. government aided an army of Cuban exiles living in the United States who attempted to attack Cuba in the BAY OF PIGS INVASION. After the failure of this mission, more than 800,000 Cuban refugees were admitted to the U.S., most of them settling

Cuban American architect in Miami in 1966. Early Cuban refugees used their middle-class education and business skills to advance quickly in American society. (Library of Congress)

in southern Florida. These refugees were at first admitted temporarily as parolees, like the Hungarians. Several pieces of legislation later enabled Cubans to become permanent residents and to apply for citizenship.

The Immigration and Nationality Act of 1965 removed the discriminatory national origins quotas and opened the gates to immigrants from Asia. It also created a more formal refugee policy by creating a "seventh preference visa" specifically for refugees. The act retained the ideological bias of earlier refugee policy, however, by identifying refugees as persons fleeing from "Communist or Communist-dominated" areas.

The Indochinese Refugee Crisis. American military involvement in the Vietnam War led to the most active refugee programs in U.S. history. In the spring of 1975, the U.S.-supported governments of South Vietnam, Laos, and Cambodia fell to Communist forces. As North Vietnamese forces took control of what had been South Vietnam, tens of thousands of South Vietnamese, many of whom had been associated with the American war effort, fled by boat and helicopter. The U.S. government hastily created a program known as Operation New Life, which moved refugees to American military bases to prepare them for temporary resettlement in the United States. In this way, about 130,000 Vietnamese, most of whom were well educated and somewhat familiar with the American way of life, became the first wave of Indochinese migrants to the United States.

During the late 1970's, Vietnamese refugees continued to leave their country by boat or by land across Cambodia to Thailand. Cambodians and Laotians also continued to flee, most of them into neighboring Thailand. In 1977, Attorney General Griffin Bell used his parole authority to admit emergency cases into the country temporarily, allowing thousands of people from Cambodia, Laos, and Vietnam to come to the United States, while President Jimmy Carter signed legislation that permitted the Indochinese to become permanent residents.

When tensions between Vietnam and Cambodia led to the Vietnamese invasion of Cambodia in December, 1978, Vietnam was attacked by Cambodia's ally, China. These events resulted in an outpouring of refugees from both Cambodia and Vietnam, including many ethnic Chinese living in Vietnam. Anti-Communism, hostility toward former enemies, and continued guilt over the failure to help Jewish victims of Nazism in World War II created pressure to help the fleeing Indochinese, who became popularly known as "boat people."

In response to the Indochinese refugee crisis, Congress passed the most comprehensive piece of refugee legislation in American history, the Refugee Act of 1980. In place of the "seventh preference category" established in 1965, which admitted refugees as part of the total number of immigrants, the Refugee Act provided for an annual number of admissions specifically for refugees. This number was to be independent of the number of immigrants permitted, and it was to be established each year by the president in consultation with Congress. References to communism were also dropped, even though the refugees who inspired the act were, in fact, fleeing from Communist countries.

Indochinese refugees, especially boat people, began entering the United States in unprecedented numbers from 1979 to 1982; by 1990 the number of Vietnamese in the country had grown to more than 615,000, the number of Laotians to more than 149,000, and the number of Cambodians to more than 147,000. The Orderly Departure Program (ODP), created in 1983 by an agreement between the American and Vietnamese governments, enabled Vietnamese political prisoners and Amerasians (half-Vietnamese children of American soldiers and Vietnamese women) to leave Vietnam legally for resettlement in the United States, further swelling the ranks of Indochinese.

At the same time that the flow from these Asian nations was reaching its peak, the United States received another mass migration of refugees from Cuba. In the spring and summer of 1980, Castro announced that Cubans wishing to go to the United States could leave from Mariel Harbor. Over the next five months almost 130,000 Cubans arrived in Florida as part of the Mariel boat lift. Known as Marielitos, many of these new arrivals were detained in military camps since there were too many to be immediately resettled.

Closing the Gates. The late 1970's and early 1980's saw a dramatic increase in people seeking refuge in the United States from Haiti and Central America, as well as from Cuba and Indochina. An estimated fifty thousand Haitians, fleeing from the dictatorship of Jean-Claude Duvalier, arrived illegally on the coasts of Florida in hastily constructed, overcrowded boats between 1972 and 1980. Unwilling to accept this influx of refugees from a country whose government was not hostile to the United States, the Reagan Administration claimed that the Haitians were not true refugees but "economic migrants" from one of the poorest countries in the Western Hemisphere. The administration began the practice of "interdiction" in which the U.S. Coast Guard stopped Haitian boats at sea, gave the Haitians on board interviews with U.S. immigration officials, and then returned most of them to Haiti. When another mass outpouring of Haitian

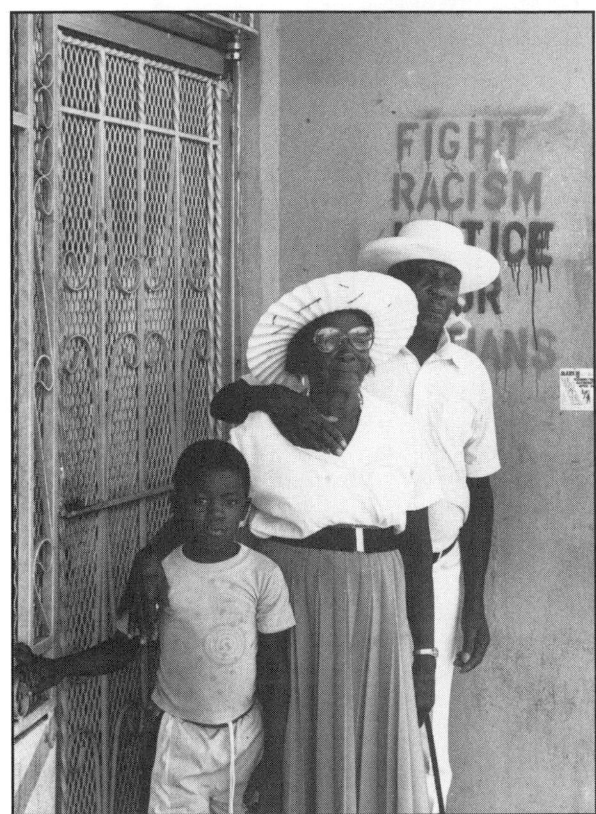

Thousands of Haitian refugees such as this family in Little Haiti, Miami, sought asylum in the U.S. in response to Haiti's political and economic woes. (L. Solmssen/UNHCR)

boat people began after the military overthrow of democratically elected Haitian President Jean-Bertrand Aristide in 1991, the Bush Administration pursued a similar policy, holding intercepted Haitians at the U.S. Guantanamo Bay military base in Cuba and returning many of them to Haiti.

Refugees from Guatemala and El Salvador in the late 1970's and 1980's were fleeing countries whose governments the United States supported. The U.S. government did not recognize them as true refugees, and most Guatemalans and Salvadorans who arrived in the United States entered illegally from Mexico. Nicaraguans fared slightly better because the U.S. government was opposed to the socialist government that ruled Nicaragua during the 1980's. About twenty thousand Nicaraguans without claims to permanent resident status were allowed to remain temporarily in the United States after 1979. Almost all Central American refugees, however, met a declining American willingness to accept new refugees. The efforts of the SANCTUARY MOVEMENT to provide Central Americans with a safe haven and application for political asylum aroused sympathy in some circles but met with legal defeat. Many Salvadorans and others who entered illegally before 1982 gained legal status with the amnesty program of 1987-1988.

Refugees and Public Opinion. Popular sympathy for refugees has generally been the result of well-publicized crises. As large numbers of refugees have arrived, however, this sympathy has frequently given way to hostility. In 1961, a reporter for the *Miami Herald* told a Senate committee that the newly arriving Cubans had been warmly received by citizens of Florida but that this support was turning to distrust as Floridians experienced living with a foreign, Spanish-speaking culture and began worrying about competition for jobs. When the Cuban community in Florida achieved relative economic success, this created resentment on the part of members of other, traditionally underprivileged groups.

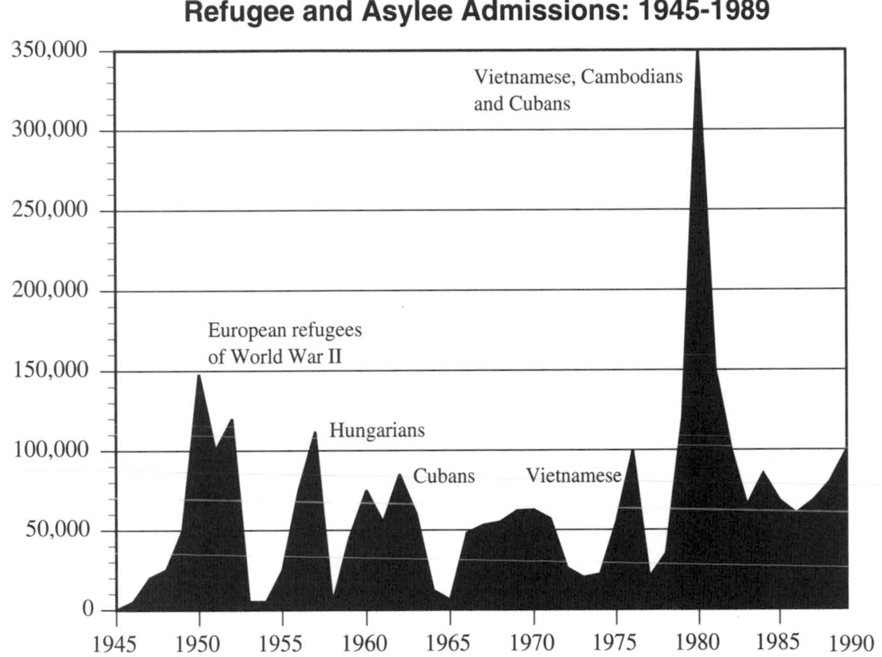

Source: Data are from Allison Landes, ed., *Immigration and Illegal Aliens.* Figure 4.1. Wylie, Tex.: Information Plus, 1991.

Newspaper and television accounts of the hardships of Vietnamese BOAT PEOPLE also evoked the sympathy of Americans. The Indochinese refugees' high rates of employment and willingness to work hard at low-paying jobs have given them the image of a "MODEL MINORITY." The Vietnamese have also often been resented as competitors for jobs or housing. In a notable incident, which formed the basis of the film *Alamo Bay* (1985), tensions between Vietnamese and local shrimp fishermen in Galveston, Texas, led to attacks on the Vietnamese by the KU KLUX KLAN.

American attitudes toward refugees became more negative in the early 1980's when it was revealed that some of the Marielitos had been criminals in Cuba. When Marielitos who had been confined in American military installations, such as Fort Chaffee, rioted to protest being held as prisoners, many Americans began to question the wisdom of allowing large numbers of refugees into the country. By the early 1990's, with the end of the COLD WAR that had provided motivation and support for a massive refugee policy, it appeared that the United States would become much less open to seekers of refuge.

SUGGESTED READINGS. One of the best books on American refugee policy is *Calculated Kindness: Refugees and America's Half-Open Door* (1986) by Gil Loescher and John Scanlan. Ellis Cose's *A Nation of Strangers* (1992) provides a readable overview of American attitudes toward immigrants. *Latin Journey* (1985) by Alejandro Portes and Robert L. Bach offers a comparison of Cubans and Mexicans in the United

States and is the authoritative description of the Cuban refugee economy in Florida. *The Boat People and Achievement in America* (1989) by Nathan Caplan, John K. Whitmore, and Marcella Choy describes how their culture and family values helped Indochinese refugees adapt successfully to American life. *Refugees in the United States: A Reference Handbook* (1985), edited by David Haines, compares the adaptive experience of various modern refugee groups.—*Carl L. Bankston III*

Regents of the University of California v. Bakke (1978): U.S. Supreme Court case that helped to clarify the distinction between AFFIRMATIVE ACTION, which seeks to rectify discriminatory practices of the past against racial minorities, and REVERSE DISCRIMINATION, which unduly penalizes white individuals.

The "Bakke case" grew out of the CIVIL RIGHTS MOVEMENT of the 1950's and 1960's. President Lyndon Johnson issued executive orders in 1965 and 1967 that called for affirmative action to ensure that African Americans and other underrepresented populations would have equal opportunity in EMPLOYMENT and EDUCATION. He spoke in 1965 of the need for "equality as a fact and as a result."

In 1968, African Americans composed 2 percent of medical school students but 12 percent of the nation's population. To attract minority students, the University of California, Davis, Medical School, in 1969, voluntarily reserved a certain number of places in each year's class for minority applicants. In 1972, sixteen out of one hundred available places were reserved for minority applicants.

Allan Paul Bakke, a thirty-two-year-old engineer with strong credentials, applied to the Davis medical school and was rejected. The following year, he reapplied and was rejected again. Knowing of the special admissions program, Bakke believed that he was discriminated against for being Caucasian and that those sixteen places may well have been given to less qualified individuals by virtue of their race.

On June 20, 1974, Bakke filed suit in state court against the Regents of the University of California, charging that his constitutional right to equal protection under the law had been violated. The university admitted that the special admissions program accepted students with lower test scores, grade point averages, and overall performance, but argued that such individuals were the victims of a legacy of DISCRIMINATION that required redress.

The state court granted Bakke's suit, but the University countersued and the case ultimately reached the U.S. Supreme Court. It stirred much controversy and publicity, and sixty individuals and organizations filed *amicus curiae* briefs. Civil rights advocates feared that a decision for Bakke would erase decades of CIVIL RIGHTS advances. Their opponents believed that validation of the university's special program would lead to mandatory admissions QUOTAS and forced integration in all walks of life.

The case was argued in the Supreme Court on October 14, 1977. The following June 28, more than six years after Bakke had first applied to the university, the Court delivered two decisions in the case. By a vote of five-to-four, it ruled that Bakke had indeed been discriminated against on the basis of race. Again by a five-vote majority, however, the Court held that affirmative action is constitutional if applied on an individual basis without numerical quotas. In short, the Bakke case struck a precarious compromise, recognizing reverse discrimination as a concern in civil rights policy-making but reiterating the ongoing need for affirmative action to balance past injustices.

SUGGESTED READINGS. A thorough account of the Bakke case is found in Allan P. Sindler's *Bakke, DeFunis, and Minority Admissions* (1978). Terry Eastland and William J. Bennett trace the case's historical underpinnings in *Counting by Race* (1979). A statistical approach is found in the Rockefeller Foundation's *Bakke, Weber, and Affirmative Action* (1979), and Mary Ten Thor's *The Bakke Symposium* (1977) records a symposium on the case and its impact.

Rehabilitation Act (1973): Provided grants to states "for VOCATIONAL REHABILITATION services, with special emphasis on services to those with severe handicaps." It created a Rehabilitation Services Administration to oversee programs that offered services and job training to people with disabilities and to solve rehabilitation problems. It also promoted use of the International Accessibility Symbol, required federal employers or those with federal contracts to hire people with disabilities, and studied methods for eliminating physical barriers in public buildings and transportation. This act replaced the earlier Vocational Rehabilitation Act.

The Rehabilitation Act included a number of sections intended to afford extended CIVIL RIGHTS protection to people with disabilities. Section 502, for example, established a board to monitor compliance with laws requiring that certain facilities be made accessible to people with wheelchairs. Section 504 was the most sweeping, stating that no "program or activity" receiving federal financial assistance could discriminate against people because they have a disability. The federal government, unsure about how business and the public at large would react to the measure, as well as how best to draft guidelines for its implementation, delayed Section 504 for four years. In 1977 (after considerable pressure from DISABILITY RIGHTS activists that included demonstrations in Washington, D.C.) it finally issued a regulation describing how Section 504 should be applied.

Religion: Just as the population of the United States includes people from every part of the globe, so the religions practiced in the United States range from large denominations with millions of worshipers to tiny sects that are barely known. The many different tribal groups of American Indians had their own religions before European explorers ever set foot in the New World. Immigrants from western and eastern Europe brought their religions with them, predominantly Christianity and Judaism. Africans kidnapped and brought here as slaves brought their religions, such as the beliefs of the Yoruba people. Then came immigrants from Asia, bringing with them Buddhism and Hinduism.

As time passed, particularly American variations began to emerge. Moreover, new religions were created in the United States, among them variants of traditional Christianity such as Mormonism, Christian Science, and the JEHOVAH'S WITNESSES. In a multicultural society, understanding and tolerance of the beliefs of others is crucial. Yet in order to study any religion, certain obstacles must be overcome.

Among the difficulties that arise in the comparative study of religion are the tremendous variety in religious beliefs and the need to overcome one's own (sometimes invisible) assumptions and biases. Nevertheless, scholars have identified elements that seem to be common to most religions. Among these is the fact that religions involve human interaction with "the sacred," although this is not necessarily a formal concept of God. Other aspects that are central to religious belief and practice are myth, ritual, and community.

The complexity of religion becomes apparent in any attempt to define the word itself. To a participant in any of the major American religions, religion may be the basis of all human experience, a way of perceiving and expressing human relationship to the sacred, and a way of structuring one's social actions and inner life to allow for that sacred reality. To a nonreligious person, religion is a system of thought, belief, and action related to a "sacred" realm that does not actually exist. For such a thinker, religion is best understood in secu-

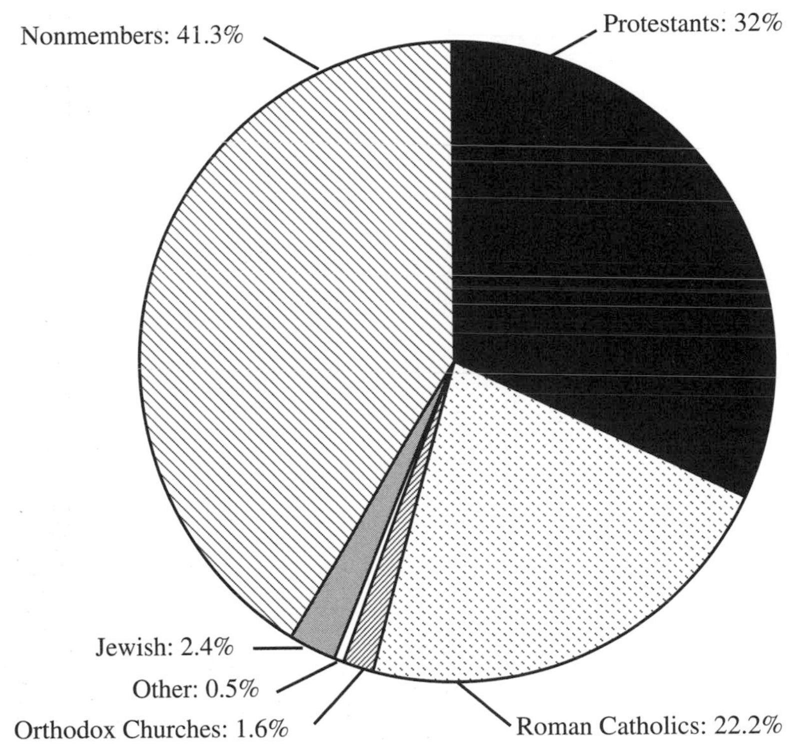

Source: From William C. Lowe, *Blessings of Liberty: Safeguarding Civil Rights.* Human Rights series, p. 23. Vero Beach, Fla.: Rourke Corp., 1992.

lar terms as a social, historical, or psychological phenomenon. To an agnostic, religion is an open question, a puzzle, and an enduring unknown.

The Multicultural Challenge. Studying religion in a multicultural framework becomes even more complex. Definitions and experiences of religion vary considerably from culture to culture, within cultures, and across time. A Buddhist, for example, would probably say something different about Islam than would a Muslim interpreter. A modern African American habits of Judeo-Christian thought when they try to understand religion in other cultures. Hinduism as it is understood in the Judeo-Christian West may be quite different than Hinduism as it is understood in India. Similarly, forms of Buddhism, Islam, Judaism, Hinduism, Baha'i, and Christianity found in the United States can differ profoundly from other forms of those same religions in other parts of the world. The use of general terms such as "American Indian religion" or "West African religion" can be convenient, but it

Muslim religious procession in New York City. Islam is among the least understood minority religions in the United States. (Richard B. Levine)

Baptist studying the influence of West African Yoruba religion on African American Christianity may be affected by Christian bias.

The challenge of understanding complex religions from both inside and outside the tradition is central to the multicultural study of religion. Most human cultures are deeply conditioned by religious worldviews. Even those people who reject the dominant religions in their culture have had to grapple with the worldview that religion itself offers. For example, in the United States, it is difficult for many people, regardless of religious belief (or lack of it), to put aside the masks the remarkable diversity and variance among religions within these larger groupings.

As a working cross-cultural definition, religion can be called a way of viewing and acting in the world that creates meaning for human life in relation to "the sacred." This religious worldview can be private and informal, or social and highly structured, and it should be understood in its own terms.

Any interpretive approach to religion is situated within its own cultural framework—people tend to think about the world with habits of thought formed in their own culture. Yet it is important to try to understand religious worlds in the ways that people within those religious cultures understand themselves. To think multiculturally is to try to see Islam through the eyes of Muslims, to see Judaism as Jewish believers experience Judaism, and to see within the broad category of American Indian religion how HOPI religious experience is distinct from Lakota tradition, which is distinct from NAVAJO, and so on.

Many people unintentionally use their own religious or nonreligious worldview as the norm for the study of other religious cultures. Scholars call this habit "centrism," or the placing of one's own worldview at the center and seeing all other traditions only in relation to one's own truth. Other religions are then defined essentially by what they are not. History is full of the tragic consequences of such uncritical "centrism," in which one culture is unable to understand and accept the culture of another people. At the very least, those who attempt a multicultural perspective on religion should be aware of their own interpreter's bias.

The Sacred. The sacred has been defined as that reality which a person or culture infuses with extraordinary power and meaning. In some cultures, this reality is perceived as completely separate from the realm of secular human experience; the sacred must be reached, or appealed to, across a gulf that separates the human from the holy. In other cultures, people perceive the sacred as pervasively present in all of nature and human experience. Despite these different conceptions of the nature of the sacred, all religious cultures share the presumption of the sacred's special power.

Mircea Eliade, a scholar of comparative religion, offers a way of looking cross-culturally at the diversity of ideas of the sacred through an exploration of "sacred space" and "sacred time." Most Americans are familiar with some form of sacred space: the synagogue, the temple, the church, the mosque, the sweat lodge, or any of the many versions of a sacred building. These structures mark off a location as special: Religious people gather there with an understanding that what occurs inside the building is qualitatively different than what occurs outside. The boundaries of these structures thus mark a sacred space. Within them, human beings focus their attention and energy "toward" or "with" the sacred. Thus, sacred spaces provide a place of heightened human connection with the sacred.

Sacred spaces can range from a small Vietnamese Buddhist or Mexican Catholic altar in a private home, to the elaborate churches, synagogues, mosques, and temples that are found in most American cities. What sacred spaces share is their function as what Eliade calls "the center of the world": They provide a place of "breakthrough" between humanity and the sacred. It is important to note that many religions do not have special sacred buildings but mark off sacred space through ritual. In addition, for some cultures, sacred space is the geography of a particular region; to leave a geographical area is to leave sacred space, and thus to leave sacred reality. This was true for many West African peoples who were forcibly removed from their homelands during the Atlantic slave trade; for American Indians forced from their traditional lands; and for recent Southeast Asian refugees who left the place of their ancestors. The personal and cultural trauma that resulted from such violent breaks in sacred space cannot be overstated.

Ethnic churches such as St. Augustine Roman Catholic Church, founded as a black parish in Washington, D.C., in 1858, have traditionally served as both sacred spaces and community centers that reinforce group identity. (Library of Congress)

Another important way of experiencing the power and reality of the sacred is through the marking of sacred time. Probably the most familiar sacred times for many people are the Sabbaths, holy days, or longer periods of religious observance such as the month of Ramadan in Islam, PASSOVER in Judaism, or Lent in Christianity. A weekly Sabbath, or sacred day, is central in all three of the major Western religious traditions: Islam, Judaism, and Christianity. For example, the Jewish Sabbath is observed from sunset Friday to sunset Saturday. This period is marked by Jews as a sacred time, a time for intensified religious observance and experience. On Friday evening, families and friends gather to light the Sabbath candles, recite blessings, and share a festive meal. Some attend synagogue services. During the Sabbath, observant Jews refrain from work in order to pray and study Jewish Scripture. At the close of the Sabbath on Saturday evening, worshipers extinguish a candle with wine in a ceremony called *havdalah*, literally, "separation" of the Sabbath from the weekdays.

As scholar William Paden suggests, "Ritual time constructs its own space. It is time that can be 'entered' by participants . . . the Jewish Sabbaths have been called 'cathedrals in time.'"

Concepts of the sacred vary profoundly from culture to culture, and within cultures across time. Many religious traditions include the concept of gods or God: the "one God" (monotheistic) traditions such as Christianity, Islam, and Judaism; the "many gods" (polytheistic) religions such as some forms of Hinduism; and the "all is God" (pantheistic or monistic) religions such as Buddhism and many mystical traditions. Specific ideas about God(s) or godliness are very complex and easily misunderstood by people from outside of the religious culture. For example, it may be difficult for many people in Western culture to understand the monistic sacred world of some Eastern traditions, while some Eastern Buddhists or HINDUS may have difficulty understanding the monotheistic and dualistic ideas about the sacred in the major Western traditions. The sacred, then, is the ultimate power and reality within a religious world, but the precise conception of that sacred power or reality varies profoundly from culture to culture.

Myth. In the multicultural study of religion, myth means a story, or stories, that explain the most basic ways that the world works. In a very fundamental sense, religious myth creates a religious world and provides a structure of meaning that allows people to understand their experience. Myth organizes reality, including sacred reality, into foundational stories; through these stories, people are able to conceptualize meaning for their existence. Myth, in this sense, is not "false," but is actually a very central part of the "truth" of a particular culture. Within this framework, New Testament stories about Jesus, Hopi Indian creation stories, and stories about Buddha are all myths. Note that here, the term "myth" does not carry any claim regarding the truth of these stories. For a Buddhist, the stories of Buddha illustrate the path to Essential Truth just as for Jew, Moses' encounter with God on Mount Sinai and the giving of the Torah are the foundational stories of a deeply held faith. In the comparative study of religion, what matters is not evaluating whether myths are "true" or "false," but rather understanding how a myth is true for a particular person or culture, in a particular time or place.

One excellent example of the dynamic nature of myth is illustrated by comparing the Exodus story in Jewish tradition with the Exodus story in early African American Christianity. In both cases, the story of Moses is central to a people's understanding of itself and its place in the order (or disorder) of life, but in each case the Moses story has its own distinct cultural meanings and implications.

For Jews of every branch of Judaism, the story of Moses from the Hebrew Bible (Tanakh) is foundational to Jewish identity, individually and collectively. In this story, Moses leads the People Israel from bondage in Egypt to liberation and a special covenant with God in the promised land of Canaan. Central to the story is God giving the written and oral Torah ("learning" or "law") to Moses on Mount Sinai on two stone tablets. After much trouble and deep struggle over the nature of faith, this sacred word becomes the bond that seals Israel's identity as God's chosen people. In Jewish life, the religious myth of Moses, the People Israel, and their journey from bondage to liberation, marks the beginning for a complex religious culture and thus is foundational to Jewish identity and self-understanding.

It is not surprising that the Moses story, with its emphasis on liberation from bondage, had particular appeal to African American slaves in antebellum North America. Beginning in 1619, with the first arrival of enslaved Africans in Jamestown, Virginia, white Christian slaveholders selectively introduced some of the basic Judeo-Christian myths to their slaves. Although slaves were prohibited by law from learning to read English, many of them heard the Exodus story passed on in secret slave religious gatherings, where elements of Christian tradition were sometimes fused with remnants of African religious tradition. Later, as slaves did learn to read and the first independent black churches formed in the North, African American communities began to develop their own understanding of the Moses story as it applied to the experience of suffering under American SLAVERY.

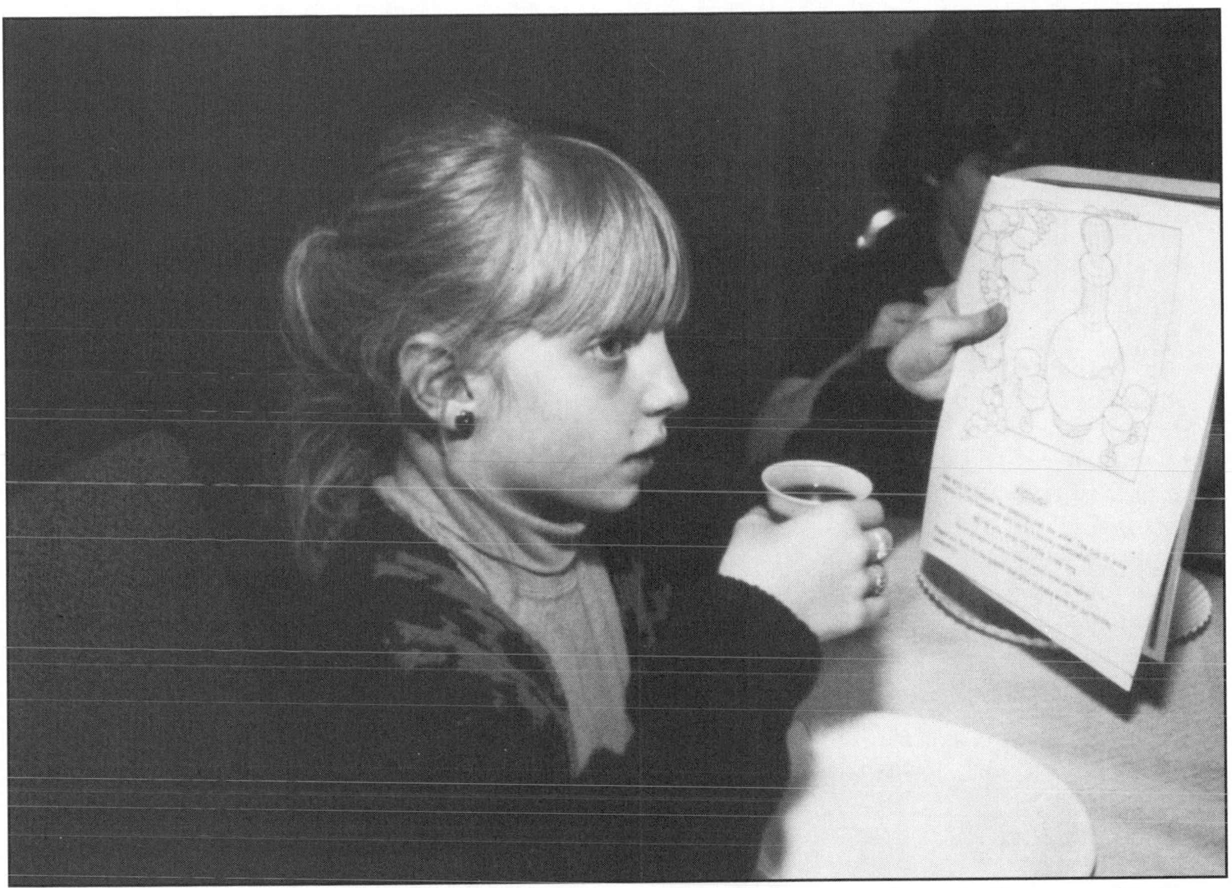

The biblical story of Moses leading the Jews from slavery to freedom is retold every spring at the Passover seder. Here, a girl holds a child's version of the service and a ritual cup of wine (or grape juice). (Frances M. Roberts)

The parts of the Moses story that took on special importance were those emphasizing the journey from bondage to freedom and the special relationship with God that is claimed for those who suffer under oppression. African Americans used the Moses story to create a religious worldview that sanctified black experience and provided a way both to understand slavery and to fight for liberation. The Moses story persists in African American Christian culture, where it provides one way (among many) of talking about the continued need for confronting racial PREJUDICE and the challenges of African American identity in American culture. This can be seen, for example, in the imagery of black spirituals, gospel music, sermons, and oratory, such as civil rights leader Martin Luther KING, Jr.'s, reference to having "been to the mountain top" in his mission for racial justice. Thus, as is the case with Jews, the Exodus story is foundational to African American identity and self-understanding.

This example illustrates how religious myth creates the world for people who tell and retell the story. Some religious people understand the Exodus story of Moses allegorically or symbolically. Within this framework, the story is not claimed to be literally true but spiritually true—the truth that matters most in religion. The events in the myth represent deeper spiritual connections between human beings and God, not necessarily actual events in the historical world. For other Jewish and Christian readers, it is imperative to claim the historical truth and literal accuracy of the biblical account of Moses. For these believers, the lit-

Special chants, icons, and blessings accompany this annual Greek Orthodox name day procession through the streets of Astoria in New York City. (Odette Lupis)

eral historical truth of the myth is central to its authority as the founding truth of religious tradition.

In oral religious traditions where stories also work to explain and organize the cosmos, cultures convey myths through speech rather than through written text. Some oral traditions are relatively fluid, while others are quite fixed and consistent over time. There are many examples of world-creating myths among the many groups of North American Indians.

Ritual. Almost all religions involve ritualized human action. Whether performed privately or publicly, rituals create sacred reality by combining human "intention" with patterns of using voice, action, and particular objects. Through the motion of ritual, a new state of being is created that did not exist prior to the ritual. In this sense, ritual is deeply existential: It is an act of creating the existence of a person or of a community.

In cultures where time is conceived in linear terms as moving forward, religious ritual also creates a bond between the past, present, and future. For example, one of the reasons that changing the wording of the Catholic Mass from Latin to vernacular languages was (and is) so controversial is that for many believers, a fixed and unchanging ritual practice ties together a community of faith across generations. In this view, rituals provide deep religious and spiritual continuity within a tradition, despite profound social changes that occur over time. Attempts to eradicate gender bias in religious language are similarly complicated in many religions, as people grapple with the tension between the desire to express change religiously and the desire to maintain ritual continuity.

In cultures where time is conceived as more circular or "simultaneous," religious ritual allows people to participate fully in the "eternal present" of sacred reality. In many traditions, ritual allows people to re-create a time of sacred "origin"—not only symbolically, but for believers, in actuality. It is easier to understand this idea by looking at examples of how ritual actually functions in various religious cultures.

In 1947, a Lakota Oglala Indian spiritual leader known as Black Elk gave an oral account of many of the traditional rituals of his people. His words were translated from Lakota to English by his son, Benjamin Black Elk, and recorded by Joseph Epes Brown in a book titled *The Sacred Pipe* (1953). Black Elk's account of a Lakota "Inipi" ritual, the rite of purification in a sweat lodge, provides a good example of how religious ritual creates sacred reality.

Black Elk's opening description illustrates how the ritual uses the elements of nature and human "intention" to sanctify the world:

> The rite of the *onikare* [sweat lodge] utilizes all the Powers of the universe: earth, and the things which grow from the earth, water, fire, and air. The water represents the Thunder-beings who come fearfully but bring goodness, for the steam which comes from the rocks, within which is the fire, is frightening, but it purifies us so that we may live as Wakan-Tanka wills, and He may even send to us a vision if we become very pure. When we use the water in the sweat lodge we should think of Wakan-Tanka who is always flowing, giving his power and life to everything; we should even be as water which is lower than all things, yet stronger than the rocks.

This short excerpt reveals many of the common elements of religious ritual: Humans gather in a special place (the *onikare*), with special intention (to purify themselves and the world), and perform a highly patterned set of actions (the complex Inipi ritual) with objects that are infused with special meaning (sacred fire, steam, water, pipe, sticks, tobacco). Through the ritual, people re-create the order of the sacred cosmos and purify (sanctify) themselves and their community. They create and participate in sacred reality.

Another important ritual is prayer. Prayer is performed across many cultures, and at times in profoundly different ways within religious traditions. In prayer, ritual creates or expresses the relationship between the person praying and the "prayed-to," whether this be a god, ancestor spirit, or internal and nonpersonal state-of-being. Through prayer, the world is sanctified. Some prayer rituals are private, such as the "wordless" prayers of the mystics or the private meditations of QUAKERS. In other settings, prayer can be a highly structured and social ritual in which whole communities collectively appeal to God or gods. Observant Muslims, for instance, arrange their working lives so that they can pray five times daily and attend public prayers at a mosque on Friday afternoons. Ritualized prayer may be embedded within a complex multilayered public ritual. Within Christianity, for example, many churches conduct a ritual pattern that allows for silent prayer, public and collective prayer, ritualized interaction between worshipers and the priest or pastor, and the very intensely focused ritual of the Eucharist. Prayer expressed through music gives rise to an astonishing diversity of ritual from the chanting of Buddhist monks at a Thai temple to the rousing GOSPEL hymns at a black Pentecostal church.

Community. One final cross-cultural aspect of religion is its role in creating or expressing community. Because religious worldviews comprise distinct and culturally varied ways of understanding reality, they have a significant effect on people's actions and social perceptions. In this sense the social role of religion is very important: religion both creates and expresses community structure and deeply influences the experiences of individuals within the community.

Critics of religion have raised important questions about the ways that religions form communities. They are concerned about an "insider vs. outsider" mentality and a tendency toward conformity and social control to the exclusion of diversity and dissent. Examples of racial and gender bias within some traditions illustrate the social and psychological consequences that "exclusion" from religious experience can have on individuals and communities. Controversy over the admission of women to Catholic priesthood is a familiar example. In Catholic tradition, women are denied access to the full range of religious expression available to men. Feminist theologians, female and male, contend that such exclusion damages the religious identity of individual women and thus fractures the spiritual community of the church. In response, defenders of the Catholic tradition argue that to break a "fixed" part of religious tradition will itself fracture the community. Similar arguments, pro and con, have been expressed on the question of allowing female ministers and rabbis, or admitting gay people to positions of Christian or Jewish leadership.

In many American Christian denominations,

Mennonites are among the many religious sects that have created their own relatively isolated communities in rural America. (Robert Maust, Photo Agora)

autonomous African American congregations have formed in order to define religious—and thus social, political, and cultural—truth in ways that reflect African American experience. Some black Christians wished to separate from the destructive and longstanding racist practices of many predominantly white congregations. In this case, black theologians claim that RACISM in white-defined churches damages the spiritual integrity of individual African Americans, thus splitting black communities and compromising the spiritual and political freedom of black people. Here, the existential power of religion and its role in defining communities is understood as critically important. Clearly, religion allows the positive and liberating formation of individual identity and community, yet it also provides a potentially destructive source of social conflict and individual suffering.

SUGGESTED READINGS. It is best when pursuing further study on religion to do a bibliographic search on specific subjects, such as "African American Islam," "Mormonism," or "Jewish Feminist Theology." For general study of comparative and multicultural approaches to religion, consult William Paden's *Religious Worlds: The Comparative Study of Religion* (1988) and *Interpreting the Sacred* (1992), which offer cross-cultural models for researching religion. Paden's ideas are applicable to many different religious traditions, but his perspective is based on primarily Western assumptions about the nature of scholarship and religion. Similarly, Mircea Eliade's *The Sacred and Profane* (1959) and the multivolume study of world religion that he edited, *The Encyclopedia of Religion* (1987), provide a wealth of information. Finally, for a discussion on the comparative anthropology of religion, see Clifford Geertz's *The Interpretation of Cultures* (1973), especially the essays entitled "Religion as a Cultural System" and "Ethos, World View, and the Analysis of Sacred Symbols."—*Sharon Carson*

Religion and mythology—American Indian: Among the first nations of North America, religion was an integral part of life, not distinct from other aspects of daily living such as child rearing, food production, political and social relations, and even entertainment. As with other aspects of culture, religion was intimately bound with the people's relationship to their environment, as reflected in the extraordinary variety of religious expression on the continent.

Mythology and Doctrine. The great creation myths explain both how the world came about and the origins of the people's relationship to their land. They reflect intimate bonds with particular landscapes as well as complex accounts of clan origins and migration traditions. Thus there are actually hundreds of creation stories, many varying from teller to teller and family to family within specific groups; however, scholars have identified several pervasive themes that recur throughout wide geographic areas. Two widely distributed creation themes are the earth-diver story and the emergence story.

An example of the earth-diver motif occurs in a creation account of the Western Mono, a people whose home is the Sierra foothills of eastern California and western Nevada. Earth-diver myths begin with a flood. In this one, Prairie Falcon and Crow send first Duck, then Coot, and finally Grebe to dive beneath the water and bring up sand from the bottom. Duck and Coot have dreamed of the numbers three and four, respectively, but are unable to bring up the sand before their allotted number of days expire and they pass out of their dreams. Grebe, who has five days, also dies, but when Prairie Falcon and Crow bring him back to life they find grains of sand under his fingernails; these grains, flung in every direction, become the present world. The birds involved in this story are native to the Mono Lake region; their presence in the myth is typical of American Indian mythology, which represents the natural world and the human world as an integrated whole with no division between them. In "the time immemorial" when the world was being formed, animals were powerful beings; they assumed their present forms as part of the creation process, and as that process is continually being renewed, actual animals can be thought of as embodiments of the powerful mythological figures. Dreaming is a highly respected psychological process: In some tribes the belief is that humans dream virtually all significant knowledge, from how to construct artifacts and tools to composition of poems and visionary communication with natural creatures or those who have died.

Emergence creation stories are common throughout the Southwest (and found in other parts of the continent as well). One version from the HOPIS, who live in pueblos in northern Arizona, emphasizes a division between men and women that occurred in the first or lowest world. Women and men separated on either side of a river, according to this story, because their leaders could not find another solution to anarchy and dissoluteness. Things went no better after the separation, especially for the women, who could neither farm as well as the men nor hunt at all. Finally, after a period of extreme want, corruption, and unhappiness, the men and women discussed their dire problem and decided to live together. After this they sought a way out of their lower world; finally, with the assistance of emissaries Locust and Badger, they ascended through a hollow reed to the upper or present world.

Emergence stories are clan origin stories, and are linked in PUEBLO tradition to the *sipapu* (hole) in the floor of the *kiva* (a circular building or subterranean structure used for the esoteric portions of religious rituals). The symbolism of emergence stories is obviously related to themes of birth and maternal earth; in this one, conflict between agricultural and hunting

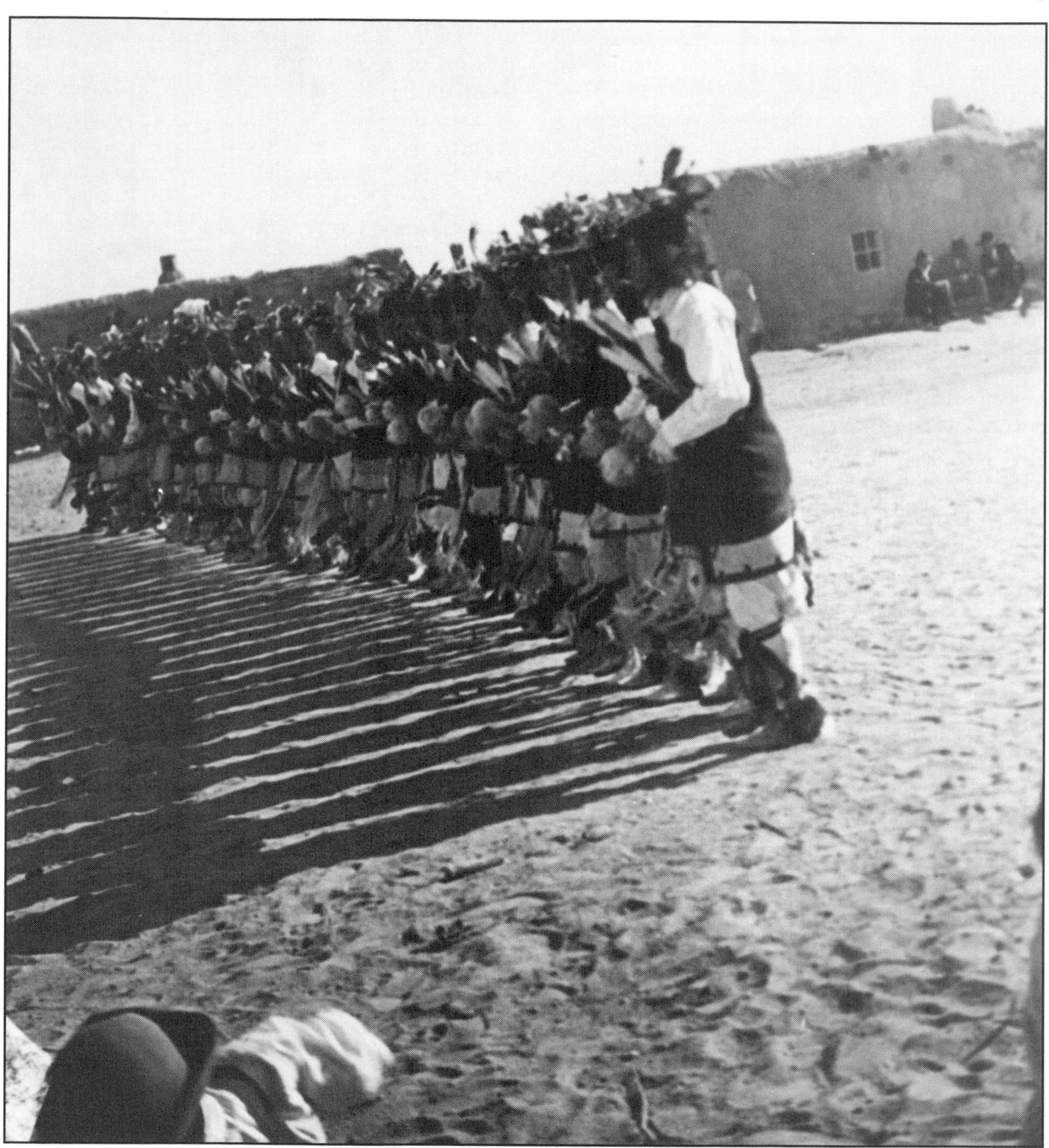

Kachina dancers at Cochiti Pueblo in 1908. (H. F. Robinson, Museum of New Mexico)

modes of production is characteristic of a tension which pervades many Pueblo myths and which suggests a historical conflict in the change from a hunting and gathering economy to sedentary agriculture. The resolution of the problem through discussion and agreement is also characteristic of the deeply pacifist orientation of the Hopis.

Emergence and earth-diver motifs represent a minute portion of the great myths that explain the origins of the universe to American Indians. Indians' reluctance to explain such myths is evident in their remarks that the meanings of stories are clear and need no explanation, or become clear through being applied to actual life situations. Hence it is risky to attempt to extract dogma apart from specific texts. Hopi KACHINAS, for example, are in some cases ancestral spirits, and reverence for them has been called ancestor worship; however, this is not the case with all kachinas, nor is it necessarily important in stories of kachinas, composition of kachina songs, or the appearance of the kachinas during the half-year when they are physically manifested in the pueblos through participation in ceremonies and dances.

Ritual and Ceremony. In few things is religion as integral to traditional life as in ritual. Indian ritual ranges from the elaborate healing ceremonies of the NAVAJOS—up to nine consecutive days and nights of song, prayer, body painting, vomiting, production of sand painting and prayer objects, feasting, dancing, and even construction of a special *hogan* or house for the ceremony—to the everyday tasks of beginning the day or gathering plants. Such traditions offered constant reminders of the sacredness of the universe and the importance of alertness to a correct relationship with it.

The vision quest was a highly personal ritual by which an individual defined his or her relationship with the divine. Fasting, isolation, and prayer might, if carried out correctly, bring on a vision in which the person would receive a visit from a guardian spirit and possibly a song or name that would carry with it spiritual and physical power. The vision quest rite is best known from the Plains and Eastern Woodlands but was practiced elsewhere as well. Visionary experience could also be spontaneous, as in the well-known case of Black Elk. This Oglala spiritual leader experienced a tremendous vision at the age of nine; the relationship of the private vision to communal tribal life is detailed in his autobiography, *Black Elk Speaks* (1961), in which he recounts how the entire tribe enacted his vision throughout several days, bringing it to life and creating a new ritual from his dream. This twentieth century autobiography replicates the many myths that describe the origin of a ritual in a journey or experience: after receiving guidance and power from supernatural beings, an individual then makes that power available to the community through ritual.

Experience of the supernatural through vision quest, spontaneous vision, and apprenticeship characterizes the initiation of the shaman in American Indian life. Shamanism involves a highly individualistic relationship of a person with a supernatural power to heal the sick or influence events, and the holder of such access to power was often suspect and dangerous. Anything out of the ordinary—good or bad—might be attributed to a person with shamanic power, and the shaman who was successful or became wealthy was especially feared. Shamans practiced in many tribes, from the Arctic to the Southwest.

Contrasted with the highly personal, even shamanic, nature of the vision quest are the seasonal, communal ceremonies of the PUEBLOS of the Southwest plateau. Responsibility for these rites rests with clan societies, sometimes called clan priests, who undertake the organization and direction of the rites as well as their continuance through initiation and education of new society members. Although many of the ceremonies (sometimes called dances, as dancing is the most spectacular element of the portions that are performed in public) are performed only every other year, the general purpose of the ceremonies is closely tied to the agricultural year and especially to the production of corn. The region is arid, and the object of most of the ceremonies is to call down rain. While some ethnologists have called such rites compulsive magic, a form of coercion of the natural forces, Indian commentators more often speak of reciprocal obligations between the human community and the natural world.

Religion in the Post-contact World. The earliest contact between Europeans and American Indians included missionary activity. In North America the Jesuit Relations document efforts of dozens of priests to convert tribes of the far-flung Spanish empire and the French fur-trading territories of Canada and the Mississippi. Kateri Tekakwitha, a pious Iroquois woman of the seventeenth century, is entered in the Roman Catholic roster of "Blessed" individuals—one step from official sainthood. Protestant MISSIONARIES arrived with the first Pilgrims, and the earliest writings in English by American Indians are poems of Harvard University divinity students from the 1600's and letters from New England Indians who were serving as missionaries less than a hundred years later. Conversion to Christianity was frequently not a benign process, as indicated, for example, in the mission records of California, which note the harsh treatment of Indians and coercive tactics used to keep them at mission sites. Many apparent converts maintained inner resistance to the imported religion; others sought a synthesis of traditional and Christian doctrine.

Corn Dancers enter ceremonial kiva at San Ildefonso Pueblo, N. Mex., c. 1905. (Edward S. Curtis, Museum of New Mexico)

A convert to Christianity and a catechist to his people, Black Elk sought to synthesize Oglala and Christian beliefs. In *The Sacred Pipe* (1953), which he dictated shortly before his death, he describes seven holy rites of the Lakota, commenting occasionally on the parallels and harmony between Oglala and Christian sacred belief. Black Elk's career as a religious teacher carried on a tradition going back to Eleazer Wheelock in the 1700's, who sent Indian students out to villages to proselytize. In the nineteenth century notable Indian Christian missionaries and activists included the Pequot William Apess and the Ojibwas Reverend Peter Jones and George Copway.

One widespread ritual that includes Christian elements is the PEYOTE religion. Both testimonials of Indian participants like Crashing Thunder and accounts by non-Indians suggest the influence of Methodism in practices such as public testimonials to conversion and strict prohibition of alcohol. The peyote ritual also draws on the Protestant, especially Methodist, communion service.

The Yaquis of the Southwest are immigrants from the northern area of Mexico who came to the United

States to escape persecution and land expropriation during the Mexican Revolution, which began in 1910. They brought with them a religious tradition that blends Catholicism and indigenous beliefs. Evangelized by Jesuits in the sixteenth century, the Yaquis adapted not only elements of Catholic belief but also Spanish folklore and history. The traditional "flower world" of Yaqui spiritual reality is most intensely embodied in the Deer Dance, while Spanish Catholic influences predominate in a series of EASTER rites that include dramatized conflict between "Moors" and "Christians."

Contemporary Indians belong to various Christian denominations and practice a variety of traditional religions, including the NATIVE AMERICAN CHURCH. The late twentieth century has seen a revival of many traditional religious rituals and societies.

SUGGESTED READINGS. A good introduction to further study of American Indian religions is *Seeing with a Native Eye: Essays on Native American Religion*, edited by Walter Holden Capps (1976), which contains a helpful bibliography. Ake Hultkrantz is foremost among scholars of American Indian religions; his *The Religions of the American Indians* (1979) is indispensable. Joseph Epes Brown's *The Spiritual Legacy of the American Indian* (1982) expands on work that Brown initiated with his interviews of Black Elk. *The Encyclopedia of Religion*, edited by Mircea Eliade (1987), contains several relevant introductory articles.—*Helen Jaskoski*

Religious discrimination. *See* **Discrimination—religious**

Religious organizations: All religious organizations interrelate with political, social, and economic institutions of the larger society. Even in the United States and Canada, there is no full separation of church and state: There is simply a carefully and legally prescribed relation between the two. Religious organizations influence and are influenced by all the other social structures with which they come in contact. As these organizations evolve and develop, their relationships with the wider culture change. They either continue to function or stop functioning, according to their ability to meet the sociocultural needs of specific eras and environments. In the United States, new religious organizations have formed and new social action programs have been established by churches in response to the challenges of CULTURAL PLURALISM.

The Impact of Multiculturalism. Groups that create religions have been associated traditionally with particular cultures. The trend in a global village, a world grown small, however, is to find religions that increasingly cross cultural barriers and religious adherents that come from a wide variety of cultural backgrounds. Some religions in the twentieth century developed theologies largely based on the idea of MULTICULTURALISM: The Unitarian Universalist and the BAHA'I faiths are prime examples. The first of these was founded in the United States, while the second was founded in the Middle East. Each celebrates the variety of religious thinkers and prophets other religions have produced, and each acknowledges the value of all world faiths. Both of these multicultural religions appeal to people who represent differing nationality, racial, ethnic, and class groups, although UNITARIANS tend to attract formally educated class groups that are tolerant of competing cultures.

The trend toward CULTURAL RELATIVISM in religions can be found, as well, in some historic belief systems. The United Church of Christ in the United States, an example of liberal Protestantism, and some congregations within Reform Judaism teach the validity of other religious expressions. Most world faiths have liberal components that emphasize how religions are not exclusive and how multicultural influences alter religious belief systems. For these liberal religionists, multiculturalism is not a threat but, rather, a means toward positive religious changes.

World religions have traditionally been associated with one particular culture. For example, Islam came from the Arab world, Judaism was identified with the Israelites, Shinto came from Japan, and Confucianism was Chinese. Even Roman Catholicism was based in Latin cultures of Europe and the Americas, while Protestantism had an Anglo-Germanic orientation in Europe and North America. In the twentieth century especially, these monocultural orientations have expanded dramatically. Zen and other Buddhist sects are widely practiced in the Americas. Evangelical Protestantism has challenged traditional Catholic influences throughout Latin America. Jewish congregations include converts from various ethnic and racial backgrounds. One criterion for the survival of a major religion today is its capacity to be culturally inclusive.

Religious Structures in Pluralistic Societies. There are four types of religious institutions that function in multicultural societies: ecclesia, denomination, sect, and cult. The first is the official state church or ecclesia, as in Islamic Iran or Anglican Britain.

The second type, the denomination, is predominant in societies such as the United States that have no state religion and sanction religious pluralism. Denominations are large, socially acceptable institutions that compete with one another for adherents in the religious marketplace. Some religions that are state churches elsewhere, such as Judaism in Israel, are denominations in the United States. Denominations often are formed by ecclesia members who have sociocultural reasons for withdrawing from a state religion. For example, the BAPTISTS in the Americas appealed to middle- and lower-middle-class groups that required emotive religious services as a therapeutic release from the struggles of migration or discrimination. By contrast, the Episcopal denomination attracts upper-income groups and the Presbyterian denomination emphasizes education as a mandatory component of religious culture. Black-oriented Pentecostal denominations have appealed to disfranchised groups that sanctioned themselves as holy communities when the larger society claimed they were unacceptable. Because of the strength and size of these religious groups, they were denominations rather than sects. Each, however, had a distinctive cultural profile in their membership and expressed a social as well as a religious culture that distinguished them from adherents of other denominations.

Palmer Hayden's painting "Baptism Day" shows the full immersion experience as practiced by many African American Baptists. (National Archives)

As denominations expand their memberships and become more culturally inclusive, groups withdraw and form the third type of religious organization; the sect. Their formation is usually the result of class rather than theological differences. Sects are small in membership and often have less well educated clergy. They encourage congregational participation in religious worship, and stress the importance of separation from the larger society's culture. Most are not long-lived, because they cannot compete successfully with the larger society's values. If they do continue to function, it is ordinarily because they have become more culturally inclusive and, therefore, have lost some of their unique sectarian culture. American METHODISTS, Baptists, and PENTECOSTALS all began as sectarian groups; conversely, the Church of Christ, Scientist (CHRISTIAN SCIENTISTS) and JEHOVAH'S WITNESSES have become more denominational than sectarian in Western societies. Unlike sects, cults (the fourth type of religious organization), develop radically different theologies, rituals, and holy books. They often have a charismatic leader who presents himself or herself as a messianic figure, and they furnish codes of obedience that may be in direct contradiction to the laws or morals of the larger society. Cults provide an in-group culture that remains clearly distinct from other groups. Cults tend to be separatist, claiming that relations with the larger society are the source of contamination. This separatism, however, must often be compromised in a pluralistic society.

Social Activism. Western religions such as Christianity may be compared generally with Eastern faiths as being more activist in addressing social problems. This is not new: In the nineteenth century, the classical social historian Ernst Troeltsch traced the history of the Protestant commitment to social change. More recent analysts such as H. Richard Niebuhr have shown how religious social activism was intensified in North America and how American religious organizations have had an impact on diverse ethnic and cultural groups. This is true even of sectarian or separatist groups. For example, others are affected when the Amish struggle to keep their children out of public school systems, when Christian Scientists decline to immunize their children or receive blood transfusions, or when Jehovah's Witnesses refuse to pledge allegiance to the U.S. flag or enter the military. All these acts seek to protect the rights of these groups in the face of the dominant culture, but they are sometimes interpreted by others as hostile or antisocial acts.

Some religious organizations are especially known for their social action commitments. The so-called peace churches, including the Society of Friends (the

Quaker educator Prudence Crandall went against a state law in admitting blacks to her school for girls in the 1830's. Quakers have long been known for their application of religious beliefs to social action. (The Associated Publishers, Inc.)

QUAKERS) and the MENNONITES in both the United States and Canada, have made local and world peace a prime religious commitment. The Quakers, through their international organization the American Friends Service Committee, send people of all cultural backgrounds to communities throughout the world to initiate social service projects, including programs on American Indian RESERVATIONS and in the INNER CITIES of the United States. Seventh-day Adventists, although not a traditional peace church, do comparable work in medical areas: They are known for establishing health care institutions in Third World countries and in low-income regions of North America. These organizations are not rigid about whom they serve or the religious responses to their work; their services are geared toward meeting broad human needs rather than acquiring converts.

Non-Christian religious organizations, such as Jewish congregations, have shown commitments to issues such as intergroup tolerance and interfaith religious understanding. American Jews established the Anti-Defamation League (ADL), which actively publicizes HATE CRIMES, conducts workshops on multicultural tolerance, and assists in the legal defense of victims of DISCRIMINATION. The ADL cooperates with other religious groups that share these goals, such as the Unitarian Universalist Fellowships, a liberal Protestant denomination. During the 1950's and 1960's, Reform Jews and Unitarians were among the few nonblack religious groups directly supporting CIVIL RIGHTS MOVEMENT activists in the southern United States. They frequently joined African American ministers and students in sit-ins and marches. In the 1980's and 1990's, Unitarians in particular have actively supported newer human rights movements, including the GAY AND LESBIAN RIGHTS MOVEMENT organized to prevent continued discrimination in employment, housing, and the military.

Some more conservative American religious denominations share a commitment to meeting human needs, although the causes they support may not necessarily include issues such as gay rights. The Salvation Army has shown a historic identification with the homeless and the hungry in North America as well as internationally. The Salvation Army's network of feeding stations and housing sites is found in most American cities. Comparable urban missions are operated by other evangelical Protestant organizations that may be supported by a variety of fundamentalist churches rather than one denomination. Generally, these social

Antiabortion demonstration in Washington, D.C., uses crosses to represent aborted fetuses. Although the religious right supports the pro-life movement, other church groups have been more divided in their response. (Sally Ann Rogers)

services differ from those offered by groups such as the UNITARIANS by emphasizing religious worship and/or instruction of clients. This is rationalized as an attempt to recover or reform the whole person rather than as an attempt simply to acquire members for a specific religious group. Conservative religious social agencies have provided refuge to battered women and dysfunctional families long before these causes were of interest to most liberal churches and secular movements.

All regional organizations of the Roman Catholic church in North America, such as dioceses and archdioceses, have designated clergy who are trained in and hired for directing specific social action activities. These usually include homes for the aged; health care institutions including hospitals and rehabilitation centers; charitable institutions that feed, house, and sometimes offer medical care for the homeless; and, especially in the Southwest, social service centers for migrant workers. The latter group is particularly important for Catholic agencies since many migrants in the United States are Latinos of Catholic backgrounds.

In a less officially sanctioned way, some Catholic as well as Protestant groups such as the United Church of Christ supported the SANCTUARY MOVEMENT to aid illegal immigrants from Central America. Churches involved in this movement not only supplied food and housing but also offered safe houses and transportation to help immigrants avoid detection by immigration officers. The sanctuary movement is an example of religious organizations supporting causes that are in direct conflict with federal authorities and laws.

Religious groups may also be active in controversial movements that do not have the consensual support of the American populace. For example, "right to life" (antiabortion) organizations are supported by many

Catholic clergy and laity as well as fundamentalist PROTESTANTS. "Pro-choice" (favoring women's right to abortion) groups receive at least indirect support from more liberal Protestant organizations, which help staff offices and join in legal suits supporting a woman's right to choose abortion. Churches are often split within their own denominational organizations about what roles to take regarding controversial issues. Many Catholic and Jewish groups are debating whether homosexuals can be members of their clergy; while traditions such as the Roman Catholic faith condemn homosexuality, there are organized groups of Catholic homosexuals that encourage changes in religious law and practice as they attempt to remain within the church.

The Black Church. African American churches have one of the strongest traditions of social activism in the United States. Unlike many of their nonblack counterparts, black churches have always been educational, social, and political centers that organized the larger black community for participation in civil and human rights issues. Also unlike many other ethnic religious groups, African American clergy have routinely sought political office without general criticism from their constituencies: Jesse JACKSON is one of the more recent and best-known examples of the preacher-politician. Some African American academics have even claimed that black churches are primarily social rather than theological agencies, promoting justice and human welfare under the guise of religion (Joseph Washington) or as the main function of religion (Albert Cleage).

The black church, in the absence of other durable, dependable, and black-directed institutions, has historically acted as that community's main social service and political institution, and a new theology has developed to support this involvement. "Black liberation theology," espoused by thinkers such as James Cone, attempts to interpret prophets and even Jesus as advocates of disfranchised groups. It also claims that the main mission of churches is to overcome oppression wherever and whenever it occurs. Black liberation theology is a clear departure from both black and white traditional Christian dogma, which sometimes encouraged adherents to expect rewards only in an afterlife. For black liberation theologians, rewards must be obtained "here and now."

The social activism of American religious groups is reflective of the activism of the broader American society. Both religious culture and the general culture of North America are influenced by the traditional Calvinist "Protestant ethic." This tradition encourages both religious and nonreligious people to improve present social orders, to make society more functional, and to realize social values here and now.

SUGGESTED READINGS. For further information on religion in a societal context, see Ronald L. Johnstone's *Religion and Society in Interaction* (1975), Andrew M. Greeley's *The Denominational Society* (1972), and Meridith B. McGuire's *Religion: The Social Context* (3d ed., 1992). For sociological perspectives on the relationship between religion and social disagreements, see *Religion and Social Conflict* (1964), edited by Robert Lee and Martin E. Marty.—*William T. Osborne*

Removal and relocation of American Indians: Recurrent feature of federal Indian policy. The U.S. government has used the forcible moving of Indian tribes as a means of defining the relationship between Indians and the larger American society. Such policies have done much to determine the geographical distribution of the American Indian population and to fuel Indian hostility toward the U.S. government.

Origins of Removal Policy. The removal of Indian tribes first became federal policy in the early nineteenth century. A number of factors helped to bring this about. Of primary importance was the desire of white settlers for Indian land. Many settlers saw American Indians as barriers to settlement to be removed as quickly as possible. Disputes over land had long been a source of conflict between whites and Indians. Since the United States recognized the right of Indian occupancy, removal by treaty provided a legal means of clearing Indian title to the land so that it could pass into other ownership. Removal was also favored by many who were genuinely concerned about protecting Indian interests. Traditional tribal cultures were viewed as backward and incompatible with modern civilization; in any competition, even many sympathetic whites believed, the Indians would be doomed to extinction. To prevent this, it was argued, they should be moved beyond the point of contact with settled society. At a distance they might gradually acquire the values, habits, and agricultural skills that would allow them eventually to assimilate into American society.

Though the idea of eastern Indians exchanging their ancestral lands for new territory acquired in the LOUISIANA PURCHASE was first suggested by Thomas Jefferson in 1803, it was only in the 1820's that action was taken. During the previous decade, the War of 1812 had done much to weaken militarily the tribes east of the Mississippi River, as well as to discourage them from expecting British assistance. During the mid-1820's, the Monroe Administration began to try to persuade various tribes to exchange their eastern lands voluntarily in return for territory west of the Mississippi, where Secretary of War John C. Calhoun marked out a tentative INDIAN TERRITORY (originally the area of the Louisiana Purchase between a line drawn south from the headwaters of the Mississippi to the hundredth meridian). A number of tribes, mostly in the former Northwest Territory, signed treaties.

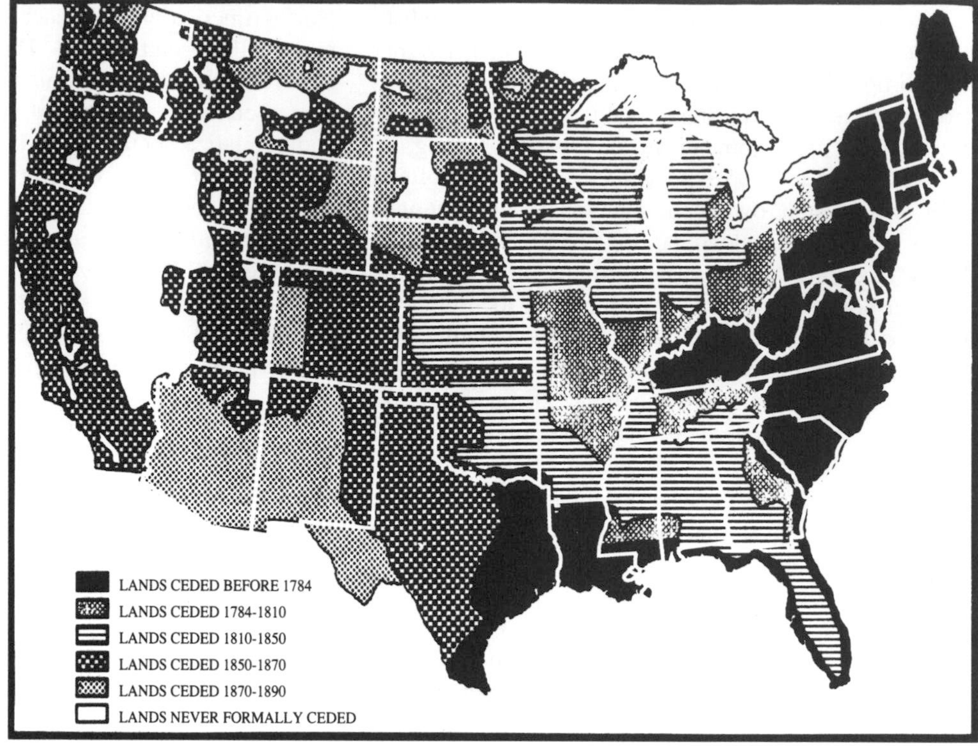

LANDS TRANSFERRED FROM NATIVE AMERICANS TO WHITES

Source: Redrawn from *Atlas of the North American Indian*, 6.6.

The Age of Removals. The great age of tribal removals came after Andrew Jackson was elected president in 1828. Though he had made his reputation in part as an Indian fighter, Jackson was not an Indian hater. He believed, however, that tribal life could not coexist with white settlement, and he thought the policy of dealing with tribes as separate nations was ridiculous. If Indians wished to stay in the rapidly growing areas between the Appalachian Mountains and the Mississippi, they could do so as individuals subject to the laws of the states in which they might reside. He saw no place for organized tribes in such an arrangement. Moreover, the federal government was under heavy pressure from eastern states to get Indian removal underway. Georgia was especially insistent, having sold its western claims to the United States in 1802 on the understanding that all Indian claims in the state would be bought by the federal government.

At Jackson's behest, Congress passed the INDIAN REMOVAL ACT OF 1830. This measure allowed the president to designate unsettled land in the West as Indian Territory and to negotiate exchanges of lands with eastern tribes. Congress appropriated $500,000 to provide inducements for the Indians in the form of moving expenses, reimbursement for improvements on lands given up, and annuities. Though the act did not specifically state that tribes would be coerced into accepting treaties, there was a clear implication that more was intended than the strictly voluntary removals of the 1820's and that most eastern Indians would move. In all, the Jackson Administration signed ninety-four treaties with various tribes.

Not all tribes wanted to move west. The matter came most directly to a head in the South with regard to the position of the FIVE CIVILIZED TRIBES (the CHEROKEES, Chickasaws, CHOCTAWS, Creeks, and Seminoles). The Cherokees, largest of the tribes and the one that had done the most to adopt an "American" lifestyle, were already resisting Georgia's encroachments by going to court. They argued that they were a separate nation, independent of the laws of Georgia and other states. After gold was discovered in northern Georgia in 1829, pressure on the Cherokees mounted as the state prepared for the division of Cherokee lands. Though the Supreme Court found in the Indians' favor, defining the Cherokees as a domestic dependent nation subject to federal but not state jurisdiction, the decision proved unenforceable. In 1835, a faction within the tribe was persuaded to sign a treaty that the federal government accepted as binding on all. Except for a small group that escaped into the mountains of western North Carolina, the Cherokees were moved by the U.S. Army in 1838 to their new home in the INDIAN TERRITORY (Oklahoma). There they joined most of the rest of the Five Civilized Tribes. The removal was badly managed and characterized by much suffering; ultimately about a quarter of the sixteen thousand Cherokees died on what became known as the "TRAIL OF TEARS."

Events in the Old Northwest followed a similar though less dramatic pattern. The northern tribes were smaller and more migratory by nature. While a few managed to remain east of the Mississippi by moving onto reservations in northern Wisconsin and Minnesota, most of the tribes north of the Ohio River signed treaties and moved into the part of the Indian Territory that would eventually become Kansas and Nebraska. (Most would be moved again when these areas were opened for settlement in the 1850's and 1860's.)

A few tribes violently resisted removal. In 1832, the Sac (or Sauk) and Fox Indians, led by their revered chief Black Hawk, attempted to return to lands they had given up in Illinois. In the Black Hawk War that followed, they were pursued by federal and state forces and eventually forced to surrender after much loss of life. Consequently they were pressured into giving up most of the lands they had earlier claimed in Iowa. The most spirited opposition to removal came from the Seminoles, a tribe that included numbers of runaway slaves. It took the Army seven years to break Seminole resistance in the Second SEMINOLE WAR (1835-1842) and move the bulk of the tribe to the Indian Territory. (A few hundred managed to escape to the Everglades, where they were eventually given a reservation of their own.)

By 1840, the number of American Indians east of the Mississippi had been drastically reduced. Many had been killed in battle or had succumbed to disease; most of the rest had been removed. Only a few small tribes managed to remain, usually on remote reservations on land that whites found undesirable.

Reservations and Removals. No sooner did Indian Territory begin to take shape than westward expansion again raised the prospect of Indian removal. The annexation of Texas (1845) and Oregon (1846), as well as the Mexican War (1846-1848), brought the United States vast new lands, peopled in part by diverse groups of Indians. Access to the Pacific coast and settlement of the interior of the continent seemed to demand greater control of native peoples whose lifestyles would be threatened by railroads and white settlement. The result was the policy of concentration: The various tribes would be confined to reservations to allow corridors of expansion through the West.

The more nomadic tribes of the Great Plains, whose way of life required access to the herds of buffalo that roamed the land, found such arrangements intensely confining. Moreover, as Indian lands became more attractive to miners, farmers, and ranchers, RESERVATIONS were often reduced in size. Some tribes were assigned reservations in the now smaller Indian Territory (reduced to Oklahoma), where half the original lands of the Five Civilized Tribes had been lost because of their alliance with the Confederacy during the CIVIL WAR. Not surprisingly, during the 1860's and 1870's the concentration policy helped to spark the fiercest period of warfare between the United States and the Plains Indians.

Added to concerns about the fighting, episodes such as the forced movement of the Poncas to a reservation in the middle of the Indian Territory in 1877 and the unsuccessful attempt of the Cheyennes to return to the northern plains the following year won considerable sympathy for the Indians in the East and in Congress. This helped to ensure that the next major phase of Indian policy—allotment—did not have removal and relocation as specific goals. Embodied in the DAWES ACT (1887), the new policy emphasized making citizens and farmers of Indians by allotting some tribal lands to individual tribal members and selling the rest. Viewed as more humane than concentration (and again as an alternative to American Indian extinction), the policy did not work as planned: It substantially reduced the quantity of land under Indian control. By 1934, when the allotment policy ended, Indian land had decreased from 138 million to 52 million acres. Not only had "surpluses" been sold off, but many Indians obtained land in their own name and eventually sold it off or leased it to whites, necessitating many individual relocations.

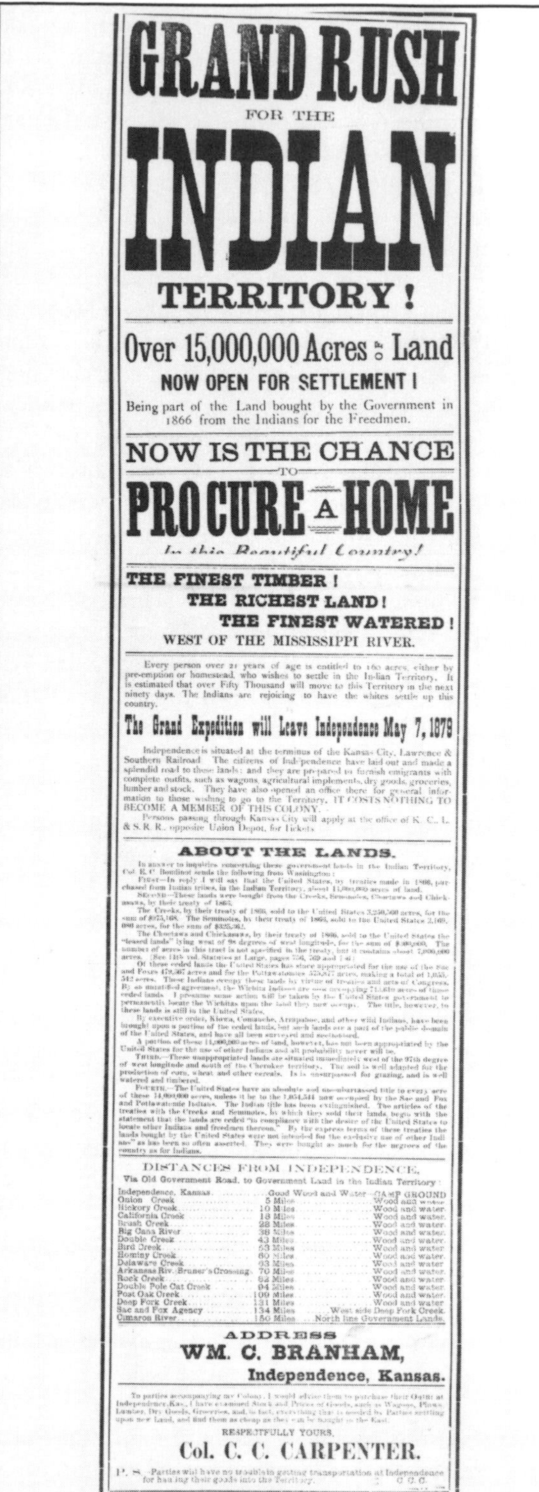

The Indians' loss was seized upon as the white people's gain in rushes to settle in Indian Territory after the Civil War. (Library of Congress)

Relocation in the Twentieth Century. The allotment policy was ended by the INDIAN REORGANIZATION ACT of 1934, which ushered in the "Indian New Deal." This sought to revitalize the tribes and allow them more control over what remained of Indian lands. It appeared that the government had given up its efforts to move the Indian population. During the 1950's, however, a new form of relocation emerged in tandem with a policy known as TERMINATION. Termination was really a new form of the old idea that Indians could only survive through ASSIMILATION into American society. It called for "freeing" the Indians from their dependence on the federal government by dissolving tribes as legal entities and helping American Indians into the mainstream of American life with the proceeds from the sale of tribal assets. This would be accompanied by a new relocation program, this time aimed at encouraging the Indians to move to the cities.

Though termination and urbanization were often seen as two sides of the same policy, they had different roots. The urban relocation program was most immediately intended to reduce unemployment on what were perceived as overpopulated RESERVATIONS. As proponents of the program pointed out, the urban Indian was already a reality, especially after World War II. A relocation division was established within the BUREAU OF INDIAN AFFAIRS (BIA), and soon its agents were encouraging Indians to relocate in one of a number of cities, offering free transportation and money for moving and living expenses. Many found the shift to city life a difficult adjustment.

Though the termination policy was ended in the 1960's, relocation continued as an employment assistance program. By 1972 it had attracted more than 100,000 Indians to urban areas. A larger number, distrustful of the BIA, relocated on their own. Relocation continues to have a major influence on Indians. The U.S. CENSUS OF 1990 found a majority of American Indians living in urban areas, while most of the rest lived on reservations or in areas such as Oklahoma where earlier generations had been relocated.

SUGGESTED READINGS. The best overall account of federal Indian policy, including removal and relocation, is Francis Paul Prucha's *The Great Father: The United States Government and the American Indians* (2 vols., 1984), which is also available in a one-volume paperback abridgment. A readable, brief survey of nineteenth century developments may be found in Philip Weeks's *Farewell, My Nation: The American*

Indian and the United States, 1820-1890 (1990). More detailed treatment of the removal era is provided in Ronald N. Satz's *American Indian Policy in the Jacksonian Era* (1975). Grant Foreman's *Indian Removal: The Emigration of the Five Civilized Tribes of Indians* (1972) describes the consequences. Donald L. Fixico's *Termination and Relocation: Federal Indian Policy, 1945-1960* (1986) discusses the last major effort at relocation.—*William C. Lowe*

Reno, Janet (b. July 21, 1938, Miami, Fla.): First female U.S. attorney general. Reno came to the nation's highest legal post in 1993 after serving as a Dade County, Florida, prosecutor. She won easy confirmation after attempts by the Clinton Administration to push through the nominations of two other women, both of whom had legal irregularities with the employment of domestic help. Reno is considered liberal on social issues, such as broad-based crime-prevention programs, and tough on crime per se. She was widely admired, both within government and by the public, for her straightforward handling of the April, 1993, incident at Waco, Texas, in which an armed standoff between the Federal Bureau of Investigation (FBI) and a religious cult led to the deaths of more than eighty cult members. Reno took full responsibility for the FBI's operation, saying that she had ordered it out of concern for children in the cult compound.

Reparations for Japanese American internment. *See* **Japanese American internment—reparations**

Repatriation program: Mexican laborers residing in the United States have frequently become unwelcome during times of economic recession. During the severe but short-lived recession of 1921-1922, a large-scale campaign designed to repatriate Mexican immigrants was conducted by U.S. government agencies in conjunction with local communities and various charities.

For its part, the Mexican government created a special department within the Ministry of Foreign Relations to facilitate the repatriation of its citizens. Free transportation and food assistance was provided as a follow-up to the delivery of migrants to assist their return to communities in Mexico's interior. It is estimated that approximately 20 percent of the Mexicans then residing in the United States were sent back to Mexico in 1921 alone. By 1923, the repatriation wave had subsided and the repatriation programs were largely phased out.

Six years later, the Great Depression triggered renewed United States efforts at repatriation. The principal motivation for this was the desire to alleviate the burden that migrant workers posed for local, state, and federal public assistance programs. Moreover, there was widespread popular support among organized labor for eliminating migrants from competing for jobs in the shrinking United States labor market.

The Mexican government created a national repatriation program to assist in the return of its citizens, a process that it had always supported as a matter of national principle. Mexican authorities generally acknowledged that emigration northward was a symptom of poor economic conditions, which the Mexican Revolution had sought to transform. Thus, returning migrants were included in Mexico's agrarian reform efforts to redistribute land to peasant farmers. Public education campaigns in Mexico warned that migrants were frequently abused in the United States and stressed that laborers should never migrate without a contractual agreement specifying the conditions of work.

This time, however, the Mexican government openly expressed its concern over the expectation that their country could easily absorb the flow of returning laborers during a recessionary period when its own economy had difficulty generating employment. Mexico wanted the United States to consider assuming greater financial responsibility for the repatriation of returning Mexican laborers.

The United States responded by orchestrating a well-publicized series of community raids that rounded up illegal aliens for immediate deportation, prompting many others to leave voluntarily with their possessions intact. Although Mexico had requested as early as 1929 the negotiation of a bilateral labor migration agreement with the United States, the offer was never met with a tangible response until the *bracero* program was created during World War II.

Suggested Readings. Abraham Hoffman's *Unwanted Mexican Americans in the Great Depression: Repatriation Pressures, 1929-1939* (1974) describes the dynamics of the repatriation program. *Mexican Workers in the United States: Historical and Political Perspectives* (1979), edited by George C. Kiser and Martha Woody Kiser, and Stanley Ross's *Views Across the Border* (1978) both provide background information concerning the changing tides of Mexican immigration. Leo R. Chavez's *Shadowed Lives: Undocu-*

mented Immigrants in American Society (1992) examines the social implications of immigrants who lose their legal status.

Republican Party: The GOP (Grand Old Party), one of the two dominant political parties in the United States, symbolized by the elephant. It is often called "the party of Lincoln," referring to Abraham Lincoln, the first president elected on the Republican ticket. The name actually derives from Thomas Jefferson's political theory of republicanism, which placed national interest over states' rights.

The party was established in 1854 by diverse political groups united in their opposition to slavery. After the Civil War, the Republican Party prevailed in American politics, winning fourteen of eighteen presidential elections between 1860 and 1932. Republican influence declined after 1929, primarily because of the party's resistance to President Franklin D. Roosevelt's New Deal policies during the GREAT DEPRESSION. The Republicans' power was reestablished during the COLD WAR years under Dwight D. Eisenhower, in part because of a strong anticommunist stance in foreign policy, but diminished again with the election of Democrat John F. Kennedy as president. After the turbulent 1960's, dominated by the VIETNAM WAR and the progressive social programs of President Lyndon B. Johnson, the Republicans regained the White House, relinquishing their executive power only once in sixteen years until the defeat of George Bush in 1992.

The modern Republican Party has traditionally espoused a conservative political philosophy emphasizing individual initiative and minimum government interference. It has promoted a probusiness, antilabor, laissez-faire approach to industry and commerce; a strong commitment to military strength; lower taxes (particularly for the wealthy); and a resistance to progressive policies such as welfare and social reform. Since the 1970's, the party has evolved into a coalition of social conservatives, religious fundamentalists, antitax populists, and proponents of deregulation and supply-side economics.

The Republican Party of the 1980's derived its power from Ronald Reagan's ability to unite a white middle class and blue-collar class with the more affluent upper class to forge an indomitable political force. The establishment of the New Right (conservative activists) led to calls by some outspoken members for a "cultural war" against liberals, intellectuals, artists, and feminists. Entities targeted by various right-wing Republicans included the National Endowment for the Arts, the NATIONAL ORGANIZATION FOR WOMEN, the American Civil Liberties Union, National Public Radio, and the Public Broadcasting Service.

In the 1992 presidential election, voters rejected the divisive rhetoric of Republican convention speakers such as Reverend Pat Robertson, columnist Patrick J. Buchanan, and Texas Senator Phil Gramm. The party's platform called for a ban on ABORTION, voluntary prayer in schools, and legislation aimed at curbing the CIVIL RIGHTS of homosexuals.

Ronald Reagan led the Republican Party to a tougher, more conservative stance in the 1980's. (White House Historical Society)

SUGGESTED READINGS. For a general history of the Republican Party, read Fred Schwengel's *The Republican Party: Its Heritage and History* (1988). For a conservative's reaction to the Reagan-Bush years, see Kevin Phillips' *Boiling Point* (1993) and *The Politics of Rich and Poor* (1990). Hunter S. Thompson's *Generation of Swine* (1988) is a scathingly comical account of the 1980's while Peggy Noonan's *What I Saw at the Revolution: A Political Life in the Reagan Era* (1990) provides a sympathetic insider's view of the Reagan-Bush White House.

Rescate, El: Nonprofit organization established in Los Angeles in 1981 by the Santana Chirino Amaya Central American Refugee Committee. Its stated mission is to serve and advocate on behalf of Central American REFUGEES seeking safe haven in Los Angeles and to work for a just peace in El Salvador. El Rescate provides legal services, cultural orientation seminars, and training programs in leadership and employment for refugees and maintains a human rights department. It also publishes a bilingual domestic and international newsletter. El Rescate is Spanish for "the rescue."

Research centers. *See* **Museums and research centers**

Reservations, American Indian: Areas set aside and reserved by the U.S. government for Indian use. Not all Indian land is included in reservations, and reservations have a significance beyond simply being Indian land. Since the middle of the nineteenth century, when the federal government began to establish reservations, these areas have been the central focus of the government's Indian policy.

Though agriculture was alien to some Indians who were forced to live on reservations, the Navajo and other southwestern tribes had farmed for centuries. This photograph from the 1940's shows a Navajo sheep flock near Shiprock, N. Mex. (Museum of New Mexico)

There were 296 reservations in twenty-nine states in 1990, mostly in the trans-Mississippi West, according to the BUREAU OF INDIAN AFFAIRS. These areas included about 44 million acres of tribally owned land.

Colonial Antecedents. The "praying towns" established by the Puritan government in seventeenth century New England were the first precursors of the reservation system. The first such town was authorized by the General Court of Massachusetts Bay Colony in 1646. Potential Indian converts to the PURITAN religion were required to move to the praying towns, where they were expected to dress and farm according to Puritan norms and where they were punished for such cultural lapses as long hair worn by men. This emphasis on control combined with ASSIMILATION would be shared by the later American reservation system.

The experiment was not successful. Few of the "praying Indians" were accepted into the Puritan church, and in 1675 many of them abandoned their towns and joined other New England Indian people in fighting the Puritans in KING PHILIP'S WAR.

About a century later in California, Franciscan MISSIONARIES gathered an estimated maximum of about twenty thousand people in their mission system, which also stressed control and assimilation. Military force was used to collect mission "neophytes" and escapees were severely punished. As in New England, the results were not entirely satisfactory, and Indian people frequently rebelled against missionary abuses.

Early U.S. Policy. The first treaties the United States negotiated with Indian nations after independence drew boundaries between areas taken for white settlement and areas where Indians could continue to live, but did not establish reservations in the modern sense. The government aimed Indian policy mainly at getting land cessions and regulating trade under the aegis of the War Department.

In the later reservation system, Indian agents would be the chief administrators in the field, but the first Indian agents were managers of government trade "factories." Congress took the initial step toward providing teachers and instructors in AGRICULTURE in an 1819 act appropriating $10,000 annually. The money was used to fund private organizations that set up Indian schools, however, rather than on the direct government efforts to promote assimilation that would characterize the reservation system.

Beginning in 1817, the U.S. government made treaties with Indian nations in the Old Northwest with provisions for "reserves" for groups and sometimes individuals located within the areas ceded to the United States. These areas were not originally reservations in the modern sense because they were not administered by the federal government. The government would absorb the reserves that still existed into the reservation system that came into being after the new Interior Department took over administration of Indian affairs in 1849.

First Reservations. In 1848, William Medill, the last commissioner of Indian affairs in the War Department, suggested a tentative version of the reservation concept. He called for the establishment of two Indian colonies on the Great Plains, one on the headwaters of the Mississippi and the other on the western borders of Missouri and Arkansas. He suggested training in agriculture and other aspects of civilization, and argued that concentration of the Indian population would save money because fewer agents would be required. Such colonies would also reduce conflicts with whites because they would leave more land for the settlers to occupy.

Luke Lea, commissioner of Indian affairs in the Fillmore Administration, suggested in his report for 1850 that Indian peoples should be compelled to settle on permanent, well-defined reservations and encouraged to become farmers. According to historian Robert A. Trennert, Jr., makers of Indian policy during this period developed "a definite reservation psychology."

Lea's successor, George Manypenny, said in his 1853 annual report that "the new plan" had been tried in New Mexico "with an encouraging degree of success." Manypenny recognized that setting up reservations for Indian people "would be attended with considerable cost at the outset, as will any other [plan] that can be suggested for their safety and permanent welfare." He expected, however, that reservations would soon be self-supporting, and he argued that no other plan would save the western Indians "from dire calamities, if not entire extermination." Manypenny's three principles for the reservation system were concentration of the population, isolation from white settlers, and training in agriculture.

In his 1854 report Manypenny said the new system was "in progress in California with some prospect of success" at Tejon Pass. He said in 1855 that "the policy of fixed habitations I regard as settled by the government, and it will soon be confirmed as an inevitable necessity," adding that soon there would be "no pretext for a change, as there will be no place to remove the Indian population."

Problems of the Reservation System. The reservation concept was flawed from the beginning by the refusal of policymakers to recognize that little of the land that was being set aside for reservations was usable as farmland. According to Indian service statistics in 1887, only about 8.6 percent of reservation land was considered tillable, and only a little more than .2 percent was actually being cultivated.

Moreover, the government gave management of the reservation system to political appointees whose qualifications and honesty were often questionable. The first agent at the Siletz agency in Oregon, for example, was appointed immediately after he had fought as a volunteer in the Rogue River War of 1855-1856 against the very people who were sent to the reservation after the war; he selected his staff from among his fellow Indian fighters. He was said to have pocketed $60,000 (about $1.2 million in 1992 terms) after serving for only three years.

The Grant Administration attacked the management problem through the "peace policy," begun in 1869, which allocated each reservation to a specific religious denomination. Reformers expected agents nominated by churches to be more conscientious than political appointees. This policy did not produce conspicuously better management than the former system, however, and the government had discontinued it by 1882.

Many tribal groups were reluctant to stay on the

lands which had been set aside for them. The government often expected Indians to settle outside their homelands, sometimes sharing their reservations with former enemies. Efforts to keep people on reservations generated many of the INDIAN WARS in the latter half of the nineteenth century. For example, the Modoc War in Northern California developed in 1872-1873 when white soldiers and vigilantes attacked camps of Modocs who had left the Klamath reservation in Oregon, complaining of bad treatment, to return to their former homeland. The war on the northern Great Plains in 1875-1877 during which Lakotas and CHEYENNES destroyed the command of George Armstrong CUSTER began when the U.S. government ordered Lakotas living on lands in Montana and Wyoming that still belonged to them to leave those lands for their designated reservations.

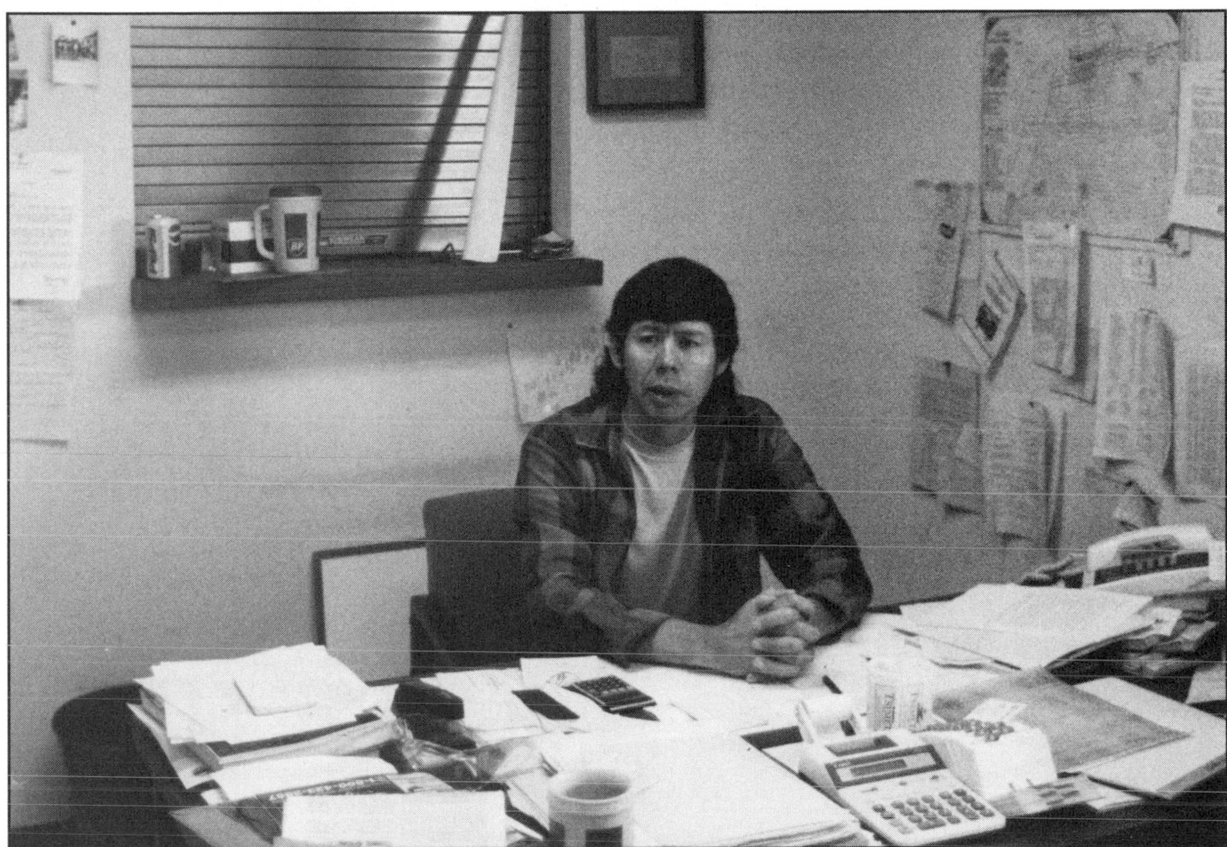

Some young Indians like this Hupa return to or remain on the reservation to assist with tribal government or economic development projects. (Ben Klaffke)

Constant scandals, the failure of the reservation system to end warfare with Indian nations, and the case of the Ponca leader Standing Bear all contributed to demands for reform in the early 1880's. In the winter of 1879, Standing Bear returned to his homeland in Nebraska after being removed to a reservation in INDIAN TERRITORY. A federal district judge ruled that he and his followers could not be returned to Indian Territory without their consent, calling into question the right of the federal government to use force to maintain the system.

Allotment. Reformers promoted allotment, or the division of reservations into individual plots of land, as the solution for the problems of the reservation system. They expected individual ownership to encourage ASSIMILATION and break down tribal ties. Under the principal allotment legislation, the DAWES ACT of 1887, however, most of the land that was not given to individuals when reservations went through the allotment process was bought by the federal government with the expectation that it would be distributed to white settlers. This feature of the allotment policy was the main reason for the disastrous decline of the Indian land base from 138 million acres in 1887 to 52 million acres in 1934. So-called surplus land purchased by the government during the allotment process made up almost 70 percent of the land lost during this period.

The government also gradually shifted reservation management to the control of superintendents of Indian service schools, who were appointed under CIVIL SERVICE, and politically chosen agents were phased out entirely during the administration of Theodore Roosevelt. Reformers had long argued for civil service in Indian administration, but the change did not produce any notable improvement in conditions.

Modern Reforms. During the "Indian New Deal" under the administration of Franklin D. Roosevelt, reformist Indian affairs commissioner John Collier ended allotment and the loss of reservation land and, in the INDIAN REORGANIZATION ACT of 1934, created a basis for reservation self-government. Because the new governments had to conform to white concepts of democracy, however, they tended to favor more assimilated members of tribes and to promote Indian factionalism. Collier was sympathetic to maintaining at least superficial versions of indigenous cultures, and under his management ASSIMILATION ceased to be an official goal of the reservation system.

In 1953 assimilationist sentiment, coupled with congressional demands for economy, threatened the continued existence of reservations when Congress passed House Concurrent Resolution 108, which called for an end to federal responsibility for Indian affairs. Twelve acts for the TERMINATION of federal relationships with tribes were passed between 1954 and 1962, beginning with the Menominees in Wisconsin. During the same period the government sought to reduce reservation populations through programs that relocated Indian people in cities.

Although living conditions on most reservations were poor and federal services minimal, reservations had long since become essential to tribal identities. Termination affected only about 3 percent of reservation and other Indian lands, and 3 percent of federally-recognized Indians. Sponsored relocation affected even fewer people. Nevertheless, the threats these measures posed to the continued existence of tribes

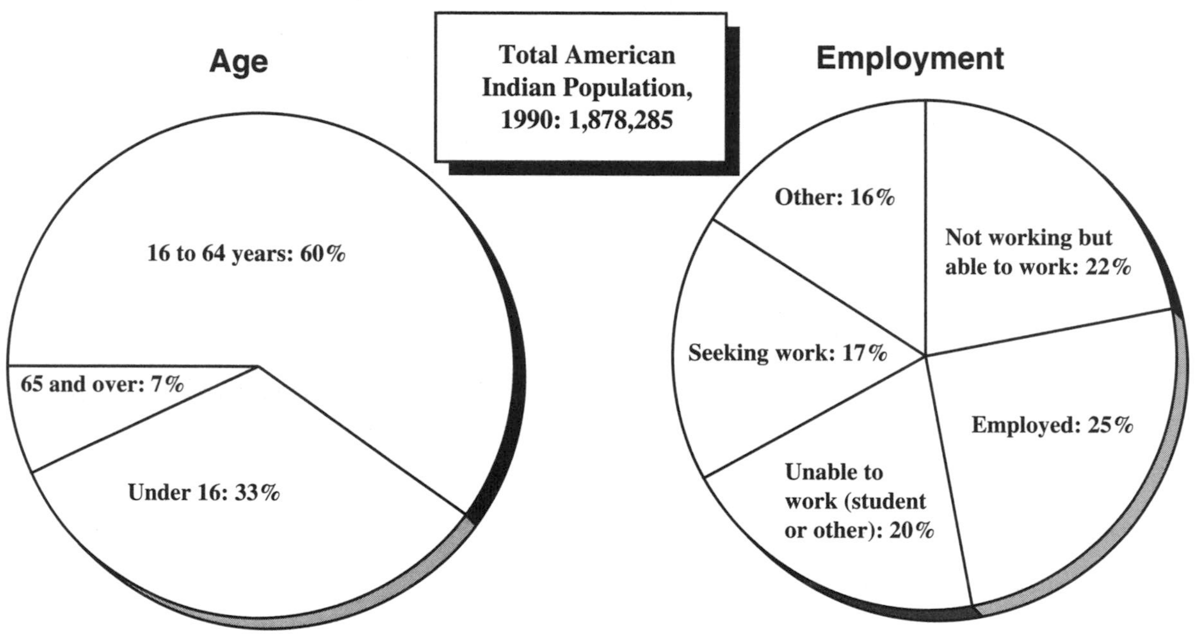

Source: Data are form Carol Foster, ed., *Minorities: A Changing Role in America.* Table 2.4. Wylie, Tex.: Information Plus, 1992.

led Indian people to organize to fight the acts. The Kennedy Administration responded by ending termination and relocation policies and emphasizing economic development on reservations. Federal antipoverty programs during the Johnson Administration improved reservation conditions somewhat. The confrontational activism of organizations such as the AMERICAN INDIAN MOVEMENT (AIM), organized in 1968, encouraged the government to make further changes.

Under the INDIAN SELF-DETERMINATION AND EDUCATION ASSISTANCE ACT OF 1975 tribal governments began taking responsibility for administering some federal programs previously managed by the BUREAU OF INDIAN AFFAIRS. Several community colleges were established on reservations under the Tribally Controlled Community College Act of 1978. Since 1976 Congress has given federal recognition to a number of terminated tribes. Federal recognition of formerly terminated and previously unrecognized tribes increased the number of reservations by about 10 percent between 1985 and 1990. The late 1900's also saw the phenomenon of some nonreservation Indians such as the elderly returning to live on the reservation for emotional support and social services.

Although the majority of Indian people no longer live on reservations, most of those whose Indian status is recognized by the federal government maintain that status through their membership in reservation-based tribes. The exceptions to this trend are in Oklahoma and Alaska, where circumstances produced different forms of organization for most Indian groups.

SUGGESTED READINGS. For an account of relations between the Indians and the European colonists in colonial New England, see *The Invasion of America: Indians, Colonialism, and the Cant of Conquest* (1975) by Francis Jennings. The California mission system is discussed by Sherburne F. Cook in *The Conflict Between the California Indians and White Civilization* (1976). Francis Paul Prucha's *The Great Father: The United States Government and the American Indians* (1984) is a comprehensive study of U.S. Indian policy.

Robert A. Trennert, Jr., describes the beginnings of the modern reservation system policy in *Alternative to Extinction: Federal Indian Policy and the Beginnings of the Reservation System, 1846-51* (1975). In *The Dispossession of the American Indian, 1887-1934* (1991), Janet A. McDonnell considers the results of allotment. Vine Deloria, Jr., and Clifford M. Lytle give an account of John Collier's administration of the BIA in *The Nations Within: The Past and Future of American Indian Sovereignty* (1984). Donald Fixico describes post-World War II Indian policy in *Termination and Relocation: Federal Indian Policy, 1945-1960* (1986).—*E. A. Schwartz*

Reservists. *See* **Veterans and reservists**

Restrictive covenants: Form of housing DISCRIMINATION that forbids or restricts the ownership of property by certain minority racial or ethnic groups. An example of restrictive covenants were the clauses added to property deeds in wealthy urban and suburban neighborhoods in the 1920's to ban residence there by JEWISH AMERICANS. Official or unofficial covenants have also been used to uphold the SEGREGATION of all-white neighborhoods. U.S. SUPREME COURT RULINGS in 1945 and 1953 held aspects of restrictive covenants based on race unconstitutional, but the practice continued unofficially until stronger fair housing laws were put in place in the 1960's largely as the result of pressure brought to bear by the CIVIL RIGHTS MOVEMENT.

Reverse discrimination: Political phenomenon first publicized during the 1970's. It refers to alleged DISCRIMINATION against whites as an outgrowth of legal remedies won by racial minorities since the CIVIL RIGHTS MOVEMENT of the 1960's.

Reverse discrimination asserts that unfair treatment of whites can result from programs or formal selection processes such as AFFIRMATIVE ACTION designed to assist minorities in achieving full racial equality. Lawsuits that charge reverse discrimination argue that such practices have the effect of discriminating against whites not directly implicated in racist behaviors, simply on the basis of their race. In fact, antidiscrimination laws in the United States have always reflected social tension regarding the correct legal remedy for historical oppression, with debate centered around the issue of who should pay the price for implementing social reforms designed to rectify past injustices.

The most famous reverse discrimination case was *REGENTS OF THE UNIVERSITY OF CALIFORNIA V. BAKKE* (1978). Allan Bakke, a white medical school applicant, was rejected by the University of California, Davis, in both 1973 and 1974. During the same years, nonwhite applicants with significantly lower entrance exam scores were accepted through a special admissions program designed to increase the school's racial diversity. Bakke argued that his rejection, alongside the acceptance of less qualified applicants, amounted to discrimination based on his race and thus constituted a violation of his rights as protected under the FOURTEENTH AMENDMENT and Title VI of the CIVIL RIGHTS ACT OF 1964.

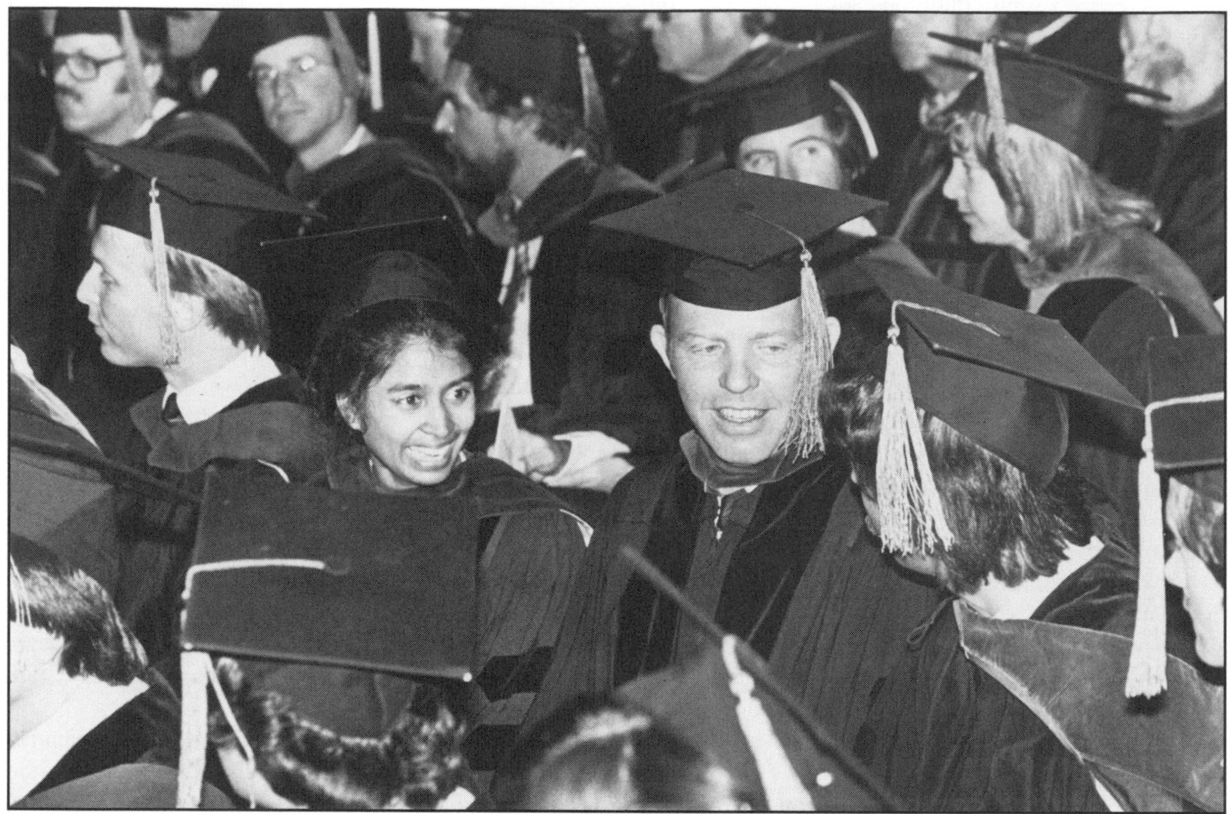

Alan Bakke (center) at his medical school graduation. The Bakke case ignited a stormy debate on reverse discrimination. (AP/Wide World Photos)

The Supreme Court ruled in favor of Bakke's claim of unfair discrimination and ordered him admitted. In doing so, the Court established a legal precedent that became a major setback to civil rights activists who have supported special admissions programs. All programs mandating "crude racial quotas" that denied inclusion to whites solely on account of their racial background were henceforth considered unduly harmful. The legal recognition of reverse discrimination essentially complicates the enactment of any reform requiring whites to pay a price for rectifying discrimination which they themselves did not specifically commit.

In the wake of the Bakke case, increasingly conservative courts have generally upheld reverse discrimination suits filed in EDUCATION, EMPLOYMENT, and other areas. By fueling the popular white slogan of "racism in reverse," the moral purity of antidiscrimination reforms has become clouded, thus undermining their popular support. Many legal experts have pointed out that reverse discrimination suits have simply drawn attention to the inherent limitations of antidiscrimination law as thus far enacted. Racial inequality cannot be genuinely eliminated unless more far-reaching means are devised to address the institutionalized nature of discrimination.

SUGGESTED READINGS. Derrick Bell's *Race, Racism, and American Law* (1992) presents a comprehensive legal analysis of reverse discrimination as well as the limitations of antidiscrimination litigation. An overview of early affirmative action policies can be found in John C. Livingston's *Fair Game? Inequality and Affirmative Action* (1979). Nathan Glazer's *Affirmative Discrimination: Ethnic Inequality and Public Policy* (1975) argues for affirmative action policies to be seen as reverse discrimination, while Roy L. Brooks's *Rethinking the American Race Problem* (1990) explores alternatives to traditional antidiscrimination approaches.

Reynoso, Cruz (b. May 2, 1931, Brea, Calif.): Mexican American lawyer, judge, and public official. In 1958, Reynoso received his law degree from the University of California, Berkeley. He went on to a varied career in law, academia, and public service. Reynoso has been an associate justice for the Third Appellate Court in Sacramento as well as a justice of the California Supreme Court, and has also had a private law practice. He served as assistant chief of the Division of Fair Employment Practices for the California Department of Industrial Relations, associate general counsel of the EQUAL EMPLOYMENT OPPORTUNITY COMMISSION (EEOC), and director of the California Rural Legal Assistance. He also taught at the New Mexico School of Law.

Rhythm and blues music: African American blues-influenced music, using electrified instruments, that thrived in the 1950's and 1960's. The term "rhythm and blues," or "R&B," was adopted by the music trade newspaper *Billboard* as a replacement for "race music" and "sepia," terms which had previously been used to trace the sales of records in the African American market. The most prominent form of BLUES related to rhythm and blues was the blues of the Mississippi Delta as it was reshaped in Chicago and other midwestern cities. The big band, shout, scream and cry, and combo styles of blues were also influential. Rhythm and blues was a term that identified the singer and primary audience as African American.

Most rhythm and blues was vocal, and the music was performed by a group typically consisting of a lead singer or singers, a lead instrumentalist, a rhythm section (drums, double bass or electric bass guitar, piano or organ, and electric guitar), and a backup vocal group. Rhythm and blues songs were related to the song styles of Tin Pan Alley and GOSPEL, with the notable addition of a dance rhythm. Often the lyrics dealt with the same subjects as mainstream popular music—such as love—but rhythm and blues also addressed the more biting or ironic themes found in the blues.

Booker T. and the MGs were popular rhythm and blues performers during the 1960's. (AP/Wide World Photos)

Independent record companies in New York, Chicago, and Los Angeles released most rhythm and blues recordings, though a number of smaller record labels in southern cities such as Houston and New Orleans also produced R&B records. In the 1950's, important rhythm and blues performers who recorded mainly in New York and Los Angeles included T-Bone Walker, Wynonie Harris, Joe Turner, and Ruth Brown. Southern guitar-dominated rhythm and blues styles were, and still are, represented by artists such as B. B. King, Little Walter, Muddy Waters, and Howlin' Wolf. Most of these singers had a raucous style that depended upon loud, emphatic rhythms and a heavy back beat. Another important blues singer was John Lee Hooker, whose style was somewhere between the rough bar-blues and a smoother boogie style.

Rhythm and blues was the inspiration for and immediate forerunner of ROCK AND ROLL; it influenced both the development of white rock and roll in the 1950's and the pop music revolution of the 1960's. Undoubtedly, a direct link exists between African American rhythm and blues and the music of black rock and rollers Little Richard and Chuck BERRY, as well as white rock and roll superstar Elvis Presley. Another strand of the legacy of rhythm and blues can be heard in American SOUL MUSIC.

SUGGESTED READINGS. For a study of New Orleans rhythm and blues, see *I Hear You Knockin'* (1985) by Jeff Hannusch. *Up from the Cradle of Jazz* (1986) by Jason Berry, Jonathan Foose, and Tad Jones is an overview of New Orleans music since World War II and includes portraits of some of the most important rhythm and blues artists. Robert Pruter's *Chicago Soul* (1991) is a history of the rhythm and blues era in Chicago. *The Sound of the City* (1983) by Charles Gillett documents the evolution of rhythm and blues and the rise of rock and roll.

Rich, Adrienne (b. May 16, 1929, Baltimore, Md.): Poet and feminist. Rich's first book of poetry, *A Change of World*, was published in 1951 with a foreword by W. H. Auden. In 1969 she published Leaflets, which included political poetry opposing the Vietnam War. She is most recognized for her books that center on women's issues; her Diving into the Wreck (1973) won the National Book Award. Other works include *Of Woman Born: Motherhood as Experience and Institution* (1976, essays), *On Lies, Secrets, and Silence: Selected Prose 1966-1978* (1979, essays), *The Dream of a Common Language* (1978), *A Wild Patience Has Taken Me This Far* (1981), and *An Atlas of the Difficult World* (1991).

Ride, Sally (b. May 26, 1951, Encino, Calif.): Astronaut. Ride attended Swarthmore College but dropped out to pursue what could have been a successful professional tennis career. In 1970 she put tennis aside and enrolled in Stanford University. In 1978 she went through astronaut training after having been chosen by NASA to enter the astronaut corps. In 1983 she was aboard the space shuttle *Challenger* as it took off from Cape Canaveral, Florida; thousands of people waved signs reading "Ride, Sally, Ride." Ride emphasizes that she is an aerospace professional and is not particularly interested in the prestige of being the first American woman in space.

Rivera, Geraldo Miguel (b. July 4, 1943, New York, N.Y.): Latino broadcast journalist and talk show host. After graduating from Brooklyn Law School and the Columbia School of Journalism, Rivera spent two years as an attorney for a small activist law firm in New York's Harlem neighborhood. In 1970 he became a reporter for WABC-TV's *Eyewitness News* in New York. During the next two decades, Rivera variously hosted, produced, and/or reported for that program and national television newsmagazines such as *Good Morning America* and *20/20*, as well as news specials such as "Miguel Robles: So Far" (1972) and "Puerto Rico: Island of Contrasts" (1974). In 1987, Rivera began hosting his own popular daytime talk show *Geraldo*, which became known for

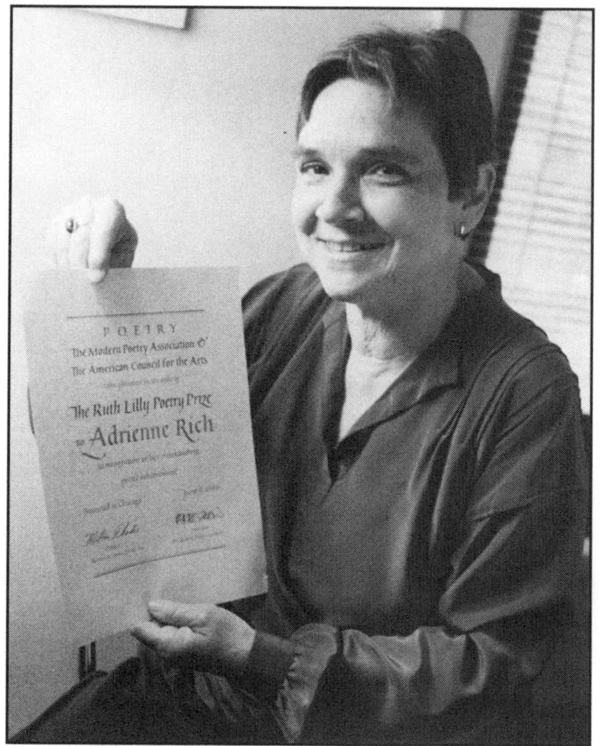

Adrienne Rich has won accolades not only for poetry but also for feminist political essays. (AP/Wide World Photos)

its frank, sometimes sensational treatment of celebrities and lifestyle issues. He has received seven local and three national Emmy Awards.

Robeson, Eslanda Cardoza Goode (Dec. 15, 1896?, Washington, D.C.—Dec. 13, 1965, New York, N.Y.): American writer and anthropologist. Of a mixed background that included Spanish, Jewish, and African forebears, Eslanda Goode had a varied career. After marrying actor Paul Robeson, she left medical school in New York City to manage his career; her first book was a biography of him. After 1928 she studied at the London School of Economics and took up photography. Her book *African Journey* (1945) attacked colonialism; *American Argument* (1949) was a collaboration with novelist Pearl S. Buck. In 1945, the Robesons moved to Connecticut, where Eslanda ran for office as a Progressive.

Paul and Eslanda Robeson traveled extensively on behalf of his artistic career and their political interests. (AP/Wide World Photos)

Robeson, Paul (Apr. 9, 1898, Princeton, N.J.—Jan. 23, 1976, Philadelphia, Pa.): African American actor, singer, and activist. An honor student and athlete at Rutgers University with a law degree from Columbia University (1923), Robeson became a famous stage and film actor and a concert singer from 1924 through the 1950's. Roles in *Porgy and Bess, Show Boat, Othello*, and *The Emperor Jones* brought him awards; at the same time, his liberal politics made him suspect during the McCarthy era of the 1940's and 1950's among white conservatives and led the U.S. government to withhold his passport. His later career included travel, writing, and belated recognition for effective civil rights activism. His autobiography is entitled *Here I Stand* (1957).

Robinson, Jackie (Jan. 31, 1919, Cairo, Ga.—Oct. 24, 1972, Stamford, Conn.): African American baseball player. After playing at the University of California, Los Angeles (UCLA), Robinson broke the color barrier in major league baseball. Black athletes in other sports had made gains, but baseball remained segregated until the Brooklyn Dodgers bought Robinson's contract in 1945 from the Kansas City Monarchs, a black team. Robinson moved up to the majors in 1947 to become rookie of the year (1947), the league's most valuable player (1949), and the first black player in the Baseball Hall of Fame (1962). His impressive ten-year career in the majors paved the way for other blacks in the sport.

Rock and roll: A style of popular music that emerged in the 1950's and became enormously popular among teenagers. Rock and roll combined the elements of various musical styles, including GOSPEL, BLUES, FOLK MUSIC, JAZZ, boogie-woogie, and COUNTRY music. All these styles had been more or less influenced by the African American musical tradition.

Prior to the 1950's, the style of music which became rock and roll was called RHYTHM AND BLUES MUSIC and was played and listened to predominantly by African Americans. After the late 1940's, however, an increasing number of white teenagers became dissatisfied with the popular music of the time, the crooning style typified by Perry Como and Frank Sinatra. They began to listen to black radio stations and to purchase records by black musicians. Discovering white teenagers' interest, Cleveland-based disc jockey Alan Freed started a radio show called "Moondog's Rock and Roll Party" in 1952. Independent record companies continued to market rhythm and blues records for white teenagers as well as African Americans while major record labels issued records on which white artists recorded ("covered") the same songs. With Elvis Presley's recording debut in 1954 and a film, *Blackboard Jungle* (1955), which made Bill Haley and the Comets' "Rock Around the Clock" a number-one hit, rock and roll swept the United States.

While Presley and Haley were two of the genre's most successful white musicians, black musicians largely shaped the rock and roll style. Vocal groups such as the Crows ("Gee"), the Chords ("Sh-Boom"), the Penguins ("Earth Angel"), the Charms ("Hearts of

Stone"), and the Platters ("Only You" and "The Great Pretender") not only introduced rhythm and blues to the white audience but also developed a style known as "doo-wop." Popular solo musicians included Fats Domino, whose "Blueberry Hill" was one of the most frequently recorded songs of the era; Ray CHARLES, who effectively combined gospel and rock and roll (as heard in "I've Got a Woman"); and Bo Diddley, known for his distinctive rhythmic style. Little Richard's flamboyant style influenced those who followed him, most notably white musician Jerry Lee Lewis. The most important and talented musician was Chuck BERRY, whose songs, including "Johnny B. Goode," "Rock and Roll Music," and "School Days," epitomized the feelings of teenagers as well as the spirit of rock and roll. Berry was the first rock and roll poet. He also established the standard of rock and roll guitar style.

The emergence of rock and roll coincided with the rise of the CIVIL RIGHTS MOVEMENT, and black musicians made Americans aware of African American contributions to American musical and cultural traditions. During the early 1960's, as a result of a folk music revival and a wave of English bands, led by the Beatles, rock and roll diversified and was transformed into ROCK MUSIC, which remained the dominant form of American popular music in the late twentieth century.

SUGGESTED READINGS. For the development of rock and roll, see Ed Ward, Geoffrey Stokes, and Ken Tucker's *Rock of Ages* (1986). Charlie Gillett's *The Sound of the City* (1970) is the first scholarly book written on rock and roll. For the biographical information of individual musicians, see *The Rolling Stone Illustrated History of Rock & Roll* (1976), edited by Jim Miller.

Rock music: Heavily rhythmic American popular music that began in the 1960's for a mostly white, middle-class audience. Rock combines traditional American musical forms such as BLUES, FOLK MUSIC, and COUNTRY AND WESTERN with more exotic styles, such as Asian chord compositions, gothic ballads, Middle Eastern and Caribbean rhythms, and baroque fugues. Without completely abandoning its roots, rock manages to transform RHYTHM AND BLUES music into a distinctive sound that relies on amplification, extensive overdubbing, electronic special effects, and distortion. Rock lyrics range from social activism to libertine escapism, at times depicting graphic sex and violence, other times describing drug experiences or mystical and surreal states of mind. Rock captures a wide range of emotion: campy cynicism, sentimental posing, the edginess of teenage rebellion.

Jimi Hendrix became one of the legends of rock music with his extravagant musical style and stage presence. (AP/Wide World Photos)

Politically, rock has had a significant impact on American culture, provoking both reverence and lawsuits. During the 1960's movement against the VIETNAM WAR, rock music became the vehicle of protest and outrage of a whole generation. Janet Podell writes that rock is "the principal means by which a formerly unfocused group of people suddenly pulled themselves together and generated that vortex of hedonism called the counterculture."

Even though rock began as a white artists' synthesis of traditional African American musical styles, its roots go back to bluesmen such as Howlin' Wolf, Lightnin' Hopkins, and John Lee Hooker. Rock also owes a debt to African American rock and roll legends like Bo Diddley, Little Richard, and Chuck BERRY.

One of the most influential musicians in the history of rock was black guitarist Jimi Hendrix. Hendrix derived his style from a heady mix of MOTOWN SOUL MUSIC and bizarre electrified guitar riffs, combined with a wild persona, outlandish fashion, and a raunchy, hard-driving, strobe-lit stage show that became the quintessential rock experience.

While rock is basically a mainstream art form, it manages to absorb a wide range of multicultural styles and concerns. For example, in Los Angeles in the 1980's, young Cambodian Americans formed rock bands and Garifuna immigrants from Belize played punta rock based on a Caribbean dance form. Because rock is so accessible, it expresses and defines the spirit of a young, consumer-oriented generation. Thus it has become a perfect medium for both reflecting and shaping the ideology of youth culture.

SUGGESTED READINGS. A good sampling of diverse essays on social, political, and stylistic aspects of rock can be found in *Rock Music in America* (1987), edited by Janet Podell. One of the most complete collections of writing on rock is *Rock of Ages: The Rolling Stone History of Rock and Roll* (1986), edited by Ed Ward. For a good discussion of the commercialization of rock, refer to *Rock 'n' Roll Is Here to Pay: The History and Politics of the Music Industry* (1977) by Steve Chapple and Reebee Garofalo. For a general study of the African American influence in rock, see *White Boy Singin' the Blues: The Black Roots of White Rock* (1992) by Michael Bane.

Rodríguez, Richard (b. July 31, 1944, San Francisco, Calif.): Mexican American author and journalist. Rodríguez studied at the University of California, Berkeley, and was a 1972 Fulbright Fellow and a 1976 National Endowment for the Humanities Fellow. A full-time writer since 1981, he has reported for the *Los Angeles Times* and the Pacific News Service. His autobiographical *Hunger of Memory: The Education of Richard Rodríguez* earned the 1982 Anfield Wolf Award for Race Relations. In 1992, Rodríguez published *Days of Obligation: An Argument with My Mexican Father*, a personal meditation on Mexican history, American bigotry, and homosexuality. His opposition to AFFIRMATIVE ACTION and BILINGUAL EDUCATION, as well as his other idiosyncratic views, has added greatly to the diversity of Latino voices in American society.

Roe v. Wade (1973): Supreme Court decision successfully challenging state laws which restricted a woman's right to ABORTION. The decision in this historic case, delivered by Justice Harry Blackmun, held that the right of privacy extended to "a woman's decision whether or not to terminate her pregnancy."

Before the 1800's childbirth was a woman's domain, with midwives in charge; abortion in the early weeks or months of pregnancy was common. It was not until the late nineteenth century that women's terminations of their pregnancies became criminalized under the law. As the male medical profession sought to "professionalize" childbirth, doctors pushed to make abortions illegal. In states where abortion was permitted to save a woman's life, doctors' discretion could allow a few, usually upper-class, women to get "therapeutic" abortions.

In the years immediately before *Roe v. Wade*, a number of states had already passed more liberal abortion laws. These were supported by the medical establishment as well as the American Bar Association; the social climate was also favorable. As the Court noted, the health risk to the woman from abortion was no longer an issue. Emphasis had shifted to the issue of abortion as a means to prevent the birth of deformed babies. The danger of fetal deformities was dramatized by the plight of an American woman, Sherri Finkbine, who was unable to get a therapeutic abortion in 1962 after taking thalidomide, a widely prescribed tranquilizer that caused severely deformed limbs and internal organs in the developing fetus. A rubella (German measles) epidemic in the early 1960's also increased pressure for reforming abortion laws.

Roe v. Wade was initiated by two lawyers, Linda Coffee and Sarah Weddington. They were committed to using their legal skills to help women and wanted to challenge Texas' abortion law, which permitted abortion only to save the mother's life; it was not even allowed in cases of incest or rape. They learned of Norma McCorvey, a single woman with little income who was living in Texas; she wished to terminate her pregnancy but legally could not under Texas law. Although McCorvey would not personally benefit by bringing suit, she agreed to be the plaintiff under the pseudonym "Jane Roe" in order to help other women. (Her anonymity was preserved until she herself disclosed it some years after the case.)

In overturning the Texas law, the Court stated that being forced to have a child may result in a "distressful life and future" and may cause psychological harm to a woman and all concerned. The Court did not grant an unlimited right to terminate pregnancy, however;

in the first trimester of pregnancy, the decision was left to the woman and her doctor without interference from the state. In the second trimester (third to sixth month), however, the state could assert a legitimate "interest in the health of the mother" by regulating medical aspects of the procedure, such as licensing clinics. Only during the final trimester might the state, if it chose, regulate or prohibit abortion in the interest of preserving human life, but not if abortion was necessary to preserve the mother's life or health.

SUGGESTED READINGS. For a fascinating account of the trial and persons involved see Marian Faux's *Roe v. Wade: The Untold Story of the Landmark Supreme Court Decision That Made Abortion Legal* (1988). For additional discussion of the topic see Lawrence Lader's *Abortion II* (1973). Rosalind Petchesky considers social and political movements leading to liberalization of laws in *Abortion and Woman's Choice* (1984). For a balanced presentation of the social movements pro and con see Kristin Luker's *Abortion and the Politics of Motherhood* (1984).

Roman Catholics. *See* **Catholics, Roman**

Roman Nose [Woquini] (1830-1868): Southern Cheyenne chief who led the attack at Beecher's Island on the Arickaree River against General George Forsyth (1868). Roman Nose was reputedly invulnerable in battle because of his magic headdress—a power that proved to be a great inspiration to CHEYENNE warriors. If, however, Roman Nose broke the taboo of eating anything taken from a pot with an iron instrument, his medicine would be broken. During the summer of 1868, he inadvertently ate some fried bread taken from a pot with a fork. Later, at the battle at Beecher's Island, he explained that he knew he would be killed that day. He was shot from his horse and died near sunset.

Romanian Americans: The Romanians have been in the United States since colonial times, yet because of various factors, their position and influence have been overshadowed by other Eastern Europeans such as the Hungarians and Poles.

Origins. Romanian Americans claim the geographical regions of Bukovina, Moldovia (which includes Besserabia), Walachia, Transylvania, Banat, Oltenia, and Dobruja as their homeland. Some of these regions have been or are still divided politically. For example, in the early 1990's, Moldovia was divided between Romania and the Republic of Moldovia. These shifting boundaries make it difficult to count Romanian immigrants exactly. Ethnic Romanians also originate from what are now Bulgaria, Yugoslavia, Macedonia, and Greece. U.S. immigrants were classified according to their specific political place of origin rather than their ethnic identification. Between 1901 and 1910, only 3.5 percent of Romanian immigrants who came to the United States were from Romania, while 93 percent were from the Austrian province of Banat and the Hungarian provinces of Transylvania and Bukovina.

ROMANIA

Politically, Romanian Americans claim the country of Romania as their homeland. Many Romanians trace their origins to the Dacians, a group that evolved from the Hittites of Anatolia, who infiltrated the Danube region and merged with local tribes. Romanians claim descent from the Roman/Dacian offspring that resulted from the occupation of the area by the Roman legions.

Romanian history is characterized by a two-tier society of nobles and peasants, ruler and ruled. Most of the ruled peasants were Romanians, while Hungarians, Turks, and other outsiders dominated the nobility. The poverty of Romanian peasants under various rulers was caused partly by a land inheritance system that divided the holdings among all a family's sons rather than giving the whole estate to one son. Small farms and dense population exerted growing pressure on the Romanian peasants, driving many to emigrate during the late nineteenth and early twentieth centuries.

Between World War I and World War II, economic conditions improved, emigration declined, and Bucharest, the capital, was acclaimed as the "Paris of the

East." After World War II, when most of Eastern Europe came under Soviet control, emigration from Romania to the United States increased, dominated by displaced persons and refugees. Between 1945 and the revolution in Romania in 1989, Communist rulers required that all people who left the country had to have the approval of the dreaded Romanian Security Police. Those Romanians in the United States during this period, whether they were refugees, visitors, or scholars, had no way of knowing who was sending information about them back to Romania or what effect that information would have on them and their families. Some immigrants were actually agents for the Security Police.

Immigration. Initially, Romanian immigration to the United States was sporadic. There are recorded visits of Romanians; Johann Kelp (Kelpius) came in the mid-eighteenth century, and Samuel Damian visited Benjamin Franklin in 1748 to learn about electricity. Richard Henderson founded a Transylvanian Colony in the United States in 1774-1775. Romanians fought in both the American Revolution and the Civil War.

Romanians started becoming prominent in the immigration stream in 1870. By 1900, eighteen thousand Romanians, mostly Jews from Moldovia, Russian-controlled Besserabia, or Austrian-held Bukovina, had come to the United States. They were primarily tradesmen and merchants who arrived with their families. Peasants from Transylvania immigrated after 1895, fleeing land shortages and discrimination by Hungarian rulers. Magyarization policies led to the unfair treatment of these Romanians in the schools, civil service, and commercial life of their homeland; forced them into military service; and attempted to convert them to the Roman Catholic (rather than Eastern Orthodox) faith. These "push" factors, along with the "pull" factors of letters from immigrants and agents from steamship companies glorifying American life, encouraged Romanians from Transylvania to leave.

Married men often came alone with the goal of "a thousand dollars and home again." They left their wives and children in Romania, because their goal was to earn money, return home, and buy land to start farming in their homeland. From 1900 to 1920, two-thirds of the Romanian immigrants actually did return home. The return rate was especially high after World War I, when many of their native provinces were incorporated into the Romanian Kingdom. By 1920, the estimated number of Romanian-born nationals in the United States was 85,090, with an additional 5,400 American-born. There was a surge of Romanian immigrants just before the enactment of the Immigration Act of 1924, which set a meager annual Romanian quota of 603. After 1921, the nature of Romanian immigration changed once again. There was a decrease of unskilled laborers and a marked increase in skilled laborers and professionals.

Because of restrictive immigration laws, the Great Depression, World War II, and the Communist takeover of the Balkans, emigration from Romania between 1930 and 1970 was merely 215 persons annually. By World War II, there were 115,940 Romanians in America, with about another ten thousand arriving after 1945 under the Displaced Persons Act. With the changes brought in by the Immigration and Nationality Act of 1965, the number of Romanian Americans swelled to 315,258 in 1980 and 365,544 in 1990.

Settlement in the United States. Romanian settlement was primarily in the urban industrial heartland of the mid-Atlantic and Great Lakes states, especially in cities such as New York, Chicago, Philadelphia, Detroit, Pittsburgh, and Cleveland.

During the late 1800's and early 1900's, many Romanians followed the traditional chain migration pattern in which one or two men left a village and others followed when they learned of the early immigrants' success. Typically, those who went first helped the later arrivals. About 10 percent of the immigrant chains were from these village groups, with an average of five emigrants per village. They formed enclaves based on common origins in Romania. Village mates sometimes lived in the same area as others with a common culture and established their own ethnic neighborhoods, societies, churches, and clubs.

At the beginning of the twentieth century, most Romanians, like their eastern European compatriots, worked in factories, providing cheap muscle for the United States' growing industrial might. By the start of World War I, some of those who remained in the United States had accumulated sufficient capital to establish small entrepreneurial enterprises such as restaurants, boardinghouses, pool halls, or immigrant banks.

Being part of the industrial work force, many Romanian Americans were union members, but they were not especially active. There were a few dedicated socialists who joined the Roumaniani Socialist Workers of the United States, which was affiliated with the Industrial Workers of America and the Socialist Party;

however, this group did not gain the support of many Romanians in America.

By the 1920's, many of the offspring of the first generation had obtained membership in white-collar professions. Some second-generation Romanians visited ethnic neighborhoods and kept in contact with their people. Third-generation Romanians of the 1950's became absorbed and knew little about either Romania or its culture. With the post-1965 influx, however, Romanian ethnicity in America began to assert itself again.

Social and Religious Life. The boardinghouse, the saloon bar, benevolent societies, and the church were all crucial institutions that helped Romanians adjust to American life. Boardinghouses were often crowded, with twenty-five to thirty bachelors in a two-story frame house. Meals were bought cooperatively. These houses served as social centers for poetry and story readings, musical performances, and camaraderie. The boss of the house also acted as a banker, because the immigrants distrusted the American banking system. This institution lasted until the 1930's.

Bars were also early social centers where Romanians of common background gathered to relax after work. Sometimes bars even served as places of worship. Benevolent societies and churches often developed from bar talk. For example, the Carpatina (Carpathian Society) was founded in Homestead, Pennsylvania, in 1902 to provide insurance to Romanian workers who suffered accidents at work. Later it expanded into a cultural organization with programs of dance and song to promote the immigrants' heritage. Initially, societies competed with one another, but after 1930 they began to merge because of their common functions and heritage. The numbers of such societies have considerably decreased in the late 1900's, with original insurance functions replaced by the goal of promoting Romanian culture.

After 1930, the Romanian Orthodox Church gradually gained prominence and became the institution reflecting Romanian ethnicity. In due course, dissension crept in, and Romanian Americans became Eastern Rite Catholics, Baptists, Nazarenes, Adventists, Pentecostals, Jehovah's Witnesses, and Unitarians. Within the Romanian Orthodox Church itself, controversy developed as to whether to support the state church of Romania that was aligned with the oppressive regime of Nicolae Ceausescu.

In the past, Romanian Americans have supported an active Romanian-language press. Up to thirty-seven weeklies and monthlies were regularly published at one time. They tended to be political, working-class, anticlerical, and pro-American in their orientation. In the 1990's there were no Romanian-language periodicals, but there were several Romanian publications in English, ranging from the literary quarterly, *Drum* to the more political *Dreptatea*.

Nicolae Ceausescu dictated harsh conditions for life in Romania until his overthrow and execution in 1989. (AP/Wide World Photos)

Assimilation and Cultural Contributions. Romanians rapidly lost their distinctiveness as a community and were assimilated into American life. Reasons included their relatively small numbers, their diverse regional origins in the Balkans, their religious and political fragmentation, dispersed residence in the industrial cities, a lack of established church schools (they preferred the American public education system), and their enthusiastic support of American capitalism. Since the ethnic heritage revival of the 1970's and increased post-1965 immigration, Romanians, like many other American ethnic groups, have placed a strong emphasis on their ethnic heritage. They have created an ethnic heritage center in Grass Lake, Michigan, and some organizations, such as the Maniu Foundation of New York, provide scholarships and sponsor folk festivals. About nineteen American universities offered Romanian language classes or area studies in the 1990's. The best organized archival source is the Immigration History Research Center at the University of Minnesota. Sadly, much of the story of Romanian Americans remains unresearched and undocumented.

Suggested Readings. For an autobiographical account of a Romanian's experiences in America, see M. E. Ravage's *An American in the Making* (1971). Christine Avghi Galitzi's *A Study of Assimilation Among the Roumanians in the United States* (1929) is the classic sociological study on which most scholars build. Recent articles include Gerald Bobango's "Romanians," in *Harvard Encyclopedia of American Ethnic Groups* (1980), edited by Stephan Thernstrom, and Louis M. deGyrse and Anne R. Kaplan's "The Romanians," in *They Chose Minnesota* (1981), edited by June Drenning Holmquist. Gerald J. Bobango's *The Romanian Orthodox Episcopate in America: the First Half Century, 1929-1979* (1979) includes two introductory chapters on the Romanian American community between 1895 and 1920.—*Arthur W. Helweg*

Ronstadt, Linda Marie (b. July 15, 1946, Tucson, Ariz.): Latina popular singer. Ronstadt began recording professionally in 1967 with her group the Stone Poneys, going solo in 1969. Her more than twenty albums include *Heart Like a Wheel* (1974), *Living in the U.S.A.* (1978), *Canciones de Mi Padre* (1987), and *Mas Canciones* (1991). Successfully mixing various musical styles and honoring her Mexican American heritage through her music, Ronstadt had garnered an array of honors including Grammy Awards for Best Female Pop Vocalist (1976, 1977), Best Country Performance (1987), Best Mexican American Performer (1988), and Best Duo (1989, 1990). In addition she starred in *The Pirates of Penzance* and *La Bohème* on New York stages.

Roosevelt, [Anna] Eleanor (Oct. 11, 1884, New York, N.Y.—Nov. 7, 1962, New York, N.Y.): Social reformer and activist First Lady. At seventeen she did volunteer work in various settlement schools. In 1905 she married her cousin Franklin Roosevelt, with whom she had six children. She spent a lifetime as an energetic and outspoken crusader for labor unions, women's rights, desegregation, world peace, and other liberal causes—concerns which she continued to pursue after her husband was elected president in 1932. She was both admired by those she tried to help and reviled by politicians who resented her influence on the Roosevelt Administration. In 1945 President Harry Truman appointed Roosevelt a delegate to the United Nations, where in 1948 she helped draft the Universal Declaration of Human Rights.

Rosh Hashanah: Jewish New Year, which usually falls in September (depending on the Jewish lunar calendar). Orthodox, Conservative, and Reconstructionist Jews observe Rosh Hashanah (Hebrew for "head of the year") for two days, and Reform Jews for one day. It begins the High Holy Days (High Holidays), a solemn ten-day period of prayer, introspection, and penitence. This day, also called the Day of the Sounding of the Shofar, summons Jews to pray for God's forgiveness and thus begin the New Year with a clear conscience.

The blowing of the shofar (ram's horn) heralds the start of the Jewish New Year on Rosh Hashanah. (Frances M. Roberts)

The blowing of the shofar (ram's horn), as ordained in Leviticus 23, is a hallmark of the holiday. According to twelfth century scholar Moses Maimonides, the shofar rouses Jews from their lethargy and inspires them to reflect on wrongdoing, to search their souls for life's true spiritual purpose, and to repent. Maimonides admonished Jews to remember their Creator and not go astray in pursuit of vanity and trifles. Worshipers' prayers thank God for sustaining them in the past year and beseech God for communal redemption. The shofar accentuates the connection to the Torah passage read during the Rosh Hashanah morning service (Genesis 22), in which God calls upon Abraham to offer his beloved son, Isaac, as a burnt offering; when Abraham proves his devotion to God in being willing to sacrifice Isaac, an angel of the Lord instructs Abraham to offer a ram instead. This story of the Jewish patriarch not only explains God's blessing him and his descendants but also epitomizes Rosh Hashanah's emphasis on God's power and mercy.

The shofar's shrill blasts mark the beginning of the ten Days of Awe, in which God sits in judgment on humanity and inscribes each person's fate in either the Book of Life or the Book of Death. Sincere repentance affects these decisions before God seals the books on Yom Kippur, the Day of Atonement.

Rosh Hashanah has rich traditions of symbolic greetings, clothing, foods, and rituals. Friends and relatives are sent cards with the Hebrew greeting *L'shanah tovah tikatevu* ("May you be inscribed for a good year"), as well as best wishes for good health, happiness, peace, and prosperity. In the synagogue, rabbis wear white robes, signifying purity. In the home, special round bread loaves (challot) symbolize a year of uninterrupted health and happiness, and apple slices dipped in honey represent a sweet year. New fruits of the season are eaten, and bitter or sour foods are avoided. Some observant Jews perform the ritual of *Tashlikh* (casting off) by going to a river or seashore, reciting Scripture about repentance, and throwing bread crumbs into the water to symbolize casting off sins.

SUGGESTED READINGS. For more information on this holiday (variously spelled Rosh Hashana, Rosh Ha-Shanah, and Rosh Hashonoh), see Harold M. Schulweis' *In God's Mirror: Reflections and Essays* (1990), meditations on the High Holy Days; *Thoughts for Rosh Hashonoh* (1980), by Bahy a ben Asher ben Hlava, translated by C. B. Chavel; and Philip Goodman's *Rosh Hashanah Anthology* (1970).

Ross, John [Coowescoowe] (Oct. 3, 1790, Turkey Town, Ala.—Aug. 1, 1866, Washington, D.C.): Cherokee Indian chief who resisted removal of his people from their ancestral Tennessee lands. A CHEROKEE minority ceded the area to Georgia in 1835, and in 1838-1839, Ross led his people on the displacement of the Cherokees to Oklahoma Territory known as the TRAIL OF TEARS. In Oklahoma Territory, Ross became chief of the United Cherokee Nation.

Cherokee chief John Ross led his people from Tennessee to Oklahoma along the Trail of Tears. (Smithsonian Institution)

Roybal, Edward R. (b. Feb. 10, 1916, Albuquerque, N.Mex.): Latino politician. Roybal worked for the Civilian Conservation Corps in 1934-1935 and as social worker and director of the California and Los Angeles Tuberculosis associations from 1935 to 1949. In 1949, he became the first Latino elected to the Los Angeles City Council in eighty-one years; in 1962 he moved on to the U.S. House of Representatives. As a member of Congress, Roybal has served on the Appropriations Committee and the Committee on Aging, and he has taken deep interest in health issues. A founder of both the Congressional Hispanic Caucus and the NATIONAL ASSOCIATION OF LATINO ELECTED AND APPOINTED OFFICIALS, he has helped other Latinos win public office.

Rudolph, Wilma (b. June 23, 1940, St. Bethlehem, Tenn.): African American track and field star. The only American woman runner ever to win three Olympic gold medals, Rudolph became known as "the world's fastest woman." Despite having had a physical disability as a child, she broke Tennessee state records in basketball and track while in high school. In the Olympics, Rudolph won golds for the one hundred and two hundred meter dashes and the four hundred meter relay. In 1960 Rudolph was named U.S. Female Athlete of the Year by the Associated Press, and Athlete of the Year by United Press. She has been an assistant director of athletics in Chicago for the Mayor's Youth Foundation.

Olympic gold medalist Wilma Rudolph was once known as "the world's fastest woman." (AP/Wide World Photos)

Rural life and culture: Social scientists define rural communities as places having twenty-five hundred inhabitants or less, which may be incorporated villages, towns, or settlements. Residents of the rural United States come from a variety of racial or ethnic backgrounds, including diverse European Americans, African Americans, Latinos, and American Indians, as well as smaller groups of Asian Americans. For example, the AMISH people maintain strong, separatist farming communities in states such as Iowa, Illinois, Indiana, Ohio, and Pennsylvania. One of the heaviest concentrations of nonfarming rural whites is found in the Appalachian Mountain area, where most of them are involved in the coal mining industry. Rural blacks still live in large numbers in the South and parts of the Southwest, such as Texas, where they were forced by the domestic slave trade to migrate westward to provide agricultural labor. MEXICAN AMERICANS have settled in rural parts of Texas, New Mexico, Arizona, and California. AMERICAN INDIANS who live on reservations or in adjacent rural areas are mostly found in states such as Oklahoma, the Dakotas, New Mexico, and Arizona. Since the 1980's, many Southeast Asians, such as HMONG AMERICANS, have settled in Texas and California to work for commercial farmers.

Historically, American immigrant groups such as the Mennonites in Kansas, the Germans in Illinois, or the Dutch in Ohio and Pennsylvania often settled together in the same rural area, reproducing their traditional lifestyles. Many of these communities remain today, celebrating their ethnic heritage in festivals and fairs and, in some cases, translating heritage into a profitable tourist industry, as with the Swedish communities found in parts of Ohio, Pennsylvania, or Kansas. Some Russian MENNONITE farmers have contributed significantly to the advancement of American agricultural productivity. For example, they introduced the Russian red winter wheat, a crop far more suited to agricultural conditions on the Great Plains than either spring wheat or corn. Rural social activities include church picnics, barn dances, auctions, and county fairs where people compete for prizes in agricultural activities such as tractor pulls, vegetable and livestock production, or log chain-sawing. American Indians from a wide area come together for POWWOWS or religious festivals that sometimes go on for days, depending upon the nature and purpose of the occasion being celebrated. All of these activities help to enrich the American cultural diversity.

Studying Rural Life. The scientific study of rural life and culture as a specialized area of sociology is a development of the twentieth century. This study involves ecological, cultural, and behavioral activities with a focus on the interrelationships of social systems within the rural society. To a great extent, knowledge concerning rural Americans is governed by definitions of residence groups adapted by the Bureau of the CENSUS. Social scientists agree that it is difficult to come up with a uniform definition of the term "rural." This is so because, in many cases, characteristics of rural

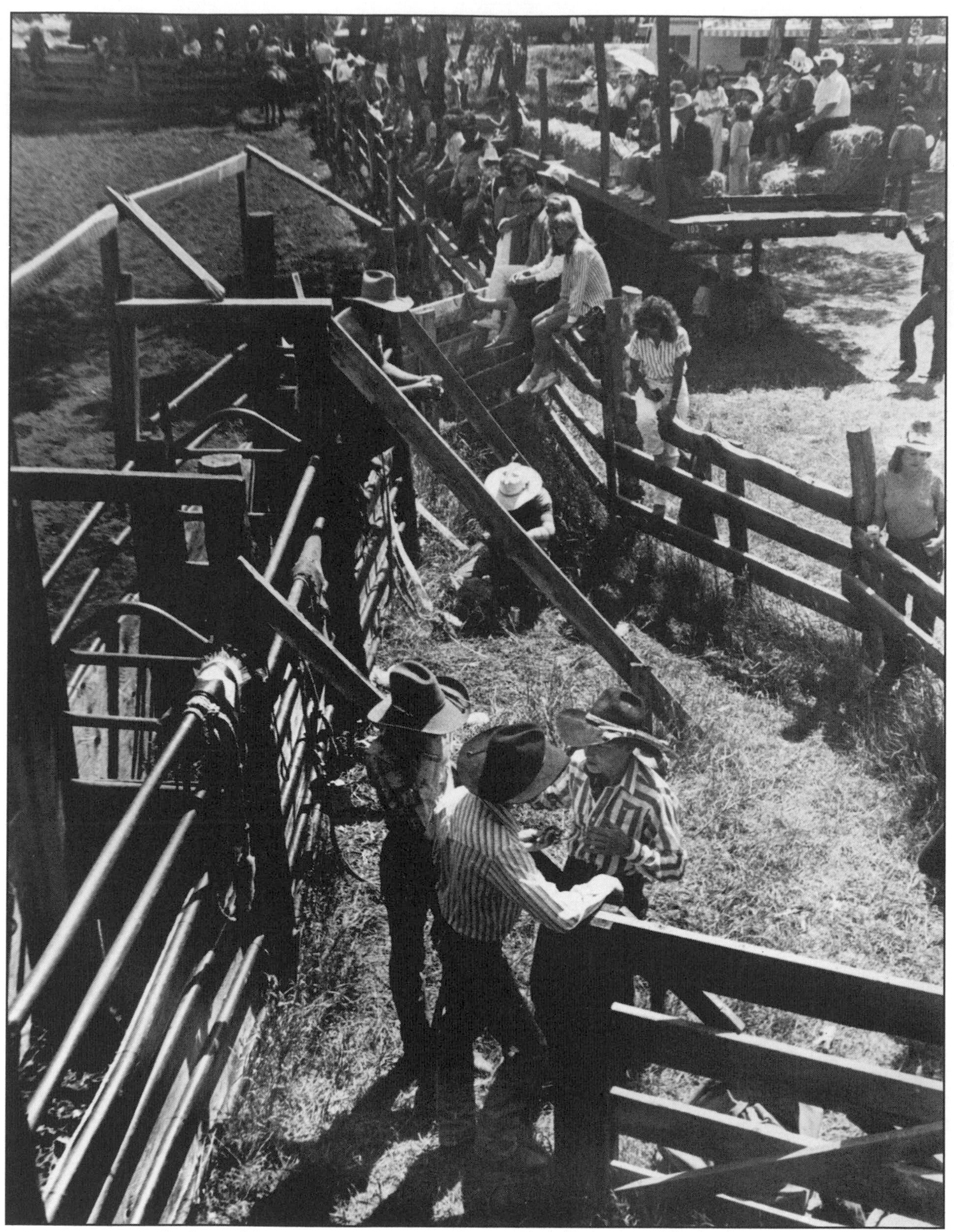

Anglos and Latinos participate in a rodeo in Costilla, N. Mex. (Elaine S. Querry)

society may also be found in urban communities. An example of this is close personal primary-group relations, which can be found in both urban and rural communities. Rural-urban differences have also been further reduced by linkages such as the interchange of people through large-scale migration, the powerful influence of urban-centered mass media, and increasing interdependence of rural and urban economies. Even though there is a general agreement that the term "rural" refers to populations that live in low-density areas, there is a difference of opinion in the cutoff point used to distinguish between rural and urban cultures. Sociologists have also found that occupational criteria cannot be used to define the rural population; in some cases, farmers are a minority within their local rural communities. One accepted pattern is to use population, size, and density of a given settlement in an attempt to define the term rural.

The Role of Rural Communities. Rural communities play several important functions in American society. Traditionally, they have been responsible for food and other raw material production. Even at the end of the twentieth century, the survival of people in urban areas depends on this function. Rural society has also served as a supplier of city people's manufactured material goods. A third important function of rural society is serving as a custodian of natural resources such as forests, minerals, oil, land, and water. Some rural communities serve as "bedroom" residential areas for people who work in urban areas. Finally, rural communities have acted as a "security zone" in times of crisis, drawing urbanites who seek to escape from the problems of big-city life.

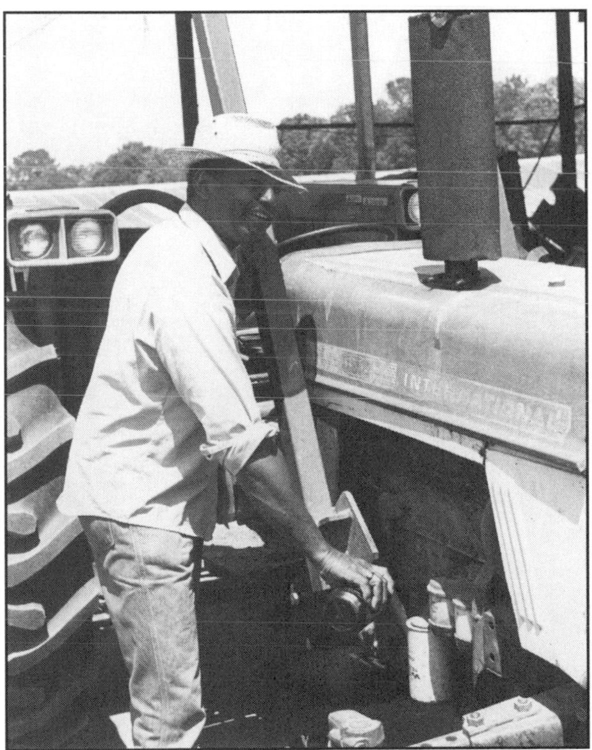

Mississippi farmer works on his tractor. New technologies, the growth of agribusiness conglomerates, and economic changes have all threatened the survival of the family farm. (Dale D. Gehman)

Social Interaction. Rural social interaction and organization are determined by the unique characteristics of rural life, such as population density and community size. Patterns of social interaction involve relatively few contacts per individual at any given time, but the connections people forge are close ones. Second, in rural cultures, there is a limited division of labor, since there is a limited range of occupations and social roles. This means that there is relatively little heterogeneity at the community level, as compared to urban societies. Third, in rural cultures, social roles tend to be more personal and less segmented, but more diffused. Social class identification in rural communities tends to be based on the individual's attributes rather than on general and achieved attributes, mainly because of the limited variety of occupational and social roles. Thus social mobility is more restricted in rural cultures than in urban ones. Finally, because rural people are better known to their neighbors, they are less likely to exhibit deviant behavior.

Changes in Rural Life. Many programs have been developed to equalize social conditions in rural areas. Examples range from government income support programs for farmers and the electrical improvements of the Tennessee Valley Authority to better rural mail delivery, library systems, medical care, and educational facilities. As urban expansion puts pressure on rural areas at the edge of cities, rural and urban centered systems are increasingly interacting, either cooperatively or in conflict as they try to maintain system boundaries.

In the area of AGRICULTURE, new technologies and economic forces have led to increased specialization of agricultural activities. This can be seen in the increased dependency of farmers on purchased inputs in farm production, the development of new types of farm credit systems, the ever-growing numbers of farmers' markets and cooperatives, and major changes in the marketing system for farm products. With the use of more efficient farm equipment, the need for many farm workers has declined; increased farm worker productivity has resulted in fewer but larger farms. This reduction has led to a decrease in population density in all areas where farm population losses were not offset by growth of the rural nonfarm population, and to the virtual disappearance of the traditional family farm.

One consequence of these changes has been in migration patterns. For example, net rural to urban migration is rather selective as to who leaves and who remains. Migration from rural to urban communities is generally done by young adults. Sociological studies have also revealed that relatively more females than males migrate from rural to urban areas. At the same time, because of technology, people who continue to live in rural areas have become less isolated, benefiting from developments in media communication that greatly enlarge their fund of knowledge and contact with a broader worldview.

Rural Poverty. It is generally agreed that the redundant supply of labor in agriculture is largely responsible for low incomes and underdevelopment in the rural United States. For millions of rural people, the adaptation to changes in rural life has been strained by POVERTY and its unfortunate attributes. The availability of educational and medical services in rural areas compares unfavorably with those in urban areas, as does the choice of social and cultural activities. Housing conditions are frequently substandard.

Migrating in search of EMPLOYMENT usually intensifies unemployment, underemployment, and financial problems for workers and their families. Every year, workers fan out from Texas and Florida through the central and western states and along the Atlantic Coast in search of seasonal employment. Other groups flow from Arizona and New Mexico to California, Washington, and Oregon. The workers are rarely covered by health insurance or workers' compensation, and their annual wages are usually far below the poverty

Migrant farm workers such as these women detasseling corn in Illinois are among the poorest Americans. (Joel Dexter, Unicorn Stock Photos)

line. With this kind of migratory life, it is very difficult, if not impossible, for MIGRANT WORKERS' children to get a sound formal education.

Some of the rural people who are most hard-hit by poverty are AMERICAN INDIANS. They live on or near RESERVATIONS that are usually located in sparsely populated areas with few natural resources and job opportunities. To be eligible for basic BUREAU OF INDIAN AFFAIRS services, such as health care, an individual must live on or near a reservation or trust land that comes under the jurisdiction of the bureau and must be a member of a tribe, band, or group of Indians recognized by the federal government.

The causes of Indian rural poverty are complex, rooted in a history of exploitation by the federal government, the reservation system, and the social welfare system that may encourage dependence. Some traditional Indian cultural values favor the community over the individual, discouraging competitiveness and materialism and otherwise distinguishing some Indians from members of the dominant culture's work force. Moreover, many rural Indians are impeded by social problems such as poor education, diabetes, or ALCOHOLISM in their efforts to improve their standard of living. Signs of hope are tribal colleges established since the 1970's and increasing business initiatives by tribal councils and individuals.

Another group of rural Americans at risk for poverty are those people who live in the Appalachian region of the Southeast. Many of their ancestors came from Scotland, Ireland, and central or eastern Europe to settle in coal mining and steel mill communities. The region lacks the environment and facilities to attract and support significant economic growth. With less demand for commodities such as coal, Appalachians have found themselves without meaningful jobs. Like their American Indian counterparts, the average rural Appalachian person's annual income and level of education lag far behind those of average urban Americans. They also suffer from inadequate educational and medical services.

In spite of rural poverty that affects certain regions and populations, rural life in the United States is far more advanced than rural life in other countries. The average standard of living, as well as the level of health care services, transportation systems, media technology, and literacy are second to none, according to various studies.

SUGGESTED READINGS. For a general discussion of rural life see the *International Encyclopedia of the Social Sciences* (1968), edited by David L. Sills. *The Development of Rural America* (1974), edited by George Brinkman, gives a good historical account. A discussion of changes in rural life can be found in Lorraine Garkovich's *Population and Community in Rural America* (1989). For data on the rural American population, see Priscilla Salants' *A Community Researcher's Guide to Rural Data* (1990).—*K. Paul Kasambira*

Russian Americans: Russian Americans are an East Slavic people who are, after the Polish Americans, the second-largest Slavic national group in the United States. Even after the breakup of the Soviet Union in 1991, its core, Russia, remained the world's largest country in area and fifth largest in population (145 million in 1989). Determining precisely what proportion of the U.S. population is of Russian ancestry is a difficult task because the Russian empire and its successor state, the Soviet Union, were multicultural entities consisting of more than one hundred ethnic groups. Coming to the United States from this empire were mixed-ethnic immigrants as well as Russians, Germans, Jews, Ukrainians, Belorussians, Lithuanians, and dozens of other nationalities such as Georgians and Circassians. U.S. immigration officials routinely assigned the term "Russian" to any person originating in that country. By 1980 the U.S. Bureau of the CENSUS estimated that there were 1,378,446 Russian Americans in the single ancestry group. There were approximately half a million foreign-born Russians in the U.S. population.

History. Except for the U.S.-Soviet alliance during World War II, Americans and Russians for much of the twentieth century have been bitter adversaries. Locked in ideological, economic, and military competition, the United States and Soviet Union until the mid-1980's engaged in a long and burdensome COLD WAR.

Thus, it is difficult to recall that these two great powers once shared in the settlement of the North American continent. The Russian presence in North America began with Vitus Bering's voyages on behalf of the Russian monarchy in the 1720's. From Siberia, the Danish explorer crossed west through the strait now bearing his name and reached present-day Alaska. The first permanent Russian settlement was founded in 1784, and by the early 1800's the Russian American Company had established a network of colonies from Kodiak Island to Fort Ross, north of San Francisco. Far from the Russian capital of St. Petersburg, these

RUSSIAN FEDERATION

settlements were small and sparsely populated. In 1841, the Russians sold their interests in Fort Ross to John Sutter for $30,000.

Several hundred Russians remained behind in North America after the United States bought Alaska from Russia for the sum of seven million dollars in 1867. Thus, in contrast to most European patterns of settlement and immigration, the first modest Russian presence started in Alaska and worked its way down the West Coast. In places such as Sitka, Alaska, vestiges of those earliest settlements are preserved in a few Russian Orthodox churches attended by descendants of those pioneers.

Immigration. Between 1820 and 1990, more than 3.5 million immigrants from Russia and the Soviet Union came to the United States. The earliest of these immigrants fled economic hardship in the empire. In the 1880's and 1890's, hundreds of thousands of former serfs (peasants tied to the land and owned by the landed gentry until their emancipation in the 1860's) emigrated to the rapidly industrializing United States. They took up unskilled positions in the expanding mining and manufacturing industries, especially in the Northeast. As with overall U.S. immigration, the peak decade for eastern European and Russian immigration was 1901-1910, when 70 percent of the record 8.8 million arrivals originated in southern and eastern Europe. This swelling tide included Jews, Germans, and Poles as well as ethnic Russians.

A consistent feature of both Russian and Soviet emigration has been the Jewish component. Under both systems, JEWS were subjected to persecution, originally in the form of periodic pogroms (organized massacres) or deportation to Siberia, later in the form of DISCRIMINATION and suppression of religious life. In the post-World War II period, U.S. legislation made improvements in U.S.-Soviet relations contingent upon the lifting of restrictions on Soviet Jews' emigration to Israel and the United States. As a result of these policies and internal Soviet emigration reforms, by 1992 thousands of RUSSIAN JEWS had emigrated to the United States either directly or via transit countries.

Another component of the early mass migration in

the twentieth century was the exodus of religious sectarians such as the Molokans and Old Believers, who settled primarily in Los Angeles, San Francisco, and Oregon. The Bolshevik Revolution in 1917 and ensuing civil war in Russia (1918-1921) sent a distinctive wave of immigrants to the United States. In contrast to earlier arrivals, many among the thirty thousand immigrants were nobles, intellectuals, professionals, and clergymen.

After World War II, Russians were one of the many nationalities in the group of REFUGEES admitted to the United States under the provisions of the DISPLACED PERSONS ACT. In the 1980's, both Jews and Armenians were prominent among immigrants from the Soviet Union, admitted to the United States under special quotas.

Geographic Distribution. Like millions of other immigrants from Europe, Russians originally established communities in their ports of entry, primarily New York, Boston, and Philadelphia, or in nearby cities such as Jersey City and Newark, New Jersey. These communities centered around the traditional institutions of the Russian Orthodox church and Russian Catholic church and associated supporting fraternal and social organizations. Later, Pittsburgh, Chicago, and Los Angeles became centers of Russian American communities.

Owing to mutual hostility and fear between the Soviet Union and the United States, which reached its height in the MCCARTHYISM of the 1950's, being Russian in the United States was often a dubious distinction. As a result, in contrast with other Slavic nationalities, many Russian immigrants sought ethnic anonymity, and many of the communities lost their identity. Russian Americans moved to the suburbs and were assimilated into American society. One rather conspicuous exception to this process was Brighton Beach, near Coney Island in Brooklyn, where a vibrant Russian Jewish community developed in the 1960's and 1970's.

Bolsheviks seize power in 1917 during the October Revolution in Russia. As a result, thirty thousand Russians emigrated to the United States. (Library of Congress)

Cultural Contributions. Russian Americans and Russians of mixed ethnic origin have enriched not only the branches of American art, science, and culture, but the roots as well. Ballet and music have clearly benefited the most from an extraordinary infusion of spectacular artistry, both through traditional immigration and the sudden defection of artists while on tour. Some of the twentieth century's most brilliant ballet dancers, Rudolf Nureyev (1938-1993), Natalia Makarova (b. 1940), and Mikhail Baryshnikov (b. 1948) for example, sought asylum and new opportunities to excel with the New York City Ballet and the American Ballet Theatre.

multicultural environment from which they came, many of these artists were also Jewish, Ukrainian, Belorussian, or Georgian.

Russians have been among America's best music directors and conductors. Foremost among them was Serge Koussevitzky (1874-1951), director of the Boston Symphony Orchestra from 1924 to 1949. The maestro enthusiastically promoted the revolutionary works of the illustrious Russian American composer Igor Stravinsky (1882-1971) and the early works of American composers Aaron Copland and Samuel Barber. Continuing in this tradition, Russian American Mstislav Rostropovich (b. 1927) was named music director of the National Symphony Orchestra in 1977 and transformed it into one of the country's finest orchestras. In 1992 the virtuoso cellist/conductor received the nation's highest tribute for performing artists, the Kennedy Center Award for a lifetime of artistic achievement. Since their inception in 1978, several of these coveted awards have been bestowed

Russian delicatessen in Brighton Beach, Brooklyn, a prominent enclave of Soviet Jews. (Frances M. Roberts)

The most significant contribution to the development of classical dance in the United States was the work of Russian choreographer George Balanchine (1904-1983). Directing the New York City Ballet from 1948 until his death in 1983, he transformed it into one of the world's premier troupes.

Many Russian virtuosos made the United States their home and performing base. Sergei Rachmaninoff (1873-1943) and Vladimir Horowitz (1904-1989) were two of the century's finest concert pianists, performing to sell-out crowds at Carnegie Hall and elsewhere. For cello and violin their celebrated equivalents were Gregor Piatigorsky (1903-1976) and Jascha Heifetz (1901-1987), both of whom later taught at the University of Southern California. Personifying the on Russian-born or Russian-descended Americans: Balanchine, Jerome Robbins (b. 1918), and Alexandra Danilova (b. 1907) for ballet and dance; Danny Kaye (1913-1987) for stage and screen performances; and Isaac Stern (b. 1920), Yehudi Menuhin (b. 1916), and Nathan Milstein (b. 1904) for violin.

The opening up of relations between the United States and the Soviet Union allowed this Russian singer to perform at the Festival of American Folklife in Washington, D.C., in 1988. (Smithsonian Institution)

In popular culture, Russian Americans have made major contributions to many of the most popular American television series, such as *Candid Camera* (Allen Funt, b. 1914), *All in the Family* (Norman Lear, b. 1922), and *Star Trek* (Leonard Nimoy, b. 1931). The compositions of prolific songwriter Irving Berlin (1888-1989) include "God Bless America" and "White Christmas."

In literature, the United States has been a traditional refuge for outstanding Russian writers and poets. At ease writing in Russian, French, or English, Vladimir Nabokov (1899-1977) created a stir with his novel *Lolita* (1959) and controversial lectures on Russian literature while on the faculty of Cornell University. In the 1970's two Nobel laureates, both forced into exile from the Soviet Union, continued writing critically acclaimed works in the United States. In *The Gulag Archipelago*, Alexandr Solzhenitsyn (b. 1918) chronicled the horrors of life in Soviet concentration camps, and Joseph Brodsky (b. 1940) became Poet Laureate of the United States in residence at the Library of Congress (1991-1992). The list of distinguished Russian American and Russian Jewish American literary figures includes science fiction master Isaac Asimov (1920-1992) and novelists Saul Bellow (b. 1915) and E. L. Doctorow (b. 1931).

Two Russian Americans have won the Nobel Prize in Economics: Wassily Leontief (b. 1906) and Simon Kuznets (1901-1985). Eugene Rostow (b. 1913) and Walt Rostow (b. 1916) were presidential advisers and prominent academics. One of the twentieth century's preeminent linguists was Roman Yakobsen (1896-1982).

Measured in terms of EDUCATION, occupation, and income, Americans of Russian and Russian Jewish stock have been one of the highest achieving ethnic groups in the United States. Some have pioneered new directions in their fields, including William Paley (1901-1990) at Columbia Broadcasting System (CBS), Armand Hammer (1898-1990) at Occidental Petroleum, and Arnold "Red" Auerbach (b. 1917) with the Boston Celtics. Following in the tradition of Russian American Civil War general John Turchin, Admiral Hyman Rickover (1900-1986) became known as the father of the U.S. nuclear navy. These figures join the ranks of earlier famous Russian Americans such as Prince Matchabelli (perfumes) and businessman-railroad builder Peter Demyanoff-Demens, who co-founded and christened the city of St. Petersburg, Florida. A Russian American, Vladimir Zworykin (1889-1982), invented the iconoscope and cathode ray tube, innovations that promoted developments in two key twentieth century technologies, television and the computer.

With the easing of travel and emigration restrictions in the late twentieth century, Russians by the thousands formed a new wave of immigrants to Israel and the United States. In fact, in the late 1980's and early 1990's, concern was voiced in the former Soviet Union over the "brain drain" or emigration of unemployed or underemployed top scientists and specialists to Israel, Europe, and the United States. As in the past,

The collapse of the Soviet Union in the early 1990's, symbolized by these toppled statues of former heroes, was followed with great interest by Russian Americans. (AP/Wide World Photos)

the United States appeared to be playing its traditional role as a land of opportunity for Russians and Russian Jews liberated by the collapse of the Soviet totalitarian state.

SUGGESTED READINGS. Two basic general texts on the topic are Nancy Eubank's *The Russians in America* (1986) and *The Russians in America: A Chronology and Factbook* (1977), edited by Vladimir Wertsman. Paul Magosci's "Russians" in *The Harvard Encyclopedia of American Ethnic Groups* (1980), edited by Stephan Thernstrom, provides an excellent overview, and an annotated bibliography-essay "Americans from Greater Russia" is found in *A Comprehensive Bibliography for the Study of American Minorities* (1976).—*David McClave*

Russian Jews: In the half century after the Civil War, no fewer than thirty-five million immigrants settled in the United States; the period constituted the largest wave of immigration in American history. More than two million of the immigrants were Russian Jews. In addition to political oppression and pogroms under the czarist regime in Russia, the dominant cause of their mass immigration was POVERTY and overpopulation. Nearly all middle-class Russian Jews managed to survive in different regions of their homeland while the poor as well as the lower middle class of artisans, peddlers, and tailors left the country.

The majority of Russians were YIDDISH-speaking immigrants. Thus, they differed from the central European and German Jews who settled in the United States during the pre-1880 period and from the SEPHARDIC JEWS who constituted the majority of American Jews until the early part of the eighteenth century. They were also different from other immigrant groups of the post-1880 period. Virtually all immigrants, irrespective of ethnic or religious origin, regretted the loss of the national and family ties that had kept them together in Europe. The Irish and the Italians, for instance, were devoted to maintaining their ethnic identity more than most other groups. Yet both groups understood that the old values, if transplanted, would obstruct their desire to reach the highest socioeconomic levels of American life. They were determined to assimilate. The Russian Jews, on the other hand, held on intensely to their cultural separateness.

Although the Russian immigrants prior to the 1920's were not oblivious to the necessity of conforming to American values, they continued to believe that Jewish values and heritage had to be maintained. Clinging to their Jewishness was the result of a siege mentality, of centuries of being an embattled minority in a hostile environment under czardom, where the only avenue for survival was the use of one's wits. Thus, even in a far less hostile land, Russian Jews were determined to excel by relying only on their "Jewish head" and virtues.

An interesting contrast emerged between Sephardic and central European/German Jews on the one hand, and the Russian/east European Jews, on the other. The older groups had developed within American society when there was an open and expanding frontier. It was easy for them to view themselves as different from the rest of society only in religious matters. The Russians came to urban America after 1880, when society needed laborers for its factories, and they competed with millions of other immigrants for jobs. Though the ASSIMILATION of Russian Jews would take longer, their children and grandchildren would constitute the majority of an American Jewish population that by the 1990's was heavily intermarried with and almost indistinguishable from the dominant culture.

SUGGESTED READINGS. For the most thorough accounts on Russian Jewry in the United States see: Arthur Hertzberg's *The Jews in America: Four Centuries of an Uneasy Encounter* (1989); Nathan Glazer's *American Judaism* (1972); John Higham's *Send These to Me: Jews and Other Immigrants in Urban America* (1975); and "Jews in the United States," in volume 15 of *Encyclopedia Judaica* (1972), edited by Cecil Roth.

S

Sabin, Florence Rena (Nov. 9, 1871, Central City, Colo.—Oct. 3, 1953, Denver, Colo.): Medical researcher. Sabin was the first woman to study and teach at The Johns Hopkins University. In 1901, as a student, she constructed a three-dimensional model of the brain, "An Atlas of the Medulla and Mid-brain," which was later adopted for textbooks. From 1925 to 1938 she established and ran the Department of Cellular Studies at the Rockefeller Institute for Medical Research in New York, where she studied blood cells in relation to tuberculosis. In 1938 she returned to Colorado, where she pushed the passage of a series of health improvement bills.

Florence Sabin was the first woman to study and teach at The Johns Hopkins University. (AP/Wide World Photos)

Sacagawea (c. 1788—Dec. 20, 1812, Fort Manuel, Dakota Territory): Shoshone Indian who was the sole woman and guide on the Lewis and Clark expedition. Sometimes called Bird Woman, she had been taken captive from her people and traded to Toussaint Charbonneau, interpreter for the expedition. In the upper Missouri River region, her knowledge as a guide and interpreter was indispensable. On the return journey, she and Charbonneau remained with the Mandan Indians.

Sacco and Vanzetti: Italian immigrants accused of being part of a gang of bandits who murdered two guards during a payroll robbery in South Braintree, Massachusetts, on April 15, 1920. Nicola Sacco (1891-1927) and Bartolomeo Vanzetti (1888-1927) were anarchists devoted to the overthrow of the United States government as well as all other forms of political control. Such a viewpoint is always unpopular, but it was considered especially dangerous during the RED SCARE which followed World War I and the Russian Revolution. At that time, civil liberties were often ignored in the United States, and many foreign-born citizens were deported because of hysteria over Bolshevism and other political ideologies which challenged American democracy. Many Americans assumed that all anarchists were violent and likely to commit robbery to finance their activities. Thus public opinion was firmly against Sacco and Vanzetti before their trial began.

Although eyewitnesses were not conclusive in placing the two Italians at the crime scene, Sacco and Vanzetti had lied when first questioned upon their arrest, thus suggesting their guilt. Both men were carrying guns when apprehended, and the prosecution produced ballistic evidence that showed that a bullet taken from the body of one of the slain guards had come from Sacco's pistol. The evidence against Vanzetti was more flimsy. Both men were convicted in July, 1921, and sentenced to die.

Many thought that the pair was really convicted for having the wrong political beliefs, and a worldwide effort involving people from many nations and cultures was organized in their defense. Communists and other radicals were particularly vigorous in aiding Sacco and Vanzetti, an element that may have had a negative impact. Some theorized that a gang of immigrant thieves from Providence, Rhode Island, had actually committed the crime, and a man already jailed confessed to being part of this group and participating in the robbery and murders, but none of these developments had any effect. Despite numerous legal appeals and demonstrations on their behalf around the

Public opinion against Sacco and Vanzetti (center, hatless) led authorities to place them under heavy guard during the course of their trial. (Culver Pictures, Inc.)

world, Sacco and Vanzetti were electrocuted in August, 1927.

Suggested Readings. The Sacco and Vanzetti case has generated many studies that continue the debate regarding the men's culpability. While the men were still alive, Harvard law professor and later Supreme Court Justice Felix Frankfurter wrote *The Case of Sacco and Vanzetti* (1927), which disputed the procedures of the prosecution and judge. Upton Sinclair's novel about the case, *Boston* (1928), appeared only a year after the two were executed. Osmond K. Fraenkel's *The Sacco-Vanzetti Case* (1931; reissued with new material, 1969) exhaustively reviews the evidence and history of the case. Robert H. Montgomery, in *Sacco-Vanzetti: The Murder and the Myth* (1960) supports the contention that both men were guilty. William Young and David E. Kaiser reexamine the ballistic evidence in *Postmortem: New Evidence in the Case of Sacco and Vanzetti* (1985) and conclude not only that both men were innocent but also that the state faked evidence. Katherine Anne Porter in *The Never-Ending Wrong* (1977) gives the perspective of one of those who tried to save the men.

St. Augustine, Fla. (founded 1565): Oldest continuously occupied city in North America settled by Europeans. Founded in 1565 by the Spanish explorer Pedro Menendez de Avilés, St. Augustine was the capital of the territory called "La Florida." This initially was bounded in the west by the present-day state of Mississippi and in the north by the state of Virginia. Spanish activities in other parts of Florida were initiated, organized, and administered from their base in St. Augustine. Like modern Miami, the settlement also served as a conduit for Spanish Florida's connections to the larger Latin American and European world.

St. Augustine was the only European town in the region until Charleston, South Carolina, was established in 1670. The older town was also the largest in the South other than Charleston until 1763.

St. Augustine attracted invaders from its earliest decades. The Englishman Sir Francis Drake looted and burned it in 1586, as did the English pirate John Davis in 1668. In 1702 the town was taken and burned by a group of Carolinians. General James Oglethorpe, the British governor of Georgia, led an unsuccessful joint expedition of Georgians and Carolinians against St. Augustine in 1740. The Spanish built Fort Mantanzas in 1742 to counter further British intrusions—not a moment too soon, since the following year, Oglethorpe again attempted to take St. Augustine and again was defeated. Twenty years later the town came under British control by treaty, and St. Augustine thrived as an export center. In 1783, the town reverted back to the Spanish, who controlled it until Florida was ceded to the United States in 1821.

This 1673 engraving captures St. Augustine's thriving commercial activity as a Spanish-controlled port city. (Culver Pictures, Inc.)

During the SEMINOLE WARS in 1835, Major General Francis L. Dade and a force of 139 were ambushed at St. Augustine by the Seminoles. He and 135 of his troops were killed in the battle. Confederate troops controlled St. Augustine during the Civil War from January, 1861, to March, 1862, when the Union Army occupied the town. The wealthy Henry Flagler developed St. Augustine into a thriving resort in the 1880's, and it remains a popular vacation destination.

In spite of its importance in the history of the southeast, St. Augustine has always been a small town on the margins of the centers of wealth and power. It has a population of 25,000 and an economy based on tourism sparked by interest in the city's history.

SUGGESTED READINGS. For a further look into the establishment of St. Augustine, see Edward Chaney and Kathleen Deagan's "St. Augustine and the La Florida Colony: New Life-Styles in a New Land," in *First Encounters: Spanish Explorations in the Caribbean and the United States, 1492-1570* (1989). Early St. Augustine is also described in Verner Crane's *The Southern Frontier* (1928); Irene Wright's "The Odyssey of the Spanish Archives of Florida," in *Hispanic American Essays* (1942), edited by A. Curtis Wilgus; and *The Oldest City* (1983), edited by Jean Parker Waterbury.

St. Patrick's Day (Mar. 17): Religious holiday celebrating the life of St. Patrick, the patron saint of Ireland, known for his conversion of the Irish people to Christianity. Celebration of the day in the United States began as early as the eighteenth century and coincided with the arrival of Irish immigrants. On this day it is customary for Irish Americans to wear shamrocks or green articles of clothing. In some cities of the United States, the holiday is celebrated with a parade. The annual Fifth Avenue Parade in New York City is one of the nation's largest. Saint Patrick's Day is also a national holiday in Ireland.

Salinas lettuce strike: In 1970, seventy lettuce growers in Salinas, California, signed five-year contracts with the International Brotherhood of Teamsters under which the Teamsters would represent farm workers. The organizing committee of the UNITED FARM WORKERS (UFW) objected that this "sweetheart deal" deprived the workers of being able to choose their own union. Led by César CHÁVEZ, the UFW went on strike. It also began a lettuce boycott on September 17, 1970, urging consumers not to buy lettuce. In March, 1977, the UFW and the Teamsters finally agreed on a five-year pact. Chávez ended the lettuce boycott in January, 1978. A year later, in January, 1979, UFW members began another strike and boycott, this time for higher wages. After Chávez led a march from San Francisco to Salinas, contracts were signed. The second strike and boycott ended in August, 1979.

Salsa music: Style of dance music which has its roots in Afro-Cuban popular and folkloric music enhanced by jazz phrasing. The term, which literally means sauce, as in the spicy Mexican condiment of the same name, was first used in the 1960's. Salsa is sometimes used in place of the term "Latin music"; indeed, it is popular with a broad spectrum of Latino Americans. According to Charley Gerard, "salsa is best distinguished from earlier styles in Latin music by defining it as a New York sound developed primarily by Puerto Rican New Yorkers, known as Nuyoricans."

Cuban musical influences have been present in the United States since the beginning of the twentieth century through a French-influenced dance known as the *danzon*. The African-inspired rhythms found in the rhumba, a drum form with many variants, took firm hold with musicians and consumers in the 1930's. Since the 1920's, Latin musicians had used the expression *echale salsita* ("give it some spice").

Salsa drew much of its form from the music of Arsenio Rodriguez, who lived in the United States from 1950 until his death in 1970. He played an important role in the development of the *conjunto*, a band based on the black carnival parade groups of the Americas. The ensembles consisted of voices, trumpets, conga drums, piano, and bass. Rodriguez also helped popularize the mambo, an Afro-Cuban form derived from Congolese religious cults. The music of Rodriguez, along with the Afro-Cuban big band sounds of Machito and Mario Bauza, and the mambo bands of Tito Puente, set the foundation for American salsa in the 1960's.

Salsa percussionist and band leader Tito Puente, shown here with singer Celia Cruz, receiving his star on the Hollywood Walk of Fame, in 1990. (AP/Wide World Photos)

By the late 1960's and early 1970's, young Nuyorican musicians were drawn to the Cuban music of Rodriguez and others. Gerard has written, "The feeling was that the Cuban way of playing was not only the correct way, but the only way." Nevertheless, musicians of various Latin countries have left their own distinct mark on the music. Largely through the efforts of Charlie Palmieri, the traditional salsa sound took on jazz phrasing as well as a strong horn section, and modern salsa was born.

The basic salsa ensemble consists of one or two lead singers, two to five brass instruments, piano, bass, a pair of conga drums, timbales, bongos, a cowbell, and various hand-held percussion instruments. Lead singers are supported by a *coro* (chorus) in the call and response pattern typical of much African-based music. Interestingly, in a style dominated by Nuyorican and Puerto Rican musicians, folkloric music from Puerto Rico has had little influence. Yet, salsa has drawn from other musical sources such as Brazilian and American rhythms. Some of the representative salsa and salsa-influenced artists include Rubén Blades, Willie Colon, Celia Cruz, Johnny Pacheco, and Eddie Palmieri.

Suggested Readings. For additional information, see *Salsa!: The Rhythm of Latin Music* (1989) by Charley Gerard with Marty Sheller, and John Storm Roberts' *The Latin Tinge* (1979).

Salt War (1866-1877): Conflict between Mexican Americans and Anglo Americans over public access to salt deposits located east of El Paso, Texas, on the U.S.-Mexican border. Mexicans on both sides of the border had free access to the salt until Samuel Maverick of San Antonio, Texas, acquired claim to much of the area. After an unsuccessful attempt by a group of Anglo Americans, dubbed the Salt Ring, to claim the rest of the deposit, it was acquired by Charles Howard in 1875. He promptly charged fees for taking salt. Rioting resulted, and Howard was held captive and later killed by a Mexican American. More violence erupted but was quelled by U.S. troops.

Salvadoran Americans: The Salvadoran population in the United States expanded drastically during the twelve-year civil war that began in El Salvador in 1980. Fewer than 20,000 Salvadoran immigrants arrived between 1967 and 1976. By 1990, however, the Salvadoran American community was estimated at one million.

The most densely populated of the Central American countries, El Salvador covers a mere 8,260 square miles. Unlike its northern neighbor, Guatemala, El

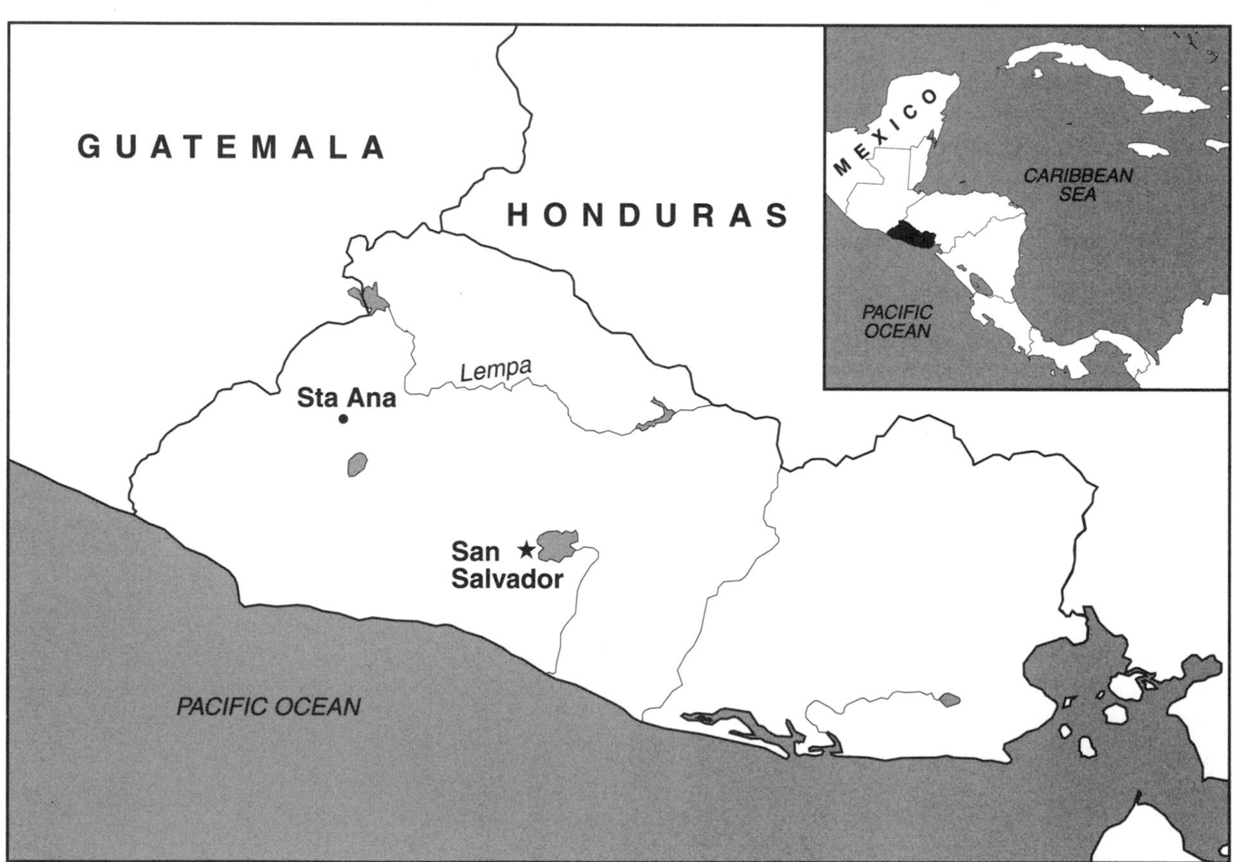

El Salvador

Salvador does not have a flourishing Indian culture, though it shares a similar history of settlement by Mayan peoples and conquest by stronger Aztec-related tribes. The assimilated people the Spanish conquistadores encountered were the Nahuatl-speaking Pipils who survived the conquest better, perhaps, than other peoples in the region but were reduced to modest numbers by the end of the nineteenth century. In 1932 resistance by Indians and peasants to the growing power and wealth of the oligarchy was crushed in the genocidal atrocity known as *la matanza*. Estimates of the dead range between ten and thirty thousand. Indians survived by dressing like mestizos (people of mixed European and Indian ancestry) and by abandoning the public use of their language. Indian culture in El Salvador remained relatively obscure until the end of the century.

Considered the wealthiest Central American country by the 1950's, El Salvador's coffee-based economy grew throughout the 1960's and 1970's. A thriving middle class and an ostentatious oligarchy presented an image of tropical glamour, though the disparity between rich and poor increased. A challenge to the U.S.-supported government by the Farabundo Martí National Liberation Front (FMLN) in 1980 resulted in a brutal civil war during which one quarter of the country's population was displaced. A devastating earthquake in 1986 compounded the problem of refugees seeking homes, stability, and an escape from the violence.

Although large concentrations of Salvadorans settled in Honduras and Mexico, the largest number sought refuge in the United States. Helped by the SANCTUARY MOVEMENT and organizations such as the CENTRAL AMERICAN REFUGEE CENTER (CARECEN), an estimated three to four thousand refugees applied for political asylum every year; chances for approval, however, were slim since the government being charged with repression was supported by the United States. Illegal immigration, therefore, caused the greatest swelling of the U.S. Salvadoran community. By 1990, 160,000 Salvadoran immigrants had applied for amnesty under a government program to legalize the status of many who had entered the country illegally. After the peace settlement that ended the civil war, a cautious attempt was made to restore stability to the country, and the number of refugees declined.

About half of all Salvadoran Americans live in Los Angeles, where their presence can be felt in the Pico-Union district's shops, restaurants, churches, parks, and schools. Salvadorans there have formed their own cultural and social organizations, and sponsor a large parade for their homeland's independence day in September. Other large Salvadoran communities can be found in Washington, D.C., and Houston, with considerable numbers also in Dallas, San Francisco, New York, and the Nassau-Suffolk area in New York state.

San Francisco, Calif. (founded Mar. 28, 1776): Cultural and commercial center in northern California located on a hilly peninsula situated on three bodies of water: the Pacific Ocean, the Golden Gate, and the San Francisco Bay. In 1776 Spanish settlers came there from Monterey to build a military post and establish the Mission San Francisco de Asis, commonly referred to as Mission Dolores. By 1846, the city had a Caucasian population of 375, mostly of Spanish descent, and an additional eighty-three residents who were black, American Indian, and Hawaiian. With the discovery of gold in California in 1849, the city became a boom town and financial center.

The gold rush made many San Franciscans rich as merchants. The city's permanent population grew rapidly. Although the Panic of 1857 and the great fire of 1906 slowed San Francisco's economic growth, immigrants flocked to the city from France, Italy, Germany, Japan, and China. Each group established ethnic enclaves in separate parts of a city that was quickly becoming one of the most cosmopolitan in the United States, often referred to as "Baghdad by the Bay." These groups were joined by Latin Americans, American Indians, Pacific Islanders, and other smaller concentrations of foreign settlers.

Many of the ethnic enclaves of the early period continue to exist: San Francisco's Chinatown is the largest Chinese community outside China; the Japanese Cultural Center reflects the culture of a people temporarily dispossessed when they were sent to government relocation camps in 1942; North Beach, once a predominantly Italian community, now has a large Chinese population; a substantial Filipino community exists south of Market Street; and a large Spanish-speaking community occupies the Mission District. San Francisco's largest non-English-speaking minority is Chinese, although the growing Spanish-speaking population may overtake it in size by the early twenty-first century.

In 1941, the San Francisco Bay area had about 20,000 black inhabitants, some 4,000 of whom lived in the city proper. With the growth of shipyards and

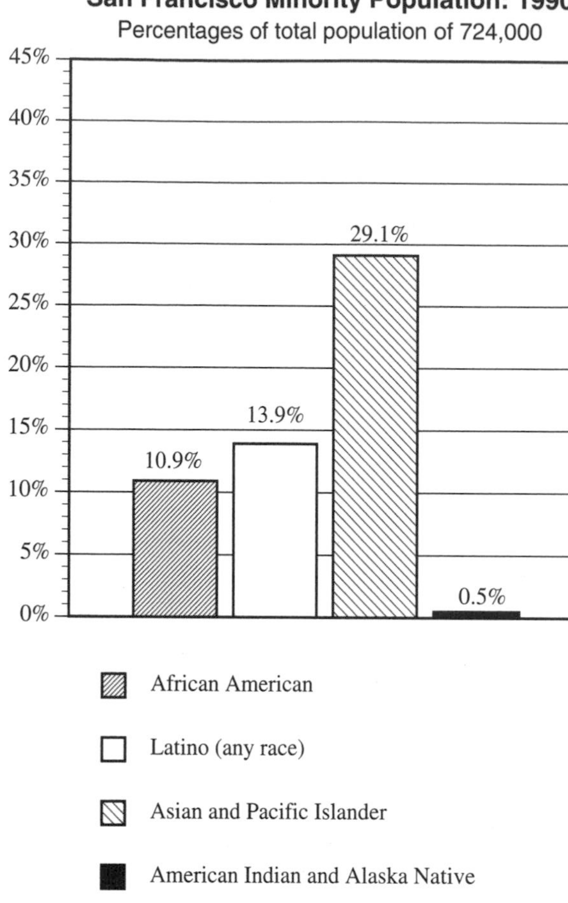

Source: Data are from *Statistical Abstract of the United States, 1992.* Table 38. Washington, D.C.: Government Printing Office, 1992.

other defense installations during World War II, 500,000 black workers from the South came to the area as defense workers.

San Francisco is also known for the diversity of lifestyles that it spawns and supports. Its Haight Ashbury area was the center of the 1960's counterculture and a mecca for American hippies. The city has a large gay community and continues to be a major center for the gay rights movement. The overall population of San Francisco—723,959 in the 1990 census—makes it the fourth-largest city in California. Its location on a peninsula inhibits the city's expansion severely.

SUGGESTED READINGS. Anita Loos writes spiritedly about the city in *San Francisco* (1978), as does Morton Beebe in *San Francisco* (1985). Particular aspects of the city's ethnic diversity are examined in Victor Nee and Brett de Bary Nee's *Longtime Californ': A Documentary Study of an American Chinatown* (1986) and Richard H. Dillon's *North Beach: The Italian Heart of San Francisco* (1985).

San Joaquin cotton strike (1933): Dispute in central California over wages, abolition of the labor contract system, and hiring union members. About 80 percent of the ten to twelve thousand striking workers were Mexican. Cotton growers were supported by businesspeople, the Chamber of Commerce, newspapers, the Farm Bureau, elected officials, and police. The Workers International Relief of the Communist Party aided the strikers with food and money. Consequently strikers were labeled communists; some were arrested, and the strike's leaders were deported. At least nine workers were murdered by growers. The strike ended when the government recommended a compromise and ordered relief payments stopped.

Sanctuary movement: Organized civil disobedience by certain American religious groups that offered their churches as asylum for Central American refugees in the 1980's. The sanctuary movement in the United States was both a protest movement and a response to an international refugee crisis caused by civil war in Central America. The controversy surrounding the sanctuary movement was fuelled by the heavy involvement of churches and synagogues throughout the United States, which publicly proclaimed their intention of violating U.S. immigration laws by granting safe refuge to refugees from Central America, mainly Salvadorans. The organized effort went beyond the provision of shelter, food, and clothing to refugees arriving from the border separating Mexico and the United States. Those involved in the organization of relief efforts clearly associated their humanitarian actions with criticism of American foreign policy in relation to Central American states, specifically El Salvador.

The Political and Historical Context. El Salvador is a country no larger than the state of Massachusetts. In the late 1970's and 1980's, it was dominated by a wealthy oligarchy in league with the military. Official repression of the large Indian and peasant population reached levels of shocking cruelty.

In the early 1980's, nearly two million people were displaced within Central America as a result of political unrest. Although thousands remained in refugee camps in Central America, thousands more streamed into Mexico, and from there made their way into the United States. Of the 750,000 refugees who entered the United States—roughly comparable to the number of Southeast Asian refugees who arrived after the Vietnam War—nearly 500,000 were Salvadoran. This figure represented nearly a tenth of the entire population of El Salvador.

The Salvadoran refugees were visible results of U.S. foreign policy in El Salvador. Since the United States officially supported the government of El Salvador, it was official policy under the Reagan Administration (1980-1988) to prevent admission of most Salvadoran refugees, rejecting the pleas that these refugees faced political repression or personal danger. The arrival of numerous refugees, however, and their highly publicized testimony brought attention to the repressive and unpopular regime in El Salvador, leading a large number of Americans to question openly the wisdom of American support for the Duarte government in El Salvador.

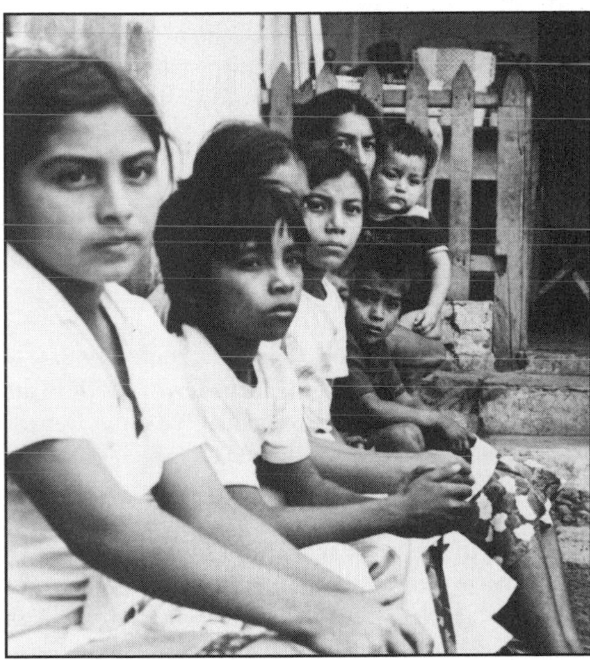

Violent civil warfare in El Salvador between government troops and guerrilla fighters trapped civilians, such as this family, in the middle, prompting many to seek refuge in the United States. (AP/Wide World Photos)

Social Reform in the Catholic Church. At the same time as authoritarian political developments in many Latin American states, the ROMAN CATHOLIC CHURCH was being transformed by an internal reform movement that came to be known as "liberation theology." This form of theology shifted the church's major attention and mission to the needs of the poor masses in developing countries, emphasizing such biblical messages as the Exodus of the Israelites from Egyptian slavery as the basis for involving the church in social projects, and becoming an outspoken advocate for the rights of the poor and landless.

The Catholic church took these dramatic turns in the 1970's, partly as a result of the liberalization of church doctrine in Vatican II, and also influenced by Marxist social analysis of the exploitation of the poor. Advocates of liberation theology maintained that despite their interest in social issues, their central concerns were decidedly Christian, rooted in the more compassionate and reforming strains of Christian history.

The response of ruling military-oligarchical regimes to liberation theologians was brutal. Sixteen Catholic leaders were assassinated in El Salvador alone; March 24, 1980, saw the public assassination of Archbishop Oscar Romero, whose outspoken attitudes on behalf of the poor could no longer be tolerated. It has furthermore been estimated that some 40,000 noncombatant civilians were killed in El Salvador before 1984. During this time a violent civil war broke out, bringing displaced and persecuted people to desperation in their search for escape.

The sanctuary movement, then, was a significant movement of both political and religious protest in the United States that cannot be clearly understood apart from a number of important factors. These included civil war in El Salvador (with the United States supporting one side with arms, financial assistance, and military advisers); a significant swing to the right in American foreign policy with the election of Ronald Reagan; a significant swing to the left in many churches, particularly in the Catholic church with liberation theology; and a well-organized campaign of civil disobedience in the border states of Arizona, California, Texas, and New Mexico.

Asylum in American History and Politics. The sanctuary movement began among Christian clergy, both Catholic and Protestant, who responded to the needs of Salvadoran refugees who began arriving in the early 1980's in high numbers. Clearly, in helping Salvadorans to enter and settle in the United States, and in giving the refugees asylum in their churches, the sanctuary movement was violating U.S. policy as determined by the IMMIGRATION AND NATURALIZATION SERVICE (INS). There was a conflict between the traditional religious concept of asylum and the legal definition of asylum as permitted by the U.S. government. Movement leaders claimed that the granting of legal asylum to foreign nationals had long been a tool of political ideology rather than humanitarian aid to persecuted people. According to Ann Crittenden, a historian of the sanctuary movement, 90 percent of the more than two million refugees granted asylum by the United States since World War II have come from officially recognized "communist" countries, particularly Eastern Europe. While such states disgorged a large percentage of the world's postwar refugees, in the 1980's the number of applicants from these countries declined significantly.

Between 1983 and 1986, for example, the United States approved more than 50 percent of the eight hundred refugees from Romania who requested asylum, and nearly 45 percent of the two hundred Czech applicants. During this same period, however, only 14 percent of seventeen thousand Nicaraguans, and a mere 2.6 percent of twenty thousand Salvadorans who officially applied were granted asylum. One of the clear differences from the Eastern European refugees was that the United States officially supported the regimes from which the Salvadorans escaped, and the pre-Sandanista Nicaraguan government as well. Another difference, however, was the economic gap between the Latin American and the Eastern European refugees, which led many INS officials to publicly suggest that economic, rather than humanitarian, issues were really the motivating factor for the Central American refugees.

The Sanctuary Movement: 1980-1987. When large numbers of Salvadoran refugees began entering the United States with horrific stories of conditions in their homeland, clergy in Arizona and New Mexico were moved to become involved. At first, they provided housing and other assistance on an ad hoc basis, as they were able. They justified helping refugees enter the United States with the claim that refugee applications for asylum were far more effective when made from within the United States than from outside—an argument the INS could not deny.

The Rev. Jim Fife, a Presbyterian minister and one of the first clergymen involved, brought an activist background to his concerns about the refugee population. The theoretical leader of the movement, however, was the QUAKER rancher and former teacher Jim Corbett. He drew parallels between the need for organized aid for the Salvadoran refugees and the strong QUAKER involvement in the ABOLITIONIST MOVEMENT against African American SLAVERY in the nineteenth century. He particularly stressed the importance of a linked chain of safe-houses known as the UNDERGROUND RAILROAD, which helped to guide escaped slaves to the free northern states. Advocates of sanctuary came to see their movement as a means of guiding Salvadoran refugees safely away from the civil strife in their own homeland to freedom in the United States.

Corbett's ideas led to a national campaign of churches and synagogues providing "sanctuary" to arriving refugees. Members of a few hundred American congregations took part in coordinated volunteer networks, helping the refugees with English skills and medical problems as well as basic needs. Congregations often voted on whether to support or fully participate in sanctuary—a controversial question even in liberal groups because of the legal implications. The concepts of legal asylum, sanctuary, and a modern underground railroad were the symbolic foundations that lent the sanctuary movement its unique character as a religious, social, and protest movement of the 1980's.

Official Investigation. The growing national and international media attention given to the sanctuary movement made Corbett an especially well-known figure. The coverage included a widely seen segment on the CBS television program *60 Minutes* and an illustrated article in *People* magazine. This attention to an organized campaign of civil disobedience was perceived by the INS as a politically calculated attempt to embarrass the Reagan Administration. In 1983, an investigation was launched by the INS in the southwestern states. By November, 1984, the Department of Justice in Washington, D.C., gave permission to INS authorities to begin "Operation Sojourner," an undercover infiltration of the sanctuary movement, which led to the arrest and trial of several of the leaders of the movement, including Fife and Corbett.

Not unexpectedly, the trials of sanctuary workers in Tucson, Arizona, became media events, further embroiling the American public in divisions between the political left and right during the highly ideological presidency of Ronald Reagan. By the time of the trials in the mid-1980's, however, the movement itself was showing signs of instability. Churches began to make specific "requests" for refugees of a particular type or experience. Some members of the movement expressed concern that only those refugees with particularly newsworthy or politically acceptable stories should be encouraged to speak or appear as representatives of the movement. Such sophisticated attention to marketing the movement began to alienate more humanitarian-minded leaders and church members, and lent credence to government claims that the movement had more to do with liberal and leftist political agendas than genuine compassion for refugees.

All of these complications contributed to the unusual level of emotion that surrounded an already politicized trial. The trial opposed the interests of the INS in enforcing immigration law against the defense's interest in addressing the human plight that the refugees faced, the religious motivations of the defendants, and the problems with U.S. Central American policy. The sanctuary trial was also of sensational public interest as the first federal court case in which the government used paid informers to infiltrate churches. Clearly, issues of separation of church and state also added to the drama of the celebrated case.

The trial provoked a national response. In January, 1985, Santa Fe declared itself a sanctuary city; the governor of New Mexico also declared his open support for the sanctuary movement. National politicians openly questioned the Justice Department's case, and accused the INS of political interests in prosecuting the movement's leaders. In the end, the trial resulted in the conviction of some sanctuary leaders, including Fife, and the acquittal of others, including Corbett. On July 1, 1986, presiding judge Earl Carroll stunned the court by sentencing five of the defendants to probation and suspending the sentences of all the others.

The disruptive trial hurt the morale of the sanctuary movement. Although the concerns which propelled the movement to national and international attention continued beyond 1986, greater attention to human rights in El Salvador and a new U.S. immigration law slowly brought changes in the movement. By 1987, Central American refugees were no longer "going public." Some took part in the amnesty offered to illegal immigrants in the late 1980's. Although illegal immigration continued to be controversial in American policy and public opinion, it was no longer the center of a nationally recognized, effective sanctuary movement.

Many Salvadoran refugees who ultimately sought sanctuary in the United States lived first in refugee camps like this one across the Salvadoran border in neighboring Honduras. (United Nations High Commissioner for Refugees)

Suggested Readings. The best chronicle of the

movement remains Ann Crittenden's journalistic work, *Sanctuary* (1988). Other works include Robert Tomsho's *The American Sanctuary Movement* (1987). To gain a sense of the movement from the activist's perspective, see Gary MacEoin's *Sanctuary: A Resource Guide for Understanding and Participating in the Central American Refugee's Struggle* (1985). Finally, movement leaders themselves published a variety of writings in magazines and church publications. A good summary of the thought of Jim Corbett is his work, *Sanctuary Church* (1986).—*Daniel L. S. Christopher*

Sand Creek Massacre (Nov. 29, 1864): One of the most tragic of the many atrocities resulting from conflicts between American Indians and European Americans. The incident at Sand Creek, Colorado, has been called the "Battle of Sand Creek" by those who would ignore the fact that it was a massacre, and "Chivington's Massacre" by those who would emphasize the ultimate responsibility of the man who led a force of more than seven hundred Colorado Volunteers in the dawn attack on an encampment of some six to seven hundred CHEYENNE and ARAPAHO Indians.

Colonel John M. Chivington commanded the five battalions, which were heavily armed with artillery consisting of four twelve-pound mountain howitzers. Previous to that morning, Chivington had instructed his troops to "kill all Indians you come across," and, in a speech in Denver, publicly advocated the killing and scalping of Indians—even infants. Chivington is reported to have proclaimed, "Nits make lice!"

Eyewitness accounts of the massacre are as many as they are varied in their specifics. One soldier present at the scene testified later that he had personally observed "450 dead Indian warriors," and another that he had "counted 130 bodies, all dead"; yet another reported that he "visited the battlefield one month afterwards [and] counted sixty-nine, but a number had been eaten by the wolves and dogs." While the reports of the numbers of dead vary greatly—Chivington himself reported that "between five and six hundred Indians were left dead upon the field"—it is clear that the mounted force of well-armed soldiers stormed a peaceful village of Indian families and murdered a great number of people. The most consistent reports indicate that upward of 133 Indians were killed, only twenty-eight of whom were men. In what has been described as "a few hours of madness," Chivington's mob scalped and otherwise mutilated the bodies of their victims.

Horrible events occurred that morning: one junior officer was reported to have killed and scalped three women and five children, who had surrendered and were screaming for mercy; a small girl was seen to have been shot and killed as she walked toward the soldiers carrying a white flag: and, according to Major E. W. Wynkoop of the First Colorado Cavalry, "the dead bodies of females profaned in such a manner that the recital is sickening."

SUGGESTED READINGS. A thorough, unbiased account of what is surely one of the most controversial events in the history of U.S.-Indian conflicts is Stan Hoig's *The Sand Creek Massacre* (1961), which contains excerpts from testimony taken during the exhaustive congressional investigations that followed the massacre. For an insider's view of the massacre and the events that followed, see *The Life of George Bent* (1968) by George E. Hyde. Accounts of the event are included in Angie Debo's *A History of the Indians of the United States* (1970), and Dee Brown's *Bury My Heart at Wounded Knee* (1971).

Sand painting: Highly developed art form created by the NAVAJO and PUEBLO Indians and to a lesser degree

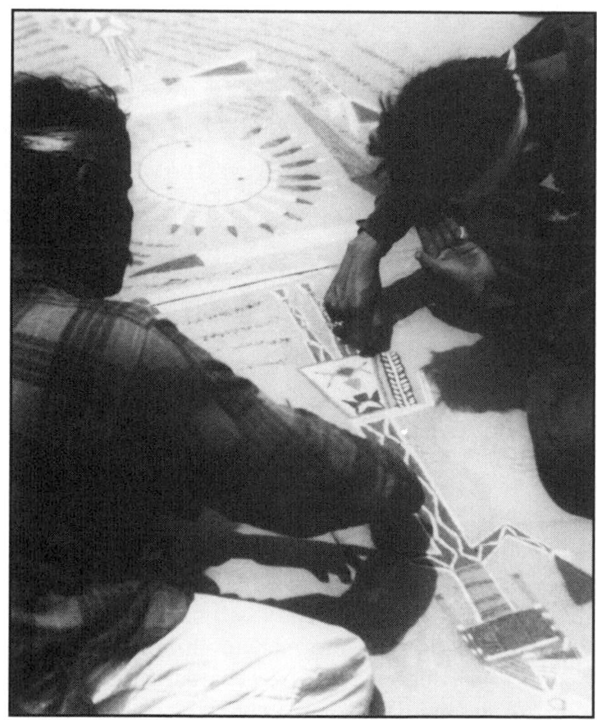

Two Navajos combine their artistic talents with their knowledge of the religious rituals surrounding ceremonial sand painting. (Museum of New Mexico)

by the Plains Indians. To American Indians, the main function of sand painting is religious rather than artistic. Sand paintings are stylized, symbolic pictures connected with healing ceremonies. The paintings are made by trickling small amounts of crushed, colored sandstone onto a background of clean, smooth sand. There are more than six hundred different pictures, with representations of various deities, animals, and other symbols that are described in the chants performed in the healing rituals. When the entire ritual is completed, the painting is destroyed and no permanent, exact copies of paintings are allowed to be made. When designs are copied into rugs, an error is deliberately made so that the original design will maintain its power.

Sanger, Margaret (Margaret Louis Higgins; Sept. 14, 1879, Corning, N.Y.—Sept. 6, 1966, Tucson, Ariz.): Birth control advocate and reformer. In 1914 Sanger published *The Woman Rebel,* a journal that was declared unmailable according to the Comstock Act of 1873, which banned the circulation of information on contraception and abortion. In 1921 she founded the American Birth Control League. In 1927 she organized the First World Population Conference in Geneva, from which came a national lobby group. The first president of the International Planned Parenthood Federation (1953), she was responsible for the establishment of more than three hundred birth control clinics in the United States.

An outspoken advocate of birth control and reproductive rights for women, Margaret Sanger was the first president of the International Planned Parenthood Federation. (AP/ Wide World Photos)

Sansei: Third-generation JAPANESE AMERICANS, that is, those whose grandparents were born in Japan and settled in the United States. Speaking very generally, Sansei enjoy greater opportunities in education and business than did their Nisei parents or Issei grandparents, because they have not had to face the same levels of discrimination. Since power and authority are in the hands of the older generations, Sansei have the least influence and respect within the Japanese American community. Nevertheless, because they are more ASSIMILATED, Sansei have more power and influence in American society at large.

Santa Fe, N. Mex. (founded 1610): New Mexico's capital since 1912, the year in which the state joined the Union, and one of the oldest cities in the United States. Santa Fe was established in 1609-1610 by Pedro de Peralta, the third Spanish governor of the Province of New Mexico, then a part of Mexico. The city was named *La villa Real de la Santa Fe de San Francisco de Asis* (The Royal City of the Holy Faith of St. Francis of Assisi). Its name was soon shortened to the present form.

Situated in the Sangre de Cristo Mountains some 60 miles north of Albuquerque, Santa Fe has an elevation of 7,000 feet. Its moderate climate and cool, crisp air have long attracted people to the area. The vivid colors and the desert landscape have enticed artists for two centuries, making Santa Fe a major art center of the Southwest.

The town retains much of the Spanish and Indian atmosphere established by its early settlers. Many of its government buildings are of Spanish territorial or colonial design; many of its commercial and residential buildings are constructed of the adobe that the Anasazi Indians used to build their pueblos. A number of functioning Indian villages lie within 10 miles of the town's central plaza, around which Indian craftspeople and merchants cluster every day to sell their wares.

Archaeological excavation reveals that Santa Fe and its environs were sites of American Indian settlements dating, perhaps, to prehistoric times. The modern city contains the Mission of San Miguel of Santa Fe, thought to be the oldest church in the United States, dating to 1621. The oldest continuously operated restaurant in the United States is near the central plaza.

Indian craftspeople market their handiwork on the sidewalks surrounding Santa Fe's historic plaza. (Justine Hill)

Contemporary Santa Fe, with a population of 55,859 in 1990, represents a commingling of Anglo, Latino, and American Indian cultures. The city is trilingual, with Spanish and Navajo used along with English. Many local restaurants serve food derived from Navajo cuisine, a mainstay of which is tortillas made from blue corn.

Drawn by its charm, cosmopolitan atmosphere, and cultural attractions (such as a world renowned opera company and fine museums), thousands of travelers from around the world visit Santa Fe every year. The city has also become a popular retirement community and a mecca for those interested in "new age" health and spiritual movements. Its population increased by fifteen percent between the 1980 and 1990 census.

Suggested Readings. Jack Parson's *Santa Fe and Northern New Mexico* (1991) provides reliable information about the city and the surrounding area, discussing culture, archaeology, and history. Arrell Morgan Gibson's carefully researched *Santa Fe and Taos Colonies* (1983) focuses on early Indian settlements and their impact upon present-day northern New Mexico. Ernest Knee's *Santa Fe, New Mexico* (1942), although dated, is beguilingly written. Christine Mather's *Santa Fe Styles* (1985) emphasizes Santa Fe's art and architecture.

Santa Fe Fiesta: Celebration in early September that dates back to 1712. It was originally a religious festival stemming from the vow of a Spanish general and focused on the restoration of a memorial cross to the Plaza of Santa Fe. Today the Santa Fe Festival includes a procession, crowning of a Fiesta Queen, a Conquistadores Ball, and various parties and celebrations. A new feature was added in 1926 when Will Shuster created a large grotesque figure, named Zozobra (Old Man Gloom), which was publicly burned during the festivities.

Santana, Carlos (b. July 20, 1947, Autlan de Navarro, Jalisco, Mexico): Mexican American rock musician. Santana began his career by playing guitar in clubs in Tijuana, Mexico, and recording with Mike Bloomfield and Al Kooper. He moved to San Francisco in 1962 and four years later founded the band Santana. Santana's more than thirty albums with Columbia Records and Polygram include the debut *Santana* (1969), *Caravanserai* (1972), *Amigos* (1976), and *Viva Santana!* (1988). His style has gradually moved from rock music toward jazz, always flavored with African and Latin rhythms. He and his band have toured internationally and received numerous awards, including a Gold Medal Award in 1977 and a Grammy Award in 1989.

Santayana, George (Dec. 16, 1863, Madrid, Spain—Sept. 26, 1952, Rome, Italy): Spanish philosopher and writer. Santayana came to the United States in 1872. He studied at Harvard University, receiving his Ph.D. in 1889, and became an instructor in the university's Department of Philosophy. Santayana began writing poetry in 1894, soon moving on to such philosophical works as *The Sense of Beauty* (1896), *The Life of Reason* (1906), and *The Realms of Being* (1927). He returned to Europe in 1912 and spent the rest of his life in Oxford, Paris, and Rome. Through his extensive writings, he developed a speculative and detached philosophy known as critical realism. His most popular work was his 1944 autobiography *Persons and Places*.

Guitarist Carlos Santana. (AP/Wide World Photos)

Santería: Afro-Cuban religion that combines elements of the African Yoruba religion with folk Catholicism. It began in the nineteenth century when Yoruba people from Africa were brought to Cuba to work in sugar fields. Santería means "the way of the saints" and is based on devotion to Yoruba spirits called *orishas*. After the 1959 revolution, Cuban immigrants spread the religion throughout the Caribbean and the United States. Music, especially ritual drumming, plays an important role in the religion and is associated with certain saints. In the early 1990's, Santería appeared to be thriving in Cuba, Venezuela, Puerto Rico, and Cuban American communities in the United States, but the size and spread of the religion is difficult to document because a history of oppression and misunderstanding has resulted in secrecy among its members. Nevertheless, increasing numbers of non-Cuban musicians and others have been drawn to the religion. In 1987, the city of Hialeah, Florida, attempted to suppress Santería by banning ritual animal sacrifice; in 1993, the U.S. Supreme Court ruled in favor of the religion on First Amendment grounds.

Saudi Americans: Saudi Arabia occupies four-fifths of the Arabian peninsula, which is one of the most sparsely populated areas on earth. The Saudi Arabians are a tribal people who trace their lineage to a son of the biblical Noah named Shem. Ancient tribal loyalties still influence their behavior, as in rivalries that persist between northern and southern tribes.

The prophet Mohammed united Arabia when he founded Islam in the year 622. Arabs were so ener-

SAUDI ARABIA

gized by their new faith that within the next hundred years they conquered central Asia, northern Africa, and Spain. Yet, soon after, Arab unity disintegrated and their power became diffused. Saudi Arabia remains important to world Muslims as the site of Mecca, Mohammed's birthplace and a holy shrine, to which the faithful are urged to make a pilgrimage at least once.

Early in the twentieth century, Abd al-Aziz Ibn Saud, the father of Saudi Arabia, captured much of the Arabian peninsula from the Turks. Out of this land he formed a new kingdom, which was named Saudi Arabia in 1932. Modern Saudi Arabia is governed by a king and a council of ministers. It has no constitution or representative government. It is ruled by Islamic law, which means that alcohol is forbidden and the activities of women are legally circumscribed.

Saudis had little reason to emigrate to the United States in the early half of the twentieth century. The country lacked the mosques that provide essential support for the Muslim lifestyle. This involves fasting every day during the month of Ramadan, observing the Sabbath on Fridays, and praying five times a day toward Mecca.

After World War II, well-off Saudis began to send their sons to the United States to get a good education. These students often stayed on because their economic prospects were better in their adopted country and because they had become accustomed to a more liberal way of life than they would have had in their homeland. The IMMIGRATION AND NATIONALITY ACT OF 1965, with its clause stating a preference for certain professionals, induced some educated Saudis to emigrate to the United States. In fact, from 1965 to 1976, all Arab countries experienced a serious brain-drain.

Saudi Americans are generally well-educated and live in cities near their professional jobs. They maintain amicable relations with other Americans, particularly after the cooperation between the United States and Saudi Arabia in the 1990 Persian Gulf War.

Since the 1967 Arab-Israeli war, Arab Americans including those of Saudi background have become more vocal and politically visible as a group while promoting pride in their heritage. Muslims among them have built many mosques and revived the Arabic language, both of which are necessary for the strict practice of Islam.

Saund, Dalip Singh (Sept. 20, 1899, Chhajalwadi, near Amritsar, India—Apr. 23, 1973, Hollywood, Calif.): Asian Indian American politician. Having been graduated from the University of Punjab in 1919, Saund came to the United States to study food preservation at the University of California at Berkeley. In 1925 he moved to California's Imperial Valley to farm and write a

In 1957, Dalip Singh Saund became the first person of Asian Indian descent to be elected to the U.S. House of Representatives. (AP/Wide World Photos)

memoir, *My Mother India* (1930). He organized the Indian Association of America in 1942 and traveled to Washington, D.C., to overturn laws denying citizenship to Indian immigrants. Naturalized in 1949, Saund ran his own fertilizer business and, in 1957, became the first native of India elected to the U.S. House of Representatives. During a goodwill tour of Asia that year, he addressed a joint session of the Indian Parliament.

Scandinavian American women: Women from Sweden, Norway, Denmark, and Finland arrived with their families in significant numbers after treaties in 1851 opened Minnesota to settlement. As the railroads advanced, further settlement opportunities opened in Illinois, Iowa, and Wisconsin.

Harsh natural conditions in the Scandinavian countries had created a people who were hardy, persistent, and industrious—qualities necessary for the rugged life of pioneer agriculture in the United States. Women worked at heavy farm labor and took care of the house and children. Overwork, severe weather, and poor housing contributed to sickness and death among adults, while diphtheria and typhoid claimed many more children's lives.

Proud of their rich ethnic heritage, Scandinavian American women such as this folk singer have worked to preserve their ancestral traditions. (James L. Shaffer)

In addition to harsh physical conditions, many Scandinavian-born farm wives suffered profound loneliness. Their husbands could not afford to sit idly all winter and often sought work far from home in the lumber industries. There are numerous records of hunger, cold, childbirth, and death while the men were gone. Some pioneer women retreated into a private world of madness.

Scandinavian American family life was dominated by the husband, whose authority was absolute. Geographical isolation perpetuated paternal dominance. Even when children made other contacts through the public schools, the mothers usually remained isolated on farms.

Conditions improved slowly after the beginning of the twentieth century. Scientific farming allowed women to give up field work, and the rising status of many Scandinavian American families was marked by the acquisition of household appliances such as an indoor pump, a hand-cranked washing machine, and a gasoline stove. Access to birth control lightened the burden of many urban women, but Scandinavian men often resented this development. Rural families, including those of Scandinavian Americans, remained large, and constant childbearing was considered one of the hardest burdens of frontier mothers, even into the twentieth century.

Despite these hardships, there were always women who achieved. In 1850, Jenny Lind, the "Swedish Nightingale," sang her way to national acclaim. In the early years of film, one of the very first to switch from theater to motion pictures was Anna Q. Nilsson, a Swedish actor who appeared in about two hundred films. Later, she was followed by Greta Garbo, Ingrid Bergman, Gloria Swanson, and Susan Hayward.

Scandinavian women also made their mark in literature. Kathryn Forbes, who wrote *Mama's Bank Account* (1943), was the best known. The story, a memoir about Norwegians in California, was retitled *I Remember Mama* and won great acclaim on stage and in the 1948 film version.

A new national origins quota system brought Scandinavian immigration to a virtual standstill after 1925. During the 1930's and 1940's Scandinavian Americans grew more distant from the customs and languages of their countries of origin. By the 1970's, Scandinavians lived throughout the United States and were difficult to identify as a separate ethnic group except in regions with large communities such as the Northwest and Upper Midwest. Conditions for women had become the same as for any other group of American women.

Suggested Readings. For a fascinating study of Scandinavian immigrant life reflected in literature, see *The Divided Heart* by Dorothy Burton Skardal (1974). *Swedish America: An Introduction* by Nils Hasselmo (1976) focuses on one group. A carefully documented chronology, *The Scandinavians in America, 986-1970* by Howard B. Furer (1972), is a good choice. *The Scandinavian Element in the United States* by Kendric Charles Babcock, Ph.D. (1969) offers a more general discussion.

Scapegoat: Group or person blamed for a situation or event actually caused by others. Prejudice and bigotry are often involved in the process of scapegoating, because it is convenient for one group to make a scapegoat of another group that is already disliked or distrusted. It is common, for example, for a particular racial or ethnic group to be falsely blamed for increases in unemployment or crime. Scapegoating arises from the general desire not to see oneself as being at fault for a bad situation as well as from oversimplifying the complex factors that cause social or economic conditions.

Schlafly, Phyllis (Phyllis Stewart; b. Aug. 15, 1924, St. Louis, Mich.): Profamily, antifeminist activist. The mother of six children, Schlafly was an extremely influential figure in the defeat of the EQUAL RIGHTS AMENDMENT in 1982. A delegate to the Republican National Convention since the 1950's, she became the first vice president of the National Federation of Republican Women in 1965. In 1964 she published her first book, *A Choice Not an Echo,* and three years later began her newsletter, *The Phyllis Schlafly Report.* She founded Stop ERA in 1972 and the Eagle Forum in 1975. Schlafly is a powerful and dedicated force in the profamily movement.

Founder of the Stop ERA movement in 1972, Phyllis Schlafly was a key figure in the campaign to defeat the passage of the Equal Rights Amendment. (AP/Wide World Photos)

Schomburg Center for Research in Black Culture: One of the world's foremost collections of materials on the history and culture of people of African descent. It holds more than five million items in all forms of media and is used by researchers and scholars from the United States and abroad.

Arthur A. Schomburg (1874-1938), born in Puerto Rico to a black mother and a white father, was a bibliophile and historian. His name has been associated with the collection since 1926, when he added his personal holdings to the Division of Negro Literature, History, and Prints of the 135th Street Branch of the New York Public Library. In Schomburg's collection were more than ten thousand books, manuscripts, and pamphlets, and some two thousand etchings and paintings. He served as curator of the Negro Division from 1932 until his death in 1938. Four years later, the collection was named after him. Designated one of the Research Libraries of the New York Public Library, it became the Schomburg Center for Research in Black Culture in 1972. In 1980, the collection was moved to its current home in the center of Harlem at 135th Street and Lenox Avenue.

In his best-known essay, "The Negro Digs up His Past," Schomburg wrote, "the American Negro must remake his past in order to make his future." He believed that it was through the study of the history of peoples of African descent, a study firmly based upon documentary sources such as those he collected, that assumptions about racial superiority and dominance could best be refuted. He worked tirelessly toward that goal, collecting materials from the United States and abroad. His collection and the research center which bears his name stand as irrefutable testimony to the myriad achievements and distinctions of people of African heritage. Schomburg hoped that the materials he had assembled would serve as both a source of information and inspiration for all members of his race. Indeed, many AFRICAN AMERICAN thinkers, writers, and artists turned to Schomburg and his collection for support during the HARLEM RENAISSANCE of the 1930's. "Though it is orthodox to think of America as the one country where it is unnecessary to have a past, what is a luxury for the nation as a whole [is] a prime social necessity for the Negro," he wrote in 1925.

Schomburg is the subject of an excellent biography, *Arthur Alfonso Schomburg: Black Bibliophile and Collector* (1989) by Elinor Des Verney Sinnette, which discusses his life and work within the social, cultural, and historical framework of his time. Schomburg also is often included in studies of the rich period of African American artistic activity known as the Harlem Renaissance.

SUGGESTED READINGS. Nathan Huggins' *Voices from the Harlem Renaissance* (1976), for example, contains a reprinting of Schomburg's essay "The Negro Digs up His Past." *A Dictionary Catalog of the Schomburg Collection of Negro Literature and History* (authorship is listed as Schomburg Collection of Negro Literature and History, 1962) is a useful guide to the holdings of the center. On the occasion of its sixtieth anniversary, the Schomburg Center published an informative booklet detailing its history, *The Schomburg Center for Research in Black Culture: Sixtieth Anniversary Tribute* (1986).

The Schomburg Center for Research in Black Culture sponsors exhibits, conferences, and roundtable discussions on African American culture, such as this one attended by artists Lois Mailou Jones (left), Selma Burke (center), and Georgette Powell (right). (Roy Lewis Photography)

Science: The sciences in the United States have benefited extensively from the participation of immigrants and members of many minority groups. This has been true throughout the country's history, but particularly in the years since World War II as racial barriers became less insurmountable. Science, as a study and a profession, historically has not been immune to general trends in American society, including PREJUDICE and DISCRIMINATION. The attitude of the scientific community toward diversifying and integrating its ranks has essentially followed the patterns of other social institutions. Those people considered outsiders have had to persevere in long, difficult struggles to achieve full-fledged participation.

On the other hand, in science there is a somewhat greater chance for an individual to achieve based on intellect and perseverance alone than there is in such fields as the business world. A scientist can win a Nobel Prize, for example, for the merit of the work itself; in the world of business, subtle institutional discrimination is more likely to create a glass ceiling keeping members of certain groups from reaching top-level positions. Yet prejudice still remains in the sciences, often in very subtle forms; one example is the prejudice against women, particularly in certain fields such as engineering, physics, and astronomy.

Virtually every ethnic and racial group represented in the U.S. population, whether American Indian or people of African, European, or Asian descent, has produced distinguished scientists. Any of these could be examined in detail, but the experiences of a few groups—JEWS, AFRICAN AMERICANS, and women—can be seen as representative of the variety of challenges and achievements of many others.

Historical Background. In fifteenth century Europe, which is considered the birthplace of modern science, there were few Jewish scientists. Social exclusionary practices kept Jews out of certain activities and academies. In addition, Jewish intellectual traditions often found the study of natural sciences to be at variance with the teachings of Jewish law. Jewish scholarship was more centered on theology than natural science at this time. Gradually, some Jews began to hide their identity in order to succeed as scientists. In eighteenth and nineteenth century Europe, Jews often converted, became baptized, and acquired documents forged to a new identity. In the United States, Jews often changed their name with immigration, as from Abraham to Allendale.

By the mid-1700's, a few European women such as Gabrielle-Émilie du Châtelet had started to engage in scientific study and research, and wrote and published works in mathematics, astronomy, and natural history. A woman's route into science was often through progressive male mentors such as her father, brother, uncle, or lover.

A few black people pursued science in eighteenth century Europe, but African Americans made only small contributions to science prior to the Civil War because of SLAVERY. A notable exception was Benjamin BANNEKER, who published an almanac in 1792 and various studies of insects. Enslaved blacks invented a number of devices and medical techniques to enhance their well-being, but these inventions were often credited to the slaveowner since slaves were not considered citizens.

Charles Drew, an African American surgeon and medical researcher, pioneered the collection and processing techniques necessary to provide blood plasma for transfusion. (American Red Cross)

Following the Civil War, African Americans slowly became a larger force in the sciences. In 1876 physicist Edward Bouchet became the first African American to receive a doctorate in the United States. Although he was a graduate of Yale University and the first African American in Phi Beta Kappa, the only job he could find was teaching high school science. In 1895 black doctors formed the National Medical Association as an alternative to the American Medical Association, which continued to bar most African Americans from membership until the 1950's.

Science in the Early Twentieth Century. Funding played an important role in the growing African American involvement (or lack thereof) in science in the early 1900's. African Americans had previously received no systematic outside support for scientific work. The first major help came through National Research Council (NRC) fellowships. In the 1920's, the chair of NRC's Division for Biology and Agriculture proposed establishing long-term support for scientific research at African American institutions to replace the piecemeal fellowship approach. African American scientists' careers remained tied to black colleges and universities, except for seasonal research in laboratories such as the Marine Biological Laboratory at Woods Hole, Massachusetts, until World War II.

In the early 1900's, ANTI-SEMITISM prevailed at American academic institutions, although they were not totally exclusionary. A quota system served to limit, but not bar, Jewish admissions to graduate and medical schools as well as the hiring of Jewish faculty at major universities and research institutions. The brilliant contributions and reputations of the physicists Albert Einstein, Albert Michelson, and others who supported them helped more Jewish students and scientists find places in academia and research. Some served in key scientific and administrative roles. Many maintained a tradition of social awareness and moral energy generated by their personal experience with ethnic intolerance.

Meanwhile, in the late nineteenth and early twentieth centuries, women in the United States slowly became more visible participants in science. They often were graduated from and held positions at WOMEN'S COLLEGES but rarely achieved a rank comparable with their male peers. For the most part, they were relegated to adjunct or research associate posts until after World War II.

Post-World War II Era. Following World War II, and partially because of the war, science became more open to women and racial and ethnic minorities. Jews became much more established in American science and academia by the end of World War II as the result of the influx of European émigré scholars and sympathy for the victims of Nazism. The war also brought limited public notice to African American scientists because of their work on the development of the atomic bomb.

At the end of World War II, a few white universities opened up opportunities for black faculty members and graduate students. Other problems, however, lingered in the African American community, limiting the access to science. These included a lack of access to high quality elementary and high school science programs, weak undergraduate curricula in black colleges, exclusion from admission to many white universities, and the high cost of graduate training.

The CIVIL RIGHTS ACT OF 1964 marked a milestone in educational opportunities for African American and other minorities. Many white colleges and universities created openings for blacks and Latinos at both the undergraduate and graduate levels. Academic and industrial careers in science became a more viable option for minority students.

In the 1990's, an increasing number of minority students were choosing careers in science and technology in the corporate world, or in academia as professors and administrators. Academia had more African American science and technology faculty members, deans, and college presidents than ever before. Some were serving in the nation's major universities. Approximately 75 percent of all black science doctorate holders, however, were employed by predominately African American colleges and universities where opportunity for serious scientific research is limited. The most notable yet least appreciated contribution made by African American scientists has been teaching the sciences at black colleges, where most of them received their undergraduate training.

Asian Americans. The contributions of Asian Americans to the sciences in the United States, especially since the 1960's, have been impressive. They have been active in fields including mathematics, computer science, chemistry, physics, and medicine. Chinese American scientists Chen Ning YANG and Tsung-Dao LEE shared the Nobel Prize for Physics in 1957. Physicist Samuel Ting won the Nobel Prize in Physics along with Burton Richter in 1976. Ting studied at Columbia University, where his teachers included Chinese American scientists such as Tsung-Dao Lee and C. S. Wu. Another renowned Chinese American scientist is chemist Yuan T. Lee, who helped revolutionize the field of molecular reaction dynamics in the 1970's and 1980's.

Har Gobind Khorana, an Indian-born biochemist who moved to the United States in 1960, won accolades including the 1968 Nobel Prize for his work with nucleic acids. Another scientist born in India, Subrahmanyan Chandrasekhar, moved to the United States to study at Harvard in 1938. His work in the field of astrophysics led him to a new theory about white dwarf stars and to what is now known as the

Born in India, astrophysicist Subrahmanyan Chandrasekhar was awarded a Nobel Prize in Physics in 1983 for his theoretical work on the structure, evolution, and life cycles of stars. (The Nobel Foundation)

"Chandrasekhar limit." Among the many highly respected Japanese American scientists are chemist Jokichi TAKAMINE, pathologist Hideyo Noguchi, and aerospace engineer Ellison ONIZUKA, who was one of the astronauts killed in the 1986 *Challenger* explosion. Molecular biologist Susumu Tonegawa won the Nobel Prize in 1987 for his important work with antibodies in the field of immunology.

Modern Women in Science. Black women have received a smaller proportion of their science degrees in the fields of engineering, mathematics, and physical sciences than women of any other racial or ethnic group. This is particularly troubling since within the African American population, women receive an overwhelming majority of high school diplomas and bachelor's degrees. These young women must be reached in order to increase the total number of African American scientists. Recommendations on how to recruit and retain more African American women in the sciences have come from African American women educators and scientists such as mathematicians Sylvia Bozeman and Etta Falconer, who were involved in such projects at Spelman College. Historically, Spelman has been one of the major producers of African American scientists and physicians. In 1991, thirty-seven percent of its female students had majors in the sciences.

The U.S. National Institutes of Health (NIH) has expanded its new women's health initiative to try to topple some of the barriers that women face in medical research. Reasons for this include the fact that men on average receive larger grants although the number of women applying for biomedical grants is growing. A 1990 government study found that women were badly underrepresented in NIH-sponsored clinical trials. That, along with a string of women's health scandals over devices such as the Dalkon Shield and breast implants, prompted Congress to give the agency $30 million for new research on women's health. This advance also helps the women in medical schools who make up 39 percent of the students, 21.5 percent of the faculty, but only 4 percent of department chairs.

Women earn 40 percent of the doctorate degrees in the biological sciences and 30 percent of the doctorate degrees in chemistry, but only 10 percent of the doctorate degrees in physical sciences. The conventional wisdom for this is that fewer girls develop an interest in physics and the necessary math while in high school and college. More women also leave the sciences to start a family. Women in physical sciences also complain of a subtle and elusive "chilly climate" which can leave them feeling undervalued, ignored, or alienated and keep them from pursuing a physics or astronomy career. For example, 40 percent of the women surveyed in a study by the American Astronomical Society had experienced discrimination in the category "general social treatment," mostly women astronomers over thirty-five who had had problems in

After pursuing medical research in hiding during World War II, Rita Levi-Montalcini left her native Italy in 1947 to teach and conduct neurobiological research in the United States that eventually led to her selection as a Nobel laureate in 1986. (The Nobel Foundation)

the past. The loss of female talent in physical science when the nation is facing a shortage of scientists and engineers has spurred debate on how to increase the numbers of women scientists. Women scientists themselves are divided as to whether AFFIRMATIVE ACTION programs are needed to help reduce the male domination of physical science or whether such programs would further demean women.

Representation of African Americans in scientific careers is 2 to 3 percent. In 1986, women made up 15 percent of all scientists and engineers, up from 9 percent in 1976. The 1970's and 1980's saw efforts by scientific organizations, universities, and learned societies to make their membership more inclusive. For the first time, the American Association for the Advancement of Science elected a woman president, Sheila Widnall, and an African American president, Walter Massey. These leaders symbolize powerful messages about the makeup of the scientific community.

SUGGESTED READINGS. For a general overview of the multicultural aspects of science, the article "The Complexion of Science" by Kenneth R. Manning in *Technology Review*, November/December, 1991, is excellent. Portia P. James's *The Real McCoy: African American Invention and Innovation, 1619-1930* (1989) portrays the hardships and achievements of African American scientists and inventors. Vivian Ovelton Sammons' *Blacks in Science and Medicine* (1990) is a comprehensive directory. *The Astronomers* by Donald Goldsmith (1991) introduces the reader to the careers of astronomers and the achievements they have made in a multicultural field.—*David R. Teske*

Scots-Irish Americans: Scots-Irish, or Scotch-Irish as they are sometimes termed, are usually considered the descendants of those Scots who migrated to Ulster (Northern Ireland) in the seventeenth century and then to North America in great numbers in the eighteenth century. Yet modern scholarship suggests that this is a simplistic interpretation. While Ulster was a primary provider of immigrants to America, other Celtic areas also provided colonists. Ulster Scots were joined by Scots as well as Welsh and English people from the border region with Scotland to collectively form what is called Scots-Irish. The vast majority of Scots-Irish Americans came to the colonies before the AMERICAN REVOLUTION, although immigration from those Celtic areas of Britain has continued to the present day.

The inhabitants of the areas around the Irish Sea are known collectively as Celts, a cultural rather than racial term. During the medieval period, the political and cultural development of those areas was markedly different from that of England. Linguistically, various Gaelic dialects composed the language of the Celtic areas. Despite their differences, Celtic cultures resembled one another more than they resembled that of the English. Geographically, the two most important Celtic areas, Ireland and Scotland, are only twelve miles apart at their closest point, and extensive contacts between the two areas had existed for centuries. During the fifteenth century, English monarchs extended their political and military control over Ireland. When James VI of Scotland acceded to the throne of England as James I, he was determined to civilize Irish Catholics by introducing Presbyterian Scottish settlers into the area. It was believed that the idea would be attractive to Scots because the availability of arable farm land in Ulster was far greater than that available in Scotland. In 1610, "plantations" of Scots were established in Ulster, and over the course of the next two decades, perhaps 20,000 Scots emigrated there. The English Civil War (1643-1660) demonstrated that little ASSIMILATION had occurred and that two separate societies had formed, one Irish Catholic and the other Scottish Presbyterian. At the end of the war, emigration into Ulster was again encouraged. An estimated 300,000 Scots from all parts of Scotland had moved into Ulster by 1715. While the original purpose of the plantations had failed, the economic success of the emigrants posed new problems for England.

Despite being numerically inferior to the original inhabitants, the immigrants had prospered in the seventeenth century. In an effort to attract settlers, the English Parliament had passed special legislation to aid strong woolen and linen manufacturing concerns in new towns such as Belfast and Lisburn. Their very success, however, resulted in the recision of the acts in 1699; Ulster goods were thereafter treated as imports from a foreign country. Periodic business depressions caused by competition with English manufacturers led to widespread economic misery in Ulster. A second major economic problem for the Scots-Irish occurred as the result of Ulster procedures for land tenure, which ultimately drove large numbers of Scots-Irish to emigrate.

Immigration. It has been estimated that more than 250,000 Scots-Irish emigrated to British colonies in North America between 1715 and the AMERICAN REVOLUTION. Some were motivated by concerns over religious discrimination in Ulster. In 1703 an act of Parliament banned non-Anglicans from holding office. This resulted in Presbyterian ministers being barred from performing their duties and Presbyterians being barred from government positions. While some of the most onerous provisions were eliminated within a decade, the Test Act was not fully repealed until 1782, long after Ulster Presbyterian ministers had taken many of their congregations to North America. Yet the most important stimulus for Scots-Irish emigration was, as usual, economic. Economic problems, both urban and rural, were major elements in Scottish-Irish dissatisfaction with their life in Ulster. When business depressions coincided with poor harvests, the flow became a flood. There were five such periods when emigration numbers escalated sharply: 1717-1718, 1725-1729, 1740-1741, 1754-1755, and 1771-1775.

The first wave was probably the smallest, although it was the most important. More than 5,000 Scots-Irish migrated to the colonies in this initial surge. Their destination, primarily frontier Pennsylvania, was determined by reports from earlier emigrants who wrote of cheap and fertile land, religious toleration, and non-interfering government officials. This first wave not only established settlement patterns but also provided glowing pictures of life in colonial America to those left behind. Famine in Ireland from 1725 to 1729 led to a massive outflow of emigrants to Pennsylvania. Famine in 1740 resulted in a third major exodus. This time, the destination shifted to the Shenandoah Valley of Virginia, and, from there, to the backcountry of western North Carolina. While the fourth and fifth waves resulted primarily from hunger, mass evictions, and the collapse of the linen industry in Ulster, propaganda from several Scots-Irish governors of North Carolina also encouraged the immigrants.

The backcountry of the southern English colonies, while initially fertile, was quickly exhausted because of primitive agricultural methods. Scots-Irish settlers moved westward, settling the south central and the southwestern areas of the United States. By 1860, the descendants of the Celtic immigrants of the eighteenth century had become the largest white ethnic group in the American South. Their way of life would define many things southern.

Cultural Contributions. The impact of an immigrant group in a new homeland is usually determined by the numbers of immigrants in relation to the size of the resident population. This made the impact of the Scots-Irish on American life enormous. If the number of 250,000 immigrants is accepted, then the Ulster Scots-Irish made up more than 10 percent of the white population of the American colonies in 1775. The percentage would be substantially higher if other Celtic groups were included in this figure. A high percentage of those immigrants settled along the frontier, especially in the South, where the population density of European immigrants was lowest. As the descendants of the original Scots-Irish settlers moved westward, their numbers gave them power. Andrew Jackson, the seventh president of the United States, and John C. Calhoun, South Carolina senator and vice president under Jackson, are but two examples of notable Scots-Irish Americans.

Andrew Jackson, military hero of the War of 1812 and seventh president of the United States, is one of many notable historical figures of Scots-Irish descent. (White House Historical Society)

The Scots-Irish American society that evolved in the eighteenth century was largely rural, agricultural, and individualistic. Ancestral folkways were adapted to the realities of the American frontier. Few immigrants from other European areas tended to settle in the South, and Scots-Irish isolation on the frontier of North America and throughout the Old South tended to preserve traditional cultural mores, habits, and values. The language of the Celtic areas of settlement is a distinctive dialect of English that still reflects speech patterns of a Celtic past. Other traditions and folkways such as farming practices, arts and crafts, music, and folk tales in the region continue to show their Celtic roots. In the South the extended family has always played an important role, a fact that may be related to the significance of home and family to the original Scots-Irish immigrants. A Fundamentalist attitude toward religion and rigid male attitudes regarding women are other inheritances from the Calvinist Presbyterianism that the Celts brought with them. The same heritage led to an ambivalent attitude toward education: a basic education was considered necessary for activities such as Bible reading, but higher education was seen as a luxury.

SUGGESTED READINGS. An excellent introduction to Ulster, as well as an important, if controversial, interpretation of the Scots-Irish in North America, can be found in David Hackett Fischer's *Albion's Seed: Four British Folkways in America* (1989). An overview of emigration to the British colonies in North America that includes significant data pertaining to the Scots-Irish is Bernard Bailyn's *The Peopling of British North America: An Introduction* (1986). Two excellent works that deal specifically with the Scots-Irish in North America are R. J. Dickson's *Ulster Emigration to Colonial America, 1719-1775* (1966) and James G. Leyburn's *The Scotch-Irish: A Social History* (1962). Grady McWhiney's *Cracker Culture: Celtic Ways in the Old South* (1988) offers insight into the cultural patterns of the Old South and their links with Celtic Britain.—*William S. Brockington, Jr.*

Scott v. Sandford (1857): Ruling by the U.S. Supreme Court (often called the "Dred Scott decision") that Congress had no authority to limit SLAVERY in federal territories. As the United States was expanding westward, the question of whether slavery would be permitted in the new territories was extremely important. If slavery were prohibited, slaveholding Southerners would not be able to migrate westward with their slaves. Northerners hoped to keep slavery out of the territories, both on moral grounds and because they wanted to increase their own power by expanding westward without competition from Southerners.

Dred Scott was a slave born in Virginia, the property of the Blow family. He was later sold to an army surgeon, Dr. John Emerson, who, from 1834 to 1838, worked both in Illinois, a free state, and in the Wisconsin Territory, a free territory. Scott accompanied him to these posts.

When Emerson died, his widow left Scott in St. Louis with Henry Blow, the son of his original owner. Blow was actively opposed to the extension of slavery. He encouraged Scott to file suit to be declared a free man on the grounds that he had become free when he entered Illinois and the Wisconsin Territory with Emerson and could not be made a slave again.

The suit, originally filed in 1846, eventually made its way to the U.S. Supreme Court in 1856. Finally, on March 6, 1857, the Court announced its ruling against Scott. The vote was seven-to-two in favor of the decision, with all five of the justices from slave states voting in favor.

Chief Justice Roger Taney of Maryland, a slave state, wrote that no slave or descendant of a slave could ever become an American citizen. Since Scott was not a citizen, he had no right to bring a suit in federal court. Taney also declared that the Missouri Compromise which declared Wisconsin Territory free was unconstitutional, because the document told citizens that they could not transport their own property—that is, their slaves—into federal territories. Further, it was up to each federal territory to make its own decision about whether or not to permit slavery.

The ruling widened the gulf between slavery and antislavery forces in the United States. Northerners were furious over the decision; they could not accept the allowance of slavery in the territories, and they found Taney's explanations indefensible. Ultimately, the strong feelings on both sides became one of the major factors leading to the Civil War.

Suggested Readings. The most complete analysis of the case is the Pulitzer Prize-winning *The Dred Scott Case: Its Significance in American Law and Politics* (1978) by Don E. Fehrenbacher; an abridged version is titled *Slavery, Law, and Politics: The Dred Scott Case in Historical Perspective* (1981). A book that tries to understand, but not to pardon, the Court's decision is Vincent C. Hopkins' *Dred Scott's Case* (1951). Finally, *Black Mondays: Worst Decisions of the Supreme Court* (1987) by Joel D. Joseph devotes an illustrated chapter to the case and includes an insightful introduction by Justice Thurgood Marshall.

Scottish Americans: Scotland, a kingdom now united with England, Wales, and Northern Ireland to form Great Britain, is located at the northern end of the main island of Britain. It is a small country of only 30,114 square miles, about the size of South Carolina. The Highlands, which comprise the northern and western two-thirds of the country, and which include thousands of wind-swept islands, cannot support a large population. Most of the arable land lies to the east and south in an area known as the Lowlands. The cool, cloudy climate has always made farming difficult.

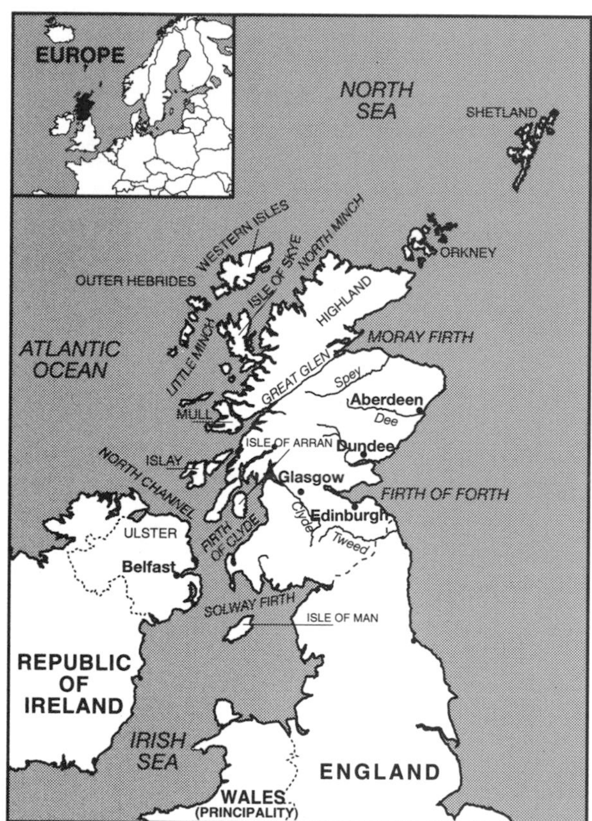

SCOTLAND (UK)

In the preindustrial era, the vast majority of Scots survived through subsistence farming. With inhospitable weather and terrain against them, Scots compounded their difficulties through deforestation and poor farming techniques, leading to extensive erosion. This, coupled with a population surge, resulted in famines occurring with alarming regularity by the late sixteenth century. Between 1500 and 1700, domestic instability compounded these economic problems. Few Scottish monarchs were able to control the Highlands, and Scottish nobles developed strong personal armies based on familial interrelationships, or clans. Noble factionalism, coupled with blood feuds and a violence-prone honor code, frequently resulted in interclan warfare and feuds. A combination of these factors prompted many Scots to seek their livelihood elsewhere, often within the British Isles or in Continental Europe.

The cultural legacy of the Highland Scots in the United States is kept alive by marching bagpipe and drum groups such as this one from western New York. (Don Franklin)

The eighteenth century was the most significant era for Scottish emigration to North America. The Scottish Rebellions of 1715 and 1745 led to the destruction, by British military and legislative action, of the traditional clan structure in the Highlands. The enclosure movement, an altered land-rent system, and the consolidation of farm holdings led to "the Clearances," during which entire communities of Scots were evicted to make way for new large farms. Thus, when settlement in North America became a viable alternative, and when pressures or crises necessitated a move, tens of thousands of Scots emigrated to North America.

Immigration. Immigration to North America resulted from various "push" factors prompting Scots to leave Scotland. The most frequently cited factor, the failure of the 1715 and the 1745 rebellions, was perhaps the least significant of all. While some Scots who had the misfortune of being on the losing side were expelled from Scotland, compulsory emigration was a small part of the Highland settlements of North America. The economic changes which were occurring throughout Scotland were of far greater significance and resulted in an estimated 50,000 Scots settling in the Appalachian mountains between the 1730's and the 1820's. Agricultural changes in Scotland meant a declining need not only for farm laborers but also for estate managers, known as tacksmen. In Highland society, when a tacksman who was unwilling to accept a lowering of status in Scotland decided to emigrate to North America, he would take his tenants with him.

While large numbers of Highland Scots settled in what is now Canada as well as along coastal areas of the thirteen Colonies, the most important settlements were in the backcountry of the southern colonies. Landing in Virginia or Pennsylvania, Scottish Highlanders made their way to the valleys of Appalachia. Backcountry Virginia, western North Carolina and South Carolina, and northern Georgia were settled by Highland Scots. Among the primary reasons were that the landscape was most similar to that which they had left, and there was free or cheap land available.

The earliest recorded mountain settlements date to the 1730's. For three decades the numbers were not substantial, perhaps because of the European and colonial wars of the period. At the end of the French and Indian War in 1763, there was a flood of Scottish immigrants. Accounts of cheap and fertile land by earlier settlers, the granting of land in North America to Scottish soldiers who had served during the wars, and the active recruiting of settlers for the frontier all stimulated emigration from Scotland. Between 1763 and the American Revolution an estimated 25,000 Scots, of whom perhaps 20,000 were Highlanders, came to North America. A famine in Scotland in 1783, coinciding with the end of hostilities between England and the colonies, led to the emigration of another 25,000 Highlanders over the following decade. After the French Revolution and the Napoleonic Wars, another wave of perhaps 10,000 Highlanders came from 1815 to 1825. Thereafter, emigration from the Highlands spread to areas within the British Empire as well as to the United States.

While the most visible Scottish emigrants to the Colonies and later the United States were the Highlanders, lowland Scots also emigrated in great numbers. It is very difficult, however, to quantify their numbers, since many went first to Ulster and from there across the Atlantic. According to the 1790 U.S. census, approximately 190,000, or about 15 percent, of Americans were of Scottish origin. A relatively high percentage of this figure should be considered Scots-Irish, however. The total number of Scots who emigrated to the United States from 1820 to 1970 is probably over 800,000. While these numbers are small compared to those of other immigrant groups, Scots have bequeathed to their chosen country a legacy far out of proportion to their numbers.

Cultural Contributions. The most visible area of Scottish cultural contribution is the southern Appalachian region. When Highlanders came to this area, they brought with them not only their meager human possessions but also the cultural baggage of their history. Since most of the Scottish Highlander migrations occurred before the Industrial Revolution in Great Britain, the Scots tended to be closer to their ancestral customs and habits than later, more urbanized generations. Moreover, as the vast majority of nineteenth century immigrants from other countries tended to avoid the South, the Scottish culture predominated in the Southern mountains. Together with the Scots-Irish, it was Scots who made up the bulk of the "plain folks" of the Southern backcountry. It was they who gave to the South language, culture, and values that today still largely define the word Southern.

While the Highland legacy to the American South is difficult to quantify and assess, it certainly would include speech patterns, social structure and propensities, economic tendencies, and cultural contributions. Appalachian speech patterns, often described as Elizabethan English, are actually Scottish in origin with added northern English, Welsh, and Ulster Irish elements. Mountain family names indicate their Scottish roots. The Scottish clan propensity to defend honor and individualism with violence and feuds was continued in the United States. The dour Calvinist Presbyterian Scots brought with them a legacy not only of religious fundamentalism but also of rigid male attitudes toward women. Finally, as would be expected, mountaineer music, folk tales, and arts and crafts betray their Scottish origins.

Although Appalachia is the most distinctively Scottish part of the United States, most Scottish emigrants, especially those who emigrated after the American Civil War, have blended into American society and contributed as Americans rather than as Scots. With their religion being an integral part of their life, and with a reading knowledge of the Bible being requisite for their faith, Scots were active both in the propagation of Presbyterianism as ministers and in the spread of learning as schoolteachers. Calvinism also stimulated Scots in economic endeavors, for their religion taught them that a godly person should strive for earthly success. Scottish names may be found in virtually every American industry, but certainly the most famous was that of Andrew Carnegie (1835-1919), who made his fortune in steel. One of the wealthiest men of his age, Carnegie not only provided Scots with work opportunities in his many businesses but also furthered education by providing free "Carnegie Libraries" throughout the United States and Scotland. Scots have contributed to the United States in virtually every facet of American life from government and the military to the arts. Finally, Scots have left their mark on the geography of the United States, as a survey of place names in an atlas will quickly demonstrate.

While Scots have generally been assimilated into the greater American culture, they have never forgotten their roots. The popularity of Scottish bagpipes, clans and tartans, and Highland games in Scottish American communities has never been greater, stimulated in part by the ethnic heritage revival of the 1970's.

SUGGESTED READINGS. In ethnic studies, Scots are frequently included with the Scots-Irish. An excellent introduction to Scottish emigration is presented in Gordon Donaldson's *The Scots Overseas* (1966). Ian C. C. Graham's *Colonists from Scotland: Emigration to North America, 1707-1783* (1956); John P. MacLean's *A Historical Account of the Settlements of Scotch Highlanders in America Prior to the Peace of 1783* (1978); and Duane Meyer's *The Highland Scots of North Carolina, 1732-1776* (1961) are three important studies of Scottish immigration patterns in North America. Three other works, while somewhat controversial, offer important reinterpretations and insights into the cultural accoutrements brought from Scotland to North America: Rodger Cunningham's *Apples on the Flood: The Southern Mountain Experience* (1987); David Hackett Fischer's *Albion's Seed: Four British Folkways ln America* (1989); and Grady McWhiney's *Cracker Culture: Celtic Ways in the Old South* (1988).
—*William S. Brockington, Jr.*

Scottsboro Nine: Group of nine AFRICAN AMERICANS accused of rape in a series of infamous trials in the

A courtroom scene from one of the series of trails held in Alabama in the 1930's to determine the fates of nine young African American men alleged to have raped two white women. (National Archives)

1930's. Because they were African Americans, the Scottsboro Nine suffered through one of the greatest miscarriages of justice in twentieth century American history.

On March 25, 1931, several male youths, at least nine blacks and five whites, and two Anglo girls were "hitching" an illegal ride on a freight train traveling from Chattanooga to Memphis, Tennessee. A racial fight ensued, and the African Americans threw the white boys off the train. After walking to Stevenson, the white youngsters aroused the town, saying that they had been assaulted and that the two white girls were still with the black youths aboard the train. After the Stevenson station master telegraphed ahead, authorities stopped the train at Paint Rock, Alabama, and arrested nine African Americans, who became famous as the Scottsboro "boys."

When the white girls claimed that the black youths had raped them, the nine African Americans were all charged with the crime. Tried within days, eight were given the death penalty, and one was sentenced to life in prison. Both the NATIONAL ASSOCIATION FOR THE ADVANCEMENT OF COLORED PEOPLE (NAACP) and the International Labor Defense (ILD), a Communist organization, intervened, each willing to appeal the case. The parents of the youths allowed the ILD to take the case, which the Communists turned into an international cause. Samuel Liebowitz of New York handled the appeal, in which the U.S. Supreme Court in 1932 ruled for a new trial because the defendants had not had adequate counsel in the original case. Next, one of the girls withdrew her testimony. It was later revealed that Paint Rock doctors who first examined the two girls had found evidence only of intercourse, not rape. Moreover, although one girl claimed to be cut and bleeding, such evidence was not substantiated by the doctor's examination.

A second trial resulted in another guilty verdict, although the presiding judge was so outraged that he condemned the proceedings and granted the defense a new trial. In November of 1933, a third trial also found the defendants guilty, but the Supreme Court again overturned the verdict in 1935 because African Americans had been excluded from the jury. Still, the local authorities showed a dogged determination to retry the case.

The Scottsboro Defense Committee was formed in December of 1935 as the ILD, the AMERICAN CIVIL LIBERTIES UNION, the NAACP, and several other groups came together to represent the defense. The noted lawyer Clarence Darrow was added to the defense team. In 1937 before the new trial, the prosecution began offering a series of "deals." The one accepted was to free four men and to prosecute the remaining five for assault. Although four men were, indeed, freed, the prosecution violated its word and tried the remaining five men for rape. One man received the death penalty, while the others received lengthy prison terms.

Although the defense got the death sentence commuted, further action came slowly. In 1943 two of the Scottsboro Nine received parole; in 1948 another was legally freed, while yet another escaped from prison, only to be arrested by the FBI in 1950. The last man, Andy Wright, was freed on June 9, 1950. The Scottsboro Nine lived through their ordeal, but their lives had been ruined by white RACISM in a country that prided itself on such values as freedom, democracy, and guaranteed rights for all.

SUGGESTED READINGS. A good, detailed account of the Scottsboro Nine is Don Carter's *Scottsboro: A Tragedy of the American South* (1969); a shorter account is found in Milton Meltzer and August Meier's *Time of Trial, Time of Hope: The Negro in America, 1919-1941* (1966). The case is briefly discussed in George Tindall's *The Emergence of the New South, 1913-1945* (1967) and John Hope Franklin and Alfred A. Moss, Jr.'s *From Slavery to Freedom* (1988).

Sedition Acts. *See* **Alien and Sedition Acts**

Segregation, desegregation, and integration: In U.S. history, Americans of Anglo-Saxon ancestry have used law and custom to keep various ethnic groups separate, such as American Indians, EASTERN EUROPEAN JEWS, Irish Catholics, and JAPANESE AMERICANS. The most complete and rigid segregation, however, has been practiced against AFRICAN AMERICANS, and the history of segregation and integration is basically a story of white-black relations.

Historically, there were two broad types of segregation in the United States. *De jure* (by right) segregation was mandated by city ordinance, state statute or federal law while *de facto* (actual) segregation was (and is) separation by custom and tradition.

Segregation was institutionalized in the South in a system called "Jim Crow." In their heyday in the middle of the twentieth century, JIM CROW LAWS separated whites and blacks in hotels, restaurants, theaters, schools, libraries, museums, parks, swimming pools, beaches, auditoriums, neighborhoods, public transportation, hospitals, and cemeteries. At its most absurd, the system sometimes called for separate Bibles for swearing witnesses in court and separate soft drink vending machines for the two races.

Segregated entrances such as this stairway for "colored" patrons at a Mississippi motion picture theater were a common sight in the decades before the Civil Rights movement of the 1950's and 1960's. (Library of Congress)

The 1950's and 1960's saw efforts to dismantle Jim Crow as a system, followed by efforts to eliminate various forms of discrimination that kept blacks and whites separate. When some African Americans saw the barriers of official segregation fall only to find themselves still the victims of RACISM and more subtle forms of discrimination, they began to lose faith in the ideal of integration. Thirty years after the lunch counter sit-ins of the 1960's, many African Americans wondered just how much improved their situation really was with desegregation. Most observers in the 1990's agree that the United States remains far from a fully integrated society, with people of color disproportionately represented among the poor and the imprisoned. The debate continues.

Segregation Before 1954. Prior to the CIVIL WAR, slavery kept southern blacks in a separate caste, and southern leaders believed segregation laws were largely unneeded. A few larger cities in the South passed laws keeping free blacks separate from the rest of society; in the North, some states passed laws forbidding the education of blacks and whites together, outlawing miscegenation, even limiting the right of blacks to enter the state. Immediately after the Civil War and emancipation of the slaves, southern state governments attempted to keep blacks in a separate caste by passing BLACK CODES, but Congress responded with the FOURTEENTH AMENDMENT and several civil rights acts that protected the rights of African Americans and their access to public places. Southern Republican governments during and just after RECONSTRUCTION preserved these black rights, in part because of the Fourteenth Amendment's promise of equality before the law for all citizens.

The United States Supreme Court soon eviscerated the federal civil rights laws. In the *Civil Rights Cases* (1883), the Court considered the situation of a number of black citizens who had been denied equal access to theaters, restaurants, and the like. The complainants argued that the Civil Rights Act of 1875 had forbidden racial segregation in public places. The Court, however, held that the Fourteenth Amendment forbid discrimination by states but not by individuals or companies. In other words, while blacks' civil rights might be protected, mere "social rights" would not be. In the landmark decision *Plessy v. Ferguson* (1896), the Court ruled that separate facilities for the two races, in this case on the railroads, were not unconstitutional as long as the facilities were equal in quality.

Coincident with the *Plessy v. Ferguson* "separate but equal" doctrine was a flood of new state and local laws aimed at separating the races in public places. Typically, lawmakers mandated segregation on streetcars and railroads first, then began expanding the list of places to be legally segregated. Championing such laws gave new popularity to such virulently racist politicians as James K. Vardaman in Mississippi and Jeff Davis in Arkansas. Meanwhile, few voices in the North raised concerns about the plight of southern blacks. The generation that had pushed abolition and black rights was giving way to a generation more interested in reconciliation between North and South. Northern blacks continued to be segregated, by law or custom, in housing, schools, and in most public places.

The National Association for the Advancement of Colored People (NAACP) was founded in 1909 to defend the rights of African Americans. Over the next four decades, elite black and white Americans quietly engaged in the organization's work of lobbying and litigation. While the lobbying produced little in the way of results, the NAACP was more successful before the U.S. Supreme Court. In *Buchanan v. Warley* (1917), for example, the Court overturned a city ordinance that segregated neighborhoods by race. Soon NAACP attorney Charles Houston began to attack separate facilities by proving that black facilities were not equal to the ones provided for whites. Houston hoped to make separate educational systems too expensive for southern state governments to maintain. Later, NAACP attorney Thurgood Marshall argued before the Court that separate facilities were inherently unequal, and the Court finally agreed in the case of *Brown v. Board of Education* (1954).

Brown v. Board of Education was certainly not the end of segregation in the schools. In setting a timetable for desegregation, the high court ruled that the process should move forward "with all deliberate speed," a vague phrase that, as it turned out, could be translated as "very slowly." Only after federal troops were deployed in the Little Rock crisis in Arkansas in 1957 was that city's Central High School integrated; nine black students attended for one year, under military guard, and then the school closed. Virginia, too, closed many of its schools rather than integrate. Mississippi made virtually no effort to comply with desegregation laws. Even six years after the *Brown* case only a tiny handful of black students were attending integrated schools in the deep South. Still, *Brown* was a landmark case that lay the groundwork for the eventual dismantling of *de jure* segregation.

Desegregation Since 1955. Although President Harry S Truman's desegregation of the armed forces in 1948 and the *Brown* case in 1954 provided some early victories, the movement for desegregation began in earnest in 1955 with the Montgomery bus boycott, which lasted more than a year. The boycott was initially sparked by an unplanned act of resistance—the refusal of a tired black woman named Rosa Parks to relinquish her seat on the bus to a white man. The protest soon became highly organized under the leadership of Martin Luther King, Jr., and others. The bus boycott ushered in the modern era of the Civil Rights movement in several ways. First, it was a mass movement, involving thousands of participants from many walks of life. Second, it was the first showcase for the nonviolent tactics that would be used by civil rights protesters. Finally, the boycott exploded white southerners' cherished myth that southern blacks preferred Jim Crow segregation to a more integrated society.

Similar protests followed in other cities. In the late 1950's, the tactic of the sit-in by African Americans seeking to integrate public places was pioneered in Oklahoma, Kansas, and Florida. These early sit-ins were largely successful but went unnoticed by the national press until a successful sit-in at lunch counters in Greensboro, North Carolina, in 1960. Typically, polite, well-dressed black college students sat down and tried to order lunch. When they were told that blacks would not be served, they sat and waited until closing time, then came back the next day, and persevered until they prevailed.

The protests in Montgomery, Greensboro, and elsewhere were effective for a number of reasons. Anyone could participate, so protest activity was no longer restricted to lawyers and other elites. Further, the idealistic young people who participated contrasted markedly with white hoodlums and toughs who harassed and sometimes attacked them, so the nation's sympathy was often with the protesters. Most important, the protests had economic costs for southern cities. Montgomery's city-owned bus service was brought to a standstill by the boycott, and shoppers began to stay away from downtown areas where sit-ins were occurring, waiting for calmer times. Cities that brutally suppressed peaceful protesters found it difficult to attract new industries because of the adverse publicity.

Protests against segregation in southern cities were anything but nonviolent. Although the civil rights activists themselves were almost invariably peaceful in the early 1960's, they evoked an angry and violent response from many southern whites. Civil rights leaders knew this violent response was likely; on several occasions they even admitted that their protest would succeed only if whites responded violently. The KU KLUX KLAN and other white hate groups sometimes attacked and even killed civil rights leaders; these killings often went unnoticed unless the leader killed was white. Attacks on white and black civil rights activists in Anniston, Birmingham, and Montgomery, Alabama, and in Neshoba County, Mississippi, helped fuel national support for new federal laws, most notably the CIVIL RIGHTS ACT OF 1964.

Southern whites believed that they were justified in their continuing defense of segregation. They pointed, first of all, to the South's traditional support of the states' rights ideology. Voter qualifications and pupil placement had always been state prerogatives, and white southerners recoiled at the efforts of Congress, the president, and the Supreme Court to interfere with their traditions and laws. They also asserted that segregation was a long-established tradition that could not

Lunch counter sit-ins such as this one in Jackson, Miss., often provoked vicious attacks from bystanders that helped generate sympathy for the cause of desegregation. (AP/Wide World Photos)

be abolished overnight. This point was debatable since full *de jure* segregation had not appeared until about 1900. Moreover, white southern leaders tended to blame "outside agitators" for civil rights protests; they argued that if the outsiders would only go home, peaceful and pleasant race relations would return immediately. For their part, southern black protesters denied that whites or Northerners were the driving force in the movement.

By 1963 and 1964 the Civil Rights movement was moving in new directions. Instead of emphasizing the fight against Jim Crow segregation, the new focus was on voting rights for blacks in the South. Leaders believed that blacks would never be treated as equals in southern society until they wielded more power, and the ballot was the clearest route to a more powerful voice. The federal VOTING RIGHTS ACT OF 1965 helped achieve a huge advance in the number of southern blacks registered to vote. For example, in Alabama, the number of blacks registered to vote increased 279 percent between 1960 and 1966.

In the mid- to late 1960's, many black activists downplayed the importance of desegregation. These leaders, typified by MALCOLM X and H. Rap BROWN, stressed that white society would always be a racist society; they often called for a new separatism and a new pride in African American heritage and achievement. Instead of sit-ins and voter drives, violent confrontations in northern cities became the rule, as activists promoted BLACK POWER through control of their own neighborhoods and schools, an end to police brutality and—in some cases—armed resistance. The assassination of Martin Luther King, Jr., in 1968 and the massive riots that followed symbolized the move-

African Americans in Albany, Ga., in 1962, pledge their support for a mass protest march on city hall to call for desegregation of all public facilities. (AP/Wide World Photos)

ment away from nonviolence.

Segregation and Integration in the late 1900's. For African Americans, the biggest revolution since 1960 has not been the war on segregation but the winning power of the ballot in southern states. By the 1990's southern state legislators, Congress members, and sheriffs must listen to their black constituents or face the very real possibility of defeat at the next election. Mississippi offers a clear example of this increase in black political power. In 1960, the state had only 22,000 black voters. Thirty years later, it had more African American office-holders than any state in the country.

"Nuisance segregation," such as that once found in restaurants and city parks, has largely disappeared in the United States, although many African Americans find that patterns of discrimination continue. Two very important types of segregation still exist, however. One is residential segregation. Though expressly forbidden by law, it has proved very durable in American society. Even middle-class and upper-class African Americans tend to be segregated in their own neighborhoods. Related to residential segregation is the segregation of public schools. Once again, this is not segregation by law but an outcome of school district lines being based on neighborhood lines, which are generally segregated. Suburban areas have a high percentage of the white population, while the inner city is often predominantly black. Suburban schools, then, tend to be overwhelmingly white, while the inner city schools have very few whites enrolled. Since the suburban counties have a much stronger tax base, whites generally attend better schools, as in the first half of the twentieth century, while blacks attend schools woefully underfunded. Thus, the legacy of segregation still impacts the daily lives of black and white Americans wherever they live, learn, or work, in spite of legal progress on the issue.

Suggested Readings. The standard history of southern segregation is C. Vann Woodward's *The Strange Career of Jim Crow* (3d rev. ed., 1974). An excellent collection of essays on individual southern cities is *Southern Businessmen and Desegregation* (1982), edited by Elizabeth Jacoway and David R. Colburn. For an insightful memoir by a rank and file participant in the Civil Rights movement, see Anne Moody's *Coming of Age in Mississippi* (1968). See also James E. Blackwell's *The Black Community: Diversity and Unity* (2d ed., 1985) and Manning Marable's *Race, Reform, and Rebellion* (1991).—*Stephen Cresswell*

Seminole Wars: Three conflicts between the Seminole Indians of Florida and the United States. The first Seminole War, 1817-1818, was started because U.S. authorities were trying to recapture runaway slaves hiding within the Seminole bands. While invading the area, U.S. military forces scattered the Seminole villagers and burned their towns. The second Seminole War, 1835-1842, began with the refusal of the Seminoles to leave the reservation that had been established for them. Wanting the land for their own, whites sought to displace the Seminoles under the authority of the Indian Removal

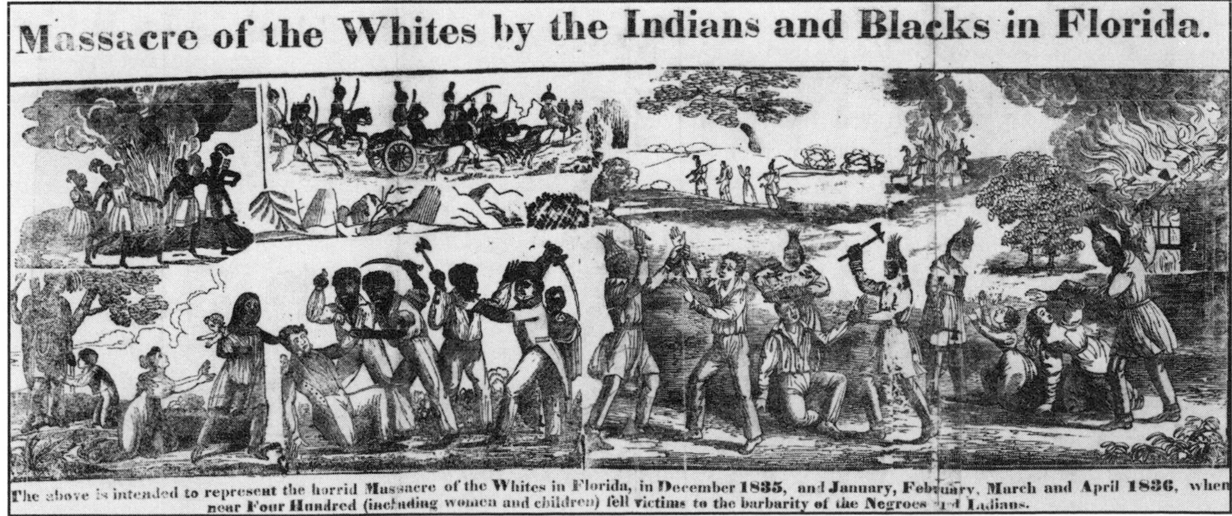

Viewed from the perspective of white Americans, this engraving depicts events that occurred during the second Seminole War in Florida. (Library of Congress)

ACT OF 1830, relocating them west of the Mississippi River. While hiding their families in the Everglades, Seminole warriors fought to defend their homeland; during the war, the U.S. government incurred damages and expenses estimated between 40 and 60 million dollars. The third and final Seminole War, 1855-1858, began while U.S. troops were tracking down the remaining Seminoles in Florida. It ended with the U.S. government paying indemnities to force the Seminoles to leave.

Seneca Falls Convention (1848): First large, public meeting to discuss and promote the rights of women. Five women including abolitionists Lucretia MOTT and Elizabeth Cady STANTON decided to call a meeting to discuss the rights denied to women. Approximately three hundred people met for two days in the Wesleyan Chapel in the small town of Seneca Falls in upstate New York. At the end of the convention, the women wrote a Declaration of Independence with a list of grievances and claims. Among the claims listed were the right to vote, the right to own and sell property, and the right to remain guardian of one's children. The location has been named a national historic monument.

Sephardic Jews: Jews of Spanish or Middle Eastern origin. The term Sephardic is derived from the Hebrew word *Sepharad* (Spain). For centuries, Sephardic Jews contributed to the culture and economy of Muslim Spain, bringing Jewish learning to unprecedented heights, only to be expelled in 1492 during the Spanish Inquisition. Some of the 100,000 Jews who left the Iberian Peninsula settled in The Netherlands, where their descendants subsequently became active in the Dutch and English colonies of the New World. These were the first Jews to settle in America, preceding the larger-scale immigrations of central and eastern European Jews. Several of them were part of the historic contingent of twenty-three Jews who came to New Amsterdam in 1654 by way of Brazil. Other expelled Spanish Jews and their descendants settled in the Ottoman and Sharifian empires of the Mediterranean basin, where they joined older Jewish communities.

The Sephardim emerged as a small, though influential, group in the thirteen colonies. They established themselves rapidly as a financially affluent stratum in Charleston, South Carolina; Savannah, Georgia; Newport, Rhode Island; and New York.

Sephardic immigration to America from the Ottoman and Sharifian empires gained momentum in the years immediately before and after World War I. These Mediterranean Sephardim constituted the most important reservoir of non-Ashkenazic Jewish immigrants to the United States. The collapse of the Ottoman Empire in 1917-1918 and the rise of nationalistic regimes raised fears among Ottoman Jews as to their future. Important centers such as Salonica and the island of Chios were seized by Greece; Rhodes was occupied by the Italians; and Monastir, a bustling Jewish center, became an integral part of Serbia and, later, Yugoslavia. To escape the possibility of pogroms and economic hardships, as many as 55,000-60,000 Sephardic Jews came to the United States between 1917 and 1924. This flow was severely curtailed by the IMMIGRATION ACT OF 1924.

New York City has the largest concentration of Sephardic Jews in the United States; here, members of the Yemenite Federation participate in a parade celebrating Israeli independence. (Odette Lupis)

The vast majority of American Sephardim arrived later than the large waves of eastern European Jews, who had already formed their own extensive network of communal organizations. The Sephardim set out to organize themselves into societies that were analogous to the Ashkenazi central/east European *landsmannschaften*, based on common birthplace. Though most of the new immigrants chose New York City as their home, others either landed directly in other American ports, such as Seattle, or relocated from New York to other areas. By the 1920's, small Sephardic communities existed along the eastern seaboard, each with its own character. For example, the Sephardic community of Boston is composed mostly of Syrian, Iraqi, Egyptian, North African, Iranian, Turkish, and Greek Jews, while the Sephardim of Hartford, Connecticut, are mainly from Turkey and Greece.

Midwestern Sephardim have been settled since the 1920's in Chicago, Indianapolis, Detroit, and Cincinnati. They include Egyptian, Turkish, and Yugoslavian Jews as well as those from the Dardanelles. Just as the GERMAN JEWS already settled in the United States initially treated the newer Russian/eastern European immigrants with contempt, the Sephardic Jews arriving in Chicago after 1908 were initially despised by both the German and RUSSIAN JEWS, who were not inclined to accept the Judeo-Spanish and Arabic-speaking Jews. Since the end of World War II, the Chicago Sephardic community has been divided into several congregations: the Sephardic congregation of the Portuguese Israelite Fraternity, the majority of whom originated in Iraq, Morocco, and Egypt; the Iran Hebrew congregation, established in 1960 in the northern suburb of Skokie; and the newer Moroccan congregation, immigrants who arrived in the 1970's.

In the West, the original Sephardim of Seattle arrived from the islands of Marmara and Rhodes. Later immigration brought North African Jews, especially Moroccans, into the Seattle Sephardic community, which was estimated at 2500 in the mid-1980's. The Sephardic community of Los Angeles began after 1900 with immigrants from Rhodes and Turkey. They organized themselves into congregations based primarily on their common native communities. It was only during the 1970's, with a general population boom in the area and new Jewish immigration, that the Los Angeles community expanded to include Middle Eastern/North African Jews as well as Israeli Sephardim and Iranians fleeing from Ayatollah Khomeini's Islamic republic. This period witnessed heightened levels of Sephardic communal consciousness and cultural activity in Southern California.

Whereas the Sephardic community of Los Angeles is approximately 150,000 strong (out of a total Jewish population of at least 600,000), the total proportion of the Sephardim is estimated at between 14 and 20 percent of the American Jewish population, or about 1,200,000.

SUGGESTED READINGS. For extensive accounts of the American Sephardim, see Joseph M. Papo's *Sephardim in Twentieth Century America* (1987); Marc D. Angel's "The Sephardim of the United States: An Exploratory Study," in *American Jewish Yearbook* (1973), edited by the American Jewish Committee; and Daniel J. Elazar's *The Other Jews: The Sephardim Today* (1989).

Sequoya (1776, Taskigi, Tenn.—Aug., 1843, Mexico): Half-blood CHEROKEE Indian renowned for creating a written Cherokee alphabet and persuading the Tribal Council to adopt it for general use. One of the most remarkable figures in nineteenth century American history, Sequoya exemplified how one person's ideas can shape a society's destiny.

His mother, Wurteh, was a chief's daughter and a half-blood Cherokee of the Pain clan. His father was probably Colonel Nathaniel Gist, a white officer in the American Revolution. Sequoya was also called Sogwill, derived from *Tsikwaya*, meaning Sparrow. After injuring his leg in a hunting accident and acquiring a limp, he became known as "Lame One."

Sequoya started life as a hunter and trader. Settling down in his twenties, he became a competent silversmith; through his work, he made friends with white people. Long before he could speak or write English, he was impressed by what he called the "talking leaves" of the whites. In 1809, he began experimenting with pictorial symbols like those used in Oriental languages to represent the sounds of Cherokee. Encountering problems with this, he turned to the English, Greek, and Hebrew alphabets in mission school books and devised a Cherokee syllabary of eighty-six simple characters.

In 1821 Sequoya organized a practical demonstration of his system before the Cherokee Tribal Council. He dispelled the doubts of the tribal leaders by showing how his young daughter could understand his written messages and answer him in writing. Three years later, the Bible was translated into Cherokee with the help and approval of missionaries. Sequoya traveled in Arkansas and Tennessee, sending letters to friends and fellow Cherokees to promote his Cherokee alphabet and writing system. Many of his people enthusiastically accepted the system and supported its universal teaching.

The tribal newspaper *Cherokee Phoenix and Indian Advocate* appeared in 1828. It flourished for seven years until it was banned by the Georgia State Legislature for demanding Cherokee land rights.

Sequoya garnered much respect for his contributions to Cherokee education and was granted a lifetime pension by the Tribal Council. He was a staunch land rights advocate and served as an Indian envoy in Washington, D.C., to represent Indian claims. Late in life he became interested in the fate of Cherokee migrant groups driven west during the American Revolution and organized a search for them. He traveled to the Mexican border with a group of followers and his son Tessee. The "lost" Cherokee proved elusive, however, and Sequoya developed dysentery and died.

Some of Sequoya's working documents can be seen at the Museum of the American Indian in New York City. A statue commemorating him was erected in the state of Oklahoma's Capitol Statuary Hall in the late 1940's. California's giant redwood trees were named after Sequoya, as was a national park of 604 square miles in central California.

SUGGESTED READINGS. For further reading see Frederick J. Dockstader's *Great North American Indians* (1977), Grant Foreman's *Sequoyah* (1938, reprinted in 1970), and George E. Foster's *Se-quo-yah, the American Cadmus and Modern Moses* (1979).

Serbian Americans: Serbs belong to the South Slavic family of nations, occupying the central regions of the Balkans, to which they immigrated in the sixth century from an area beyond the Carpathian Mountains. Serbs had their own state from the ninth to the middle of the fifteenth century, then they fell under the occupation of the Ottoman Empire until the beginning of the nineteenth century. From 1918 to 1989 they constituted the central part of Yugoslavia, together with the Croats, Slovenians, and Macedonians. They formed the new Yugoslavia in 1989 with the Montenegrins. Most Serbs belong to the Serbian Orthodox Church, a circumstance that has played a crucial role in the history not only of their homeland but of their American experience as well.

Waves of Immigration. The immigration of the Serbs to America started in the early 1800's. There have been five more or less distinct waves of immigration. The first lasted from 1815 to 1880, when the sailors and fishermen from the southern Adriatic coast arrived in search of adventure and a better life. Most Serbs flocked to coastal regions of the United States, such as California and Louisiana, because of their own coastal origin.

The second wave, between 1880 and 1914, saw a far greater number of immigrants, this time coming mainly from the interior areas controlled by the Austro-Hungarian Empire. These Serbs left their homes in Lika, Slavonia, and Vojvodina primarily for economic reasons and to escape serving in the army of a foreign ruler. Instead of going to the coast, they tried their luck in the industrial centers around Chicago, the mining regions of Pennsylvania, and as far north and west as Minnesota, Montana, Colorado, and Utah. Because most of these immigrants were semiliterate peasants with no knowledge of English, they tended to band together for self-protection and preservation of their cultural heritage. This was the period of the first fraternal organizations and Serbian Orthodox churches in America.

The events during and after World War I contributed to significant changes in Serbian immigration during the third wave between 1914 and 1941. Many American Serbs returned to their homeland to help "defeat three empires"—the Ottoman, Austrian, and German—as they romantically boasted. The fact that they fought on the same side as their adopted country made this endeavor both easier and more meaningful. Many of those who returned never resettled in the United States. Moreover, restrictions in the immigration laws after World War I significantly decreased Serbian immigration. The interwar period was a time of consolidation as thousands of earlier immigrants reared their children and developed increasing pride in being American.

This process was somewhat slowed down with the fourth wave of immigrants, after World War II, when thousands of Serbs who opposed the Communist takeover of Yugoslavia, and were therefore stranded in European refugee camps, were admitted to the United States. Most of them were well-educated, in striking contrast to the previous immigrants. They swelled the number of new Americans through INTERMARRIAGE. They reinforced the militant anti-Communism of the American Serbs. They also brought with them political divisions acquired in their native country.

The fifth wave, after 1965, consists of even better-educated immigrants—doctors, engineers, scientists, and other professionals. They generally do not mix with older immigrants. The tragic events in the Balkan wars of the early 1990's brought the two groups somewhat closer in their unanimous efforts to help their Serbian brethren back home, but there is still little religious or cultural interaction.

Population. The number of Americans of Serbian origin is difficult to establish. According to the 1970 census, 89,454 Americans declared themselves to be of Serbian origin, either Serbian-born or the child of at least one parent born in Serbia. When the third- and fourth-generation Americans with some Serbian background are added, the above number could easily be doubled or even tripled. Many American Serbs have Americanized their names, so the exact number of Americans of Serbian origin will probably never be fully ascertained. It can be assumed, therefore, that close to half a million Americans have some Serbian background. There are more than a hundred Serbian centers across the country, with prominent communities including Chicago and Pittsburgh, Pennsylvania.

Organizations. The two main institutions that have helped the American Serbs preserve their ethnic tradition are the Serbian Orthodox church and fraternal organizations. The church became an important factor as early as the second half of the nineteenth century; the church was able to reinforce Serbs' sense of belonging and to prevent a quick melting into a faceless mass. The fact that most Serbian immigrants prior to World War I were conservative peasants facilitated this process. Serbs struggled to establish their religious identity after being long under the jurisdiction of the Greek and Russian Orthodox churches.

The most painful episode in the history of the Serbian Orthodox Church in the United States was the schism that began in 1963 and lasted thirty years. The split came over ties with the mother church in Yugoslavia, which a number of church communities rejected as being dominated by the Communist rulers. This created bad blood among parishioners and led to bitter divisions in communities, and even in families, that were not healed until 1992.

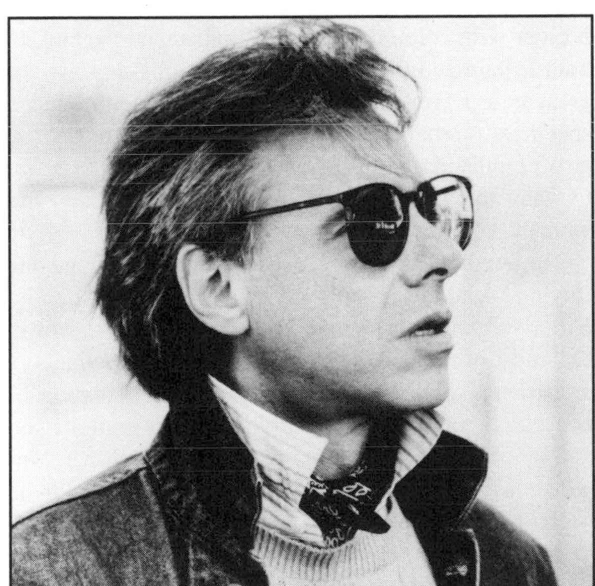

Film director, producer, and screenwriter Peter Bogdanovich is one of many distinguished Americans of Serbian descent. (Columbia Pictures)

Serbian immigrants began to establish fraternal organizations early, primarily to protect themselves but also to preserve ethnic identity. Out of many such groups that existed in the nineteenth century, the Serb National Federation emerged as the dominant association in 1901. Its official voice, *American Srbobran*, is the largest Serbian weekly newspaper, reporting on religious, social, and cultural activities. Of other organizations, four deserve to be singled out: Serb National Shield, organized primarily to defend Serbian political and national causes; Serbian Sisters Circle, a women's organization supporting church and social activities; Serbian Fraternal Aid, devoted to humanitarian aid for needy Serbs; and the North American Society for Serbian Studies, an academic association for the advancement of Serbian studies in North America.

Cultural Contributions. American Serbs have produced important scientists and inventors in several fields. The greatest among them is Nikola Tesla (1856-1943), the inventor of more than seven hundred patented devices in electronics. One of his inventions was the Tesla coil. His pioneering work in the fields of alternating current, wireless transmission of electricity, magnetic fields, and other projects led to his being nominated for the Nobel Prize in Physics; he refused the award because he would have had to share it with his scientific rival, Thomas Edison. Another famous physicist, Columbia University professor Michael Pupin (1858-1935), also worked in electronics, especially in telephone and telegraph systems and X rays. There are many other recognized Serbs in the academic world; among them are Michael B. Petrovich, the author of several books on Balkan history; Dimitrije Djordjevi, another historian and a member of the Serbian Academy of Sciences; and anthropologist Traian Stoianovich.

American Serbs have made valuable contributions to literature and other arts. Among the older writers, two distinguished poets, Jovan Dui and Rastko Petrovi, gained fame in Yugoslavia but spent a few years in America and wrote or published important works. Proka Jovki and Stephen Stepanchev are other poets active in the United States. Of the younger writers, Charles Simic has achieved the greatest success. A Pulitzer Prize winner, he ranks among the leading American poets today. Another successful writer is Steve Tesich, the author of plays, screenplays, and novels.

In other arts, actor Karl Malden has had a distinguished career, as has film director Peter Bogdanovich. Miodrag Mihailovi has achieved success with his paintings. Numerous American Serb musicians, such as the Popovitch brothers of Chicago, have helped preserve Serbian folk music and dancing, which remain an integral part of Serbian American cultural heritage.

Numerous Serbian Americans have served with distinction in Congress and local politics; in the military (including several Congressional Medal of Honor winners); in commerce and trade unions; and in all other sectors of American life. There have been many newspapers and journals devoted to Serbian affairs through the years. *American Srbobran* is the leading Serbian newspaper. *Sloboda*, the organ of Serb National Shield; *Serbian Studies*, the quarterly journal of the North American Society for Serbian Studies; and the independent bimonthly *Serb World U.S.A.* are among other leading publications. There are also numerous television and radio programs, most of them on the local level, broadcasting material for Serbian audiences.

SUGGESTED READINGS. Michael B. Petrovich and Joel Halpern wrote a brief but informative article, "Serbs," in the *Harvard Encyclopedia of American Ethnic Groups* (1980). Jerome Kissinger's *The Serbian Americans* (1990) traces the history, culture, emigration, and immigration of American Serbs and their acceptance as an ethnic group. Djuro Vrga's excellent study, *Changes and Socio-Religious Conflict in an Ethnic Minority Group: The Serbian Orthodox Church in America* (1975), discusses the schism. Branko M. Colakovic's *Yugoslav Migrations to America* (1973) has good statistics on the subject. An excellent bibliography by Robert P. Gakovich and Milan M. Radovich, *Serbs in the United States and Canada: A Comprehensive Bibliography* (1976), lists monographs and selected articles, both in Serbian and English.—*Vasa D. Mihailovich*

Sert, José Luis (July 1, 1902, Barcelona, Spain—Mar. 15, 1983, Barcelona, Spain): Spanish American architect and urban designer. Sert studied architecture in Barcelona before going to Paris in 1928 to work with the Swiss architect Le Corbusier. He came to the United States in 1939 and cofounded Town Planning Associates, which designed plans for established cities and new towns in Cuba, Colombia, Peru, Venezuela, and Brazil. Naturalized in 1951, Sert taught at Yale and Harvard, opening his own firm in 1955 in Cambridge, Massachusetts. Among his important designs are the U.S. Embassy in Baghdad, Iraq; Harvard's Holyoke Center; and the Foundation Maeght in St. Paul de Vence, France. Sert also authored *Can Our Cities Survive?* (1942) and *Antoní Gaudí* (1960).

Seton, Elizabeth Ann Bayley (Aug. 28, 1774, probably New York, N.Y.—Jan. 4, 1821, Emmitsburg, Md.): Founder of an American religious order and first American-born ROMAN CATHOLIC saint. In 1805 Seton converted to Catholicism, receiving much criticism from her Unitarian friends. In 1808 she started a school for Catholic girls in Baltimore, Maryland, to which was added the Sisters of Charity of St. Joseph, a house at Emmitsburg occupied by the teaching sisters. Mother Seton compiled textbooks, translated religious books, and helped the local poor. Because many of her students were from wealthy families who paid to keep the school going, her school is often considered the first American PAROCHIAL SCHOOL. She was canonized in 1975.

Settlement houses: Reformist organizations set up in poor urban neighborhoods to help immigrants and minorities with cultural adjustment and social welfare. In both Britain and the United States, the rapid growth of great industrial cities in the nineteenth century produced specifically urban problems for the new urban poor. It also stimulated a compassionate awareness and a desire to help among well-educated middle-class men and women.

These educated young people sought to mend the fraying social fabric—indeed, to knit society back into a more organic community—by placing themselves in the midst of the poor, living among them as neighbors and friends, and thereby overcoming the isolation of one class from another. They did so for complicated and often confused reasons: religious commitment, intellectual curiosity, dissatisfaction with other available social roles, empathy, paternalism, and even the need to confront their private demons. The success of their efforts is similarly ambiguous, in part because they never explicitly defined their original goals; nevertheless, the institutions that they created in the process—settlement houses—have continued to affect the lives

HULL HOUSE, WITH THE NEW CHILDREN'S BUILDING.

Hull House, founded by Jane Addams in Chicago in 1889, was devoted to improving the lives of the city's growing immigrant community. (Culver Pictures, Inc.)

drawn from the writings of English essayists Thomas Carlyle, John Ruskin, and William Morris, that stressed self-sacrifice and a more organic, less utilitarian concept of community. Most crucially, Americans who came of age in the 1880's were ready for something like the settlement idea. A generation of college-educated young women sought a social role in which they could use the skills they had learned for the good of society. Young men, imbued with the theology of the "social gospel," matched them in their fervent desire to make a difference.

of both the urban poor and the liberal middle class and to influence public policy.

Origins of the Settlement Movement. The English Victorians who founded the first settlement houses asserted that change must come through a recognition that all in society, rich and poor alike, are inextricably bound together. Nineteenth century church leaders such as Samuel Barnett initially saw a vigorous Christianity as the answer to urban problems, but his failure to win the souls of his parishioners in London's East End eventually led him toward "practicable socialism," a program of moderate public welfare. Still, he insisted that true reform must come "one by one." To this end, he recruited idealistic young men from the University of Oxford to live and teach with him in the slums. In 1884, they established a permanent "settlement"' in East London, named Toynbee Hall in memory of a charismatic young volunteer. Within five years of its founding, Toynbee Hall had inspired several Americans to found settlements of their own.

The settlement idea migrated to the United States so quickly for several reasons. Both countries faced similar problems of urbanization and industrialization. They also shared a common language of idealism,

Easier transatlantic travel enabled young Anglo Americans to gain both a new perspective on urban problems and insight into how they themselves could take action. At home, they might have turned a blind eye on the squalid conditions in which immigrants from Eastern and southern Europe lived, but seeing English people living in similar conditions shocked them. For the first time, some felt compelled to consider poverty as a broad social problem as well as a personal misfortune. Visits to Toynbee Hall showed them how they could personally become part of the solution.

Early Settlement Houses in the United States. Settlements quickly sprang up in several large U.S. cities. Following a three-month stay in London, Stanton Coit established the Neighborhood Guild on New York's Lower East Side in 1886 (the Guild became the University Settlement in 1891). In 1887, Vida Scudder organized alumnae of eastern women's colleges into the College Settlement Association, which opened the College Settlement in New York in 1889. That same year, Jane ADDAMS and Ellen Gates Starr, classmates from Rockford Female Seminary, opened Hull House on Chicago's Halsted Street. Two years later, Robert A.

Woods, after studying social movements in England, returned to Boston's South End as the first head resident of Andover House. Pittsburgh, Philadelphia, Cleveland, and other eastern and midwestern cities soon had settlements as well.

Settlement workers initially had few specific programs to implement. Instead they trusted that their own presence in poor neighborhoods would contribute to healing social divisions through reciprocal education. The early settlement workers usually had the grace to recognize how little they knew about the lives of their new neighbors. Though often frustrated, they were willing to let their neighbors' experiences set the agenda for confronting local problems. Nevertheless, settlement workers never lost faith in one educational gift that they had to offer—Americanization.

This singing class at Hull House helped improve immigrants' English skills while encouraging their musical talents. (Culver Pictures, Inc.)

Americanization: Assimilation, Anglo-Conformity, and Cultural Pluralism. Immigrants from southern and eastern Europe—the so-called new immigrants—made up a very large proportion of the urban population in U.S. cities in the late 1800's. Driven by economic and political disruption in their homelands, Italians, Greeks, Bohemians, Slovaks, Hungarians, Poles, Russians, and eastern European Jews were among the ethnic groups seeking better lives in America's cities. Many had come from rural areas and had limited urban or industrial skills; few spoke English. These factors left them easy prey for economic exploitation and ensured that many would live in the poorest urban neighborhoods. Their poverty, their unfamiliar languages and customs, and their apparent clannishness aroused fear and antagonism among native-born Americans and earlier immigrant groups.

While some Anglo Americans promoted the simplistic solution of excluding members of certain ethnic groups, settlement workers saw Americanizing the newcomers as a central part of their mission. The workers differed, however, in their vision of what this meant. Some, like Israel Zangwill, author of the drama *The Melting Pot* (1909), saw Americanization as the eventual obliteration of ethnic distinctions through INTERMARRIAGE and cultural blending, and the evolution of a new American ethnicity—virtual genetic ASSIMILATION. Others asserted that immigrants would be Americanized once they had shed their traditional customs, language, and ethnic identities in favor of well-established Anglo American norms—a notion which has since been called Anglo-conformity. Still others argued that American society already represented a broad range of cultural influences and that the defining quality of the American national identity was its very diversity. This view, known as CULTURAL PLURALISM, saw in differences the potential for a richer national identity; therefore, diversity should be nurtured, not suppressed.

Most settlement workers walked a fine line between Anglo-conformity and cultural pluralism, reflecting their ambivalent goals. On the one hand, they wanted to give their neighbors the skills to "make it" in the United States. To succeed in school, find better jobs, and live more comfortable lives, immigrants and their children would have to learn English, dress and act "like Americans," and, in short, conform to the cultural mainstream. On the other hand, they should not have to deny fundamental truths about themselves or destroy the community ties that sustained them. To accomplish these somewhat contradictory goals, settlement workers taught English while simultaneously stressing the "contributions" of the immigrants' native cultures; they encouraged American standards of housekeeping while organizing European-style festivals and encouraging traditional crafts. To a degree, they endorsed cultural pluralism as a way to ease the transition to Anglo-conformity. At the same time, many truly appreciated the richness of various European traditions, within limits. For example, they extolled the glories of Greek and Italian culture, which they knew from study of the classics and art, but had little to say about the legacy of eastern Europe; the only famous Russian pictured at Hull House was a contemporary, Leo Tolstoy.

For immigrants, this sort of Americanization had mixed appeal. Children and young people, eager to cast off old country ways, responded quite positively. Immigrant women likewise participated more enthusiastically than men, for several reasons. First, settlements drew women in with services that appealed to them, such as child care. Second, women often played dominant roles in many settlements; the reversal in gender power relations may have alienated immigrant men whose self-esteem was threatened by their lack of power in a new country. Third, settlement workers seriously underestimated immigrants' commitment to building and supporting their own community organizations, especially those based on religion; in these organizations, immigrant men found more satisfying roles than settlements could offer.

Overwhelmingly Protestant (more than 70 percent METHODIST, by one estimate), settlement workers had little understanding of the part Catholicism and Judaism played in immigrants' evolving American identity, both emotionally and socially. Strong, religion-based community organizations facilitated their members' integration into American society by means of their own schools, hospitals, and other institutions. These allowed newcomers to define an American identity on their own terms. Though settlement workers continued to offer what they could, immigrants by and large Americanized themselves.

Settlements and Reform. Settlement workers discovered other important work to do soon enough, however; the depression of the 1890's hit poor urban neighborhoods hard, and settlement workers quickly involved themselves in community relief as case workers, investigators, and advocates. They learned the extent of distress by doing detailed street-by-street, house-by-house neighborhood surveys, compiling copious statistics on housing, sanitation, health, education, unemployment, and work conditions.

In educating themselves about neighborhood needs, they acquired information that stimulated political change. Here the settlement workers' middle-class status and contacts were crucial, because they ensured easy access to policymakers such as state legislators, as well as to other influential citizens such as newspaper editors. For example, Hull House workers Julia Lathrop and Florence Kelley played a key role in passing Illinois's first factory act in 1893. Armed with stories and statistics gathered firsthand in their neighborhood, they successfully pressured the legislature for a law to regulate factory inspections, child labor, limited hours for women, and control of tenement sweatshops. Settlement workers thus helped to educate not only their immediate neighbors and themselves but also the wider society.

In the process, they nurtured the nascent progressive movement and participated in virtually every progressive reform for decades to come. They worked for municipal reform to clean up waste, fraud, and corruption in city government. With their growing awareness of the problems of industrialization, they opened their doors to labor unions while continuing to press for legislative solutions. They demanded improved sanitation and housing standards as a matter of public health and safety. When they learned that African Americans in northern cities lived and worked in conditions every bit as bad as those of their immigrant neighbors, they established settlements among them as well; settlement workers Mary White Ovington, Henry Moskowitz, Lillian Wald, and others were founding members of the NATIONAL ASSOCIATION FOR THE ADVANCEMENT OF COLORED PEOPLE (NAACP). They all but invented the field of youth work, from opening kindergartens to sponsoring playgrounds and youth clubs to demanding reform in the juvenile court and probation systems. During the presidential administrations of Woodrow Wilson and Franklin D. Roosevelt, they brought their knowledge and skills to federal agencies as well.

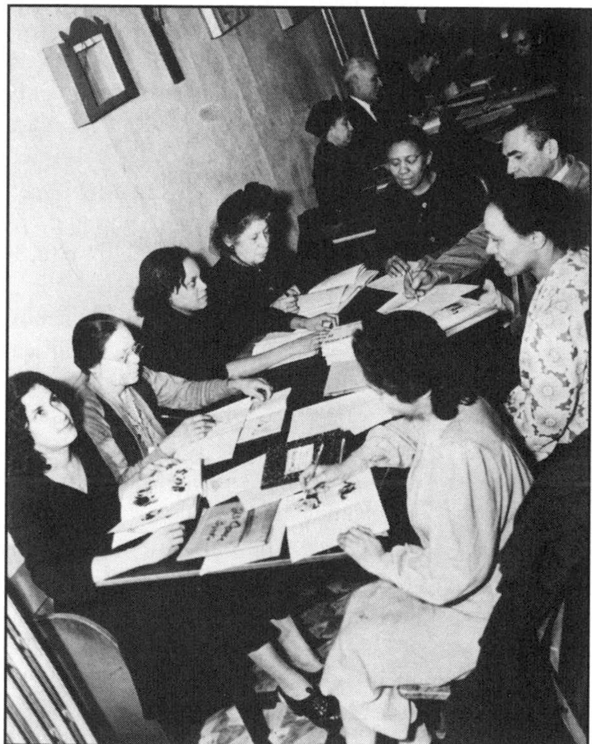

During the New Deal era, settlement houses such as this one in the Little Puerto Rico section of East Harlem continued to help immigrants find employment and learn English. (AP/Wide World Photos)

After World War I, settlement houses declined, continuing to provide local services but no longer pressing for reform. The development of NEW DEAL agencies and the Community Chest movement in the 1930's also diminished their prominence. Settlements have continued their work through the Great Society programs of the 1960's and into the 1990's, although with an increasingly professional staff. Their influence continues in the reforms they helped to enact in federal programs such as Volunteers in Service to America (VISTA), in the development of the SOCIAL WORK profession, and in the vision of the United States as a more compassionate society.

SUGGESTED READINGS. Judith Ann Trolander's *Settlement Houses and the Great Depression* (1975) and *Professionalism and Social Change: From the Settlement House Movement to Neighborhood Centers. 1886 to the Present* (1987) offer an introduction to the topic. Mina Carson's *Settlement Folk: Social Thought and the American Settlement Movement 1885-1930* (1990) emphasizes what the movement meant to its workers, while Rivka Shpak Lissak's *Pluralism and Progressives: Hull House and the New Immigrants, 1890-1919* (1989) provides a more critical assessment by examining the effect of settlements on particular immigrant groups. Finally, *One Hundred Years at Hull House* (1990), edited by Mary Lynn McCree Bryan and Allen F. Davis, vividly re-creates the settlement experience in the participants' own words and pictures.—*Susan Wladaver-Morgan*

Seventh-day Adventists: Health-conscious religious group that believes in the imminent second coming of Christ. The term "Seventh-day Adventist" came into official existence in 1860 when a general conference of Adventist Christians decided to adopt it as the appropriate designation for their growing religious organization. The theological roots of this American-born religion, however, are found in a longstanding Christian perspective known as premillennialism. Relying on biblical passages such as Mark 13 and the millennial prophecy in Revelation 20, premillennialists since the first century have preached a new "advent," or imminent second coming of Jesus, which will bring a final, catastrophic end to the present evil age and usher in a millennium (a thousand-year period) of peace, righteousness, and Christian goodness.

From colonial times, millennial thinking captured the religious imagination of Americans. The sense that God had led the peoples of Europe to a new continent to prepare a setting for the "new Advent" fueled the colonial effort. Later, the same belief offered purpose and promise to pioneers struggling to tame what they saw as an uncompromising wilderness.

The premillennial spirit began to take institutional

form in response to the adventist preaching of William Miller (1782-1849). Miller ignited a fire of premillennial excitement when, after studying the prophetic books of the Bible, he pronounced that Jesus would return sometime between March 21, 1843, and March 21, 1844. Millerites, as his followers were called, sold their belongings and donned "ascension robes" in preparation for the event. When Jesus did not materialize, Millerites disbanded to live with what they called the "Great Disappointment."

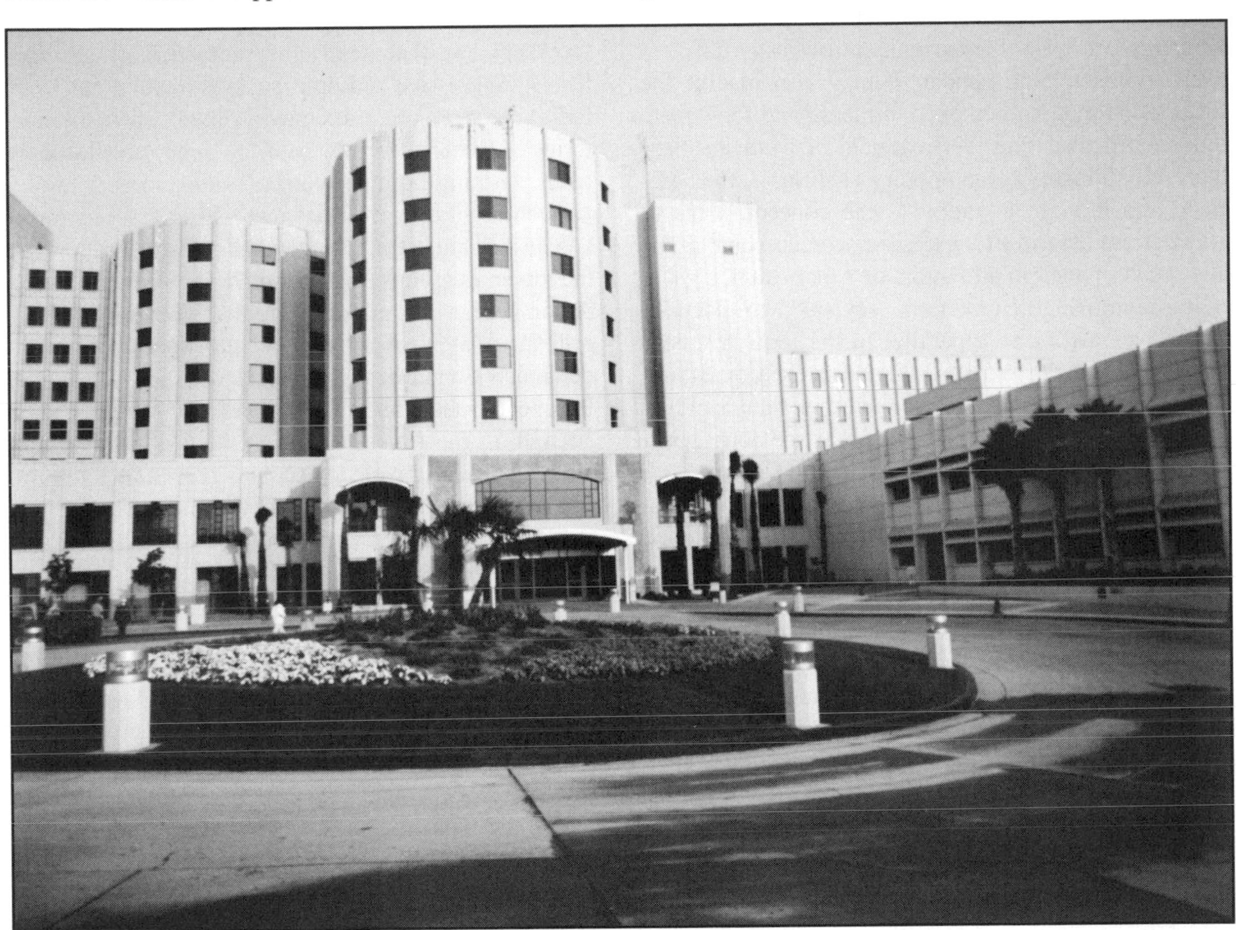

Loma Linda University Medical Center, one of several hospitals run by Seventh-day Adventists, has received media attention for its organ transplant programs. (Loma Linda University Medical Center)

Adventism might eventually have died out had it not been for the efforts of Ellen Gould White (1827-1915). The virtual founder of the modern health-minded cause of Seventh-day Adventism, White was a charismatic religious visionary who was able to rally the "disappointed" and give institutional form to premillenial yearnings. Inspired by more than two thousand visions, White articulated Adventist views on a wide range of topics, including Sabbatarianism (keeping the ancient Jewish Sabbath on Saturday, the seventh day, as the day for worship), dietary reform and health care; child rearing; education; world missions; and church organization. Somewhat paradoxically, given the group's focus on the next age, White initiated the building in this age of what would become an empire of Adventist religious, medical, and educational organizations found in Adventist enclaves such as Loma Linda, California, and Battle Creek, Michigan, as well as in other countries around the world. Because Adventism began as a sect (a religious organization that maintains a separate and exclusive identity apart from other institutions in society), the organization managed to escape much of the RACISM that infected more mainstream religious groups in American culture.

SUGGESTED READINGS. Two excellent historical accounts that chronicle the rise of the Adventist movement are *The Rise of Adventism* (1974), edited by Edwin Scott Gaustad, and *The Disappointed: Millerism and Millenarianism in the Nineteenth Century* (1987), edited by Ronald Numbers and Jonathan Butler. Also see Ronald Numbers' *Prophetess of Health, A Study of Ellen G. White* (1976). For students who would like to place Adventism in a broader historical context, see Martin Marty's *Pilgrims in Their Own Land* (1984).

Sexism: Attitudes or practices that discriminate against or disadvantage women because of their sex. Generally sexism implies a belief in the superiority of men over women or, at least, the assignment of vastly different social roles to each gender. It may also involve the assumption that women exist to please and serve men, thus tacitly accepting the treatment of women as less than fully human. Contemporary FEMINISM, which defined and brought attention to the concept, seeks to eradicate sexism in order to give women equal rights and greater power in all sectors of American life.

It is significant that the term "sexism" was first used in the late 1960's as a parallel to the term "RACISM" by activists in the WOMEN'S LIBERATION MOVEMENT. Like racism, sexism is deeply rooted in American history and society. Women of color bear the double burden of being victims of both racism and sexism. Both sexists and racists have justified the unequal treatment of women and minorities on the basis of presumed biological differences between men and women or between whites and nonwhites. Organized efforts to oppose these forms of discrimination began in the mid-1800's, culminating in the social change movements and legislative reforms of the 1960's and 1970's. One example of such reforms was AFFIRMATIVE ACTION programs to redress a history of discrimination against both minorities and women. This led to charges of REVERSE DISCRIMINATION as well as reverse sexism, in which white men were suddenly at a disadvantage. In spite of progress, many observers, including many sociologists, argue that RACISM and sexism have become institutionalized and are hard to eradicate.

Like racism, the charge of "sexism" in contemporary American life remains highly controversial. For example, most Americans would concede that it is sexist and wrong to pay women only a fraction of what men are paid for doing equal work. Yet fewer are comfortable with requiring (or allowing) women in the military to perform combat duty as part of equal treatment, and even fewer would completely agree with radical feminists that rape, pornography, or restrictions on abortion are also forms of sexism.

Sex Roles. Sexism is both a cause of and a product of beliefs about socially appropriate behavior for the sexes. Virtually all societies assign men and women different social roles, often with the man dominating the public sphere and the woman relegated to the private or domestic sphere. The origins of this pattern are complex and are the source of much debate, yet it appears that they lie in perceived biological differences. Because men are generally larger and more muscular, and because women are equipped to bear and nurse children, women came to be seen as the "weaker" sex that needs the protection of stronger males. Aggressive activities such as hunting and warfare were most often assigned to men, while the nurturing activities of child care, cooking, and in some cases, farming became women's domain.

Each culture evolved its own particular version of and justification for this general pattern, influencing the diverse groups that peopled the United States. Among American minority groups, women were subordinate to men's rule but were still expected to shoulder much of the heavy physical work. For example, European traders and missionaries were struck by the strength of the American Indian women they encountered, and their travelers' accounts perpetuated the image of the unfeminine, submissive squaw. The biblical story of Adam and Eve presented woman as evil and declared that as punishment for eating the forbidden apple, women would be condemned to bear children in pain and men would rule over them. This story was fundamental to the Calvinist notion of Original Sin, as believed by the Puritans, and became part of the Judeo-Christian heritage shared by many Americans.

Ancient views about the nature of and proper division of labor for the sexes persist in modern STEREOTYPES and behaviors. For example, as recently as the nineteenth century, prominent doctors and educators warned against female academies and colleges on the grounds that women were too delicate for extensive study. Devotion to one's nurturing role as wife and mother was the ideal for American middle- and upper-class white women from the age of industrialization to at least the 1960's. In the 1990's, women remain primarily responsible for the care of children, whether at home, in day care facilities, or in school, while men remain primarily responsible for the leadership of government, business, and war. Leaders of the men's movement and others have noted the price of sexism for men as well as women in men's lower life expectancy, high rates of stress, dangerous jobs,

232 LYNCHBURG BUSINESS DIRECTORY.
LYNCHBURG FEMALE SEMINARY,
Corner of 4th Street and 6th Alley,
LYNCHBURG,
M. & C. S. GORDON, PRINCIPALS.
This is one of the largest and most flourishing Institutions in this part of the State—can accommodate one hundred and fifty scholars.

Concerns about the health and mental endurance of women led some nineteenth century doctors and intellectuals to discourage parents from sending their daughters to colleges and female academies such as this one in Lynchburg, Va. (Library of Congress)

and death through war—as well as the restrictions on individual freedom that come from the need to conform to rigid sex roles.

Contemporary American feminists have challenged traditional sex roles of domesticity and passivity from the boardroom to the bedroom. Since the 1970's, it has become increasingly acceptable for women to express opinions, make decisions, and take assertive action—in short, to behave as independent individuals. They have entered nontraditional occupations as mechanics and physicians while pioneering new domestic arrangements, such as single motherhood or open LESBIAN relationships, and portraying their strength and individuality through the arts and literature. Most important, women have begun to rear their daughters to take a greater role in society and to live economically independent lives.

Historical Background. Until the mid-1900's, sexism was unquestioned as the norm for the treatment of women in most social arenas. Abigail Adams' plea to her husband, colonial politician John Adams, to "remember the ladies" in framing the laws of the new republic, went unheeded. The U.S. CONSTITUTION was essentially a document concerning the rights of white males. A handful of individual women broke precedent by getting an education, entering the professions, gaining recognition for their talents, or serving in public office before the late 1800's, but these opportunities were not routinely available to all, and especially not to women of color.

Most early progress on women's rights related only to white women. After the AMERICAN REVOLUTION, for example, they were finally allowed to claim full inheritance of their husbands' property; not until the 1860's, however, would they be allowed to keep their wages or buy property in their own name. American women of every ethnicity, except the most privileged, were expected to work hard and bear many children, but no group was more exploited than were enslaved African American women. They lacked the rights of marriage and motherhood as well as citizenship and were commonly sexually abused by their white masters.

Gradually, more women began to work outside the home because of economic necessity. Young rural white women flocked to New England textile mills in the 1820's, later followed by waves of female immigrant workers. Female seminaries were founded beginning in the 1830's to train women as schoolteachers, a profession previously dominated by men. As women became better educated and had some experience of the working world, they became increasingly concerned with improving American society.

After the GREAT AWAKENING of the 1700's, women began to volunteer in church and charity work. This, along with their involvement in the later ABOLITIONIST MOVEMENT and temperance societies, became an important training ground for gaining political experience and organizational skills. As women encountered frustration in their social welfare and reform efforts, they realized that they needed to be able to vote in order to influence public life. For example, when attending the World Anti-Slavery Society Convention in London in 1840, Elizabeth Cady STANTON was appalled to find that women delegates were required to sit behind curtains and were not allowed to speak. The cause of abolishing slavery was soon wedded to the campaign for women's suffrage. The GRIMKÉ sisters astonished American society with the rare act of speaking in public on both issues, as did the eloquent African American woman Sojourner TRUTH. Her famous "Ain't I a Woman" speech in 1851 testified to women's strength and neglected potential.

In 1848, the Woman's Declaration of Independence was issued at the SENECA FALLS CONVENTION in New York, officially marking the start of the SUFFRAGE MOVEMENT. Slavery was abolished in 1865, and black men were given the right to vote in 1870. Yet it would take seventy-two years of organizing, lobbying, and protesting to achieve passage of the NINETEENTH AMENDMENT guaranteeing women the right to vote in 1920.

The women's suffrage movement protested for more than seventy years before passage of the Nineteenth Amendment in 1920 guaranteed women the right to vote. (AP/Wide World Photos)

By 1900, American women's lives were greatly transformed. Women's colleges had opened in the 1870's and historically African American colleges saw a boom during the Reconstruction period; by 1900, about half of all women were getting college educations. Black women could be mistresses of their own homes but were struggling to earn a living to supplement the meager wages of their husbands. About twice as many minority women worked outside the home (40 percent) as did white women (20 percent), the majority in poorly paid jobs such as laundry work, factory work, domestic service, and agriculture. White women were increasingly involved in service occupations such as nursing, which had opened to women with the Civil War, but tended to work only as long as they were single. Landmarks for women's progress in the early 1900's were the establishment of settlement houses by Jane ADDAMS and other reformers, the campaign for liberalized birth control by Margaret SANGER, and the election of Jeanette RANKIN to Congress.

In the 1920's, more women moved into the work force, most notably those single women who lived seemingly carefree, independent lives as FLAPPERS. During the GREAT DEPRESSION, however, twenty-six states passed laws banning the hiring of women. This policy was based on the belief that when jobs were scarce they should go to men, who needed to support their families. Such policies represented a setback for thousands of women. At the same time, the national achievements of First Lady Eleanor ROOSEVELT and Secretary of Labor Frances PERKINS were an inspiration to women who hoped to make a contribution to society.

Women took part in World War II in unprecedented numbers in newly created women's divisions of military units. Thirty-six percent of all women joined the civilian work force, including minority women who could take advantage of new opportunities. Their jobs in the defense and other industries were often nontraditional, highly skilled, and well-paid. Women's work in wartime was portrayed in the media as a form of patriotic service. It stopped abruptly, however, after the return of servicemen in 1945. Women were urged to go home, have children, and fulfill themselves with advanced methods of homemaking.

The contemporary feminist movement that arose in the 1960's was largely a response to the closing of options for women during the conformist 1950's. With the growth of suburbs and the rise of new technologies for housework, housewives were more isolated than ever before. Women's magazines and other media of the day encouraged them to conform to the ideal of woman as the attractive, homemaking, childbearing helpmate of the breadwinning male. This situation created tension and unhappiness for many well-educated women, who believed their talents and abilities were being wasted in the domestic sphere.

The Women's Movement. Betty FRIEDAN wrote *The Feminine Mystique* in 1963 as a critique of domestic expectations for women and a call to the struggle for equal rights. Two years before, President Kennedy had created the Commission on the Status of Women. Through the 1950's and 1960's, many black and white women had become involved in the CIVIL RIGHTS MOVEMENT. Just as the abolitionist movement in the mid-1800's had given women the tools to demand their own rights, so, too, the various rights movements of the period helped give birth to the women's liberation movement. Some female activists became disillusioned when their work for peace or civil rights went unacknowledged by male leaders. Some of them, mostly white women, banded together to form organizations such as the NATIONAL ORGANIZATION FOR WOMEN (NOW) in 1966; many women of color, however, opted to focus their attention on liberation for their people first, their sex second.

The CIVIL RIGHTS ACT OF 1964, the nation's most sweeping piece of CIVIL RIGHTS LEGISLATION, included for the first time a provision in Title VII barring discrimination in employment on the basis of sex. NOW pressed government agencies to enforce this with policies such as a ban on sex-specific job advertisements, which had been standard practice until that time. The election of Shirley CHISHOLM, the first black woman in Congress, in 1968 was a breakthrough for both the civil rights and women's movements.

The 1970's were a watershed decade both in strides made to overcome sexism and in the promoting of greater public awareness of sexism by the women's movement. In 1972, TITLE IX OF THE EDUCATION AMENDMENTS outlawed sex discrimination in the schools, leading to changes such as the creation or expansion of girls' and women's athletic programs. Four years later, military academies began to accept women. Clerical workers formed the organization 9 TO 5 to push for better pay and working conditions in traditional female occupations, while flight attendants filed sex discrimination suits regarding unfair expectations for female employees. An amendment to Title VII in 1978 banned employment discrimination against pregnant women. In 1970, the EPISCOPAL church began to ordain women, followed by the JEWISH REFORM movement and other sects and religions. In 1973, the Supreme Court legalized ABORTION in *ROE V. WADE*. This decision, combined with their lifting of the eighty-six-year ban on contraceptives in 1965 and scientific advances in methods of birth control, opened new options to American women of every background. Women-staffed women's health clinics were established as an alternative to the patronizing practices of the male-dominated medical profession, and attention was brought to female diseases such as anorexia nervosa, brought on by sexist STEREOTYPES about women's bodies. Thousands of women met in consciousness-raising groups to analyze the system of male dominance that they felt had historically oppressed women and to discuss their newfound identities and dilemmas as liberated, independent women. They found their voice in *Ms.* MAGAZINE, founded by Gloria STEINEM in 1972, which made journalism history by refusing to accept advertising that was exploitive of women.

In 1971, Congress passed an EQUAL RIGHTS AMENDMENT (ERA), which stated, "Equality of rights under the law shall not be denied or abridged by the United States or any state on account of sex." This amendment, first proposed in 1923, had taken nearly fifty years to win congressional approval. Feminists mounted an aggressive campaign to convince a majority of state legislatures to ratify the amendment, which they believed was necessary to strengthen protections for women's rights beyond just the workplace. At the same time, Phyllis SCHLAFLY and others organized STOP-ERA groups in every state. ERA opponents charged that the amendment would actually worsen life for women by removing special protections, as in mixed-sex public bathrooms, a military draft for women, and an end to child support by divorced fathers. While many of their charges were mere alarmism, the anti-ERA groups rallied conservative concern about fundamental changes in sex roles in American life. ERA supporters failed to meet the 1982 deadline for state ratification, and the amendment was abandoned.

Women's groups were greatly disappointed by the defeat and by what seemed like back-stepping on abortion rights and social legislation during the Reagan and Bush Administrations in the 1980's. The women's movement continued to press for the opening of nontraditional jobs to women and the smashing of the glass ceiling that prevented their promotion to top positions. Americans became used to seeing women police officers, college presidents, and corporate vice-presidents. At the same time, the NATIONAL WOMEN'S POLITICAL CAUCUS and other groups promoted women candidates for public office and lobbied on "women's issues" in continuing efforts to combat sexism. In 1984, Geraldine FERRARO became the first woman to run for a top national political office as a major party candidate for vice president. Yet women were still grossly underrepresented in politics and dramatically underpaid in the workplace. Although discrimination laws and affirmative action laws were in place, wages tended to go down when women dominated a profession (as in the history of secretarial wages) and up when men dominated (as in elementary school principal positions after the 1950's). Efforts by some states to set standards for equal pay based on comparable worth proved difficult to enforce or defend in court.

From its inception, minority women had criticized the women's movement as a white middle-class women's crusade. They felt excluded from the leadership of organizations such as NOW and believed that the priorities of most women's groups neglected the needs of women in their communities. While some women of color persisted in efforts to be included in mainstream feminist groups, others formed their own organizations. These groups explored their own avenues for addressing sexism in different historical, cultural, and socioeconomic contexts, such as the issue of African American women becoming the economic backbone of families in a society that denied full manhood to black males. Like white women activists, many women of color found their springboard to leadership in civil rights work. For example, Sara Winnemucca Hopkins became prominent in the INDIAN RIGHTS MOVEMENT, and Dolores HUERTA became an inspiration for supporters of the UNITED FARM WORKERS UNION and the CHICANO MOVEMENT. The confluence of the ethnic heritage revival and the women's movement in the 1970's and 1980's led some minority women to seek out the stories of their mothers and grandmothers as seen in Asian oral history projects or the rediscovery of early twentieth century African American writer and anthropologist Zora Neale HURSTON.

By the late 1980's and early 1990's, the women's movement was a less vocal force in American society. Many of its assumptions about combatting sexism had become incorporated into law, education, employment, family life, and even language. For example, the usage of the title "Ms." rather than "Mrs." or "Miss" had become accepted on government forms, and child rearing manuals and other publications routinely alternated the use of the masculine and feminine pronouns. An entire generation, the children of the baby-boomers, was growing up with seemingly more equal treatment and more equal prospects—again with the exception of members of ethnic and racial minority groups.

Sexism in the 1990's. Like racism, sexism has been lessened in American life but is far from entirely eliminated. It is institutionalized, some believe, into the basic structures of society, from how parents raise children to how employers treat workers. For example, SEXUAL HARASSMENT of women has long been accepted practice in the workplace, as the stories of many women in the aftermath of Anita HILL's 1991 congressional testimony revealed; more governments, businesses, and schools have since drawn up guidelines to punish such behavior. A brief review of statistics suggests the persistence of the unequal position of American women, and the ways in which policy and institutions have not kept pace with the changes in women's lives.

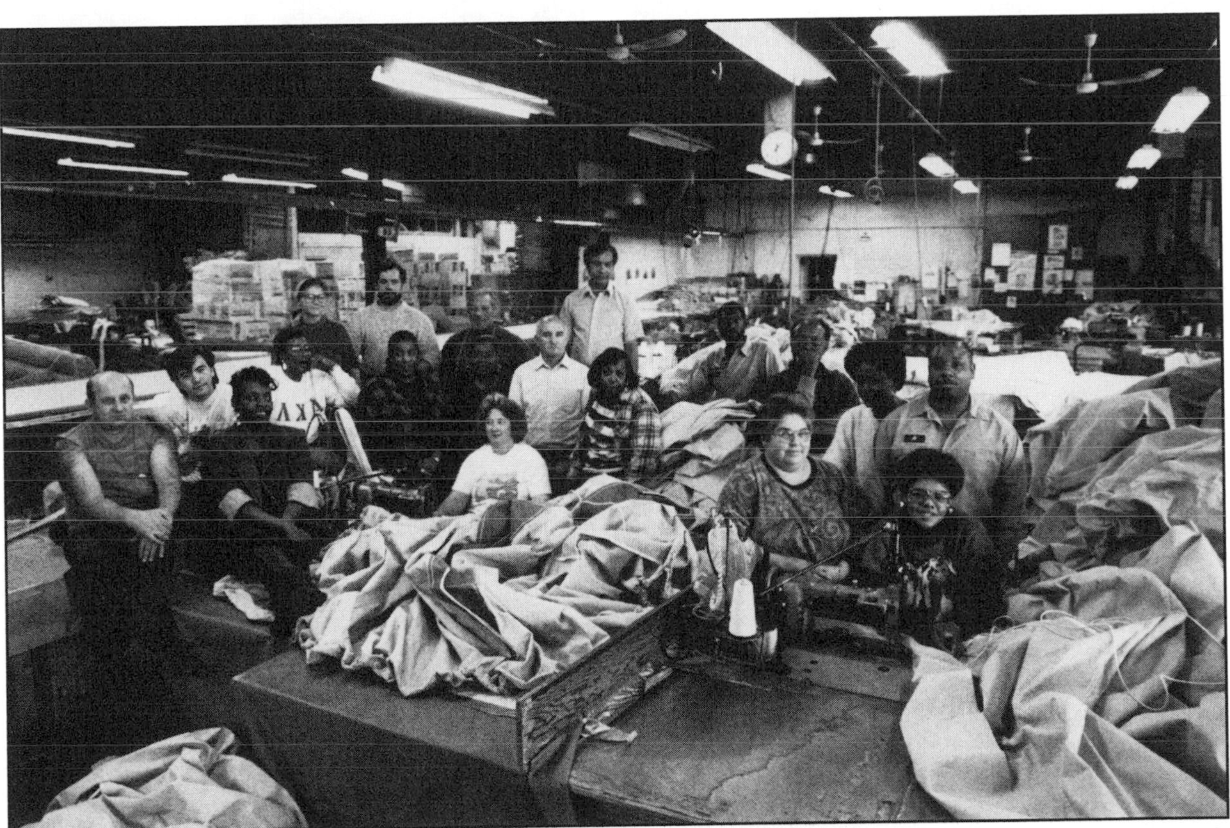

Despite their entry into a greater variety of industrial jobs, as at this canvas manufacturing plant, women still earned only seventy cents for every dollar earned by men in 1990. (Jim West)

In 1990, women constituted 45 percent of the American work force, nearly their percentage in the working-age population. In 1960, fewer white women worked (41 percent) than nonwhite women (54 percent), but by 1990, about 57 percent of both black and white women worked, compared to 52 percent of Latinas. The proportion of divorced women and single mothers has risen steadily since the 1970's, yet women's role as primary or active secondary earners has not won them fair pay and work opportunities.

In 1970, women earned only fifty-eight cents for every dollar earned by men; they still earned only seventy cents to men's dollar in 1990. According to the Bureau of the Census, only part of this 25 to 30 percent wage gap can be explained by differences in education, work experience, or occupational segregation (the channeling of women into traditional female jobs and denial of entry into nontraditional jobs). More than half of all working women in the early 1990's still worked in traditional female occupations such as retail clerks, food servers, child care workers, teachers, and nurses, with more than one-fourth of working women in administrative support (secretarial) jobs. Latinas on average earned 21 percent less than all other women, perhaps because of their consistently lower educational attainment. Yet according to census studies, American women with college degrees generally earned the same as white male high school graduates, while women high school graduates on average earned the same as men with elementary level educations; minority women earned consistently less at all levels of education. Studies of the country's largest corporations found that women and minorities made up less than 5 percent of top managerial positions. Women owned 30 percent of all businesses in the United States in 1987, but brought in only 14 percent of the receipts—partly because of the relative newness of such businesses, partly because they tend to be concentrated in the service and retail sectors where women are most experienced. It would appear that slow progress in closing the wage gap has much to do with continuing patterns of sex discrimination.

The wage gap, along with rising rates of divorce and single motherhood, as well as cuts in social programs, contributed to the feminization of POVERTY that began to receive media and political attention in the 1980's. It became apparent that women and children made up the majority of the poor in the United States, especially among minorities and single mothers. Female-headed households increased dramatically in number since the 1960's, making up half of all poor families in 1990. Whereas such households represented less than half of all poor white and Latino families, they made up 75 percent of all poor African American families.

Lack of affordable child care that would permit single mothers to work also compounds the problem of poverty among these families. Mothers worked in 52 percent of all American families with children under age six and in 60 percent of families with children under eighteen in 1990. Yet quality child care is still hard to find and too expensive for many families, and child care workers (mostly women) are among the poorest paid workers in the nation. Some employers began providing subsidized child care on site for their employees' children or making innovative arrangements such as job sharing to permit mothers of young children to work part-time, but in general, American society has made few accommodations to the fact that most women work. Women also continue to do the bulk of the housework, whether or not they work outside the home and in spite of more help from men.

If it is true that sexism begins with how children are raised, the schools do not present a promising picture. Eighty percent of elementary school teachers, but only 12 percent of the principals, are women. Studies show that teachers consistently call on boys more often in the classroom, and that girls are often discouraged from mathematical or scientific pursuits; girls still score about fifty points lower than boys on college entrance examinations in math. School and

Studies have shown that women and minorities hold less than 5 percent of top managerial positions in large American corporations. Here, an African American supervisor explains a task to her secretary at a New York investment bank. (Hazel Hankin)

college athletic budgets for females remain about 20 percent that of athletic budgets for males. Although women are slightly more likely to graduate from high school and college, they are less likely to pursue graduate and professional degrees. White women make up only 27 percent of American college and university faculties, black women less than 3 percent. One hopeful sign is the burgeoning field of women's history and the spread of WOMEN'S STUDIES PROGRAMS. The more students and scholars know about women's place in history, psychological sex differences, and related topics, the more they will be prepared to understand and oppose sexism.

SUGGESTED READINGS. An introduction to the history of sexism for teenage readers is Trudy Hanmer's *Taking a Stand Against Sexism and Sex Discrimination* (1990). Betty Friedan's classic work is *The Feminine Mystique* (1963), followed by her assessment of the contemporary women's movement in *The Second Stage* (1981). Susan Faludi's *Backlash: The Undeclared War Against American Women* (1991) updates the status of American women to the early 1990's. For minority perspectives, see Bell Hooks's *Ain't I A Woman: Black Women and Feminism* (1981) and Paula Gunn Allen's *The Sacred Hoop: Recovering the Feminine in American Indian Traditions* (1986). *Women's Changing Role* (1992), edited by Alison Landes et al., is a useful compilation of statistics. For a feminist man's critique of the women's movement's view of feminism, see Warren Farrell's *The Myth of Male Power* (1993).—*Susan Auerbach*

Sexual harassment: Unwanted, inappropriate sexual attention. It takes many forms and can include sexual comments, jokes, looks and gestures, and sexual assault.

Sexual harassment is a form of sex discrimination that is illegal under Title VII of the CIVIL RIGHTS ACT OF 1964 for employees and under TITLE IX OF THE EDUCATION AMENDMENTS of 1972 for students. Unwelcome sexual advances, requests for sexual activity, and verbal or physical conduct of a sexual nature are considered harassment if under certain conditions. These prevail when submission to this behavior is made either explicitly or implicitly a term or condition of an individual's employment or academic standing; acceptance or rejection of the behavior is used as the basis for employment decisions or decisions affecting the individual's academic life; or the behavior interferes unreasonably with an individual's work or academic performance or creates an intimidating, hostile, or offensive working or learning environment. Since these guidelines include not only the occurrence of unwanted behavior but also the impact that the behavior has on the work or academic environment, the creation of a hostile climate may be considered a form of sexual harassment.

Victims and Harassers. Typically, the victims of sexual harassment are women, while the harassers are men. While men can be sexually harassed by women, and men and women can be harassed by members of the same sex, these pairings are less common. Although harassment often takes place between individuals with different levels of power (supervisor/supervisee, teacher/student), an increasing amount of peer-to-peer harassment (such as student/student, colleague/colleague) is being reported. Some of the most serious forms of peer harassment involve groups of men harassing individual women.

Sexual harassment is considered an assertion of hostility or power expressed in a sexual manner. Harassment is not considered a sexually motivated act; rather, sexuality is used to control the actions of others. Research shows that it is women with lower status or power who are more likely to be the victims of harassment. Lower status women include those who are of relatively young or old age; those who hold a marginal position in an organization; and those who are divorced, single, LESBIAN, or members of ethnic minorities.

There is some evidence that women of color are

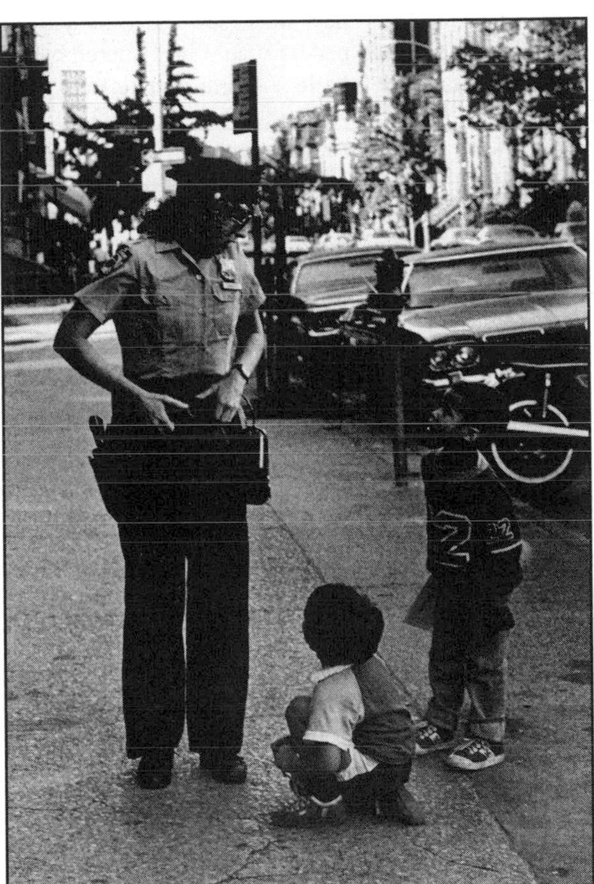

Women in male-dominated professions, such as police work, have been found to report a greater incidence of sexual harassment on the job. (Hazel Hankin)

among the most vulnerable to sexual harassment. Women of color typically possess little status and power in work and academic settings. In addition, racial and gender STEREOTYPES and myths—that ethnic minority women are sexy and exotic, for example—abound in American society. Thus, there appears to be a convergence of RACISM and SEXISM—double discrimination—in the way some men view and interact with women of color.

Studies of women in work and academic settings have revealed that sexual harassment is a serious and common problem. A variety of surveys in the late 1970's and 1980's revealed that between 20 to 30 percent of women students experienced sexual harassment. Both a 1981 and a 1988 nationwide survey of sexual harassment in the federal workplace revealed that about 40 percent of the respondents had been harassed.

Harassers tend to interpret their behavior differently than the victims. They may see their actions as friendly, or think the person would be flattered by the attention. Some men believe that a woman says "no" but actually means "yes"; therefore, her refusal may not always be accepted. Research on faculty men reported that they were less likely than women to define sexual harassment as including jokes, teasing of a sexual nature, and unwanted suggestive looks. Men at work were likely to feel flattered by sexual overtures from women, while women facing the same behavior from men were often threatened or offended.

Legal History and Implications. The term "sexual harassment" was developed in the mid-1970's. Before that time sex discrimination was seen as a personal problem and therefore was not given much legal attention. Many states now have laws or regulations that make sexual harassment illegal. In addition, the EQUAL EMPLOYMENT OPPORTUNITY COMMISSION (EEOC), the federal agency that enforces employment discrimination laws, adopted guidelines in 1980 which further clarified the concept of sexual harassment. In a 1986 decision, *Meritor Savings Bank v. Vinson*, the U.S. Supreme Court unanimously ruled that sexual harassment was a violation of the law. The Civil Rights Act of 1991 allowed financial damages for victims of job discrimination. In 1992 the Court ruled that under Title IX of the 1972 Federal Education Act monetary damages could also be provided to students who were harassed.

African American women have been in the forefront of the movement against sexual harassment. Lawsuits filed by African American women have resulted in several important judicial decisions, including the legal definition of sexual harassment, prohibition of sexual harassment under Title VII, recognition that sex discrimination includes sexual advances while at work, and employer liability for sexual harassment by supervisors. Some scholars explain the disproportionate number of cases filed by African American women as the result of their massive oppression in American society. As some of the lowest paid workers and often the last hired and first fired, African American women may have the least to lose by taking action against sexual harassment.

In October, 1991, Anita HILL, an African American woman attorney, charged Clarence THOMAS, an African American nominee for Supreme Court justice, with sexual harassment. Although Hill's allegations

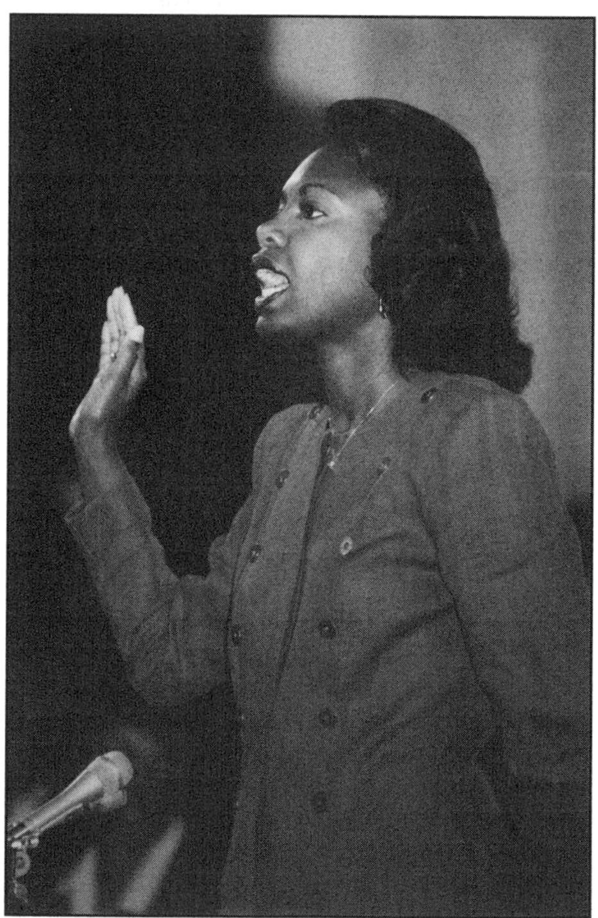

Allegations made by Anita Hill during 1991 Senate hearings on the confirmation of Clarence Thomas to the U.S. Supreme Court helped bring greater attention to the complex issues surrounding sexual harassment. (AP/Wide World Photos)

did not block Thomas' confirmation, the televised Senate hearings and the resulting discussions helped to raise the level of awareness and to change the attitudes of many Americans about sexual harassment. After the Thomas-Hill hearings, sexual harassment charges in the first half of the 1992 fiscal year increased by more than 50 percent from the same period in 1991 (4,754 complaints as compared to 3,135) according to EEOC reports.

The military and Congress have also had to respond to allegations of sexual abuse. The 1991 Tailhook scandal involved twenty-six women who alleged that they were forced to run through a gauntlet of male naval aviators who touched and fondled them against their will. At first there was an attempt to cover up the incident, but as the allegations became substantiated, several high-level officers resigned or were reassigned. Individual members of Congress have also been charged with harassment, and these allegations have received a great deal of media coverage.

Persistence of the Problem. In spite of the EEOC guidelines, court decisions, and a growing level of sensitivity, sexual harassment remains a complex, confusing social issue. It is difficult to accurately define sexual harassment or to determine the distinction between what is harassment and what is acceptable social interaction. Because of different cultural and gender norms as well as diverse personal styles, what is considered unwelcome, hostile, and offensive to some may be considered neutral or even friendly to others. In certain Latino cultures, for example, an attitude of "MACHISMO" is expected and valued among men. According to several studies, Latino men are expected to engage in seductive, sexual behavior toward women who are not related to them; women are expected to be in a subservient role. This type of culture-specific interaction between genders might lead Latinas to submit to and not question inappropriate sexual behavior when working in mainstream settings.

Sexual harassment continues to occur even when policies and procedures are in place. Furthermore, victims rarely report incidents of sexual harassment. The harasser's behavior may be subtle and cumulative and therefore difficult to pinpoint or document. A person who openly files harassment charges may be ridiculed, blamed, or even lose her job. She is often not believed, as it is her word against that of the harasser, often a higher ranking employee. Yet research does not support the notion that most harassment claims are false. Indeed, there is little for a victim to gain from making false charges, since her private life will become open to public scrutiny.

The Impact of Sexual Harassment. Victims have very different strategies for coping with sexual harassment. Some try to ignore the situation, which often leads to continued harassment at the same or even higher levels. Some blame themselves or fear that if they did report sexually inappropriate behavior they would suffer retribution. They may change their dress or their style of interaction. Others may even leave their jobs or classes.

Obviously, the impact of sexual harassment can be emotional, physical, and/or financial. Victims may experience confusion about what happened to them and whether it is sexual harassment. They may feel embarrassment, guilt, humiliation, degradation, helplessness, anxiety, anger, and depression. They may be fearful of receiving a poor grade or losing their employment. Their self-esteem and confidence may be lowered. They may feel sympathy toward their harasser. Their other personal relationships may be affected if they withdraw and isolate themselves. They may suffer from insomnia, difficulty concentrating, low energy and motivation, headaches, stomachaches, and other somatic manifestations of stress. Achievement, future career aspirations, and earnings may be affected by absenteeism and decisions to drop out of school or leave a job.

Sexual harassment, often by male coworkers or peers, has been used against women who attempt to enter nontraditional majors or jobs. The result is often that women leave and the male domain is protected. Sexual harassment may also affect bystanders who witness the harassment. They may experience a lack of confidence in the organization or institution and feel a sense of helplessness or cynicism.

Action. Sexual harassment is a complex issue, with sociocultural, psychological, and interpersonal causes and effects. As such, there are no simple solutions.

To combat the problem, business and academic settings need to write and disseminate clear policy statements that define sexual harassment, give examples, and include written grievance procedures and sanctions. These statements should identify individuals within the organization who are designated to receive complaints. Publicity and education about these policies must follow.

Sexual harassment is maintained by silence. Employers, supervisors, and others in authority must express strong disapproval when sexual harassment occurs, quickly following up the complaints. They must investigate thoroughly, no matter what level of worker or management is involved. Since many alleged offenders are in a position to hire and fire their victims, there must be procedures in place that can bypass these immediate supervisors. There must be no retaliation against the complaintant, and the due process rights of the alleged perpetrator must be protected.

Most American workplace and educational settings had both informal and formal procedures for dealing with sexual harassment complaints by the 1990's. Often informal, confidential mediation is attempted first because it can save time, money, and energy. An attempt is made to solve the problem, eliminating the harassment, without judging or punishing the harasser.

When informal steps are not successful, formal grievance procedures are often pursued. These usually involve a written complaint, coming before a board,

At school and in the workplace, Americans have begun to institute programs to educate people about what constitutes sexual harassment and about how to report complaints. (James L. Shaffer)

some determination of the offender's guilt or innocence, and punishment. Depending on the severity of the harassment and the disciplinary measures of the setting, sanctions might range from a letter of reprimand or a requirement for therapy, to dismissal from a job or suspension or expulsion from school. Formal legal complaints are often settled out of court in order to avoid lengthy, usually expensive lawsuits.

The development and application of sexual harassment policies is only a first step. If the prevention of sexual harassment is the ultimate goal, change must be directed at the value system of organizations. Since sexual harassment is considered to be abusive behavior fostered by power differentials, working relationships must be built on mutual respect, equality, and trust. Traditional sex role expectations must be challenged. Men and women of any age, race, ethnicity, marital status, or religion should have the right to work and study in an atmosphere of safety and comfort. Clearly, there will be fewer harassment complaints in settings where diversity is valued and gender equality (equal opportunities for men and women) is advocated and supported.

Suggested Readings. For more information about sexual harassment at work, see Barbara A. Gutek's *Sex and the Workplace* (1985). Sexual harassment in academic settings is the focus of Billie Wright Dziech and Linda Weiner's *The Lecherous Professor: Sexual Harassment on Campus* (2d ed., 1990) and Michele A. Paludi's *Ivory Power: Sexual Harassment on Campus* (1990). Specific techniques for preventing and eliminating sexual harassment are found in Michele A. Paludi and Richard B. Barickman's *Academic and Workplace Sexual Harassment: A Resource Manual* (1991).—*Ricki Ellen Kantrowitz*

Shakers: Members of Protestant religious sect marked by celibacy and communal settlements. The Shaker movement came to the United States from England, peaking in the mid-nineteenth century with the great religious revivals of that period. Originally known as "Shaking Quakers" for their trembling during worship, Shakers shared the Friends' belief in the spiritual equality of all souls and the validity of each person's "inner light" or "gift." In practice, this belief meant that women played at least an equal, and sometimes a dominant, role in the sect.

Ann Lee, known as Mother Ann, brought her version of Shakerism to the American colonies in 1774. Her involvement in the sect had changed after her four children all died in infancy; she took their deaths as a sign that people should turn away from the world and particularly from sexuality. Her vehement and popular preaching, combined with the Shakers' ecstatic dancing and speaking in tongues, prompted accusations of witchcraft as well as mob violence and imprisonment. Following her release from prison, she and seven fellow Shakers emigrated to America, settling near Albany, New York. By 1779, they had won their first converts following a Baptist revival, and they soon set up other settlements throughout New England. The great revivals in the early nineteenth century produced prosperous Shaker settlements west of the Appalachians (Ohio, Kentucky) as well. Unlike many sects based on a charismatic leader, the Shakers clearly survived the death of Mother Ann in 1784.

Shaker religious views both resembled and differed from those of other Protestants. Shakers believed that the Second Coming was imminent; therefore, all effort should be directed toward heavenly goals. They also believed, however, that God had a dual nature, that Christ had embodied the masculine side, and that Mother Ann was an incarnation of the feminine side. Their worship continued to focus on communal dancing, music, and speaking in tongues.

Shaker social life was unusual, though well within the spectrum of other nineteenth century religious/philosophical communities. All land and possessions were held in common, and all shared the work under strict discipline. They simplified their houses, furnishings, and clothing to free their minds for contemplating holy things. They called their settlements "families," where the dominant relationship was expressed as that of brothers and sisters. All members had to remain celibate, giving their "hands to work and hearts to God." Their families grew through conversions and the adoption of orphans; by 1990, they had all but died out. This life was not for everyone, but for some, especially women, it offered liberation, because Shaker beliefs upheld the primacy of one's spiritual gifts, regardless of gender, race, or class.

Suggested Readings. The Shakers are often compared with other groups, as in Raymond Lee Muncy's *Sex and Marriage in Utopian Communities* (1973), Lawrence Foster's *Religion and Sexuality* (1981), and Sally L. Kitch's *Chaste Liberation* (1989). Two works that focus on them alone are Edward Deming Andrews' *The People Called Shakers* (1953), and Priscilla J. Brewer's *Shaker Communities, Shaker Lives* (1986). One gains deeper insight into their religious experience from *Gifts of Power: The Writings of Rebecca Jackson. Black Visionary. Shaker Eldress* (1981), edited by Jean McMahon Humez.

Shamanists: Practitioners and followers of a religious practice based upon the belief that certain individuals (male or female) called shamans possess physical and mental abilities that enable them to communicate with the spirit world, heal the sick, and perform other important spiritual functions. The term shaman is derived from

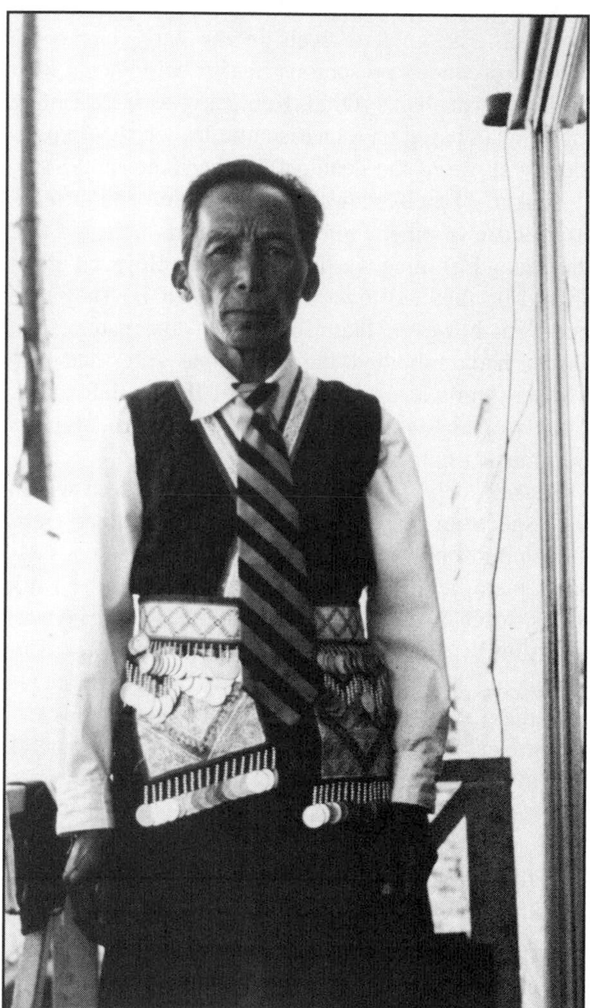

Hmong Americans often employ the services of shamans such as this man to preside over funerals and ensure the proper passage of souls of the dead. (Eric Crystal)

the Tunguso-Manchurian word *šaman* which means literally "he who knows." Shamanism is a religious phenomenon most commonly associated with indigenous peoples in Asia, India, Australia, and North and South America. There are different theories as to when and how shamanism first developed. Many scholars believe that shamanism evolved as the earliest form of religion among hunting and gathering peoples.

The classical form of shamanism is based on the practices found among the peoples of northern Asia. Basically these practices involve a belief in a multidimensional spirit world that is inhabited by various gods, spirits, and souls. Among these spirits there may be wicked or harmful deities as well as benevolent gods. The shaman journeys to the supernatural realm in order to communicate with the spirits. The actions of the shaman may result in either good or harm depending upon the kind of spirits the shaman contacts.

The shaman is obligated to possess knowledge of things that human beings are unable to comprehend because of their limited capabilities. For example, the shaman can foresee the future, locate lost possessions or animals, and predict hunting or fishing success. He or she may also assist in increasing the harvest. Other important functions of the shaman involve the three great life events: birth, marriage, and death.

At births, the shaman may quiet a crying infant or aid in its growth and development. Since illness is believed to be caused by spirits, the shaman may intervene on behalf of the patient and offer sacrifices to the spirits in order to appease them. At deaths, the shaman catches the departing soul and escorts it to the realm of the dead.

Since the shaman does not engage in productive activities such as hunting and fishing, he or she must be supported by the community. This support traditionally took the form of gifts of furs, animals, or the best food. Because shamans are figures of power and authority, they often hold the position of leader of the tribe or clan among some peoples.

Shamans are chosen by the spirits before birth and thus do not voluntarily assume the role. An initiate does not study to become a shaman as one would study to become a priest but rather enters the profession by accepting the call of the spirits. Shamans wear ceremonial dress that is often based upon the image of some animal such as a deer, bird, or bear. They may also have a ritual drum decorated with drawings of the supernatural worlds. When beaten during ceremonies, the drum is used as a kind of map to the spirit realm. Shamanistic rituals often involve drumming, the singing of songs to the spirits, and a dance performance as the shaman makes a journey to heaven.

Although many peoples have been converted from a belief in shamanism to religions such as Christianity or Islam, shamanism continues to be practiced in various regions throughout the world, particularly among tribes in northern Asia and Arctic Siberia. In the contemporary United States, various forms of shamanism are practiced by some Indian tribes, HMONG AMERICANS, and KOREAN AMERICANS, among others.

SUGGESTED READINGS. Mircea Eliade's *Shamanism: Archaic Techniques of Ecstasy* (1964) offers a thorough examination of shamanism in Central and Northern Asia, North and South America, Southeast Asia, and Oceania. John A. Grim's *The Shaman: Patterns of Siberian and Ojibway Healing* (1983) compares the religious activities of the shaman with developments in the world's great religious traditions. In *Dreamtime and Inner Space: The World of the Shaman* (1988), Holger Kolweit presents a comprehensive account of the practices and experiences of many types of tribal healers from diverse regions of the world.

Shange, Ntozake (Paulette Williams; b. Oct. 18, 1948, Trenton, N.J.): African American poet and playwright. Shange gained attention for her play *for colored girls who have considered suicide/ when the rainbow is enuf* (1976), a "choreopoem" that celebrated the strengths and struggles of black women. A BARNARD COLLEGE graduate (1970) with an M.A. from the University of Southern California (1973), Shange has been on the faculty at various colleges. She published numerous novels, plays, and collections of poems in the 1980's, many with unusual titles. Typically her dramas fuse dialogue with poetry, African American dance, and jazz music. Shange's awards include an Obie (1977).

Obie Award-winning playwright Ntozake Shange. (AP/Wide World Photos)

Sharecropping: A tenancy system in which landowners provide a plot of land as well as farming implements and supplies to agricultural laborers in exchange for a portion of their future crops. In U.S. history, the term "sharecroppers" refers to tenant farm workers in the South from Reconstruction (1867-1877) to the 1930's, about half of whom were AFRICAN AMERICAN.

The sharecropping system functioned as a form of quasi slavery in which newly freed slaves were quickly made dependent on former plantation owners. Following the Civil War, many wealthy landowners retained their vast estates but could not afford to hire wage laborers to farm them. At the same time, most poor white farm workers and newly freed slaves had agricultural experience but could not obtain land to cultivate. The result of this supply-and-demand relationship was a system in which credit was extended to laborers in the form of tools, seeds, fertilizer, and mules if they farmed plots of 20 to 40 acres and agreed to forfeit a portion of the resulting crop, usually cotton, to the landowner. Sometimes, clothing and food were also provided to the sharecroppers, also on a credit basis. The portion of the crop to be turned over to the landowner, as well as the amount of supervision to which the sharecroppers were subject, depended on their need for credit. Thus, sharecroppers who could contribute some of their own supplies or equipment were more independent than those who accrued greater debts.

Such a system was ripe for exploitation, and many landowners took advantage of the debts incurred by sharecroppers. A landowner could charge extremely high interest rates on advances in credit and confiscate part of the crop for payment. Sometimes, an increased portion of crops was seized so that the landowner could pay banks and suppliers. The annual contracts between landowners and sharecroppers were verbal and easily broken at the end of the year; the plenitude

A colleague of Susan B. Anthony, Anna Howard Shaw served as national lecturer and vice president of the National Woman Suffrage Association in the late nineteenth and early twentieth centuries. (Library of Congress)

of unskilled labor in the South gave the landowners no incentive to keep on unwanted tenants. African American sharecroppers were especially vulnerable to such exploitation, as it was coupled with the racism and hatred to which they were subjected in the South. Sharecropping was largely phased out by the 1930's; increased mechanization meant that fewer workers were needed to farm large estates, and many landowners turned to wage laborers in order to minimize their costs. Moreover, many African American and white agricultural workers had left the cotton belt.

Shaw, Anna Howard (Feb. 14, 1847, Newcastle-on-Tyne, England—July 2, 1919, Moylan, Pa.): Minister and SUFFRAGIST. The Shaw family immigrated to Massachusetts in 1851. In 1871 Shaw became a licensed METHODIST preacher, despite complaints from her UNITARIAN parents. She had difficulty financing her divinity school education at Boston University because such funds were not given to women. In 1885 she joined the Massachusetts Woman Suffrage Association; she addressed the International Council of Women in 1888. In 1891 she became the national lecturer of the NATIONAL WOMAN SUFFRAGE ASSOCIATION. She also served as the organization's vice president under Susan B. ANTHONY (1892-1904) and president (1904-1915).

Sheppard-Towner Act (1921): Federal law which provided funds for maternity and infant care. This piece of legislation was the first major policy victory of newly enfranchised women. Its passage is widely attributed to the successful lobbying of the Women's Joint Congressional Committee, a coalition of ten major women's organizations, and to male legislators' fears of repercussions from the "women's vote." Opposition to the act by the American Medical Association and the Woman Patriots almost blocked the re-funding of the policy in 1927. It was permanently defeated in 1929.

Shima, George (Kinji Ushimura; 1864, Fukuoka Prefecture, Japan—Mar. 27, 1926, Hollywood, Calif.): JAPANESE AMERICAN agriculturist and businessman. Shima came to California in 1887. He began picking potatoes near Stockton but soon acquired acreage of his own. Converting San Joaquin River Valley swampland into potato fields, Shima became the undisputed "Potato King" of California. By 1920, he owned an estimated 85 percent of the state's potato crop and was worth $15 million. As president of the Japanese American Association and the Empire Navigation Company, Shima was a strong example for Japanese Americans of the possibilities for success in the United States.

Shintoists: Adherents to the indigenous religion of Japan, which is marked by its reverence of holiness in all living things as well as its emphasis on life cycle rituals and community celebrations. Various forms of Shinto were practiced, either informally or officially, by many Japanese Americans until World War II. For example, immigrants had small Shinto shrines in their homes, and large public shrines in Seattle, San Francisco, Los Angeles, and Hawaii became the site of marriages and annual festivals. Concerns about Imperial Shinto, which revered the emperor of Japan, helped fuel the U.S. government's policy on JAPANESE AMERICAN INTERNMENT during the war, and Shinto leaders were singled out for harsh treatment, including deportation. Since the war, many Japanese Americans continue to observe Shinto practices, such as marriage customs and the Japanese New Year, and several thousand belong to official Shinto religious organizations, of which the best-known is the Tenrikyo sect.

Sierra, Paul Alberto (b. July 30, 1944, Havana, Cuba): Cuban American artist. Sierra received his training at the School of the Art Institute of Chicago. Beginning as a minimalist, he moved into a more expressionist style during the 1970's, when he began exploring images and subjects from Cuba and Africa. His work is hung in major collections including the Museum of Contemporary Art in Chicago and the Anheuser-Busch Corporate Collection. Sierra was included in *Cuba-U.S.A.: The First Generation*, the first traveling group exhibition of Cuban and American artists. He was a member of the Illinois Arts Council from 1988 to 1990 and received a CINTAS Fellowship in 1990.

Sign language: System of manual and facial symbols used by deaf and hearing-impaired people to communicate among themselves and with members of the hearing population. For centuries, deaf people were believed to lack language skills by virtue of their hearing impairment. Communication with them relied on indicative gesturing, but the deaf were considered incapable of leading "normal" lives.

In France in 1761, Abbé Charles Michel de L'Épée founded the first public school for the deaf. His follower Laurent Clerc joined with Thomas Hopkins Gallaudet to found a similar school in the United States in 1817. The informal sign languages developed at these schools became standardized and codified. French Sign Language appeared first; American Sign Language (ASL) and other variations emerged from it. Other sign languages have developed independently among deaf people in many cultures.

A Korean American teacher instructs a special education class on the basic symbols of American Sign Language. (Don Franklin)

During the nineteenth century, education of the deaf deemphasized signing and encouraged oralism, whereby deaf people are taught to speak vocally and to read lips. Alexander Graham Bell, inventor of the telephone, was a key figure in the oralist movement. Eventually people recognized the unfairness and difficulty of expecting deaf people to adapt to spoken language. Many hearing-impaired people were simply not able to articulate sounds or distinguish lip movements.

During the twentieth century, the oral/manual controversy became a central issue of deaf rights, and sign language became much more widely accepted. A turning point came in 1965, when William Stokoe, Jr., published his *Dictionary of American Sign Language on Linguistic Principles.* Unlike other manuals, Stokoe's volume classified sign language not according to alphabetical English or subject matter, but rather by hand shapes. In treating the language according to its basic elements—the visual correlates of sounds and phonemes—Stokoe proved the linguistic values of sign language.

American Sign Language is the primary sign language used by the estimated 9 percent of Americans who suffer some form of hearing impairment. Far from being a gestural form of English, American Sign Language has its own grammar and syntax, and a vocabulary that is as metaphoric, economical, stylized, and flexible as it is visual. Deaf poets create poems in it; the National Theatre of the Deaf, founded in 1967, performs original and translated plays in it; and classes are conducted in it at Gallaudet University, a college for the deaf that was founded in Washington, D.C., in 1864.

Suggested Readings. For more information on sign language in America, see Arden Neisser's *The Other Side of Silence: Sign Language and the Deaf Community in America* (1983). *Deaf In America: Voices from a Culture* (1988) by Carol Padden and Tom Humphries provides an inside view of deaf culture from two deaf authors. In *When the Mind Hears: A History of the Deaf* (1984), Harlan Lane offers a historical account of deaf education through the eyes of Laurent Clerc. A powerful fictional view of deaf culture and sign language is found in Mark Medoff's award-winning play *Children of a Lesser God* (1980).

Sign language—American Indian: System of fixed hand and finger positions symbolizing ideas. The sign language of the Plains Indians was one of the most extensively used systems. The many tribes living in the Plains region were designated by the language they spoke. There were six distinct language families within the Plains area; each family was broken down further into distinct tribal languages. Sign language provided a limited but common means of communication between speakers of different tribal languages.

Singh, Jag Jeet (b. May 20, 1926, Rohtak, India): Asian Indian American physicist. Singh studied at Punjab University and the University of Liverpool before coming to the United States in 1958. He taught and conducted research at several American universities and worked for the National Aeronautical and Space Administration (NASA) from 1964 to 1980. Singh has received numerous awards from NASA for technical utilization and outstanding performance as well as its 1990 Medal for Exceptional Scientific Achievement. Among his achievements are the establishment of radiation damage thresholds for semiconductor devices and the development of techniques for safety monitoring in aerosols, polymeric materials, and aviation fuels.

Sioux: Northern Plains Indian group best known historically for their material culture—tipis, war bonnets, buffalo hunting, and equestrian lifestyle. Among themselves, the people use the term Dakota (or its variant Lakota), which means "friends" or "allies." The term "Sioux," which dates back to the seventeenth century when the Dakota were living in the Great Lakes area, comes from the Ojibwa "Nadouwesou" meaning "adders." This term, shortened and corrupted by French traders, resulted in retention of the last syllable as "Sioux." Among the various Sioux divisions there are important cultural, linguistic, territorial, and political distinctions.

Originally located in the Great Lakes or Woodland area, the Sioux were allied in what was known as the Seven Fireplaces. These consisted of the Santee division (Dakota speakers) with four groups, the Middle division (Nakota speakers) with two groups, and the Teton or Western division (Lakota speakers) with one group. These subdivisions were not originally culturally distinct from one another, but they became more separate as the people moved westward. All the groups were semisedentary with a Woodland economy based on fishing, hunting and gathering, and some cultivation of corn.

By the mid-seventeenth century, the Sioux were pushed westward by tribes who obtained guns through the French fur trade. The Teton and Middle divisions moved westward to the Great Plains where they acquired horses and became dependent on the buffalo for food and material needs such as housing, clothing, and implements. The Middle Sioux settled along the Missouri River while the Tetons pushed further west into the Black Hills and beyond to present day states of Nebraska, Wyoming, and Montana. Although they too were pushed westward, the Eastern Sioux remained essentially woodland people in territory and culture, settling in the area of southwestern Minnesota. By the early nineteenth century, political and cultural differences between the Sioux groups became pronounced, and true Eastern, Middle, and Teton (Western) divisions emerged.

The Sioux negotiated treaties and agreements with the U.S. government beginning in 1851. Constant broken promises, unresolved issues, and encroachment on tribal lands brought the various Sioux divisions into direct conflict with the United States between 1862 and 1877. These encounters, famous in American history, are known collectively as the Sioux wars.

This warrior was a member of the Hunkpapa Teton Sioux, the Plains Indian tribe led by the famous Sitting Bull in the late 1800's. (National Archives)

Eventually the Sioux were moved onto reservations in North and South Dakota, Montana, and southern Canada where they continue to live. The Sioux regard their reservations as homelands and draw strength from their past, maintaining strong commitments to preserve their languages, spiritual beliefs, and cultural traditions.

SUGGESTED READINGS. A good history of the Eastern Sioux is Roy Meyer's *History of the Santee Sioux* (1967), while Royal Hassrick's *The Sioux: Life and Customs of a Warrior Society* (1964) is informative on the Teton Sioux. Interesting accounts from a Sioux perspective include Luther Standing Bear's *My People the Sioux* (1928) and *Land of the Spotted Eagle* (1933); Charles Eastman's *Indian Boyhood* (1902) and *Soul of the Indian* (1911); and Ella Deloria's *Speaking of Indians* (1944).

Sit-ins: Form of social protest pioneered by AFRICAN AMERICANS. The development of sit-ins was an indispensable part of the CIVIL RIGHTS MOVEMENT of the 1950's and 1960's. Although sit-ins are known to have occurred as early as the 1940's, they remained isolated occurrences until around 1957, when the NATIONAL ASSOCIATION FOR THE ADVANCEMENT OF COLORED PEOPLE (NAACP), along with the CONGRESS OF RACIAL EQUALITY (CORE) and the SOUTHERN CHRISTIAN LEADERSHIP CONFERENCE (SCLC), began to sponsor organized sit-in protests.

Carefully organized sit-in protests such as this one at the lunch counter of a Chattanooga, Tenn., department store, helped generate public attention for the Civil Rights movement. (AP/Wide World Photos)

Rather than being spontaneous outbursts of civil disobedience, the sit-ins of the late 1950's were the result of careful strategies planned by civil rights organizations. Surveys were conducted to determine those public facilities most dependent upon African American customers. Support from black churches was solicited by civil rights organizations as they established protest headquarters and devised numerous contingencies in anticipation of concerted and often violent responses from the targeted businesses, racist whites, and the police.

In mid-1958, the NAACP led a series of sit-ins at various lunch counters that refused service to African Americans in Wichita, Kansas, and Oklahoma City, Oklahoma. These efforts were followed by the February, 1960, sit-in at a Woolworth's lunch counter in Greensboro, North Carolina, conducted by four members of the NAACP Youth Council. Although sit-ins had occurred elsewhere in North Carolina as early as 1957, the Greensboro action acted as a catalyst for the subsequent proliferation of sit-ins.

The widespread publicity generated by the "Greensboro Four" led to an explosion of sit-ins in more than sixty southern cities during the weeks following their arrest. In Greensboro itself, hundreds of students from nearby African American colleges quickly joined in the protest and the store decided to close in an attempt to quell the mushrooming movement. Instead, the actions spread to other North Carolina cities as well as to Nashville, Tennessee.

In each case, the sit-ins became increasingly better organized as the African American community mobilized to confront the opposition of the white establishment. Legal, financial, communication, and basic support networks were formed to optimize the success of the nonviolent actions in each new target city. The civil rights organizations sponsoring these actions had little difficulty recruiting support from college students who displayed relentless energy and endurance in the face of mass arrests, harassment, and intimidation mounted by local authorities. The actions launched in Nashville succeeded in desegregating lunch counters at various downtown shopping establishments. Before long, white-dominated peace organizations opposing the VIETNAM WAR began to stage sit-ins of their own, building on the successes of black civil rights activists. Later, American Indian activists as well as other mobilized communities adopted sit-in tactics.

SUGGESTED READINGS. Howard Zinn's *SNCC: The New Abolitionists* (1964), Donald Mathews and James Prothro's *Negroes and the New Southern Politics* (1966), and Louis E. Lomax's *The Negro Revolt* (1962) provide early accounts of the civil rights struggle when sit-ins began to play a crucial role. Kirkpatrick Sale's *SDS* (1973) describes how white student protesters adopted the technique of sit-ins.

Sitting Bull [Tatanka Iyotake] (Mar., 1831, Dakota Territory—Dec. 15, 1890, Standing Rock Agency, S.Dak.): Leader of the Hunkpapa (Dakota) SIOUX Indi-

Although Sitting Bull was not a war leader at the Battle of the Little Big Horn, many of his followers attributed their victory to his magical powers as a spiritual leader of the Hunkpapa Sioux. (Library of Congress)

ans in their resistance after 1866 to removal to reservations. He helped defeat General George Armstrong Custer in the Battle of the Little Bighorn (1876). He escaped to Canada and was later pardoned. In 1885, Sitting Bull appeared in Buffalo Bill's Wild West Show. He was killed during the Ghost Dance uprising shortly before the Wounded Knee Massacre.

Six Nations: Confederacy of the six Iroquoian-speaking tribes in New York and Ontario, Canada. The Mohawks, Oneidas, Onondagas, Cayugas, and Senecas (the Five Nations) are among many Iroquoian tribes who have been in this region since ancient times. The sixth tribe, the Tuscaroras, entered the confederacy about 1720 as refugees from an eastern North Carolina border war. Their language, although classified as Iroquoian, is quite different from that of the Five Nations.

Archaeologically, the separate tribes of the Five Nations can be traced back to about 1200, when population increase was having disastrous effects on the many large towns along the area's waterways. Murder and infanticide accompanied the abandonment of the exposed low-lying villages as the inhabitants moved into fortified towns on higher ground and then to tiny communities hidden away in the hills and on islands. These sites, usually fortified single houses, reveal a society torn apart by internecine warfare and cannibalism.

Shortly before 1400 a great prophet, Deganaweda, appeared among the Mohawks. His eloquence and intelligence attracted a small band of reformers who set out to rebuild the fabric of these tribes. Beginning with the Mohawks and the Oneidas, they built a unique society based on a concept of extended kinship (based on both marriages and adoption) that related people to others in different tribes. They spread their reforms among the Onondagas and the Cayugas before 1450 and to the Senecas about 1450. These five peoples became a closely knit supertribe known as the Iroquois League, with refined legal systems, social orders, and political structures. They drew in many other nearby tribes. This large group continued to wage war on other tribes, seeking to establish an enforced peace.

Many later prophets and political leaders continued to reshape the league. The greatest of these was Handsome Lake, who, in the late eighteenth century, created the Longhouse Religion, a blending of traditional Iroquois values and Quaker principles. This religion, which strengthened family ties and disapproved of drinking, helped the Iroquois maintain traditional ways as the white population grew. The Iroquois League still exists and is known for its refusal to ally itself with any foreign power. The Six Nations claim to be an independent, autonomous nation that has illegally been denied membership in such bodies as the League of Nations and the United Nations.

Taken as a whole, the Iroquois today are one of the largest groups of Indians in North America. Because of U.S. policies of removal and relocation, the Six Nations are now scattered geographically, with reservations and populations in New York State, Canada (including the Six Nations Reserve, near Brantford, Ontario), Wisconsin, and Oklahoma. Nevertheless, there are bonds between the Iroquois in their various locations, including those of language, kinship, land claims, religious movements, and ceremonials.

Iroquois tribes have been extensively involved in Indian activist movements since the 1960's and have protested U.S. and state government policies regarding them. More recently, with varying success, they have pressed land claims in the courts for the return of Indian lands. They have also tried to resist further encroachment onto Indian lands. In 1990, for example, the town of Oka, Quebec, wanted to expand its golf course onto land that contained a Mohawk burial ground. After legal means failed, Mohawks occupied the land and constructed barricades. Canadian forces used ground forces, helicopters, and tear gas in attempts to remove the Mohawks, who held their ground. Many violent incidents occurred. The tense standoff lasted for nearly three months before the Mohawks finally relented and took down the barricades.

There are bitter divisions within Iroquois communities between traditionalists and those who have accepted white culture. On the Six Nations Reserve, one group adheres to the native religion and traditional method of appointing chiefs and opposes taxation, military conscription, and the uses of non-Indian police forces and courts. The other side accepts Christianity, general elections, government taxation, and external legal institutions. Similar conflicts exist on reservations in the United States. There is also a vocal minority that advocates withdrawal from the U.S. or Canadian government and complete independence for Indian nations.

SUGGESTED READINGS. For an overview, see *Handbook of North American Indians* (vol. 15, 1978), edited by Bruce T. Trigger. Two books by Laurence Hauptman present information on the Iroquois in the twentieth century: *The Iroquois and the New Deal* (1981) and *The Iroquois Struggle for Survival: World War II to Red Power* (1986). See also *The Iroquois Book of Rites* (1963) by Horatio Hale and *Parker on the Iroquois* (1968) by Arthur C. Parker.